THE GREAT DIVIDE

Lord Mountbatten, Pandit Nehru, Liaquat Ali Khan and Field
Marshal Auchinleck at Palam (Delhi) Airport on Lord Mountbatten's
arrival in India, 22nd March 1947.

THE GREAT DIVIDE

Britain - India - Pakistan

H. V. HODSON

Hutchinson of London

HUTCHINSON & CO (*Publishers*) LTD
178–202 Great Portland Street, London W1

London Melbourne Sydney
Auckland Bombay Toronto
Johannesburg New York

First published 1969
Second impression November 1969

Printed in Great Britain by litho on antique wove paper
by Anchor Press, and bound by Wm. Brendon,
both of Tiptree, Essex

09 097150 7

Contents

PART FOUR   THE AFTERMATH

PART FIVE   RETROSPECT

Illustrations

Lord Mountbatten's arrival   *frontispiece*

*Unless otherwise indicated, all illustrations are reproduced by
courtesy of the Press Information Bureau, Government of India.*

Author's introduction

The Great Divide, of which the title speaks, was the simultaneous breach between Britain and her Indian Empire, and between India and Pakistan. Britain had been suzerain of the whole sub-continent for a hundred years, of large parts of it for a century longer; Hindus and Muslims had shared it, ruling or ruled according to time and place, for a millennium, and had mingled as subjects or subordinates of the British raj from its earliest days. The severance of 1947 was thus a great recoil of history. Partition and independence arrived together, the one as the price of the other. Two new great sovereign States arose, the self-liquidation of the British Empire began.

How did this happen? Why did it happen thus? Whose decisions, or indecision, brought about this double revolution? This book aims to give, if not answers to such questions, at least material for answering.

It owes its inception to two men, each of whom played a great part in the story it tells, General Lord Ismay and Mr. V. P. Menon. Both, to their countries' sad loss, have died since work on the book began. Menon, an old colleague and friend, had often urged me to write the history of the end of the British period in India, but I had to say I was much too busy with other things. Then, in 1962, Lord Ismay begged me, in Lord Mountbatten's name as well as his own and Menon's, to take on the task. Though time for writing was still scarce and precious, I agreed, on the understanding, first, that the book should not deal merely with the events of 1947 but should go back far enough to trace how the condition of India came to be as it was when Lord Mountbatten took up his charge as last Viceroy; secondly, that I might need several years to complete the book, since it could not be written superficially, and I already had an exacting full-time post as Provost of Ditchley; thirdly, that Lord Mountbatten's India papers should be available to me without reserve; further, that neverthe-

ix

less the book should be my own independent enterprise and that
I should be under no obligation or commitment to Lord Mountbatten or anyone else. To all this Lord Ismay and Lord Mountbatten generously agreed.

First and foremost of my thanks, therefore, are offered to
Admiral of the Fleet Earl Mountbatten of Burma, who entrusted
to me all the papers that he brought back from India, encouraged
me, was patient with me, talked with me in complete frankness,
answering my questions or volunteering recollections, and finally
read my manuscript and made many valuable comments, yet
without attempting to alter my conclusions or to press any amendment, save on verifiable fact. For any defects in the book, and
for any judgments made in it, I am solely responsible; but it
could never have been written without the unstinting help and
confidence of the last Viceroy of India.

At Lord Mountbatten's request the Government of India
consented to his including, among the documents which he
allowed me to use or quote, papers of his period as Governor-
General of independent India, on the express understanding that
the Government of India was not on any account to be taken as
approving any particular use made of such documents or any
statement or opinion recorded in the book: for all these the author
takes entire responsibility. I am grateful to the Government of
India for their liberal attitude in this regard.

The Mountbatten India archive includes, besides many other
documents of great interest, four series of papers which together
give a unique personal picture of Lord Mountbatten's experiences,
ideas and policies as Viceroy and Governor-General: (i) the
minutes of his almost daily meetings with his staff, (ii) records
(mostly dictated by himself) of all his important conversations
with Indian political leaders, Princes and Governors and others
in high places, (iii) files of his weekly letters and accompanying
reports to the Secretary of State for India while he was Viceroy,
copies of which went to His Majesty the King and certain other
Ministers concerned with Indian affairs, and (iv) files of his
monthly reports as Governor-General to His Majesty the King.
Both the Viceroy's and the Governor-General's reports were used
by Lord Mountbatten as the basis of final despatches in which
the whole story was brought together in a more ordered and
consecutive way, as the *Report on the Last Viceroyalty* and the

Report of the Governor-General of India. All these I have used freely, both by way of quotation and as the foundation of my own writing. No great man could have provided more handsome, more personal or more liberal material for a contemporary historian.

Certain of the documents included or quoted in this book are reproduced with the permission of the Controller of Her Majesty's Stationery Office.

By gracious permission of Her Majesty the Queen, I have quoted from the Governor-General's reports to the Sovereign after independence, these having been, unlike the personal communications of other Governors-General in the Commonwealth, in the nature of demi-official reports continuing the series of confidential reports of successive Viceroys of India, and having clearly been intended, not for the King's eyes alone, but also through His Majesty for the confidential information of United Kingdom Ministers.

Further, I was most fortunate in being allowed by his widow to see some of the late Sir Stafford Cripps' private letters, written to her during his visit to India with the Cabinet Mission in 1946. To Dame Isobel Cripps I am indeed grateful; as I am, too, to Lady Ismay for the loan of her late husband's India papers— few in number, alas! though often of high interest; for, accustomed to carry countless secrets of great affairs of state, he was habitually most discreet in his writing.

Other original material included my own diary of 1941–2 when I was Constitutional Adviser to the Viceroy, correspondence with various people concerned in the events, and tape-recordings of many conversations that I had for purposes of the book both in England (with Lord Mountbatten, Lord Ismay and others) and in India and Pakistan, where I paid a special visit during my summer holiday in 1964, unhappily just after the death of Pandit Jawaharlal Nehru, whose recollections I would dearly have liked to record. These conversations included many hours spent with V. P. Menon, then living in retirement in Bangalore, and a long talk with Mohamed Ali Choudhury, first Secretary General of Pakistan and at one time its Prime Minister. I owe a heavy debt of thanks to all those who gave me so much of their time and goodwill for this purpose, and to other participants in the events here recorded who generously commented on sections of the draft or proofs, including Sir George Abell, Field Marshal Auchinleck, General

Sir Roy Bucher, Sir Olaf Caroe, Sir Conrad Corfield, Sir Evan Jenkins, Sir Gilbert Laithwaite, Sir Penderel Moon, Sir Francis Mudie, Viscount Radcliffe, the Earl of Scarbrough, Sir Ronald Wingate and others; also to Lord Glendevon and the Earl of Birkenhead, then engaged on biographies of the late Marquess of Linlithgow and the late Viscount Monckton of Brenchley.

Many further original sources on the period, I am well aware, exist to be tapped, among them the India papers of two previous Viceroys, Lord Linlithgow and Lord Wavell, and much material in the archives of the Indian and Pakistani Governments and parties and the papers of such men as Mahatma Gandhi, Jawaharlal Nehru, Mahomed Ali Jinnah or Vallabhbhai Patel. This book would have been that much better if I had had the time and means to use all that is or could be available. In particular, I am conscious that the sources and the outlook are predominantly British, though Britain was only one party among two or three to the events recorded. But I reflect that every historian, however impartial and careful of the truth, as I have tried to be, must have a personal point of view, without which history is anaemic, and my viewpoint cannot but be British; and that only an Indian or a Pakistani could write from the viewpoint of his own people and leaders.

Fortunately there already exist many secondary sources on the period—books published in India, Pakistan or Britain. First among them are V. P. Menon's monumental volumes, *The Integration of the Indian States* and *The Transfer of Power in India* (Longmans 1956 and 1957), on which I have freely drawn for the background story. I am also particularly indebted to Professor Coupland's Report on the Constitutional Problem in India (published in two volumes by the Oxford University Press in 1942 and 1943), John Connell's *Auchinleck* (Cassell, 1959), and Sir Penderel Moon's *Divide and Quit* (Chatto and Windus, 1962).

Last but far from least, I pay my grateful tribute to my wife for all her encouragement, her stimulus and her tolerance of the sacrifices of time and temper endured for the sake of this enterprise. A six-year pregnancy is longer than any spouse should have to suffer.

PART ONE

Background to the drama

I

British policy in India

The broad history of British policy in India, which culminated in the events described here, is too familiar to need a long account. From the time of Sir Thomas Munro and Thomas Babington Macaulay there was threaded in that policy a strand of aspiration to lead the peoples of India to a condition in which they would be able to govern themselves and grow out of imperial tutelage; in the same liberal vein it was a Scotsman who with official benevolence formed the Indian National Congress in 1885. But it would be quite wrong to suppose that the persistent purpose of British rule in India was to accomplish its own end, or even that the idea of trusteeship, so much in vogue in the latter days of British imperialism, always dominated British attitudes in India. Consciously or unconsciously, there was in them a strong element of self-interest, which a powerful nation finds it hard to forgo.

The material self-interest was economic and strategic. India was a captive market, for long prevented by a system of counter-vailing excise duties from protecting its cotton-manufacturing industry from the products of Lancashire. Even after the Fiscal Convention of 1920 had thrown out this system, and established that when the Government and Legislature of India, acting for the benefit of India and in response to Indian opinion, were agreed on fiscal policy, the Secretary of State would not exercise his overriding power on behalf of any British interest, it remained true that British control of Indian government conveyed substantial economic advantages. At least it prevented the development of Indian economic policy on autarkic lines which most British people honestly believed to be harmful to India—and which would certainly have been harmful to Britain. Strategically, India became the trunk of a systematic corpus of imperial defence whose limbs stretched from Hong Kong to the Middle East, from East Africa to the northern passes of Burma. Apart from the Indian forces themselves, it was an essential overseas training-ground and cantonment for the British Army. And for this India paid. Such benefits were not lightly yielded to political pressure.

A less tangible but nevertheless very powerful interest was the prestige and authority that Britain gained in world affairs from being master of an immense empire of which India was the heart. Without that empire and the naval power that cemented it she was but a medium-sized European country. With it, she was great among the greatest, boasting a world-wide Pax Britannica. Without India, the subordinate empire would be scarcely more than a string of colonial beads. Pride is less easily sacrificed than even major material interests.

British policy progressed to the point of offering India national independence under the influence of three broad secular forces. One was the development of public opinion along liberal lines both in Britain itself and in countries whose goodwill was important to her. (Diplomatic pressure from the United States has been popularly supposed to be more significant than it actually was; only in 1942 does it appear to have had a determinable effect. Nevertheless the climate of world opinion was undoubtedly important.) Another was the growth of Indian political consciousness and solidarity, with all that this implied for the problems and conduct of a paternal autocracy, governing a great oriental empire with a few thousand soldiers and civil servants, and thus essentially dependent on the passive consent of the people. A third was the natural evolution of imperialism itself. All these were linked together.

The classic interpretation of imperial evolution runs on these lines: 'To rule successfully is to rule well, to raise and educate the subject people, who thus become imbued with the ideas of the governing race; and these ideas at length supplant their willingness to submit to alien authority, while education has rendered their submission unnecessary.' This theme can indeed be read plainly in the Indian story. But the evolution of modern empires has another aspect. In the enlightened self-interest of the rulers, as well as the ruled, the subject country develops social and economic structures and needs which pass beyond the competence of an alien power. Imperial authority reaches the point at which it can no longer assume the popular consent, upon which its stability rests, to social reforms rendered necessary by changing needs or standards but opposed by many on deep religious, social or atavistic grounds; nor can it strain any further, for the sake of the masses,

the support of the vested interests on which such a regime inevitably relies—the aristocracy, the landed classes, the well-to-do and
the seekers after office. Radical reforms can be shouldered only by
representatives of the people who will bear the conflict with those
whom they offend. This, too, was true of India; for the most
benevolent and far-seeing imperialism was incapable of those
profound changes in economic structure, agrarian law, caste
division and native monarchy which were required if the country
was to keep up with the twentieth century.

Policies, however, are changed not by cloistered reflection on
historical trends or ingestion of political theory but by particular
events and forces which lead to particular decisions. The problem
which actually faced British administrators and the British
Parliament was rather how best to continue to govern India in
face of new movements and new difficulties. Repression always
proved a short-lived remedy, unless it were far more bloody and
severe than a British electorate could tolerate. If the shooting at
Jallianwalabagh (Amritsar) in 1919 quelled the Punjab disorders
it solidified Indian political opinion and shocked British political
opinion. On either side nothing was ever the same again. If the
non-co-operation and civil disobedience movements of the 1920s
failed in their immediate purpose, they produced Viceroy Lord
Irwin's famous foreshadowing of Dominion Status in 1929[1] and
the Irwin-Gandhi pact of March 1931, whereby the Government
agreed to release the political prisoners and the Congress to
suspend civil disobedience—a truce regarded by many British as
compounding with the enemies of law and order. If the Indian
parties boycotted the Simon Commission, and its report fell flat
in political India, it did lead to the Round Table conferences and
thence to a new constitution which with all its limitations gave
considerable opportunity and satisfaction to Indian democracy for
a dozen years from 1935 until the final transfer of power.

All this could be seen as a story of reluctant concession to
unremitting agitation, but behind it lay a steady advance of British
thought, much affected by the healthy growth of national indepen-

[1] 'In view of the doubts which have been expressed . . . I am authorised on
behalf of His Majesty's Government to state clearly that, in their judgment, it is implicit in the Declaration of 1917 that the natural issue of
India's constitutional progress as there contemplated is the attainment of
Dominion Status.' 31st October 1929.

dence in the colonised parts of the Empire, and by the transmutation of the old imperial idea of a White Man's Burden into
that of trusteeship of the stronger for the weak. The advance was
towards a new concept, or rather an early-nineteenth-century
concept sprung to fresh life: that it was not only the historic role
or the pragmatic requirement but the political duty of an imperial
power to grant self-government to its wards to the fullest possible
extent.

A remarkable expression of this concept, partial as it was, came
at the very start of the inter-war period in India, namely the
Montagu-Chelmsford Report of 1918 and the new constitution or
reforms to which it gave birth in the following year:

> Indians must be enabled in so far as they attain responsibility to
> determine for themselves what they want done. The process will
> begin in local affairs . . . it will proceed to the complete control
> of provincial matters, and thence, in the course of time and
> subject to the proper discharge of Imperial responsibilities, to
> the control of matters concerning all India.[2]

Despite the paternalist caution and the note (not discordant fifty
years ago) of overriding imperial duty, from then on it was a
question of time and method, not of ultimate objective.

In India, however, self-government to the fullest possible extent
meant taking into account not only the poverty and backwardness
of its masses but also the divisions of its communities and castes.
This was a genuine difficulty, as almost every page of this book
confirms. That many British people clung to Hindu-Muslim and
other internecine conflicts in India as a reason for not granting
democracy and independence cannot be denied. That such divisions and conflicts should be used as practical aids to imperial
government was only to be expected; for who with the daunting
task of governing, with absurdly small force, an Indian district or
province or all India would not use such helpful means as lay to
hand? But that the British raj deliberately provoked or fostered
these conflicts in its latter decades is not true. It was far from its
interest to do so. Broad political aims apart, its prime responsibility
was peace and order, and the last thing that it sought was to promote forces that would have left it the helpless spectator of violence
and chaos.

[1] Cmd. 9109. *Report on Indian Constitutional Reforms*, p. 148.

The plain fact is that in latter times British rule in India ran on its own momentum rather than the impulse of any imperialist ideology. Day by day and year by year, its agents from Viceroy to newly-joined police officer, and their subordinates, did the work that lay before them; whatever their private aspirations or fears, they had to obey orders, to take decisions, and to see that the decisions were carried out. This meant obedience by those from whom obedience was due, but more often it was a far more complex business. All had to be done within a framework of policy, of institutions and of law. In such a system there is a vast inertia, like that of a heavy flywheel. From judges to village *chowkidars*, from army commanders to government clerks, the agents and servants of the Raj went on doing as they had been wont to do, while political storms raged around them. It is only when too many decisions fail to be carried out, too many orders are not obeyed, that the system begins to weaken. Once this happens, deterioration is self-accelerating and must before long end in collapse unless it is checked. That process of decline had begun before the British left India, but even at the end it was far from complete. Government as such still had enormous prestige and authority. So long as it was firm government, it was still good government, and the mass of people obeyed or played their parts in making it work. Like the management of a giant company, remote alike from shareholders and customers, it had become very largely government for its own sake, following the law of its own nature. British policy in India had ceased to serve extraneous interests; it had become British policy for India.

Nowhere in the story told here is any part of the struggle between British and Indians recorded in terms of race or colour. There was, of course, still an aroma of racial superiority about the British in India long after the Kipling era had faded; but it clung most to the memsahibs, the underlings and some in the Army, and lingered longest in the more distant cantonment towns. It was of little or no account, at this period, among those in positions of administrative or political power—indeed, nonsensical as it always was, it became a total anachronism when Indians held many of the highest posts in government, up to governorships of provinces and membership of the Viceroy's Executive Council. Of course imperialism always has an aspect of racial arrogance: different ways of life, too, raised barriers, and intermarriage was deplored from both sides. Of course the British led their own social life, and as part of it had their exclusive clubs; of course some Indians were rightly affronted at being made to feel, by exclusion not only from club membership but even from entry, second-class social persons in their own country. Many were the stories of cultivated Indians, once acquiescent and pro-British, being turned sour and hostile by such snubs. Not all of them were authentic. But this was mere froth on the flowing tide of nationalist feeling, and if for fifty years every European club had been wide open, and if neither colour nor religion nor social customs nor food taboos nor any other difference had caused any human barriers or segregation, the broad story would have been varied scarcely more than in footnotes. The problem of India was essentially one of imperialism, nationalism and internal disunity, not of race or colour.

In the end, the divisions of India, with the British obligations arising from them, reduced themselves to two major parameters of the equation to be solved in the transfer of power: the Muslim minority (and its lesser corollary, the Sikh-Hindu minority in the Punjab) and the Princely States. Before embarking on the later story it is therefore desirable to take an historical look at these two problems.

2

The Muslims

The transfer of power in India from British hands to the two successor States was the end of a story the preface of which was the annexation of the Punjab by Mahmoud of Ghazni in A.D. 1018, and which began in earnest with the defeat of Prithviraj by Mahommed Ghori in 1192, followed by the conquest of the Ganges Valley and Bengal. The tale that ended in 1947 can be said to have had its beginning eight or nine centuries earlier, not because thereafter a large part of India was ruled by alien empires, for the later Muslim conquerors became absorbed by the land they ruled, and Akbar the Great was as much an Indian as Pandit Nehru; but because the last days of the British raj were the climax of a double struggle, at the same time for national independence by Indians generally and for self-assertion by the Indian Muslims, descendants of the Turk, Afghan and Persian invaders or of the native peoples whom the conquerors converted to Islam. Had it not been for Muslim nationalism the story would have been quite different, and far simpler. The struggle was three-sided, and the creation of Pakistan was its most extraordinary result. That India should become independent had been long striven for by Indians as a goal and long conceded as a principle by British statesmen. Even the question 'When?' could have been answered within narrow limits years before the event. It was the question 'How?' that could not be answered, basically because of the problem of the Muslims, and it was over this question that the leaders of both Britain and India strove so intensely and for so long.

That a nation should be split in twain by a religious conflict was not new in the contemporary world. But the conflict of Hindu and Muslim had a far deeper quality than that of, say, Catholic and Protestant in Ireland. Hinduism is much more than a religion as we in the West know religion—as a matter of transcendental belief, circumscribed dogma and occasional observance; it is a way of life, pervading every corner of daily existence, social relations and personal thought. Marriage in Hindu society, for instance, is not merely sanctified by a religious rite, it is regulated by a complex of social rules inextricably entangled with religious belief. Religion prescribes attitudes towards certain animals, certain objects, certain occupations. It provides its own fabric of personal law. The caste system is integral to Hinduism. No Hindu but has his caste, low or high, which is part of him from birth to grave, to which he succeeds without choice and from which he cannot escape without exchanging his religion for another; and his caste regulates his religious observance, his social relationship, and in a general way his occupation and livelihood. Indian Mohammedanism also had some of the character of the religious society in which it had been embedded. It, too, was a way of life, more rigid than Hinduism in some ways, such as fasting and respect for holy writ, less rigid in others—concerning caste, for instance, which though faintly reflected in certain practices among some Indian Muslims is in principle alien and heretical to Islam. Mohammedanism also had its own system of personal law, and its own code of conduct from birth to burial. It, too, prescribed certain attitudes towards ordinary creatures and events, besides enjoining observances, practices and taboos, some of which were repugnant to Hindu neighbours, as Hindu customs were to Muslims.

So here were two great groups of people, living together in one country, often in the same villages, sharing the same fortunes, under the same government, ethnically not distinct (for most Indian Muslims sprang from the same racial stocks as their Hindu neighbours), yet separated not only by religious creed and ritual but by whole modes of life and attitudes of mind, each a permanent hereditary group, without intermarriage (save most exceptionally at the highest and lowest social extremes) or mutual absorption.

Of course there were other religious minorities—Sikhs (embracing a reformed religion of Hindu ancestry with its own unique rules of daily conduct), Christians, Parsees and many sects of the Hindu family. These, too, are part of the story. But none of them presented, in India as a whole, problems comparable with the problem of the Muslim minority. (The Sikh-Muslim conflict was in a sense the inverse of the Muslim-Hindu conflict, the same object seen in a diminishing mirror, without, however, its nation-wide spread, its long political intensity or its dramatic constitutional climax.) These other minorities were not only much smaller in numbers but also—again, bar the Sikhs of the Punjab—far more scattered. The Muslims, moreover, could nourish their communal pride and resistance on the consciousness of being part of a great religious brotherhood spanning the world, though it is true that in our present times this Islamic internationalism played but a small part in the outlook of the mass of Indian Muslims, or in the activating political concepts of their leaders, save on certain occasions like the Khilafat movement (of protest against the impending overthrow of the Ottoman Caliphate) after the First World War. It was essentially the size of the Muslim community and its majority status in the provinces of the north-west and north-east, taken with its historical memories of lordship over a vast Indian empire, that gave it such special importance in the Indian constitutional problem. Of that past autocratic supremacy certain Princely States, like Hyderabad, with Muslim rulers over Hindu majorities, were a living residue and reminder.

There was a strain in Indian Muslim attitudes which gave the communal division a peculiar political importance and objective (using 'political' in the largest sense). From its earliest days Islam had been a conquering and proselytising faith. Its tradition in India was one of conquest and empire. The tides and currents of invasion and warfare had flowed to and fro, and great Hindu kingdoms had risen in the wake of periodic Muslim retreats, up to the time of the Mahratta empire, which was finally broken by the British; but for many hundreds of years no Hindu raj had lorded it over Muslims either in all-India or in the great basins of the Indus and the Ganges. When the British first became territorial sovereigns in India, though the Mogul Empire was in decay, there were Muslim monarchies or satrapies not only in all that is now Pakistan but also in present Uttar Pradesh, Bihar, Hyderabad, West Bengal and Mysore and much of Madhya Pradesh and Madras State; and a Muslim titular suzerain reigned in Delhi. In their folk-memory the Muslims of India had been rulers, not subjects. A few men living in 1947 could as infants have known the last Mogul court. For Muslims, to roll back history by removing the European invader could not mean a restoration of Hindu rule but rather a revival of their own.

Yet the distinctness, self-consciousness and historical yearnings of the Muslim community did not necessarily predetermine its political status or power in the years with which this book is concerned, let alone the eventual birth of a new nation state. Those were the outcome of political events in which many people and interests took part: the Muslim leaders, the politicians of other parties and communities, the British Government and its agents high and low in India. If there is a sense of mounting inevitability in the progress of Indian constitutional history as the moment of independence and partition approaches, it would be quite wrong to conclude that things must have been as they were, no matter what decisions had been taken, or by whom, in the preceding decades, or that the figures who appear on the stage from act to act of the final drama—Linlithgow and Wavell, Mountbatten and Cripps, Gandhi and Jinnah, Sikander Hyat Khan and Jawaharlal Nehru, and all the others—were mere puppets moved by historical forces which they had no power to deflect. It is the historian's task to discern which were the fateful decisions that determined the course of history, who took them and why.

Especially is it requisite to do so in regard to the emergence of the Muslim League as the third side of the triangular conflict which was resolved only by the partition of India. The other two major parties to the conflict—the British Government, and the Indian National Congress as representative of the political and communal majority—were already striding the scene when the present story begins, with their fundamental policies already defined and plain, subject to such modification (especially on the British side) as the passage of time and external events like the Second World War might impose. Whereas the position that the Muslim League under Mahomed Ali Jinnah held in 1947, its ability and even its desire to enforce a carving of historic India into two nations, would have seemed to most people in 1937 a fantastic dream.

The roots of this strange development, however, lie much further back.

After the Sepoy Mutiny of 1857 the Muslims were not looked on favourably by the British in India, for they were regarded as having been the mainspring of the rebellion. Moreover, among the Indian educated and commercial classes, who were coming to play an increasing part in the public life of the country, in association with the British, Muslims were few in proportion to their place in the population. In the old India their best elements had been characteristically soldiers and administrators, occupations for which the opportunities were greatly diminished by the supremacy of the British, their emasculation of the States and their later suspicion of the Muslims. For reasons of Indian social and regional history, in addition, the frustrated Muslim community fell into neglect of higher education, now deliberately based on English, whereas the traditional language of the Muslim *literati* and of the Mogul court had been Persian. Consequently, when the Indian Councils Act of 1892, by enlarging the legislative councils set up by Lord Canning in 1861, and including in them nominees of such bodies as municipal and district boards, chambers of commerce and universities, gave, in Lord Dufferin's words, 'a still wider share in the administration of public affairs to such Indian gentlemen as by their influence, their acquirements, and the confidence they inspire in their fellow-countrymen are marked out as fitted to assist with their counsels the responsible rulers of the country', relatively few of such Indian gentlemen turned out to be Mussulmans. Aware of the risk that one class or community might, by virtue of its superior numbers, wealth or education, come to dominate India's nascent political life and the counsels of government, successive Viceroys supported the policy of separate communal or class representation.

It should be emphasised, however, that in this period there was no question of transferring executive or legislative power to Indian hands, or of establishing representative government in India. It was for the British rulers, who kept the ultimate authority firmly in their own control, to choose their Indian advisers and subordinates, whether by nomination or group representation or otherwise. No question of the political domination of one Indian community by another could arise until some effective political authority was granted to Indians, or at least the prospect of such a grant became substantial. The greater the authority to be transferred, the more real the question became, though it would always retain a relative character so long as the transfer, in any theatre of affairs, was still subject to the presence of an ultimate arbiter, the British raj. As a final transfer of power, even over a part of the political domain, loomed nearer, so the question must take on its acute and decisive form. That is the background to half a century of Indian political life.

A fateful stage was reached with the Minto-Morley reforms of 1909. The rights of the central and provincial legislative councils were enlarged, including the right to discuss the budget; and although small official majorities were retained (save in Bengal, where the non-official European members were counted on to support the official bloc) the council memberships were substantially enlarged and the principle of election of the unofficial members was conceded. Separate electorates and reserved seats were granted to the Muslims.

Behind these developments of British policy lay the growing political awareness and ambition of the educated classes in India. The Indian National Congress had been formed in 1885; although the moderate wing had asserted their control after a struggle early in the twentieth century, its declared object was responsible self-government for India, and it included men who demanded direct action to assert this claim. Many Muslim leaders were alarmed by these developments. Though the Congress was non-communal, its leadership—men like Gokhale, Surendranath Banerjea and Tilak, of both the moderate and extreme wings—was predominantly Hindu. Government by territorial election would, it was felt, give the Muslims representation weaker than their relative numbers and importance prescribed. A deputation led by the Aga Khan waited upon the Viceroy, Lord Minto, to express these views, and to press the Muslims' claim to favour, through separate electorates and otherwise, on the ground of their contribution to the defence of the empire and their traditions of past political greatness.[1] The Viceroy expressed himself entirely in accord. 'I am as firmly convinced,' he said, 'as I believe you to be, that any electoral representation in India would be doomed to mischievous failure which aimed at granting personal enfranchisement, regardless of the beliefs and traditions of the communities composing the population of this continent.'

So, for good or ill, the die was cast. Separate electorates re-

[1] The occasion gave rise to one of the undying myths of Indian politics. In her diary, which was later published, Lady Minto described the impressive delegation, the Princes with jewelled turbans, and exclaimed: 'Quite a Command Performance!' To an English reader, the allusion was to the presence of everybody who was somebody, in their finest garments and regalia, as at a Royal Command Performance at the opera; but to Indians unfamiliar with English social custom and idiom the phrase was taken to imply that the delegation was performing by command—a set of puppets summoned and animated to justify a policy already determined in the Government's own interest. This myth became part of the inevitable stock-in-trade of Indian opponents of communal representation.

mained an integral part of the constitution of India right up to the transfer of power. Most Hindu political leaders and writers, and many Muslims who were nationalists first and foremost, have blamed the system of communal electorates for perpetuating and exacerbating inter-community conflict in the political field, and preventing the growth of a national spirit and of national parties characterised by social or economic beliefs rather than religion. They have charged the British with riveting upon India this system, with all its consequences up to partition, in pursuit of the principle of 'divide and rule'.

There is admissibly some force in these criticisms. If electors vote as members of a minority community they will not only be bound to elect fellow communalists, but will be persuaded to vote for 'good' fellow communalists, those who will put the interests of their community first and assert its differences from other communities and its interests in contrast to theirs. This does not always happen but it is likely to happen, as Indian experience showed. And undoubtedly ulterior motives reinforced the honest belief of British Viceroys and Secretaries of State that by giving the minorities, especially the Muslims, separate electorates they were doing justice and assuring fair play in the conditions of India. At the time of the Minto-Morley reforms, and later up to the end, the Muslims were regarded and from time to time employed as a counterpoise to the Hindu majority, and the Muslims' resistance to majority rule as a counterpoise to the swelling demand for democratic self-government. Lady Minto, whose opinions probably reflected her husband's, described his reply to the Muslim delegation as 'nothing less than the pulling back of sixty-two millions of people from joining the ranks of the seditious opposition'.

Nevertheless, the system of communal electorates, and the policies of successive Governments, have to be judged, not by abstract theory, nor by motives which were not necessarily evil because they distorted formal Indian democracy, for that begs the whole question whether untrammelled Indian democracy was then a good objective in itself. They have to be judged in terms of the actual facts at the time at which they were applied. The position of the Muslim minority being as it was, and the relationships of the chief communities being as they were, to establish separate electorates appeared as necessary as it was logical, if the pattern of Indian life was to be truly represented in the counsels of government, and justice was to be done to the underdog in the tangle of class and caste and religion in India. It is not possible to divide and rule unless the ruled are ready to be divided. The British may have used the Hindu-Muslim rivalry for their own advantage, but they did not invent it. They did not write the annals of India's history, nor prescribe the conflicting customs of her communities, nor foment the murderous riots that periodically flared between Hindus and Muslims in her villages and cities. They were realists, and if they did use India's divisions for their advantages, the divisions themselves were already real.

Nor were separate electorates regarded by all nationalists as hostile to the movement for *swaraj* or home rule for India. Mahomed Ali Jinnah, who was destined to become the un-challenged leader of the Muslims of British India, and who plays a more decisive role than any other man in the story to be told in this book, made his first excursion into politics as private secretary to the Hindu veteran Dadabhai Naoriji at the 1906 session of the Indian National Congress in Calcutta. He became the devoted disciple of another great Hindu and Congress leader, Gopal Krishna Gokhale, with whom he travelled to England in 1913. He identified himself with the Congress, and for long held back from the Muslim League, because its purpose was too sectarian. When he formally joined it, in 1913, he required his two sponsors 'to make a solemn preliminary covenant that loyalty to the Muslim League and the Muslim interest would in no way and no time imply even the shadow of disloyalty to the larger national cause, to which his life was dedicated'.[1] It was this unswerving nationalist who said about separate electorates, in a speech at Ahmedabad in October 1916:

> As far as I understand the demand for separate electorates is not a matter of policy but a matter of necessity to the Muslims, who require to be roused from the coma and torpor into which they have fallen for so long. I would therefore appeal to my Hindu brethren that in the present state of position they should try to win the confidence and trust of the Muslims, who are, after all, in the minority in the country. If they are determined to have separate electorates, no resistance should be shown to their demands.

[1] Mrs. Sarojini Naidu: *Mohamed Ali Jinnah: An Ambassador of Unity.*

Two months later he played a leading part, as president of the Muslim League and at the same time a prominent member of the Congress, in negotiating the so-called Lucknow Pact, which was intended as the basis of understanding between the two bodies on which their common effort for all-Indian self-government could be securely founded. He himself had engineered the simultaneous meeting of the two bodies at Lucknow to further their unity in a common cause. The Lucknow Pact provided for the representation of the Muslims through separate electorates, in proportions which gave them 'weightage' beyond their numbers in provinces in which they were a minority and in the imperial legislative council, where they were to have one-third of the seats.

That separate electorates were an unnecessary creation of the British or inimical to Indian self-government is therefore questionable. To what extent their imposition was the cause, or their retention the consequence, of Hindu-Muslim political conflict in the years of struggle for independence is a matter incapable of proof. The fact is that they were an integral part of the Indian constitution from 1909 onwards, that in the Lucknow Pact they were freely accepted by the Congress in the interest of Indian nationalist unity, and that to have abandoned them at any time up to the partition of the country would have been to court an almost universal outcry and insurrection from the Muslims of India.

But long before the transfer of power such mechanistic devices for mitigating majority rule had ceased to satisfy Muslim militancy. Communally self-conscious for long past, as the reality of independence approached the Muslims found a new and revolutionary ambition, the story of which belongs to a later chapter.

The Sikhs of the Punjab

Neither as individuals nor as a community had the Sikhs played any noteworthy part in Indian national politics before 1947. In the Punjab, however, where the great majority of them lived, and where they formed 14 per cent of the population, they held a position comparable in importance for a settlement to that of the Muslims in all India.

The Sikh faith is by religious origin a purified and protestant development of Hinduism, rejecting idolatry, caste and Brahminical dominance, though remnants of caste and untouchability persisted in the community to the present time. To the Hindus, Sikhs were and are a kind of Hindu, however separate, casteless and dissenting. On the other hand, as believers in a revealed religion of one God, as foes of caste and the worship of idols, who had had to fight for their religious creed against the pervading pantheism of Hindu India, it might be thought they had much in common with the followers of Mahomet. However, as with the Muslims themselves in their reaction to the Hindu raj, it was not the niceties of religious dogma but the call of historical memories that stirred the Sikhs, as the prospect of democratic rule and the division of India drew nearer.

The fifth of the founding Gurus of the faith paid the penalty for supporting an unsuccessful revolt against the Mogul Emperor Jehangir, and was tortured to death in 1606, after enjoining his heir to maintain his authority by arms, and thereafter the Sikhs were almost constantly at war with the Mogul power or other Muslim rulers. The ninth Guru was executed by the zealot Aurangzeb in 1675 for refusing to accept Islam, and the tenth and last had his two sons cruelly put to death by the Governor of Sirhind. In the eighteenth century the Sikhs formed a shapeless military theocracy, which by 1767 was master of the whole of the Punjab from the Jumna to the Indus. Their time of greatest power followed when the soldier Ranjit Singh suppressed the Sikh confederacy in 1808, established an hereditary monarchy, and brought Kashmir, Peshawar and some of the hill states into his Empire. Though outwardly tolerant of Islam, the Sikh rulers relentlessly suppressed their Muslim subjects, and the name of Hari Singh, who took the Sikh dominion to the Khyber Pass, became and remains a byword for violence and tyranny throughout the Muslims of the north-west. The Sikh hegemony of the Punjab was finally overthrown not by the Muslims but by the British in the 1840s, and it was in the service of the new rulers of India that the Sikhs last warred against the Muslims, at the siege of Delhi in 1857–8.

It is therefore not surprising that enmity between the two communities should have been reawakened as the time for British withdrawal loomed nearer. Less than a hundred years had passed since they had fought in battle, and their previous history for two

and a half centuries had been one of bitter and bloody war, first
for communal survival and then for the mastery of the Punjab.

During a period of about 70 years after the Mutiny, the Sikhs
had lost much of their old militancy. Their Gurdwaras (temples)
were under no common authority and were often not unlike Hindu
shrines. Strict Sikhism was kept alive and vigorous largely by the
Sikh element in the Indian Army. Civilian Sikhs observed the
rules laid down by the Tenth Guru, of which the most conspicuous were the long hair and beards, but the prescribed sword
or *kirpan* was usually a token, a charm worn on a watch-chain.
There were signs that the Sikhs were slowly being reabsorbed
into Hinduism. Sikhs and Hindus of the same castes could marry,
and some families had both Sikh and non-Sikh members.

Until the coming into force of the Government of India Act,
1919—the Montagu-Chelmsford Reforms—the Punjab, like the
rest of British India, was administered by British officials, leaving
very little scope for legitimate political activity. The enlarged
opportunities thereafter were, however, taken seriously by all three
communities. The Sikhs concentrated on a plan which was
ostensibly religious, but had important political consequences.
Between 1919 and 1926 they took advantage of a largely spontaneous revivalist movement to campaign for the 'liberation' of the
Gurdwaras. There were emotional meetings; visions were seen
of the Tenth Guru's hawk and of his war-horse; and there were
mass conversions and baptisms. The organisers, in a quasi-
military emulation of Congress methods, developed a system of
successive daily demonstrations directed against a stated objective.
The demonstrations were not always non-violent. A riot at
Nankana Sahib, a famous Sikh shrine, led to further encounters,
the most important being the Guruka Bagh agitation of 1921–2
in Amritsar district. In 1925 the Sikhs secured control of the
Gurdwaras and the right to wear full-sized swords without
licences. The Gurdwaras Act set up democratically elected
Committees to administer the Gurdwaras, the Central Committee
being thus a kind of representative Sikh Assembly. The Sikhs
had established themselves much more firmly as a distinct community, with access to substantial religious funds.

Politically, Sikhs were an essential element in Mr. Fazl-i-
Husain's Unionist Party, the all-community governing group. But
those who took part in ordinary politics tended to be 'safe' men

with less power in the community than those who belonged to the
Central Committee. On the approach of the transfer of power the
Sikhs who mattered were not those in ordinary politics, but the
men with influence in and through the Gurdwaras. They had
neither the training nor the experience to cope with the problems
of partition. Unversed in national politics, divided in their
attitude towards the British—the soldiers and the moderates
leaning on British authority, the militants hostile and suspicious—
the Sikhs reverted to a historical posture of communal defence
and defiance. They began to recoil from the hardening prospect
of Muslim raj in the north-west even as the Muslims recoiled
from the hardening prospect of Hindu raj over the whole of
India, and for the same basic reason of hate-laden folk-
memory, sharpened and prolonged by religious and cultural
distinction.

The reaction was peculiarly dangerous, for a number of reasons.
The Sikhs of the Punjab, especially of the central area of the
province, were mostly tough country people, hard and fearless, and
bloodthirsty when roused. They formed a disproportionately
large element in the Indian Armed Forces and in the police of
many areas beyond their home province. Adaptable and vigorous,
they had spread all over northern India as cultivators, craftsmen,
mechanics and drivers, so that there was hardly a place of any
size, from Calcutta to a country town, without a colony of Sikhs
to be victims or instruments of communal violence. Though
possessing a religious solidarity unrivalled by any other community, a strong martial tradition, and a discipline under leadership
which rendered them, even in small numbers, much more formid-
able than their neighbours, they were divided into factions which
made it extremely difficult for either central or provincial Governments to deal with them as a community, or to be sure that an
understanding reached with an acknowledged Sikh spokesman
would be honoured by his people.

Time and again, in the present story, the powers-that-were
in the central governance of India complained of the political
incompetence of the Sikhs. Outside the Punjab there were no Sikhs
in high places in the civil administration where strong influence on
policy could have been exerted. They were essentially a provincial
community: peasants, artisans, soldiers and traders. Their
aristocracy was the ruling houses of the Sikh States, who could and

did support them in violence but gave them little or no constructive leadership in a crisis. Feeling themselves in danger, and seeing
the end of British authority nigh, they reacted with a solidarity
and temper none the less dangerous for lacking clear political
purpose.

3

The problem of the States

The Indian States presented a unique problem, and a highly complex one, in the progress to independence. They varied enormously, from principalities the size of France to petty estates unworthy to be ranked as political entities yet neither part of British India nor subordinate to any other government than the Crown itself. Their citizens were not British subjects, but, in international status, 'British protected persons'. Some of the States were ancient monarchies whose history went many centuries back beyond the advent of European power; some had been former feudatories or satrapies of the Mogul Empire which had asserted their independence of the Delhi throne; others were fragments from the break-up of Mogul dominion after the death of Aurangzeb in 1707, or of the more limited empires of the Mahrattas, the Sikhs, or the Muslim overlords of the Deccan and the south; a few were deliberate creations of the British. Their existence alongside the provinces of British India was the fruit of two centuries of history with all its accidents and variety, in a continent as large as Europe and even more divided by language, religion and dynastic ambition.

Four main waves of British policy went to form the speckled and incoherent pattern of princely India as it was in the twentieth century. The first was the early period of East India Company rule, when trade was the primary motive, complicated by war with France and by the need to repel local threats and safeguard the hinterland of the main trading ports. Though Clive and Warren Hastings increased the area under Company rule, or subservient to it, British power did not pretend to any general suzerainty, nor aim to extend its alliances with the indigenous monarchies beyond its immediate territorial or military needs.

The second wave began in 1798, when the Marquess of Wellesley became Governor-General, enjoying the supreme powers given him by Pitt's India Act of 1784. Disregarding his instructions from London, Wellesley set out to make Britain the paramount power throughout India, as the only solution to the problem of its political chaos and internecine warfare. A principal instrument of this policy was the system of subsidiary alliances with the Indian rulers, whereby, in return for guaranteed protection, a State concluding such an alliance undertook neither to make war nor to negotiate with any other State without the Company's knowledge and consent, and accepted in its capital a British Resident representing the Governor-General's authority. Among the greater States brought under subsidiary alliance within the seven years of Wellesley's rule were Baroda in the west, Mysore and Travancore in the south, and Gwalior and Hyderabad in the Deccan. Later Governors-General, especially the Marquess of Hastings, continued this policy, until by the time Hastings departed in 1823 every State in India outside the Punjab and Sind was under the Company's control, and the fiction of Mogul suzerainty was no longer paid even official lip-service.

The policy was given a further twist by Governors-General after the Charter Act of 1833, which abolished the Company's trading function and ratified its function as government of India, above all by the well-meaning but over-ambitious Lord Dalhousie; in administrative and social reform one of the greatest, in understanding of others' feelings or institutions one of the most deficient of British Viceroys, a great Victorian, energetic, progressive and calamitous. The twist, characteristic of this third phase, was to take advantage of the weakness of the Indian Rulers to conquer fresh territory and to annex dependent states on the excuse of maladministration or want of natural heirs (the Doctrine of Lapse). This process culminated in the annexation of the Muslim kingdom of Oudh, a sickening blow to Muslim pride throughout India and one of the chief proximate causes of the war known in Britain as the Indian Mutiny (or even the Mutiny in the Bengal Army)[1] and in India as the Great Revolt. The Mutiny brought to an end the third phase of British policy towards the States and ushered in the fourth.

Not only had annexation had its nemesis in the desperate reaction of all the threatened forces of the old India,[2] but the earlier

---

[1] See e.g. *The Cambridge Shorter History of India*, p. 741.
[2] 'All the leaders of the rebellion came from among the great dispossessed: but all were united in the object they had in view: the expulsion of the British and the recovery of national independence.' 'The dispossessed

policy of subsidiary alliance had proved itself triumphantly. Only the passive acquiescence and in some cases active aid of Princely States from the Punjab to Hyderabad saved the British raj from irretrievable disaster in 1857. This was never forgotten in either country, and was a contributory factor in subsequent attitudes for ninety years. Queen Victoria's proclamation of 1858 declared:

> We desire no extension of our present territorial possessions, and while we will permit no aggression upon our dominions or our rights to be attempted with impunity, we shall sanction no encroachment on those of others. We shall respect the rights, dignity and honour of Native Princes as our own; and we desire that they as well as our own subjects should enjoy that prosperity and that social advancement which can only be secured by internal peace and good government.

The syntax may be imperfect, but the purport is clear, and thenceforward British policy towards the States was governed by two main principles: a territorial and constitutional standstill, and an intent to bring the States along with British India in social and economic advance, subject to the Ruler's rights of internal autonomy.

The first of those principles froze the political map of India (bar the most marginal changes) in the pattern of 1858, when the fragmentation consequent upon the collapse of the Mogul Empire and the subjugation of its successor powers by the British (invaluably aided by their own jealousies and conflicts) had had little or no time to turn to a new consolidation through the survival of the fittest; it also decreed that the States were to have no dealings with each other on any political matter, so that even the processes of administrative or dynastic merger, which might have rationalised the position a little in adjacent or related States, were barred.

classes still had great prestige with the masses. The Muslims of upper India felt that from a ruling class they had in one generation become a dispossessed and uninfluential population. . . . The Marathas in North India had also not contemplated this transfer of power with equanimity. . . . It was the annexation of Satara, Nagpur and Jhansi'—all grasped by Dalhousie on dynastic pretext—'that they felt as irretrievable blows to their prestige.' K. M. Panikkar, *A Survey of Indian History* (Bombay), 1947, pp. 253–4.

The Government of India in some cases grouped minor States in a region for its own administrative purposes, but their individual sovereignty, such as it was, remained intact. Both the guarantee of the Ruler's right to his throne and internal autonomy, and the enforced isolation of the States, handicapped the carrying out of the second principle, though a fortuitous leverage was sometimes obtained through the temporary assumption of government by the Raj when the Ruler left a minor heir or was deposed, pending a due succession, on account of gross misrule or personal obliquity. Several of the States, indeed, with adequate resources and enlightened Rulers or outstanding Dewans, advanced as far in terms of economic progress and of education and public services as their British Indian neighbours; but others, including large as well as small States, remained socially and economically backward, sometimes with scandalous contrasts between the luxury of the Ruler and the poverty of the subjects; and even at its best the achievement of progress was the fruit of benevolent paternalism rather than popular self-government.

It is not surprising, therefore, that even during the long period of stability between 1858 and 1916 there should develop tensions between the States and the Government of India. British Indian administrators chafed at the limitations on reform and good organisation set by the existence of States large and small whose frontiers bore no relation to natural obstacles or linguistic or other divisions, and which were sometimes embedded, or partly so, in British Indian provinces. Indeed the development of communications, including the railways, trunk roads, posts and telegraphs, had often made nonsense of political frontiers, and the Rulers could not and did not withhold consent to bringing central administration into their States in such respects. Currency and international Customs were other central functions which inevitably overlapped the States. On the other hand the States were aware of a growing presumption—based partly on such changes, but more on the habitual arrogance of superior power—that the supreme authority in their internal as well as external affairs rested with the Crown operating through the provincial and central Government of India, and that their treaty rights and status were essentially conditional and frequently obsolete. As Mr. Montagu and Lord Chelmsford said in their joint report on Indian constitutional reforms in 1918,

Practice has been based on the theory that treaties must be read as a whole, and that they must be interpreted in the light of the relations established between the parties not only at the time when a particular treaty was made, but subsequently. The result is that there has grown up around the treaties a body of case law. . . . The Princes, viewing the application of this case law to their individual relations with the Government, are uneasy as to its ultimate effect. They fear that usage and precedent may be exercising a levelling and corroding influence upon the treaty rights of individual States.[1]

The Montagu-Chelmsford report recommended that a Council of Princes be formed as a permanent consultative body, meeting ordinarily once a year under the presidency of the Viceroy, and that the Council in turn appoint a Standing Committee, to which the Viceroy or the Political Department (which had been set up to conduct the States business of the Government of India directly under the Governor-General, with its own administrative corps, the Indian Political Service) could refer any particular question on which they needed composite advice from the Princes' point of view. These recommendations flowered in the creation, by Royal Proclamation, of the Chamber of Princes, including 108 rulers in their own right and 12 representatives of a further 127 lesser States, together with its Standing Committee.

Mr. Montagu's and Lord Chelmsford's views on the development of relations with the Princes were, of course, coloured by their purpose of advancing responsible self-government in British India. They had proposed a division of powers between provinces, which were to be governed under a system of partial devolution of power known as dyarchy, and the Centre, where British authority was to remain unqualified. This plan they regarded as transitional, with further steps to responsible government following in due course. They saw that the States must somehow be fitted into this picture of the future: yet, bearing very much in mind the support which the Princes had given the King-Emperor in the war,[2] as

[1] Cd. 9109 (1918), para. 304.
[2] The debt was symbolically acknowledged in the summoning of the Maharajah of Bikaner to the Imperial War Cabinet in 1918: the absence, indeed the highest improbability, of such a gesture in the Second World War was a sign of how much attitudes towards the States had changed in the intervening years.

well as the need for preserving elements of stability in a politically turbulent India, they did not want to frighten them with anticipations of democracy. 'We need not conceal our conviction,' they wrote, 'that the processes at work in British India cannot leave the States untouched and must in time affect even those whose ideas and institutions are of the most conservative and feudal character. But in that respect there can be no intention or desire to accelerate growth by artificial means.' They expected that British India would eventually become a federation of self-governing provinces, with the Centre confined to matters of common concern to them all (and incidentally to the States too) such as defence and communications.

> The gradual concentration of the Government of India upon such matters will therefore make it easier for the States, while retaining the autonomy which they cherish in internal matters, to enter into closer association with the central Government if they wish to do so. But . . . the last thing we desire is to attempt to force the pace.[1]

The recommendations they made to assist 'the natural developments of the future' included joint sessions of the Council (or Chamber) of Princes and the Council of State—which were never in fact organised—and the concentration in the Political Department of those relations with the States which had hitherto been conducted by the provinces. The latter course, however valuable in simplifying the long-term problem of relating the States to a progressively self-governing British India, for the time being increased their isolation from the stream of democratic and social advance under dyarchy; and it tended to make them the jealously guarded protégés of a single central department, itself separate from the Governor-General in Council, and to make their preservation its vested interest.

The report also recommended a review of the whole condition of relations between the States and Government, 'not necessarily with a view to any change of policy but in order to simplify, standardise and codify existing practice for the future'. No such thorough-going enquiry was in fact undertaken until nearly a decade later, when a committee of three headed by Sir Harcourt Butler was appointed at the time of the Simon Commission to

[1] op. cit., para. 300.

inquire into the relationship between the States and the paramount power. The deliberations of the Butler Committee embraced a great debate, conducted largely in writing or by examination *in camera*, on the fundamental status of the Indian States—as to whether they were inherently subordinate, their treaties, engagements and *sanads* being in the nature of self-denying ordinances of the supreme power, or were inherently sovereign, their sovereignty being limited only by such treaties or Acts, construed as between equals according to the principles of international law, which would always interpret narrowly any voluntary restriction of sovereignty. Champions of the latter view (like Sir Leslie Scott, K.C., who was engaged to argue the case for most of the Rulers before the Committee) further deduced that such bilateral treaty relations between Crown and States implied mutual obligations, including 'the duties which lie upon the Crown to ensure the external and internal security of the States and to keep available whatever armed forces may be necessary for these purposes'.

This fascinating controversy,[1] which divided lawyers, civil administrators, historians and lay publicists, had a considerable bearing on the claims of the Princes and the policy of the British Government towards them when the time came to plan a transfer of power in British India in 1946 and 1947. The Butler Committee did not determine it, for their rejection of the Princes' thesis on historical status was balanced by their acceptance of a fundamental point for the Rulers in relation to the future. They held that the relationship of the paramount power with the States was not merely contractual but a living, growing relationship shaped by changing circumstances and policy. They declined to lay down any definition of paramountcy, but in a famous sentence asserted that

> paramountcy must remain paramount; it must fulfil its obligations, defining or adapting itself according to the shifting necessities of the time and the progressive development of the States.

On another aspect of the controversy, however, namely, Sir Leslie Scott's argument that 'the paramount power is the British Crown and no one else', and that consequently 'the agency and machinery used by the Crown for carrying out its obligations must not be of such a character as to make it politically impracticable for the

[1] See, e.g., Sirdar D. K. Sen, *The Indian States*, Sweet and Maxwell, 1930.

Crown to carry out its obligations in a satisfactory manner', the Committee found in effect for the Princes. They proposed that the Viceroy, not the Governor-General in Council, should be the agent of the Crown in all dealings with the States; and it was following this recommendation that the Government of India Act of 1935 divided the powers and titles of the Viceroy into those of Governor-General and those of 'His Majesty's Representative for the exercise of the functions of the Crown in its relations with Indian States',[1] commonly known as the Crown Representative. By explicitly providing that one person could fill both offices the Act plainly implied that they might be held by different proconsuls, an option permitting certain forms of solution for the States problem in 1946–7 which were never in fact pursued. The Butler Committee went further:

> If any government in the nature of a Dominion Government should be constituted in British India, such a government would clearly be a new government resting on a new and written constitution. . . . We feel bound . . . to record our strong opinion that, in view of the fact of the historical nature of the relationship between the paramount power and the princes, the latter should not be transferred without their agreement to a relationship with a new government in British India responsible to an Indian legislature.

This proposition, obvious and unexceptionable as it might seem, now as then, to most British eyes, excited deep offence among the politically conscious in British India. According to that faithful servant of his country and of the Government in India both before and after the transfer of power, Mr. V. P. Menon, it 'laid the foundation of a policy whereby, in later years, a wedge was to be driven effectively between the States and British India'.[2]

The Nehru Committee, under the chairmanship of Pandit Motilal Nehru, father of Jawaharlal, appointed by the All-Parties Conference in 1928 to frame a Dominion constitution for India, denounced what they described as 'an attempt to convert the Indian States into an Indian Ulster by pressing constitutional theories into service'. Its report argued that the Government of a Dominion of India 'will be as much the King's Government as the

[1] Part I, Sections 2 and 3.
[2] *The Integration of the Indian States*, p. 24.

present Government of India is, and that there is no constitutional objection to the Dominion Government of India stepping into the shoes of the present Government of India'. (This argument might not have seemed so convincing, even to its authors, a few years later, when Dominion Status had come to include, by general admission, the right to secede from the Crown, but by that time independence, not Dominion Status, had become the avowed goal of the Congress.) The Nehru Committee protested, in effect, that the States were being given a veto on India's aspiration to achieve independence within the Commonwealth. Five years earlier, it is true, Pandit Motilal Nehru himself, in reply to a challenge as to whether the Dominion Status demanded by the Swarajists was to be extended to the Indian States as well, had declared that if the States wanted to come in their representatives would be welcome, otherwise not; and this offer to the States to join a hypothetical federation was repeated in the Nehru Report, with the proviso 'that it would necessitate, perhaps in varying degrees, a modification of the system of government and administration prevailing within their territories'. But the nub of the matter was the claim that paramountcy should be transferred from the Crown advised in Britain to the Indian Dominion. The Report's draft constitution provided that

> The Commonwealth (i.e. of India) shall exercise the same rights in relation to, and discharge the same obligations towards, the Indian States, arising out of treaties or otherwise, as the Government of India has hitherto discharged.

Remembering what those rights were often claimed to be by interventionist Viceroys or Political Department apologists, it is small wonder that the Princes viewed that demand with the utmost apprehension.

When the heat of the struggle for independence had cooled, and in the calm collected language of an official publication, the independent Government of India challenged the outwardly banal and obvious opening paragraph of the Butler report:

> Politically there are . . . two Indias. . . . The problem of statesmanship is to hold the two together.

Were there really two Indias, it asked. Geographically, India was one and indivisible; communications, common economic interests, and close ties of cultural affinity, linked States and provinces. Only two things separated the Indian States from the rest of India, the historical factor that the States had not been annexed by the British, and the political factor that the States maintained the traditional monarchical form of government.

Did these factors, however, really segregate the States from the Provinces and create an impassable political barrier between them? The freedom of the Indian States from foreign subjugation was only relative; the paramount power controlled the external affairs of the States and exercised wide powers in relation to their internal matters. The whole of the country was, therefore, in varying degrees under the sway of the British Government. Besides, in the context of the demand for India's freedom the degree of control exercised by the British power ceased to have any meaning. Nor was there any reason to over-emphasize the political difference between the States and the Provinces. There was nothing incompatible between the systems of governance in the Provinces and the States provided the supremacy of the common popular interests was recognised and representative and responsible Governments were established in the States.[1]

The last proviso was of crucial political importance, and had become so at the time of the Butler Report. Although by the 1920s the Indian National Congress was a non-violent revolutionary organisation, it adhered in principle to the policy of non-intervention in the internal affairs of the States, laid down at the Nagpur Congress in 1920, and had no organisation worth anything in Princely India. Nevertheless, democratic agitation in imitation of the Congress increased in the States, for the most part clandestinely, since there were not many in which it was openly tolerated. The Indian States' Peoples Conference was formed in 1927, aiming at 'responsible government for the people of the Indian States through representative institutions under the aegis of their Rulers'. The Congress, at its 1928 session, assured the Indian States' people 'of its sympathy with and support in their legitimate and peaceful struggle' for responsible government.

It was not, however, until the thirties, and particularly until the triumph of the Congress at the 1937 elections in British India,

[1] White Paper on the Indian States (Delhi), 1948, Foreword, para. 7.

that the principle of impotent non-intervention was transmuted into the practice of active involvement. The demands of States' subjects—catching both the ideals of democracy and the methods of agitation from the example of British Indian politics—led to unrest and repression in a number of States, large and small. At the Haripura session of the Congress in 1938, Congress policy was re-defined. Acknowledging the States as integral parts of India, it called for the same political, social and economic freedom in the States as in the rest of the nation. Nevertheless, in existing conditions 'the burden of carrying on the struggle for freedom must fall on the people of the States', not on the Congress, which could not operate within their borders, though Congressmen were free to assist them in an individual capacity and the Congress itself gave them its moral support. Events and emotions, however, became too strong for this equivocal policy.[1]

Meanwhile the Round Table Conference of 1931–2, which had adumbrated a federation of British India and the States, and the Government of India Act, 1935, which had given it constitutional though provisional form, had opened a new chaper in the story of relations between the States and the paramount power. The Simon Commission had asked for its terms of reference—originally confined, in effect, to the working of constitutional reforms in British India—to be extended to include the whole country, and had cautiously recommended a tripartite conference of representatives of the Imperial Government, British India and the States to consider its report; but its approach both to Indian federation and to extension of popular responsible government at the Centre was so timid that it had no concrete proposals of any weight to make concerning relationships with the States. All it envisaged was a consultative 'Council for Greater India', representing British India and the States, to 'bring more nearly within the range of realisation other steps which are as yet too distant and too dim to be entered upon and described'. Those dim and distant steps began to seem plain and imminent less than a year later, when the India Round Table Conference met in London.

---

[1] See below, p. 57.

4

Two great personalities

1 *Mr. Gandhi and the Congress*

For thirty years before the transfer of power the history of the
Indian National Congress and the life and personality of Mahatma
Gandhi were plaited in one inseparable coil. This can be explained
only in terms of human relations, not of structural hierarchy; for
Mr. Gandhi was President of the Congress for the last time in
1924, and after 1934 he held no office whatever in it. Yet such was
his magnetic power, and such the veneration in which he was held
by his fellow leaders of the Congress, indeed throughout political
India, that he was always its supreme figure, and when he chose to
insist his word was virtually law among Congressmen. Time and
again, when massive action was to be taken, it was resigned to his
leadership, as in the non-co-operation movement of 1920, civil
disobedience in 1928, or the Quit India revolt of 1942. In 1931 the
Congress entrusted to him alone the representation of its views at
the Round Table Conference in London. Time and again, though
he was not a member of the Congress Working Committee, its
debates were settled by his opinion, for example in 1937 when the
Congress agreed to take provincial office, or in 1942 when it
rejected the Cripps Offer.

A few exceptions only proved the rule—one in particular. In
1939 the revolutionary left-wing leader Subhas Chandra Bose was
re-elected Congress President by a small majority against Mr.
Gandhi's wishes. He asserted himself through the All-India
Congress Committee and Mr. Bose was obliged to resign. Over
the whole period it was the one instance of fundamental challenge
to his view of the spirit, policies and methods of the Congress, and
the challenge failed. Though there were other instances of difference on particular issues, in not all of which his view prevailed, the
philosophy of the Congress was Mr. Gandhi's philosophy, and its
leaders were men who respected his opinion above any other. One

of the last acts of his life was to reconcile two sharply different characters, Pandit Jawaharlal Nehru and Sardar Vallabhbhai Patel, when the latter had resigned from the Indian Cabinet in a fury because of Pandit Nehru's allegedly high-handed actions: Lord Mountbatten, learning of this, and fearing a disastrous left-right split in the Government at a moment of grave external crisis, at once sent a message to Mahatma Gandhi; for he alone, as the Governor-General knew, could heal the breach, and he succeeded.

By that time, of course, the Mahatma had acquired a semi-divine aura, and to flout him had assumed the nature of a religious renunciation. But it was not only the saintly simplicity of his mode of life and attire, nor his devotion to the causes of the poor and down-trodden, that had earned him this political halo. His personality was one of remarkable power. Few Englishmen who met him were not charmed by him—by his melodious voice, his sense of humour, above all by the spirit of calm and peacefulness that hung about him. To the British, even so, he was always an enigma—as indeed he remained even to his closest Indian associates—and many of them thought him two-faced and hypocritical. They contrasted his cult of non-violence with the violent consequences that his *satyagraha* movements were bound to entail. (More than once he publicly fasted to expiate such consequences, after the milk was spilt.) They observed how often he had entered upon fasts unto death without dying. They contrasted his vast presumption of political influence with his total lack of political pragmatism. He was a man with whom they had to negotiate but with whom it was almost impossible to settle. To the administrator his philosophy seemed negative, even nihilist, and remote from reality.

But Mahatma Gandhi was an Indian, not a European, and to Indians, especially Hindus, his philosophy had a powerful natural appeal. Though India is a land of wars and warriors, there is in the mass of its people a strong spirit of quietism. Parcelled by religions and castes and languages, it yet has an overall sense of Indian-ness, of belonging together not only over vast spaces but over centuries of time. To the mass of its people, living in villages and small towns, the endless cycle of seasons and the ties of family and small community mean far more than remote, incomprehensible issues of politics and economics. Its leaders of thought have been more

often men of words than men of action. Government and war were
for the few. To such a country the Gandhian philosophy had a
pervasive appeal. The contradictions which it bore to Western
eyes did not trouble Indians. As with fasting mystics, to people
starved alike of political responsibility and economic well-being
dreams assume the power of reality, and ideals have virtues, like
the attributes of gods, irrespective of practical application or
incidental wrongdoing. Unity as a god-like ideal can be wor-
shipped amid the facts of human disunity. To Mahatma Gandhi it
had supreme validity. He loved and worked for the Untouchables
—the Scheduled Castes in the prim official phrase—but within the
Hindu family. He loved and worked for the Muslims, but within
the unity of all India in whose name he claimed to speak. His one
great stroke of political opportunism—wedding the Congress to
the Khilafat movement in 1919 when the European powers seemed
to be violating the ancient structure of the Muslim world—was a
move to weld Muslims and Hindus in a revolt against the West.
His cult of spinning was a symbol, not only of reviving village
industries, but still more of linking the townsman with the country-
man and the rich with the poor.

His central political creed was simple and was expressed in the
first article of the Congress constitution which he himself reframed
in 1921:

> The object of the Indian National Congress is the attainment of
> Purna Swaraj (complete self-rule) by all legitimate and peaceful
> means.

To this formula could adhere people of all classes and widely
different interests—poor peasants hoping for land reform or the
lightening of taxes, rich merchants and industrialists eager for
reversal of the protection the British had given to their own economic interests, middle-class men and women eager to replace the
existing rulers in their positions of power and affluence. The all-
inclusive spectrum of the Congress was a great source of strength
in its days of opposition, a source of weakness in its days of office.
To play upon unity, to minimise those policies or decisions which
might disunite, was part of the Gandhian system. Inability to
sustain Hindu-Muslim unity within one national political organisation was its greatest failure, but it was one that became obvious and
irretrievable only in the last decade of the period. Until after 1937

the Congress was so far ahead of every other political party, in organisation from top to bottom, in communication with the people, in coherent policy and national prestige, that it almost monopolised genuine political power; and, much as the British might dislike it, if they were to come to terms with anybody about the future of India it would have to be with the Congress.

Like all political parties it was a compound of democracy and oligarchy. Every accredited member, paying four annas a year, had a vote for provincial Congress committees and for a delegate conference which in turn elected the All-India Congress Committee. The President of the Congress was elected by the annual All-India Congress. But the Working Committee, to which was entrusted the whole executive authority of the party, consisted of the President and thirteen members appointed by himself from among the A.I.C.C. and a Treasurer who was also his nominee.

Self-government was to be attained 'by all legitimate and peaceful means'. Though legitimacy and peacefulness were viewed differently by Congressmen and the rulers of India, it was well for the British raj that it was the Gandhian rather than the violent side of the Indian character that dominated the Congress, and political India generally, in the generation before the transfer of power. So few could never have governed so many with so little bloodshed if the prevalent national philosophy had been fierce and forcible, even though the institutions of the Raj—the enlistment of the martial classes in the Army, the cultivation of the Indian Rulers, the grant of subordinate powers to innumerable Indians holding traditional offices—had themselves done much to suborn or neutralise the militant strains in the nation. Nothing is more remarkable in those years, looking back on them, turbulent as they seemed then, than the absence of violent revolution. The revolt of 1942, though dangerous, was a desperate and ill-prepared campaign, swiftly quelled. Given its revolutionary purpose, the Congress was remarkably tame and non-revolutionary in practice. Apart from Subhas Chandra Bose, its Presidents for twenty-five years up to the transfer of power (some of them holding the office several times) were peaceable bourgeois with no stomach for a bloody fight—Mr. Gandhi himself, Maulana Abul Kalam Azad, Mrs. Sarojini Naidu, Srinivasa Iyengar, Dr. M. A. Ansari, Motilal

Nehru, Jawaharlal Nehru, Vallabhbhai Patel (probably the toughest, but no man of the barricades), Seth Kanchhodlal, Madan Mohan Malaviya, Rajendra Prasad, Acharya Kripalani. Not all were unquestioning disciples of the Mahatma, who had many critics both in the leadership and in the rank and file of the party; but on all he exercised an influence which at critical moments could be decisive.

Pandit Jawaharlal Nehru, after the Mahatma the most important Congress figure in the present history, was in many ways poles apart from him. Thoroughly Westernised in outlook, urban and upper class in upbringing and mentality, radical in his opinions in quite a different sense from the Gandhian delving to the roots of Indian life and tradition, impetuous and excitable, capable of hate and of sudden inflammatory outbursts, he often found himself vexed, frustrated or bewildered by his hero's attitudes. Yet again and again he submitted to obedience, moved by the sort of faith that a son has in a beloved father with whom he can still disagree. The story of the Congress' rejection of the Cripps Plan of 1942, and of its destructively qualified acceptance of the Cabinet Mission plan in 1946, can be told in terms of the relations between these two personal forces. There were other big men in the Congress too—the hard-boiled Patel, the statesmanlike Rajagopalachari, the idealistic, fluffy Azad, the politically strong Pant or Prasad. All had their parts in the drama. But the director of their acting, in the wings of the stage, was that frail, bony figure in the spectacles and homespun garments who lived his life for the twin ideals which he could not separate, Indian independence and Indian unity.

2 Mr. Jinnah and the Muslim League

Of all the personalities in the last act of the great drama of India's re-birth to independence, Mahomed Ali Jinnah is at once the most enigmatic and the most important. One can imagine any of the other principal actors (not counting Mahatma Gandhi, who makes but fitful and inconclusive appearances from the wings) replaced by a substitute in the same role—a different Congress leader, a different Secretary of State, a different representative of this or that interest or community, even a different Viceroy—without thereby implying any radical change in the final dénouement. But it is barely conceivable that events would have taken the same course, that the last struggle would have been a struggle of three, not two, well-balanced adversaries, and that a new nation State of Pakistan would have been created, but for the personality and leadership of one man, Mr. Jinnah. The irresistible demand for Indian independence, and the British will to relinquish power in India soon after the end of the Second World War, were the result of influences that had been at work long before the present story of a single decade begins: the protagonists on this side or that of the imperial relationship were tools of historical forces which they did not create and could not control, pilots of vessels borne by winds and tides set in motion long before they took the helm. Whereas the irresistible demand for Pakistan, and the solidarity of the Indian Muslims behind that demand, were creations of that decade alone, and supremely the creations of one man.

Jinnah is enigmatic in two ways. By nature, and in his conduct of life, he was cold, aloof and lonely. The scrupulous elegance of the Western clothes that he always wore, the monocle that he employed to transfix an audience of one or thousands, seemed deliberately to signal his apartness from the rest of the Indian world. Little is known of his early life and background except that he came from a Sindi family of the Khoja sect, who had the reputation of being good business men, good masters, ambitious, resourceful and epicurean. He spoke familiarly no other language than English: even his broadcast announcing to the Muslims of India that he had achieved for them their national goal had to be translated for him into their Urdu tongue. A prodigious worker, he would shut himself up for day after day and night after night with his briefs or his political papers. No intimates shared his secrets. No disciples watched his moods or tracked the straws in the wind of his thinking. No family, at this time, knew him relaxed and off guard. No collaborator of equal stature tempered his opinions or divided his responsibility. He walked alone.

But it was not only his inscrutable nature that made Jinnah enigmatic. How did it come about that the respected Congress leader, the idol of young nationalists in the 1920s, the 'ambassador of unity' between Hindus and Muslims, as Mrs. Sarojini Naidu called him in a eulogy of passionate fervour, became the single-minded leader of his community, the scourge of Congress and the hammer of the Hindus, the man who framed and accomplished the colossal ambition of destroying India's unity by carving from her body a new Islamic nation? One thing is certain: it was not for any venal motive that he changed. Not even his political enemies ever accused Jinnah of corruption or self-seeking. He could be bought by no one, and for no price. Nor was he in the least degree a weather-cock, swinging in the wind of popularity or changing his politics to suit the chances of the times. He was a steadfast idealist as well as a man of scrupulous honour. The fact to be explained is that in middle life he supplanted one ideal by another, and having embraced it clung to it with a fanatic's grasp to the end of his days.

It is easier to say of the change when it happened than why. The dividing line is commonly said to be the period that he spent in England from 1930, when he came to London for the first and second sessions of the Round Table Conference, after which he settled in England, voyaging to and fro for several years before he decided to make his home again in India. But his self-exile itself sprang from sources further back, causing in him the disillusionment which was observed in him at the Conference and which he expressed by shaking the dust of his own country from his feet. The date of his conversion (neither ecstatic nor sudden, like St. Paul's, but gloomy and protracted) can be pinned with fair assurance to the late 1920s.

At this period two strands of disappointment and depression entwine the thread of Jinnah's life; the one private, the other political. When he was fifteen or sixteen years old—so content was he to allow his early days to remain obscure that even the year and date of his birth are disputed—he was married to a child bride, who died some two years later while he was in England studying law. Thereafter he remained unmarried and seemingly indifferent to women until in 1918, when he was forty-one (to accept his own version of his birth-date—Christmas 1876), he married a beautiful, gay, social and extravagant Parsee girl, Ruttenbai, daughter of Sir Dinshaw Petit. This union of opposites was foredoomed to failure. Early in 1928, Mrs. Jinnah left her husband; the following year she died, and Mahomed Ali Jinnah was once more alone. A sense of human failure must have overhung his life. He was too honest a man not to blame his own character as well as his wife's for the breakdown of their marriage; 'It is my fault,' he told a friend who tried to reconcile them; 'we both need some sort of understanding we cannot give.' A man with an unquiet and unhappy home is apt to project private disillusionment upon his public business and opinions.

Outside the law, in which he had made a great reputation and fortune as a peerless court advocate, Jinnah's public business and opinions were still concerned above all with Indian unity and the part which his community of Mussulmans were to play in it. In May 1924, addressing a meeting of the Muslim League in Lahore, he had used these words:

> The advent of foreign rule and its continuance in India is primarily due to the fact that the people of India, particularly the Hindus and Muslims, are not united and do not sufficiently trust each other. . . . I am almost inclined to say that India will get Dominion Responsible Government the day the Hindus and Muslims are united.

A student of our times might consider Jinnah's 'almost inclined to say' an excess of caution. But what was to be the political foundation of Hindu-Muslim trust and unity? Jinnah held to the basis of separate electorates and reserved seats in the Legislatures for Muslims as the essential assurance that they would not be swamped by the Hindu majority. In the Congress, where Gandhi was at the height of his power, his pleas for special recognition of the Muslims fell upon stony ground. The Lucknow Pact, which he had helped to negotiate in 1916, had been thrown into the discard. Jinnah at this time held an élitist view of politics: sophisticated leaders should decide for the masses. This too was contrary to the ruling Congress philosophy of mass involvement.

In 1928, responding to a caustic challenge by Lord Birkenhead, Secretary of State for India, while the Simon Commission was at work, an All-Parties Conference was called to draw up the outline of a constitution upon which the Indian leaders could all agree. It gave rise to what came to be known as the (Motilal) Nehru Report. Jinnah was abroad when the so-called Unity Conference was held at Lucknow, and had no hand in the Nehru Report, but he attended the All-Parties session at Calcutta in December 1928, which considered it. The Muslim League had submitted amendments, inserting safeguards for the Muslim community, which the Nehru Committee had ignored, and which the Calcutta Conference again rejected. Jinnah described the Report as 'neither helpful nor fruitful in any way', and gave warning that the inevitable result of leaving minorities with a sense of insecurity would be 'revolution and civil war'. His speech went unheeded. Sir Tej Bahadur Sapru, the Liberal leader, while scornfully recommending that the Muslim demand, wrong-headed as it was, should be appeased, called its spokesman 'a spoilt child'. As he left Calcutta for his home city of Bombay, Jinnah declared to an old Parsee friend: 'This is the parting of the ways.'

Years afterwards (in a speech to the students of Aligarh Muslim University, in 1938), Jinnah described the mood of disillusionment in which he decided to make his home in England after the first two sessions of the Round Table Conference. He saw no hope of unity in India. The Mussulmans were led by 'either the flunkeys of the British Government or the camp-followers of the Congress'. He had begun to feel that he could neither help India, nor change the Hindu mentality.

In England, Jinnah was visited by Nawabzada Liaqat Ali Khan, a young landowner from the United Provinces, who had already shown his political zeal anc organising talent in the Muslim League, and was destined to become Jinnah's right-hand man for a quarter of a century, the first Prime Minister of Pakistan, and the victim of a still mysterious political assassination. Liaqat Ali Khan and his eager, newly-wed Begum pleaded with Jinnah to return to lead his community and the League, which was then, in the Begum's later phrase, 'in a degraded state'. He took two years to make up his mind, but in October 1935 he returned for good. Speaking in March 1936 in Delhi he used words with a different ring from those of his earlier years:

> We must think of the interests of our community. . . . The Hindus and Muslims must be organised separately, and once they are organised they will understand each other better.

A year and a half later, in a speech at Lucknow which is generally regarded as Jinnah's decisive challenge, he spoke significantly of the Muslim 'nation' that would emerge from the struggle with the majority community, who had 'clearly shown their hand that Hindustan is for the Hindus'. Mahatma Gandhi dubbed this utterance 'a declaration of war'. In March 1940, at its conference at Lahore, the Muslim League passed the historic 'Pakistan Resolution' calling for the divorce of the Muslim-majority provinces from the rest of India as a separate nation.[1] Meanwhile, however, after the inauguration of the new constitution under the Government of India Act of 1935, many contributory events had occurred in Indian politics which belong to the main stream of this book's story.

Jinnah's estrangement from the Congress and his emergence as a purely communal champion were evidently due both to personal causes and to political conviction. His Muslim nationalism had become paramount above his Indian nationalism. His pride had been wounded by the disdain with which the Congress and Liberal leaders of the late 1920s had treated him. Jinnah never submitted to a slight: anecdote after anecdote tells of his cutting rejoinders to anyone who snubbed him intentionally or unintentionally, whoever he or she might be—a judge, a Governor-General, a Secretary of State, a noble lady. Neglect was a slight, rebuff an insult. The grievance of his rejection by the Congress leaders would not be assuaged until he had finally frustrated their purpose, twenty years later. Mahomed Ali Jinnah was always a man of principle, but he was supremely a man of pride.

For the Muslims, as the heaven-sent leader of their 'national' cause, he had two supreme qualities. The first was his single-mindedness. Having set his hand to the task of uniting his community behind a demand for recognition as a nation, nothing deterred him, least of all the practical difficulties of separation, which he declined to discuss, and which he time and again averred would be settled once the principle had been accepted. His aloofness, his detachment from detail and the in-fighting of parliamentary politics, even his lack of Muslim roots which might have labelled him as Shia or Sunni or partisan of this or that Mohammedan tradition, such as Punjabi aristocracy, all contributed to the power of his national leadership. His second great quality was unrivalled tactical skill. He knew how to take advantage of every situation, however unpromising, above all how to delay commitment, leaving opponents to make their mistakes—and they made many. A point once gained was never lost: it became the starting-ground for the next point to be demanded. The counter-tactics that

---

[1] See below, p. 79.

could have defeated Mr. Jinnah's tactics seem obvious enough: but neither in respect of personalities and singleness of leadership, nor in respect of its refusal to compound its claim to represent all Indians, was the Congress capable of adopting them.

PART TWO

How the rift widened

5

The Act of 1935

The Government of India Act, 1935, opened a new era in Indian constitutional progress. It was born of long gestation and heavy travail, beginning with the Simon Commission of 1929, continuing through the Round Table Conferences of 1931–2 and a Joint Select Committee which had all the weight of a Royal Commission, and concluding with a hard-fought passage through Parliament against the opposition of Mr. Winston Churchill and his right-wing friends. Four names will always be respectfully linked with it: Sir Samuel Hoare,[1] its champion as Secretary of State for India; Mr. R. A. Butler,[2] his Parliamentary Under-Secretary, upon whom fell much of the heat and burden of piloting it through the Commons; the Marquess of Linlithgow, Chairman of the Committee of Lords and Commons on the White Paper that preceded the Bill, who was destined to become its first chief administrator as Viceroy and Governor-General; and Sir Maurice Gwyer, its principal legal draftsman, later Chief Justice of India. Politically and constitutionally the new Act was a remarkable feat, even though its highest intention was never fulfilled. Under it, India had her first taste and practice of parliamentary self-government, in the eleven provinces; although the all-India federation embodied in it was never created, the bones of a federal system, including a detailed separation of powers, were formed and exercised; under the Act, including its fall-back provisions for the Centre pending federation, an interim Government of a wholly popular-political kind eventually came into office; under it, with relatively few amendments, power was transferred entirely from British to Indian hands; and, as thus amended, it served as the working constitution of independent India for three years and of independent Pakistan for nine years[3] while they were debating and

[1] Later Viscount Templewood.
[2] Later Lord Butler of Saffron Walden.
[3] And then large portions of it were borrowed.

adopting their own new constitutions. In the history of Indo-British relations it is an edifice deserving admiration, though Mr. Winston Churchill called it 'a gigantic quilt of jumbled crochet work, a monstrous monument of shame built by pigmies'.

The core of the Act was the establishment of autonomy, with a representative parliamentary system of government, for eleven British-Indian provinces, within their defined provincial powers; it intended these provinces to become, willy-nilly, components of an all-India federation including Princely States. The federation itself was also to have a representative parliamentary system, and a large degree of autonomy in the federal sphere, but the Viceroy would retain supreme powers, including the appointment of his own Executive Council or Government and the whole control of defence and foreign affairs and the ultimate responsibility for law and order.

In clearing the way for this constitutional system, however, three other important decisions were embodied in the Act. First, Burma and Aden were constitutionally separated from India, with which they had previously been governed under one Governor-General; and Sind (previously part of Bombay) and Orissa (previously joined to Bihar) were made separate provinces; secondly, the authority of the Crown in respect of the Indian States was removed from the Government of India and placed in the hands of a Crown Representative, who could also be, and in practice always was up to independence, the Governor-General of India; after 1935 the Viceroy wore two hats, one for British India and one for the States, and the Political Department was separated from the Government of India secretariat, to become distinctly and directly responsible to the Crown Representative. Thirdly, a decision was taken as to communal representation in the new legislatures. The Communal Award for the provinces, announced by the British Government in April 1932, gave separate electorates and reserved seats to Muslims, Europeans, Sikhs, Indian-Christians and Anglo-Indians, and weightage to minorities. Thus in Bombay, where the Muslims were less than 10 per cent of the population, they had 30 reserved seats in the Assembly out of 175, a proportion of 17 per cent; whereas in the Punjab, where they were 57 per cent of the population, they were awarded only 86 seats out of 175, two fewer than a majority. An award for the Centre, made in November 1932, gave Muslims one-third of the seats in the central legislature, though they were only a quarter of the British Indian population. It was these numerical arrangements—imposed because the communities and parties in India could not agree among themselves—which set the pattern of representation, especially in the provinces, on which partition and the transfer of power was to go forward.

The federal construction was to be set up only when one-half of the States by weight agreed to federate: this never happened.[1] Meanwhile an interim system of government at the Centre was provided, broadly on the lines that already existed under the Montagu-Chelmsford Reforms, but with a revised legislature, with States affairs separated, and with its legislative powers limited to a federal list of subjects and a 'concurrent list' on which both the Centre and the provinces could legislate, the provinces usually acting as administrative agents for the Central Government. The central legislature had no powers over a list of subjects, including defence and foreign affairs, which were reserved to the Governor-General. Moreover, both at the Centre (whether federal or interim) and in the provinces many safeguards for British authority were worked into the fabric—powers in the hands of Governors and the Governor-General to disallow Bills, to certify Bills or financial requirements, to legislate by ordinance and to control the higher public services. It was the intention of the framers of the Act that the provinces should be genuinely self-governing within their allotted sphere, and that under federation there should be a genuine dyarchy, or sharing of powers, between parliamentary representatives and British-controlled authorities; but the self-government was unmistakably in leading strings. This was the price of prudence—or of pacifying the British Conservative Party.

In exercising their reserved powers the provincial Governors were subject to the Governor-General, and he in turn was subject to the general direction and control of the Secretary of State. As terms of art—familiar to lawyers and administrators who had to interpret and work the Act but esoteric to everyone else—the occasions on which a Governor or Governor-General was empowered or obliged to exert his autocratic powers were distinguished between those on which he could act 'in his discretion' and those on which he would act on 'his individual responsibility'. Broadly, discretionary powers applied to the working of the con-

[1] See Chapter 6 below.

stitution in relation to the Indian legislatures and executives, individual powers to prerogative or other matters that were reserved from these authorities, thus reflecting the intention on the one hand to set up a system of Indian self-government, but with safeguards and tutelary qualifications, and on the other to withhold from India altogether certain areas of political decision.

One particular form of discretionary power must be mentioned both because it fundamentally affected provincial parliamentary responsibility and because it played a vital part in political developments over the ten years between the Act's entry into force and the transfer of power. Under Section 93, if at any time the Governor of a province was satisfied that a situation had arisen in which the government of the province could not be carried on in accordance with the provisions of the Act, he might by proclamation declare that his functions to any specified extent should be exercised by him in his discretion, and assume to himself all or any of the powers vested in or exercisable by any provincial body or authority except High Courts. In doing so he had to get the concurrence of the Governor-General, and his proclamation had to be laid before the British Parliament and periodically renewed. The political effects of this breakdown clause were far-reaching. If, for instance, in an autonomous Dominion, the Governor-General were to find it impossible to form a Ministry having majority support in the legislature, the position would have to be resolved by political means, such as a general election or even a series of general elections, the onus falling on the politicians and the electors to find a way out; but in India under the Act of 1935 the Governor of a province could 'go into Section 93' and govern autocratically until a solution was found. Only one province, Sind, escaped any period of Governor's rule under Section 93, and that rather because of the opportunism of its politics than because of any steadfastness or skill in operating parliamentary government.

6

The failure of federation

At the very first full working session of the Round Table Conference, on 17th November 1930, an all-India federation had suddenly become a realistic and central item of the agenda. One of the most respected spokesmen for British India, Sir Tej Bahadur Sapru, came out unequivocally for a federal system of government in which he invited the Rulers to participate, and he was backed by the chief Muslim representatives. In response, the Maharajah of Bikaner identified the Princely Order with 'that passion for an equal status in the eyes of the world, expressed in the desire for Dominion Status, which is the dominant force amongst all thinking Indians today'. He assured the conference that the Rulers would come into a self-governing federation of India provided their rights were guaranteed; and in this he had the strong support of the Nawab of Bhopal, a Muslim Ruler of great influence. Another group of Princes, led by the Sikh Maharajah of Patiala, and supported by a number of smaller States who feared submersion in an all-India federation, argued that the States themselves must first confederate before linking up with British India. As the sessions of the Round Table Conference wore on through 1931 and 1932, the initial enthusiasm waned, and all kinds of particular objections or conditions were raised by Rulers who evidently had cold feet about committing their fate to a self-governing and predominantly democratic Dominion; nevertheless the concept of all-India federation was never abandoned, and was firmly embodied in the British Government's proposals published after the Conference had ended, in the report of the Joint Select Committee, and in the Bill submitted by the Government to Parliament.

Under the eventual Government of India Act, 1935, accession of the States to the federation of India set up by the Act was to be voluntary, by way of separate instruments of accession, each executed by a Ruler and accepted by His Majesty the King; the area of federal powers assigned was to be defined in each instrument and could be less than that compulsorily applicable to the provinces of British India. Moreover, the Princes as a group were given a virtual veto over the whole federal scheme, on which depended the extension of dyarchy to the Centre. Not until the States acceding were enough to fill half the States' quota of seats in the Federal Upper House, and also included half the total population of all the States, could His Majesty's Government take steps to proclaim the inauguration of federation.

The Federal Upper House, or Council of State, was to consist of 156 members from British India and not more than 104 from the acceding States. The House of Assembly, the Lower House, was to consist of 250 representatives of British India and not more than 125 of the States. States' representatives in both Houses were to be appointed by the Rulers. As the total population of the States was less than a quarter of that of all India, whereas their quotas in the federal legislature were 40 per cent and 33⅓ per cent respectively, they were being given heavy weightage. The provision that all 'powers connected with the exercise of the functions of the Crown in its relations with Indian States' should in India be discharged by a distinct Crown Representative reflected a decision that paramountcy was not to be transferred to the federation of India. The federation could enjoy in the several States only those powers and functions which they had agreed to confer on it by their instruments of accession.

In retrospect these provisions appear so strikingly favourable to the States, touching both the disproportionate influence they were awarded in the federation, and the maintenance of their status, their relations with the Crown and the personal autocracy of their Rulers amid the growth of democratic government in British India, that it seems astonishing that the British Parliament and Government should have favoured them to such an extent, especially in giving them a veto over the federal scheme which had cost five years of intense effort to evolve; and still more astonishing that the Princes and their advisers should not have seized the opportunity of taking their part in an Indian Dominion on terms much more advantageous than they were ever likely to be offered again. In fact, as to the attitude of His Majesty's Government, these two astonishments cancel each other; for the Government believed that they had so temptingly baited the federal scheme as to ensure the entry of the leading Princes, at least in sufficient numbers to fulfil the preliminary condition. On the British side it is illusory to ascribe to a Conservative Government in 1935 the states of mind, let alone the past experiences, of a Labour Government in 1947, or for that matter a Conservative Opposition at that later date. Before the Second World War the great majority in Parliament at Westminster viewed the presence of the States in a federal India as a vital element of stability in a country ravaged by civil commotion, and as a counterpoise against political parties, especially the Congress, which if unrestrained might have fatally undermined the strength and security of India, a pillar of British imperial power in a dangerous and darkening world.

On the side of the Rulers a foretaste of trouble had been given by sharply critical objections raised by a special Committee of the Chamber of Princes, and by a conference of Rulers and States' representatives held in Bombay in February 1935, during the passage of the Government of India Bill through Parliament. The Bombay meeting showed that, although some of them may have paid lip-service to federation, the Princes generally had not yet accepted its fundamental principle of a limitation of powers of the federating units, involving a permanent resignation of part of their internal sovereignty to the federation, in return for a share in its government.[1] The meeting also revived the old pretensions of the States in regard to paramountcy. It complained that 'usage and sufferance' were coupled with 'treaties' in the draft text of instruments of accession, and demanded that what it would prefer to call 'treaties' of accession between His Majesty's Government and the States should lay upon the former a counter-obligation 'to preserve and safeguard the whole of their sovereignty and internal autonomy . . . from any encroachment in future'. The Secretary of State refused to be drawn on paramountcy or to extend the debate with the Princes beyond the limited problem of their place in the projected federation.

It was thus with some ominous clouds overhead, though with confident hope of success, that the Marquess of Linlithgow, who succeeded the Marquess of Willingdon as Viceroy in 1936, set about persuading the principal Rulers to accede to federation. He had been Chairman of the Joint Select Committee on the Bill, he

[1] *Views of the Indian States on the Government of India Bill* (1935), Cmd. 4843.

was deeply committed to the federal scheme, and he was resolved upon launching federation during his Viceroyalty, which would normally end in 1941. His failure in this effort set the scene for the political and constitutional troubles that culminated in the wreck of Indian unity, and the eventual ousting of the Princes from all independent power in the governance of India.

Lord Linlithgow's first main move was to send three personal emissaries—Sir Arthur Lothian, Sir Courtenay Latimer and Sir Francis Wylie, all high officials of the Political Service, chosen by himself—to tour the principal States in the winter of 1936-7 and explain to the Rulers and their advisers the effect of federation and of the terms of accession, embodied in a draft instrument. This procedure, though having obvious merits, especially for a Viceroy who wanted to keep the whole negotiation under his hand, had also certain disadvantages. The Rulers and their Dewans, faced with what appeared to them concentrated high-level pressure, enlisted constitutional experts from England and even the United States to advise them, with the result that broad policy tended to become lost in detailed legal controversy. Some of those who knew the States well, including Sir Conrad Corfield, who was to be Political Adviser in the crucial Viceroyalties of Lord Wavell and Lord Mountbatten, believed that a quiet individual approach to the Rulers by the British Residents or Political Agents, whom they knew, would have been much more likely to convince them on the issues about which they really cared—their personal status and the integrity of their States. Be that as it may, the three emissaries' reports to the Crown Representative, though full of the multifarious details raised by the different States, showed two common factors throughout Princely India; a strong reluctance to federate under the Act, and a determination to bargain for every possible concession as the price of overcoming that reluctance. Not only did the Rulers shrink from committing themselves irrevocably to a national system of government under democratic forces hostile to their personal power; they demanded that the offset be a limitation of the paramountcy that they resented, and a guarantee of the sovereignty that they claimed. When it came to particular terms, the concessions which they wished to exact were mostly financial, including permanent guarantees of the revenue enjoyed by certain of them from sources that would become federal subjects, such as customs and excise, salt tax or the match monopoly.

Concessions of this sort would have involved statutory amendment of the new Government of India Act. It was not only for that reason, however, that the Secretary of State, Lord Zetland, opposed the Viceroy's anxious wish to grant enough favours of this order to induce some leading States—he had in mind particularly Kashmir, Baroda and the Kathiawar States—to agree to enter the federation and thus to encourage others by their example. Lord Zetland feared that every concession gained by one State would be demanded by all, with fatal results for the whole structure and prospects of federation. He disliked the method of individual and piecemeal negotiation, whereas the Viceroy felt that only by keeping up the momentum of the parleys with the Princes could the issue of federation be kept alive. His correspondence with the Secretary of State shows how unremitting was his drive to induce the States to make federation a reality. His attitude was considerably influenced by that of the Political Department and its officers, who had close relations with the several States and in pursuing the accepted imperial policy of upholding the treaty system were experts on the States' special interests and the interests of the Princely Order generally, often different from those of British India and especially of its advancing political democracy. They had even less personal contact with Indian political leaders than had British civil servants in other departments or in the provinces; for such contacts would have aroused the gravest suspicions among the Princes whose confidence they cherished. As agents for the Viceroy in negotiating with the States they could not be expected to become hard and unyielding bargainers on behalf of all-India, against the Rulers whom they had advised and protected. The negotiations, in retrospect, seem thus to have had a certain unreality.

They dragged on for over a year, while the Viceroy and Secretary of State expressed to each other their respective anxieties, the one lest all the effort be wasted, the other lest an essentially one-way conciliation produce results fatal to a proper federation. At last Lord Linlithgow decided to make a comprehensive effort to bring matters to a head. In January 1939 he addressed a circular letter to the Rulers of all salute States, enclosing a revised draft of the proposed instrument of accession and associated documents, emphasising that there was no prospect of any substantial variation of the general terms for accession, and asking for a yea or nay to those terms within six months. He did not have to wait so long. A few weeks later a conference of Rulers and States' Ministers in Bombay passed the following resolution:

> The Conference . . . having considered the revised draft of the instrument of accession and connected papers, resolves that the terms on the basis of which accession is offered are fundamentally unsatisfactory . . . and are therefore unacceptable. At the same time, the Conference records its belief that it could not be the intention of His Majesty's Government to close the door on all-India federation.

The States proceeded to express this facing-both-ways resolution in practice by resuming their pressure for concessions. When world war broke out in 1939 not a single big State had agreed to enter the federation. On 11th September the Viceroy announced in an address to the central legislature that, while federation remained the objective, the need to concentrate on the emergency left 'no choice but to hold in suspense the work in connection with preparation for federation'. Whether or not Lord Linlithgow had no other choice—a point on which some of those associated with the States disagreed—this was the death-knell of federation under the 1935 Act. Under its transitional provisions, the Centre continued to be governed under a modified form of the Montagu-Chelmsford constitution. It is proof of the skill and farsightedness of the draftsmen both of the 1921 Act and more especially of the 1935 Act, with its quasi-federal division of powers between Centre and provinces, that they provided a constitutional structure for India which absorbed provincial autonomy, was viable both in peace and through six years of war, became the essential instrument of the transfer of power, and was the initial basis of independent government in India and Pakistan.

It may well be asked why, after the apparent enthusiasm of the Round Table Conference, the Princes with one accord failed to take this opportunity, which was never to recur, of associating themselves with an all-India federation on terms highly favourable to them, in that they were given a heavily-weighted place in the federal government while retaining their privileges and internal sovereignty intact. Commentators on the period[1] agree that there

---

[1] e.g. Menon, *The Integration of the Indian States*, and Coupland, *Indian Politics 1936–42*.

were two broad reasons. First, faith in federation faded fast when the Princes and their keenly calculating senior advisers looked more closely at its meaning for their future. Their status as sovereigns in their own States was to them supremely precious. Circumscribed though it had been by British paramountcy, they hated to yield any fraction of it to an Indian power, even if that power was to be partly themselves. So they tried to exact the highest payment in financial and other such concessions for what they viewed not as a potential opportunity but as a certain sacrifice.

Secondly, they had been taught by the development of Congress policy to fear the politicians and democratic politics more than ever. The classical Congress attitude towards the States, expressed in a resolution adopted in 1928 and reaffirmed in 1935, was one of solidarity with the States' peoples in their demand for democratic government, combined with non-intervention. No branches of the Congress were established in the States. 'Any attempt at interference,' said Mr. Gandhi, 'can only damage the cause of the people in the States.' But this policy was not to the liking of the militant wing of the Congress which was gaining strength in the thirties.

No doubt, in retrospect, the correct policy for the Congress would have been to placate the Princes; for in the long run the politicians stood a good chance of controlling the States' representatives through the progressive democratisation of their régimes, while the Muslims were still weak, had not formulated a Pakistan policy, and would have had to accept any terms approved by the Government. But this was wholly contrary to the spirit of the Congress at that time, which was to demand nothing less than complete democratic self-government.

After the general elections in British India in 1937 had placed Congress Governments in office in eight provinces, the situation developed further. Those Governments tolerated and indeed connived at agitation in neighbouring States conducted from bases in the provinces. Individual Congress leaders took part in subversive State politics. In several States, Congress committees were formed. Non-intervention, though reiterated as Congress policy in 1938, became a formality rather than a fact. Mr. Gandhi himself, though still a moderate in this sphere, began to change his tune. In December 1938, acclaiming the popular awakening in the States as due to the 'time-spirit', he declared that there was no halfway house between full responsible government in the States and their total extinction. After warning the Princes that the Congress policy of non-interference might have to be abandoned, he advised them to cultivate friendly relations 'with an organisation which bids fair in the future, not very distant, to replace the paramount power— let me hope, by friendly arrangement'. It is small wonder that their Highnesses were reluctant to submit themselves to a constitution in which the Congress would apparently have the predominant political power. And who is to say, in the light of what happened to the States after 1947, that they misjudged their own likely fate?

It is a commonplace of comment on Indian political history that the failure of the Princes to enter the federation under the 1935 Act—or the failure of the Viceroy to persuade them to do so—cost India the peaceful establishment of a national government and parliament which, on the historical analogy of the old Dominions, would steadily have gained in autonomous power, notwithstanding the restrictions of the Act, until they became self-governing under the Crown. India would, it is supposed, have become constitution- ally united as never before, with a democratic apparatus to enlist its people and its will in the war effort of 1939–45; the communi- ties and parties would have learnt to work together through the necessary compromises and coalitions imposed by the nature of the Act; Indian leaders would have gained invaluable experience of government (including especially defence) under gradually relaxing tutelage before being called upon to control and administer an independent nation; the transfer of power, progressively made effective through convention and practice, could have been legally ratified by simple amendments of the Government of India Act and extension of the Statute of Westminster to India; and partition, with all the turmoil and bloodshed which it brought, would have been avoided. It is a rosy dream, not without substance; but commonplaces are not always correct, and it is well to examine a little more closely the premise upon which those glowing prog- nostications have been based.

If States' Rulers governing one half of the total population of the States had acceded, and the federation been proclaimed, what would have been the political position? The Congress was radically opposed to the 1935 constitution: it took part in the subsequent provincial elections only with the aim of subverting it, though success in the formation of provincial Governments brought a

change of mind so far as the provinces were concerned; its basic
policy was non-co-operation with a British raj which stood in the
way of Indian freedom. Total non-co-operation in the federal part
of the 1935 constitution was thus to be expected of the Congress,
and the more the Princes adhered to it the less acceptable to the
Congress it would become. The attitude of the Muslim League was
not much more promising. At its session in Bombay in April 1936
it passed a resolution utterly condemning the new constitution as
anti-democratic (a 'monstrosity', the League's President called it),
though grudgingly consenting to use the provincial scheme 'for
what it is worth'. Non-co-operation in the federation by the
Muslim League, though not quite so certain as with the Congress,
was thus also to be expected. Nor would the entry of the Princes
improve matters in this quarter; for the overwhelming majority
of States' Rulers were Hindus, and the greater the number of
adhering States the smaller proportionately would become the
communal Muslim minority in the federal legislature.[1] It seems
highly improbable that a federation boycotted by the two main
political parties, and opposed by them with every form of peaceful
if not violent resistance, could ever have worked at all.

Even if Congress and League non-co-operation had not extended
to boycotting the federal elections but had been confined to refusing to enter a federal Government, the possibility of successfully
forming such a Government would have been thin. In the winter
of 1934–5 elections to the central Legislative Assembly had been
held under the old Act; of the 77 elected members other than
Europeans, 44 were Congressmen, 11 Congress Nationalists
(mainly belonging to the Hindu Mahasabha), 19 Muslims under
various banners and 3 non-Muslim Independents. Even with
the aid of the European, official and nominated blocs, the
Government had no majority unless it could muster some of the
Muslims and Independents. The likely picture under the 1935
federal constitution would have been an Assembly of perhaps 120

[1] Without Hyderabad and Bhopal, both of which were among the most
reluctant States in 1947, Muslim representation in the States bloc in the
federal assembly would have been virtually nil. Towards the end of 1938
the Executive Council of the League passed a resolution denouncing the
federation and significantly declaring that the main objective of the
Congress in the States was to secure an elective system which would send
their representatives to the federal legislature and thus give the Congress
a majority.

Congressmen and over 30 members of the Muslim League[1] out of 250 representatives of British India, together with, say, a minimum of 70 members from the States. A Government of States' Rulers (or Dewans), Europeans and Indian-Christians, non-League Muslims, Independents, and members from reserved seats for labour and for commerce and industry, might, on a favourable calculation, have had a bare majority; but it would hardly have been the kind of representative Government that could have carried India through the war, healed the communal rift, or become the heir of Dominion Status. Nor could its stability have been more than highly precarious. One is forced to the conclusion that if the federal part of the 1935 Act had been put to the test by the sufficient adherence of the States it might well have proved un- workable without a massive and continuous use of the special powers reserved to the Governor-General.

Immensely important and invaluable as the 1935 Act was, in general as marking a critical stage in the development of British policy towards Indian self-government, and in particular as afford- ing a viable structure of provincial self-government from 1937 to 1947, it was far behind the times for which it was legislating. Its origins went back to the appointment of the Simon Commission in 1927. By the time it came (or, as regards the federation, could have come) into effect, a decade had passed, a decade of vital development in the political life of British India and in less degree of the Indian States. Political power, subordinate as it was, which up till then had been largely diffuse, was becoming concentrated in organised parties. The political consciousness of the masses was awakened. Politicians became revered national figures. With these developments the Government in London, including the India Office, and British political opinion except for a few left-wing specialists, were largely out of touch. British officials in the field in India were doubtless aware of them, but their instinct and often their duty were hostile to the trend, and in any case their know- ledge could reach London only through provincial Governors and the departments and Governor-General of India, whose business it was to govern rather than to be political assessors or the eyes and ears of Westminster and Whitehall. It was not until provincial governments, most of them dominated by the Congress, began to operate from 1937 onwards that a truer understanding of political

[1] Judging from results in the provincial elections of 1937.

India grew in the high places of British power. Even then, contact was remote and ignorance substantial. Before Lord Mountbatten went out as Viceroy in 1947, he was briefed at great length by the India Office, but he found on his arrival a very different state of affairs from that which had been depicted in London.

7

Provincial autonomy

In the cold weather of 1936–7, elections to the provincial legislatures were held throughout India under the new constitution embodied in the 1935 Act. The electorate had been greatly enlarged and now exceeded 30 million men and women, of whom perhaps one half were illiterate. Over 54 per cent went to the poll. Voting was assisted for the uneducated by the use of symbols and in some places coloured voting boxes, a system which gives great advantage to organised parties against independents and small groups. The Congress contested the elections explicitly in order not to work the Act but to combat and destroy it. The Muslim League, while equally opposed to the federal provisions, fought in order to use the provincial part of the Act 'for what it was worth'.

The League's successes were patchy, totalling only 108 out of 485 Muslim seats, and in no province did it come near to having a majority or even being in a position to form a Government with minor allies. The successes of the Congress, however, were widespread and decisive. Out of 1,585 seats in the 11 provincial lower houses it won 711, of which no fewer than 494 were in 5 provinces (Madras, the United Provinces, the Central Provinces, Bihar and Orissa) in which it secured absolute majorities of the seats. In Bombay, too, though just short of an absolute majority, it was capable of forming a stable Government with the aid of a few sympathisers ready to toe its line. Its victories throughout India included 26 of the 58 Muslim seats which it had contested, but some of these were in the North-West Frontier Province, where for a number of reasons its hold was exceptional.[1] In this province, though without an initial majority, it held a commanding position, its opponents being divided, and it was able to form a Government.

The triumph of the Congress, at least in the 'general' or Hindu seats, was to have been expected. Not only did the party have a

[1] See below, p. 277.

virtual monopoly of national political organisation at that time, but there was also another reason, thus expressed by the then Governor of the United Provinces:

> The sense of impending change awakened the villages. The Government, which had in past agitations opposed the Congress with the weight of its authority, now stood inactive. It was too much to expect that the villager would understand the constitutional necessity for this attitude. He felt that the British Raj was weakening, that the Congress Raj was coming, and, as so often happens, threw himself definitely on what seemed to be the winning side.[1]

This was a phenomenon destined to be repeated with decisive effect at later points in the story of the transfer of power.

The Congress victories in the Hindu-majority provinces precipitated a great debate on whether the party should accept office. The radical wing of the party was hotly opposed to this course, which indeed was inconsistent with the declared policy of entering the legislatures only in order to destroy the constitution. 'It would be a fatal error,' Pandit Jawaharlal Nehru had said; for it 'would involve co-operation with British imperialism'. On the other hand, the provincial Congress leaders wanted to take office: the lure of power is always sweet, and, besides, they were anxious to begin the social and agrarian reforms which were part of the Congress platform and which they knew came much closer to the life of the masses than the struggle for constitutional independence. But they were not free agents. The Congress was not a congeries of autonomous provincial parties but a tightly disciplined national organisation, controlled by an All-India Committee elected, like its President, by the annual All-India Congress. Between sessions of the A.I.C.C., control was exercised by a powerful working committee of fourteen members nominated by the President himself. This structure, combined with the party's claim to represent all Indians, gave rise to charges, within India as well as beyond, of Congress 'dictatorship' and 'totalitarianism'. These were particularly dirty words in democratic countries in the 1930s, but if they did apply to the Indian National Congress they applied in a fundamentally different sense from the totalitarian dictator-

[1] Sir Harry Haig in the *Asiatic Review*, July 1940, quoted by Coupland in *Indian Politics, 1936–42*.

ships of Europe, for the Congress ethos, if not always its practice, was essentially democratic.

Those who wanted acceptance of office managed to postpone a decision by the A.I.C.C. until after the elections. Victory had then softened the opposition. On 18th March 1937 the Committee passed a resolution reiterating the Congress policy of combating the 1935 constitution and demanding that it be withdrawn, and concluding that, in pursuance of this policy,

> the All-India Congress Committee authorises and permits the acceptance of offices in Provinces where the Congress commands a majority in the legislature, provided that Ministerships shall not be accepted unless the leader of the Congress party in the legislature is satisfied and is able to state publicly that the Governor will not use his special powers of interference or set aside the advice of Ministers in regard to their constitutional activities.

Such an assurance the Governors were obviously unable to give, for it would have been contrary to their statutory duties, and when asked to give it upon their inviting Congress provincial leaders to form Ministries they refused. Their only immediate resort, in Congress-majority provinces, short of imposing direct Governors' rule under Section 93 of the Act, was to appoint caretaker Governments from minority parties to hold office until defeated in the legislatures, or until the Congress changed its mind; and this they did.

Whether or not the spectacle of others enjoying Ministerial offices which Congressmen could claim, and of popular Governments effectively administering non-Congress provinces, affected the attitude of the Congress, it did eventually change its mind. Mr. Gandhi, declaring himself the sole author of the clause on acceptance of office in the resolution of 18th March, said he had not intended to lay down an impossible condition, but one which the Governors could easily have accepted. A proposition around which the feelings on both sides—Congress and Government—in favour of a compromise formula could crystallise was provided by the Marquess of Lothian, who had been Chairman of the Indian Franchise Committee, in a letter to *The Times* (of London) in April. The history of responsible government in Britain and the Dominions, he argued, showed that a Governor's decision to differ from his Ministers depended on whether they could count on the support of the electorate in the event of a dissolution. 'Is not the most promising way out of the present difficulty to recognise that once responsible government is in being the ultimate "arbitration" will almost inevitably be exercised by the electorate?' This doctrine was welcomed in India, even by Pandit Nehru, one of the most obdurate of the Congress leaders and then its President. The Working Committee, however, continued to demand specific assurances.

On 22nd June, when time was running out because the legislatures had to be called within six months of the elections, the Viceroy, Lord Linlithgow, issued a long statement. Experience had shown the people of India, he said, that a Governor's special responsibilities did not entitle him to intervene at random. They had been restricted to the narrowest possible scope, and each represented a response to demands from legitimate interests in India. Governors were anxious not merely not to provoke conflicts with their Ministers but to leave nothing undone to avoid or resolve such conflicts. If conflicts arose, resignation of Ministers was more constitutional than dismissal, but in any event the question at issue would have to be one on which Ministers felt that their position was hopelessly compromised. 'You may count on me,' concluded Lord Linlithgow, 'in face even of bitter disappointment, to strive untiringly towards the full and final establishment in India of the principles of parliamentary government.'

This generous statement by the Viceroy had cost him a hard struggle with the Government in London, in which he had come close to resignation when they lost their nerve and wanted to back out of agreement to what he proposed to say. Though far from accepting the Lothian doctrine, it ended the deadlock. On 7th July the Congress Working Committee, strongly influenced by Mr. Gandhi,[1] resolved that Congressmen be permitted to accept office when invited, but that office was to be utilised 'to further in every possible way the Congress policy of combating the new Act on the one hand and prosecuting a constructive programme on the other'. The caretaker Ministries in the Congress-majority provinces then resigned and Congress Governments took over.

The efforts of the British authorities, from the Secretary of State to the provincial Governors, in bending and stretching the

[1] Azad, *India Wins Freedom*, p. 15.

new Act in order to secure the co-operation of men pledged to overthrow it presented a strange paradox. But they and the provincial Congress leaders were realists, pitted against ideologues obsessed by the pursuit of a Holy Grail—total Indian political freedom under a constitution framed by Indian democracy, that is to say, in the last resort by the Indian majority. In 1937 the realists won; in 1939, when the Congress Governments were forced by the 'High Command' to resign, they were defeated. Unfortunately, their victory in 1937 was achieved at the cost of heightening the anxieties of minorities for whose benefit some of the safeguards in the Act, now so conspicuously played down, had been inserted. While the Congress had learnt that responsible government, once established, grows organically and cannot easily be upset whatever the constitutional provisions, the Muslims and others had drawn the lesson that majority power, once established, likewise grows in security and self-confidence, and cannot easily be countered whatever the constitutional safeguards for minority interests.

There followed an episode still more tangibly and permanently damaging to the confidence of the Muslims. Before the elections it had been expected that Muslim League members would be brought into coalition with the Congress in forming Governments in provinces in which there was a substantial Muslim minority, such as the United Provinces and Bombay. In their Letters of Instruction, Governors had been told that, while Ministries must have collective responsibility, they should include so far as practicable members of important minority communities. The election manifestoes of the Congress and the League differed scarcely at all in their practical programmes of social and agrarian reform, or in the principle of opposition to British rule and to the federal part of the constitution. Their sharpest difference lay in the League's implicit stress on maintaining the safeguard of separate electorates for minorities, which were anathema to the Congress, and in its anxiety for protection of Urdu as a national language; but provincial Governments were not much concerned, at least with the former issue. The achievement of clear majorities by the Congress alone changed the picture. The Governors' requirement of minority representation could be fulfilled with Congress Muslims without bringing in the League.

In the United Provinces, where the Muslims formed one-sixth of the population and had influence and solidarity beyond their numbers, and where there had been an unwritten understanding that two Ministers would be Muslims from the League, the latter won 26 of the 64 reserved Muslim seats against only one gained by a Congressman. Notwithstanding the independent majority won by the Congress in the legislature, it was still expected to implement the understanding. But its terms for admission of Muslim Leaders to office—pronounced, significantly, not by the provincial Congress leader but by Maulana Abul Kalam Azad, a member of the three-man Parliamentary sub-committee which had been appointed to exercise central Congress control over the provincial Ministers and legislators—were in effect that the League in the United Provinces should dissolve itself in the Congress. The League group in the legislature should cease to function as a separate group; U.P. League members should become part of the Congress party, subject to its control and discipline; all decisions in the party should continue to be taken by majority vote. Such suicidal conditions were totally rejected by the League. The United Provinces Ministry was formed with two Muslims, one the only Congress Muslim elected, the other a deserting League member. In the Central Provinces the Congress Government also included a renegade Muslim Leaguer, and in Bombay a Muslim Independent. The League was thus left in the wilderness in six provinces. But it had been taught a lesson, and thenceforward accepted the Congress as its mortal foe.

In the light of its consequences, the Congress policy, though politically understandable, was a blunder of the first order. It is often attributed to Pandit Nehru, but it was clearly the joint *diktat* of the Congress High Command, specifically the Parliamentary sub-committee of Maulana Azad, Sardar Vallabhbhai Patel and Dr. Rajendra Prasad, and it expressed more plainly than any speeches the ideology that the Congress alone spoke for India. To Muslims this meant submitting to Hindu rule. The cry of 'Islam in danger' was raised, and 'Congress raj' to the Mussulmans became a worse bogy than British raj had ever been. In correspondence with Mr. Jinnah early in 1938, Pandit Nehru adopted a conciliatory tone, but the clash between the latter's ideal of a united secular India under one banner and the former's demand for recognition of the League as an equal with the Congress was incapable of being settled by formulae or by compromise on specific issues.

The Congress formed Governments of its own complexion in seven provinces of the eleven. There remained the Punjab, Bengal, Assam and Sind. In all these, non-Congress Governments were formed. After an interval, in September 1938, a Congress-led combination took office in Assam; and in Sind the solidarity of the Congress block enabled it, though a small minority in opposition, to exert critical influence on patched-up Governments. Politics in Sind and Assam remained, throughout the period of provincial self-government, highly complex, personal and unstable.

In Bengal Mr. Fazl-ul-Huq, a resourceful and experienced Muslim politician, formed a coalition Government based mainly on the Muslim League, his own Proja Party (mainly Muslim), the independent Muslims—together holding 116 seats out of 250—and the Scheduled Castes; when it lost the support of the latter it was kept in office by the European vote (twenty-five seats), though it also had a few caste Hindu supporters. Mr. Fazl-ul-Huq was not initially averse to a coalition with the Congress, and there were rumours of its having been arranged. But in April 1938 the provincial Premier announced that, if he had accepted the Premiership of a coalition Ministry, which the Congress had more than once offered him, he would have 'signed the death-warrant of Islam'. He continued to hold the reins, and even after a split in the Muslim ranks in 1941 between the full-blooded Leaguers, headed by Sir Nazimuddin, and his own more eclectic followers he managed to keep office with a Muslim-Hindu coalition. Although on a communal show-down the Muslims could always outvote the Hindus in Bengal, the allocation of seats, together with the force of provincial politics and personalities, prescribed some sort of inter-communal pact for a viable Government. Bengal could belong neither wholly to the League nor wholly to the Congress.

The same was true in the Punjab. Here, however, there was a stable combination to build on. The National Unionist Party, representing rural interests of all three communities, led by Sir Sikander Hyat Khan, won 96 out of 175 seats in the election of 1937, and could further count on the support of the Khalsa Sikhs. Though Hindu and Sikh support tended to fall away as Indian politics grew ever more communal, Sir Sikander stayed at the head of an all-community Ministry until his untimely death in 1942, when Sir Khizar Hyat Khan Tiwana formed another Unionist

Ministry. The stability and loyalty of the Punjab Government were of immense value to the rulers of India throughout the war; for the Punjab provided over half the fighting men of the Indian Army.

The experiences, achievements and difficulties of the autonomous provincial Governments, whether Congress or non-Congress, before and during the war, need not be related here. At the time, and right up to 1945, they seemed more important to the constitutional future of all India than they appear in retrospect; for provincial autonomy under the 1935 Act was regarded, in Britain and by many Indians, as a laboratory of Indian political freedom and an experiment whose extension to the central or federal plane would open a progressive path to full Indian nationhood. Up to the outbreak of war it worked, in fact, much as parliamentary democracies generally do: not without internal political vicissitudes or personal intrigues, nor without mistakes, nor without the occasional subordination of broad public interests to narrower party ones, but on the whole successfully, and, most important, in amicable co-operation with the Provincial Governors and with the established Services representing the British raj. No Governor had to use his reserve powers to demand the resignation of a Ministry or to force a showdown on a major issue,[1] though this is far from saying that the existence of those powers had no effect in guiding and moderating Ministerial policies. On the contrary, there were many occasions on which Congress Ministers, anxious to avoid such conflicts, heeded advice from departmental Secretaries that proposed courses might attract the Governor's special responsibilities. Only four Bills throughout India were vetoed by a Governor or the Governor-General in the first five

---

[1] In February 1938 the Governor-General, Lord Linlithgow, using his power under the Act for 'preventing any grave menace to the peace or tranquillity of India or any part thereof', instructed the Governors of the United Provinces and Bihar to reject the advice of their Congress Premiers, given under pressure from the 'High Command' and their own left wing, to release the two-score remaining hard-core 'political prisoners' in those two provinces, and the Ministries thereupon resigned. But at the Haripura session of the Congress later that month the moderates, led by Mr. Gandhi, won the day, and the ex-Ministers withdrew their resignations on an assurance from the Governor-General that the Governors still desired to carry on the policy of progressive release, case by case, which had hitherto been agreed.

years of provincial autonomy, two of them in the North-West Frontier Province; and only on one occasion, in Sind in order to strengthen the forces of law and order, did a Governor legislate by ordinance over the heads of his Ministry.

In social and economic reform, which was the substantive purpose of provincial self-government from the popular Indian viewpoint, the Ministries were handicapped by financial stringency as well as the need to balance the interests of different sections of their supporters, but the advances made were considerable, and could not have been made by an alien Government dependent, as such must be, on the support of vested interests. Law and order was a provincial subject, and the Ministries had a fair taste of its difficulties in the shape of communal riots, strikes and subversion;[1] there was nothing here to bear out the charge, sometimes levied in India, that the British for their own purposes had allowed or fomented inter-communal disorder, or the claim that self-government would relieve workers and peasants from the need for direct action, but rather the contrary. If, however, the new Governments were sometimes weaker or more partisan in face of disorder than British authority might have been, there were no great disasters in this period, and all storms were weathered. Governors did indeed suffer anxieties about the morale of the public services, including the police, against whose officers high and low many Congressmen could not refrain from trying to pay off old scores. But the Ministries gradually learned how much they depended on the services, and the damage done, though substantial, was not irreparable, as the conduct of the police and civil administrators under later assaults, like the 'Quit India' revolt of 1942, was to show.

In its bearing on the broad political and constitutional future of India, the great importance of the first phase of provincial self-government lay in the reaction of the Muslims, and particularly the Muslim League, to Congress rule in seven provinces and the

---

[1] For instance, the Shahidganj agitation in the Punjab, the Khaksar troubles in the Punjab and the United Provinces, the Dacca communal riots of 1940–1, the Digboi strike in Assam, the Sukkur fighting in Sind, the no-rent agitation in the United Provinces, the great strikes in Ahmedabad, Bombay and Cawnpore. In the two years beginning October 1937 there were eighty-five serious communal outbreaks, causing casualties of about 2,000, of which about 170 were fatal.

impact of Congress 'dictatorship' from the Centre. The refusal to
admit Muslim Leaguers to Ministries in Congress-majority
provinces, save on terms of surrender, was followed by a great
Congress effort, of which Pandit Nehru was the leading exponent,
to rally the support of the Muslim voters themselves, especially in
the United Provinces—the key area, with a substantial Muslim
minority, whose example might well be followed in the less-
promising Muslim-majority provinces. The arguments behind this
'mass-contact' movement were, first, that otherwise the Muslims,
where in a minority, were condemned to permanent opposition;
secondly that the Congress alone could deliver the goods of social
and economic reform by which the masses regardless of community would benefit; and thirdly that genuine minority interests were
safe in the hands of the Congress as the great all-India non-
communal body. In October 1937, stung by an attack by Mr.
Jinnah, the Congress Working Committee passed this resolution
at its Calcutta session:

> The Congress has solemnly and repeatedly declared its policy
> in regard to the rights of minorities in India and has stated that
> it considers it its duty to protect those rights and ensure the
> widest possible scope for the development of those minorities
> and their participation in the fullest measure in the political,
> economic and cultural life of the nation. The objective of the
> Congress is an independent and united India where no class or
> group or majority or minority may exploit another to its own
> advantage and where all the elements in the nation may co-
> operate together for the common good and advancement of the
> people of India.

At its Haripura session the following February the Congress, on
the motion of Pandit Nehru, confirmed the Calcutta resolution,
and added a significant and challenging paragraph:

> The Congress welcomes the growth of anti-imperialist feeling
> among the Muslims and other minorities in India and the grow-
> ing unity of all classes and communities in India in the struggle
> for India's independence which is one and indivisible and can
> only be carried on effectively on a united national basis. In
> particular the Congress welcomes the large numbers of members
> of the minority communities who have joined the Congress

during the past year and given their mass support to the struggle for freedom and the ending of the exploitation of India's masses.

In short, the national objectives of political freedom and social reform were to be achieved, not by alliance with non-Congress minority forces, but by their absorption into a single Congress fold, or by their liquidation, through seduction of their mass support.

The Muslim reaction was equal and opposite—and was to prove far more successful. The Muslim politicians outside the Congress realised that their power, or their prospect of any power, was at peril from two causes: their own disunity, and their lack of organisation to reach and hold the mass voters. These two weaknesses they set about remedying, under the leadership of Mr. Mahomed Ali Jinnah, who from being one among a number of prominent Muslim figures, President of a League which could win fewer than one quarter of the Muslim provincial seats, now swiftly emerges as the acknowledged and supreme national leader of the community. The strength afforded by his detachment not only from provincial politics but also from administrative responsibility was an asset which he was to exploit to the end, declining to take any office in the Interim Government of India in 1946 and choosing rather to be constitutional head than first Prime Minister of the Pakistan he had created. At the Lucknow conference of the League in October 1937 he pronounced a diatribe against the Congress, which he charged with pursuing a Hindu policy and thus playing into the hands of British imperialism by exciting communal antagonism—a remarkable case of stealing one's opponent's clothes. Muslims, he said, could expect neither justice nor fair play under Congress rule.

The first great success of this new militant regime was achieved at that time, when Sir Sikander Hyat Khan and shortly afterwards Mr. Fazl-ul-Huq and Sir Muhammed Saadulla, the Premiers of the Punjab, Bengal and Assam, announced that they were advising their Muslim supporters to join the League. This move enormously enhanced both the strength of the League and the ascendancy of Mr. Jinnah at its head. Sir Sikander's decision was all the more remarkable in that the League had failed dismally in the Punjab elections; but he sensed the danger that a section of his Muslim followers, inspired by the growing communalism and seeking to be on the right band-wagon, might split away to join the League, and he preferred to retain his own leadership both of the Muslims and of the Unionist Party by bringing its Muslim members into the League *en bloc*.[1]

The second great success was in the constituencies. Within three months of the Lucknow Conference over 170 new branches of the League had been formed, 90 of them in the United Provinces, and it claimed to have enlisted 100,000 new members in that province alone. This was its retort in kind to the Congress mass-contact movement. Before long the effect was being shown decisively in by-elections.

The attack on Congress raj in the provinces now became more and more bellicose. At the Patna session of the League in December 1938, Mr. Jinnah declared that all hope of communal peace had been wrecked on the rocks of 'Congress fascism'. Shortly afterwards there was published the report of a committee appointed by the League's Council to enquire into Muslim grievances in Congress provinces, known from the name of the committee's chairman as the Pirpur Report. This comparatively restrained document was followed in March 1939 by a much more lurid account of 'some grievances of Muslims in Bihar' by a provincial League inquiry committee (the Shareef Report) and by an equally intemperate account of 'Muslim Sufferings under Congress Rule' put out by Mr. Fazl-ul-Huq in December 1939. These charges were scornfully repudiated in the Hindu Press, and, in the case of the Pirpur Report, rejected in a reasoned reply by the Bihar Government. At this distance their truth or untruth matters less than their nature.

On the one hand there are the religious or quasi-religious provocations familiar throughout Indian history since Hindus and Muslims lived alongside each other—cow worship, prevention of the call to prayer, desecration of mosques and music in their vicinity, personal assaults including rapes and abductions. On the other hand there are new political and administrative accusations, especially in the reasoned Pirpur Report. Urdu is being suppressed in favour of Hindi, the police and magistrates are biased, Muslims are denied their fair share of public appointments, they have no hope of equity from Congress Ministries, let alone the 'parallel

[1] Moon, *Divide and Quit*, p. 17. This critical incident is referred to again on p. 270 below.

governments' established by local Congress committees; Congress rule means Hindu rule, exemplified in the flying of the Congress flag everywhere, the singing of the allegedly anti-Islamic 'Bande Mataram' as the national anthem, and the 'Wardha Scheme' of village education, a typical concept of Mr. Gandhi's, based on non-violence and the crafts of spinning and weaving, and eschewing religion, to the revolt of the Muslims whose primary education had always been founded on the Koran.

Behind all this smoke there was undoubtedly some fire. British Governors of Congress provinces at the time generally formed the opinion that while their Ministers for the most part genuinely tried to be communally non-partisan, the sense of power among Congressmen in the districts and villages often led them into arrogant and provocative behaviour. This tendency was worsened by the phenomenon of 'parallel government' whereby some Congress Ministries sought to operate simultaneously through the official administrative machine and through the party organisation and leaders in the districts. Here at least they were, perhaps unwittingly, taking a leaf out of the book of the European dictatorships. The tendency may, on the other hand, have been mitigated by that other, much stricter and more pervasive non-constitutional feature of Congress government in the provinces—control from the Centre by the All-India High Command, either the Congress Working Committee or its Parliamentary sub-committee. Early in 1939 the Working Committee sent to all Congress Ministries unexceptionable instructions on the treatment of minorities, and Sardar Patel, a member of the Parliamentary sub-committee, revealed that at his instance every Congress Premier had invited his Governor to intervene if he thought his Ministers were not dealing correctly with minorities.

The main effect of 'dictatorship' by the High Command, however, in the present context was to heighten Muslim fears. Appointments and resignations of Ministers were controlled—in the Central Provinces the Congress Premier himself was eliminated, though he still commanded a majority in the legislature—programmes and legislation were so far as possible uniform throughout the seven provinces; procedure such as flag-flying and anthem-singing was prescribed; and sometimes even subordinate political appointments were supervised. (The Muslim League began to imitate the Congress centralism; in the summer of 1939 its Working Committee instructed provincial branches not to come to terms with the Congress on their own account but to refer all such proposals to the Working Committee. No doubt the League would have gone much further in the same direction but for the resignation of the Congress Ministries as a result of the war.) This monolithic regime was sustained by strict party discipline not only over Ministers but also over Congress members of the legislatures, with the result that parliamentary debates often became formal and unreal.

However necessary all this was for a party whose primary goal and *raison d'être* were national, and dependent in the eyes of its leaders upon unqualified unity and coherence, its appearance to those outside the party, especially the Muslims, was odious. Provincial parliamentary debate or local agitation was seen to be useless in face of orders delivered from Delhi or Wardha. Pacts and alliances which would have given opposition groups political leverage were barred. The value of provincial autonomy, and of reservations and guarantees written into provincial constitutions, was debased. Above all, for the future, majority rule was seen to be Congress rule, exerted from a Centre dominated by the Hindu majority through an organisation which brooked no opposition and refused to share its power. There is no doubt that the conduct of provincial self-government from 1937 to 1939 was a major cause of the spread of the two-nation theory and the Pakistan movement. Yet its achievements were considerable and without it the way could hardly have been open to a peaceful and orderly transfer of power to responsible Indian hands a decade later.

8

The war and the Pakistan movement

On 3rd September 1939 the Viceroy issued a proclamation that war had broken out between His Majesty and Germany, and that a state of war emergency existed in India. That India should be 'dragged into war against her will', or at least without consulting her people's representatives, was then and continued to be a loudly trumpeted grievance of Indian politicians, especially in the Congress. But it was not a grievance that appeared at the time to be felt with deep and unqualified emotion, and this for two reasons. The constitutional correctitudes were understood and accepted, however much resented and opposed; senior Indian leaders knew well that, while Canada and other Dominions could demonstrate their freedom to choose whether 'His Majesty' was at war for them, this right had been legally ratified but a few years earlier in the Statute of Westminster—and, even then, only implicitly. They did not really expect suddenly to be granted a freedom in this vital respect which they did not possess in others less momentous. Secondly, and more important, Indian opinion on the war itself was divided.

Hostility to 'imperialist war', it is true, had been vehement from 1936 onwards. In August 1939 the Congress Working Committee declared, in the context of foreign policy, that 'India cannot associate herself with democratic freedom which is denied to her'. Congress members of the Legislative Assembly at Delhi were ordered to absent themselves from attending the next session, the provincial Congress Governments were warned 'to assist in no way the war preparations' and to be prepared to resign. But, when war came, opinion was far from unanimous even in the Congress, still less elsewhere. Helped by the absence of the Congress members, a Defence of India Bill granting emergency powers was passed by the central legislature without a division on its final reading. The Punjab and Bengal Ministries, headed by members of the Muslim League, and backed by their legislatures, promised complete support for the war. The Liberals—the Old Guard of moderate co-operators—and the Hindu Mahasabha endorsed the war effort, though calling for pledges for India's future on their own political or communal lines. Among Congressmen, detestation of Hitler's aggression struggled with hostility to helping Britain while she kept India subject. The Working Committee of the Congress, on 15th September, passed a resolution condemning Fascism and Nazism, attacking the proclamation of war and the emergency powers, declaring that a decision on co-operation could not be long delayed, and calling on the British Government 'to declare in unequivocal terms what their war aims are in regard to democracy and imperialism and the new order that is envisaged, in particular how those aims are going to apply to India and to be given effect to in the present'.

This bargaining resolution, drafted by Pandit Nehru, was not to the taste of Mr. Gandhi, who had told Lord Linlithgow two days after the outbreak of war that his own sympathies were with England and France from the humanitarian standpoint, and that he could not contemplate without being stirred to the very depth the destruction of London. 'I was sorry to find myself alone,' he wrote in his paper *Harijan* after the Working Committee's resolution, 'in seeking that whatever support was to be given to the British should be given unconditionally', though he always made clear that in accordance with the principle of non-violence it could only be moral support. But soon afterwards he changed his mind. On 10th October the All-India Congress Committee spelt out the demand for giving effect 'in the present' to war aims for India: 'India must be declared an independent nation, and present application must be given to this status to the largest possible extent.'

Mr. Jinnah, following a tactic that he often repeated, waited for the Congress move before making his own. If they were bargaining, so could he. On 18th September, three days after the Congress Working Committee resolution, the Muslim League Working Committee, while taking the same line on the justice of the war against German aggression, warned the Government of India that it could count on solid Muslim support only on two conditions: in the present, 'justice and fair play' for Muslims in the Congress provinces; for the future, an assurance that no declaration or constitutional advance for India should be made, nor any Indian constitution framed or adopted, 'without the consent and approval of the All-India Muslim League'. So the terms were plainly stated: by the Congress, immediate independent status; by the Muslim League, its right of veto as 'the only organisation that can speak on behalf of Muslim India'. These were terms mutually antagonistic, and such as no British Government could possibly grant in the conditions of September 1939. The triangle of forces that was to endure until partition and the transfer of power was already set up.

On 17th October, after a series of talks with political leaders, including Mr. Gandhi, Pandit Nehru, Mr. Jinnah and Sardar Patel, Lord Linlithgow issued a statement as eloquent as it was hazy in respect of Indian political demands. Dominion status for India remained the objective of His Majesty's Government. They would, at the end of the war, be prepared to modify the scheme of the 1935 Act in the light of Indian views, giving full weight to the opinions and interests of the minorities. The immediate situation must be faced in terms of the world scene and Indian political realities. The best way of associating Indian public opinion with prosecution of the war seemed to the Viceroy to be 'the establishment of a consultative group, representative of all major political parties in British India and of the Indian Princes', over which the Governor-General himself would preside. If this offer was seriously intended to placate the Congress it was a wide misjudgment. The Muslim League, certainly, was no worse than lukewarm: the stress on the rights of minorities was for them a point gained. But the Congress Working Committee denounced the Viceroy's statement as 'an unequivocal reiteration of the old imperialist policy'. In the circumstances the Congress could not possibly give any support to Britain, and as a first step the Committee called upon the Congress Ministries to resign. In many cases reluctantly, but without revolt, one by one they did so. Seven provinces thereupon went into government under Section 93 of the 1935 Act, that is to say, direct rule by the Governor.[1]

A further plank was hammered firmly into the constitutional platform of the Congress when, in March 1940, it adopted on Pandit Nehru's motion a resolution again condemning a war 'for imperialist ends' to which the Congress could not in any way be party, and continued:

[1] In 1941–2 there was a temporary reversion to parliamentary government in Orissa, thanks to the defection of a group of Congress members.

Indian freedom cannot exist within the orbit of imperialism, and Dominion or any other status within the imperial structure is wholly inapplicable to India. . . . The people of India alone can properly shape their own constitution and determine their relations to other countries of the world through a Constituent Assembly elected on the basis of adult suffrage . . . the rights of all recognised minorities will be fully protected by agreement, as far as possible or by arbitration if agreement is not reached on any point. . . . The Congress cannot admit the right of the Rulers of the Indian States or of foreign vested interests to come in the way of Indian freedom. Sovereignty in India must rest with the people, whether in the States or in the Provinces.

A popularly elected Constituent Assembly, safeguards for minorities by agreement or arbitration, no Dominion status, no voice for Princes or the British commercial community—these remained in the Congress creed right up to the last phase.

Almost simultaneously the permanent Muslim League platform was defined. In February 1940 Mr. Jinnah publicly proclaimed that any constitutional settlement must recognise that India was not one nation but two, and that the Muslims would not accept the arbitrament of any body, Indian or British, but would determine their destiny themselves. In March, at Lahore, the League adopted its famous Pakistan resolution:

Resolved that it is the considered view of this Session of the All-India Muslim League that no constitutional plan would be workable in this country or acceptable to the Muslims unless it is designed on the following basic principle, viz., that geographically contiguous units are demarcated into regions which should be so constituted with such territorial readjustments as may be necessary that the areas in which the Muslims are numerically in a majority, as in the north-western and eastern zones of India, should be grouped to constitute 'independent States' in which the constituent units shall be autonomous and sovereign. . . .

Both the syntax and the import of these phrases are obscure, but the intended meaning was clarified in a later paragraph authorising the Working Committee 'to frame a scheme of constitution in accordance with these basic principles, providing for the assumption finally by the respective regions of all powers such as defence, external affairs, communications, Customs and such other matters as may be necessary'. That is, the contiguous Muslim-majority regions were 'finally' to become fully sovereign States.

No doubt a certain vagueness and lack of clarity were present by design. As his later conduct showed, Mr. Jinnah had no intention of offering a focus for opposition, either within the Muslim ranks or beyond, by spelling out the details of the 'Pakistan' idea, details which were bound to expose both its general difficulties and its particular effects on areas or interests, but was content to leave it as a broad aspiration to which it was politically easier to adhere in principle than to object in application. The Working Committee of the League in fact never did produce its constitutional blueprint. In February 1941 the newspapers published a scheme attributed to a committee which was reported to have studied the various proposals for Pakistan. Two sovereign states should be created, one comprising the Punjab, Sind, the North-West Frontier Province, Baluchistan and Delhi (the area controlled from the Centre under a Chief Commissioner) with their existing boundaries, the other Bengal and Assam but with some territorial adjustments, *minus* in west Bengal, *plus* in east Bihar. The independence of Hyderabad and other States with Muslim rulers must be recognised, and Princely States adjacent to the two Muslim-majority areas might federate with them. For a transitional period a Centre would be required to co-ordinate policy on foreign affairs, defence, communications, customs and minority safeguards and, significantly, for encouraging communal migration. Mr. Jinnah, however, was swift to deny the authority of this scheme. He and the League remained uncommitted to anything more precise or authoritative than the Lahore resolution until they were obliged to take a position in face of the Cabinet Mission of 1946.

The adoption of the Pakistan goal by the Muslim League, though sudden and by most observers unexpected, had as its background the organic growth of a new ideology. Its first apostle is usually claimed to be the Urdu poet and Punjabi leader Sir Mohammed Iqbal, who in his presidential address to the Muslim League in 1930 declared:

> . . . I would like to see the Punjab, the North-West Frontier Province, Sind and Baluchistan amalgamated into a single State. Self-government within the British Empire or without the

British Empire and the formation of a consolidated North-West Indian Moslem State appears to me to be the final destiny of the Moslems at least of North-West India.

But it is clear from the context of Sir Mohammed Iqbal's speech that he was thinking not of total partition but of the structure of a confederal India. He spoke of the need for other 'autonomous states' in India, obviously not all Muslim, based on language, race, history, religion and identity of economic interests, and he declared:

A unitary form of government is simply unthinkable in a self-governing India. Residuary powers must be left entirely to self-governing States, the Central Federal Government only exercising those powers which are expressly vested in it by the free consent of the Federal States.

Clearly this was neither the two-nation theory nor the true idea of Pakistan.

Mr. C. Rahmat Ali claims, with evident reason, to be the founder of the Pakistan movement.[1] In 1933 he and three other young Muslim Indians in England circulated a leaflet declaring that 'on behalf of our thirty million Muslim brethren who live in PAKSTAN —by which we mean the five northern units of India—viz., Punjab, North-West Frontier Province (Afghan Province), Kashmir, Sind and Baluchistan' they protested against the federal constitution then being adumbrated at the Round Table Conference, and repudiated the claim of the Indian Muslim delegation— which of course included Mr. Jinnah—to speak for their community. They rejected Sir Mohammed Iqbal's federal ideas as inadequate. India, they wrote, was not the name of one single country, nor the home of one single nation. The Muslims of PAKSTAN, a distinct nation, 'demand the recognition of a separate national status'.

Delegates of the Muslim League and the All-India Muslim Conference, asked about a scheme 'under the name of Pakistan' when giving evidence to the Joint Select Committee of Parliament, dismissed it as 'only a students' scheme' and 'chimerical and impracticable'. But Mr. Rahmat Ali and his friends were not

[1] In 1935 he described himself as Founder-President of a body called the Pakistan National Movement, with an address in Cambridge, England.

silenced. In 1935 they found a new argument in the separation of Burma from India. If Burma, why not Pakistan, as it was now spelt?[1] In 1940, in a presidential address to his Movement, Mr. Rahmat Ali elaborated the plan. The *millat* of Islam (a term which can be translated as community or nation) could be saved only by severing all ties with India. North-West India must constitute the nation and sovereign state of Pakistan. But to it should be added Bengal and Assam, dubbed Bang-i-Islam (Islam in Bengal), which must be allowed self-determination, and Hyderabad, dubbed Usmanistan; and these three independent nations should form a triple alliance.

Meanwhile other propagandists had fired their broadsides, notably Dr. Syed Abdul Latif and Sir Abdulla Haroon, both supporters of the Muslim League, and Sir Mohammed Shah Nawaz Khan. Dr. Latif allowed for a minimal All-India Centre, with one-third Muslim representation and a 'composite stable executive' subject to communal ratio, but advocated a wholesale though voluntary transfer of population, such that the Northern Muslim zone would eventually become 'a permanent home for all the Muslims living at present in the United Provinces and Bihar'. Sir Abdulla was for dividing India into two federations, but he neglected Bengal. Sir Mohammed's plan is interesting because it envisages a three-tier system such as was to play such a key part in the Cabinet Mission phase of the post-war story. He wanted India, including the Princely States, divided into five regional federations, two of them, in the north-west and north-east, with Muslim majorities, and together forming a confederation without taxing power.

The most significant contribution, however, came from Sir Sikander Hyat Khan, Premier of the Punjab, significant not only because of his status as a distinguished Muslim political leader who had subscribed to the League but also because of its motive. In July 1938 Sir Sikander drafted a scheme later published as a pamphlet under the title 'Outlines of a Scheme of Indian Federation'. This scheme envisaged a three-tier system of provinces, regions and Centre. The powers of the provinces should be enlarged to the maximum. The regions should include Indian States as well as parts of British India. Seven were provisionally suggested, two of them corresponding broadly with Pakistan; the first

[1] Fortuitously, but happily, Pakistan means in Urdu 'land of the pure'.

grouped Bengal States and Sikkim with Assam and most of Bengal, and the second grouped Kashmir, Punjab States and two western Rajput States with the Punjab, Sind, North-West Frontier Province and Baluchistan. The Regional legislatures would collectively constitute the Central Assembly, whose powers would normally be confined to defence, foreign affairs, Customs, currency, and communications, though it could be entrusted with additional concurrent powers at the option of the Regions. Sir Sikander had invited Mr. Moon, i.c.s.,[1] Secretary to the Governor of the Punjab, to help him with editing the pamplet. When Mr. Moon asked him why he was anxious to lay such a complex scheme before a sceptical public, 'he replied with a wry smile that unless positive proposals such as his were put forward for consideration other people would come out with "something worse". The "something worse" to which he referred was the idea of Pakistan.' Some months later, Mr. Moon suggested to the Punjab Premier that the Pakistan concept might after all be the best solution. Sir Sikander turned upon him, his eyes blazing with indignation, and exclaimed:

> How can you talk like this? You have been long enough in Western Punjab to know the Muslims there. Surely you can see that Pakistan would be an invitation to them to cut the throat of every Hindu *bania*. . . . I do hope I won't hear you talk like this again. Pakistan would mean a massacre.[2]

Nine years later, Pakistan did mean a massacre. But Sir Sikander was dead. For tactical reasons he had subscribed to the Lahore resolution of the League, hoping to keep his followers together while the mad dream, as he saw it, of total partition faded and less drastic proposals such as his gained favour. Reason, however, is not the ruler of mass movements, and it was the dream, the chimera, the students' scheme, that was to become reality.

All these developments happened in the period of the 'phoney war' in Europe. In April 1940 Germany invaded Denmark and Norway; in May Mr. Winston Churchill became Prime Minister, with Mr. L. S. Amery as his Secretary for State for India; in June France fell; in July Britain had her back to the wall, expecting invasion. Indian political attitudes, though emotionally affected, did not change. 'While India is completely opposed to the idea of

[1] Later Sir Penderel Moon.
[2] Moon, *Divide and Quit*, p. 20.

the triumph of Nazism,' said Pandit Nehru, 'it is no good asking
her to come to the rescue of a tottering imperialism.' Mr. Gandhi
preached pure pacifism, but the Congress did not agree. The
Working Committee, on 7th July, demanded a declaration of the
full independence of India and

> as an immediate step to giving effect to it, a provisional National
> Government . . . at the Centre which, though formed as a
> transitory measure, should be such as to command the confid-
> ence of all the elected elements in the Central Legislature and
> secure the closest co-operation of the responsible Governments
> in the Provinces. . . . The Working Committee declare that, if
> these measures are adopted, it will enable the Congress to throw
> its full weight into the efforts for the effective organisation of the
> defence of the country.

Whatever the Congress demands and offer meant, they met
another obstacle besides the certain British objections. In a fresh
series of talks and correspondence between the Viceroy and Mr.
Jinnah the latter laid down two conditions for the Muslim League's
participation in government. First, the British Government must
undertake to adopt no constitution, temporary or final, 'without
the previous approval of Muslim India'. Secondly, in any wartime reorganisation 'Muslim India must have an equal share
in the authority and control of the Governments, central and
provincial'.

Immediate independence and majority rule: Muslim veto and
Muslim equality—such were the rival demands, conflicting, extravagant and unreal. Amid such revolutionary trumpeting the
cautious tune of Government seemed thin and uninspiring. On
8th August the Viceroy issued a statement which became known as
the August Offer. Lord Linlithgow declared:

> It is clear that earlier differences which had prevented the
> achievement of national unity remained unbridged. Deeply as
> His Majesty's Government regret this, they do not feel that they
> should any longer, because of those differences, postpone the
> expansion of the Governor General's Council, and the establish-
> ment of a body which will more closely associate Indian public
> opinion with the conduct of the war by the Central Govern-
> ment. . . .

... There is still in certain quarters doubt as to the intentions of His Majesty's Government for the constitutional future of India, and . . . as to whether the position of minorities, whether political or religious, is sufficiently safeguarded. . . .

... It has already been made clear that my declaration of last October does not exclude examination of any part either of the Act of 1935 or of the policy and plans on which it is based. His Majesty's Government's concern that full weight should be given to the views of minorities in any revision has also been brought out. . . .

... They could not contemplate transfer of their present responsibilities for the peace and welfare of India to any system of government whose authority is directly denied by large and powerful elements in India's national life. Nor could they be parties to the coercion of such elements into submission to such a Government.

... There has been very strong insistence that the framing of the new constitutional scheme should be primarily the responsibility of Indians themselves. . . . His Majesty's Government are in sympathy with that desire and wish to see it given the fullest practical expression, subject to the due fulfilment of the obligations which Great Britain's long connection with India has imposed on her and for which His Majesty's Government cannot divest themselves of responsibility. It is clear that a moment when the Commonwealth is engaged in a struggle for existence is not one in which fundamental constitutional issues can be decisively resolved. But His Majesty's Government authorise me to declare that they will most readily assent to the setting up after the conclusion of the war with the least possible delay of a body representative of the principal elements in India's national life in order to devise the framework of the new Constitution, and they will lend every aid in their power to hasten decisions on all relevant matters to the utmost degree. Meanwhile they will welcome and promote in any way possible every sincere and practical step that may be taken by representative Indians themselves to reach a basis of friendly agreement, first upon the form which the post-war representative body should take and the methods by which it should arrive at its conclusions, and,

T.G.D.—D

secondly, upon the principles and outlines of the Constitution itself. . . .

Whatever might be said of the substance of this declaration, its structure and terminology were such as to make it as unattractive as possible in India. Had it been left to the Viceroy, it might well have been better phrased; but he was plagued with innumerable drafting amendments from London, most of them of a dampening character. Hardly a sentence is without a qualifying or balancing clause, so that the general impression was one of taking as much with one hand as was given with the other. The note of boldness or imagination or generosity is wholly absent.[1]

Later events, it is true, especially the Cripps Mission of 1942, do not confirm the supposition that a great opportunity was lost in August 1940. Writing to Mr. Amery, the Secretary of State, in July, Lord Linlithgow had said that he doubted whether anything was likely to bring in the Congress short of their full demands, for their leaders, in his opinion, were determined not to be responsible for government at that difficult time; and in this all the evidence supports him. But the fact is that imagination, decisiveness and clarity in expression of British policy towards India in the war period were handicapped by three accidents besides the complexity of Indian affairs themselves: the cautious character and public reserve of Lord Linlithgow, whose native deliberation was reinforced by the immense responsibilities he bore during the war, and whose heaviness of style belied the vigour of his mind; the out-of-date imperialism of Mr. Winston Churchill, who saw in the Indian party leaders a political clique opposed by large masses (Muslims, other minorities, depressed classes, the States) adding up to a big majority who could therefore be reckoned on Britain's side—a truly naive calculation; and the existence in the British Cabinet of an unprecedented number of influential Ministers

---

[1] This is not being wise after the event. The author, as head of the Empire Division of the Ministry of Information, had the task of projecting the August Offer upon world opinion, both Commonwealth and foreign, as a stroke of war statesmanship. Handed it a few days before publication, he went at once to the Permanent Secretary of the Ministry to ask whether, without of course altering its policy, its drafting could not be altered in a public-relations sense, for his task with its present phrasing was very hard, but was told that every word had been hammered out and agreed by the War Cabinet and the Viceroy.

previously linked with India,[1] together more powerful than the Secretary of State himself, a man of liberal and far-seeing ideas who nevertheless, as a Tory and the embodiment of British control, was deeply suspect by Indian opinion. Between Delhi and Westminster, therefore, there was always a complex and ponderous system of negotiation rather than a simple and direct understanding. After Mr. Churchill became Prime Minister he initiated a direct correspondence with the Viceroy, which Lord Linlithgow resented as interference with the proper responsibilities of the Secretary of State and himself, but which he was bound to answer and which added a further complication.

A fortnight after the 'August Offer' the Congress Working Committee declared that the British Government's

> refusal to part with power and responsibility in favour of the elected representatives of the people of India . . . is a direct encouragement and incitement to civil discord and strife. . . . The issue of the minorities has been made into an insuperable barrier to India's progress. . . . The rejection of the Congress proposals is proof of the British Government's determination to continue to hold India by the sword. . . . The desire of the Congress not to embarrass the British Government at a time of peril for them has been misunderstood and despised.

The whole conception of Dominion Status for India, said Pandit Nehru, was dead as a doornail.

If the Congress saw no good in the offer, the Muslim League recognised that it had implicitly given them half their demand, the Muslim veto on the form in which power might be transferred. But they continued to press for the other half, the principle of Muslim equality with non-Muslim India, and, while not forbidding co-operation in the war administration, refused to offer it. The All-India Congress Committee, meeting in mid-September at the height of the Battle of Britain in the sky, re-adopted the policy and leadership of Mr. Gandhi. For him, the immediate issue was not independence—'India can become independent only if she can hold her own when the British go out'—it was freedom of

---

[1] They included Mr. Attlee (a member of the Simon Commission), Viscount Simon himself, Sir John Anderson (former Governor of Bengal), Sir James Grigg (former Finance Member of the Governor-General's Executive Council) and later Sir Stafford Cripps.

speech. If this were not granted, a campaign of non-violent civil disobedience must be launched. Patiently Lord Linlithgow explained that Indian pacifists could not be treated more favourably than British conscientious objectors, who were allowed to profess and carry out their faith but not to try to persuade soldiers from their allegiance or munition workers from their work. This was not enough for Mr. Gandhi. On October 17th the civil disobedience campaign began under his direction. First, a few leaders, starting with Mr. Vinova Bhave and Pandit Nehru, were hand-picked to make anti-war speeches;[1] then more, including members of the Working Committee and former provincial Ministers, among them Maulana Abul Kalam Azad, President of the Congress, and Mr. C. Rajagopalachari, ex-Premier of Madras. The public utterance of the approved anti-war slogans, followed by arrest, conviction and sentence to varying terms of imprisonment, became a ritual. Some polite Congressmen, on good terms with the police and magistrates, even consulted the convenience of these officers before performing the duty the Mahatma had laid upon them. At a third stage, lesser Congress figures were drafted to the task, and in April 1941 the rank and file were enlisted. The peak figure of nearly 14,000 *satyagrahis* in prison was reached in May. By October it had fallen to about 5,600. Few of those released courted further arrest. To all save Mr. Gandhi and his close supporters, the civil disobedience movement seemed to have petered out.

The more the Congress became committed to its terms for co-operation, the more the Muslim League became likewise committed to contradictory terms. At the Madras session of the League in April 1941 the Lahore resolution, demanding Pakistan, was written into the League's constitution. Mr. Jinnah reiterated the fifty-fifty claim for Muslim representation at the Centre, and he was soon to prove that he meant business. In July the Viceroy enlarged his Executive Council (or Government) and enlisted eight Indian members, only four posts besides that of Governor-General being held by British members, though these were the crucial portfolios of Defence (the Commander-in-Chief, then Lord Wavell), Home, Finance and Communications. Lord Linlithgow had not, of course, been able to recruit any active members of the two main

---

[1] Pandit Nehru was sentenced by a local magistrate to three consecutive terms of sixteen months' imprisonment. But his offence was sedition, not that of formal disobedience.

political parties, but the new Law member, Sir Sultan Ahmed, did belong to the Muslim League. Mr. Jinnah ordered him to resign his office, and when he refused he was expelled from the League.

At the same time Mr. Jinnah displayed his authority still more imperiously. When the Viceroy formed his new Council he had announced that he was also setting up a National Defence Council of about thirty members, with purely consultative functions, to associate non-official opinion as far as possible with the conduct of the war, and among those who accepted his invitations to join the Council were the Muslim Premiers of the Punjab, Bengal and Assam. Led by Mr. Jinnah, the Working Committee ordered them to resign. All three did so, though Mr. Fazl-ul-Huq made clear that he obeyed against his better judgment, in order to maintain Muslim solidarity; and he resigned his membership of the League's Working Committee and Council in protest against Mr. Jinnah's 'arrogant and dictatorial line'. The Begum Shah Nawaz, another Muslim League member who had joined the Defence Council, refused to resign and, like Sir Sultan Ahmed, was expelled from the League for five years. Sir Sikander Hyat Khan, in tamely complying, showed a streak of weakness; for as leader in the Punjab he was the most committed to the war, and he had the most to gain by resisting Mr. Jinnah. Only a few months previously, in the Punjab Legislative Assembly, he had explained in a momentous speech that the Lahore resolution meant for him that there could be a Centre with limited powers enjoying the confidence of two autonomous units, and he declared:

We do not ask for freedom, that there may be a Muslim raj here and Hindu raj elsewhere. If that is what Pakistan means I will have nothing to do with it. . . . If you want real freedom for the Punjab . . . then that Punjab will not be Pakistan, but just Punjab, the land of the five rivers; Punjab is Punjab and will always remain Punjab whatever anybody may say. This then, briefly, is the political future which I visualise for my province and for my country under any new Constitution.

By capitulating to Mr. Jinnah tactically over membership of the National Defence Council, and thus demonstrating his subservience, Sir Sikander capitulated strategically to the totally different concept of Pakistan which Mr. Jinnah championed, and which was to eventuate in dismemberment of his beloved Punjab.

9

The Cripps offer

On 7th December 1941 Japan struck at Pearl Harbor. On 15th February Singapore fell to the Japanese conquest, Rangoon on 7th March. Among countries not yet occupied by the new enemy, for none did this devastating advance mean more than for India. Not only was the gate wide open for an invasion of India from the sea or overland; British prestige had received a blow which threatened its whole authority everywhere in Asia. If Britain could not defend Malaya, Singapore or Burma for more than a few weeks, how could she claim to be the permanent defender of India? Japanese radio propaganda, calling upon Indians to rise in revolt, poured into millions of ears. It is an extraordinary comment on qualities in the Indian character and on the inherent strength of the regime that, apart from a refugee movement from Calcutta, the country remained calm and everything went on much as before—including politics.

Neither the Congress nor the League changed its stance, though once more the Congress showed that it could not swallow Mr. Gandhi's total pacifism. More vehemently than ever it demanded immediate independence so that India could organise her own resistance. More vehemently than ever did the militant Hindu Mahasabha—the largest political organisation officially co-operating with Government—react with a demand for handing over the whole administration to Indians, let minority threats be what they might. Amid the political tumult, a few cool voices were heard, most clearly that of Mr. Rajagopalachari, formerly Congress Chief Minister of Madras, calling for a settlement between League and Congress, but they died upon the air. What mattered more was that military recruitment, and work for the great industrial effort that was supplying much of the needs not only of the Indian Army but also of the whole Allied forces between the Mediterranean and Australia, went on unabated. Throughout India, too, government servants, high and low, did their accustomed duty. Not all India was politics, nor all Indians politicians, nor all politicians extremists.

There were other pressures, however, upon the British Government to make some *démarche* in India. The United States was now Britain's ally, and American opinion, not least that of President Franklin Roosevelt, had been critical of British imperialism and specially anxious for a display of liberal aims in India, a move which it now believed to be essential if the sub-continent were to be saved from Japan. China was also an ally, and in February 1942, when Marshal Chiang Kai-shek visited Delhi to confer with the Viceroy and Commander-in-Chief and with the Indian political leaders, the Generalissimo expressed the hope that Britain would as rapidly as possible give real political power to the Indian people, to whom he appealed for help in the war.

Pressures mounted in Britain, too. The Labour and Liberal Parties, partners in the National Government since May 1940, had long been uneasy about the British posture in India, which the Japanese advance drove to the forefront of public attention. In a Cabinet reconstruction Sir Stafford Cripps had become Lord Privy Seal and Leader of the House of Commons: he had been deeply interested in India, having acquired many contacts among Indian nationalists. He would certainly have been one to urge upon Mr. Churchill a positive reply to a cabled appeal which Sir Tej Bahadur Sapru, the most distinguished and respected of the older, more conservative Indian leaders, had sent him at the turn of the year pleading that 'the heart of India must be touched to rouse her on a nation-wide scale to the call for service'. Sir Stafford, during his visit to Delhi in 1942, told the present author that when he came back from Moscow, where he had been Ambassador, almost the first thing he had said to the Prime Minister was: 'This Indian problem must be solved.' As soon as he became a member of the War Cabinet Mr. Churchill had asked him to start drafting his ideas.

On 11th March 1942 Mr. Churchill, after lengthy interchanges between Delhi and London, announced that the War Cabinet had come to a unanimous decision on Indian policy, and that Sir Stafford Cripps would go as soon as possible to India in order to explain it, and 'to satisfy himself upon the spot, by personal consultation, that the conclusions . . . which we believe represent a just and final solution, will achieve their purpose'. This statement could only imply, in the light of the relative positions of the Viceroy and His Majesty's Government, that the Viceroy had too little confidence in the new policy to commit himself before it had been tried out in consultation, and that H.M.G. had too little confidence in the Viceroy's enthusiasm for its policy, or in his persuasive power with the Indian politicians, to let him conduct those consultations himself. So indeed it was. The announcement of 11th March had been preceded by exchanges of telegrams which reflected a wide difference in assessment and approach between London and Delhi. While British Ministers may have thought that Lord Linlithgow was dragging his feet, the Viceroy thought they were losing their heads. He had no faith in the power of any clever formula to bring the leaders of the Congress and the League together. He was in no grave immediate trouble and wanted any decision held back until the military scene was clearer—that is to say, until Britain and her allies had recovered from the disasters of the first weeks of the war with Japan. He knew that Indian opinion cared much more about the immediate situation than about hypothetical solutions to be applied in a post-war future of which they were sceptical.

The basic political situation in India had two simple ingredients. The Congress demanded power immediately, together with its natural consequence, a free representative assembly to frame the ultimate constitution. The Muslim League, not too discontented with the power already within its grasp, insisted that nothing either in the immediate extension of power to Indian hands or in pledges for future constitutional arrangements should obstruct its goal of Muslim nationhood; and this policy was expressed in a demand for Muslim equality now and a Muslim veto on the future. In these circumstances, Lord Linlithgow held that the wise course was to play down the long-term constitutional aspect, not going beyond the terms of pledges already given, and to tempt the parties into co-operation by the bait of a practical instalment of transferred power forthwith, with the least upset to the existing system of government. Ministers in London thought otherwise.

The first round in a heavy exchange of long-range artillery had been delivered by the British Prime Minister himself. Mr. Churchill proposed to make a broadcast appeal to the Indian people to unite in face of the enemy. While no far-reaching changes in the executive government could be contemplated at that time, he intended to say, an Indian Council of Defence would be set up, its members to be elected by proportional representation by the provincial assemblies, together with representatives of the Indian States in due ratio. During the war this Council of all parties would be charged with helping the civilian war effort, besides nominating a representative of the people of India to serve as a member of the Governor-General's Executive Council, and attend meetings of the British War Cabinet and the Pacific War Council. After the war, it would send representatives to the peace conference and also work out a new constitution for India. Since its main constitutional conclusions would in their nature express the desire of the people of India as a whole, His Majesty's Government would accept a constitution so arrived at and would negotiate with the Council in regard to the fulfilment of British obligations.

The Viceroy was quick to shoot down this crackbrained scheme, which was conceived in apparent ignorance not only of the political forces at work in India but also of the actual operation of Indian government, and in an understandable obsession with the higher strategy of the war. Lord Linlithgow pointed out that if the new Council were ineffective its creation would be useless; if it were effective it would challenge or sap the authority of his Executive Council and the other regular organs of government, on which the internal order and war administration of India depended. Moreover, by identifying the wartime body with the post-war constitution-making the plan would do the very thing which he was above all anxious to avoid—import the whole communal conflict into the conduct of the war, with the risk of infecting even the Army with communal fever.

Having fired this destructive salvo, Lord Linlithgow realised that he must offer his own alternative plan, and this after a short delay he did. The key to it was an offer to try again to bring the party leaders together in order that the central as well as provincial governments should enjoy the overwhelming support of the people of India. The position of the Commander-in-Chief must remain unimpaired, but otherwise all possibilities would be open for discussion, and an unofficial member of the Viceroy's Council might hold a portfolio of co-ordination of defence. Secondly, the control of the India Office would be exercised with a progressively lighter hand, and India's representatives at the War Cabinet, the Pacific War Council and any peace conference would be instructed from

India—in other words, so far as possible without major statutory change, the representative Indian Government, with the Governor-General at its head, would be treated as the Government of a Dominion. Thirdly, as to a post-war constitutional settlement, Lord Linlithgow wanted a declaration that His Majesty's Government drew a clear distinction between British interests, which could be dealt with by negotiation and need not be provided for in a constitution, and British obligations, which required them to see that full power was transferred to a Government under which different races, communities and interests in India could live without fear. They would undertake in advance to accept any constitution framed by a representative Indian body and representing the will and desire of the people of India as a whole.[1]

The Viceroy succeeded in intercepting Mr. Churchill's intended broadcast, but not in wresting the initiative from London. Indeed the effect of his report was the setting up of a powerful India Committee of the Cabinet under Mr. Attlee's chairmanship whose deliberations it was very difficult to upset. The Committee now put up its own plan, of which the chief new features were an explicit acknowledgement that a future Indian Dominion would have the right to secede from the Commonwealth, and the grant to any province of the option to stand out of the constitution to be framed after the war by an Indian constituent body. The draft plan also incorporated Lord Linlithgow's distinction between British interests and British obligations. The Viceroy, backed by the opinion of the Commander-in-Chief, Lord Wavell, and the provincial Governors, objected strongly to the 'provincial option' clause, which, he argued, while being no substitute for safeguards for Muslims in Hindu-majority provinces, would be taken as acceptance of Pakistan as regards the Muslim-majority provinces, and would have a particularly disruptive effect in the Punjab, above all among the Sikhs, and would grievously damage the war effort. In London, however, the 'package deal' was no longer negotiable; for it represented armistice terms in a fierce Ministerial dispute which had threatened to split the War Cabinet. The Viceroy could have argued with the Prime Minister or the Secre-

---

[1] This scheme was based on a draft (which went somewhat further as regards immediate quasi-Dominion Status) prepared by the present author as Constitutional Adviser.

tary of State; with the India Committee argument was almost impossible. Lord Linlithgow's criticism, backed on the key points by Field Marshal Lord Wavell, had little or no effect on the 'final' document which Sir Stafford Cripps brought out and tried to get the Indian leaders to accept.

This basic lack of agreement between the Viceroy and the British Government haunted Sir Stafford's mission, but his tactics were his own. Lord Linlithgow scrupulously stood aside from his negotiations. The Lord Privy Seal and his staff had their own residence and headquarters, at a considerable distance from the Viceroy's house. As things turned out, it might have been better if they had not, but at least the separation made the lines of responsibility clear.

Lord Linlithgow disclosed his mind to his Reforms Commissioner[1] at one of the latter's official interviews on 14th March. Asked how he saw the tactical position he replied:

I try not to form pictures in my mind. It's dangerous. But I'll tell you what I think. I think Cripps is coming here out of public spirit. No one would choose this way of becoming Viceroy, if that were his ambition. And if he wants to be Prime Minister, what sensible politician would take the immediate risks of failure over this just when his stock is very high? No, I think he realised that India might take things from him which they wouldn't take from anyone else, and he is coming out here in a genuine public-spirited attempt to solve the problem. And I think he will go off very quickly unless he is confident of succeeding. It would be fatal to his reputation to hang around here while opinion hardens more and more against his offer—like hawking rotten fish. Personally, I think he'll fail with H.M.G.'s policy, don't you? . . . Of course the Congress and the Hindus are jubilant. They think they've scored with the British Government and that Cripps is their man. . . . I don't know how he will proceed, but I think he'll work with a pretty free hand. On our side we must avoid at all costs any suggestion that we are standing in his way or forcing evidence on him. And I agree with you that it would be disastrous to assume in advance that we were parties to a dispute with him or H.M.G. . . . The danger that I see is that if Cripps feels himself to be failing he may telegraph home

[1] The present author, from whose diary this account is taken.

to H.M.G. asking for this and asking for that. If so, I'm sure he'll soon be out of my depth.

There's another point of danger—the point about participation in government now. I can't have Cripps making my Council for me. He can clear the ground but only I can do that, and he must have gone before I begin.

It was a remarkably prescient forecast.

Sir Stafford Cripps, with a substantial entourage, arrived in Delhi on 22nd March and at once began his talks, first with the Viceroy, then with members of the Executive Council, who were critical and suspicious, next with high officials and political leaders of all the main parties and communities, including Mr. Gandhi, Mr. Jinnah and Pandit Nehru. On 29th March he addressed the Press, released a draft declaration, and took part in a frank exchange of questions and answers.

The draft declaration embodied three main points:

1 Immediately after the end of the war an elected body would be set up in India with the task of framing a new constitution. After fresh provincial elections had been held, the entire membership of the lower provincial houses would elect by proportional representation the British Indian members of the constitution-making body. The States would be invited to send representatives proportionately to their populations, with the same powers as members from British India.

2 His Majesty's Government undertook to accept and implement forthwith the constitution so framed subject only to

[i] The right of any province that was not prepared to accept the new constitution to retain its existing constitutional position, provision being made for its subsequent accession, should it so decide. His Majesty's Government would be prepared to agree with a non-acceding province a new constitution, arrived at by a similar representative process, and giving it the same status as the Indian Union itself.

[ii] The signing of a treaty between H.M.G. and the constitution-making body. The treaty would cover all necessary matters arising out of the transfer of power; it would provide for the protection of minorities in accordance with British undertakings, but would not restrict the power of the Indian Union to decide

its future relationship to the British Commonwealth. Treaties with Indian States would have to be reviewed.

3 During the war and until the new constitution could be framed the British Government must control and direct the defence of India as part of their world war effort, but the task of organising the military, moral and material resources of India must be the responsibility of the Government of India with the co-operation of the peoples of India. His Majesty's Government invited the immediate and the effective participation of the leaders of the principal sections of the Indian people in the counsels of their country, of the Commonwealth and of the United Nations.

The final drafting of the third point, concerning immediate policy, owed a good deal to the efforts of the Viceroy and his staff. But the long-term policy was essentially that of the British Government, and neither Lord Linlithgow's doubts nor Lord Wavell's intense hostility had shifted them from their faith in provincial option as the key to the communal deadlock: not even the meaningless phrase 'retain its existing constitutional position' could be amended. A further point that was strongly but vainly made by official advisers was that a treaty could not provide for the protection of minorities unless it provided for British intervention on their behalf, which was out of the question after Dominion independence, and that accordingly the treaty should be a quittance for British obligations, not a perpetuation of them. Sir Stafford had neither the wish nor the authority to alter his brief.

At his Press conference he dotted some i's and crossed some t's. The Constituent Assembly, he said, would be completely free to decide whether or not the new Indian Union would remain in the Commonwealth: it could, if it wished, start with a declaration of independence. This was the first time that this word, unqualified, had been used by a representative of the British Government about India's promised future. The new Executive Council, or Government of India, would have to work within the present constitution, but a good deal could be done by convention to make it more like a Dominion Government. It could function like a Cabinet—a point outside Sir Stafford's brief which the Viceroy never accepted; for apart from political reasons he knew that the sub-structure of administration was quite different in India from that lying beneath Cabinet Government at Westminster. But on one point which was to cause great friction Sir Stafford at this stage was unexceptionably clear: the responsibility for the defence of India must remain with the British Government during the war, and 'it would be dishonest to say that an Indian Defence Minister would be responsible for the defence of India'.

Within a day or two the negotiations fell into the pattern they were to follow to the end. The minor groups all rejected the long-term plan—the Hindu Mahasabha, though eager for present office, because it threatened the unity of India, the Depressed Classes because it failed to safeguard them, the Sikhs because they would 'resist by all possible means the separation of the Punjab'. The Muslim League held its hand, waiting for the Congress: it had gained most, through the implicit acceptance of Pakistan, and it certainly could not afford to let the Congress agree to participate in government while it refused, but if the Congress refused it might well gain still more by also holding out. As for the Congress, on 2nd April its Working Committee passed a resolution rejecting the offer: it strongly objected both to provincial option and to including representatives of the Princes, not of the States' peoples, in the constitution-making body. But the Working Committee, while showing Sir Stafford a copy of their adverse resolution, decided not to publish it while they negotiated on the interim plan, thus demonstrating, what had been clear from the start in India though not in London, that the point they were really interested in was an immediate *de facto* transfer of power. For more than a week Sir Stafford did virtually nothing but negotiate with the Congress on this point, especially in respect of defence.

It was a dangerous enterprise because he was treading on ground which the Viceroy had marked out as exclusively his own, in consultation especially with the Commander-in-Chief. A day or two after his arrival Sir Stafford Cripps had handed Lord Linlithgow a draft sketch for a new Executive Council. The Viceroy glanced at it, sufficiently to see that all seats except those of the Governor-General and Commander-in-Chief were allocated to Hindus or Muslims, and handed it back, saying, 'That's my affair.' It should have been enough warning, but Sir Stafford was tempted by the Congress attitude to do exactly what Lord Linlithgow had foretold—'bait the trap with my cheese'—by offering immediate power in a National Government. One idea, which he broached to the author, was that the Viceroy should be relieved of much of his burden of presiding over the Executive Council by appointing a deputy Viceroy for certain functions: he thought Sir George Schuster[1] was the kind of man for the part. But all this was over-taken by the tangled negotiations over the position of an Indian Defence Member of the new Council.

Already complicated enough through the lack of underlying agreement between the Viceroy, Sir Stafford Cripps and the War Cabinet in London, these parleys were further confused by the intervention of Colonel Louis Johnson, a personal representative of President Roosevelt, who had just arrived in Delhi as head of the American Technical Mission. Colonel Johnson, who struck officials in Delhi as being completely ignorant both of Indian problems and personalities and of the structure of government in India, made himself a go-between with the Congress, especially Pandit Nehru, whose views he uncritically accepted. Nevertheless Sir Stafford showed no objection to the role he played. *133747*

The author was present at a fateful meeting between the two men on 8th April, when Colonel Johnson brought a draft formula about the functions of a Defence Member which he said Pandit Nehru believed the Congress would accept, and they worked to-gether on it without the least sign of resentment or aloofness on Sir Stafford's part. (Nehru had told Colonel Johnson that at an earlier stage, before these negotiations had proceeded thus far, he would have had only five votes in the Working Committee for co-operation.) Sir Stafford made a number of amendments and then gave the revised draft to secretaries to be typed. When the typed copies were ready, Colonel Johnson took the original draft with Sir Stafford's amendments, saying, 'I would like to be able to show them this in your own handwriting.' No objection was made, nor in the course of the conversation was the question whether the new formula would be acceptable to the Viceroy ever posed. Sir Stafford, however, asked the Reforms Commissioner to take copies to the Viceroy and the Commander-in-Chief, and his recognition that the whole exercise was *ad referendum* was shown by his telling Colonel Johnson that he must put off his Press conference next

[1] Sir George Schuster had been Finance Member of the Government of India.

morning as the matter would certainly not be settled by then. He himself telegraphed the formula to the Prime Minister.

The original proposal, to which the Viceroy and the British Government had assented, was that an Indian representative member should be added to the Executive Council to take over specified defence matters which would be separated from the Commander-in-Chief's War Department, together with the Defence Co-ordination Department and certain other broad defence functions such as denial policy. The specified matters were an unexciting, semi-civilian list. The Johnson-Cripps formula inverted the definition, declaring that the Defence Department would be placed in charge of an Indian representative Member, but certain functions relating to the conduct of the war—specified as 'governmental relations of General Headquarters, Naval Headquarters and Air Headquarters'—would be exercised by the Commander-in-Chief, who would be Member of Council for the War Department in control of the armed forces of India.[1] The inversion owed something to informal discussions at official level, but the formula now proposed had never been referred directly or indirectly to the Viceroy or the Commander-in-Chief.

They received it at 7.30 that night, after a meeting of the Executive Council. The Viceroy's first reaction was to refuse to be hurried and to defer his comment until the morning, and Lord Wavell was so informed. But later Lord Linlithgow decided to send for Sir Stafford Cripps and Colonel Johnson. He put it to them that the most natural thing for the Congress to do, after losing at a blow, through rejection of the draft declaration, the laboriously built-up sympathy of the American people, was perhaps to try to enlist the sympathy of President Roosevelt's envoy, and to engineer a split between him and the British side, and that it would be wise to watch this danger. 'Ah!' said Colonel Johnson, 'but I think the Congress are going to settle.' 'On what basis?' Johnson then revealed that the Congress were even now working on the formula—in Cripps's handwriting—which the Viceroy had only just seen. The Viceroy asked Colonel Johnson to retire and tackled Sir Stafford alone. How had this happened? Sir Stafford answered that the pace was getting hot, and something had to be done; anyway Hodson, the Reforms Commissioner, had been

[1] The full texts of the successive drafts are given in Menon, *The Transfer of Power in India*, pp. 127–30.

present when he and Johnson had agreed on the formula. 'With all respect,' retorted His Excellency, 'Hodson is not the Governor-General.'

Later that evening he sent for his advisers, including the Reforms Commissioner, and told them of these conversations, saying that he had been put in an impossible position. If he rejected the formula he might precipitate a split in the Cabinet, or a row between the British and American Governments. On the other hand, if he accepted it, fatal harm might be done. No personal considerations would weigh with him, though he had been treated very badly indeed. He sought their counsel, and on the strength of it he sent a long telegram to the Secretary of State and Prime Minister, reporting the whole episode, emphasising his objections to the Johnson-Cripps formula and those of the Commander-in-Chief. By next morning Sir Stafford had received a return telegram to the effect that the British Government backed the Viceroy and Commander-in-Chief in their view that the latter's powers could not be materially reduced during the period of the war.

But this was not the last word. The next day a revised version of the formula was sent to Sir Stafford by the Viceroy, incorporating certain minimum amendments approved by the Commander-in-Chief and his Deputy, General Hartley. Moreover, Sir Stafford, though sore that the Viceroy by telegraphing to the Cabinet in London had 'gone behind his back', was not downcast. Two days after the affair of the Johnson-Cripps formula, he closely questioned the author as to the line the Viceroy was likely to take about the structure of his Government if the negotiations were successful, and elaborated certain ideas of his, including the formation of an inner War Cabinet and the appointment of two Vice-Presidents of the Executive Council, one a Hindu and the other a Muslim. Evidently he was still hoping for success. Moreover, Mr. V. P. Menon has shown[1] that the actual breakdown was not on the formula about defence responsibilities but on the Congress demand that 'the National Government must be a Cabinet government with full power and must not merely be a continuation of the Viceroy's Executive Council'. Those words were used in a long letter to Sir Stafford from Maulana Abul Kalam Azad, the President of the Congress, dated 9th April. Sir Stafford, unprompted by the Viceroy, replied on the same day to the effect that

[1] *The Transfer of Power in India*, pp. 130–1.

this demand—which he described in his broadcast next day as having been raised at the last moment—amounted to asking for constitutional changes which were impossible in wartime, and that if it were accepted the proposed Cabinet, nominated by political parties, would be responsible to no one but itself and would constitute 'an absolute dictatorship of the majority'. He regarded Maulana Azad's letter as a definite rejection of the offer, and concluded that negotiation was at an end.

The next day, the Congress Working Committee published their resolution declaring their inability to accept either the long-term or the short-term parts of the offer. They regretted that the promised self-determination in an 'uncertain future' was fettered and circumscribed by provisions which gravely imperilled the establishment of a democratic State. They insisted 'that an essential and fundamental prerequisite for the assumption of responsibility by the Indian people in the present is their realisation as a fact that they are free and are in charge of maintaining and defending their freedom'. As soon as the Congress decision was known, Mr. Jinnah published a resolution of the Muslim League Working Committee also rejecting the offer, but in vaguer terms and with emphasis on the long-term plan, which they claimed was unfair to Muslims in obliging them to take part in a constitution-making body whose main object, contrary to theirs, was the creation of an all-India Union. They found themselves unable to consider the interim offer for want of any precision, nor need they do so because, according to Sir Stafford, they were not at liberty to accept one part of the package having rejected the other. Mr. Jinnah complained, with some cause, that 'the talks had been carried on over the heads of the Muslims, and other parties had been utterly ignored'.

That same evening, 11th April, Sir Stafford broadcast on All-India Radio explaining, in hard-cut words, why it had been impossible to accept the Congress demands either on defence or on so-called Cabinet government. 'For the moment,' he declared, 'past distrust has proved too strong to allow of present agreement.' To the surprise of many Indian politicians who thought that this three-cornered exchange of negatives was the preliminary to real bargaining for a compromise, the Lord Privy Seal then packed up and flew back to England the next day.

The story of the Johnson-Cripps formula and its fate has been told at some length because the myth persists that Sir Stafford's mission was frustrated by the intervention of Mr. Churchill. This is not true. On a delicate point on which Sir Stafford had been given no brief by the War Cabinet, the latter was consulted both by him and by the Viceroy; Mr. Churchill and his colleagues had no option but to back Lord Linlithgow and Lord Wavell on a matter which they had advised could vitally affect the conduct of the war by themselves as Governor-General and Commander-in-Chief. The fault clearly lay with Sir Stafford in negotiating on such an issue to a point of virtual commitment without the clearest understanding with the Viceroy. (The busybody Colonel Johnson obviously made matters worse.) But the blame did not rest with him alone; for the War Cabinet, especially the India Committee, made a fundamental mistake, strange in a body so experienced, when they sent an emissary to promote a policy in India which had not been fully agreed with the Viceroy, though he would have to carry it out. It was not even fully disclosed to him. Sir Stafford told the author, soon after he arrived in Delhi: 'You must realise that the Cabinet has quite made up its mind that India shall have everything in the way of *de facto* Dominion Status and complete Indianisation of the Executive Council except for defence.' But in telegrams to the Secretary of State the Viceroy had explicitly reserved his right to appoint officials or unofficial British people to his reconstructed Council, and had not been denied.

The draft declaration, or Cripps Offer, was a compromise which had been accepted to avert a Cabinet crisis, but not all Ministers hoped with equal fervour that it would succeed: to some it had been primarily a public-relations exercise to appease American opinion, a section of British opinion, and moderate Indian opinion, rather than an all-out attempt to bring the Congress and other parties into Indian government. When Mr. Churchill learned of the breakdown of the Delhi negotiations he put on an act of sham tears and sorrow before his guests at Chequers, not troubling to conceal his own pleasure. But this is very different from the allegation that he sabotaged the mission.

Granted the difficulties of his position, Sir Stafford Cripps made his task more difficult by his method of negotiation. From a very early stage he went to the limits of his brief, or even beyond it, with the result that when it came to negotiation in detail he had nothing further to offer, and no room for constructive manoeuvre.

He could then only subtract. This was most conspicuous in regard to 'Cabinet government'. The procedure baffled Indians, who could not believe that he had nothing more up his sleeve which bargaining could extract, and who therefore concluded either that he had deceived them initially or that he had been pulled back by the British Government.

More fundamentally, the War Cabinet had misjudged the mood of India. For them, the crisis in the war called for swift action to break the Indian political deadlock in the face of the Japanese, and they believed that the only way to do this was to offer self-determination and independence (on terms acceptable to both the main parties and communities) after the war had been won, assuming that with this aim before them the Indian leaders and people would do all they could to help win the war within the existing constitutional structure. This was a very natural conclusion in the conditions of wartime Britain, where many social and political ambitions had had to be shelved 'for the duration' as a sacrifice to war necessity and National Government. But that was not the state of mind in India. Many Indians were doubtful of the victory of Britain and her Allies: most were apathetic about the war itself. There was little mood of sacrificing communal or political ambitions for the time being, but rather one of using the war situation to press them. The demand was for popular power now, or at least a very big instalment of it. The long-term proposals by which the War Cabinet had set such store, though almost universally spurned, were little debated: the negotiation almost at once concentrated on the immediate plan. In the light of all this, the timing that seemed so right in London was wrong in Delhi. It would have been better to proceed more slowly, waiting until the crisis of nerves after the loss of Malaya and Burma had subsided, and pressure had built up for taking office on such terms as could be granted.

In the Congress camp there were three schools of thought. Mr. Gandhi and his close disciples were essentially pacifists. They wanted power, not in order to fight, but in order that India should pursue her own non-violent policy towards the war. Opposed to them were 'moderates' who wished to co-operate in the war provided that they had real responsibility and power: such were Mr. Rajagopalachari and Maulana Abul Kalam Azad. In between was a group of hardened politicians like Sardar Vallabhbhai Patel who, while not opposed in principle to taking part in the conduct of war, were determined that this should not come about by any sacrifice of long-term policy, but only as a big step towards bringing that policy into effect. Pandit Nehru, though seeming a co-operator to Colonel Johnson, vacillated between one attitude and another. Sir Stafford Cripps, who had believed that through his personal friendship and understanding with Nehru he could soon gain the latter's agreement and that the Working Committee would follow, was grievously disappointed in him. He thought Pandit Nehru weak and uncertain. The disenchantment was mutual; Nehru said to Sudhir Ghosh about Cripps a year later: 'The more you see of him the less you know him.' In the end it was the voice of the Mahatma that proved the most influential, even though Mr. Gandhi, taking a stand of principle, had absented himself and refused to take any direct part in the negotiations. This experience may well have led Sir Stafford to his equally fruitless and frustrating concentration on Mr. Gandhi during the Cabinet Mission's visit four years later.

Though nothing came immediately of the Cripps Offer, things could not be the same after it had been made as they were before. The British Government could not resile from its promise of complete independence as soon as possible after the war under a constitution framed by an elective Indian Assembly, nor from its pledge to accept such a constitution with certain provisos, nor from its commitment to afford the Muslims at least the equivalent of provincial option. The Muslims had seen the door opened by the latter device to the principle of Pakistan. Moreover, they had even seen this commitment vaguely endorsed by the Congress in the words of the Working Committee's resolution opposing provincial option: 'Nevertheless the Committee cannot think in terms of compelling the people in any territorial unit to remain in an Indian Union against their declared and established will.' It was a hole in the dyke which Mr. Jinnah was determined to widen.

On the Congress side the net effect of the Cripps Mission was to enlarge the gulf between the Congress and the Government, which they believed had finally demonstrated its refusal to part with any power. A temper of disgruntlement gave way to one of frustration and reaction. In such a mood men are apt to forsake their better judgment. In July the Congress Working Committee met at Wardha and passed two resolutions, the first calling upon the people to refuse compliance with military requirements such as

requisitioning in certain circumstances, the second demanding
that British rule in India must end immediately, in default of
which the Congress would be compelled to use all its non-violent
strength in a widespread struggle, to be led by Mr. Gandhi. These
policies, the fruit of a 'Quit India' campaign waged for weeks
beforehand by the Mahatma, were to be referred to the All-India
Congress Committee for final decision.

The resolutions caused an outcry in non-Congress quarters.
Mr. Jinnah described them as 'blackmailing the British and
coercing them to concede a system of government and transfer
power to that government which would establish a Hindu raj
immediately under the aegis of the British bayonet'. The British,
through the mouth of the Secretary of State, made it quite clear
that they were not to be blackmailed and would not advance
beyond the Cripps Offer.

The All-India Congress Committee met in Bombay on 7th
August and approved the Working Committee's policies. In the
interval, plans—many of them most unlikely to prove non-violent
—had been laid throughout the country for conducting the all-out
campaign. Of most of these the Government was aware through its
intelligence sources. The counter-blow—approved in London and
endorsed by the Governor-General's Council[1]—was ready. Soon
after dawn on 9th August Mr. Gandhi and all the members of the
Congress Working Committee were arrested. They were soon
followed into custody by other Congress leaders, and Congress
committees everywhere were declared unlawful associations. No
other action made sense for a wartime Government in the conditions of India in 1942.

Serious disturbances followed immediately, and mounted
rapidly. The extent of the disorder was played down at the time,
for reasons of war morale at home and abroad. For two weeks or
more, the writ of Government did not run in most of Bihar and
some districts of the United Provinces. Land passage between
Delhi and Calcutta was cut—a very serious matter, for the rail
link was a vital strategic line of communication. It was as much as
a European's life was worth to venture into the old city of Delhi

---

[1] On 2nd July the Viceroy reconstructed his Council, expanding its
membership to fifteen, of whom three were officials, including the
Commander-in-Chief, one a non-official European, and eleven Indians,
one being in charge of a new Defence Department.

unless in an armed force, though life went on almost normally in the new capital beyond its gates. Troops to back the civil power were scarce because most trained units had been deployed for the outer rather than the inner defence of India. The Auxiliary Force (India) was embodied. Nevertheless, within about three weeks the situation was everywhere under control and it was clear that the insurrection had failed.

Its failure had shown how great was still the power of the existing order, if it acted resolutely and decisively, so long as the mass of the people were indifferent and so long as it could count on its side against the revolutionaries (not too strong a term) most of the minorities and the bulk of the official, professional and commercial classes. The police and the civil administration as well as the Army stood firm. There was comparatively little trouble in the north-west or Bengal or in the south. The weakness was in areas where the administration was already known to be weak, and even there the rebellion, with its leadership decapitated, soon petered out. Thenceforward, for five years to its end, the power of the British raj was never challenged on a grand scale. The presumption is that but for its own will to the contrary it could have continued for a long while longer. But the will to stay had gone, and after the Cripps Mission it could not be revived.

The chief immediate result, however, was that the Congress leaders great and less were in gaol and its organisation was hamstrung. One of its few former heads at liberty was Mr. Rajagopalachari, who had been obliged to resign from the Congress when its High Command repudiated his attempts to restore Hindu-Muslim unity by offering to acknowledge the Muslim's right to separation if they should demand it when the time came for free constitution-making. On the other side Sir Sikander Hyat Khan continued to try to make Punjabis realise that Pakistan would mean the dismemberment of the Punjab. But Sir Sikander died in December 1942, and Mr. Jinnah and his adherents, fortified by their strengthened tactical position, and given a clear field by the ban on the Congress, not only pressed but heightened their demands. They were willing to co-operate in a 'provisional government' on two conditions: not only that their claim to national homelands in the north-west and north-east was not thereby prejudiced, but also that the League had 'parity' in such a Government. The second great obstacle to Hindu-Muslim solidarity had appeared.

On 9th February 1943 Mr. Gandhi began a twenty-one day fast.[1] The object, unless it was to secure his own unconditional release, was obscure to everyone not of Gandhian persuasion, but such was his unique charisma that his self-inflicted danger aroused, both in India and elsewhere, great pressure on the Government to set him free. They had in fact offered to release him while he fasted, but he had retorted that if they released him he would not fast. As the reasons for keeping him in gaol had not disappeared, led by an imperturbable Viceroy they steadfastly resisted all the pressure, and when the fast ended on 3rd March their prestige and self-confidence had increased—though three timid members of the Executive Council resigned rather than be parties to a policy that might lead to the Mahatma's death. (They had agreed to a decision to let him fast, and face the consequences, but a few hours later returned with second thoughts—too late to intercept the orders.) A year later Mr. Gandhi was unconditionally released on medical grounds.

In October 1943 Lord Linlithgow's Viceroyalty ended. He had been Governor-General of India for seven and a half years, longer than any other Viceroy in history except Lord Dalhousie (Governor-General 1848–56). His protracted stay was not due to clinging to office: he carried probably a greater burden than any of his predecessors since the Mutiny, and the Government in London had to beg him to continue to bear it when they repeatedly prolonged his term. Their principal problem was finding the right successor. Various names were canvassed: Sir Samuel Hoare,[2] Mr. Anthony Eden,[3] Sir Roger Lumley,[4] the Duke of Devonshire, Viscount Cranborne,[5] Sir Archibald Sinclair,[6] Mr. R. A. Butler,[7] Sir John Anderson,[8] Sir Miles Lampson[9] and others. The Secretary of State, Mr. Amery, is believed to have put forward the

---

[1] He was detained, not in prison, but in the Aga Khan's palace, but he characteristically headed letters written there 'Detention Camp, Poona'.
[2] Later Viscount Templewood.
[3] Later Earl of Avon.
[4] Later Earl of Scarbrough.
[5] Later Marquess of Salisbury.
[6] Later Viscount Thurso.
[7] Later Lord Butler of Saffron Walden.
[8] Later Viscount Waverley.
[9] Later Lord Killearn.

name of Lord Louis Mountbatten[1] (then Chief of Combined
Operations), but he preferred to recommend Lord Louis for the
post of Supreme Allied Commander, South-East Asia, to which
he was eventually appointed. But the longer Lord Linlithgow
stayed the more difficult it became adequately to replace him. He
had built up an immense knowledge of Indian affairs, not merely
by sitting at their head for so long, but by indefatigable work in
correspondence with provincial Governors and others. A newcomer would have been seriously handicapped by ignorance, and
might have made mistakes which however venial in peace would
have been grave in war. The post in such times needed, too, great
administrative experience, power of work and adamant resolution.
These Lord Linlithgow had proved he had.

Though British people knew little of him, and most Indian
people could not fathom him personally, respect him as they
might, he will rank in history as an outstanding Viceroy. Politically, his achievements seem on the surface negative. He failed to
get the Princes into the federation which he had come out determined to launch; he left the country more divided politically than
he found it, with provincial self-government in abeyance over
more than half of India, and with communal attitudes hardened.
But it must not be forgotten that he more than anyone else got
provincial self-government working with the co-operation of the
Congress, and that he restored friendly Viceregal relations with
Mr. Gandhi. He had the power neither to create nor to prevent
the underlying conditions that had brought about the negative
face of affairs in 1943. They were twofold—the impact of the war,
and the approach of independence. India was divided not by the
want of self-government but by the prospect of it. In face of the
war, first at a distance and then at India's gates, and of the greatly
heightened political tension, Lord Linlithgow's achievement in
holding the country steady and enabling it to raise and largely
equip an army of two million volunteers, and to supply much of
the needs of other war theatres, is a sufficient monument to his
proconsulship. From 1939 onwards, he conceived his paramount
duty as being to ensure India's help in winning the war: he was
not much concerned with long-term speculative solutions, for he
argued that 'If we do not win the war, they are futile; if we do win,
there will be a new situation which the Government of the day

[1] Later Earl Mountbatten of Burma.

must cope with.' And this paramount duty he succeeded in performing against many political odds.

What he may have lacked in imagination he made up for in reliability: if he was cautious in movement, he planted his feet firmly. Naturally shy, and somewhat forbidding in appearance, with his great height, his long face and his way of appearing almost pontifically throned, he was frank and easy in intimate conversation. Indisputably master in his own house, whether the house were the Governor-General's Executive Council, or the central governmental apparatus, or the array of provincial Governors, he was always open to advice, which he would debate without ceremony, often matching his advisers in knowledge of their subject; for he worked with enormous energy to keep himself informed of what went on in the departments or the provinces. He had a deep interest, deeper probably than that of any other Viceroy, in Indian agriculture, public health and education. If he was slow, he was often subtle, and by the end of his Viceroyalty he knew the people he was dealing with through and through, and his judgment of persons was penetrating. Nor must it be forgotten, on his political record, that during his reign, beginning with the implementation of provincial autonomy, and running through the August Offer, the Cripps Mission—to which he had a more liberal alternative— and the almost complete Indianisation of his Executive Council, India advanced not only to the inexorable promise but also to the political capability of independent nationhood at a moment which could not be more than a few years away.

10

Lord Wavell and the Simla conference

No one was more surprised than Field Marshal Lord Wavell, who was then in London, when he was offered the Viceroyalty, though the possibility had been the subject of gossip in inner circles for some time.[1] From the British Government's point of view his appointment ended the search for someone who knew India well and could be securely entrusted with the continuance of her defence and her war effort until victory opened a new scene; one, moreover, upon whom they could count to continue the existing policy towards the Congress and its leaders, since Lord Wavell had shared in framing and imposing it as Commander-in-Chief in 1942. From the Indian point of view these same qualifications seemed conversely ominous. If the Muslim League was at first less displeased than others it was set back by Lord Wavell's insistence, in the first important speech that he made as Viceroy, that 'India is a natural unit' within which the two great communities, the lesser minorities and the States should decide how they were to live together.[2]

Lord Wavell was not in fact a clear political thinker, nor at home with politics and politicians. He was a brilliant soldier, with a strong artistic streak, and the imagination to see beyond the day-to-day horizon, but without the diplomatic skill or political experience needed to master the events and personalities that beset his path. If Lord Linlithgow's Viceroyalty ended in negation Lord Wavell's ended in despair. He was not helped, in dealing with men in public life to whom words were their sword, and argument their battlefield, by his forbidding single eye and his habit of prolonged silences. Among those who worked closely with him he was greatly and affectionately admired, but to the end of his term he remained an enigma to the Indian politicians, though they all respected him for his palpable fairness and integrity. He was closer to them

[1] See *Chips*, the diaries of Sir Henry Channon, M.P., pp. 356–65
[2] Speech to the Central Legislative Assembly, 17th February 1944.

than his predecessor, however, in one respect: he disliked the pomp and panoply with which the Viceroy had been traditionally surrounded, and preferred the informality, directness and quick movement to which as a soldier and commander of armies he had been accustomed. One of his first acts as Viceroy was to fly with a miniature staff to Calcutta (and later to other centres) to see for himself the conditions of the great famine that raged in Bengal and some other areas—the result of the cutting off of Burmese rice, the weight of military demands and the hoarding effects of inflation. When Lord Linlithgow or any previous Viceroy had travelled to Calcutta, it had been in the long white Viceregal train with a retinue running into hundreds, from private secretaries to chaprassis. Lord Wavell preferred seeing to hearing, and hearing to reading.

His rule began with a reiteration of the stiff policy towards the Congress leaders. He refused to release either Mr. Gandhi (whose wife Kasturba died in February 1944, while sharing his incarceration) or the others. His stand was that the Congress must not merely rescind its 'Quit India' resolution but repudiate it, 'not in sackcloth and ashes—that helps no one—but in recognition of a mistaken and unprofitable policy'. Meanwhile, he believed the Congress was hindering rather than advancing India's progress to self-government by its attitude. When on 27th July 1944, Mr. Gandhi wrote to him offering to advise the Congress Working Committee to renounce mass civil disobedience and to co-operate fully in the war effort, provided that an immediate declaration of India's independence was made and a national government responsible to the Central Assembly were formed, he repeated all the arguments that had been used against such policies at the time of the Cripps Mission. The sign thus pinned to Viceregal policy was 'No change: business as usual.'

But Lord Wavell was now looking ahead to a different prospect. The war seemed already to be in its last phase, after a chain of Allied victories in both the Eastern and Western theatres. The Viceroy felt that stagnation could not continue, and that a new effort must be made to prepare India for the birth of independence, the time for which must soon come. Unable to make any direct advance, he watched attentively a series of attempts made by individual Hindu and Muslim leaders to bring together their communities, or the Congress and Muslim League, in a united front.

Mr. Rajagopalachari, who from Madras could view the facts and problems of northern India with a certain detachment, had already, concluded that some form of partition had to be granted if India was to reach constitutional freedom. When he was allowed to see Mr. Gandhi during his fast, Mr. Rajagopalachari had taken the opportunity to get the Mahatma's blessing for a formula he had drafted as the basis of a Congress-League settlement. Over a year later, in April 1944, he published the formula. The Muslim League would co-operate with the Congress in working for independence and in a provisional national government; after the war, a commission should demarcate those contiguous districts in north-west and north-east India where the Muslims were in a majority, and in those areas there would be a plebiscite for or against separation from Hindustan. In the event of partition, a mutual agreement would be entered into for essential common purposes such as defence, communications and commerce. These terms should be binding only if Britain finally transferred her power. Mr. Jinnah agreed to place this scheme before the League, but without committing himself.

On 30th July the League's Working Committee gave Mr. Jinnah full authority to negotiate with Mr. Gandhi, who had meanwhile suggested that they should meet.[1] Jinnah had thus gained two strong psychological points: acknowledgement of equality of status with the holy hero of the Congress, and admission of Pakistan in some form to the Congress-League agenda. Characteristically, he at once demanded more. In his speech to the Working Committee he denounced the Rajagopalachari formula in a phrase which was to echo and re-echo; it offered, he said, 'a shadow and a husk, a maimed, mutilated and moth-eaten Pakistan'.

The official mouthpiece of the Muslim League, the Delhi newspaper *Dawn*, came out with a reasoned case against the 'moth-eaten Pakistan'. The principle of creating separate sovereign states should first be accepted: then their frontiers should be drawn so that each could be economically self-supporting and nationally

[1] Mr. Gandhi had been released earlier in the year, the doctors having given the Government a gloomy view of the risk of his dying in captivity. Lord Wavell asked leave of the Secretary of State to have a political talk with the Mahatma, and was turned down. Lord Mountbatten, to whom he related this, was astonished that he should have sought permission, when he knew what Mr. Churchill's attitude was. 'After all,' said Lord Mountbatten, 'if you had seen Gandhi and then telegraphed a report of your meeting they could hardly have sacked you.'

solvent in a sense embracing all aspects of sovereignty. Mr. Rajagopalachari turned this argument round: if the conditions for an independent State were lacking in a Muslim-majority area, that would be a good reason for advising its inhabitants against separation, not one for enlarging the separated territory. Areas incapable of economic self-sufficiency must remain in a larger State, since they could not aspire to independent sovereign status. The mothholes in this form of Pakistan were thus obvious enough.

In September 1944 Mr. Gandhi and Mr. Jinnah met in the latter's house in Bombay for a series of confidential talks, and wound up with an exchange of correspondence which they agreed to publish. Mr. Gandhi's offer had been on the same lines as Mr. Rajagopalachari's. He was willing, he wrote, to recommend to the Congress and the country acceptance of the claim for separation contained in the League's Lahore resolution of 1940, subject to certain conditions. Areas in the north-west and north-east, where it appeared that Muslims desired to live in separation from the rest of the Indian family, should be demarcated by a commission approved by the Congress and the League, and the wishes of the inhabitants then ascertained through a plebiscite. If they voted for separation, an independent State would be formed as soon as possible after India was free, under a treaty of separation providing for administration of matters of common interest such as defence, foreign affairs, Customs and so on, and for protection of minority rights. As soon as these terms had been agreed by the Congress and the League, they would adopt a common course of action to achieve India's freedom, with an escape clause for the League in respect of direct action in which it did not want to share.

Mr. Jinnah's reply rejected this solution in principle and in detail. The scheme denied the fundamental theme of the Lahore resolution, since it refused to acknowledge that the Muslims were a nation with the right of self-determination; the proposal that all the inhabitants even of the admittedly Muslim-majority areas should vote for or against separation was unacceptable. On such terms the existing boundaries of Bengal, Assam and the Punjab would be mutilated beyond redemption. Mr. Gandhi's proposal deferred separation until after India was free, whereas the Muslim League wanted a complete and immediate settlement between the two parties, who would then work together to secure the independence of India on the basis of Pakistan and Hindustan. Foreign affairs, defence, Customs, communications and other matters for which a treaty-bound joint administration had been proposed were the lifeblood of any State and could not be delegated to any common central body.

Mr. Gandhi's mild comment was that the talks and correspondence seemed to 'run on parallel lines and never touch one another'. The so-called breakdown, he said, was only an adjournment *sine die*. But the effect of his going so far to meet the demand for Pakistan was immediately felt. On the one hand, Mr. Jinnah's prestige was greatly enhanced. On the other, opponents of partition were incensed: Mr. V. D. Savarkar of the Hindu Mahasabha protested that 'the Indian provinces were not the private property of Gandhiji and Rajaji so that they could make a gift of them to anyone they liked'.

Lord Wavell was now convinced that the deadlock in India could be broken only by a *dèmarche* by the third party, the British Government or himself as its proconsul. A conference of provincial Governors which he called in August 1944 unanimously supported his view that, with the end of the war and all the consequences of military and civil demobilisation in sight, a positive move was essential, and that its basic form should be the politicalisation of the Central Government and the restoration of responsible government in those provinces which were under Governor's rule. Thus fortified, Lord Wavell submitted his plan to the Secretary of State. He proposed to call a conference of the principal party leaders and representatives of the lesser minorities and discuss with them the formation of a transitional Government at the Centre. Besides carrying on the war against Japan (which was expected to continue after the defeat of Germany) and governing India under the existing constitution, its task would be to consider, in consultation with leaders of Indian opinion, the formation of a Constituent Assembly or similar body which would draw up a constitution for India's independence and negotiate with the British Government a treaty for the transfer of power. As to the composition of this transitional Executive, he had in mind an equal number of caste Hindus and Muslims, with one representative of the Scheduled Castes and one of the Sikhs, together with the Governor-General and the Commander-in-Chief. Another of its tasks would be to consider the best means of restoring popular government in all the provinces.

The Secretary of State was not convinced by this plan. He sapiently foresaw difficulties in composing the transitional Government: for instance, was Mr. Jinnah to be allowed to nominate all the Muslim leaders? More fundamentally, Mr. Amery was sure that, unless there were prior agreement between the major parties as to the constitutional future, the new Executive Council would be paralysed by internal tension. Here was the old hen-and-egg controversy which had bedevilled the Cripps Mission. The Secretary of State had his own alternative proposal. While the existing Executive Council continued for the duration of the war, the Viceroy should call a conference representative of more co-operative and less irreconcilable elements than the Congress and the Muslim League to frame proposals for a future constitution. It might be based on the existing National Defence Council. There was much to be said, Mr. Amery argued, for bypassing the Congress and the League; if that could not be done, they might be invited to participate, on a relatively small scale. They would, of course, be represented on the elected body to which no doubt the draft constitution would have to be referred.

Lord Wavell swept aside this project, which showed a profound neglect of the facts of Indian political life. The Congress and the League, he replied, could not be bypassed. They held the keys to the situation, and would sweep the polls in any elections. Preliminary agreement about the future constitution could not be made a condition because it was manifestly impossible; on the contrary, if the party politicians could be induced to work together in a Government they might come to a greater sense of realism.

The Secretary of State now propounded a brave new plan of his own, not for immediate acceptance but for consideration, since it had no Cabinet authority. His theme was that India's main grievance was really control of India's government from Westminster and Whitehall. This encouraged irresponsibility and extremism. At the back of their minds Indian politicians were always thinking that if they pitched their demands high they would get something more out of the British Government, which would eventually take the constitutional decision; for they could not believe that the British would really accept and implement a settlement made by the Indians themselves. To that extent there was something in Mr. Gandhi's argument that until the British quit India the Indians would never come to an agreement.

Accordingly Mr. Amery suggested that His Majesty's Government should announce that they recognised India as enjoying full Dominion Status under the Statute of Westminster, and that thenceforward the British Parliament should have no power to legislate for India save at the request of an Indian Government.

The Amery Plan, at once simple and imaginative, never saw the light of day. It might conceivably have provided a solution that would have avoided all the struggles and calamities of the next three years and bequeathed a united India when the British departed. For the attractions of office in a Government having real and immediate sovereign power, even though presided over by a British Viceroy, might well have been too great for rejection by either of the two great parties, notwithstanding the positions of principle to which they were committed, and the temptation would have been offered at a time when neither the Congress nor the League was as overwhelmingly strong and entrenched as they became after the release of the Congress leaders, the sweeping of the board by Congress and League in the post-war provincial elections, and the defeat of Muslim leaders in the Punjab and Bengal who were ready to work with Hindus and Sikhs for the unity of their provinces.

The Amery Plan was lost because it was submerged by two processes, in Britain and India respectively, which distracted attention and delayed decision. Had the Secretary of State and the Viceroy been agreed in principle, either on the former's Dominion Status project or on the latter's call for a conference to set up a transitional Government, some clear-cut action might have followed in 1944; but as they were not pulling together the boat of British policy drifted before wind and tide. In India, at the instance of Sir Tej Bahadur Sapru, with the support of Mr. Gandhi, the Standing Committee of the Non-Party Conference met in November and decided to set up a committee of people from none of the main political parties to 'examine the whole communal and minorities question from a constitutional and political point of view'. To the Viceroy, this was an ineffectual distraction, and he pressed for a Cabinet decision on his own proposals; but the British Government, unconvinced of Lord Wavell's basic theme, and clutching at straws, felt that the Viceroy should come to London for personal discussions on his plan but that these should await the outcome of the Sapru Committee. The

Viceroy demurred, and insisted that his visit should not be delayed beyond March 1945. The Sapru Committee reported in April. Its main recommendations were:

[i] A national Government to be formed at the Centre;
[ii] Hindu-Muslim parity (excluding Scheduled Castes) in a constitution-making body;
[iii] Similar parity at the Centre, conditional on joint electorates to replace separate communal electorates;
[iv] No partition of India;
[v] Decisions of the constitution-making body to require a three-fourths majority, in the absence of which His Majesty's Government would make an award.

This scheme was strongly opposed by the Muslim League because it rejected Pakistan and reverted to joint electorates; at an earlier stage Mr. Jinnah had refused to co-operate with the Sapru Committee. Hindu politicians equally opposed the parity principle. Its reception thus vindicated Lord Wavell's original attitude. The Congress and the League could not be bypassed.

Meanwhile, however, there had been another, more promising development which involved both those bodies. In January 1945 Mr. Bhulabhai Desai, leader of the Congress party in the Central Assembly, brought to the Viceroy a plan which he said he had discussed both with Mr. Gandhi, who agreed with it, and with Mr. Liaqat Ali Khan, his own opposite number in the Muslim League, who in turn had secured the blessing of Mr. Jinnah. The chief features of the Desai-Liaqat plan were:

Mr. Desai and Mr. Jinnah would be asked to form a joint interim Government under the existing constitution;
Communal proportions in the new Council would be settled by agreement, Mr. Desai himself being ready if necessary to concede Congress-League parity, with one-fifth of the seats for other elements;
There would be no commitments on the long-term problem;
There would be no general elections either at the Centre or in the provinces;
In the provinces, existing Ministries would continue; in Section 93 (Governor's rule) provinces, coalition Ministries would be formed.

This prescription almost exactly accorded with Lord Wavell's ideas and he was eager to follow it up. The Governor of Bombay was asked to talk with Mr. Jinnah on the Viceroy's behalf and find out what he thought of the Desai-Liaqat plan, and, if he felt it to be worth pursuing, whether he would come to Delhi for consultations. Mr. Jinnah denied all knowledge of the Desai-Liaqat talks, but said that he would be glad to discuss the matter with the Viceroy when he came to Delhi in March. Unfortunately, when he reached Delhi he fell ill and the talks never eventuated. Mr. Liaqat Ali Khan himself later repudiated the alleged pact, and feeling against Mr. Bhulabhai Desai rose in the Congress because he was felt to have sold the pass.

If the wind shifted back and forth in India, in England an adverse tide was flowing. After making no decisive advance in his earlier exchanges with the Secretary of State, Lord Wavell had addressed himself direct to Mr. Churchill, more than ever the dominating force in the British Cabinet, pleading for a change of spirit which would convince Indians of Britain's goodwill. The only clear result was the Cabinet's request to the Viceroy to come to London for discussions on his proposals, but they wanted to put these off, and only grudgingly did they consent to his flying home towards the end of March 1945. When he arrived in London he found it difficult to get their ear. The fact was that, whereas in 1942 they had been desperately anxious to secure Indian co-operation at a very low moment in the war, now, after the years of relative quiescence, and with victory in sight, the pressure for immediate decision in India was greatly relaxed. Internationally, the United States had other things on her mind. Politically Mr. Churchill had no need to bow to demands from the Labour wing of his Government, who might be expected in any case to leave the coalition when the war was ended or even sooner. Ministers generally were preoccupied with the war in Europe and the problems of international and national reconstruction that would follow victory. It took Lord Wavell nearly two months to get any final decision: a Cabinet whose eyes were on the advance of the western and eastern allies towards the heart of Germany, on her surrender and on preparation for the Potsdam Conference, found his persistent presence more a bore than a stimulus. Lord Wavell was determined upon some action. Mr. Churchill wanted to stand fast. In the end it was the influence of Sir Stafford Cripps and Mr. Amery, in support of the Viceroy, that carried the day, the Prime Minister grudgingly admitting that 'at any rate we aren't giving anything away'.

On 14th June 1945, ten days after his return to Delhi, Lord Wavell broadcast his proposals. He intended to call to a political conference in Simla on 25th June twenty-one political leaders, including the Chief Ministers of provincial Governments and the last Chief Ministers of Section 93 provinces; the leader of the Congress Party and deputy leader of the Muslim League in the Central Assembly; Mr. Gandhi and Mr. Jinnah, as recognised leaders of the Congress and the League; and a representative each of the Sikhs and the Scheduled Castes. The purpose would be to discuss the formation of a politically representative Executive Council. The Council would be entirely Indian except for the Viceroy and Commander-in-Chief; external affairs, hitherto the preserve of the Viceroy, would be in charge of an Indian member, so far as the interests of British India were concerned. Communally, the Council would include 'equal proportions of Caste Hindus and Muslims'. While it would function under the existing constitution, the Governor-General would not use his reserve powers unreasonably, and, as a token of India's new status, Britain would appoint a High Commissioner in India to look after British interests, which had hitherto been the responsibility of the Governor-General. One vital task of the new Government would be to work towards a long-term constitutional solution.

If his conference succeeded, declared Lord Wavell, he hoped that Ministries would again be formed in Section 93 provinces, and that they would be coalitions. Orders had been given for the release of such members of the Congress Working Committee as were still in detention—this had been a point for which the Viceroy had fought hard in London—and release of remaining *detenus* implicated in the 1940 disturbances would be decided upon by the new central and provincial Governments. In expounding the proposals to the House of Commons, the Secretary of State emphasised that the Cripps Offer of 1942 held good in its entirety, with its two principles—that no limits were set to India's freedom to determine her own destiny, and that this destiny could be achieved only under a constitutional regime framed and agreed by Indians. Mr. Amery declared that the proposals owed everything to Lord Wavell's initiative, and to his deep sympathy with India's aspirations.

The story of the Simla Conference divides into four chapters. First came preliminary discussions, by correspondence with those invited, and in person with the key men among them on the eve of the conference. Mr. Gandhi declined to appear at the conference on behalf of the Congress; he said it should be represented by its President, Maulana Abul Kalam Azad, who was accordingly invited; but he agreed to be present at Simla in the wings in case he were needed for consultation, and his repudiation of any representative capacity did not deter him from expounding his views at length, both by letter and in public. His greatest objection, on the proposed composition of the Government, was to the rule of parity between Muslims and Caste Hindus (a term which the Viceroy had to explain was not meant offensively but was short-hand for Hindus other than Scheduled Castes). The Congress had always striven to be purely political, not communal. 'I am quite capable,' he wrote, 'of advising Congress to nominate all Hindus and most decidedly non-Caste Hindus. You will unconsciously but equally surely defeat the purpose of the conference if the parity between Hindus and Muslims is unalterable. Parity between the Congress and the League is understandable. I am eager to help you and the British people but not at the cost of fundamental and universal principles.'

Mr. Jinnah was studiously non-committal; he asked that the conference be postponed for a fortnight until his Working Committee could consider the clarification of the proposals which he hoped the Viceroy would meanwhile have given him. Lord Wavell did not yield, and the conference was in fact attended without more demur by Mr. Jinnah and other members of the Muslim League.

The Viceroy had interviews with Mr. Gandhi, Mr. Jinnah and Maulana Azad on 24th June. Out of these talks three clear points emerged. Both Maulana Azad and Mr. Gandhi insisted that the Congress, without wishing to fight on the issue of parity, must have a say in the representation of communities other than Caste Hindus, and would not accept the nomination of Muslims by only one communal organisation. Mr. Gandhi also claimed that in the provinces minorities should be represented in the Government by members from their communities belonging to the Congress, to which the Viceroy tartly retorted that the vital point was that they should be represented by people they trusted. Mr. Jinnah, on the other hand, claimed that under the proposals the Muslims would always be in a minority, for the Sikhs and Scheduled Castes would vote with the Congress. He asked that no matter should be decided in the Executive Council by vote if the majority of Muslim members were opposed. And he claimed for the Muslim League the right to nominate all the Muslim members, and specifically objected to including representatives of the Punjab Unionist Party or of Congress Muslims.

The second chapter embraces the first three days of the conference. No sooner had the opening debate started than the key question of the status of the Congress and the League came to the fore. Maulana Azad declared that, while he accepted that the present proposals were only for an interim settlement, the Congress could not be a party to anything, however temporary, that prejudiced its national character, or reduced it directly or indirectly to the level of a communal body. The Viceroy assured him that there was nothing in the proposals which did so. Mr. Jinnah interjected the remark that the Congress represented only Hindus—at which Dr. Khan Sahib, the Congress Premier of the North-West Frontier Province, who, of course, was a Muslim, vehemently protested. The Viceroy skilfully averted a row by observing that the Congress evidently represented its members. 'I accept that,' said Mr. Jinnah.

When Mr. Jinnah came to speak at length he said that he looked on the proposals as a stop-gap, in no way affecting the Congress stand for independence or the Muslim League stand for Pakistan. The League could not agree to a constitution on any basis other than that of Pakistan: it was fundamentally opposed to any common central government. He recognised that framing a constitution on the basis of Pakistan was a complex business which would take time; the League did not demand Pakistan immediately. He did not doubt the sincerity behind the British Government's offer, which should be examined in no spirit of carping criticism. It was no good starting by questioning each other's representative character, though if the Congress represented 90 per cent of the Hindus the League represented 90 per cent or more of the Muslims. Mr. Jinnah gave the impression that the proposals were acceptable to him provided he had his way on communal parity.

The next day the Viceroy offered the conference a definite agenda. Part A covered general points, Part B the actual composition of the Executive Council. Under Part A, the conference agreed in principle, subject to agreement under Part B, that an Executive Council should be set up as in the Viceroy's broadcast. On the point that it should contain equal numbers of Muslims and Hindus other than Scheduled Castes there was less agreement, but the majority, including Mr. Jinnah, appeared to accept it. Maulana Azad said that while the Congress did not object to the parity proposal, it had strong views about the door through which the members would enter; the Council should be appointed on a political and not on a communal basis. The conference was therefore able to pass to Part B, comprising two questions: the strength and composition of the Council by parties and communities, and the method by which panels of names would be submitted to the Viceroy for his selection. After taking the sense of the conference on procedure, the Viceroy adjourned the meeting in order to enable the participants to consult among themselves. A further short session the following day, 27th June, was again adjourned so that Mr. Jinnah and Pandit Govind Ballabh Pant, ex-Premier of the United Provinces, whom the Congress had deputed as their spokesman, could continue their conversations.

Now followed chapter three. On 29th June, when the conference met again, it was reported that Pandit Pant and Mr. Jinnah could see no way out of their disagreement. Lord Wavell said it must be assumed that discussions between the major parties had broken down. He thought that perhaps the difficulties had arisen from trying to find an agreed arithmetical formula for party and communal quotas; accordingly he now proposed a more personal approach. He asked all the interests represented to send him lists of persons whom they would like to see included in the Executive Council, lists exceeding the numbers likely to be available to their particular interests and adding outside names if they wished. After seeing these lists, and possibly considering further names of his own, he would form on paper an Executive Council and see how the conference reacted. To avoid debating names and personalities in semi-public, the nominations would be secret and he would consult the party leaders in confidence before putting his proposed list to the conference. Neither the Congress nor the League representatives committed themselves to this procedure; they must, they said, consult their Working Committees. But, in reply to a question from Mr. Jinnah, Maulana Azad said that Muslim names would be included in the Congress list.

The Congress Working Committee duly met and on 6th July submitted a list of names. After a meeting of the Muslim League Working Committee on that day, Mr. Jinnah wrote to the Viceroy, proposing, first, that instead of the League's submitting a panel, its representatives should be chosen in personal discussion between himself and the Viceroy; secondly, that all the Muslim members should be chosen from the League; and, thirdly, that some safe-guard other than the Governor-General's veto should be provided to protect Muslim interests from majority decisions of the Council. Lord Wavell saw Mr. Jinnah, discussed these points with him, and on 9th July wrote to him saying that he could give no guarantee that the Muslim members would be selected exclusively from the League's list, any more than he could give a similar guarantee to the other parties. In that event, replied Mr. Jinnah, the League would submit no list. The Viceroy proceeded accordingly to frame his own proposed selection, to which he obtained the approval of His Majesty's Government.

On 11th July Lord Wavell saw Mr. Jinnah again, and told him that he was prepared to include in the Council four members of the Muslim League, together with a non-League Muslim from the Punjab, all of whom he named, adding that if Mr. Jinnah wanted to substitute other League names he would consider them—indeed he would be glad if Mr. Jinnah himself would serve. His team, he emphasised, embodied parity not only between Hindus and Muslims but also between the Congress and the League. He had not yet, however, consulted the Congress, who might not agree. Mr. Jinnah at once replied that the Muslim League could not co-operate unless all five Muslim members of the Council were drawn from the League, and unless there were a special safeguard for Muslims within the Council. Neither of these conditions would the Viceroy accept. He told Mr. Jinnah that this spelt the failure of his efforts and that he would so inform the conference.

Lord Wavell had in effect capitulated to Mr. Jinnah. His pro-posal for a representative of the Punjab Unionist Party—which had held office since 1924 under Sir Fazl-i-Husain, Sir Sikander Hyat Khan and Sir Khizar Hyat Khan Tiwana, and represented all three communities—in the Government was entirely reasonable, and might well have been accepted by the Congress in lieu of their own nomination of a Mussulman, for the evidence is that they came to Simla in a mood to conform. Mr. Jinnah's control of the Muslim

League was at that time far from complete. The Unionist Party was still strong, and Mr. Liaqat Ali Khan favoured a settlement. There were still many uncommitted Muslims in the country. It is arguable that if the Viceroy had been as adamant as Mr. Jinnah, the latter would have been obliged himself to give in; that the destruction of the Unionist Party, which paved the way for partition of the Punjab, would have been averted; and that an effective all-community political Government of India would have operated for the rest of the war and perhaps for some time afterwards. Right or wrong, the moment was a critical one in the whole story.

After telling his official advisers, and certain other members of the conference, as well as Mr. Gandhi, of his decision, Lord Wavell announced it to the conference on 14th July, taking on himself full responsibility for the breakdown. Though Mr. Gandhi took it philosophically, observing that, as the Congress and the League, Hindus and Muslims, were irreconcilable, sooner or later the British would have to decide between them, many others were astonished and incensed. A minority party, with insupportable claims, had been allowed to veto the whole project for advancing India's self-government. Maulana Azad refused to endorse the Viceroy's acceptance of responsibility for failure: Lord Wavell had been right in rejecting the League's demands, and there was no doubt where the blame lay.

Mr. Jinnah, in reply, said he must remind the conference of the fundamentals. The League and the Congress had entirely different angles of vision. The idea of Pakistan and the idea of a united India were incompatible. The League, while recognising that the Viceroy had to carry on the government of the country whether the parties or the communities agreed or not, would consider any proposal for an interim provisional government subject to two conditions: a declaration by His Majesty's Government giving Muslims the right of self-determination; and equality for Muslims with all other communities in the interim arrangement. The Viceroy's proposals had reduced Muslim representation to one-third; since the other minority interests could not organise independent States of their own, they were bound to take the Congress side. Hence his demand for a special safeguard procedure. Again, as the composition of the proposed Council was admittedly communal, the Muslim League must insist on selection of all the Muslim members. If the League, the representative organisation of all the

Muslims of India, was expected to take the administrative responsibility, it must choose its own men. The conference had really failed on this issue.

The whole intention of the conference, we may observe from a distance, had in fact become distorted. As one of its Joint Secretaries wrote later, it

> had been conceived as a gathering of politically eminent persons who would sit together and collectively advise the Viceroy about the formation of a new central Government. Very soon, however, it became transformed into the familiar pattern of futile discussions between the Congress and the Muslim League, and between party leaders and the Viceroy. The formal sessions of the conference served as a forum for party leaders . . . while other members functioned as the audience or drones.[1]

All this may have been inevitable, but it does not fully explain why Lord Wavell brought the proceedings to such an abrupt halt. He gave no further explanation to the conference, simply recording that when Mr. Jinnah told him that his solution was not acceptable to the Muslim League he felt it would be useless to continue. Many people, including some of his official advisers, thought he was wrong to accept Mr. Jinnah's veto without even a struggle, and that a great chance of setting India on the road to united self-government had been needlessly abandoned.

Mr. Rajagopalachari, in a statement after the breakdown, said that if it had been known that the sole purpose of the conference was to get Mr. Jinnah to agree, failing which it would have to disperse, the Congress would have told Lord Wavell at the very start that it would be a waste of energy.

The immediate effect was greatly to heighten the prestige of the Muslim League and its leader at a time when its fortunes in the provinces had not altogether prospered. In the Punjab—the crucial area for Pakistan—Sir Khizar, the Premier, had been expelled from the League for failing to toe Mr. Jinnah's line, and though his Muslim support in the Unionist Party was thereafter much reduced he was still confidently in office. In Bengal, Khwaja Sir Nazimuddin, the Muslim League Premier who had succeeded Mr. Fazl-ul-Huq, had been defeated in the Assembly in March 1945 and the Governor had taken over administration under Section 93.

[1] V. P. Menon, *The Transfer of Power in India*, p. 214.

In the North-West Frontier Province, where a Muslim League Ministry had been set up in May 1943 when most of the Congress members of the Assembly were under arrest, their gradual release in accordance with Lord Wavell's policy had destroyed its majority, and in March 1945 a Congress Ministry had been formed under Dr. Khan Sahib. Mr. Jinnah's demonstration of imperious strength at the Simla conference was a shot in the arm for the League and a serious blow for its Muslim opponents, especially in the Punjab. Some observers thought that Lord Wavell's sudden abandonment of his plan was the decisive move that made the partition of India inevitable.

Critics of the Viceroy must, however, consider what were his apparent alternative courses. They reduced, in effect, to one only; to seek to form a Government with the support of the Congress and the minor elements only, as he was obliged to do in circumstances not dissimilar only fourteen months later, after the failure of the Cabinet Mission. Within this possible course there were various options: to form an entire Council from the Congress and non-League groups; to propose to the Congress leaders such a membership as he had partly revealed to Mr. Jinnah, and then to go back to the Muslim League leader saying 'such and such places are still open to you if you change your mind'; or to appoint officials to the proposed Muslim League places pending a new attitude on Mr. Jinnah's part. But the sanction behind either of the two latter options could only have been, in effect, the threat of the first. Unless the Viceroy were willing to contemplate a Government politically dominated by the Congress he could neither proceed straight to this conclusion nor credibly use its possibility to twist Mr. Jinnah's arm. Such a result, it is clear, was not part of the plan that he had so laboriously agreed with His Majesty's Government. Their consent to proceed to it was very far from assured. In the first place, they had never been enamoured of Lord Wavell's thesis that the egg must hatch into the hen, that a politicalised Government of India was the required first step towards reaching a long-term solution, and they had accepted it only on the assumption that all the main political elements were brought into such a Government, where they could be brought to work together for a long-term end. They saw the fate of the Simla conference as proof of their own belief that the hen of constitutional agreement must lay the egg of interim government. Secondly, it must be remembered that the Congress was deeply suspect at that time. Its leaders had only recently been released—some of them specifically in preparation for the conference itself—from imprisonment imposed for their revolutionary acts or intentions at the height of the war, intentions which if successful could have cost victory itself, or at least have greatly increased the losses and sufferings of the allies before it was achieved. To hand them effective power now must have seemed to Mr. Churchill and many Ministers in London an act of political lunacy. There is nothing in Lord Wavell's subsequent actions to suggest that he differed very much. By September 1946, when he invited Pandit Nehru to form a Government, the whole situation had changed—in India itself, in Britain with a new Government of the Left, and in the outer world with the defeat of Japan.

Lord Wavell's tactics are indeed open to criticism. Having asserted the initiative at the conference by quickly presenting it with a compact agenda, he lost it for a while, perhaps necessarily, in the adjournment for private talks among the Indian leaders, regained it by developing his own draft Council membership, and then immediately abandoned it. Mr. Jinnah must have been as surprised as anybody. There was more than one hint in his final speech that he had expected further bargaining, or that the Viceroy would adopt some form of possible alternative action. There is also evidence that the Working Committee of the Muslim League had been far from unanimous.[1] On the other hand, by his straightforward procedures and his acceptance of full blame for failure, Lord Wavell acquired the goodwill of all the principal participants. The Viceroy, said Maulana Azad, had done his best and the Congress delegates were grateful, and these words were endorsed by Mr. Jinnah for the League.

In his speech to the conference announcing its end, Lord Wavell had said:

I propose to take a little time to consider in what way I can best help India after the failure of the conference. You can all help best by refraining from recriminations. The war against Japan must be carried on, and law and order must be maintained; and until I see my way more clearly than I do now it may be difficult, perhaps impossible, to suggest any new move. No Government can carry on under the daily prospect of change or dissolution.

[1] loc. cit.

... Whatever decisions His Majesty's Government may take in the near future must therefore, in all probability, hold good for some little time.

Developments outside India, however, rather than those within, moulded the pattern of events in the next few months. On 26th July, less than a fortnight after the Simla conference, the first Labour Government with an independent majority took office in Britain under Mr. Attlee. On 15th August Japan surrendered and World War II was over. These changes of fortune heightened the hopes and shortened the patience of Indian politicians. Mr. Jinnah, for one, declared that the Muslim League had offered co-operation in an interim Government only because of the war; the need now was to go ahead with plans for a permanent settlement, necessarily on the basis of Pakistan, on which the League would never surrender. Sir Stafford Cripps, now more powerful than ever on India policy, had already publicly declared that time should not be wasted in trying to arrive at a temporary arrangement, but that means be expedited to arrive at a permanent solution, in which the question of Pakistan must form a major issue; and for this purpose new elections should be held in India. The Viceroy agreed.

On 21st August he announced that elections to the central and provincial assemblies would be held in the coming cold weather, and that he would shortly be visiting England for consultations. He spent the last week of August and the first two weeks of September in London, in a very different atmosphere from that which he had endured in the previous year. His consultations largely concerned procedure for reaching a constitutional settlement. British Ministers leaned towards reliance on the provincial-option provisions of the Cripps Offer, but decision on details was deferred. On his return to India Lord Wavell announced:

His Majesty's Government are determined to do their utmost to promote in conjunction with the leaders of Indian opinion the early realisation of full self-government for India. . . .

It is the intention of His Majesty's Government to convene as soon as possible a constitution-making body, and as a preliminary step they have authorised me to undertake, immediately after the elections, discussions with the Legislative Assemblies in the provinces, to ascertain whether the proposals contained in the 1942 declaration are acceptable or whether some alternative or modified scheme is preferable. . . .

His Majesty's Government have further authorised me, as soon as the results of the provincial elections are published, to take steps to bring into being an Executive Council which will have the support of the main Indian parties.

This declaration was not well received. The Congress deplored the omission of any reference to 'independence' and characterised the proposals as 'vague and inadequate'. The League reiterated that no solution would be acceptable except on the basis of Pakistan. Criticism does not appear to have focussed on the implicit effort to bypass the all-India leadership on the constitutional settlement by consulting the new provincial assemblies.

The new Secretary of State, Lord Pethick-Lawrence, disappointed no doubt by the reaction, and alarmed by the growing threat of violence in India and the disruptive forces aroused by the trials of certain officers of the quisling 'Indian National Army',[1] decided to make a further statement. On 4th December he declared in the House of Lords that the full significance of the Viceroy's proposals had not been properly appreciated; that the holding of discussions for setting up a constitution-making body after the elections was not intended to delay progress; but that the Government indeed regarded the setting-up of such a body as a matter of great urgency. He added that they proposed to send out an all-party Parliamentary delegation to meet Indian political leaders and convey the general desire of the British people to see India speedily attaining her rightful position as an independent partner State in the Commonwealth.

This warmer and more urgent utterance had a correspondingly more cordial reception in India, though the Parliamentary delegation aroused little interest, being regarded as a stalling device. Under the leadership of Professor Robert Richards, M.P., it toured India in January 1946. Educative as it surely was for its members, and through them for Parliament, it had no measurable effect on the subsequent course of events.

Meanwhile the Congress Working Committee, meeting in September, had emphasised its demand for independence and

[1] See below, p. 248.

unity of India, but it added, recalling its similar words at the time
of the Cripps Mission:

> Nevertheless, the Committee declares also that it cannot think
> in terms of compelling the people in any territorial unit to re-
> main in an Indian Union against their declared and established
> will. . . . Acceptance of the principle inevitably involves that
> no changes should be made which result in fresh problems being
> created and compulsion being exercised on other substantial
> groups within that area. Each territorial unit should have the
> fullest possible autonomy within the Union, consistently with a
> strong national State.

The door was thus open to Pakistan, of the 'moth-eaten' variety,
even though it was intended to be a revolving door. In talks with
the Parliamentary delegation, Pandit Nehru conceded that the
British Government might have to declare for Pakistan, but that
there must be a plebiscite in border districts to confirm it. Mr.
Jinnah told them that while he insisted on prior acceptance of
Pakistan on the basis of five provinces and on the setting-up of two
constitution-making bodies, the drawing of the final frontier between Pakistan and Hindustan would be a matter for negotiation.
He did not envisage predominantly non-Muslim areas, like the
Ambala division of the Punjab, remaining in Pakistan, but
he insisted that Pakistan must be a viable national State, with
no common organs of government with Hindustan for defence,
currency, communications or other functions. He had perhaps come down to fifteen ounces of his pound of flesh, but no
less.

Both the Congress and the Muslim League fought the elections
on their full-blooded national policies. The elections were held in
three waves: first, for the central assembly, then for the assemblies
in provinces with responsible Governments, and finally for the
Section 93 provinces. The central results were the most dramatic.
Of 102 elected seats, the Congress won a clear majority, but the
Muslim League swept the board in the Muslim seats. The figures
were (numbers at the time of dissolution in brackets): Congress 57
(36), Muslim League 30 (25), Independents 5 (21), Nationalist
Party 0 (10), Akali Sikhs 2 (0), Europeans 8 (8). Mr. Jinnah's claim
that if the Congress had the support of 90 per cent of the Hindus
the League had the support of over 90 per cent of the Muslims

was not statistically vindicated, but in political terms it clearly had substance on the all-India plane.

In the provinces, however, the demonstration was not so convincing. Of the provinces claimed for Pakistan, in Assam the Congress won a clear majority and formed a Government. The same happened in the North-West Frontier Province, where the Congress actually won more Muslim seats than did the Muslim League. In Sind the League formed a Government dependent upon the European group. In the Punjab, the key province, the League won 79 of the 86 Muslim seats,[1] only 7 going to Unionists, while the Congress took 51 seats and the Panthic Akali Sikhs 22. There were 3 other Unionists and 10 Independents. After the Muslim League had failed to form a Government with a majority, Sir Khizar Hyat Khan became Premier again with the support of a Unionist-Congress-Sikh coalition. It was a fateful decision which destroyed the last hopes of rallying Muslim opposition to partition round the Unionist Party. In Bengal, the League won 113 of the 119 Muslim seats (against 87 seats won by the Congress) and formed a Government under Mr. H. S. Suhrawardy, dependent, however, on the support of the Europeans and independent groups. It must of course be remembered that weightage for communal minorities reduced the Muslim representation in the Punjab, Bengal and Sind, just as it reduced Hindu representation in Muslim-minority provinces. In Assam, Sind and the Punjab, attempts at Congress-League coalitions were made, but significantly they were all frustrated by Congress insistence on nominating non-League Muslim Ministers, which was anathema to the League. On the political level, therefore, it was not so much Hindu-Muslim communalism that frustrated unity, as rival Congress-League pretensions.

---

[1] The party figures include those who shifted their allegiance after the elections.

II

The Cabinet Mission

Now was the time for the Viceroy to implement his proposal to consult the new provincial assemblies about constitution-making, starting from the Cripps Offer, and to reconstruct his Executive Council. His masters in London, however, had a new idea. On 19th February 1946 the British Government announced in Parliament that they had decided to send out to India a team of three Cabinet Ministers, to seek an agreement with the leaders of Indian opinion on the principles and procedure to be followed on the constitutional issue: the members of the Mission, who would act in association with the Viceroy, were to be Lord Pethick-Lawrence (Secretary of State for India), Sir Stafford Cripps (President of the Board of Trade) and Mr. A. V. Alexander[1] (First Lord of the Admiralty). Those were their formal terms of reference: they were to 'seek agreement' with Indian leaders, the subject of the agreement being constitutional 'principles and procedure'. They were not enjoined to impose, or to recommend for imposition, any solution; nor were they to be concerned with the details of a future constitutional structure. They were not principals but mediators, and the limit of their intended mediation was an agreed mechanism whereby Indians themselves would frame their constitutional future.

Several glosses were put upon those intentions before the Mission started work. Speaking in the House of Commons on 13th March, the Prime Minister, Mr. Attlee, said that the Mission were going to India in a positive mood, conscious that the time had come for clear and definite action. They would use their utmost endeavours to help India to attain freedom as quickly and as fully as possible. It was for India to decide what form of Government should replace the existing regime, though he hoped that she would elect to remain within the British Commonwealth. Mr. Attlee added: 'We are mindful of the rights of minorities, and the

[1] Later Viscount Alexander of Hillsborough.

minorities should be able to live free from fear. On the other hand, we cannot allow a minority to place their veto on the advance of the majority.' Lord Pethick-Lawrence sought to allay the misgiving which that reservation had caused among the Muslim leaders by saying, at a Press conference immediately after the Mission's arrival in India, that 'while the Congress are representative of large numbers, it would not be right to regard the Muslim League as merely a minority political party—they are in fact majority representatives of the great Muslim community'. The object, he declared, was to set up quickly acceptable machinery whereby Indians could determine the form of Government under which India could realise full independent status, and to make the necessary interim arrangements. The linking of those two purposes proved, in the event, the most difficult of the Mission's task, and a cause of its final frustration; and this in turn was due, in large measure, to conflict over the status of the Muslim League as representative of the Mussulmans of India.

The Mission arrived in New Delhi on 24th March 1946, and spent their first week conferring with Lord Wavell, who was to be their full colleague in their negotiations, using a joint secretariat, and with provincial Governors and members of the Governor-General's Executive Council. The latter, British and Indian, all pressed the need for a more representative Executive as soon as possible, but according to one of those present 'almost all realised that that could not be achieved until the Pakistan issue had been settled somehow'. The Governors emphasised that the Mission must determine something or the position could not be held.

Members of the Mission were of course aware that the tactical position of the several parties had been greatly affected by the results of the Indian elections. In reading those results, they could have been misled by applying the criteria of British politics. In Britain, each general election stands by itself, giving the several parties their abiding battle-strength in Parliament until the next general election, up to five years away, by which time fresh developments may have caused them either to rise or fall in public support, in a prospective cycle of ups and downs. In India, however, the post-war elections were only the preliminary to a more vital political wrestling-match, the struggle for power when it should fall from British hands. Time would be on the side of those whose present progress was dynamic. The momentum revealed by the election results was thus even more important than their static outcome. In this light, the facts that Congress had swept all the six main Hindu-majority provinces and that the Muslim League could form Governments only in Bengal and Sind were less significant than the total elimination of Nationalist Muslims from the Central Legislative Assembly, where the League took every Muslim seat, its winning of 442 Muslim seats out of 509 in the eleven provinces combined—a landslide compared with its position nine years previously—and the reduction of the once all-powerful Punjab Unionist Party, challenging Muslim communalism, to a mere 10 seats in an Assembly of 172 members,[1] of whom 79 were Muslim Leaguers. The Pakistan band-wagon was rolling, and shifts of allegiance after the provincial elections by Muslims holding neither the Congress nor the League ticket showed that more and more Mussulmans were ready to jump on it. Mr. Jinnah had every reason to believe that the more strenuously he fought for the League's demands, and the longer he could hold out against compromise with the Congress, the greater his political power would become. His demand that only Muslims who were League nominees should be accepted as members of the Central Government was now no mere display of arrogance but a key stroke of political strategy; if it was accepted, every Muslim in India would recognise where lay the only road to office and power, and the last remaining non-League aspirants would be laid low; if it were rejected, he could stay out and continue his highly successful negative and declamatory tactics in the confident expectation that the British Government would never give full reign to Congress power alone.

Mr. Jinnah, at an early talk with the Mission, seemed both charming and reasonable. He agreed without pressure to meeting Mr. Gandhi and trying to arrive at an agreement with him. But a few days later Sir Stafford Cripps found it impossible to pin him down to anything beyond vague phrases. The Muslim leader's technique of getting the other man to make an offer so that he could turn it down and ask for more was difficult to counter, thought Sir Stafford, except by ignoring it, and that was dangerous in the existing crisis. Pandit Nehru had offered the opinion that there was no chance of getting Jinnah to agree on anything and that

[1] Excluding constituencies in which by-elections were pending,

the Mission would therefore have to impose some sort of settlement.

The Congress case had been presented by its President, Maulana Abul Kalam Azad.[1] It assumed that independence was the object and that the future constitution would be framed by an Indian constituent body. Until the new regime could come into being, an interim Government, composed of, say, fifteen members, eleven chosen by the provinces and four representing minorities, should become responsible for the governance of India. For the future the Congress contemplated a federal constitution, with a short list of compulsory federal subjects such as defence, foreign affairs and communications, and a further optional list to be adopted at the choice of the individual provinces, in whom would vest the residuary powers. It would be open to the provinces, not only to decline to federate for the optional subjects, but, if they chose, to stand out of the constitution. At the same time, the Congress would never agree to the partition of India. How those two points could be reconciled was not clear. The Mission asked the Maulana whether, if several provinces—for instance, the Muslim-majority provinces of the north-west—wished to sub-federate for an optional list of their own, they could do so. He at first objected, but on being pressed admitted it might be a matter for consideration. Thus began the idea of a three-tier structure which was to play an important part in the Mission's efforts to solve the communal problem.

They were, however, in a certain difficulty in dealing with the Congress. Its President and spokesman, though well liked, was not powerful in its hierarchy and was, moreover, a Mussulman, whom Jinnah with his claim to be the sole voice of the Muslims could never

[1] It appears that at this stage Maulana Azad was speaking personally and without authority. He wrote later: 'The Working Committee met on 12th April when I reported on my discussions with the Cabinet Mission. I described . . . the solution of the communal problem I had suggested. This was the first time that Gandhiji and my colleagues had an opportunity of discussing my scheme. The Working Committee was initially somewhat sceptical about the solution and members raised all kinds of difficulties and doubts. Sardar Patel, in particular, wanted currency and finance, trade and industry, added to the Central list. Finally the Working Committee was convinced about the soundness of the proposal and Gandhiji expressed his complete agreement with the solution.' Maulana Abdul Kalam Aazd, *India Wins Freedom*, Orient Longmans, 1959, p. 141.

accept as representative. Beyond him stood far stronger figures, notably Jawaharlal Nehru and Vallabhbhai Patel. These two were supposed to be rivals and antagonists. Mr. Gandhi told Sir Stafford Cripps that the real man to consult was Nehru. Mrs. Naidu told him that when it came to getting things done Patel was the really effective leader of the Congress. Sudhir Ghosh, an old friend of Sir Stafford's, who was an intimate of Mr. Gandhi, told him that there was a feud between Patel and Nehru, and that out of jealousy Patel would sabotage anything to which Nehru agreed. Behind these two stood the enigmatic figure of the Mahatma himself.

Sir Stafford Cripps, whose Mission in 1942 had been thwarted by Mr. Gandhi's effective veto on Congress acceptance, was now determined to make sure that he carried the Mahatma with him: this in spite of several foretastes of the Mahatma's baffling and elusive methods in negotiation, which were later to drive Cripps and the Mission to despair. Mr. Gandhi's 'almost religious passion for unity as a principle in everything', in the words of his doctor, Dr. Mehta, which must imply a fundamental objection to the division of India, was not a promising background for a negotiation with Mr. Jinnah, who by this time had an almost religious passion for Pakistan and partition.

Meanwhile the Mission had seen representatives of other minorities. The Sikh case was presented by Master Tara Singh, Giani Kartar Singh and Harnam Singh in a joint but far from concerted interview, and separately by Sardar Baldev Singh, who was later to become Indian Defence Minister. All but Giani Kartar Singh, who said that the Sikhs would feel unsafe in either a united India or in Pakistan, were strongly against partition: all were in favour of a separate Sikh State or province in certain circumstances, especially if India were to be divided, though they differed as to its minimal area, which Sardar Baldev Singh defined as the Ambala, Jullundur and Lahore divisions of the Punjab. The Sardar favoured weighted communal proportions in the legislatures in a united India; specifically, the Muslims should give up their 51 per cent majority in the Punjab legislature and be content with 45 per cent, which would leave the Sikhs with the balance of power. The Mission thought that the Sikhs 'don't know what they want but are worried and alarmed'.

For the Scheduled Castes, Dr. Ambedkar opposed the whole idea of a Constituent Assembly, which would be dominated by the

Caste Hindus, and under which all the promises given by His Majesty's Government to the minorities would go by the board. Constitutional questions proper, he said, as distinct from communal questions, should be determined by an expert commission presided over by a British or American constitutional lawyer. Communal questions should be dealt with by a conference of leaders of the different communities, failing whose agreement the British Government should make an award. He insisted that before they left the British must ensure that the new constitution guaranteed to the Scheduled Castes their human rights, restored their separate electorates and afforded them the other safeguards they demanded. Mr. Jagjivan Ram and others representing the All-India Depressed Classes League put forward different ideas. They explained the difference between their League and Dr. Ambedkar's Federation: whereas the latter held that the Scheduled Castes were not Hindus but a separate religious minority, their League and, they claimed, the Scheduled Caste masses considered themselves Hindus who needed help and protection only in order to raise them to the level of their fellow citizens. The Mission appear to have soon reached the conclusion that in conditions of Indian independence there was little that could be done for the Scheduled Castes and that it would be premature and futile to try until the main Hindu-Muslim conflict was out of the way.

Of the other leaders whom they interviewed the most constructive was the Liberal elder statesman Sir Tej Bahadur Sapru. He advised them to make the most liberal offer possible to the Muslim League, short of the partition of India. Provincial boundaries might be revised to give the Muslims stronger majorities (the reverse of the Sikh demand). There should be an equality of Muslims and Caste Hindus in the Central Government. Two constitution-making bodies would be fatal, but the Congress might be brought to agree to one body meeting in two parts.

These nostrums, however, offered little or nothing towards bridging the gap between the Congress and the League, which could be summed up as the conflict between 'Union first, then consider how far Pakistan could go by way of provincial and group autonomy' and 'Pakistan first, then consider how far union could go by way of federation or treaty for common subjects'. As Mr. V. P. Menon pointed out,[1] this contrast was much more than

[1] *The Transfer of Power in India*, p. 247.

a procedural problem which some constitutional sleight-of-hand might have solved. A key test was the Indian Army, which under the Congress formula would necessarily remain one undivided instrument of all-India defence, but under the League formula would be split into Hindustan and Pakistan forces, though both might by treaty be used for common external security.

Three weeks after their arrival the Mission had decided upon their broad initial tactics. These were disclosed in a long interview with Mr. Jinnah on 16th April. The Secretary of State told him that, while they recognised the importance of his claims, they had come to the conclusion that the full demand for Pakistan as presented by himself had little chance of securing that agreement among the parties which was essential for the future of the people of India. He could not reasonably hope to obtain both the whole of the territory and the full measure of sovereignty that he demanded. The Mission therefore placed before him two alternative schemes, neither of which they offered as definitive, or the best, but only as possible bases for further negotiation leading to agreement. Under the first, a separate State of Pakistan would be set up, consisting of, say, Sind, the North-West Frontier Province, Baluchistan and the Muslim-majority districts of Bengal, the Punjab and Assam, specifically excluding Calcutta. It would obviously be necessary for this Pakistan to enter into close treaty relations with Hindustan, including a defensive alliance. The second scheme would involve the League's accepting the principle of an all-India Union for, say, defence, foreign affairs and communications, in which the two communities or constituent elements might have equal representation. A federation might well then be constructed, within the Union, of the whole of the area demanded for Pakistan (five provinces plus Baluchistan) less the Hindu-majority portion of Assam. The right of any party to the Union to secede from it after a certain period, perhaps fifteen years, was also envisaged—a damaging proviso, one would think, since such impermanence could only lead to a fresh struggle for power, through the leverage of partition versus unity, as the period drew to an end, however long it might be. Princely States could join either Hindustan or Pakistan under the first plan; they might possibly come into the Union as a separate federation under the second, or join either member federation, but the communal balance at the Centre would in any case be preserved.

The self-same gambit of confronting Mr. Jinnah with the choice between a small Pakistan with sovereignty and a big Pakistan in an all-India Union for minimal but vital central affairs, in the hope that he would accept the latter, was employed later by Lord Mountbatten in the early phases of his negotiations.[1] But there were several notable differences. The Cabinet Mission were proposing only a possible basis for agreement with the Congress: they did not therefore have to spell out the democratic processes whereby the populations and areas concerned could decide their own fate. Seeking such agreement, they adumbrated the complex system of a three-tier constitution—provinces, federations and Union —which they thought would sweeten the unitary plan for the Muslim League without making it too nauseous for the Congress. The fundamental difference, however, was that as mere mediators the Mission had no power to make a firm offer of either alternative to Mr. Jinnah or his opposite numbers, or to impose it if they refused. They became more and more deeply implicated because, without power to insist, they felt they must succeed in persuading. 'One thing is absolutely certain. We can't leave this country without a settlement of some kind. If we did there would be bloodshed and chaos within a few weeks.' So wrote Sir Stafford Cripps. Bloodshed there was, but in anticipating chaos they underrated the inertia of the masses, the deep-seated constitutionalism of Indian thought, and the inherent strength of the regime.

Confronted with terms which his interlocutors had neither authority to offer nor power to guarantee, Mr. Jinnah's tactics were as might have been expected. After raising the Mission's hopes by showing some interest in the second alternative, he reverted to a tune he had sung before: 'If Congress want to make a suggestion to me, let them do so and I will consider it.' Two days after the Mission's interview Sir Stafford made another attempt, with the Secretary of State's approval, in a long private conversation. Mr. Jinnah was determined not to give way. Sir Stafford's impression was that Jinnah knew he could not get all he asked but still was unwilling to agree to anything less, though he might be prepared to accept it if it was imposed on him. Mr. Jinnah said he would meet Mahatma Gandhi or Pandit Nehru or anyone else (except Maulana Azad) but he did not think it would do any good at all as there was no basis on which they could negotiate.

[1] See below, p. 226.

Driven into the other court, Sir Stafford went to see Mr. Gandhi. The Mahatma did not think any good would come of his meeting Mr. Jinnah, though he was prepared to do so: it would lead nowhere. If anyone were to meet him, it should be Pandit Nehru—who the next day declined, on similar grounds. Mr. Gandhi said that the Mission must make up their minds on what would be just and equitable and then see it through.

Having received these converging opinions from opposite quarters on the need for an award rather than persuasion, why, it may be asked, did not the Mission at that stage seek further instructions from the British Cabinet to strengthen their hands? The reason might have been over-confidence in their diplomatic ability. It might have been the conviction—which was presumably shared by their colleagues at home—that, come what might, Indians must shape their own constitutional future. It might have been dread of the 'bloodshed and chaos' that could follow an imposed solution. Whatever the reason, they pinned their immediate hopes on a new formula.

After refreshing themselves in Kashmir for a few days after the heat of the plains, they offered the leaders of the two parties a plan based on the immediate formation of a representative interim Government. This Government would set up an all-India commission drawn from the elected members of the Central and provincial assemblies, charged with determining, first, the constitutional provisions to be made for the protection of minorities, and secondly whether British India would be divided into two sovereign states or remain one. They would have thirty days to settle the second question in the light of the answer to the first. Failing agreement in that time, the Muslim representatives in the provincial Assemblies of Sind, the N.W.F.P., the Punjab and Bengal (plus the Sylhet district of Assam) would vote whether or not they wanted their several provinces to be separated from the rest of India, a 75 per cent majority being needed for separation. The Frontier Province would have to be separated willy-nilly if the Punjab and Sind decided to stand out. This opportunity for Mr. Jinnah to gain the full Pakistan by popular vote, if the Muslims decided for it, was however qualified by a proviso that non-Muslims in Muslim-majority districts contiguous to the main part of India could vote to have those districts detached from the excluded provinces. Mr. Jinnah could retort that the Mission proposed to take away with one hand what they offered with the other.

With this ingenious scheme in his hand, Sir Stafford Cripps went to see Mr. Jinnah, and found him stubborn and difficult. He took the line that he would not discuss the matter any more; the Muslims had given their decision for Pakistan and the Mission had better make their award and get on with it. The next day Sir Stafford put the same scheme to Pandit Nehru, who turned it down flat.

The Mission promptly switched back to the three-tier device which they had previously put up to Mr. Jinnah as the second alternative basis of negotiation—two federations linked in a minimal super-federal centre. At this stage the negotiations became very tangled. Maulana Abul Kalam Azad was persuaded to say that the Congress would meet the Muslim League to negotiate on the three-tier basis, but he did not want anything said to Mahatma Gandhi or Pandit Nehru about this because that would make his task more difficult in putting the matter across to his Working Committee. Complications ensued because the Maulana failed to show the correspondence either to Mr. Gandhi or to his Working Committee, and the whole confusion had to be explained, with everyone emerging a little sore. On the Muslim side, Sir Stafford had a bad time with Mr. Jinnah, who adopted the attitude that nothing he had said to the Mission officially was more than his own view and that he was prepared to put up to his Working Committee things he had said he would reject. Themselves unable to promise, and negotiating with men unauthorised to accept, the Mission might well have felt frustrated. Indefatigably, they started a new round of debate.

On 27th April virtually identical letters were sent to the Presidents of the Congress and the League. They were invited to send four representatives each to meet the Mission, in one further attempt to reach agreement, to consider a scheme based on the three-tier principle, with residuary sovereign rights vested in the provinces. The replies were cautious and non-committal, but both parties agreed to confer, with four men from each. It was at the Mission's request that Mr. Gandhi was also invited to Simla to be available for consultation. The conference took place in Simla between the 5th and 12th May.

The Mission had hopefully drawn up an agenda, grouping the

subject-matter under three heads: 1. Groups of Provinces; 2. Union; 3. Constitution-making machinery. Mr. V. P. Menon records, however, that after two days of discussion on this basis the gulf between the two parties was still as wide as ever.[1] The Mission's hopes, nevertheless, were not easily dashed. They were pleased with Pandit Nehru's lucid conduct of the Congress case, but disappointed in Mr. Jinnah's inability (real or feigned) to answer questions put to him. They believed they had made some progress by implication, in that they had discussed the setting up of a Union centre without arguing as to whether there should be one or not.

Two days later the Mission's demi-hero, the Congress, had become the villain, and the demi-villain Jinnah had become the hero. The President of the Congress, Maulana Azad, had written to the Secretary of State reiterating its line about independence, withdrawal of British troops, and *de facto* freedom for an interim Government, and declaring that Congress was entirely opposed to any executive or legislative machinery for groups of provinces—the three-tier system—notwithstanding that this was the logical conclusion of its own initial proposals[2] as framed by Azad himself and afterwards endorsed by the Working Committee. The Congress was also opposed to parity between groups in the executive or legislature, and held 'that it is not open to the conference to entertain any suggestions for the division of India. If this is to come, it should come through the Constituent Assembly, free from any influence of the present governing power'. No one mentioned this daunting document when the talks were resumed and they proceeded as before.

In the light of subsequent events, it is highly significant that at this stage, according to the contemporary record, Mr. Jinnah definitely offered to come into a Union if he could have his group. Mr. Gandhi, however, in a private talk, took the line that the Mission must choose between the parties and then hand over the whole business to one or other of them to conduct entirely in their own way. But he challenged the Mission to frame a workable scheme and they accepted the challenge. Their response took the form of a list of 'suggested points for agreement' which the Secretary of State sent to the Presidents of the Congress and the Muslim League on 8th May.

[1] *The Transfer of Power in India*, p. 256.
[2] See p. 136 above.

Point 1 was that there should be an all-India Union Government and Legislature dealing with foreign affairs, defence and fundamental rights and having the correspondingly necessary powers of finance. All remaining powers should vest in the provinces (Point 2). Groups of provinces might be formed, with the option of setting up their own executives and legislatures (Points 3 and 4). Point 5 was that the Legislature of the Union should have parity of representation between the Muslim-majority and the Hindu-majority provinces, whether grouped or not, together with representatives (unspecified) of the States; and by Point 6 the Union Government would be constituted in the same proportion. Point 7 allowed reconsideration of the constitution at ten-yearly intervals. Point 8 set out the constitution-making procedure. The Constituent Assembly should mirror the party strengths in the provincial Assemblies, with representatives of States by ratio of their populations. After preliminary business the Constituent Assembly would divide into three sections, representing respectively the Hindu-majority and Muslim-majority provinces and the States. Each of the first two sections would decide on provincial constitutions, and, if they wished, a group constitution. Provinces might then opt out of groups. Thereafter the three sections would join to frame a Union constitution, provided that any major point affecting the communal issue must be voted by a separate majority of each of the two major communities.

On the eve of presenting this plan to the parties Sir Stafford Cripps had another long talk with Mr. Gandhi. They went through the document line by line, and the Mahatma said he personally looked favourably on the solution.

The Viceroy's interview with Mr. Jinnah was not quite so encouraging, but the Mission thought that if only they could get Congress to accept, or to express a willingness to settle details with Mr. Jinnah, the latter would have difficulty in refusing.

Their cheerfulness soon perished. The written responses were grudging and negative. The Congress President rehearsed the well-worn Congress case and concluded: 'If an agreement . . . cannot be achieved, we would suggest that an interim provisional government responsible to the elected members of the central Assembly be formed at once and the matters in dispute concerning the Constituent Assembly between the Congress and the League be referred to an independent tribunal.' Mr. Jinnah, in a long letter, protested that the 'suggested points for agreement' were a fundamental departure from the original formula proposed by the Secretary of State, and that no useful purpose would be served by a discussion of them.

Nevertheless the conference met on 9th May with the eight points as its agenda. Pandit Nehru proposed that representatives of the two sides should sit together with an umpire, whose decision on any points of disagreement should be final. Mr. Jinnah replied that he would meet any Hindu members of the Congress and would agree an umpire with them. The conference adjourned to allow the two protagonists to discuss this idea, but eventually Mr. Jinnah refused to accept an arbitrator, and the Mission were back at the beginning of their sisyphean task.

Meanwhile they had had further experience of the Gandhian style of negotiation. The Mahatma had written a letter to Sir Stafford Cripps saying, among other things, that he understood from Sir Stafford that whatever was now agreed could be altered later if either party wanted to do so. The reply, of course, was that both sides were bound in honour to see that as far as they could any agreement reached between them was implemented. The Mission believed that they had brought both the Congress and the League to accept the basic principle of a union with groups of provinces, and that only the detail was baffling.

But had the parties both agreed to that basic principle? Certainly not explicitly in writing, and without qualifications. To the extent that they had agreed to it, it meant different things to them. To Mr. Jinnah, the prior formation of the Muslim group was fundamental: once formed, it could negotiate with the Hindu group, on the basis of equality, for such pooling of powers for common purposes as it might of its own free will approve. To the Congress the prior acceptance of an all-India Union was fundamental: once accepted, powers not essential for its Union purposes could be devolved and might be exercised by groups. It was a clash of Pakistan-plus against Unity-minus. Yet it is certainly true that Mr. Jinnah had accepted, however provisionally, the idea of an all-India Union for certain purposes, as part of a comprehensive constitutional settlement, and this suggests that he was not yet so sure of his strength and that of the League, vis-à-vis either the Congress or the British Government, as to prefer the risk of undisputed blame for a breakdown to the risk of having to make good his word if the Congress should accept the settlement. He may have judged that the latter risk was not very high, and that since he always claimed to be negotiating *ad referendum* he could find ways of escaping from a commitment if it no longer suited his strategy.

When the conference reassembled on 11th May, and faced the failure of the arbitral plan, each of the parties was invited to submit a memorandum explaining its position on the disputed issues. The Muslim League memorandum set out certain minimum demands, which amounted to this, that the six Muslim-majority provinces should have their own constitution-making body, which should decide which powers, other than defence, foreign affairs, and communications necessary for defence, should be provincial and which should be central to what was explicitly called the Pakistan Federation; that in a joint constitution-making body with the non-Muslim group it should be open to discussion whether or not the Union should have a legislature and how it should be financed, but in any event not by means of taxation; and that no decision of the Union on any controversial matter should be taken by a majority of less than three-fourths. There were further provisos about opting out, parity in the Union, fundamental rights and other issues. The Congress memorandum proposed as a basis for agreement the formation of a Constituent Assembly to draw up a constitution for a Federal Union consisting of an All-India Government and Legislature dealing with foreign affairs, defence, communications, fundamental rights, currency, Customs and planning, 'as well as such other subjects as, on closer scrutiny, may be found to be intimately allied to them', and having power to obtain finance and raise revenue in its own right and to take remedial action in the event of breakdown of the constitution and in grave public emergencies. After this had been decided by the Constituent Assemblies the provinces, in whom would vest the remaining powers, could form groups. Any major point in the all-India constitution affecting the communal issue would require separate majorities of the communities concerned; failing agreement, such points would be referred to arbitration.

The conflict was manifest, and too fundamental to be appeased by further three-cornered debate. On 12th May the conference agreed that no useful purpose would be served by going on. Its breakdown was announced in an official communiqué, followed by a pronouncement that the Mission's work was far from ended and that they would issue a statement of their views as to the next steps. This took the form of a momentous document published on 16th May.

Faced by failure to reach agreement, the Mission felt it their duty, they declared, to put forward what they considered were the best immediate arrangements whereby Indians might decide the future Constitution of India and whereby an interim Government might meanwhile be set up for British India. Their scheme, with which the Viceroy associated himself, had the full approval of the British Government.[1]

After rehearsing the claim for a Big Pakistan (five provinces and Baluchistan) the Mission demonstrated its communal proportions and concluded:

> Every argument that can be used in favour of Pakistan can equally in our view be used in favour of the exclusion of the non-Muslim areas from Pakistan.

As to the Little Pakistan, they were convinced

> that any solution which involves a radical partition of the Punjab and Bengal, as this would do, would be contrary to the wishes of a very large proportion of the inhabitants of these Provinces. . . . Moreover, any division of the Punjab would of necessity divide the Sikhs, leaving substantial bodies of Sikhs on both sides of the border.

Apart from these communal arguments there were weighty administrative, economic, military and geographical obstacles to partition, which would also increase the difficulty of associating the Princely States with the new India. The Mission were therefore unable to recommend handing over power to two entirely separate sovereign States.

The Congress, they said, had put forward a scheme for meeting the apprehensions of the Muslims that they would be submerged in a unitary India dominated by the Hindus. This scheme, however, they regarded as unworkable; besides, it would be unfair, and a breach of provincial autonomy, to deny to provinces the

---

[1] This had not been obtained without sweat and toil. The Cabinet wanted to make many amendments and the Mission had to take a firm line in order to avoid what they considered a very grave danger of jeopardising all chance of getting the document accepted.

right to group for optional subjects which they did not wish to assign to the Centre.

The Mission then turned to the States. It was quite clear that with independence the existing relationship between the Rulers and the Crown would no longer be possible. 'Paramountcy can neither be retained by the British Crown nor transferred to the new Government'—a dogma which thenceforward governed British policy towards the States in relation to the transfer of power. The way in which the States would co-operate with the new regime, the Statement continued, would be a matter for negotiation, and might differ among them.

The recommended constitution was of the three-tier sort, and followed closely the proposals already laid before the Congress and Muslim League leaders,[1] though with certain variations. The Union would specifically embrace both British India and the States, and instead of parity at the Centre (Point 5) it was provided that any question raising a major communal issue in the central legislature should require for its decision a majority of the representatives present and voting of each of the two major communities as well as a majority of all members present and voting. The Constituent Assembly would consist of representatives of the provinces, in proportion to population, elected by the provincial legislatures and allocated between the main communities in each province according to their population, every communal representative being elected by members from his own community. Only three communities were recognised for this purpose—Muslim, Sikh and 'General', comprising all the rest—and the allocation of seats in the Constituent Assembly worked out as follows:

		General	Muslim	Sikh
Section A	(Madras, Bombay, United Provinces, Bihar, Central Provinces, Orissa)	167	20	0
Section B	(Punjab, N.W.F.P., Sind)	9	22	4
Section C	(Bengal, Assam)	34	36	0
		210	78	4

[1] See p. 144 above.

To this total of 292 for British India would be added a maximum of 93 for the Indian States. Section A would also include single representatives of Delhi Province, Ajmer-Merwara and Coorg, and Section B a representative of British Baluchistan.

A preliminary meeting of the whole Assembly would be held at which the general order of business would be decided, a Chairman and other officers elected, and a fully representative Advisory Committee set up, to report upon a list of Fundamental Rights, clauses for the protection of minorities, and a scheme for administering the tribal and excluded areas. Thereafter the three British Indian sections would meet separately and draw up provincial constitutions and, if they wished, group constitutions for each section. The sections would then reassemble, together with representatives of the States, to frame a Union constitution. There followed a clause which was destined to be one of the chief bones of contention:

> As soon as the new constitutional arrangements have come into operation, it shall be open to any province to elect to come out of any Group in which it has been placed. Such a decision shall be taken by the new legislature of the province after the first general election under the new constitution.

All this was not a mere proposal but a concrete plan to be put in motion. The Viceroy, the Statement ran, would forthwith request the provincial legislatures to elect their representatives to the Constituent Assembly and the States to set up a Negotiating Committee.

Moreover, the Mission attached, they said, the greatest importance to the immediate formation of an interim Government having the support of the major political parties. For many urgent purposes a popularly-supported Government was necessary. The Viceroy had already started discussions to that end—the members of his existing Executive Council having previously placed their resignations in his hands—and hoped soon to form an interim Government in which all the portfolios, including that of War Member (the great stumbling block in 1942) would be held by Indian leaders having the full confidence of the people.

The Mission ended with an appeal to the leaders and people of India.

T.G.D.—F

We therefore lay before you proposals which . . . we trust will enable you to attain your independence in the shortest time and with the least danger of internal disturbance and conflict. These proposals may not, of course, completely satisfy all parties, but you will recognise with us that at this supreme moment in Indian history statesmanship demands mutual accommodation . . . the alternative would be a grave danger of violence, chaos and even civil war. . . . We appeal to all who have the future good of India at heart to extend their vision beyond their own community, or interest, to the interests of the whole four hundred millions of the Indian people.

The plan adumbrated in the Statement was commended in broadcasts by the Secretary of State and the Viceroy and at a Press conference by Sir Stafford Cripps. Lord Pethick-Lawrence also held a Press conference at which he answered questions. Most of these were concerned with the States or the interim Government, on which the Secretary of State declined to be drawn; or the freedom of the Constituent Assembly from British pressure, or the apparatus of groups. One ingenious questioner posed the hypothesis that a section might decide not to have any provincial constitutions at all; what then would happen to the right of a provincial legislature to opt out of a group? He was told that such a contingency would be exceedingly foolish on the part of those responsible. Such questions betrayed the dubiety with which the grouping element in the plan, the Mission's chief key to solving the communal deadlock, was regarded, and foreshadowed the confusion that it subsequently caused. On the whole, however, the Statement was well received by the public. The task of promoting it with the party leaders remained.

The Mission were now back in Delhi, largely on the insistence of Lord Wavell, who held that work was likely to suffer if he stayed too long away from the seat of government. Maulana Azad protested to the Viceroy:

Delhi presented no difficulty for him as the Viceregal Lodge was air-conditioned and he never moved out of it. It was however otherwise with the members of the Cabinet Mission and with us. We would find it very difficult to work in the furnace which Delhi had become. Lord Wavell replied that it was a matter of only a few days. In the end, it turned out that we passed the rest of May and the whole of June in Delhi. This year the weather was unusually hot. All the members of the Cabinet Mission felt it, and most of all Lord Pethick-Lawrence, who fainted one day because of the heat.[1]

The exercise of persuading the party leaders caused a rift in the solidarity of the Mission, which, though concealed, must have weakened their assurance in the sultry weeks that lay ahead. It partly stemmed from Sir Stafford Cripps' fixation on the importance of Mr. Gandhi, whom he regarded as the only man who could persuade the Congress to acquiesce in the Mission's Statement. In his view the Mission must at all cost come to an accommodation with the Congress: they could manage without the League if they had the Congress with them, but not with the League alone without the Congress. Lord Wavell, and with less certainty Mr. Alexander, ranged themselves on the opposite side. While Sir Stafford felt he must resign if they broke with the Congress before making reasonable concessions, the Viceroy was not prepared to carry on if they gave way to Congress demands.

The defect of relying on Mr. Gandhi was soon exposed. With him, nothing was certain, nothing decisive. In a communication friendly in tone he promptly declared that the Constituent Assembly could vary the Cabinet Mission proposals if it chose to do so; otherwise it would not be a sovereign body. For example, it could alter the Union subjects, or abolish the distinction of Muslims and non-Muslims; and no province could be compelled to belong to a group against its will. Sir Stafford Cripps was naturally much put out, especially as his colleagues now insisted that they must all talk with Mr. Gandhi together, or none of them. His personal dilemma, however, was averted by his own illness, which kept him out of action for a fortnight.

Meanwhile the chief party leaders' reactions had been as characteristic as the Mahatma's. Mr. Jinnah deplored that the Mission had turned down the demand for a sovereign State of Pakistan, which alone could assure stable government and the welfare of all the peoples of the Indian sub-continent, and he criticised certain points in the statement; but he was too wary to be the first to reject the plan as a whole. He preferred, he said, to leave its consideration to the judgment of the Council and Working

[1] *India Wins Freedom*, p. 147.

Committee of the Muslim League. On 24th May the Congress
Working Committee adopted a long resolution involving many
reservations and queries about the plan, of which the most important concerned grouping of provinces, representation of Europeans
in the Constituent Assembly and the status and powers of the
Interim Government. On grouping, the Committee declared that
they read the relevant paragraphs in the Statement 'to mean that,
in the first instance, the respective provinces shall make their
choice whether or not to belong to the section in which they are
placed'. They would defer their decision on the proposals until
they could see the complete picture.

The next day, the Cabinet Mission and the Viceroy issued a
clarifying explanation. Subject to the procedure laid down in the
statement, the Constituent Assembly would be free from interference, and when it had completed its labours His Majesty's Government would recommend to Parliament the action necessary to cede
sovereignty to the Indian people, provided there was adequate
provision for the protection of minorities and willingness to conclude a treaty for matters arising out of the transfer of power. It
was true that a few Europeans could be elected to the Constituent
Assembly; it was for them to decide whether to exercise that right.
The interpretation put by the Congress resolution on the paragraph relating to the sections did not accord with the Mission's
intention; the grouping of provinces was an essential feature of the
scheme and could be modified only by inter-party agreement. The
Interim Government, which would be entirely Indian, would work
under the existing constitution and therefore could not be responsible to the central legislature, but the British Government would
give it the greatest possible freedom in the day-to-day administration of India, and of course it was open to its members to resign
if they were in conflict with the legislature.

While the Congress and Muslim League temporised, other
minority spokesmen with less responsibility were more decisive.
Dr. Ambedkar's Scheduled Castes Federation expressed their
opposition to the plan, and the Sikhs were loud in their con-
demnation. Master Tara Singh declared that under the proposed
grouping and minimal Centre the Sikhs were doomed, and at a
representative conference of his community at Amritsar on 10th
June he declared his determination, with other Sikh leaders, to
fight the Mission's plan. This bellicosity did not impress the

Mission, who persisted in regarding the Sikhs, perhaps because of their wagging beards and political naiveté, as pathetic misguided dotards, who were behaving like silly children, crying before they were hurt. Fifteen months later these impatient, pathetic children were protagonists in the holocaust in the Punjab.

Attention and controversy now began to focus, as in 1942, upon the immediate arrangements for a representative Indian Government. The Congress President, Maulana Azad, wrote to the Viceroy on 25th May seeking confirmation of a promise which he recalled Lord Wavell had given informally that he intended to function as a constitutional vice-Monarch and that in practice the Interim Government would have the same powers as a Dominion Cabinet, and adding that a convention might be established to recognise the Government's responsibility to the Central Legislative Assembly.

The Viceroy, in reply, denied that he had promised what was alleged, though he had said he was sure the new Government would be treated by His Majesty's Government with the same close consultation and consideration as a Dominion Government. He repeated the words of the Mission's amplifying statement and expressed his confidence that 'if you are prepared to trust me, we shall be able to give India a sense of freedom from external control and will prepare for complete freedom as soon as the new Constitution is made'.

A new page was turned when on 6th June the Council of the Muslim League passed by a big majority a resolution accepting the Cabinet Mission's plan, though with observations of their own. Reiterating that a sovereign Pakistan remained the unalterable objective of the Muslims, but having regard, said the resolution, to the grave issues involved and the League's earnest desire for a peaceful solution, and to the fact that the basis of Pakistan was inherent in the grouping of the Muslim areas in Sections B and C, the League accepted the scheme and was willing to join the constitution-making body. It kept in view, however, the implicit opportunity of secession of provinces or groups from the Union, and reserved the right to revise its policy at any time if the course of events so required. The League Council authorised Mr. Jinnah to negotiate with the Viceroy in regard to the proposed Interim Government and to take such decisions and action as he deemed fit and proper.

What would have transpired if the Congress had also accepted the Cabinet Mission scheme without fatal reservation must always be a matter for speculation. But many people have seen in the Muslim League's acceptance of a plan which the Congress would have given their eyes to revive a year later the last chance of establishing even a minimal Union of all-India through a simple constituent assembly. The chance, if it was real, was wasted.

The Viceroy now proceeded to negotiate about membership of his Government, on his own, with a peculiar lack of acumen and finesse. The basic issue was Hindu-Muslim parity in the new Government, a matter complex enough in itself, when minorities such as Sikhs (who could be counted upon at least to be vehemently anti-Muslim) and Scheduled Castes (who might or might not be counted in the Hindu quota) had also to be considered, but rendered far more difficult by entanglement with the far from identical issue of Congress-League parity, and by Mr. Jinnah's refusal to accept non-League Muslims in any guise. The Viceroy appears, in face of this, to have committed himself too soon and too precisely, narrowing too much his room for manoeuvre or alternatively exposing himself to the charge of going back on his word.

On 8th June Mr. Jinnah wrote to Lord Wavell claiming that the latter had assured him that the Government would be composed of five members from the League, five from the Congress, one Sikh and one Indian-Christian or Anglo-Indian: any departure from this assurance might, he threatened, cause the Muslim League to withdraw its acceptance of the plan. The Viceroy, in reply, denied that he had made such a promise but admitted that the 5 : 5 : 2 formula had been the basis in his mind. After Mr. Jinnah had first agreed to come into a joint consultation with the Viceroy and Pandit Nehru (who was acting for the Congress during the indisposition of Azad), and had then refused on the ground that Congress had not yet accepted the statement of 16th May, the Viceroy confronted Pandit Nehru with proposals conforming with Mr. Jinnah's position. Nehru objected strongly and suggested instead an apportionment amounting to 8 : 5 : 2 in terms of Hindus, Muslims and others, or to 7 : 4 : 4 in terms of Congress, League and others, the variants being due to the specific inclusion of a non-League Muslim, a non-Congress Hindu, a Congress member of the Scheduled Castes and a Congress woman (here assumed to be a Hindu). The Viceroy retorted that it was quite impossible for him to negotiate on such a basis, which would be rejected out of hand by the Muslim League. Pandit Nehru's visit was followed by a letter from the Congress President declaring that the Working Committee was opposed to parity in any form. The position, he argued, was now worse even than at the abortive Simla conference, when the parity debated had been one between Muslims and Caste Hindus: now Scheduled Castes were included in the Hindu quota and non-League Muslims were eliminated—which the Congress would not accept. Further, the requirement that major communal issues should be decided by separate block voting would lead to deadlock and breakdown.

The Viceroy's response was to put up a new formula, namely 6:5:2 in terms of Congress : League : Minorities, the Congress quota to include a Scheduled Caste Hindu. Mr. Jinnah said he was prepared to place this proposal before his Working Committee, provided Congress accepted it. But the Congress answer was rejection. Negotiation having reached an impasse, the Cabinet Mission and the Viceroy decided that, as with the major constitutional issue, the only recourse left was to make their own 'award' for final acceptance or rejection. Accordingly, they issued a Statement on the 16th June nominating a Viceroy's Executive Council of fourteen named persons: six from the Congress (including a Scheduled Caste man), five from the Muslim League, one Sikh, one Indian-Christian and one Parsee. The Mission emphasised that this 6:5:3 formula was only an expedient, to get a Government in being, and not a precedent of principle. They added that if the two major parties or either of them proved unwilling to join the proposed team, the Viceroy would proceed to form an interim Government which would be as representative as possible of those willing to accept the statement of 16th May. This ill-drafted declaration of contingent policy was destined to cause much bad blood later.

The first reaction came from the Sikhs, who bluntly rejected the proposal and refused inclusion of a Sikh in the Government. It may be assumed that this did not worry the Mission very much, in view of their condescending attitude to the Sikhs and their preoccupation with the major conflict of Congress and League. Sir Stafford Cripps was chafing under the restrictions placed by the Mission on his personal negotiation, which he believed was the right way to handle the Indian leaders.

On 15th June Lord Wavell wrote prophetically in a private letter to Lord Mountbatten, congratulating him on his Viscountcy: 'It looks as if, after many weeks of bargaining, the Congress were going to run true to form and turn down yet another offer. What will happen next is uncertain, but it will certainly be difficult and unpleasant.'

At this stage a squabble over European representation in the Constituent Assembly threatened to thwart the whole plan. The Mission, who were afraid of correcting their scheme in any particular lest this invite other demands for changes, feared that the Bengal Europeans had been influenced by the Muslims to stand their ground, but after a few days they gave way. This left the structure of the Interim Government as the last stumbling-block. The Mission's intelligence of Congress deliberations blew hot and cold. Their hopes, buoyed up by an encouraging interview with Mr. Gandhi, were dashed when they learnt that against the majority of the Congress Working Committee he was insisting on the exclusion of a Muslim League man from the North-West Frontier Province and the inclusion of a non-League Muslim in the Congress list. The next day they heard that the Working Committee, led by Sardar Patel (whose position they seem to have earlier misjudged), Maulana Azad and Mr. Rajagopalachari, had decided to reject the Mahatma's view as to a non-League Muslim and to accept the statement. Sir Stafford now thought that the only hope of an agreement at this stage, as in 1942, lay in a divorce between the Congress and Mr. Gandhi. He felt that the prospect of the Congress being in government rather than opposition made that divorce inevitable, though its repercussions could be dangerous. At the moment, he was told, the Mahatma was accepting the position philosophically, though he might return to his charge later.

Meanwhile history still to come was duplicated as well as history past. Pandit Nehru suddenly left for Kashmir to intervene in troubles between the Maharajah and some of his subjects. The Kashmir Government announced that they would prevent him from entering the State. The Viceroy tried to persuade Pandit Nehru not to go but he insisted.

It was Maulana Azad who eventually persuaded Pandit Nehru to return, speaking to him by telephone to the rest house where he had been detained, and promising himself to take up the cause of Kashmir and the imprisoned Sheikh Abdullah; and it was the

Viceroy who at the Maulana's request sent an aeroplane at once to fetch back the stray.

On 20th June it seemed almost certain that the Congress would reverse their 'decision' of three days back and turn the scheme down. Mr. Rajagopalachari sent a message begging the Mission to try to reinforce Maulana Azad, who was still holding out against Mr. Gandhi. Sir Stafford Cripps found Azad exhausted, and feeling that he could not go on fighting to save the situation. He himself regarded the long-term plan as essentially the same as his own. With the agreement of his colleagues of the Mission, Sir Stafford went to see Mr. Gandhi but had an unproductive talk. He believed that the Mahatma really wanted a break because he believed the scheme to be a bad form of government, quite apart from questions still unresolved about the composition of the Interim Government. The arguments continued, amid rumours, misunderstandings and irritations provoked by the exhaustion of all concerned after weeks of travail in the dusty hot weather of Delhi in June. On 23rd Sir Stafford recorded in a letter:

> As far as we can gather, the Congress Working Committee are now unanimous in their insistence upon including a Muslim in their quota and it is equally clear that Jinnah won't come in if they do. Congress want us to accept their demand and let Jinnah break and Jinnah wants just the opposite.

> We feel that having put forward our scheme of June 16 we can't go back on it and start negotiations all over again, and also that as the Muslim League have accepted the Constituent Assembly scheme of May 16 and Congress have not, there is no logical reason for preferring the latter to the former.

A pregnant conclusion from Sir Stafford Cripps! Mr. Jinnah was indeed now holding the best tactical cards. On 19th June he had written asking for clarification of certain points about the Interim Government; to which Lord Wavell had replied that no change of principle in forming the Government, nor any change in the total number or inter-communal proportion, would be made without the consent of the parties, and that they would be consulted before he filled any vacancy among the minorities. The contents of this letter leaked, no doubt deliberately, and the gist had to be repeated to the Congress President. The Viceroy wrote further to Mr.

Jinnah on 22nd June saying that if the Congress nominated a Muslim among their six members he and the Cabinet Mission could not agree.

On 25th June the Congress Working Committee passed an argued resolution rejecting the proposals for an Interim Government, but not before Mr. Gandhi had characteristically given the Mission another agonising day. Early on 24th June they saw Mr. Gandhi, whose day of silence it was, with Sardar Patel. All seemed to go well, but later they heard that he and Patel disagreed on what had been said. The same two came again in the evening, when the Mahatma's silence was over. The Mission let him do most of the talking, and seemed to satisfy him, though he never raised the points about the Interim Government which they thought he had come to discuss. Later that night, however, a letter arrived for Sir Stafford Cripps from Mr. Gandhi. He could not make head or tail of it except that the Mahatma was going to advise Congress to reject the whole scheme. It seemed to Sir Stafford to have no relevance to anything ever said at any meeting, nor to advance any concrete reason why the Congress should not accept. He thought it a most devastating way of conducting negotiations.

The Mission believed that twice they had had agreement with the Working Committee, about five days earlier on the whole scheme, and the previous day on the long-term proposals alone. The Mahatma notwithstanding, they may well have exaggerated the previous nearness to agreement. The Congress Working Committee's considered reply was 'Yes and no'. 'Congressmen,' declared their resolution of 25th June, 'can never give up the national character of the Congress or accept an unnatural and unjust parity, or agree to the veto of a communal group.' In communicating this resolution, Maulana Azad said that Congress accepted the statement of 16th May while adhering to their own interpretation of some of its provisions, for instance regarding the grouping of provinces.

According to the Maulana, writing retrospectively,

The acceptance of the Cabinet Mission Plan by both Congress and the Muslim League was a glorious event in the history of the freedom movement in India. It meant that the difficult question of Indian freedom had been settled by negotiation and agreement and not by methods of violence and conflict. It also seemed that the communal difficulties had been finally left behind. Throughout the country there was a sense of jubilation. . . . We rejoiced but we did not then know that our joy was premature and bitter disappointment awaited us.[1]

Maulana Azad, always a man of transparent sincerity and good will, reckoned like the other jubilants without the ill-will, suspicions and *arrières pensées* that underlay the grudging acceptance of the compromise, and were forthwith to raise their ugly heads.

The Cabinet Mission, on receipt of the Congress answer, told Mr. Jinnah that as both parties had accepted the statement of 16th May, they proposed that a coalition Government including representatives of both should be set up as soon as possible, but that there would be an interval for reflection before this was done. Mr. Jinnah hurried off to his Working Committee, which on the same day passed a resolution accepting the statement of 16th June.

Now there fell on the table that ambiguous declaration of contingent policy at the end of the latter statement: that if either of the major parties proved unwilling to join the team proposed therein, the Viceroy would form an interim Government as representative as possible of those willing to accept the statement of 16th May. Mr. Jinnah understood this to mean that if the Congress rejected the statement of 16th June, but the Muslim League accepted it, the Viceroy would form a Government from the Muslim League and such minority groups as also accepted both statements. That this intention had been in the minds both of members of the Mission and of Congress leaders themselves is suggested by Sir Stafford Cripps's quoted letter and by the fact that, talking with him at a private dinner on 12th June, Pandit Nehru had clearly contemplated that, in the absence of agreement on forming an Interim Government, the Mission would go ahead with the Constituent Assembly and perhaps ask the Muslim League to form a Government. He added he was certain there would be no major communal trouble for some months, which the Mission took to mean that the Congress, even if they did not accept the scheme, would go along with it. The Mission's idea was to explain the position, then put out a proposed list of names for the Coalition Government, convene the Constituent Assembly and 'get on with

[1] *India Wins Freedom*, p. 151.

the job'. This attitude was certainly consistent with Mr. Jinnah's interpretation.

The Viceroy, however, held to a different though also a possible meaning of the statement, namely, that, the scheme of 16th June having failed to secure the necessary acceptance, he was free to form such a Government as he chose, representing, as far as he could make it so, the parties who had accepted the statement of 16th May, whether or not they accepted the statement of 16th June. He repeated to Mr. Jinnah his intention, as announced by the Mission, to conduct further negotiations for a representative Government after an interval for cooling off. Mr. Jinnah protested that the Mission had gone back on their word. The fresh inflammation caused by this conflict of interpretations, and by subsequent glosses put upon the party acceptances of the statement of 16th May (the constitutional plan), belong, however, to another chapter of the story. A chapter full of false hopes, raised by equivocal formulae compounding basic conflicts, and doomed to disappointment, was ended when the Cabinet Mission left India on 29th June.

12

Prelude to breakdown

The position when the Cabinet Mission departed was that the Muslim League had accepted the main plan (the statement of 16th May) without qualifications, though with the express intention of continuing to work within it for secession and Pakistan; the Congress had nominally accepted the plan, but with reservations or interpretations which could have nullified its central provision of grouping provinces to form a three-tier system; the League had accepted the Mission's statement of 16th May on the Interim Government but the Congress and certain minority groups had rejected it; the Viceroy had accordingly been unable to form an Interim Government either on the lines laid down by the Mission or on any others acceptable to the two main parties. Before the Mission left he had set up a caretaker Government of officials.

To elaborate on what might have happened if events had turned out otherwise than they were is to pursue a will o' the wisp. But it is a matter of historical fact that the Cabinet Mission plan for attaining constitutional freedom, which would have retained the unity of India in the shape of a federal centre with limited but vital powers, had in June 1946 been accepted by the Muslim League and rejected, in effect though not in precise form, by the Congress; whereas when Lord Mountbatten negotiated with the leaders in March and April 1947 it was the League which totally repudiated the Cabinet Mission plan, the Congress which would have revived it if they possibly could. The reasons for that change may be apparent from the story of the intervening months. They do not encourage the widely-held view that a last chance of securing a peaceful transfer of power to a united India was missed by the accident of a few political mishaps and personal mistakes in the summer of 1946, particularly the schizophrenic policy of the Congress and the unwise utterances of Pandit Nehru. This is clearly a defensible opinion, but it discounts the many slips that can come between cup and lip. It assumes that the constitutional mechanism designed by the Cabinet Mission, when put into effect, would have operated satisfactorily; that the Interim Government would have been a genuine coalition leading to a viable national Administration; and that the avowed purpose of the Muslim League of continuing to strive for separation would not have made both the group and central structures of government unworkable. These are large assumptions. On the other hand, momentum is important in political dynamics, and if the momentum of Muslim separatism had been checked in mid-1946, and a new momentum given to all-India forces, the movement of affairs would certainly have been changed, and nothing that followed would have been quite the same as it was. It is arguable, moreover, that if the Cabinet Mission's plan had been accepted there would have been no Direct Action day, no 'great Calcutta killing', and no consequent chain of communal massacres.

The Congress Working Committee's resolution accepting the Cabinet Mission's plan subject to their own destructive interpretation was ratified by the All-India Congress Committee at Bombay on 6th July 1946 by a big majority, Pandit Nehru had just taken over the Presidency of the Congress from Maulana Azad. Although in the end he was the only candidate, behind the scenes there was great debate as between Nehru and Sardar Vallabhbhai Patel, the successor clearly indicated on internal party grounds. There is evidence that Mahatma Gandhi determined the choice, and that his reason for preferring Nehru was the latter's greater fitness to negotiate with the British for the transfer of power.[1] The decision was fateful both for the events leading to independence and partition and for those that followed in India; for if Patel had been President of the Congress Lord Wavell's choice might have fallen on him as Prime Minister in the Interim Government.

At the final session of the All-India Committee, and afterwards at a Press conference, Pandit Nehru declared that the Congress had not accepted any plan, long or short; it had committed itself to participation in the proposed Constituent Assembly, but to no more. The Assembly would be a sovereign authority, and the grouping scheme would probably never function; for the North-West Frontier Province and Assam, and perhaps Bengal, would

[1] See Brecher, *Nehru, a Political Biography*, pp. 314–5. A different, indeed opposite, account is given by Maulana Abul Kalam Azad in *India Wins Freedom*, p. 153.

frustrate it. Moreover, the scope of the Centre would have to include (as the corollary of foreign affairs, defence and communications) defence industries, foreign trade, currency and credit, and adequate taxing power. The Mission's proviso about proper arrangements for minorities was a domestic Indian problem: 'We accept no outsider's interference with it, certainly not the British Government's.' Asked at the Press conference whether he meant that the Cabinet Mission's plan could be modified, Nehru replied that the Congress regarded itself as free to change or modify the plan in the Constituent Assembly as it thought best.[1]

Whether this public and contemptuous rejection of the whole implied basis of the Cabinet Mission's plan, as a delicate compromise between all-India nationalism and Muslim separatism, was a hard-headed recall to realities or a crass error of political judgment, its outcome was predictable. Mr. Jinnah at once protested against 'a complete repudiation of the basic form on which the long-term scheme rests', and demanded that the British Government should make it clear beyond doubt that the Congress had not accepted the scheme. Ministers in London failed to grasp the proferred nettle. In debates in Parliament on 18th July Lord Pethick-Lawrence emphasised that the parties, having agreed to the Statement of 16th May, could not go outside its terms in the Constituent Assembly, and Sir Stafford Cripps explained that the right of provinces to opt out of the groups could be exercised only after the first elections under the new constitution, when the matter could be made a straight election issue; but these footnotes to the plan implicitly assumed that it was accepted in the spirit and the letter as a means of reconciliation between rival parties and communities. This was not the fact. The plan was at best a formula on the basis of which co-operation could begin, step by step, if the spirit had been willing, or alternatively if an unwilling spirit had been relentlessly fought by exercise of imperial authority.

Mr. Jinnah and the League were not mollified. The All-India Council of the League passed a resolution at a meeting in Bombay on 27th July, proclaiming with chapter and verse that the Congress intended to use its majority to upset the clear intentions of the Cabinet Mission's plan in the Constituent Assembly, revoking the League's acceptance of the statement of 16th May, authorising the

---

[1] Menon, *The Transfer of Power in India*, pp. 280–1; Brecher, pp. 316–17; Azad, pp. 154–5.

Working Committee to draw up a plan of 'direct action', and calling upon all League members to renounce any titles received from the Government. Though many a rumour of reprieve was to keep hope alive among the friends of the condemned, this was the death sentence on the Cabinet Mission's plan.

Mr. Jinnah accused the Cabinet Mission of bad faith and playing into the hands of the Congress, and condemned the latter's 'pettifogging and higgling attitude'. Although the League had gone to the limits of concession, he said, the Congress had shown no appreciation: the League had now no alternative but to revert to the national goal of Pakistan. According to those close to Mr. Jinnah, he evinced a deep sense of relief upon this return to his old tactical position, and upon his no longer bearing responsibility for a strategic compromise—the Cabinet Mission plan—which he had accepted only because he feared that if he rejected it the Congress would be left not only in British favour as the time for independence approached but also in actual power as the Interim Government of India.

On 22nd July the Viceroy had written confidentially to Mr. Jinnah and Pandit Nehru, as presidents of the League and the Congress, proposing the formation of a Government of fourteen members, six to be nominated by the Congress (including one from the Scheduled Castes), five by the League and three by the Viceroy to represent minorities, including a Sikh. The Congress and League would each have an equitable share of the most important portfolios. The Viceroy would welcome a convention, as freely offered by the Congress, that major communal issues could be decided only by the assent of both major parties, though he himself had never thought it essential to make this a formal condition, since a coalition Government could work on no other basis. As to the status of the Interim Government, the assurances he had given Maulana Azad on 30th May held good—in effect, that he would give the greatest possible freedom to the Government within the constitution in the exercise of the day-to-day administration of the country.

This offer was rejected by both Pandit Nehru and Mr. Jinnah. The former demanded full independence for the Interim Government: the Governor-General should function only as a constitutional head, nor was it proper for him to select representatives of the minorities. Mr. Jinnah did not reply until after the Muslim

League Council had resolved to repudiate the Cabinet Mission plan. He then complained that the offer had discarded important conditions favourable to the League in respect of the Interim Government: no parity, liberty for the Congress to nominate a Muslim, equity rather than equality in portfolios, no communal vote. The Viceroy did not parley at that point with Mr. Jinnah, but he had a long talk with Pandit Nehru, especially on the Congress attitude to grouping and the Constituent Assembly, begging him to reassure the League, but without effective response. After consultation with the Secretary of State, who seems to have taken the view that the Muslim League's repudiation of the Cabinet Mission plan ruled them out of court, Lord Wavell, with much misgiving, invited Pandit Nehru on 6th August to form a Government on the basis of his assurances to Maulana Azad. If, he told Pandit Nehru, the latter could discuss the proposals with Mr. Jinnah and reach agreement with him, that was highly desirable.

The Viceroy next replied to Mr. Jinnah, telling him of this decision, reminding him that the 6:5:3 ratio had been accepted by the League at the end of June, and expressing the hope that if the Congress made a reasonable offer the League would join a coalition. On 8th August the Congress Working Committee agreed to accept the invitation to its President to form a Government. It also passed a long resolution designed to appease the League, glossing its attitude towards the Constituent Assembly, though still insisting that each province had the right to decide whether or not to join a group, and that the Assembly would be sovereign. Mr. Jinnah declared that but for its phraseology this merely repeated the old Congress stand, and 'the situation remains as it was'. Pandit Nehru asked the Viceroy to issue a communiqué announcing his invitation: the Congress could then seek the co-operation of the League. After the public announcement had been made, Mr. Jinnah and Pandit Nehru had a long discussion, described as amicable, but neither appears to have budged from previous positions, and nothing came of it.

There followed further conversations between the Viceroy, Pandit Nehru and Maulana Azad, largely concerning the proposed Congress nomination of Nationalist Muslims—on which point the Viceroy wanted Muslim seats left vacant, to tempt the League to come in, while Pandit Nehru argued, with logic, that having been charged with forming a Government he had the duty to make it as strong and representative as he could. The Viceroy gave way, and on 24th August the composition of the new Government was announced. It contained six Hindus (Pandit Nehru, Sardar Patel, Dr. Prasad, Mr. Sarat Chandra Bose, Mr. Rajagopalachari, and Mr. Jagjivan Ram, a Scheduled Caste man), three Muslims (Mr. Asaf Ali, Sir Shafaat Ahmad Khan and Mr. Syed Ali Zaheer), a Sikh (Sardar Baldev Singh), a Parsee (Mr. C. H. Bhabha) and an Indian-Christian (Mr. John Matthai). Two Muslim seats were left vacant.

Meanwhile an event had occurred which radically altered the background both of political manoeuvre and of peaceable government in India. After the Muslim League's Council had passed its resolution calling on its Working Committee to prepare a plan of 'direct action' Mr. Jinnah proclaimed:

> Never have we in the whole history of the League done anything except by constitutional means and by constitutionalism. But now we are obliged and forced into this position. This day we bid goodbye to constitutional methods.

In the negotiations with the Cabinet Mission, he said, the British Government and the Congress had each held a pistol in its hand, the one of authority and arms, the other of mass struggle and non-co-operation. 'Today,' he declared, 'we have also forged a pistol and are in a position to use it.'

The Working Committee followed up by calling on Muslims throughout India to observe 16th August as 'Direct Action Day'. On that day, meetings would be held all over the country to explain the League's resolution. These meetings and processions passed off—as was manifestly the central League leaders' intention—without more than commonplace and limited disturbances, with one vast and tragic exception. In Calcutta the League Ministry under Mr. Suhrawardy, who had adopted a much more bellicose attitude than Mr. Jinnah, declared 16th August a public holiday, an extremely dangerous thing to do when communal passions were inflamed, Satan would find work for idle hands to do, and any gathering or group in a crowded city might invite reactions from hostile bystanders. What happened was more than anyone could have foreseen. In the next three days some 20,000 people were killed or seriously injured in Calcutta. Whole streets were strewn with corpses—men, women and children of all communities—

impossible to count, let alone identify. If the Muslims gave the provocation and started the holocaust, they were certainly its worst victims, for they were in a minority in the city, and the Sikhs in particular, a comparatively small community in Calcutta but tough and armed and largely motorised, being the mechanics and drivers of Bengal as of so many places, swept furiously through the Muslim quarters slaying mercilessly as they went. The police were inadequate and not wholly reliable. The provincial Government under Mr. Suhrawardy, which had mischievously opened this deadly Pandora's Box, was indecisive in trying to close it and control the demons that had emerged. The Governor, Sir Frederick Burrows, could have over-ridden his Ministers in calling in the Army earlier, but declined to do so until his Government demanded it, which they did at noon on 17th August. The military command was forearmed, for the force available in Calcutta had been recently reinforced, but no better forewarned than the civil authorities, for the trouble they expected was, like previous outbreaks, anti-government rather than Hindu-Muslim, and correspondingly amenable to concentrated action, for which adequate forces were ready. When the military power was called in, the G.O.C., General Bucher, who personally toured the city with Mr. Suhrawardy, refused to scatter his men in small numbers in the alleys and byways to stop individual violence, which would have endangered their lives without achieving any durable result, but ordered them on close patrols on the main thoroughfares and crossroads in the worst-affected areas, with short sallies into the side-streets.[1] This display of force was sobering and effective: by 19th August the mass violence had ceased and the city was under control. The commission set up to investigate the events of 16th–18th August in Calcutta was dissolved, by mutual agreement, nearly a year later before it had completed its task, so there is on the record no complete account nor impartial distribution of blame. But what is certain is that the Great Calcutta Killing set in train a sequence of catastrophes which did not end until many more thousands had died of communal violence and revenge

---

[1] The Army also helped indispensably in clearing corpses, rescuing the beleaguered, relieving the police of static guard duties, and coping with refugees. The author has had the benefit of seeing the report on these events by the then G.O.C. in C., Eastern Command, General Sir Roy Bucher.

throughout India and Pakistan, indeed which might be said even now to be continuing in the Indo-Pakistani confrontation.

Soon after the Interim Government had been formed the Viceroy flew to Calcutta to see and hear for himself the terrible things of which the city still reeked. He returned convinced that only agreement between the leaders of the two communities could save the whole country from disaster. In a broadcast on 24th August he said that his 6 : 5 : 3 offer was still open to the League, and that the Interim Government could be reconstituted whenever it decided to come in. Meanwhile, he said, the formation of the new Government was a momentous step forward on India's road to freedom. The War Member would be an Indian, 'and this is a change which both the Commander-in-Chief and I warmly welcome'. It was desirable, he said, that the work of the Constituent Assembly should begin as soon as possible. (The elections for the British-Indian seats had been completed by the end of July. The Congress won all the general seats except nine, the League all the Muslim seats except five. The Sikhs at first declined to take part, because they regarded the Cabinet Mission plan as unjust to their community, but after the Congress meeting at Wardha in August had promised support in removing the Sikhs' legitimate grievances and in securing safeguards for their just interests in the Punjab the Panthic Board reluctantly accepted the Statement of 16th May and the responsibility of electing Sikhs to the Constituent Assembly.) Lord Wavell went on to assure the Muslims that the procedure laid down for framing provincial and group constitutions would be faithfully adhered to, that there could be no question of a decision on the main communal issue without a majority of both major communities, and that any interpretative dispute could be referred to the Federal Court, as the Congress had agreed. He sincerely hoped that the League would reconsider its decision not to take part in a plan which gave them so wide a field in which to protect the interests of the Muslims of India and to decide their future.

After Lord Wavell had seen the horrors of Calcutta his determination to secure a coalition Government hardened. He at once invited Mr. Gandhi and Pandit Nehru to meet him, and handed them a formula about groupings of provinces which he thought would satisfy the Muslim League. The Mahatma's reply was not helpful, amounting as it did to this admonition: 'Trust the Congress Government, and withdraw British arms; if you do not trust it, form a Government of your own which you do trust.' The answer which Pandit Nehru eventually returned was equally negative. The proposal was contrary to the declared policy of Congress, which was that interpretative questions, including grouping, should be left to the Federal Court. To change that policy because of intimidation was not the way of peace but an encouragement to further violence.

There ensued a complex pattern of negotiations involving the Viceroy, Pandit Nehru, Mr. Jinnah and the Secretary of State. Lord Pethick-Lawrence differed from Lord Wavell in attaching greater importance to keeping the co-operation of the Congress and allowing the Nehru Government to work; the Viceroy, who was being pressed by the Congress to call the Constituent Assembly, felt he would rather lose their co-operation than go ahead with constitution-making on a one-party basis. He therefore went on urging Mr. Jinnah to bring the League into the Government. Mr. Jinnah, without committing himself, listed nine points to be elucidated—he carefully did not state them as conditions. On the majority the Viceroy, after consulting Pandit Nehru, was able to accept Mr. Jinnah's position, or enough of it to bridge the gap, though he would not agree that the Congress must not include a Muslim among their nominees. In the upshot, the most important of the nine points was the last:

9 The question of the settlement of the long-term plan should stand over until a better and more conducive atmosphere is created and an agreement has been reached on the points stated above and after the Interim Government has been reformed and finally set up.

To this the Viceroy replied:

9 Since the basis for participation in the Cabinet is, of course, acceptance of the Statement of 16th May, I assume that the League Council will meet at a very early date to reconsider its Bombay resolution.

All the other points concerned the immediate structure and operation of the Interim Government. By this exchange, therefore, Mr. Jinnah had scored a very important tactical advantage: he had acquired a satisfactory option on entry into the Government, not with a cash payment of acceptance of the Cabinet Mission plan, which had been the stated price, but with a post-dated and un-signed cheque. He could of course claim that he had merely equalised the bargain as between himself and the Congress, who had paid in currency debased by stultifying interpretations. But the fact remains that he was able to take up the short-term option without incurring any strict long-term obligation.

Nevertheless, there is evidence that Mr. Jinnah's mind at that time was not wholly set upon frustrating the long-term plan while taking all the short-term advantage he could. On 18th September he asked Sir Benegal Rau, who was serving as constitutional adviser to the Constituent Assembly, for clarification of a number of points concerning its procedure and rules.[1] Other such points, he said, might occur to him later: he would like to have all of them examined carefully. The nature of the points raised, and the tone of the letter, plainly implied that Mr. Jinnah was at that time seriously pondering participation in the Assembly—unless, in-deed, it was all a deliberate subterfuge to deceive the authorities, a trick unlike Mr. Jinnah, who preferred to be inscrutable rather than deceptive. Among the questions which he posed to Sir Benegal were:

6 In view of the confusion that has arisen about the 'grouping clause', would it not be possible to set out its meaning in clear and unmistakable terms?

7 Is it open to the Union Constituent Assembly to modify in any way the group or provincial constitutions as settled by the sections?

To these Sir Benegal replied:

Question 6 The confusion regarding the grouping clause has been removed by paragraph 3 of the Viceroy's letter to Maulana Azad dated June 15, 1946,[2] and that position has now been

---

[1] The exchange of correspondence is fully quoted in B. N. Rau, *India's Constitution in the Making*, Orient Longmans, 1960—Introduction (by B. Shiva Rau) pp. *xlv* to *lii*.

[2] This letter is not quoted in V. P. Menon's comprehensive account of all these events, but it presumably did not differ much from the statement issued by the Cabinet Mission and the Viceroy on 25 May (see p. 152 above).

accepted by the Congress, and the acceptance has been emphasized by Sri Jawaharlal Nehru in his broadcast of September 7, 1946. Any fresh explanation might start a fresh dispute as to the meaning of the explanation.

Question 7 Broadly speaking, the answer is in the negative, provided the group and provincial constitutions confine themselves to their legitimate spheres.

The second answer might well have appeased Mr. Jinnah, but he could hardly have been satisfied by the first.

On 13th October he wrote to the Viceroy in the following terms:

The Working Committee of the All-India Muslim League . . . do not approve of the basis and scheme of setting up the interim Government, which has been decided by you, presumably with the authority of His Majesty's Government.

Therefore, the Committee do not and cannot agree with your decision already taken, nor with the arrangements you have already made.

We consider and maintain that the imposition of this decision is contrary to the Declaration of August 8, 1940, but since, according to your decision, we have a right to nominate five members of the Executive Council on behalf of the Muslim League, my Committee have, for various reasons, come to the conclusion that in the interests of Mussulmans and other communities it will be fatal to leave the entire field of administration of the central Government in the hands of the Congress. Besides, you may be forced to have in your interim Government Muslims who do not command the respect and confidence of Muslim India, which would lead to very serious consequences; and lastly, for other very weighty grounds and reasons which are obvious and need not be mentioned, we have decided to nominate five on behalf of the Muslim League in terms of your broadcast dated August 24, 1946, and your two letters to me dated 4 October 1946 and 12 October 1946, respectively, embodying clarifications and assurances.

This unpromising missive had at least the virtue of telling truthfully why the League was joining the Government. Its motives, unless subsumed under the unspecified 'other very weighty grounds and reasons which are obvious', were neither to avert a communal war in India nor to prepare the way for reconciliation in a Constituent Assembly, nor even to discharge a duty to share in the good governance of the country, but to avoid leaving the Congress with a monopoly of central executive power or giving an opportunity for non-League Muslims to appear as national figures and powerful Ministers. Once again Mr. Jinnah had shown that his perennial tactics had two faces: the obverse, refusal of any compromise or commitment while negotiations were proceeding and while the opposition could be counted upon, out of frustration if for no other reason, to make concessions or commit mistakes; the reverse, to accept less than the whole loaf, though without remitting any jot of claim, when negotiation could achieve no more and the alternative would be to leave the opposition in a situation of long-term advantage.

On 15th October it was announced that the Muslim League had decided to join the interim Government; that Mr. Sarat Chandra Bose, Sir Shafaat Ahmad Khan and Mr. Syed Ali Zaheer had resigned; and that Messrs. Liaqat Ali Khan, I. I. Chundrigar, Abdul Rab Nishtar, Ghazanfar Ali Khan and Jogendra Nath Mandal would join the Government. The last of those five League nominees was not a Muslim but a Scheduled Caste man,[1] and his nomination could only be taken as a deliberate riposte to the Congress retention of a Nationalist Muslim.

It may well be asked why Pandit Nehru and the Congress leaders tamely accepted a result which, if it gave Mr. Jinnah nothing in the immediate composition of the Government, which he could not have had by agreement with them once the 6:5:3 formula had been accepted,[2] deprived them of their position as the Government

[1] He held the Law portfolio, though he knew nothing about law. 'What a fall from Macaulay,' exclaimed Sir George Spence, the Secretary of the Department. It was a good illustration of the primacy of politics over efficiency that inevitably followed the change in the character of the Executive Council.

[2] Indeed he was rather worse off than he might have been earlier in regard to the distribution of portfolios; for the Congress had pre-empted External Affairs and the all-important Home Department—Sardar Patel threatened to resign if he were deprived of it—the Defence Member was a Sikh, and only Finance of the key portfolios went, after some tough exchanges with the Viceroy, to the Muslim League in the person of Mr. Liaqat Ali Khan.

of India, qualified only by inclusion of a few amenable minority representatives. Had they threatened to resign rather than take in the Muslim League until it had accepted the Cabinet Mission plan and have agreed to take part in the Constituent Assembly, they would have forced the Viceroy either to abandon his negotiations with Mr. Jinnah, or to substitute the League for the Congress in office, or to return to a nominated quasi-official Government. Mr. Sudhir Ghosh, an intimate and courier of Mr. Gandhi, put the decision down to a 'mere loss of temper' by Mr. Nehru. The latter, he records,[1] told him on 2nd October that the Viceroy had been pestering him to take in the Muslim League, and that a few days previously he had said to the Viceroy 'in sheer exasperation' that he was not going to talk to Mr. Jinnah: if Lord Wavell was so keen, he should talk to Jinnah himself. 'Next morning he started negotiations with Jinnah.' Mr. Ghosh, who had talked with Sir Stafford Cripps and Lord Pethick-Lawrence, the Secretary of State, in London shortly before this, told Mr. Nehru that according to those Ministers the Viceroy had clear instructions that the responsibility for securing the co-operation of the Muslim League in the Government belonged entirely to Mr. Nehru. 'Why,' he asked, 'did you not tell the Viceroy that if he was going to interfere with your responsibility he could have your resignation?' Pandit Nehru replied: 'Well, I have told you all I know about it.' He looked, wrote Mr. Ghosh, tired and worried and unhappy.

While there is no reason to doubt that such a conversation took place, it clearly is not the whole story. The Viceroy had opened his negotiations with Mr. Jinnah more than a fortnight earlier, as Mr. Nehru was aware, for from then on Lord Wavell turned alternately to Mr. Jinnah and Pandit Nehru in an endeavour to reconcile their differences. Moreover, Pandit Nehru was not the dictator of the Congress; strong-minded colleagues like Sardar Patel could soon have outweighed a passing 'loss of temper', though such an exasperated response was certainly in character.

Three motives must have weighed with the Congress chiefs; they could see the deterioration of order and the spread of violence all over India, above all in Bengal and the Punjab, where the Muslims were in a majority: they may well have quailed at the task of one-party and largely one-community government in such circumstances. Secondly, they could not be sure that their resigna-

[1] *Gandhi's Emissary* (London, 1967), pp. 25–6.

tion would not have been accepted by the Viceroy. The British Government, more favourable to the Congress, would probably have checked him from substituting the League for the Congress in Central authority, but his most likely decision—so it seems in retrospect and so it might have occurred to them—was to give up the attempt at popular political government until the two parties came together. The Congress would then lose not half but all the advantage and achievement they had gained by forming a Government of India. Finally, they may well have been induced by the Viceroy to place more confidence in Mr. Jinnah's oral long-term commitment than in fact it was meant to be worth.

When Lord Wavell saw Pandit Nehru on 14th October and reported Mr. Jinnah's agreement to bring the League into the Government, he said he had explained to Mr. Jinnah that his entry must be considered as conditional on his acceptance of the long-term plan: Mr. Jinnah had undertaken, in reply, to call a meeting of the Muslim League Council to reverse its decision against the statement of 16th May as soon as he was satisfied that the statement would be observed. In the upshot, the Working Committee of the Muslim League was not summoned until more than three months later, and then declined to call the League Council to reconsider its decision of July 1946. But meanwhile much water had flowed under the bridges.

The entry of the League into the Interim Government was generally received with relief, but any hope that the combination would prove a genuine coalition and lead to a narrowing of differences soon proved false. The Viceroy made no progress whatever in persuading Mr. Jinnah to call his League Council together in order to re-accept the statement of 16th May. It would be futile, said Mr. Jinnah, for him to do so in the light of declared Congress policy on provincial autonomy as to grouping, or of such utterances as this of Mr. Gandhi on 23rd October:

> The Constituent Assembly is based on the State paper. That paper has put in cold storage the idea of Pakistan. It has recommended the device of 'grouping' which the Congress interprets in one way, the League in another and the Cabinet Mission in a third way. No law-giver can give an authoritative interpretation of his own law. If, then, there is a dispute as to its interpretation, a duly constituted court of law must decide upon it.

While the Congress leaders were demanding that the Constituent Assembly be called, Mr. Jinnah insisted that to do so would lead to disaster. Lord Wavell told him that the right course for the League was to come into the Constituent Assembly and negotiate, with the option of walking out if it did not get satisfaction. On the Assembly's procedure, apart from the guaranteed meeting of provinces in sections, the British Government could not enforce its views on the Assembly, though these views were quite clear: but it could refuse to recognise a constitution which had not been arrived at in accordance with its essential requirements. Thus the Congress could not make a constitution for India without the Muslim League, nor the League force a constitution on an unwilling Congress. The alternative to agreement was civil war. But the British could not stay indefinitely in India until the parties were agreed. Mr. Jinnah replied that agreement between the two communities was impossible. If the British were going, they had better go at once, or else draw up a constitution and make an award. They should give the Muslims their own bit of country, however small, where they would live if necessary on one meal a day.

After consulting Pandit Nehru, the Viceroy warned the Secretary of State that India was approaching open civil war between the communities and that the calling of the Constituent Assembly might precipitate the outbreak; nevertheless action could not be further delayed without changing the whole policy, and the risk must be taken. On 20th November Lord Wavell issued invitations for a meeting of the Constituent Assembly on 9th December. Mr. Jinnah described this as a grave and serious blunder, and accused the Viceroy of appeasing the Congress in blindness to the realities of the situation. He called on Muslim Leaguers not to participate in the Constituent Assembly and emphasised that the League still rejected the Cabinet Mission plan.

The Viceroy thereupon sent for Mr. Liaqat Ali Khan and told him that he could not agree to keeping the League members in the Government unless they accepted the long-term plan. Nothing, however, would shift the Nawabzada from his demand that His Majesty's Government should declare not only that the provinces would meet in groups (as the Congress had now agreed) but also that the representatives in sections would decide, by a majority if necessary, whether there should be group constitutions and what these should be (a point which the Congress refused to accept). The League members of the Interim Government were otherwise ready to resign whenever His Excellency wanted them to go.

The Viceroy was now in a cleft stick. He laid his problem before the Secretary of State, pressing the Home Government to give an assurance that the sections would reach decisions by majority vote. If, he argued, they surrendered to the Congress point of view the result would be something approaching civil war, threatening the break-up of the Indian Army and chaos throughout India. Lord Pethick-Lawrence, the Secretary of State, held a different opinion. To impose rules and procedural interpretations on the Constituent Assembly would be contrary to the basic policy. Moreover, if a stable constitution was to emerge it must carry the agreement of the two major parties, however this was arrived at. For the British Government to intervene as the Viceroy proposed would only cause the minorities to rely on it for support, rather than on discussion and adjustment in the Constituent Assembly. The Secretary of State felt that one more effort should be made to bring the major parties together and that this could best be done by inviting two representatives of each to come to London to discuss with His Majesty's Government how best the Constituent Assembly could be made effective. Lord Wavell accepted this plan, with the addition of a Sikh representative, and on 26th November, against a background of further mutual threats, accusations and counter-accusations, he issued on behalf of the British Government the invitations to London.

Mr. Jinnah and Mr. Liaqat Ali Khan agreed to come, but Pandit Nehru refused. He and his colleagues, he said, were convinced that such action would be interpreted as making them parties to abandonment or variation of the Cabinet Mission plan by the British Government at the instance of the League, and this concession to violence and intimidation would have disastrous consequences. Mr. Attlee then sent a personal message urging Mr. Nehru to take this opportunity of trying to make the Constituent Assembly successful. The intention was not to abandon either the calling of the Assembly or the Cabinet Mission plan, but rather to see it implemented in full. Mr. Nehru responded, but another personal appeal was necessary from the British Prime Minister to Mr. Jinnah, after the latter had been shown copies of the interchange with Mr. Nehru and had thereupon withdrawn his acceptance. Sardar Vallabhbhai Patel declined to go as second representative of the Congress.[1]

No agreement was reached in London at meetings that stretched over four days from 2nd December. Mr. Nehru made it clear that he must return to India for the opening of the Constituent Assembly. The outcome was a statement issued by the British Government on 6th December. This declared that the Cabinet Mission's view, which had been confirmed by legal advice, had always been, in effect, that of the Muslim League as to the power of sections to decide by majority vote. This interpretation 'must therefore be considered as an essential part of the scheme of May 16. It should therefore be accepted by all parties to the Constituent Assembly'. The British Government, having thus leaned towards the Muslim League, proceeded to shift its weight to the Congress foot. If, in spite of what had been said, the Constituent Assembly (implicitly, its Congress majority) desired this fundamental point of interpretation to be referred to the Federal Court, as should be done with other interpretative questions that might arise, this reference should be made forthwith while the Assembly adjoined.

In India each party took up attitudes that were to be expected towards this equivocal and emollient statement, the League one of qualified and deferred approval, the Congress one of protest. The authoritative Congress line was expressed in a resolution of the All-India Congress Committee moved by Pandit Nehru at its meeting in Delhi on 5th January 1947. The key passages read as follows: ·

While the Congress has always been agreeable to make a reference to the Federal Court on the question of the interpretation in dispute, such a reference has become purposeless and undesirable owing to the recent announcements made on behalf of the British Government. . . .

The A.I.C.C. . . . with a view to removing the difficulties that have arisen owing to varying interpretations, agree to advise action in accordance with the interpretation of the British Government in regard to the procedure to be followed in the sections.

[1] This was not the only time that Sardar Patel, on similar grounds, objected to a meeting with Mr. Jinnah on a crucial question. See below, p. 458.

It must be clearly understood, however, that this must not involve any compulsion of a province and that the rights of the Sikhs in the Punjab should not be jeopardised.

In the event of any attempt at such compulsion, a province or part of a province has the right to take such action as may be deemed necessary in order to give effect to the wishes of the people concerned.

It was in the light of this resolution that the Working Committee of the Muslim League, meeting in Karachi on 29th January, decided, as has already been briefly noted, not to call the Council of the League to reconsider its withdrawal of assent to the Cabinet Mission plan. The Working Committee denounced the operations of the Constituent Assembly, and declared that the Congress qualifications conferred a right of veto within sections not only on provinces, but, absurdly, on parts of provinces, as well as on the Sikhs in the Punjab, and therefore completely nullified the Congress's so-called acceptance of the British Government's interpretation. Since neither the Congress nor the Sikhs nor the Scheduled Castes had accepted the Cabinet Mission's plan of 16th May, the Working Committee called on the British Government to declare that the plan had failed and to dissolve the Constituent Assembly.

The meeting of the Constituent Assembly on 9th December, though of course boycotted by the Muslim League, had not proved the signal for any serious demonstrations in the country. The most important event in its short early session was the moving of what became known as the Objectives Resolution by Pandit Nehru. This began:

This Constituent Assembly declares its firm and solemn resolve to proclaim India as an independent sovereign republic and to draw up for her future governance a constitution.

The resolution went on to declare that the 'territories' of British India and the States, with their existing boundaries or others determined by the Constituent Assembly, should 'possess and retain the status of autonomous units, together with residuary powers'. Fundamental rights, including freedom of thought, expression, belief, faith, worship, vocation, association and action, would be guaranteed, and adequate safeguards would be provided for minorities, backward and tribal areas. Pandit Nehru called his resolution 'an oath which we mean to keep'. The Constituent Assembly adjourned, to meet again on 20th January, when in the course of a six-day session it passed the Objectives Resolution and set up various committees, leaving places in them vacant in the hands of its President, Dr. Rajendra Prasad, with the intention of reserving them for Muslim League members.

All such hopes were demolished by the resolution of the League's Working Committee on 29th January. On 5th February the Congress and minority members of the Interim Government wrote to the Viceroy demanding the resignation of the League members. They observed that the League had not only boycotted the Constituent Assembly but had now totally rejected the Cabinet Mission plan and opted for a programme of direct action. This policy seemed to them quite incompatible with membership of the Interim Government. As Pandit Nehru had put it to Lord Wavell a few days earlier, the League was committed to a programme of active opposition to the Government of which it formed a part.

Again Lord Wavell found himself uncertain what to do. For his own part, he sympathised with the view put to him by Mr. Liaqat Ali Khan on 6th February that it was presumptuous of the Congress, who had never genuinely accepted the Cabinet Mission plan, and the Sikhs, who had flatly rejected it, to demand the resignation of their Muslim League colleagues. The Viceroy foresaw grave consequences if he obliged the latter to go. He asked the Secretary of State to call publicly on the Congress to confirm that its policy towards grouping and provinces did not limit or qualify its acceptance of the Cabinet Mission plan. The Secretary of State declined. On 13th February Pandit Nehru wrote to the Viceroy demanding immediate action on Muslim League membership of the Government. Delay or a wrong decision would oblige the Congress and other members to reconsider their own position. Two days later Sardar Vallabhbhai Patel publicly declared that if the Muslim League members were allowed to remain in the Interim Government the Congress members would resign.

How this cliff-hanging situation would have been resolved in the next instalment of the serial, had there not been a radical change in British policy, is a speculation hardly worth much time. For in fact, though at that date without the knowledge of the Viceroy, still less with that of the Indian leaders, the British Government had already decided upon a new and decisive pronouncement on the constitutional future of India and upon a new Viceroy to implement it. Their immediate concern in these exchanges about the Interim Government must have been to hold the situation, by whatever delays or negotiations they could devise, without throwing either the Congress or the League into political exile until their pronouncement could be made. It came on 20th February.

Its background and cause were not only the political deadlock at the Centre in India but also the grave situation that was developing in the country. The chain reaction from Calcutta had given rise to a series of explosions. In October 1946 there were serious outbreaks in Noakhali and Tipperah in East Bengal, in which the Muslim majority were the aggressors and Hindus the victims. There was evidence that this was an organised operation and not a spontaneous combustion of individual communal hatred: there were virtually no outbreaks in the larger towns, where the police and military could be more effective than in scattered villages. Reactions to Noakhali were widely distributed, but far the worst were in Bihar, where many Bengali Hindu refugees had fled, and where their tales of horror excited some of the local population to a massacre of their Muslim neighbours in November. The intervention of Mr. Gandhi in East Bengal and Pandit Nehru in Bihar helped to relieve the tension, and the trouble in Bihar, though leaving its hundreds of dead and its memory to ignite the smouldering tinder elsewhere in India, was brought before long under control. But what profoundly concerned the British Government, the Viceroy and all those responsible for law and order in India was not only the unending chain-reaction effect of these spasmodic outbreaks but also the evidence implicating minor officials and the police, at least by default of their strict duty against their co-religionists. If the police could not be wholly counted on, how soon would it be before the solidarity and inter-communal impartiality of the Indian Army, the last reserve of force against lawlessness, broke down? The words 'chaos' and 'disaster' constantly appear in the prognostications both of the Viceroy and of the rival politicians as to the outcome of particular policies or events, or of the lack of policies or of action.

This tortuous, unexhilarating and, in so many of its features, repetitive story of events in India between the Cabinet Mission and the announcement of 20th February has been told here at length for two reasons. First, the problems that faced Lord Mountbatten, and such experiences as his total failure to revive the Cabinet Mission plan, or the Congress acceptance of partition, cannot be understood without recalling how the hopes of June 1946 were transmuted into the despair of February 1947.

Secondly, the blame for that change is a matter of heated political controversy in India and Pakistan. Two broad interpretations are open. It may be argued that the whole sequence of episodes was mere byplay: that the die was cast much further back, when the Cabinet Mission persisted in seeking consent to compromise rather than imposing compromise by arbitration, or when Lord Wavell failed to secure a national Government at the Simla conference, or when the Congress rejected the Cripps Offer in 1942, or when the Muslim League adopted Pakistan as its goal in 1940, or when the Congress Governments resigned over the war issue, or when they failed to admit Muslim League Ministers in 1937, or at other dates perhaps even earlier. It is waste of time to criticise the details of navigation or oarsmanship when the boat has been driven towards the rocks by inexorable tide and tempest. Alternatively one may argue that nothing in human affairs is ever determined. Storms made by men can be mastered by men. If it was too late to undo what had already been done, it was not too late to change by degrees the direction of the drift, or for those in authority to master and shape the new events.

Since determinism makes dull history, let us at least consider why, given the facts and the continuing forces of midsummer 1947, so much that was deplorable happened in the next nine months. If, first, we contrast the goals and policies of the Congress in mid-1946 with the settlement they were obliged to accept in mid-1947, we cannot but see a vast defeat for them, which the strength of the foe was not enough to excuse. Against the chance of a national Government of all communities, which might conceivably have changed the whole course of affairs, they pitted a demand to nominate a Muslim Minister of their own persuasion, symbolising their claim to be an organisation of all communities. Against the chance of an all-India Union, they pitted the right of Assam or the North-West Frontier Province, or even parts of Bengal or the Punjab, to opt out of the groups which would have given the Muslims sub-federations of their own, a Pakistan less than sovereign but more than provincial, and geographically intact. The stakes were not matched. So pride and prejudice confounded sense and sensibility—sensibility as to the profound changes that had affected Muslim feelings and aspirations in a decade as independence approached. Pride was an understandable fault in the Congress. For half a century they had dominated the politics of India, irrespective of community: in many areas they had enjoyed a virtual monopoly of political organisation and democratic substructure. They possessed not merely a programme and a method but a code of ideals and a prophet to recall them to it. Yet one can but count the over-confidence and superbity of Congress, especially of Pandit Jawaharlal Nehru, among the fatal influences on the events that led to partition. A little greater humility, a little less certainty of righteousness, might conceivably have saved their ideal of a united India of all communities.

The faults of Mr. Jinnah and the Muslim League, though certainly no less, are not so easily epitomised. Theirs was the winning streak. They needed only to await their opponent's mistakes. Yet, if the Congress was over-confident, the League, despite Mr. Jinnah, was in a sense not yet confident enough. If in public it obstinately demanded an independent Pakistan, its leaders had clearly not made up their minds, even after 16th August 1946, that nothing less would ever do and that every sacrifice must be made and every risk taken to achieve, on the departure of the British, immediate full national sovereignty for a Muslim State. Witness their acceptance of the Cabinet Mission plan, their entry into the Interim Government notwithstanding the presence of a Congress Muslim, their repeated toying with the details of Constituent Assembly procedure. Had they already resolved upon partition as the only acceptable answer, it would have been futile for them to argue about the rights of provinces in a Constituent Assembly which would never effectively meet. Direct action was the method they had publicly announced, and on this they would have concentrated. That was totally incompatible with joining a Government whose first duty, as of any Government, was to maintain order, uphold the law and frustrate unconstitutional action. Joining the Interim Government was, explicitly, only a tactical move, but it was a risky one in such circumstances.

All Mr. Jinnah's moves may indeed have been no more than tactical expedients to delay decisive action until the British, in whose hands power still lay, and Indian Muslim opinion, with enough non-Muslim opinion to avert a total conflict in which the minority must have suffered worst, had been brought to accept the inevitability and even the desirability of total partition; but Mr. Jinnah, supreme as he was in the League, was not its only leader. If his mind was finally set, this was evidently not true of others, including Mr. Liaqat Ali Khan, Mr. Suhrawardy and Mr. Nazimuddin. Thus, as we look back over this critical period, the Muslim League presents a schizophrenic character. It had brandished its knife over the painter and cut halfway through, but it still clung to the last strands that moored it to constitutionalism and a confederal India.

Equally schizophrenic was the policy of His Majesty's Government. Their double personality was to some extent, but not entirely, identified with the attitudes of the Secretary of State and Sir Stafford Cripps, on the one hand, and the Viceroy, Lord Wavell, on the other. Ministers in London, with their closer personal contacts with the Congress than with the Muslim League, their ideological commitment to democracy and majority rule, their sense of near-success in their arduous mission to India, rudely broken by the League's repudiation of its acceptance of their plan and adoption of direct action, felt that the co-operation of the Congress must have priority, and that the pledges to Muslims and other minorities must be honoured under that umbrella. They clung too long to the idealistic hope that reason and national patriotism would defeat communalism and violent prejudice, as Indians of all parties and faiths contemplated the ever closer prospect of self-rule. Lord Wavell, on the other hand, with responsibility for law and order, living in a regime aware of its still enormous strength as the Sircar, the acknowledged ruler of India, and accustomed to regard the Congress as hostile, held a different view. Ever since he became Viceroy he had sought to create, as the essential first step towards a fair and peaceful attainment of Indian independence, a coalition Government: for him, a Government of the Congress without the League was little better, in some ways worse, than no political Government at all.

Yet, partly because of the pull between them, neither of these attitudes was uniformly and consistently expressed in action either by the Home Government or by the Viceroy. Lord Wavell did form a Government of the Congress without the League, did refuse to break with them over their right to nominate Muslims or their insistence on retaining certain key offices when the League came in, and did entrust to them real and growing power. And His Majesty's Government did at last, in December, issue a clear pronouncement in favour of the League's view of the working of sections in the Constituent Assembly which, if made in the previous July, would have had a far more timely and perhaps a decisive effect. The broad consequence of this double *motif* and indecision of British policy was that control over events was lost. Lord Wavell, determined upon an all-party Government which he at last achieved when his prime reason for wanting it had almost expired, plunges on like a sculler with his eyes on the receding view; the harder he plies his oars, the more likely he is to strike first one bank and then the other. He lacked either the political experience or the personal finesse to handle a situation, or series of situations, as delicate and complex as any in the politics of whatever nation.

On the plane of politics, as distinct from personal relations, he ends with the distrust of the Congress but without the confidence of the League. And beyond party politics he makes no impression of being the strong ruler which a great soldier might be expected to be. The communal outbreaks find him out of touch with the realities in the diverse parts of India. In fact his military training tended to have the opposite effect; for his powerful sense of discipline made him respect perhaps unduly the chain of command, under which, in his view, his own orders came from London, and beneath him others had their duties within a very broad strategy laid down for them. Provincial Governors and officials have testified to his comparative lack of interest in their affairs. Whereas his predecessor, Lord Linlithgow, required, read and often answered at great length, frequent detailed reports from all Governors about events and personalities in their provinces, so that he built up a greater knowledge of what was going on and who was who throughout India than any other man, and could advise or instruct the Governors or his members of Council with confidence at any juncture, Lord Wavell thought this no part of his task.

At the same time it must be recalled that in exercising the vast apparatus of government—civil and military—in India he was under handicaps which no predecessor had suffered since the

Mutiny. The mechanism of order and good government was gravely weakened by forces far beyond his control. The malaise that affects any country after a long war, with all its social and economic consequences, had touched even the remote masses of India. Demobilisation of an army two million strong had restored or was soon to restore to their villages vast numbers of uprooted men inured to violence and often possessing weapons. On the other side, the executants of law and order—the police, the Civil Service, the magistracy—were suffering from two weaknesses. British and Indians alike were weary after a long period of strain, when fresh recruiting had been at a minimum (no British entrants to the I.C.S. had been admitted since 1939), valuable men had been taken into the Armed Forces or war administration, and officers had had little or no leave. Instead of relief after victory they found only more strain and trouble.

The second affliction was worse. The impending demise of the British raj made everyone uncertain who would be his next master. The British, who had always relied far more upon the prestige of the Sircar than upon the force of the bayonet or the threat of civil punishment, found their authority steadily dwindling. Indian officers, too, from District Commissioners to village functionaries, from Secretaries to Government in provincial capitals to police constables in the mofussil, were beset by doubts, both in their own minds and among those over whom they exerted authority, as to how or by whom the superior power would be exerted within a matter perhaps of months, at most of a few years. They could be forgiven—especially the Indians who had to make their careers under a new regime—if they were inclined to delay difficult and controversial decisions, to keep their ears to the ground for political portents, to avoid offence rather than wield authority without fear or favour, and to be less than ruthless towards sections or persons who might soon be in a position to redress their grievances upon them.

Communal emotions had perceptibly seeped into the police forces. One particular disability was the drying-up of sources of information. A regime such as that which ruled India depends more upon secret intelligence than does one rooted in popular support and national patriotism; and in India, with its vast areas and myriad peoples governed by a thin cadre of police and military and civil officials, and given to sudden outbreaks of communal or internecine violence, the peace was kept as well as it was largely because in all communities and classes there were people willing to give warning of impending trouble, reports of secret cabals, or information about individual crimes and criminals. When the wrongdoer, the plotters and the trouble-makers might themselves soon exert power, legal or illegal, in a breakdown or transformation of the regime, more and more of these invaluable aides of law and order adopted the philosophy of the wise monkey: 'See no evil, hear no evil, speak no evil.' Lack of intelligence, such as had always reached district officers, magistrates, policemen and Criminal Investigation Departments, cost many Indian lives and much Indian substance in the disorders of 1946 and 1947.

Faced with this grim and worsening picture, some people began to think in desperate terms. Lord Wavell, the Viceroy, believed that a breakdown of the unstable equilibrium he had established at the Centre would be followed by widespread disorders and sectional oppression, of which the British raj would attract all the odium without having the power to prevent or control them. He accordingly urged the British Government to decide upon a definite programme in the event of such a political breakdown, and upon the announcement of a date by which, failing agreement in India, power would be transferred to such successors as they might choose. He himself favoured a phased withdrawal like a military retreat, outline plans for which he had prepared many months previously, beginning with southern India and concentrating the remaining British power in the more dangerous and communally divided north during the later stages of the exercise. Lord Wavell's assumed date for final evacuation was a significant one, March 1948. While rejecting this scheme, the British Government authorised the Viceroy to prepare secret plans for withdrawal, varying with the different political contingencies. A committee of senior officers set up for this purpose by the Viceroy caused the nucleus of an organisation to be formed to co-ordinate plans for the protection and evacuation of British civilians in alternative circumstances that might follow an announcement of British withdrawal. At the end of 1946, however, Mr. Attlee and his colleagues in London overcame the defeatism behind such planning, and resolved upon a new effort to achieve a constitutional transfer of power.

PART THREE

The last of the Viceroys

13

The new Viceroyalty

1 *A final policy*

It was on 18th December 1946 that Mr. Attlee, the British Prime Minister, having first submitted his intention to the King, invited Rear Admiral Viscount Mountbatten of Burma to succeed Field Marshal Lord Wavell as Viceroy. The date is noteworthy because Lord Wavell was still in London, having stayed on for consultation after the failure of the talks with Pandit Nehru, Mr. Jinnah and Sardar Baldev Singh. He was allowed to return to India on 22nd December without an inkling of what was afoot. The decision has since been the subject of much unnecessary surmise and ill-founded myth. Both speculation and legend have been concerned with three aspects: the dismissal of Lord Wavell, the choice of Lord Mountbatten, and the adoption of the policy which he was enjoined to carry out, especially the fixing of a time-limit for the transfer of power.

It is manifest from the account already given that Lord Wavell had come to the end of his resources. His Simla conference had failed. His formation of an Interim Government including both the Congress and the Muslim League had not succeeded in bringing them together except as enemies in one house, like a cat-and-dog couple staving off the divorce under the care of a well-meaning family solicitor. The London talks, which had been wished on him, had come to nothing. Writing later to the King, he said about his December consultations: 'I failed, after many hours of conference, to get any definite policy from Your Majesty's Government.' One reason for this now became clear. His Majesty's Government had already decided on a change of Viceroy. If they had a definite policy they were not going to commit it to Lord Wavell. 'I did not think,' wrote Lord Attlee[1] later, 'that he was likely to find a

---

[1] Mr. Attlee accepted an Earldom in 1955. He is here referred to as Lord Attlee when his later works are quoted.

solution.' Indeed the phrase in the Viceroy's despatch to the King implies that he was asking for a solution, not offering one. The Government had decided that there would be a new policy, and, in the Prime Minister's words, new policies called for new men.

Lord Wavell had been reduced to submitting a plan for physical withdrawal and the turning over of governmental power to provinces as they were successively abandoned.[1] 'That,' recorded Lord Attlee long afterwards, 'was what Winston would certainly quite properly describe as an ignoble and sordid scuttle and I wouldn't look at it.'[2] There seems to be some confusion, in the absence of the documents, between two such schemes, one a proposal of Lord Wavell's own, the other a contingency plan requested by the British Government, and disliked by the Viceroy.[3] It is clear from the words that he used to Lord Mountbatten about them when they met in Delhi that he had no great love for either. But he had nothing else to offer, and Lord Attlee's later judgment that he was 'pretty defeatist by then' seems justified.[4]

Ministers were also critical of Lord Wavell's personality in his Viceregal post. Though the members of the Cabinet Mission had paid high tribute to him after their return, both Sir Stafford Cripps and Lord Pethick-Lawrence had had their differences with him. There is nothing whatever to prove the claim[5] that it was pressure from the Congress leaders which caused the Cabinet in London to get rid of Lord Wavell, but they were doubtless well aware of the lack of personal intimacy and understanding between those leaders and the Viceroy. Mr. Attlee doubted whether Lord Wavell and Indian politicians 'could really understand each other', a judgment which may well have been based on the experience of British politicians. Not only the Labour Government but also their predecessors found him enigmatic and difficult to fathom. Sir Henry (Chips) Channon, who had admired him to the point of adulation, wrote of him when he died in 1950:

[1] See p. 186.
[2] *A Prime Minister Remembers* (Heinemann, 1961), p. 209.
[3] See p. 204.
[4] *Loc. cit.*
[5] By Sudhir Ghosh, *Gandhi's Emissary*, pp. 46–8. The letter from Sir Stafford Cripps there printed was written six weeks after the decision had been taken.

A curious man . . . great in his way, full of humour, with the power of shutting his mind, or almost all of it, to the assembled company. . . . He often gave the impression of being dull. . . . But if he liked someone or was amused . . . the problem was not how to make him talk, but how to stop him. He was not a politician or a statesman, and his judgement was frequently bad, even childish: but as a writer, a friend and a general he was supreme.[1]

The assessment of him by British Ministers at the end of 1946 may have been superficial and unfair, for the Viceroy had been as much the victim of Indian circumstances and the limitations of British Government policy as of his own mistakes or shortcomings, but there was enough obvious ground for it to make unnecessary any esoteric explanation for the decision to replace him.

Again, no reason has been shown for doubting Lord Attlee's account of the choice of a successor:

'I thought very hard . . . and looked all around. And suddenly I had what I now think was an inspiration, I thought of Mountbatten.'[2]

The story that Sir Stafford Cripps virtually nominated Lord Mountbatten after bringing him and Pandit Nehru together is false,[3] though it is also false to deduce from Lord Attlee's recollection that he alone made the choice in a flash. He told Lord Mountbatten, when he offered him the Viceroyalty, that senior members of the Cabinet had looked in every direction for a suitable man to make the new approach, and had reached the unanimous conclusion that it was Mountbatten alone who had the personality and qualifications required.[4]

What then were his qualifications? He was young—forty-six— and this was a job for a young man with drive and energy and the ambition to succeed. He was qualified negatively by never having been in politics nor committed himself to any public position on Indian affairs: yet, positively, he had become a popular public

[1] *Chips: The Diaries of Sir Henry Channon* (Weidenfeld & Nicolson, 1967), p. 378.
[2] *A Prime Minister Remembers*, p. 209.
[3] See letter from the author to *The Times Literary Supplement*, 27th July 1967.
[4] Campbell-Johnson, *Mission with Mountbatten*, p. 18.

figure as Chief of Combined Operations and then Supreme Allied Commander, South-East Asia, a post which had greatly enlarged his contacts with India, on whose affairs he had, in the course of duty, been intimately briefed by successive Viceroys, Lord Linlithgow and Lord Wavell. If he was suspect on the Right as being radical and even socialistic (and his wife, who had inherited a fortune, was even more so), such fears were tempered by reflection on his lineage and connections. A great-grandson of Queen Victoria, he was a second cousin of the King: there was no circle, social or political, in which he could not move with ease. If he was suspect on the Left, and in India, as being yet another military Viceroy, he was known to have liberal views, especially as to the nationalist movements which had surged up in territories under his charge as head of military government after the Japanese surrender, and as a professional naval officer promoted on his merits from cadet to Rear Admiral he had learnt to mix with men of all sorts; in the South-East Asia Command those sorts had included innumerable Asians from potentates and politicians to seamen and sepoys. He had, with all this, great personal charm and presence, readiness to listen and to talk, and sailor-like qualities of quick decision and confident command. These attributes were well and widely known in 1946; they were to be tried to the utmost in the next year, and others discovered in him, advantageous or disadvantageous to his achievement as Viceroy and Governor-General.

When Mr. Attlee talked with Lord Mountbatten on 18th December[1] he said that the Ministers concerned had concluded that a new personal approach was the only hope in India. Lord Mountbatten said that he must make it quite clear that at least up to his last talk with Lord Wavell in Delhi in June he had entirely agreed with the Viceroy's policy. The Prime Minister accepted that it was not Lord Wavell's policy in the past that was in question, but the hard fact that despite unremitting efforts it had broken down. The problem was now more one of personality: the need for closer personal contacts with the Indian leaders was paramount.

Lord Mountbatten neither accepted nor refused. He wanted, he said, to consult the King, and to know what was the policy that he would be required to implement. On this, he told Mr. Camp-

---

[1] The conversation, as narrated by Lord Mountbatten the next day, is recorded in Campbell-Johnson's *Mission with Mountbatten*, pp. 14–18.

bell-Johnson the next day that it was quite clear to him that there would have to be the earliest time-limit for the transfer of power if his mission were not to be hopelessly compromised with Indian opinion. Lord Attlee recalled much later that he had already decided upon the policy of a time-limit:

> It was, of course, a somewhat dangerous venture. But . . . inevitably the machine of administration in India was running down. It couldn't go on much longer. . . . So we decided on a time-limit. The Indians were to be told 'We are going out at a certain date'. Then I had to consider who could do it.[1]

It is evident, however, from Lord Mountbatten's account of that first interview, given when every detail of it was fresh in his mind, that so far from putting the time-limit policy in the forefront of his intentions Mr. Attlee did not mention it at all, as he would surely have done if his recollection of the sequence of events recorded above was correct. The subsequent interchanges between them confirm that it was Mountbatten who insisted on the time-limit, Attlee who hesitated about it, especially about naming a precise date.

The idea of a time-limit within which Britain would quit governing India was not, of course, new. It had been often urged by Moderate and Liberal Indian leaders, who claimed that only thus could the element of 'divide and rule' be eliminated in the framing of agreement among the parties and communities. But it had always been repudiated by British authority, on two main grounds: that it would instantly cause a deterioration in the morale and effectiveness of government officials which would grow worse and worse until government might collapse; and that it gave a bonus to intransigent elements in India who could black-mail both the Government and the majority, as the time-limit ran out, in asking a steep price for their acquiescence in a new regime. However, it was Mr. L. S. Amery, when Secretary of State, one of the ablest to hold that office, who had unofficially adopted the idea: in a Private and Personal[2] letter to the Viceroy he wrote that

---

[1] *A Prime Minister Remembers*, pp. 208–9.
[2] 'Private and Personal' correspondence was neither private nor personal in any ordinary social sense. It was filed, distributed to staff concerned, and included most of the important policy interchanges between Viceroys and Secretaries of State.

only if the British said firmly that they were going would the shock bring the squabbling Indian parties to their senses.

On 20th December Lord Mountbatten wrote to the Prime Minister:

> I am deeply honoured by the offer you have made me, to succeed Wavell. I understand you to say that you wished me to try and end the present deadlock and enable the Indian parties to agree on their future constitution.
>
> I know you would not wish me to accept your offer unless I felt I had a reasonable chance of succeeding in these tasks. And I do not feel I could tackle this job with confidence if the matter of my appointment suggested to the Indians that we wished to perpetuate the Viceregal system, or intended to exercise the right to impose our nominees to arbitrate in their affairs.
>
> In the circumstances, I feel I could only be of use to you if I were to go out at the open invitation of the Indian parties, in a capacity which they would themselves define.

Mr. Attlee did not reply in writing to this letter, but invited Lord Mountbatten to see him on 1st January.[1] He explained why it was not feasible to secure an open invitation from the Indian leaders, but agreed that there must be no suggestion of perpetuating the Viceregal system. Lord Mountbatten was most insistent that there must be a definite and specified date by which the British raj would be terminated; unless this were publicly announced, he could not accept the Viceroyalty, Mr. Attlee returned a somewhat equivocal answer. Lord Mountbatten decided that the best and most polite way of forcing the issue was to impute to the Prime Minister the proposal which he himself had made. Accordingly he wrote on 3rd January:

> It makes all the difference to me to know that you propose to make a statement in the House, terminating the British Raj on a definite and specified date—or earlier than this date if the Indian parties are able to agree on a constitution and to form a government before this. I feel very strongly that I could not have gone out there with confidence if my arrival could have been con-

[1] The Mountbatten archive contains no contemporary record of this interview: the account here is based on Lord Mountbatten's recollection, checked with two of his advisers in whom he confided at the time.

strued as a perpetuation of the Viceregal system, or of our imposing our nominee to arbitrate in their affairs. But if the statement in Parliament couples the announcement of my appointment with the announcement of the time limit we are setting to British responsibility for India, I shall not be starting under that grave disadvantage.

The picture of an insistent Mountbatten and an unconvinced Prime Minister is confirmed by Mr. Attlee's reply:

Thank you for your suggestion. As at present advised we think it inadvisable to be too precise as to an actual day, but I will bear the point in mind in case at a later stage we think it well to name a day.

Lord Mountbatten reverted to the same tactics as he had in his earlier letter:

12th January 1947

Thank you for your letter of the 9th. . . . I notice with some concern that it is now considered inadvisable to name a precise and definite day for the withdrawal of the British Raj from India.

When you first suggested to me that I should relieve Wavell, I wrote to tell you that I could only undertake this if my appointment in no way appeared to perpetuate the Viceregal system in my person. . . .

When you said that my appointment would coincide with a statement in the House, that the British Raj would be withdrawn at the latest on a precise and definite day, I agreed that the point was adequately covered.

I cannot honestly feel that any new Viceroy could hope to overcome the handicap which a renewal of this particular appointment, at so late a stage in the development of Indian affairs would create; unless the alternative you proposed, to my original stipulation, were applied categorically. For I feel very strongly that an 'escape clause' in H.M. Government's announcement would nullify its value, so far as the new Viceroy was concerned—unless it were, that any extension of the British Raj after the stated day would be by the invitation, and only by the invitation, of the Indian leaders themselves.

The Prime Minister replied:

16th January 1947

I do not think that you need worry about the question of a precise day being stated. We shall get a clear statement of timing, but an exact day of the month so long ahead would not be very wise. There is no intention whatever of having any escape clause or of leaving any doubt that within a definite time the hand-over will take place.

I should regard the insertion of a proviso for extension by invitation as just the thing which would make for incredulity as to our real intention. Such a thing might happen, but it would be a mistake to anticipate it in an announcement.

The next move was a talk between Lord Mountbatten and Sir Stafford Cripps, after which the former wrote on 26th January:

Thank you for seeing me on Friday and for being so helpful. I saw the Prime Minister at luncheon afterwards, and discussed with him the proposed statement in the House. I told him that I absolutely saw the point you had put to me, that the announced date for the termination of the British Raj, if given as a precise day, might possibly embarrass our withdrawal as the actual time approached. On the other hand, an expression such as 'the middle of 1948', covering as it does anything from two to three months, seems to me so vague that it could not fail to produce the impression of an escape clause.

I told the Prime Minister I thought that the best compromise was to take an actual month (say June 1948); and I suggested that I should then inform the Indian leaders verbally that I was going to work to the 1st June—this would in effect give me thirty days' latitude, if I found this necessary as the time approached.

I reminded the Prime Minister that my final answer could not be given until I had had an opportunity of commenting on the statement which it was proposed to make in the House, and seen my own written directive. . . .

The Prime Minister sent the draft directive and draft statement on Indian policy on 8th February. Lord Mountbatten replied in a long letter three days later.

. . . Since you say that the draft directive is no more than a cockshy and asked me to let you know how far it covered what was in my mind, I have ventured to redraft it in some respects without changing the general intention, except in regard to the date of final transfer of power, to which I refer below: . . .

I should feel very diffident in recommending amendments to a statement which you will be making in Parliament, were it not that since paragraph 1 of my directive tells me I am to take the statement issued by His Majesty's Government as my guide, that statement will in effect be an important part of my directive; and in its present form I am afraid that it is not at all what I had expected.

Lord Mountbatten then recalled all the conversations and correspondence on this topic, and continued:

The draft of the proposed statement, however, contains the phrase 'the middle of 1948': a term which I still consider so wide as not to be in keeping with your declaration that any form of escape clause must be avoided. And the vagueness of this term is underlined by certain points which could easily be misinterpreted. . . .

I hope you will not think I am pulling the document to pieces in a spirit of carping. But I am disappointed, on reading it, because in doing so I can recapture little of the enthusiasm which I felt when you told me of H.M. Government's proposal. The very length of the statement, and its phrasing, seem to me far from creating the impression I had understood we wished to give. In paragraph 6, for instance, it says: 'The failure of Indian politicians, who have all expressed an eager desire to be rid of British control, to agree among themselves, even on the machinery for deciding on the constitution to replace the existing form of government, must create an unfavourable impression on world opinion.' I believe that such phrases could not fail to antagonise Indian opinion; instead of making it feel that we are out to help, and not to score points.

The draft statement seems, also, to take great pains to establish, historically, that no new element has arisen. It is true that no reversal of policy is involved; but if it is our intention to terminate the British Raj, and withdraw the British members of the Government, by a specific month, and if a new Viceroy is being sent out specifically to implement this, these facts can combine to create the atmosphere of a 'New Deal'—and in my opinion we have everything to gain by stating them so clearly that no misrepresentation of our intentions would be possible. . . .

Rowan[1] tells me that you have not yet drafted the terms of the announcement that I am to succeed Wavell; and I have embodied a draft of this in the slightly revised and greatly shortened statement which I am taking the liberty of submitting to you, in order that my criticism shall not seem merely destructive.

The final statement, made in Parliament on 20th February, was based on Lord Mountbatten's re-draft. The correspondence ended with a letter from Lord Mountbatten, written on 17th February after he had seen copies of telegrams from India reporting communal disorders and the fears of certain Governors that the announcement of a time-limit for the transfer of power might provoke a violent struggle.

. . . Although the opinions expressed in the telegrams are very grave, a careful study of them has in no way weakened my support of your intention, of which you told me on 1st January, to couple the announcement of the appointment of the new Viceroy with that of the decision to transfer power by a specified latest time (subsequently agreed as June 1948).

As I told you at our first meeting on the 20th December, I have never supposed that the Indians would achieve self-government without the risk of further grave communal disorders.

. . . It is evident that the British authorities on the spot fear the announcement of a firm date will risk precipitating disorders and illegal seizures of power. But if they mean that attempts may be made to take advantage in this way of the fact that our intention to terminate British rule is made clear, I feel that our intention would become just as clear as a result of Wavell's plan being put into execution.

In the second case, however, where our withdrawal could be construed as a sign of weakness since it would be carried out *sub rosa*, I feel this would be more likely than if we withdraw in accordance with a liberal and realistic policy, openly and firmly stated. A public statement will 'pass the buck' to the Party Leaders in the eyes of every Indian; but a planned military

[1] Later Sir Leslie Rowan, then Private Secretary to the Prime Minister.

withdrawal of women and children would not—and might be interpreted as a preparation for fighting the thing out when they were safely out of the way.

Do you not think, moreover, that opinion in this country, as well as in the world at large, will be behind us if we are frank and realistic; but would be less likely to be so if our critics were able to claim that we were 'scuttling' without having the guts to admit it?

From all this it is perfectly plain, first that Lord Attlee deceived himself in recollecting that he had decided upon the transfer of power by a certain date and then had chosen a man to do it. The reverse is true. He chose a man to 'make a new personal approach', who then persistently demanded the adoption and announcement of that policy. Secondly, Lord Mountbatten not only approved the public terms of his own appointment and the confidential directive he received but very largely drafted them. He almost literally 'wrote his own ticket'.

It is important to remember this in judging his historic Viceroyalty. He was not serving as an agent of a policy determined by others but was performing a task which he had set himself. No blame for failure could be shifted, though praise for success was bound to be divided. Such problems as the policy created, and such advantages as it conferred, were as much his own making as the Cabinet's. The statement of 20th February contained two vital points:

1 His Majesty's Government wish to make it clear that it is their definite intention to take the necessary steps to effect the transference of power into responsible Indian hands by a date not later than June 1948.

2 If it should appear that such a constitution (as proposed by the Cabinet Mission) will not have been worked out by a fully representative Assembly before the time mentioned . . . His Majesty's Government will have to consider to whom the powers of the Central Government in British India should be handed over, on the due date, whether as a whole to some form of Central Government for British India or in some areas to the existing Provincial Governments, or in such other way as may seem most reasonable and in the best interests of the Indian people.

The second point may be regarded as no more than the corollary of the first, but it had its own imperative effect. Those in India who did not want a single nation state to succeed to British power had only to play out time, by making a fully representative Constituent Assembly impossible, in order to oblige His Majesty's Government to hand over to two or more successors; for the first alternative mentioned in the statement, 'some form of central government for British India' if the Constituent Assembly plan had failed, would most improbably be strong and representative enough in such circumstances to bear the load. In commending the statement to the House of Commons Sir Stafford Cripps elaborated the possible alternatives and concluded: 'We could not accept the forcing of unwilling provinces into a united Indian Government if they had not been represented in the making of the constitution'. The statement of 20th February 1947, in the context of Indian politics, was thus an open licence for Pakistan in some form or other.

It is odd that this vital point was not brought out in the parliamentary debates on the statement. The Opposition, denouncing the new policy as 'an unjustifiable gamble', attacked it on three main grounds: that it departed from the agreed policy embodied in the Cripps Offer of 1942, that fixing a time-limit deprived Britain of her bargaining power with India, and that so far from moderating Indian differences it would heighten them. The first criticism was irrelevant, for time had moved on and the old policy had palpably failed; the second was based on a misconception, for the idea of bargaining to limit India's independence was contrary to the promise of independence itself, which had been made five years before, and the sole condition that would enable Britain to influence the structure of that independence was not any bargaining leverage but the goodwill of the Indian leaders. The third criticism, as events were to prove, had more substance: only great skill on the new Viceroy's part prevented the already impending breakdown of the Interim Government, and brought about the consent of both the major parties and communities in India to a plan for the transfer of power.[1] The Government carried the day, in the House of Commons by a large majority, in the House of Lords with the aid of a profound speech by Lord Halifax, a former Viceroy of

---

[1] In this debate Mr. Churchill once more demonstrated the puerility of his view of India when he said: 'In handing over the Government of India to these so-called political classes we are handing over to men of straw of whom in a few years no trace will remain.'

India, who declined to oppose a policy for which, with all its faults, he could offer no alternative.

Not only was Lord Mountbatten party to the adoption and expression of the policy he was to apply: he also insisted upon other conditions before he finally accepted the Viceroyalty. He asked that he be guaranteed re-employment in the Royal Navy when he returned, in an active post commensurate with the command he was being asked to give up, and his seniority; for he had set his whole heart upon a naval career, with the First Sea Lordship as his great ambition.[1] The Lords of the Admiralty demurred, but were overruled by the Prime Minister. Lord Mountbatten said that he must be free to choose his own staff to go out with him, and that there must be no departmental scrutiny of any honours he recommended on the termination of his Viceroyalty. Both these favours were granted. Finally he demanded a condition without precedent: he must have full powers to carry out the policy with which he was entrusted, without constant reference to or interference by His Majesty's Government in London. 'But you are asking to be above the Secretary of State!' exclaimed Sir Stafford Cripps. 'Exactly,' said Lord Mountbatten. 'But,' said the Prime Minister, 'the Secretary of State will only send you instructions on behalf of the whole Cabinet. Surely you are asking for plenipotentiary powers above His Majesty's Government.' 'I am afraid I must insist,' replied Lord Mountbatten: 'How could I possibly negotiate with the Cabinet breathing down my neck?' He stood firm on his demand, and finally Mr. Attlee agreed also to this condition, which was of indispensable value to the Viceroy in all his negotiations with the Indian leaders.

A few days after Lord Mountbatten arrived in India, Pandit Nehru asked him: 'Have you by some miracle got plenipotentiary powers?' 'Why do you ask?' said the Viceroy. Nehru replied: 'You behave quite differently from any former Viceroy. You speak with an air of authority as though you were certain that what you said would never be reversed by H.M.G. in London.' 'Suppose I have plenipotentiary powers, what difference would it make?' Nehru's answer was prophetic: 'Why then you will succeed, where all others have failed.'

Lord Mountbatten's reason for demanding a definite terminal

[1] His father, the first Marquess of Milford Haven, had been First Sea Lord. Lord Mountbatten was appointed First Sea Lord in 1955.

date—by which, of necessity, some authority or authorities had to be found to whom to hand over power—was that without it his task of bringing the Indian parties together would be impossible, and the Indian people would remain unconvinced of the truth of Britain's intentions. The reason given by the British Government in the debate was different, and the correspondence with Lord Mountbatten, together with the pessimistic view taken in the Prime Minister's statement about the prospect of an agreed constitution emerging, suggests that it was indeed the paramount reason in their minds. In his speech in that debate, Sir Stafford Cripps explained at length the run-down of the British element in the Indian Services, including the Army, a run-down which was accelerating because of the suspension of recruitment during the war, and the presence of many time-expired officers. 'So far as the Indian officers were concerned,' he said, 'they naturally began to look more and more to those Indian parties which would, in the future, hold power, rather than to the British.' And he continued:

What, then, were the alternatives that faced us? Those alternatives were fundamentally two. . . . First, we could attempt to strengthen British control in India on the basis of an expanded personnel in the Secretary of State's Services, and a considerable reinforcement of British troops, both of which would have been required, so that we would be in a position to maintain for as long as might be necessary our administrative responsibility while awaiting an agreement among the Indian communities. Such a policy would entail a definite decision that we should remain in India for at least 15 to 20 years, because for any substantially shorter period we should not be able to reorganise the Services on a stable and sound basis. . . .

The second alternative was, we could . . . make a further attempt to persuade the Indians to come together, while at the same time warning them that there was a limit of time during which we were prepared to maintain our responsibility while awaiting their agreement. One thing that was, I think quite obviously, impossible, was to decide to continue our responsibility indefinitely—and, indeed, against our own wishes—into a period when we had not the power to carry it out. Those were the alternatives, and the only alternatives, that were open to us.

It was not difficult to reject the first. Of all the arguments against it, the most decisive was that the British people manifestly lacked the will to carry it out. Exhausted by the war, eager for a new world of democracy and peace, aware of great problems both at home and close at hand in Europe, recognising friendship with anti-imperialist America as a necessary pillar of British policy, and inured for years to the prospect of Indian independence, they had no stomach whatever for a long-term policy of governing India by a combination of force and the game of 'divide and rule'. Very few saw at that moment the inevitable consequence of Indian independence—the loss by Britain of the essential base and fount of all her imperial power east of Suez, a process which was to take a generation to complete but which was inexorably set in motion by the handing over of power in India. Very few foresaw a more immediate but equally inexorable consequence of the decision to announce a final date for the transfer of power; that the very forces which had impelled the decision would at once be accelerated and would impel its implementation at a much earlier date than a year and a half ahead. Power to be demitted in the future runs away like sawdust in the present. The creation of Pakistan, and the transfer of power well before the end of 1947, were implicitly but plainly written in the statement of 20th February.

2 First days

Lord Mountbatten arrived in New Delhi on 22nd March 1947. Lord Wavell was still Viceroy. This had been a break with tradition: for the outgoing Governor-General had customarily departed before his successor arrived and took up office immediately. It had been explained to Lord Mountbatten that it was impossible for two Viceroys to exist at the same time: either the departing incumbent must be His Majesty's supreme representative in India, the newcomer a private citizen, or *vice versa*. Accordingly Lord and Lady Mountbatten, on being received in Viceroy's House, bowed and curtseyed, and Lord Wavell then took Lord Mountbatten into his study for a heart-to-heart talk on the situation that he was bequeathing. The two men were no strangers. When he was Supreme Allied Commander, South-East Asia, Lord Louis Mountbatten, as he then was, had been put in a special relationship with Lord Wavell, for the latter had been nominated to represent the War Cabinet in the theatre. So Lord

Louis had frequently flown to Delhi for talks with him on the campaign in Burma and the problems of S.E.A.C.'s vital base in India. Thus, although Lord Wavell was three substantive ranks senior to the Admiral and seventeen years older the two men became real friends. Despite, therefore, the awkwardness of their relative positions—the one dismissed, the other his supplanter— they were able to talk without resentment or reserve. Lord Wavell showed the greatness of his character in betraying no bitterness or recrimination.

'I am sorry for you,' said Lord Wavell:[1] 'you have been given an impossible job. I have tried everything I know to solve the problem of handing over India to its people; and I can see no light. I have only one solution, which I call Operation Madhouse—withdrawal of the British province by province, beginning with women and children, then civilians, then the army. I can see no other way out.' Lord Wavell explained both his own plan of phased withdrawal and the 'breakdown' plan which he had prepared on instructions from London, and which amounted to giving south India immediate self-government and retaining British authority in northern India—a plan well deserving of the epithet 'Madhouse'.

An atmosphere of evacuation indeed pervaded those times. The Viceroy had reported to the India Office that the total number of British women and children in India, including military families, was over 50,000. It was thought that the demand for passages home from India in the four months March–June 1947 was likely to exceed 20,000, apart from any planned operation. Lord Wavell pressed for an announcement guaranteeing passages for all those who wished to travel in that period; he thought this essential to maintain the morale of Europeans in India. The Whitehall experts showed that such provision would mean drastically upsetting passenger shipping arrangements throughout the world. The British Government, bringing Lord Mountbatten into consultation, decided that they could do no more than promise to increase the lift as far as possible without causing world-wide dislocation, but must rely on a continuous increased lift. In the event, no emergency resources were called for, and many ships sailed for England with empty berths.

Lord Wavell went on to tell Lord Mountbatten that he had two

[1] According to an account given to the author by Lord Mountbatten in 1965.

crises on his hands. The first was the demand from Congress leaders that the Muslim League members of the Government should be expelled: this pressure he attributed to Mr. Liaqat Ali Khan's Budget imposing heavier taxes on the rich business men who were supporters of the Congress. The other crisis concerned the Indian National Army trials. Pandit Nehru was demanding that the courts martial be stopped and existing sentences quashed: the Commander-in-Chief was refusing and threatening to resign. This problem will be discussed at length later.[1] In approaching it, Lord Mountbatten started with the advantage of having had a 'preliminary round' with Pandit Nehru on the latter's visit to Singapore,[2] when he persuaded the Indian leader to cancel his intention of laying a wreath on the I.N.A. memorial. He had then told Pandit Nehru: 'The I.N.A. were not politically conscious heroes fighting for their country but cowards and traitors who betrayed their loyal friends. The people who will serve you well in your national army of the future are those who are loyal to their oath; otherwise if you become unpopular a disloyal army may turn against you.' Pandit Nehru saw the force of this but said that for political reasons he must ask for the trials to be stopped.

On 24th March, Lord Wavell having departed, his successor was sworn in as Governor-General and Crown Representative. Again breaking with precedent, Lord Mountbatten made a short speech at the ceremony in the Durbar Hall.

> This is not [he said] a normal Viceroyalty on which I am embarking. . . . His Majesty's Government are resolved to transfer power by June 1948 . . . this means that a solution must be reached within the next few months. . . .
>
> In the meanwhile, every one of us must do what he can to avoid any word or action which might lead to further bitterness or add to the toll of innocent victims.

After speaking of his many Indian friends the Viceroy continued:

> It will be no easy matter to succeed Lord Wavell, who has done so much to take India along the path to self-government. I have always had a great admiration for him, and I shall devote myself to finishing the work which he began.

[1] See below, p. 248–55.
[2] See below, p. 213.

I am under no illusion about the difficulty of my task. I shall need the greatest goodwill of the greatest possible number, and I am asking India today for that goodwill.

There can be no doubt that Lord Mountbatten received the goodwill of the Indian leaders. His appointment had been widely welcomed, as well as his mission to end the British raj. Indians of all communities were ready for new leadership and athirst for a new initiative. In Lord Mountbatten they found a man of flexible mind and strong resolution, always willing to listen but equally determined not to be distracted by conflicting arguments from making up his own mind. If his early interviews with the political leaders began cautiously they continued with friendliness.

In these personal relations Lord Mountbatten was immensely assisted by his wife. Unlike many great ladies in India—and many lesser ones too—she was wholly without prejudice as to colour, race or caste. From the start she devoted herself not only to helping her husband socially but also to working for women's causes in India, not as a distant patron but as one anxious to know the work and the problems directly and intimately. As troubles flared she showed a redoubtable personal courage in going into the turbulent areas both with her husband and alone to hospitals and refugee camps. A beautiful and gracious Vicereine on ceremonial occasions, she showed in conversation a quickness of intellect and a humanity and charm which dissolved all sense of lordly apartness. No account of Lord Mountbatten's Viceroyalty and Governor-Generalship of independent India is complete without a tribute to Lady Mountbatten and her work for the Indian people. It can be paid in the words of Pandit Nehru at the last State banquet in June 1948. After speaking of Lady Mountbatten's possessing 'the healer's touch' he said: 'Wherever you have gone you have brought solace, hope and encouragement. Is it surprising therefore that the people of India should love you?'

3 Lord Mountbatten's staff

Among the terms which Lord Mountbatten had required of the Cabinet as the price of his accepting the Viceroyalty was the stipulation that he should be allowed to choose and take out to India his own staff. In selecting them he appears to have been guided mainly by two considerations: his experience of supreme

command, which taught him the need of a hand-picked headquarters staff devoted to the Commander, including men skilled in
the recording of discussions and the care of relations with the outside world, and his realisation that to end the Empire in India was
bound to be a dangerous and hard-contested operation in British
politics, in which he would need allies and go-betweens if he were
not to be isolated from the Right and Centre, among the anti-
imperialist radicals. It was doubtless with this latter thought that
he enlisted General Lord Ismay, a former Indian Army officer who
loved the old India, was trusted by the soldiers both British and
Indian, and was a close friend and wartime collaborator of Mr.
Winston Churchill; and Sir Eric Miéville, who had been Private
Secretary to the Viceroy under Lord Willingdon and carried influence with the more conservative of the British who knew India,
with business in the City of London where he was now working,
and in those innumerable circles with which he had had relations
as Assistant Private Secretary to the King. Under the former head
he took out such men as Captain (later Vice-Admiral) Brockman,
Lieutenant-Colonel (later Major-General) Erskine Crum and
Wing Commander Alan Campbell-Johnson—one from each of the
three Services—who had worked with him in S.E.A.C. and were
his devoted aides.[1]

With such a personal entourage he was content to accept without change or challenge the staff that had surrounded his predecessor Lord Wavell in India: Sir George Abell, the Private
Secretary to the Viceroy, and his various assistants, the Military
Secretary who ran the Viceregal household, and others. Indeed
with such a weight of new men, and with such perilous revolutionary policies in his charge, it was only tactful and provident so to do.
The result was astonishingly successful, thanks largely to the
dutiful and unselfish readiness of the established staff in India to
accept the intruders and work with them as a team. Lord Mountbatten's praise of their mutual co-operation and unstinted service
to himself was unbounded. But seen from outside with an histori-

---

[1] To these three, as well as to the late Lord Ismay, the author owes a
special debt: to Admiral Brockman and Mr. Campbell-Johnson for
personal help and advice, to the latter for his diary of events published as
Mission with Mountbatten, and to Colonel Erskine Crum, the Viceroy's
Conference Secretary, for his impeccable records of a vast number of
interviews and meetings.

cal eye, in light of the events of May to August 1947, this team of advisers had one glaring omission: it contained no single Indian.

From many points of view this could be excused. The Viceroy came out with the authority of His Majesty's Government and with responsibility to them and Parliament at Westminster for the discharge of his task: if the liberation of India from British over-lordship could not be achieved with Indian assent and help in the process, it was to be a British deed, and in the doing of it decisions would have to be taken and matters debated not only of primary British concern but also of such a kind that any risk of leakage to Indian politicians might be fatal. The approach was still, and inevitably, *de haut en bas,* from We to Them. Furthermore, any Indian was, of necessity, Muslim or non-Muslim, and the problem that the Viceroy faced was dominated by the communal split. It was bad enough to preside over a Cabinet that was balanced and divided communally without having to apply similar considerations to an intimate secretariat. Lord Ismay had pointed out to Lord Mountbatten that he would be continuously dealing with the Indian leaders himself. They could not object to a purely British staff but they would be intensely suspicious of any Indians not of their community or party whom the Viceroy enlisted.

Yet these thoughts might have been set aside if Lord Mount-batten (whose previous experience of India had been mainly of wartime command, Princely entertainment and the highly Estab-lishment contacts of the Prince of Wales's tour) had known better the contemporary Government of India Secretariat, its men and its traditions. He had at his disposal such Indian administrators as Sir Chandulal Trivedi, Sir B. N. Rau, H. M. Patel, Mohamed Ali Chaudhury, and V. P. Menon. All these were to play vital parts in the eventual operation: Patel and Mohamed Ali as the administra-tive divisors, Rau as the draftsman of the new Indian constitution, Trivedi (already Governor of Orissa in 1947) as the surgeon called in to show how the living tissue of the Indian Army could be dissected, Menon as the first author of the Dominion-Status plan which Lord Mountbatten adopted, and later as the agent and inspirer of the integration of the Princely States into India.

Lord Mountbatten himself was aware of the gap. In London he had enquired whether the Viceroy had any Indians on his staff, and was told—incorrectly—that he had none, not even A.D.C.s. He immediately asked that Indian officers of the three Services be appointed as A.D.C.s, to meet him on his arrival. Very soon, in Delhi, he began to feel the need of an adviser with a real Indian mind, and enquired who might be available. Sir George Abell recalled that the Viceroy's official Constitutional Adviser—his formal title was Secretary to the Governor-General (Reforms), or Reforms Commissioner—was actually an Indian, Mr. V. P. Menon. But of course he was a Hindu, and was known to have particular connections with the Congress leader Sardar Vallabh-bhai Patel. The Viceroy, unaware of the intimate trust Menon had enjoyed on constitutional matters under Lord Wavell, and remembering Lord Ismay's advice, decided to move cautiously. He began by inviting Menon to tea, and took a liking to him. Thereafter his appreciation grew, and more than once he sent for Menon without warning for a talk alone in his study or even in his bedroom. Eventually—not without some influence by Lady Mountbatten, who became sensitively aware of Menon's frustration, and to whom he confided his feeling that as Constitutional Adviser he ought to resign, because he had outward responsibility but at that time no power to influence a policy with which he disagreed—Menon was brought into the daily staff discussions shortly before completion of the first draft plan, and Lord Mountbatten took him to Simla in May when he had retreated there after sending Lord Ismay with the plan to London. Thereafter it was Menon who did more than any other Indian, save three or four political leaders of the first rank, to construct the new nation, including the States, and in so doing served faithfully both the British-controlled Government to which he had given a lifetime's work and the free nation of India which he loved.

The Viceroy's staff appointments were criticised in India because the Civil Service element was so much associated with northern India, particularly the Punjab, thus reinforcing the experience and inclination of the soldiers, and contained not a single I.C.S. man who had learnt about India and its peoples and problems in the south or even in Bengal. This was certainly a defect, reinforced by Lord Ismay's attachment to the Army and to the north-west where he had served. He, Sir George Abell, Private Secretary to the Viceroy, who was a 'Punjabi', intimately conscious of the interests of the three communities of the province, and Mr. Ian Scott, Assistant Private Secretary, whom Lord Mountbatten regarded as the accredited 'Pakistani' spokesman on his staff, were probably his most influential official advisers, apart from Menon after a critical interval. Some people, including Menon himself, believed that the result might have been different if I.C.S. men from other provinces had been included in the Viceroy's staff, and in particular that Bengal might have remained united. But the fact was that the partition of India was compelled by political forces, not by official advice. Official 'Punjabis' like Sir Evan Jenkins—one of two or three outstanding provincial Governors at that time, accused by Hindus of being pro-Muslim and by Muslims of being pro-Hindu—were deeply opposed in their feelings to partition of the province. Yet they had to acquiesce to it. Like the soldiers, they hated the partition of the Army: yet they found it could not be prevented.

4 *Cripps and Mountbatten contrasted*

Fundamentally the same political situation in India confronted both the Cabinet Mission in 1946 and Lord Mountbatten on his arrival nearly a year later. The party leaders were the same, and so were their basic attitudes and policies, though both Congress and the Muslim League had moved on—the latter, by its Direct Action movement, to an even more militant demand for Pakistan, the former to a more resigned attitude towards partition, while yet retaining strong hopes and claims for a minimal Centre. The weight and pretensions of the parties rested on the same voting strengths, demonstrated in the general elections of the 1945–6 cold weather. The basic problem of reconciling rival communal claims to power on the departure of the British was unchanged. For Lord Mountbatten, indeed, the solution propounded by the Cabinet Mission still held the field as British official policy, which he was enjoined to revive if he could. How was it, then, that where the Cabinet Mission failed, the new Viceroy succeeded, in face of the same key facts and personalities, in obtaining a settlement accepted, however reluctantly, by both Congress and the League, as well as minor communities and interests?

The root reason, of course, was that the Mission was charged with negotiation, Lord Mountbatten with decision. The Mission came out to India to persuade and mediate, he to insist and if necessary to impose. There is much to be said for the view that if the Cabinet Mission, instead of eventually offering terms for acceptance, had dictated them for submission, their plan could have been applied with the co-operation of the parties: whether it would have turned out better than the 1947 solution, more durable, less liable to launch mass migrations and atrocities, is another question. Lord Mountbatten's fiat was more powerful than theirs because the British Government had fixed the date by which British rule must end; but it was the same Government as had sent the Mission, and it could have added that element to its policy in June 1946 as readily as in January 1947, if the Mission had asked for it as a sanction. Lord Mountbatten possessed the secondary but immense advantage of having clear and undivided responsibility in himself, as at once Viceroy in India and plenipotentiary for the Government at Westminster. The Mission were a team of three, who had frequently to reconcile differences among themselves or between them and the Viceroy, as well as those among Indian leaders, and had always to remember that, if they were responsible for negotiating, Lord Wavell was responsible for governing.

There were, however, also certain important differences in personal approach and conduct. Whereas the Mission spent three whole months single-mindedly on their constitutional discussions, Lord Mountbatten, though loaded with the cares and duties of Governor-Generalship, not only propounded his plan but secured its acceptance barely two months after his arrival. Some things can be done quickly which slow motion only makes harder. Sir Stafford Cripps was by far the most active negotiator on the Mission's behalf: if they had succeeded, the credit would have been due more to him than to any of his colleagues, and responsibility for failure must be shared in the same proportion. His experience in 1946 throws up two glaring contrasts with the record of Lord Mountbatten's negotiations. First, Lord Mountbatten concentrated his efforts on a handful of people who could deliver the political goods he wanted—acceptance of his plan by the two great parties. Open and friendly as he was to all who had claims to his ear, he did not waste time and effort on powerless men or institutional representatives. He soon saw that, apart from Mahatma Gandhi with his almost mystic influence, two men could 'deliver the goods' for the Congress—neither one nor the other, but both together— Pandit Nehru, with his appeal to the masses, Sardar Patel with his command of the party machine. Sometimes he made use of go-betweens—Krishna Menon with Jawaharlal Nehru, V. P. Menon with Vallabhbhai Patel, the Nawab of Bhopal with Jinnah—but those three leaders were his main target. Sir Stafford Cripps had the advantage, as it seemed to him, though it may well have been a handicap, of being on terms of personal friendship with a number of political Indians, not only Gandhi and Nehru but also people like Sarojini Naidu, Rajkumari Amrit Kaur, Sudhir Ghosh, B. Shiva Rau. With these he often talked at length, no doubt to some extent imbibing their views, and treating some of them as levers of influence. So far as he did concentrate his efforts, he chose a fatally wrong objective. That was the second great contrast.

Whereas Mountbatten never made the mistake of treating Mahatma Gandhi as a negotiator, Cripps to the end regarded him as the key to the whole problem. For Mountbatten he was a friendly if baffling personality to be cultivated, listened to, and kept sweet, but not one capable, even if willing, of clinching a bargain in the name of the Congress. Despite repeated disillusionment, Cripps believed Gandhi's agreement was both the condition and the guarantee of Congress compliance. It is true that the Mahatma's influence on the Congress Working Committee had dwindled somewhat between the summer of 1946 and the spring of 1947, but this was at least partly due to realisation by the other Congress leaders of the futility of the part Gandhi had played in the Cabinet Mission's efforts. Sir Stafford had, of course, good reason from his own experience for treating Gandhi as the key figure to be persuaded; for it had been Gandhi's advice to the Congress leaders which had finally turned them against the Cripps Offer of 1942, when many of them, including Jawaharlal Nehru, had been more than half-willing to accept. But the conclusion he drew was the wrong one: that the Mahatma was the man with whom positively to make a compromise settlement, one whose signature would commit him and his followers, rather than the man to be negatively persuaded not to oppose a bargain made, ratified and carried out by others.

Cripps was a lawyer and a politician, subtle in negotiation, persuasive in argument, confident in the power of reason and the rightness of democratic process. Mountbatten was a sailor and a man of action, no less persuasive but more so through personality than through professional practice, confident in himself and determined to bend the democratic partisanships of India to serve the purpose with which he had been charged.

5 *Mountbatten and Nehru*

Lord Mountbatten's first and only previous encounter with Pandit Jawaharlal Nehru may have had some bearing on later political events. In March 1946 Pandit Nehru decided to pay a visit to Singapore. He was then a private citizen, a leading member of the Indian National Congress which had achieved a sweeping victory in the non-Muslim seats in the elections a couple of months previously. His impending arrival was notified to Lord Mountbatten, Supreme Allied Commander, South-East Asia Command, with the report that everything was being done to play down this unsettling visit by a nationalist politician, and that Pandit Nehru was being neither officially received nor allowed to meet Indian troops. Lord Mountbatten instantly ordered these plans to be reversed. Here, he said, was a man who wielded great influence in an India that had been promised constitutional freedom, who might indeed become India's first independent Prime Minister. It was of the highest importance not to antagonise him, but rather by treating him with friendliness and respect for his political eminence to influence him, so far as might be, to speak and act moderately during his visit and establish a good relationship with the Armed Forces. The military and civilian officers concerned loyally carried out the Supreme Commander's wishes. Receptions were organised, Pandit Nehru addressed large gatherings of military personnel as well as civilian meetings, and had a friendly interview with Lord Mountbatten.

The two men did not meet again until Lord Mountbatten was Viceroy of India and Pandit Nehru his Prime Minister of the Interim Government,[1] and it was not until 24th March 1947 that they had their first long talk together. Almost the first question Lord Mountbatten asked was what the Prime Minister thought was the greatest problem confronting India, to which Pandit Nehru characteristically replied, 'the economic problem'. They went on to discuss Mr. Jinnah's tactics, the difficulties of running the Interim Government, and the harsh pressure of the time factor. Pandit Nehru said he did not consider it possible, with the forces at work, that India could remain in the Commonwealth. But they did not want to break any threads, and he even suggested 'some

---

[1] A story in *Gandhi's Emissary* by Sudhir Ghosh, that in December 1946 Sir Stafford Cripps brought Mountbatten and Nehru together in London is without any foundation in fact.

form of common nationality'—again a characteristic thought. Lord Mountbatten recorded: 'Pandit Nehru struck me as most sincere.'

Although the Viceroy was careful not to treat Pandit Nehru as the sole authoritative spokesman of the Congress, and to reserve every right of criticism and opposition towards Nehru's views, it is clear that there developed during the negotiations of April and early May 1947 a closer personal relationship than between the Viceroy and any other political leader, Hindu, Muslim or Sikh, and that this understanding, especially on Pandit Nehru's side, had much to do with the Congress acceptance of the plan for the transfer of power, followed by its comparatively smooth implementation between 3rd June and 15th August, with the request for Lord Mountbatten's appointment as Governor-General of independent India, and with the course of subsequent events. It was certainly a very important part of the background to the Viceroy's 'hunch' in showing Pandit Nehru, who was staying with him in Simla, the first plan for the transfer of power as amended by the Government in London, a dramatic episode that changed the fate of nations.[1]

The affinity between the two men is not hard to explain. They were both detached by their ancestry, education and place in society from the narrower, earthier prejudices and preoccupations of the grass-roots politician, the businessman or the practising lawyer. They had the aristocratic outlook which while patrician in its view of the people often breeds an imaginative radicalism. On the one hand stood the scion of royal houses, having monarchs of Britain, Russia, Germany and Greece in his nearer ancestry, widely travelled, with the global view of affairs which a maritime career encourages and which had been refreshed by his wartime command of men of many nations, Asian and Western; on the other, the Kashmiri Brahmin, born to effortless superiority and Westernised affluence, educated at Harrow and Cambridge, essentially a man of the world in the larger sense, committed to nationalism and democracy but often infuriated by the masses, and, like Mountbatten, embracing radical views highly suspect by his own social class. If in all this they were alike—'rich men furnished with ability'—in other traits they were complementary. Nehru was the philosopher and ideologue, Mountbatten the realist and man of action, though the philosopher had to turn to action in office and the sailor had to turn philosopher in comprehending the

[1] See p. 295 below.

immense political problems that confronted him in 1947. Each respected the predominant quality in the other. Though both were impulsive, Mountbatten's impetuosity was essentially pragmatic, a sailor's excitement at Action Stations, whereas Nehru's was essentially emotional, a more feminine passion. His emotional outbursts often led him into actions which, with the depressive streak in his character, he later regretted; regrets were not often in evidence in the confident, optimistic Mountbatten. Mountbatten was an individualist, a man on a pinnacle of his own eminence and ebullience; Nehru had always seemed to need a stronger figure to give him confidence, a wiser or more self-assured man whose judgment would guide or confirm his own: in the early days it was his father Motilal Nehru, for most of his life it was Mahatma Gandhi, in Cabinet and in Congress politics in these crucial days it was Sardar Patel—when they did not quarrel—and now in major affairs it was to be Mountbatten himself. Alike yet unalike, if the two men were often said to be hand in glove, it must be remembered that hand and glove are different things, and that a left-hand glove is no fit for a right hand.

6 Mountbatten and Jinnah

Early in Lord Mountbatten's considered despatch to the Secretary of State on his discharge of the Viceregal office from April to mid-August 1947 he refers to his first talk with Mr. Jinnah in Delhi and observes: 'It was clear that this was the man who held the key to the whole situation.'[1] That was true, and to recognise it was perspicacious. Yet in the subsequent relations between the two men there was little to exemplify that sympathetic diplomacy of which Lord Mountbatten was so brilliantly capable, and which he might have been expected to exercise with particular care upon so crucial a figure. Indeed it is obvious from the Viceroy's own contemporary accounts of their dealings that they often exasper-

[1] *Report on the Last Viceroyalty*, Part A, para. 17. Lord Mountbatten wrote every week a personal report to the Secretary of State, with a private and secret covering letter. Copies of these reports were also received by His Majesty the King and certain other interested Ministers. They are cited here as *Viceroy's Personal Reports* (V.P.R.) with their numbers and dates. They formed the textual basis of a considered despatch entitled *Report on the Last Viceroyalty* dated from London, September 1948, in which different subjects are dealt with more continuously.

ated each other, and, without ever breaking into conflict, found no basis for mutual understanding.

Writing immediately after that same initial interview, Lord Mountbatten described Mr. Jinnah as 'frigid, haughty and disdainful'.[1] If, however, Lord Mountbatten found Mr. Jinnah infuriating it is likely that Mr. Jinnah was equally infuriated by Lord Mountbatten. Time and again, in their early discussions, the Viceroy contended, with unassailable logic, that the arguments which the Muslim leader produced for partitioning India were equally valid for partitioning Bengal and the Punjab, and that if he was to get Pakistan he could not therefore get it on the basis of five undivided provinces. 'I drove the old gentleman quite mad,' wrote Mountbatten after such an argument, with a note of mischievous pride.[1]

This incompatibility seems to have been due, primarily, to a certain conflict of temperament. Mountbatten, born of royal blood and confident of his status, was at once out-giving and anxious to please: Jinnah, who had forced his way to eminence from obscurity less by natural genius than by industry and hard-learnt forensic and political skill, cared much more for the result he obtained than the impression he made. No one would have ascribed to him, in his sixties, that 'spirit of adventurous radicalism' which a close observer marked in 1947 as one of Mountbatten's decisive traits: for radical though his supreme objective was, in that it would uproot the established order of Indian Government, it could equally be dubbed reactionary, for its intent was to counter the democratic revolution which would give to the Hindus, through the vote, the mastery of India which they had lost by the sword; Quaid-i-Azam, as his followers called him, was adventurous only in the sense of leading his people, like Moses, into the unknown, being in the method of his advance grimly deliberate, secretive and cautious. We can see in this contrast of personalities a clash as of a Lloyd George and a Carson, of a Rupert and a Cromwell.

Like General de Gaulle, Jinnah had learnt the power, in the hands of the materially weak, of 'le petit mot non'. He knew that such power is apt to leak away with talk and to evaporate with concessions. His 'frigid' attitude was one of frozen, impenetrable obduracy in pursuit of his main chance. 'I am afraid,' wrote Mountbatten after Jinnah had said that he must consult his advisers before replying on a matter on which he clearly meant for

[1] *Viceroy's Personal Report* No. 2.

the time being to keep his own counsel, 'that the only adviser that Jinnah listens to is Jinnah'—an irritating trait to one who liked to discuss everything transparently with a whole group of advisers day by day. Jinnah could not be wheedled, neither could he be converted; his fear was of being out-manœuvred. This feat Mountbatten rarely accomplished.

Thus it was that often, when they debated together, and the argument went back and forth, the Viceroy believed he had scored a point but had only set up a resistance and reached a deadlock. There was a maddening occasion when Mountbatten tried to persuade Jinnah that it would be politically disastrous, after the fall of Sir Khizar Hyat Khan Tiwana's coalition Ministry in the Punjab, to form a one-party Muslim League Ministry in a deteriorating communal situation. Jinnah said he quite saw the point. 'I am glad you agree,' said the relieved Lord Mountbatten. 'But I don't agree,' said Jinnah; and another attempt brought them to precisely the same *impasse*. 'What can you do,' exclaimed Mountbatten, 'with a man who says he sees your point but doesn't agree?'[1]

There was, however, a deeper cause of their political incompatibility than differences of personal temperament or negotiating method. No course was ever more clearly determined by the aphorism that 'politics are about power' than Jinnah's later career. To gain and hold power, for himself, for the League and for the Muslims, was his sole and all-embracing object. When Mountbatten confronted him with the realistic choice between less power for a larger Pakistan and more power for a smaller one, they were, for once, really understanding each other. Often they seemed, in retrospect, to have been on different wave-lengths. For Mountbatten was not pursuing power: he was there to get rid of power. For him the exercise was one of diplomacy, of balance, of compromise; like a naval commander set to take part in a continental campaign, he was content to emerge victorious on the high seas but without an acre of conquered land. Sardar Vallabhbhai Patel, the realist of the Congress High Command, for whom also politics were about power, once said of Mountbatten that he 'would not govern'.[2] Everything else in his responsibility was subordinated—

---

[1] Lord Mountbatten was not the first Viceroy to be baffled in debate with Mr. Jinnah. Mr. Edwin Montagu wrote in his diary thirty years earlier: 'Chelmsford tried to argue with him and was tied into knots'.

[2] *Report on the Last Viceroyalty*, Part A, para. 116.

with reason, in the circumstances—to the transfer of power. This was inherently a short-term and self-terminating objective. But Jinnah's objective was long-term and perpetual—to seize from this moment of history, from these few months of opportunity, what might be a millennium of national identity for ninety million Indian Muslims. With such stakes a leader cannot afford magnanimity or compromises. A concession might prove a perpetual loss, suffered in exchange for an evanescent advantage.

Mountbatten wrote of Jinnah's 'megalomania': and there did seem sometimes a maniac streak to his obsession with power and his inordinate pride. When the Viceroy wanted a joint Congress-League denunciation of communal violence, Mr. Jinnah agreed to sign if Mahatma Gandhi did, but flatly refused to share sponsorship with Mr. Acharya Kripalani, the President of the Congress,[1] who was strictly his opposite number but whom he regarded as a mere transitory office-bearer without power. It seemed a petty piece of prejudice, but by such acts had Mr. Jinnah preserved his supreme authority over his weakly organised League and his disunited and bewildered community. Mountbatten, ever ready to unbend, to change his mind, to stoop to conquer, found this hard to understand. He often felt he had worsted Jinnah in a political argument without yet gaining an inch of ground, to have used his best persuasion yet to have made no headway at all.

On the other hand, when the argument was on legal or constitutional points Jinnah was almost always right—as was to be expected of a highly successful pleader before the Privy Council and the Indian High Courts—sometimes to Lord Mountbatten's subsequent discomfiture. A number of examples appear in the Viceroy's and Governor-General's correspondence, most of them concerning the Commonwealth connection. To the end, the underlying relationship between the two men was one of contest, even if it were professional contest not affecting personal respect, as between rival lawyers in a hard-fought suit. Mr. Jinnah's warmest and most emotional display of friendship for Lord Mountbatten came, significantly, when the case was over and the verdict given, in Karachi on the eve of Pakistan's independence. But the slow process of implementing the verdict, with all its consequences, estranged them once more.

[1] He had succeeded Pandit Nehru when the latter joined the Government in September 1946.

14

Talks with political leaders

Nothing is more remarkable in the Mountbatten archive than the file of notes of Lord Mountbatten's interviews with Indian political leaders. These were dictated as soon as possible after each conversation had taken place, and often purport to record verbatim some of the more important exchanges. Between 24th March and 6th May 1947 there are 133 numbered records of interviews, almost all of them with political leaders.

Lord Mountbatten decided that all such interviews must be on a heart-to-heart basis. He and his visitor sat in comfortable armchairs in his study. No documents, no note-pads nor any other signs of business were allowed to obtrude. The Viceroy's time-table allowed an hour for the actual interview, followed by fifteen minutes with a stenographer to record the important points of the discussion. Copies of these records were circulated as soon as they were typed to key members of his staff, who thus were fully informed when they met with the Viceroy each day. That was the immediate purpose, but to the historian the records are of unique value, for they recover not only the facts of what was said but also the changing atmosphere and personal reactions.

In addition, of course, the Viceroy had innumerable unrecorded but perhaps influential talks of a more casual, intimate or routine kind with members of his Executive Council (the Interim Government of India), Secretaries to Government and high civil servants, military commanders and others in the course of daily business, besides discussing developments almost every day with his senior staff, both informally and in conference. The political interviews, however, embodied the advice he received on the transfer of power from those to whom it was to pass, the policies of men who could make or break his plans, and the reactions that he observed to the questions and propositions he put to them; they therefore deserve separate study as a main moulder of his mind and an index of its changes.

The length and character of the different interviews suggest that he very soon perceived the diplomatic method he must follow. While he must be open to opinion from all quarters, everything would turn upon the co-operation of a few leaders, especially Pandit Nehru for the Congress and Mr. Jinnah for the Muslim League. Others might be interesting, and worth consideration for their ideas or their expression of particular interests, such as those of the lesser minorities, but none could 'deliver the goods' as could these few. (It was not long before he recognised the near-equal importance of Sardar Vallabhbhai Patel.) At the same time he realised that he must not set Mr. Gandhi against him but must make of him a friend. To the Mahatma he always listened patiently and responded cordially, but he regarded him rather as an eccentric and an idealist than as a politician with whom a pragmatic settlement could be made. Nevertheless a spontaneous friendship obviously grew quickly between them.

Mr. Jinnah, at his very first interview, gave Lord Mountbatten some advice about the Mahatma which the Viceroy obviously took to heart. Referring to his earlier abortive negotiations with Mr. Gandhi over the structure of the Interim Government, Mr. Jinnah claimed that whereas on the Muslim side there was only one man to deal with—himself, for if he took a decision the Muslim League would enforce it, or if they refused he would resign and that would be the end of the League—the same was not true of the Congress. Mr. Gandhi had acknowledged that he represented nobody: he could agree only to 'endeavour to use his influence'. He had enormous authority but no responsibility. Pandit Nehru and Sardar Patel, continued Mr. Jinnah, represented different points of view within the Congress: neither could give a categorical answer on behalf of the Congress as a whole. (He might have added that still less could Mr. Acharya Kripalani, the President of the Congress: Mr. Kripalani himself explained to the Viceroy that as a temporary office-holder he had no authority to speak for the Congress except to a brief from the Working Committee, nor could he give any undertakings on their behalf—to which Lord Mountbatten replied that he really could not negotiate with fifteen men.) All this, said Mr. Jinnah, went to show that even Mr. Gandhi's signature, let alone his word, was valueless.

Lord Mountbatten first talked with Mr. Gandhi on 31st March, and recorded that he 'showed no inkling of getting down to business'. The Viceroy, however, felt that there was no hurry. 'We had progressed on the path of friendship.' The next day Mr. Gandhi came again. He told the Viceroy that, while he did not hold the British responsible for the origin of Hindu-Muslim animosity, their policy of 'divide and rule' had kept the hostility very much alive. Lord Mountbatten now had to reap what his predecessors had deliberately sown. The Mahatma's advice was 'to have the courage to see the truth and act by it', even though the answer might mean loss of life on an unprecedented scale on the departure of the British. In previous talks with Pandit Nehru and Mr. Liaqat Ali Khan, the Viceroy had taken the contrary line, in an effort to bring them down from political slogans and generalities to harsh facts. He had been given, he told them in almost identical words, an appalling responsibility. Intending, he said, to approach the problem in a spirit of stark realism, he was less interested that India should be handed over on lines which might ultimately prove correct than that mechanism should be set up to avoid bloodshed after the British had left. It is tempting to suppose that Pandit Nehru had reported this to Mr. Gandhi, who in turn had taken the first opportunity to champion principle against pragmatism, though the sky fall. In this respect the two men were opposites, but each felt a great respect and affection for the other.

Mr. Gandhi went on to propound his own solution for the constitutional problem. Mr. Jinnah should be invited to form the Interim Government at the Centre, with members of the Muslim League and any others he might wish. Power would be turned over to them, and they would make of it what they could. Lord Mountbatten could hardly believe his ears. But he need not have been so astounded, for Mr. Gandhi had put virtually the same proposition to the Cabinet Mission a year earlier and had never abandoned it. Pandit Nehru pointed this out when Lord Mountbatten told him of the conversation later in the same day. The plan, said Nehru, had been turned down then as impracticable, and it was much more so now.

The Mahatma, however, was in earnest. Repeating his proposal to Lord Mountbatten the next day, he said it was essential that it should be put through quickly in order that His Excellency—who was assumed to have a mandate until June 1948—should have as long a period as possible as Viceroy and President of the Cabinet exercising control in the interest of fair play. The British, who had

long believed themselves guardians of minority rights, should become guardians of the rights of the majority until political circumstances caused the majority to take over—these are not Mr.
Gandhi's precise words, but they convey the effective meaning of
his plan, as it impressed itself on Lord Mountbatten. He added
another proposition which took the Viceroy even more aback:
that he, Lord Mountbatten, should stay on indefinitely as a 'servant
of India', at the head of an independent Indian nation. The
Viceroy was flattered by this tribute alike to his acceptability and
to his readiness for self-sacrifice, but pleaded his naval career and
his private obligations. Mr. Gandhi felt he would change his mind
when the time came.

If Mr. Jinnah refused to form a Government, continued the
Mahatma, the offer to form a Government should be made to the
Congress. Lord Mountbatten cannily suggested that this was the
real object, the initial invitation to the Muslim League being only
a tactical manoeuvre. This Mr. Gandhi denied 'with burning
sincerity', offering his whole services to make the offer to Mr.
Jinnah go through. They then discussed alternatives. When Lord
Mountbatten told him that he favoured the Cabinet Mission plan
most of all, Mr. Gandhi replied that he too would be in favour of it
if it could be revived. Lord Mountbatten mooted the possibility of
handing over power to the different areas of India according to the
wishes of the inhabitants, that is to say, presumably to a Hindu
India, a truncated Pakistan, the several larger States and groups of
small States, all under a central authority for defence, external
affairs, communications, and possibly food. (The tentative addition of the last subject, like Pandit Nehru's proposal to add
planning to central powers in the Cabinet Mission negotiations,
showed how difficult it would be to reconcile the idea of units
having genuine sovereign powers with a Centre controlling common interests; for both food and planning were open-ended
economic subjects.) On this Mr. Gandhi returned no direct
comment, beyond agreeing that whatever the decision might be it
should be taken and implemented soon, and urging that Lord
Mountbatten should in any case remain in charge of the Central
Government with a power of veto until June 1948. Talking with
the Viceroy the next day (3rd April) 'he was more than ever intense
about his scheme as being the best solution'. But if Lord Mountbatten were unable to go along with it he would support him in

any other which the Viceroy could put before him as being in the best interests of the Indian people. If the Muslim League were completely intransigent, partition might have to come, but in that event he was anxious to have as strong a Centre as possible—indeed a combination of incompatibles!

Lord Mountbatten lost no time in trying out the Gandhi plan with other consultants from the Congress, besides Pandit Nehru. Maulana Abul Kalam Azad staggered him with his opinion that it was perfectly feasible and that there was a chance Mr. Jinnah might accept it. Mr. V. K. Krishna Menon, who then held no office in the Congress, but whom Lord Mountbatten reckoned an old friend and whom he had seen twice in London between his appointment and departure to India, told him he was afraid that not even Mr. Gandhi could put this particular scheme through, even if Mr. Jinnah were to swallow it. But it was Mr. Gandhi who eventually seemed to perform the obsequies of his own plan. He wrote to the Viceroy on 11th April saying that he had been unable to persuade responsible members of the Congress and must therefore withdraw it. When Lord Mountbatten thanked him for this letter, Mr. Gandhi replied that the Viceroy himself could still go ahead with the plan if he ardently believed in it. Whether this was a Ghandhian joke or a serious suggestion, Lord Mountbatten hastened to decline the invitation: he could not, he said, possibly hope to succeed in a matter in which the Mahatma himself had already failed with the Congress.

When the two met again on 12th April Mr. Gandhi nevertheless pursued his notion by another path, which perhaps revealed his mind more frankly. His advice to the Viceroy was to go on strengthening the Interim Government, and making them function as they should for the next 14 months, after which power should be handed over to them. Lord Mountbatten recorded:

This staggered Lord Ismay and myself, and we both pointed out that that meant handing over power to one party, namely Congress, to the grave disadvantage of the other party, the Muslim League, which would not fail to produce strife, possibly leading to civil war. Mr. Gandhi, with a wily smile, pointed out that if M1. Jinnah indeed signed the paper which we were sending round to him [a joint public appeal for a truce to violence] he could not again use force for political purposes. I must say

I was speechless to find that he proposed, if Mr. Jinnah indeed meant both to sign and stick to his statement, to take advantage of this to impose a Congress Government over the Muslims. Here again I find it hard to believe that I correctly understood Mr. Gandhi.

He was not the first Englishman to be thus baffled by the Gandhian ethic.

Mr. Jinnah gave him no encouragement to take the Gandhi plan further. When eventually Lord Mountbatten cast a fly over him, on 9th April, he showed enough interest to keep the angler's hope alive, but he had long ago fixed his appetite upon solider bait. It was not until 5th April—a fortnight after Lord Mountbatten's first interview with Pandit Nehru—that Mr. Jinnah paid his initial visit to Viceroy House. But Lord Mountbatten had meanwhile talked with Jinnah's henchman Mr. Liaqat Ali Khan, Finance Member of the Interim Government, on 24th March and 3rd April, and had been given a premonitory recording of the master's voice. Mr. Liaqat Ali Khan had begun by saying that Mr. Jinnah was most anxious not to embarrass the Viceroy in any way. But when Lord Mountbatten asked whether, if he obtained the complete adherence of the Congress to the letter and the spirit of the Cabinet Mission's statement of 16th May, there was any chance of Mr. Jinnah's returning to his original assent, Liaqat replied that the communal strife had become so bitter that he felt there was now no chance of it. The Viceroy asked what his own solution would be.

> He smiled engagingly and said: 'Since my dealings with the Congress members of the Interim Government, I have come to realise that they are utterly impossible people to work with, since there is no spirit of compromise or fair play in them. . . . If Your Excellency was prepared to let the Muslim League have only the Sind Desert, I would still prefer to accept that and have a separate Muslim State in those conditions than to continue in bondage to the Congress with apparently more generous concessions.'

When Mr. Jinnah first arrived 'he was in a most frigid, haughty and disdainful frame of mind', wrote Lord Mountbatten. 'Having acted for some time in a gracious tea-party hostess manner, he eventually said that he had come to tell me exactly what he was prepared to accept.' The Viceroy replied that he did not want to hear that at that stage: the first object was that they should make each other's acquaintance. The ice was not broken until after dinner on the following day, when Mr. Jinnah stayed until well after midnight. The Viceroy explained that while his mind was not made up it was his policy to make a decision as soon as possible after he had seen all concerned. Mr. Jinnah agreed not to force the pace: the whole of India was awaiting a quick decision, but that decision must be a right one. The Cabinet Mission, in his view, had been imbued with a wrong attitude. They had come out pleading for agreement instead of laying down a solution. Lord Mountbatten observed that he was much better placed; for he did not have to obtain prior acceptance from the Indian parties to the course he would recommend to His Majesty's Government, though of course he would not recommend any solution which was patently unacceptable. His visitor seemed pleased with these remarks.

Mr. Jinnah claimed that there was only one solution—'a surgical operation' on India—otherwise India would perish; to which the Viceroy replied that an anaesthetic must precede any surgical operation. Mr. Jinnah accused the Congress leaders of constantly shifting their front. They were determined, he said, to inherit to the full all the powers of the British in India. They would stoop to anything to gain this object, even to accepting Dominion Status, rather than allow any part of India to be handed over to the Muslims.

In their next conversation, on 7th April, the Viceroy employed the tactics of constructive pressure. 'I tried by every means to bring him to the point of saying that he would accept the Cabinet Mission plan and enter the Constituent Assembly.' This course Mr. Jinnah declared quite valueless. The whole basis of the Cabinet Mission plan had been that it would be worked in a spirit of co-operation and mutual trust: now, nearly a year later, the atmosphere had become seriously worse, and it was clear that in no circumstances did Congress intend to work the plan in accordance with the spirit or the letter. India had passed beyond the stage at which any such compromise solution could possibly work. Mr. Jinnah categorically called upon the Viceroy to hand over power as soon as possible, preferably province by province, and let the provinces themselves choose how they should form into groups.

He had come to the conclusion, he said, that the defence forces must be partitioned between Hindustan and Pakistan. On no other basis would it be possible to have any form of central organisation on terms of parity—a significant observation, for it shows that Mr. Jinnah was still thinking in terms of some sort of minimal Centre, albeit of a co-operative rather than organic nature. Lord Mountbatten, who had responded to Mr. Jinnah's general plan with the comment that it could be implemented only if he had time enough for each step to be satisfactorily carried out, likewise applied the time-factor to the problem of defence forces. He recalled a recent statement by Brigadier Cariappa, the senior Indian officer in the Army, that a minimum of five years was needed before the actual Indian Army could stand efficiently on its own legs without the help of British officers. If this period were cut to little over a year, and on top of that he was 'to perform the miracle of cutting the Army in half', did Mr. Jinnah really think it could be done before he left in June 1948? Mr. Jinnah 'smiled in a cryptic way and asked, "How then do you propose to leave at that time—do you intend to turn this country over to chaos and bloodshed and civil war"?'

It was a sharp question, and Lord Mountbatten parried it with more spirit than foresight. Of one thing at least, he said, he was certain—that he was going in June 1948, and withdrawing all British personnel, unless by some miraculous event all Indian parties united to beg the British to stay, in the interests of the whole people of India. Such a request he would be prepared to consider laying before His Majesty's Government, though he could not promise what their answer would be. When the issue came up again at their next interview on 8th April Mr. Jinnah admitted it had been a shock to him to be told that he must count upon British officials and military officers being out of India by June 1948, but he quite understood the position and would accommodate to it.

He then repeated his demand for Pakistan, using arguments which by this time could be regarded as classical. He was 'absolutely adamant that it was useless to resurrect the Cabinet Mission plan'. The Viceroy's retort was also on lines well worn since Lord Pethick-Lawrence had followed them early in the Cabinet Mission discussions. If he accepted the arguments for partition as applying to all India, logic compelled him to apply them equally to the

Punjab and Bengal. Mr. Jinnah admitted the apparent logic of this, but begged Lord Mountbatten not to give him a 'moth-eaten Pakistan'. The demand for partitioning Bengal and the Punjab was all a bluff on the part of the Congress to frighten him off his claim for Pakistan. But he was not so easily frightened, he said, and the Viceroy would be making a sorry mistake if he fell for the Congress ploy. To which Lord Mountbatten replied: 'If I agree to partition it would be because of your able advocacy; but I could not let your theories stop short at the national level.' Mr. Jinnah was 'most distressed' and appealed to the Viceroy not to weaken his Pakistan by destroying the unity of the Punjab or Bengal, each of which had a common national character. Lord Mountbatten gave the merry-go-round another quarter-turn, professing himself impressed by these arguments, and therefore inclined to review his ideas about partition anywhere; for any argument against partition within the Punjab and Bengal applied with still greater force to India as a whole. 'I am afraid,' he wrote, 'that I drove the old gentleman quite mad.' As for splitting the Indian armed forces, Mr. Jinnah would, of course, be at liberty to do so—but only after he, Lord Mountbatten, had ceased to be responsible for law and order in India.

At his next interview, on 9th April, Mr. Jinnah took the initiative on this point. To have their own army was the be-all and end-all of Pakistan; nothing less would satisfy them. The Viceroy, after repeating his earlier argument about piling partition of the Armed Forces on top of their nationalisation, and his refusal to do anything to weaken their efficiency or morale while he was responsible for law and order, suggested that—if indeed he were finally to decide upon some form of partition—a committee of experts be set up to consider the steps to be taken to divide the forces and the time-table for doing so, and that meanwhile the forces should remain under the control of some neutral body presided over by himself while he remained, and afterwards so constituted that no single party could control the Army. 'To all this he agreed as being reasonable.'

Mr. Jinnah again appealed to the Viceroy not to give him a 'moth-eaten' Pakistan, and again was most distressed by the Viceroy's insistence that the logic of partition, if applied to India, must be applied also to the provinces, that is to say, the Punjab and Bengal. Lord Mountbatten seized the chance to counter-appeal for a united India. He regarded it as a very great tragedy, he said, that Mr. Jinnah was trying to force him to abandon the idea of unity. What greatness could not India achieve, as a leader of Asia and a power in the world, if she were independent and united! Mr. Jinnah outflanked this frontal movement. Nothing, he said, would have given him greater pleasure than to see such unity, and he entirely agreed how tragic it was that the behaviour of the Hindus made it impossible for the Muslims to share in it.

While expatiating on the fruits of unity, the Viceroy had re-marked that the Interim Government at the Centre was working progressively better and in a more co-operative spirit, and that it was a day-dream of his to be able to put the Central Government under the Prime Ministership of Mr. Jinnah himself. 'Some thirty-five minutes later, Mr. Jinnah suddenly made a reference out of the blue to the fact that I had wanted him to be Prime Minister. There is no doubt that it had greatly tickled his vanity, and that he had kept turning over the proposition in his mind.' Lord Mount-batten may not have overestimated Mr. Jinnah's vanity, but for a vain and rigid man there could be no doubt which was the more tempting prize, the virtual dictatorship of his own Promised Land or the temporary status of Prime Minister of an India riven by communal and party divisions which would either have overturned him or have led him into an endless chain of compromises.

'Nevertheless,' wrote Lord Mountbatten when recording their talk, 'he gives me the impression of a man who has not thought out one single piece of the mechanics of his own scheme, and he will get the shock of his life when he really has to come down to earth and try and make his vague idealistic proposals work on a concrete basis.' Mr. Jinnah's reaction to Lord Mountbatten's fore-cast about withdrawal of British personnel should have warned Lord Mountbatten against counting too much on shaking his resolve in this way. Mr. Jinnah might be shocked, but he would not be deterred.

The conversation was continued between Lord Ismay and Mr. Jinnah while the Viceroy fulfilled another engagement. Lord Ismay asked what were Mr. Jinnah's ideas, in the hypothetical event of partition, about arrangements for consultation between Pakistan and Hindustan in all essential matters of common interest—for instance, the division of assets and liabilities. That, said Mr. Jinnah, was the job of a liquidator, as in the winding-up of a company. Lord Ismay retorted that the British could not take responsibility; they could advise, but the successor Governments would have to agree among themselves. Lord Ismay recorded Mr. Jinnah's ideas as broadly these. If the British Government were to demit power by provinces, they would immediately form into groups and elect their own group federal parliaments. Group Cabinets would then meet together to consider all matters of common interest such as communications and defence. There would be no supreme authority, not even a consultative council, sitting over the group federal governments: sovereign nations did business with each other through exchange of delegates, not by setting up formal machinery. 'Mr. Jinnah said with the greatest earnestness that, once partition had been decided upon, everyone would know exactly where they were, all troubles would cease, and they would live happily ever after.'

It was most important, in Mr. Jinnah's view, that the decision should be announced as soon as possible, since the framing of group constitutions and the inter-group consultations would take a lot of time. Mr. Jinnah prayed that there would be no question of a 'moth-eaten Pakistan'. In any event, the new State could not stand alone but would need to be friends with a big power. Britain was their natural friend.

When the Viceroy and Mr. Jinnah met again, on 10th April, they went over a great deal of the old ground. Mr. Jinnah was more emphatic than ever that he would have nothing to do with the Cabinet Mission plan. There must be a surgical operation. Although, replied the Viceroy, he retained a fully open mind, the only way in which he could follow Mr. Jinnah's advice was to pursue it to its logical conclusion.

'We argued back and forth, Mr. Jinnah's main point being that I must make his Pakistan "viable". He quoted the example of the partition of Poland'—a very dubious analogy, but perhaps he meant the reconstruction of Poland after World War I—'as not having been made on the basis of counting heads or taking into account the will of the people. I told him I was not prepared to proceed on this basis, and that I must follow a course that would be generally acceptable. . . . For this purpose I had in mind an immediate announcement that I would demit power to the provinces in June 1948, and that provinces would have the right forthwith to decide whether they wished to join any group of provinces or remain entirely autonomous.[1] I presumed in fact that Sind, half of the Punjab and probably the North-West Frontier Province would form one group, part of Bengal another group, which together would form Pakistan. The remaining provinces I assumed would wish to join Hindustan. . . .'

Mr. Jinnah became more and more distressed and displeased at the turn the conversation was taking . . . threatening that in that case he would demand the partition of the province of Assam. I replied that certainly I would grant him the same rights as the Congress, and if he wished to put the Muslim-majority area of Assam in with Bengal he must let me see his proposals. I continued to stress that this scheme was very tentative, until I could see what mechanics were involved. . . . Since he denied that the scheme was in any way what he wanted, he said he could not possibly contribute anything useful to working out the mechanics.

Nevertheless, Mr. Jinnah asked to be allowed to see the Congress proposals for carving up the Punjab and Bengal, so that he could submit counter-proposals. The Viceroy decided to ask Pandit Nehru for these proposals—though he never specifically did so—and to discuss with him the tentative plan.

'Finally,' wrote Lord Mountbatten, 'I took the opportunity of Mr. Jinnah's bitter complaint about my ruining his Pakistan . . . to try and bring him back to the Cabinet Mission plan . . . which gave him . . . a really worth-while and workable Pakistan . . . the only difference between the scheme I was prepared to give him and . . . the Cabinet Mission plan was that under the Cabinet Mission plan he was obliged to accept a small weak centre at Delhi controlling defence, communications and external affairs. I pointed out that these three might really be lumped together under the heading of general defence, and that I did not see how under the new scheme he could possibly avoid joining some organisation at the Centre to take care of general defence. In fact I prophesied that he would find that he had thrown away the substance for the shadow.' (Mr. Jinnah might have retorted that it was the Viceroy who was playing with shadows, and he who was holding to the substance, a sovereign, independent Pakistan.) Added to all that, said Lord Mountbatten, he was ruining the position of India as a great

[1] This scheme was known to the Viceroy's staff as Plan Balkan.

power, and for ever pulling her down to something below a second-class power.

It is clear, however, from these records that in the course of the conversations Mr. Jinnah's attitude had if anything hardened. It was impossible to work with the Congress: the Muslims must have their own nation state with its own Armed Forces. He would have nothing to do with the Cabinet Mission plan or any other providing for a constitutional Centre. First there must be a surgical operation or partition, and then Hindustan and Pakistan would come together to deal with matters of common concern as between nation states. He rejected most strongly the partition of Bengal and the Punjab, but was not to be put off by the threat of it. Nevertheless his request to be enabled to make counter-proposals in this respect indicated that he was moving toward paying the price of accepting a 'moth-eaten Pakistan' rather than no Pakistan at all. He refused to be scared by difficulties. Though shocked by the prospect of losing all British officials and military officers, he nevertheless accepted it philosophically, at least to outward seeming. His attitude to problems raised by partition was to cross bridges when he came to them, to demand principle first and consider detail afterwards. When, in an interview on 19th April, Lord Mountbatten confided to Mr. Liaqat Ali Khan how completely impractical he and his staff thought Mr. Jinnah was, and how they had been unable to get him down to earth at all, Liaqat surprised the Viceroy by replying: 'If your staff will work out exactly what partition means and then if you present the full difficulties to Mr. Jinnah, he will of course understand them even though he has not worked them out for himself.'

In a despatch to London dated 17th April Lord Mountbatten wrote:

Although Jinnah did not lose his friendly attitude, his arguments became more and more futile, and he ended by saying 'If you persist in chasing me with your ruthless logic we shall get no-where.' . . . Until I had met him I would not have thought it possible that a man with such a complete lack of administrative knowledge or sense of responsibility could achieve or hold down such a powerful position.

Judgments appropriate to civil servants or soldiers or career politicians cannot be applied to visionaries. Mr. Jinnah and

Mahatma Gandhi, so utterly unlike in other ways, had this vision-
ary quality in common: for them, politics was the art of the
impossible—non-violence, Pakistan. In Mr. Jinnah Lord Mountbatten was dealing with a man not concerned with obstacles or
compromises or details until he was forced willy-nilly to consider
them, but dedicated to a principle which brooked no qualification,
and bent upon a purpose which he was determined to achieve.

The Viceroy's conversations with the Congress leaders other
than the Mahatma tended to lead in the same direction, that of a
'moth-eaten Pakistan', though from opposite premises. When he
saw Pandit Nehru for the first time on 24th March he was impressed by his sincerity. Pandit Nehru described Mr. Jinnah's
character and tactics: his negative outlook and methods had a
direct appeal to Muslims, and it was therefore not to be hoped that
constructive logic would prevail. Lord Mountbatten asked, what
if he were to tell Mr. Jinnah that he would be granted his Pakistan
—would that not bring him down to reality? Nehru agreed that it
might be possible to frighten Mr. Jinnah into co-operation because
of the shortness of the time available before partition must be
completed. At present the League obviously had no intention of
enabling the Interim Government to work as an independent
authority. The Viceroy stressed the time-factor, not least in
Indianising the Army—the final guarantee of law and order.

At their next recorded interview, on 1st April, Pandit Nehru
discussed at length the problem of partitioning the Punjab and—
as a necessary corollary, in his view—Bengal. He was scathing
about Mr. Gandhi's efforts to pacify communal strife by personal
persuasion, particularly his present activities in Bihar. The
Mahatma, he said, was going round with ointment trying to heal
one sore spot after another on the body of India, instead of diag-
nosing the cause of this eruption of sores and participating in the
treatment of the whole body—a metaphor recalling Mr. Jinnah's
about a surgical operation. Although, agreed Pandit Nehru, an
early constitutional decision might not affect the ultimate causes
of communal strife, it would certainly remove the immediate
cause if it were acceptable to most Indians and their communities.

A week later the Viceroy asked him directly what would be his
solution for the transfer of power. Pandit Nehru thought it would
not be right to impose constitutional conditions on any community
having a majority in a major specific area. Thus, if power were

demitted to provinces, they should have the right to decide
whether to join a Hindustan or a Pakistan group, or possibly remain independent of either—provided, of course, that Bengal and
the Punjab had been previously split each into two provinces. In
the North-West Frontier Province fresh elections should be held
after the British Government's policy had been framed.

Complete partition was not, however, in Pandit Nehru's mind.
The whole process revolved, he said, round having a strong Centre,
certainly to begin with. For that reason he favoured issuing a
statement soon and transferring power to provinces while there
was still time for Lord Mountbatten to be in charge of the Centre
and help with the negotiations between groups until June 1948.
He agreed that, if the Army were kept undivided in the hands of
the Centre, a formula would have to be found to prevent the
Congress, with the majority voting power, from imposing their
will upon it. On 11th April the discussion went further on the
same lines. The Viceroy began by giving an account of his negotiations with Mr. Jinnah. 'Pandit Nehru,' wrote Lord Mountbatten,
'was obviously pleased to find that my independent and impartial
conclusions were very much on the same lines as he would like to
see adopted, namely, a unified India with a strong Centre.' Lord
Ismay, who joined them, explained the need for working out a
programme for implementing Pakistan—still viewed, evidently, as
compatible with an all-India Centre. The arrival of Mr. Liaqat
Ali Khan cut short the conversation before Nehru could be asked
for the precise Congress proposals for re-drawing boundaries in
the Punjab and Bengal, but Lord Mountbatten did have time to
warn him that Mr. Jinnah was going to counter with a demand for
partitioning Assam: to which Pandit Nehru replied that this was a
perfectly reasonable request and could easily be accepted.

Lord Mountbatten's mind at this time must have been in a fluid
condition, for on the prospect of a united Centre he expressed
himself much more doubtfully to Sardar Patel only the next day.
At their first meeting, on 25th March, the Viceroy had been impressed by Sardar Patel's charm and sense of humour. He must
also have been impressed by the Home Member's toughness and
realism. Sardar Patel forthwith pressed the Viceroy to dismiss the
Muslim League members of the Interim Government, because the
'Direct Action' resolution, which had never been suspended, was
avowedly intended to wreck the central organisation of India.

When a week later he complained again that the Muslim League members were promoting movements of violence, Lord Mountbatten observed that the Hindus were not entirely guiltless in this respect. The Coalition Government was the only means he had of dealing with the responsible leaders of both parties together. If he did away with it, the Congress would be the sufferer. The two men did, however, agree on one point—in opposing the enquiries into the riots in East Bengal and Bihar demanded by Mr. Gandhi and others. Sardar Patel pointed out that the enquiry into the Calcutta riots of the previous August was still going on, and was futile as well as damaging to the morale of those in charge of law and order.

Confidence and realism were thus the background of their discussion of the great issue on 12th April. The Viceroy gave Sardar Patel, as he had given Pandit Nehru, a full account of his talks with Mr. Jinnah, explaining that he had never before asked Patel, or any other Congress leader, directly for their suggested solution for the transfer of power, in order to be able to tell Mr. Jinnah that his views were his own for the best future of India, without any ideas borrowed from members of Congress. Those views, said the Viceroy, were in favour of a firm Union with a strong Central Government. He would like to see the Interim Government—with the possible addition of Mr. Jinnah—operating independently, and becoming the successor authority when power was finally transferred in June 1948. The next best solution was the Cabinet Mission plan. The one course into which he did not want to be forced was unrestricted Pakistan, but if he were it would have to be a truncated Pakistan.

Sardar Patel was asked whether he thought the Congress could be brought to accept the Cabinet Mission plan without reservations. He replied that it was he who had persuaded the Congress Working Committee, at the last moment, to accept the plan, and he remained its strongest champion. He promised his support in getting the Congress to accept it as a final settlement. Maulana Abul Kalam Azad, on 27th March, had told the Viceroy that, if he had not been due to leave the Presidency of the Congress when the Cabinet Mission was in India, his party would have accepted the Mission's plan without equivocation. Blame for the non-acceptance of the plan must be laid in the first place on the Congress, though it was the Muslim League that was now intransigent. He failed to see, he said at a later interview, why Mr. Jinnah could not accept the plan, since after all it gave the Muslim areas the right of secession after ten years if they wished, and he advised the Viceroy to find out the precise points on which Mr. Jinnah had decided to withdraw his acceptance, and to try to meet them.

Mr. Jinnah, said Sardar Patel, would accept the Cabinet Mission plan only when the force of circumstances gave him no alternative. The British had repeatedly made the mistake of giving way to Jinnah in order to save his face. In his view, as soon as the Viceroy announced the prospective partition of Bengal, the Bengali Muslims would break from the League in order to preserve the province as a whole, and the same might possibly follow in the Punjab. Accordingly Sardar Patel thought there was a real chance that Mr. Jinnah would either be forced to come to terms or be overthrown by the League.

As for Lord Mountbatten's idea of giving more independence and eventually transferring central power to the Interim Government, how did he imagine, asked Sardar Patel, that they would be able to govern without control over their own top civil servants— the British Government having decided that the Secretary of State's Services (including the I.C.S. and the Political Service) could not be turned over to India until June 1948? The Viceroy replied that since it was now highly doubtful that there would be a unified India he did not see to whom the Secretary of State's Services could be justifiably transferred.

This pessimistic note had been struck in some earlier interviews. On 10th April Lord Mountbatten asked Dr. Rajendra Prasad, who had dilated on the disastrous consequences of the break-up of Indian unity, whether he thought that the Congress would voluntarily accept a decision which virtually abandoned the idea of unity if that were the only way in which power could be transferred without a risk of civil war. If that were so, replied Dr. Prasad, he was inclined to believe that the position might be accepted; for his part he did not see that the Viceroy had any option but to transfer power in any way that would avoid civil war. However, he agreed that, if a time-element could be introduced into the stages whereby partition was effected, there could be some chance for reason to prevail over communalism. At an earlier interview Dr. Prasad, whom Lord Mountbatten thought 'a most delightful man', had argued that, whatever other arrangements were made, there would have to be a central food organisation; he believed the Muslims realised that India could not do without it. On April 11th Mr. Jagjivan Ram, the Scheduled Caste member of the Government, was asked whether he thought there was any hope of getting a unified India by consent of all parties. Although, he replied, this had seemed possible earlier, and although any form of partition would be as disastrous for India as a whole as it would be for Pakistan as the weaker element, he now thought matters had gone too far to consider unity by consent. He doubted whether Mr. Jinnah himself could reverse the feeling which he had instilled in the Muslims. Mr. Rajagopalachari, the same day, 'admitted with great expressions of regret that the ideal of a unified India could not be imposed by force, and, if in fact the decision to hand over to a unified India were to lead to civil war, that would indeed be a tragic paradox'.

It was, however, the President of the Congress himself, Mr. Acharya Kripalani, who turned the hypothetical answers into a factual statement. Asked by Lord Mountbatten, on 17th April, whether he had made up his mind as to the advice he wished to offer for the transfer of power, he replied: 'The point has now been reached at which the Congress must reluctantly accept the fact that the Muslim League will never voluntarily come into a Union of India. Rather than have a battle we shall let them have their Pakistan, provided you will allow the Punjab and Bengal to be partitioned in a fair manner.' With Mr. Jinnah insisting on a sovereign Pakistan, even if against his protests the two disputed provinces had to be partitioned, and with the Congress High Command conceding Pakistan, on condition that they were partitioned, the contest was virtually over so far as advice from the effective leadership of the two main parties was concerned, though the arguments went on.

Spokesmen for the lesser minorities were all against partition either of India or of the provinces. Dr. John Matthai, an Indian Christian, told Lord Mountbatten on 4th April that the Interim Government seemed now to him for the first time a possible Centre to which power could be transferred. The strides made in Cabinet business in ten days would previously have seemed impossible: the system of Cabinet committees, which up to then had been so violently opposed, was now working with the utmost success, and problems like the Budget controversy, over which he had feared the Government would finally break up, had been surmounted by

the process of reasonable compromise in committee. Lord Mountbatten was getting the whole Cabinet more and more on his side.
Dr. Matthai believed that Mr. Liaqat Ali Khan and Pandit Nehru
could work together, though Mr. Jinnah remained the big obstacle.
The views of Mr. Jagjivan Ram, the Scheduled Caste member, on
the main issue, have been related above. On the Scheduled Castes'
own special interest, he thought the majority of them disagreed
with Dr. Ambedkar's attempt to make them into a separate
minority community. Too poor, too uneducated and too ill-
equipped to fight in the big league, they saw their only hope in
assimilation with the caste Hindus and finally the voluntary
eradication of Untouchability. He entirely agreed with Dr.
Ambedkar, however, on the need for safeguards, seats being
guaranteed to the Scheduled Castes in proportion to their numbers, though the real conflict would come when they demanded
their share of seats in all the Governments and of appointments in
the civil and fighting services. For the Anglo-Indian community
Mr. Frank Anthony protested bitterly against the blows they
had been dealt by the Cabinet Mission and Lord Wavell, and
appealed to Lord Mountbatten to look after their interests in the
transfer of power. The Viceroy, though sympathetic, held out
little hope that there was anything he could do for them.

The Sikhs were in a more advantageous position, through their
relationship to the main Hindu-Muslim conflict, especially in the
Punjab. But they were unable, thanks largely to their own political
ineptitude, to make much of it. Their first spokesman was Sardar
Baldev Singh, the Defence Member of the Interim Government,
with whom Lord Mountbatten talked regularly about defence
matters, and especially about the problem of nationalising (i.e.
Indianising) the Armed Forces in the time available before India
left the Commonwealth, as she appeared bent on doing upon the
transfer of power, even if they did not also have to be partitioned.[1]
The Viceroy had received disturbing advice about the growing
militancy of the Sikhs, and on 5th April he asked Sardar Baldev
Singh whether the Sikh leaders would be prepared to join in an
appeal for a truce to violence until he had made a decision. The
Minister thought that Master Tara Singh would certainly agree to
this but he warned the Viceroy that the situation in the Punjab was
explosive, since they had in the area a million recently-demobil-
[1] See below, page 255.

ised soldiers of the three communities, who were spoiling for trouble. On 16th April he protested his own innocence of patronising violence, denying categorically in the presence of the Governor of the Punjab that he had ever signed an appeal put out by the Ajit of Lahore declaring that he (Baldev Singh) was prepared to receive money on behalf of the Sikhs' fund, which was obviously intended to support a civil war, nor had he ever agreed to do so. At the interview the Viceroy told him that the constitutional decision would be taken in accordance with what would appear to be the will of the people; although he hoped it would be for a strong India, or at least the Cabinet Mission plan, they had to face the likelihood of its being partition. To which Sardar Baldev Singh replied that partition was now the only acceptable solution.

The next day Lord Mountbatten saw one of the chief Sikh Rulers, the Raja of Faridkot. His Highness produced a letter to himself from three Sikh leaders, Master Tara Singh, Giani Kartar Singh and Ishar Singh, inviting him to take over the entire policy, organisation and safety of life and property regarding the districts of Ludhiana, Ferozepore and portions of Lahore. The letter appealed to the Sikhs' courage and sense of glory and to the sacrifices of their martyrs. In addition, said the Raja, he had the personal assurance of Muslim League leaders in the Punjab—specifically, the Nawab of Mamdot and Sir Firoz Khan Noon—as to their wishing to include in a new Sikh State certain areas, which were precisely those which the Governor of the Punjab had warned the Viceroy would be most hotly disputed between Muslims and Sikhs. Lord Mountbatten regarded these 'beginnings of a mutual agreement on a division as a very hopeful sign'. But when His Highness told the Viceroy that the Sikhs, greatly valuing the British connection, wanted to stay in the Commonwealth, he replied that he could not possibly negotiate the point with small parts of India, and he held out no hope of supporting a separate Sikh State.

The next day the Viceroy had a visit from two of the signatories of the letter to the Raja, Master Tara Singh and Giani Kartar Singh, together with Sardar Baldev Singh, in whose presence he did not mention the letter, though he said he had seen the Raja of Faridkot. When he asked them about the situation in the Punjab they poured out a long tale of woe: how the Sikhs had been gratuitously attacked by the Muslims; how peacefully inclined they were; and how they would never again be able to live in harmony with the Muslims, and would accept no solution that would put them under Muslim domination.

Of the two specific demands they had come to make, one concerned the recruitment of police in the Punjab, who they said were at present nearly three-quarters Muslim, and the imposition of martial law. The other was that the Viceroy should announce without delay the creation of two separate Ministries for the eastern and western parts of the Punjab respectively, to carry on until the transfer of power. On this, according to Sardar Baldev Singh, Mr. Jinnah had informed him that he accepted the principle of transfer of populations in Punjab; in fact 20,000 Sikhs had already fled their homes and were refugees in the State of Patiala. The Viceroy said he would look into this, but stressed the appalling difficulties involved in partition by migration. To which the Sikh leaders replied that the establishment of Pakistan, if decided upon, would be even more difficult to effect. If, said the Viceroy, he were reluctantly to accept Pakistan, he would also agree to the partition of the Punjab, however difficult it might be; but he would resist this if the Cabinet Mission plan or anything like it were acceptable. In the Sikh leaders' opinion an agreed partition of the Punjab on that basis was not impossible, but in its absence they invited the Viceroy to arbitrate. Nothing, he replied, would induce him to give a decision that would have to be enforced by arms.

In pressing for separation they said they knew that the Hindu Jats wanted a province of their own, consisting of the Jat part of the Punjab and United Provinces, and this they did not oppose. They admitted that in no substantial part of the Punjab were the Sikhs a majority, but they were now so bitterly anti-Muslim that they would not mind forming a Hindu-Sikh province. As for the Sikh States, negotiations were afoot to bring Patiala, Kapurthala, Faridkot, Nabha, Jind and Khalsia into a Sikh States Confederation. They recognised and fully accepted that no part of British India could join up with an Indian State or confederation of States.

'They then proceeded,' wrote Lord Mountbatten, 'to shower me with leaflets and publications. These two unkempt jungly-looking old men were immensely learned in their knowledge of every point of the Cabinet Mission's negotiations and the subsequent debates in the House.' Neither Master Tara Singh nor Giani Kartar Singh was very old, and their 'jungly' appearance was probably due largely to their untrimmed beards and their long hair beneath their pugarees, according to the Sikh rule. Not for the first time, unknowing English judgments from appearances under-valued the Sikhs—'the dear old Sikhs', as Sir Stafford Cripps had called them. The chief grievance their leaders voiced to the Viceroy on this occasion was that in the Constituent Assembly, whereas the Hindus and Muslims had a communal veto, the Sikhs had none, though the Cabinet Mission had given them the status of third and only other major community. They had been advised to seek safeguards in the Constituent Assembly but the Congress were averse to any amendment of the Cabinet Mission plan lest this give the Muslims an excuse for not participating. The Viceroy having declined to press the Congress on the point, pending his final consideration, they warned him that if they were not given a communal veto they would be obliged to leave the Constituent Assembly. He begged them not to do this until he had his final discussions with the political leaders, whereupon he would recommend a solution to His Majesty's Government.

He then asked them whether they would accept the Cabinet Mission plan provided their point was met. They replied that they would give up their insistence on partition only if they secured adequate safeguards against being dominated by the Muslims. They suggested re-allocating seats in the Punjab Assembly on the basis of 40 per cent to the Muslims and 30 per cent each to the Hindus and Sikhs. Lord Mountbatten observed that he did not think anybody else would agree to such proportions, but he accepted that the question of safeguards would need careful investigation. In any case the Sikh leaders held that, even if the Muslim League did join the Constituent Assembly, negotiations would break down on the proportion not only of seats but also of offices and appointments which the Muslims would demand and the Congress would not grant.

Finally they asked that, if Pakistan and a partition of the Punjab were decided upon, they should be given the option of joining either Pakistan or Hindustan, so that they might have some bargaining power in negotiating the best terms for the Sikhs. The Viceroy agreed that this was fair.

Two more Sikh Rulers appear in the record of interviews in this phase of the debate. On 20th April the Viceroy saw the chief among them, the Maharajah of Patiala. After deploring the way in which the British were letting down their friends in the States, the Maharajah said that as to the Punjabi Sikhs he was trying to keep Tara Singh and Kartar Singh in order, but of course they were apt to be inflammatory. In his view they and the Raja of Faridkot were being extremely foolish in the schemes they were trying to hatch. He had warned the Raja that any thought that the departure of the British could be made the occasion of a nineteenth-century grab-bing match was completely unreal and could not fail to have the most disastrous repercussions on the grabbers. The Maharajah added that while he would do all in his power to preserve peace, he believed that chaotic and riotous conditions were the least that could be expected when the British departed, and that they in India would be lucky if they escaped civil war.

Talking with the Maharajah of Nabha on 25th April, Lord Mountbatten asked him if he thought the Sikhs were preparing for a war and were prepared to fight. He replied without hesitation: 'I greatly regret to report that I am convinced they mean to fight.' Asked why, he replied: 'For revenge for the wrongs they have suffered—unless the Muslims show their remorse and a complete change of heart.' Lord Mountbatten reminded hin that in war nobody gained, and in civil war both sides were doubly losers. The Maharajah could quote him as saying that if the Sikhs made any attempt to start such a war he would not hesitate to crush them with every weapon at his disposal—a threat which he repeated to others, especially to Sardar Baldev Singh, whom he warned on 6th May that in such an event he would instruct the Sardar as Defence Member to use the Army and Air Force to fight them.

Despite the sincerity and vigour of the Viceroy's warning, the fact that the Sikhs were plotting deadly resistance to any solution which left them under Muslim dominance, neither partitioning the Punjab as well as India nor giving them such safeguards in a united India as the parties would never accept, may have been the decisive make-weight in Lord Mountbatten's mind. He manifestly clung, to the bitter end, to hopes of a compromise on Cabinet Mission lines, perhaps induced by refusal of the peoples of the Punjab and Bengal to have their historic provinces divided. In all the possible options the Sikhs were a key factor.

It was to Mr. Liaqat Ali Khan first among the political leaders that Lord Mountbatten opened his mind fully at this stage of his thinking. On 19th April, after talking with the Muslim League leader about the situation in the Punjab, and telling him that unless all parties agreed to a sensible solution for the transfer of power the only possible future he saw for the provinces was partition, Lord Mountbatten said he could now tell him how his thoughts were beginning to move towards a solution. He must keep it all to himself, consulting Mr. Jinnah later but not at that stage. Lord Mountbatten then took him through various alternative plans, beginning with Pakistan and complete partition of the Punjab, Bengal and Assam. He had no doubt, he said, that the Indian leaders and their peoples were in such a hysterical condition that they would gladly agree to his arranging their suicide in this way. Liaqat Ali nodded his head and said: 'I am afraid everybody will agree to such a plan; we are all in such a state.' Lord Mountbatten replied that the worst service he could do to India, if he were her enemy or indifferent to her fate, would be to take advantage of this extraordinary mental condition to force complete partition upon her, before departing in June 1948 and leaving the country to hopeless chaos.

With that preamble he returned to the Cabinet Mission plan but was met by the response that it was useless discussing it; the Muslim League had now a phobia towards the mere words 'Cabinet Mission'. But what, asked the Viceroy, if he produced a Mountbatten Plan, very nearly the same in form and substance? This, thought Mr. Liaqat, would have a far better chance psychologically. Did he think, then, that the League would accept the Mission's Groups B and C, with safeguards for the Sikhs, and with two separate Armies under their own Army Headquarters, though under an overall Defence Headquarters? To this he replied: 'Now you are beginning to talk. But with the central authority empowered to raise taxes for defence finance the Hindus would be given a crippling hold over the economy of the whole country.' Lord Mountbatten then suggested that the groups might be assessed according to their respective populations and the size of the forces they maintained, and pay a contribution on that basis towards a Central Defence Fund for running the central activities, including joint technical schools for the Services. Liaqat Ali Khan 'jumped at' this proposal.

It would be essential, said Lord Mountbatten, that all the different parts of India should agree to remain within the Commonwealth. What did Liaqat Ali Khan think of the prospect of putting through such a plan? The recent riots and massacres, said Liaqat, had frightened everybody, and now that people had had a foretaste of civil war they realised what would happen if an acceptable solution could not be found. 'Although we are all being most intransigent now, you may find that you can bring considerable pressure on every group you meet if you are able to show them a plan which will get them out of their present impasse.' He gladly accepted the role which the Viceroy offered him of unofficial adviser from the Muslim League point of view on various alternative plans, alongside Pandit Nehru for the Congress, and promised to reflect on all that Lord Mountbatten had told him and to think out possible future lines of approach. 'I have the impression,' wrote the Viceroy at the end of his record of this talk, 'that Mr. Liaqat Ali Khan intends to help me find a more reasonable solution than this mad Pakistan.'

That was on 19th April. The sands were running out, for Lord Mountbatten was already working on a draft plan for the transfer of power, and was determined to have it ready for submission to His Majesty's Government by early May. In the event, no alternative to 'this mad Pakistan' was found. Why was this? The interviews with Indian politicians by themselves provide no clear answer. On 22nd April the Viceroy had a long talk with Mr. V. K. Krishna Menon. Since the Viceroy recorded that 'we properly let down our hair together and discussed every aspect of the plan now being worked on', it is reasonable to assume that he exposed his true intentions as they were at that time. They had talked of the world background, and of Mr. Krishna Menon's view that the object of United States policy was to create an economic, political and military vacuum in India which America would fill. The record continues:

I suggested to him a solution along the lines he himself had raised last time, namely, Dominion Status before June 1948, so as to avoid the necessity of having to make any declaration when we left, and thus leave India within the Commonwealth. My proposal was that . . . Pakistan and Hindustan should be declared independent Dominions, with a Central Defence Council, a single army (pending partition) and with myself at the head of the Central Defence Council and as Governor-General of the

two Dominions on a constitutional basis. I pointed out that the
British Army would come directly under my command, and that
that would be my personal contribution to the Defence Council.
I suggested that, in order not to imperil the sovereignty of
Dominion Status, each Dominion would voluntarily accord me
the right of a casting vote as Chairman of the Defence Council.

This scheme had three outstanding elements. The first was that of
an intermediate and early demission of power on a Dominion
Status basis, with the future after June 1948 left open. The second
was that there were to be two sovereign Dominions, Pakistan being
presumably of the moth-eaten variety. Thirdly, the central residue
had been whittled down to a tripartite Defence Council on an undisclosed constitutional basis and with a dubious future after
June 1948.

The Viceroy, clearly not entranced by this alternative solution,
made one more attempt to resurrect the Cabinet Mission's plan in
a revised form. On 25th April he suggested to Sardar Patel the
possible amendment of that plan by making the Central Cabinet
subject to a system of voting on communal questions similar to
that envisaged for the legislature. Sardar Patel replied: 'If you
raise this question of parity you will incur the everlasting enmity
of Congress: that is the one thing we have been fighting against and
will never agree to.' They went on to argue about the Congress
interpretation of the Cabinet Mission's plan, but Patel's two main
points were unequivocal. First, he was convinced that the Muslim
League would not accept it. Secondly, if they would not, Congress
wanted partition: it was a fundamental policy of theirs that there
should be no coercion.

Mr. Jinnah confirmed the first point in an interview the very
next day. 'You told me,' said Lord Mountbatten, 'that your objection to the Cabinet Mission plan was the fact that the Centre would
be controlled by a majority vote of the Congress. . . . Is that your
objection?' Mr. Jinnah nodded his head vehemently. There
followed an argument about the value of the communal veto in the
Constituent Assembly, Mr. Jinnah protesting that it would prove
valueless because rulings of the Federal Court would be dis-
regarded. 'In fact,' he continued, 'the leaders of the Congress are
so dishonest, so crooked and so obsessed with the idea of smashing
the Muslim League, that there are no lengths to which they will

Above The new Viceroy takes over: Lord and Lady Mountbatten bidding farewell to Lord and Lady Wavell at Palam Airport, 23rd March 1947.

Below Mr. M. A. Jinnah with the Viceroy and Lady Mountbatten at Viceroy's House, April 1947.

Mahatma Gandhi and the Mountbattens

not go to do so, and the only way of giving Pakistan a chance is to make it an independent nation of the British Commonwealth, with its own Army and the right to argue cases at the Central Council on this basis.' From this decision Lord Mountbatten was quite unable to shake him, and he begged the Viceroy not to ask him to reconsider the Cabinet Mission plan again.

The options open thus appeared extremely narrow. The Congress said: 'Better partition than any dilution of the Cabinet Mission plan.' The Muslim League said: 'No Cabinet Mission plan at any price.' The conclusion from those two propositions— partition into sovereign nations—was no doubt rendered more palatable and less mad in Lord Mountbatten's mind by three considerations which these political talks had exposed. First, he hoped that at least for an interim period both nations would remain in the Commonwealth. Secondly, he clung to the idea, again at least *ad interim*, of a Central Council for defence and perhaps other associated purposes. Thirdly, he may well have cherished a hope that when the key provinces of the Punjab and Bengal were faced with the naked choice for or against dividing themselves in order to divide India, one or other or both might choose unity, perhaps on the basis of separate national independence, which at that time was contemplated as one of the alternatives on which they would be asked to vote. The Pakistan concept might then itself be fatally wounded.

Certain advice the Viceroy had received from political leaders gave cause for such an expectation. Maulana Abul Kalam Azad had told the Viceroy that if he were to announce the partition of Bengal it was highly likely that the Muslims of Bengal would separate from the League; he thought it was possible, though slightly less likely, that the same would happen in the Punjab. Sardar Patel made the same prognostication, adding that Mr. Jinnah would be forced to come to terms, or else be overthrown by the League. Mr. Jagjivan Ram expressed what Lord Mountbatten described at the time as 'the very wise view' that if the Muslims were allowed to do what they wanted, particularly if their goal were restricted by the partition of the Punjab and Bengal, they would find their Pakistan quite unworkable and would voluntarily join the Indian Union.

The Secretary to the Governor of Bengal (Sir Frederick Burrows), who attended the Governor's Conference of 14th–15th

April in Sir Frederick's absence through illness, was emphatic
that the Muslim-majority part of Bengal could not stand by itself
economically, even in association with the rest of a truncated
Pakistan. In his view Mr. Suhrawardy, the Provincial Premier, and
his Muslim followers would choose Hindustan rather than accept
partition on a population basis. Khwaja Nazimuddin, another
eminent Bengali Muslim, Deputy Leader of the League in the
Central Legislative Assembly, while demanding the major partition of India, protested violently at the minor partition of the two
provinces. It was physically impossible to divide the Punjab without large transfers of population, and the Sikh problem would be
unresolved: in Bengal, and still more in Assam, partition would be
a very serious matter. Mr. Suhrawardy himself, on 26th April,
told the Viceroy that in the case of Bengal partition was far from
being the necessary corollary of partitioning India. Since the plan
of which he had been told involved a vote on whether a province
should be partitioned or not, and, if not, whether it was to join
Pakistan or Hindustan or remain independent, he could say with
confidence that given enough time he could persuade Bengal to
remain united, and that he could get Mr. Jinnah to agree that in
that event it need not join Pakistan. 'This is very good news,' said
Lord Mountbatten. The same day he saw Mr. Jinnah and reported
his conversation with the Bengali Premier. What did Mr. Jinnah
think, asked the Viceroy, about keeping Bengal united at the price
of its staying out of Pakistan? Without hesitation Mr. Jinnah
replied: 'I should be delighted. What is the use of Bengal without
Calcutta? They had much better remain united and independent:
I am sure they would be on friendly terms with Pakistan.'

That the problem was not quite so simple, however, was brought
home to the Viceroy by an interview with Mr. Kiran Shankar Roy,
Leader of the Opposition in the Bengal Legislative Assembly.
Having received a request for the partition of Bengal from the non-
Muslim members of its legislature, he asked bluntly whether Mr.
Roy was in favour of unity or partition for the province. Mr. Roy
replied that he had always been strongly in favour of unity, and
only Muslim intransigence and pressure from the Congress had
driven him into recommending partition. Unless the Muslim
League were prepared to come forward with some offer to the
Hindus the chances of keeping Bengal united were slim. Lord
Mountbatten told him he had recommended Mr. Suhrawardy to

offer joint Hindu-Muslim electorates. 'Most certainly,' said Mr. Roy, 'that would satisfy the Hindus. If they give us that you can practically count on unity.' The Viceroy was bound to tell him, however, that Mr. Suhrawardy doubted whether he could carry his party with him on this.

> Mr. Roy got more and more excited as the meeting progressed [recorded Lord Mountbatten]. I advised him strongly to go straight back to Calcutta and see Mr. Suhrawardy, and then go on to Darjeeling and see the Governor. 'You have not a moment to lose,' I told him; upon which he got up dramatically, shook me warmly by the hand, and left the room.

The drama fizzled out in the last act of the play. When all the advice about the Punjab and Bengal was sifted and examined coolly, three facts stood out. The Muslims as a whole were determined upon a sovereign Pakistan, even at the price of provincial partition. The Sikhs refused to submit to Muslim-majority rule in the Punjab. The Hindus in Bengal refused to accept Muslim-majority rule save on conditions which the Muslims were highly unlikely to grant. Was this the will of the people and the communities, when faced with a decisive choice, or only the propaganda of their few top leaders while trying to persuade the Viceroy to a conclusion favourable to their communal cause? The only way to answer this was to throw the decision to a democratic process. Such was the nature of the eventual plan. It omitted the option of independence. But the prospect of a Balkanisation of India was as oppressive as any other; for if Bengal or the Punjab could opt out for independent nationhood, why not the major Princely States, or groups of States, or even other provinces?

Whatever other criticism may be made of Lord Mountbatten's plan for the transfer of power, it certainly cannot be said that it was imposed without the fullest consultation with India's political leaders, or that it was contrary to the ultimate consensus of their views. It may truly be said that it was not he but the Indians who divided India. To the end he strove for unity on some such lines as the Cabinet Mission had planned, but the more he strove the clearer it became that this solution was dead.

15

The problem of the forces

1 *The I.N.A. trials*

As has been recorded above, when Lord Wavell and Lord Mount-batten met in New Delhi, the outgoing Viceroy told his successor that one of the most difficult problems that he left to be settled was that of the trials of officers of the Indian National Army. In his last days he had used his reserve powers to veto discussion of this matter in Cabinet. Politically, that was a position which obviously could not be held, but between the rival views of what should be done, voiced respectively by the Prime Minister, Pandit Nehru, and the Commander-in-Chief, Field Marshal Auchinleck, no middle way seemed possible.

The Indian National Army had been recruited by the Japanese after the fall of Malaya and Burma from the captured Indian soldiers and from Indian civilians who had been overrun. Proclaimed as a patriotic organ of Indian liberation, it served the Japanese better as a propaganda instrument than as a military weapon, in which capacity it was rated very low by the Allied Forces.[1] After a false start with a Sikh officer in command, they found a far more powerful leader in a brilliant Bengali politician and former Congress leader, Subhas Chandra Bose. Subhas was a natural revolutionary who had quarrelled with Mahatma Gandhi over non-violence, and who saw in the war the chance for a violent overthrow of British rule. In January 1941 he escaped while awaiting trial for sedition, and after reappearing in Berlin eventually reached Japan in March 1943. No better tool for the Japanese purpose could have been found—already famous in India as an extreme nationalist, dynamic, ruthless and zealous to the point of mania. In October 1943, with the backing of his Tokyo masters, he declared himself Head of State of Free India and Commander-

---

[1] South-East Asia Command reckoned a division of the I.N.A. to be worth one battalion of Japanese or regular Indian troops.

in-Chief of the Indian National Army, with his seat in Singapore. Of the original recruitment of 16,000 in the I.N.A., 12,000 then remained on its roll. Bose raised another 10,000 from the prisoners of war and about 20,000 from the Indian civil community, but only one combat division of some 14,000 men went into action.

During the war little was known about the I.N.A. by the Indian general public except from enemy propaganda. I.N.A. men taken prisoner were segregated in categories and many released to their homes. Nine officers convicted by court martial of spying or sabotage were executed. It was all part of winning the war, and regarded as primarily an Army matter. The reconquest of Japanese-occupied territory and the release of wartime restraint on news produced a totally new picture. Decisions had to be taken as to how to deal with the many thousands of I.N.A. men now captured, including their officers, though the most fateful decision of all was averted by the death of Subhas Chandra Bose in August 1945 when the aircraft in which he was fleeing from Singapore to Tokyo crashed in Formosa.

This event, and the publicity about the I.N.A. to which it gave rise, fired a fuse leading to the vast powder-barrel of Indian national and communal politics. The situation was ripe with nationalist opportunity. The Congress leaders had been released, and the prospective end of the war promised an early demise of the British raj. Undeserving as the I.N.A. was (for those who joined it thereby escaped the cruelties and privations suffered by captured Indian soldiers loyal to their oath, and many of them betrayed their comrades), it became a symbol of national patriotism. The Congress leadership was the first to exploit it, but soon the Muslim League, not wanting to display any less nationalist zeal, joined the cause. A rich bonus was presented to agitation by the decision to hold trials of selected groups of I.N.A. officers in the Red Fort at Delhi, the former palace of the Mogul Emperors. Only the leaders and those charged with atrocities would be tried, and there would be no attempt to punish the rank and file. To ignore the whole episode and amnesty the entire personnel of the I.N.A. seemed to the authorities unthinkable, not only for broad reasons of justice and political equity, but also for the sake of morale in the Armed Forces; for who would be true to his oath and loyal to his superior officers, at greater or less cost to himself, if,

because of political pressure, the disloyal and the defectors all
went scot free? No one stated the case more stoutly than Lord
Wavell, in a public address on 10th December 1946. It was improper for him, he said, to say anything of the trials themselves or
the men under trial. But, he went on:

> I do propose to say something for the men who were prisoners of
> war but did not join the I.N.A., who, under pressure and
> punishment, under hardships and want, stood firm to their
> ideals of a soldier's duties, a soldier's faith. They represent
> some 70 per cent of the total men of the Indian Army who be-
> came prisoners of war in Malaya and Hong Kong. Whatever
> your political views, if you cannot acclaim the man who prefers
> his honour to his ease, who remains steadfast in adversity to his
> pledged faith, then you have a poor notion of the character which
> is required to build up a nation. I say to you that amongst all
> the exploits of the last five or six years for which the world
> rightly extols the Indian soldier, the endurance of those men in
> captivity and hardship stands as high as any. As a proof of what
> they endured as a price of their loyalty to their ideals of a
> soldier's duty, I will tell you this: the 45,000 Indian prisoners of
> war who stood firm are estimated to have lost about 11,000 or
> one quarter of their number, from disease, starvation and
> murder; the 20,000 who went over to our enemy's side lost only
> 1,500, or $7\frac{1}{2}$ per cent.

The choice of the Red Fort as seat of the trials was made by
General Auchinleck himself, against the strong advice of senior
civil servants, who urged that they be held in some remote town,
where it would be difficult for the Press and public to attend or
proceedings to be widely reported. This argument he altogether
repudiated. Such attempted secrecy, in his view, not only belonged
to an outworn tradition but was repugnant in itself and not to be
defended: once the decision to hold the trials had been made
there could be no question of hushing them up. Honourable as
this attitude was, the choice proved disastrous for the image of
the regime.

If the Red Fort was convenient for Army Headquarters it was
equally convenient for every politician and lawyer in the capital.
If, as the scene of great Durbars, it expressed the might of the Raj,
as the palace of the last Indian rulers of India it was replete with

memories of great days before the British conquest, and of the Mutiny which patriotic Indian historians called the National Revolt, less than ninety years past and far from forgotten. Another error of political sense was to charge the accused with 'waging war against the King-Emperor'. True, this was their alleged offence, and the only appropriate general charge lying under the Indian Criminal Code, but no phrase could have held less political opprobrium among Indians in 1945, or echoed more succinctly the note of imperial discipline which political India believed was now fading to a whisper.

In September 1945, before any proceedings had been opened, the All-India Congress Committee passed a resolution claiming that 'it would be a tragedy if these officers were punished for the offence of having laboured, however mistakenly, for the freedom of India', and set up a defence committee. Its membership, extremely strong, ranged beyond the Congress, including Sir Tej Bahadur Sapru, the venerated Liberal leader, as well as Pandit Nehru and two other distinguished Hindu lawyers. It began by addressing to the Viceroy a general appeal for the postponement of the trials, as primarily concerning the Indian people, until after the elections and the reconstitution of the Government of India and the provincial Ministries. The Commander-in-Chief, General Auchinleck,[1] advised against this course on the ground that the administration of justice could not properly be delayed for political reasons. The trials proceeded.

The first three officers to be court-martialled were charged with murder, abetment of murder, and waging war against the King-Emperor. After nearly two months—a protraction which could only allow agitation to feed and grow—the Court conveyed its decision to the Commander-in-Chief on the last day of 1945. Two officers were acquitted of the first two charges, one was found guilty of abetment of murder, all of waging war against the King. All alike were sentenced to transportation for life (the only alternative to the death penalty for waging war) and to be cashiered and lose all pay and allowances while with the Japanese. General Auchinleck, the next day, decided in all three cases to remit the sentences of transportation while confirming the lesser sentences. He did so, he wrote, because to confirm the sentence of transportation for life on the first two officers, or commute it to a lesser term

[1] He was promoted to the rank of Field Marshal in May 1946.

of imprisonment, would make them into martyrs and intensify 'the political campaign of bitterness and racial antipathy being waged by Congress', and because there was no real difference between the third case and the other two, as the Court had presumably also thought, since they imposed the same sentences on all. (He might have added that to punish the only Muslim of the three with transportation or imprisonment would have had serious political and even military consequences.) Equally important, General Auchinleck had been instituting both a review of future action and a special enquiry into the real feelings of Indian soldiers about the I.N.A. On 22nd January he recommended, and the Viceroy agreed, that the charge of waging war against the King should in future be dropped, the indictments being confined to murder and brutality. In February General Auchinleck circulated to all Army Commanders in India and South-East Asia a remarkable memorandum reflecting on the first Red Fort trials.[1]

As he saw it, the commutation of sentences had had the following effects in India: on the general public of all opinions and creeds, intense relief, born of the conviction that the alternative would have resulted in violent internal conflict; on Indian officers, except for a few, likewise relief; on the other ranks of the Indian Army, largely indifference mixed with pleasure; on many British officers, a bad reaction and public criticism contrary to traditional standards of loyalty. 'To these officers, perhaps not very perceptive or imaginative, an officer is an officer whether he be Indian or British, and they make no allowance for birth or political aspirations or upbringing, nor do they begin to realise the great political stresses and strains now affecting this country. . . . Moreover, they forget, if they ever knew, the great bitterness bred in the minds of many Indian officers in the early days of "Indianization" by the discrimination, often very real, exercised against them, and the discourteous, contemptuous treatment meted out to them by many British officers who ought to have known better.' General Auchinleck went on to recall the circumstances affecting the Indian troops after the capitulation of Singapore, which must have seemed to them to be the end of the British raj—separated from their British officers and often seduced by Indian officers who had been suborned by the Japanese. He reminded his Commanders that

[1] The memorandum is reproduced in full in *Auchinleck*, by John Connell, pp. 945–52.

these men 'had no real loyalty or patriotism towards Britain as Britain'. For the officers there was less excuse, but 'it is no use shutting one's eyes to the fact that any Indian officer worth his salt is a Nationalist, though that this does not mean that he is necessarily anti-British. If he is anti-British, that is as often as not due to his faulty handling and treatment by his British officer comrades'. The document went on to debate and defend the decision to show clemency after the trial of the first three officers, and the holding of the trials in public in the heart of India. Although in the future the charge of 'waging war' would be omitted, the temptation to discharge all and sundry without more ado must be resisted, if grave injustice was not to be done to the innocent. The central object was 'to maintain the reliability, stability and efficiency of the Indian Army for the future, whatever Government may be set up in India'.

At the end of April 1946 General Auchinleck decided to drop all further proceedings against I.N.A. culprits. Pandit Nehru wrote him a grateful letter. Meanwhile, however, trials of some fifteen more men accused of serious offences other than 'waging war against the King-Emperor' had resulted in prison sentences, and an agitation for a total amnesty continued. When Lord Mountbatten took over the Viceroyalty from Lord Wavell, the latter had just vetoed, with the approval of the British Cabinet, his Government's wish to support an impending Legislative Assembly motion, backed by all parties, calling for immediate release of all I.N.A. prisoners. As Pandit Nehru himself admitted in an interview with the new Viceroy on 1st April, this situation confronted Lord Mountbatten with a grave dilemma. It would be impossible to delay any further the Assembly debate, already several times postponed, and now due in two days' time. If Lord Mountbatten renewed Lord Wavell's veto, he would irretrievably damage his reputation with Indian politicians at the start of his task. If he reversed it, the Commander-in-Chief might resign and Lord Mountbatten would be equally damaged in relation to the British Government.

Lord Mountbatten took Pandit Nehru through the problem slowly and deliberately.[1] He had the advantage of having had a 'preliminary round' with Pandit Nehru in Singapore in March

[1] This portion of the interview was narrated to the author by Lord Mountbatten in 1965, and tape-recorded.

1946,[1] when he had persuaded Nehru to cancel his plan to lay a wreath on the I.N.A. memorial there. He told the Prime Minister that the I.N.A. were not politically conscious heroes fighting for their country but cowards and traitors who had betrayed their loyal comrades. 'The men who will serve you well in your national army of the future are those who are loyal to their oath: otherwise the Army may turn against you politicians if you become unpopular.' However, Pandit Nehru insisted that for political reasons the trials must be stopped.

'Then the Commander-in-Chief will resign.'

'That doesn't worry me.'

'And I will resign too.'

'But why?"

'Because I was the Supreme Commander under whom the loyal Indians fought; I led them against the I.N.A.'

'That would be terrible. We cannot start again with a new Viceroy.'

'Well, you must choose.'

'You are pressing me very hard. . . . You must give me time.'

The same evening the Viceroy saw the Commander-in-Chief. He wrote shortly afterwards:

> We went through the whole history of the I.N.A. case, and although he was his usual friendly self and spoke with the utmost frankness, I detected a frame of mind which made him more difficult to deal with than I can remember at any time since October 1943. It was clear to me that he had in mind that any retreat from the position he had taken up on the advice of his staff and senior commanders would be impossible, since he would lose the confidence of the Army. He made it quite clear that once his utility had gone he would not feel justified in staying.
>
> When I pressed him about what was likely to happen with the rest of his staff and commanders, he replied that he knew that most of them would resign, because they had raised the matter with him. He had given them instructions that they were on no account to do so, or act in any precipitate manner that could be held as a threat, but that they were to indicate their desire, if necessary, for release in due course.

[1] See above, p. 213.

It was only with the greatest difficulty that I got him to see that it might be necessary to take at least one pace forward from this position if I was not to be faced with two entirely unacceptable alternatives.

The following day Lord Mountbatten called Pandit Nehru, Mr. Liaqat Ali Khan, Sardar Baldev Singh, and Field Marshal Auchinleck to a special meeting. It proved long and tense. For a long time neither the members of the Cabinet nor the Commander-in-Chief would yield an inch. Eventually, however, the Viceroy persuaded the Indian leaders to stand up to the Legislative Assembly the next day and refuse the demand for immediate release, while stating, with the consent of the Commander-in-Chief, that without creating any precedent the available Justices of the Federal Court would review the cases and recommend whether there should be any alteration in the sentences. A formula to that effect was agreed between Field Marshal Auchinleck and the Chief Justice over lunch. In the Assembly Pandit Nehru made a balanced and courageous speech, and the resolution was withdrawn. That was, in effect, the end of the I.N.A. as a political issue. It had proved a flaming torch for agitation and the cause of grave loss of prestige and self-confidence for the British in India. If it had not fatally undermined the loyalty of the Armed Forces, as many officers had predicted it would unless the public law and military code were vigorously upheld, it certainly did nothing to repair their morale and discipline at a critical time. It typified the pains and paradoxes of a period when those responsible for government were losing the power to govern, while the would-be inheritors of that power would not take on the responsibility it implied. The longer that period lasted, the more dangerous it was likely to be.

2 Partition of the Armed Forces

The future of the Armed Forces of India was manifestly one of the key questions, perhaps the key question, involved in the possible partition of the country. It was also intimately connected with the relationship between the successor state or states and the Commonwealth, for a number of reasons, most especially because they could not hope to retain the services of British officers, save as pure mercenaries, unless they continued to acknowledge the

Headship of the Crown to which those officers' loyalty was due. Therefore the problem of the Armed Forces, especially their unity or partition, could never be settled as a separate matter, but repeatedly changed its fundamental character as decisions, provisional or definitive, were taken on the two main issues bearing on it —division of India, and Commonwealth membership. This helped to explain why a policy of rapid partition of the Army and other Forces, which had at first been regarded as unthinkable, was eventually adopted and applied in great haste. Another part of the explanation was the infection of the Armed Forces with the prevailing acute communalism.

The puzzles and paradoxes of the situation were well illustrated in a talk which Lord Mountbatten had with Mr. Liaqat Ali Khan on 11th April 1947. The Viceroy had outlined to the Finance Minister, Mr. Jinnah's chief henchman, how his talks with Mr. Jinnah had gone, especially as to partitioning provinces if India was to be partitioned, with all the delays and difficulties that would be implied. Mr. Liaqat raised the question of partitioning the Army, which he always insisted was the *sine qua non* of setting up Pakistan. The Viceroy was emphatic: so long as he was responsible for law and order in India nothing would induce him to take one step that would imperil the efficiency of the Army. 'He fully accepted this,' recorded Lord Mountbatten. The Viceroy added: 'I am prepared to go so far as to put up proposals for machinery for planning a split of the Armed Forces, but the Indian parties themselves must work out the final details.'

'After June 1948,' asked Mr. Liaqat, this being the date assumed for the final transfer of power and the end of the Viceroyalty, 'who will see that the Centre, if there is one, does not use the Army unfairly?'

'Presumably you will have two Defence Ministers meeting on equal terms and giving joint agreed instructions to the Commander-in-Chief.'

'Is there any chance of the Commander-in-Chief being British?'

'That is entirely dependent on the Congress and the Muslim League getting together and saying they wish to retain sufficient connection with the Commonwealth to enable them to have the services of a British Commander-in-Chief.'

'But there is no doubt that Pakistan wants to remain a Dominion, if only because we want to keep your officers.'

'I am not prepared,' said the Viceroy, 'even to discuss the suggestion of any part of India remaining with the Empire unless the suggestion came from all parties together, and even then I could not say what the policy of His Majesty's Government would be.'

Thus at that stage, only a month before the decision on the transfer of power was taken, all the principal questions were wide open. Should partition of India be subject to creation of a Centre concerned with defence? Would the successor nation, or nations, wish to be members of the Commonwealth, able to retain the services of British officers? Would such a wish be accepted by the British Government?[1] Meanwhile there could be no question of actually partitioning the Armed Forces, though there could be contingency planning for a distant future.

Three days later the Viceroy thrashed the matter out with Field Marshal Auchinleck. The occasion was a letter he had received that morning from Mr. Liaqat Ali Khan, asking that steps should be taken, first to ensure adequate representation of the Muslims in each branch of the Armed Forces, and secondly to reorganise the Armed Forces so that they could be split when a decision on partition of the country was taken.

The Commander-in-Chief observed that the general claim of inadequate representation of Muslims in the Forces was largely unfounded. The proportion in the Army was 29 per cent against a ratio of about 27 per cent of Muslims in the population of British India. Nevertheless, Mr. Liaqat was right to this extent, that most of the Indian senior officers were Hindus, since for one reason or another many of the Muslim senior officers had faded out.

As for the reorganisation of the Armed Forces on a communal basis, it would be a very complicated and difficult process, taking many months, if not years. Field Marshal Auchinleck said he was not prepared to undertake planning for it, which would in any case need a large new staff. Lord Mountbatten told him he had in mind

[1] While Lord Mountbatten's own implied doubts on this score may have been tactical, for others at least they were real. In an interview on 14th April Lieutenant-General Sir Archibald Nye, Governor of Madras, gave Lord Mountbatten his opinion that India was about the weakest country in the world in proportion to her population, and since the nationalisation of the Armed Forces would set her back still further, she would be such a liability as a member of the Commonwealth that he doubted very much whether it would be wise to admit her.

setting up a committee of Indians to prepare the plans, in order to show fair play if Pakistan was decided on, and because one of his objects was to demonstrate that splitting the Forces was impracticable. He suggested, and the Field Marshal agreed, that the Commander-in-Chief and other senior officers should appear before such a committee as expert witnesses. Field Marshal Auchinleck then disclosed that a plan for reorganisation on communal lines was already in existence, although it had been prepared some time previously and for a different purpose.[1] It had been estimated that units in course of reorganisation would be out of action for at least a year. He was assuming the continuance of a unified India, which he and his fellow Commanders had agreed was the only possible basis of planning for such reorganisation. He reminded the Viceroy that many of the Muslim soldiers had their homes in parts of India which would not be in Pakistan.

Sir Eric Miéville, who with Lord Ismay was also present at the interview, asked what would be the effects on the Army of a decision in favour of partitioning India. They would be very serious, said the Commander-in-Chief. Muslim soldiers would not take orders from Hindu officers and *vice versa*. Any indication that the Army would be split would have appalling effects, though those would be lessened if it were made clear that the structure would remain as it was until June 1948. If things went on as they were, with no settlement and no agreement, the general situation was bound to worsen and the Army would be affected. If the Punjab were split it was doubtful whether the Muslim troops would stand steady. Already the hold of the British officers was loosening and it would continue to do so as Indian soldiers came to realise that the British were definitely leaving in June 1948. At the moment the Army was on the whole loyal. So was the Indian Navy, but any trouble in the Army was bound to spread there. The Indian Air Force officers were very politically minded. In general the situation had deteriorated rapidly over the previous three months.

The Commander-in-Chief pointed up his views on the partition of the Armed Forces, thus privately expressed, in a memorandum referring to Mr. Liaqat Ali Khan's paper. (The Defence Member, Sardar Baldev Singh, was correctly the intermediary for this correspondence: the matter, being so secret and potentially ex-

[1] Possibly Lord Wavell's evacuation plan.

plosive, was not being taken in Cabinet or in the Defence Committee.) Field Marshal Auchinleck wrote:

> The Armed Forces of India, as they now stand, cannot be split up into two parts each of which will form a self-contained Armed Force. . . .
> The formation of two separate Armed Forces is not just a matter of re-distributing certain classes of men. It is a matter of the greatest complexity and difficulty. . . . Any such drastic reorganisation would have to be carried out in stages over a period of several years, and during this period there would be no cohesive Armed Force capable of dealing with any serious defensive operations on the North-West Frontier.
> Meanwhile it has not been possible to suspend planning on the assumption that H.M.G. will hand over a unified Armed Force. . . .
> As it is likely that any rumour concerning a proposal to divide the Armed Forces would have an immediate and unsettling effect on the morale of the Muslim soldiers, ratings and airmen, it is urged that this matter should not be discussed except on the highest level.
> I wish to stress that in the present state of communal unrest in India any publication of such discussions might well be disastrous to the continued morale and efficiency of the Armed Forces.

Sardar Baldev Singh added his own strong support as Defence Member. He was, of course, as a Sikh, bitterly opposed to Pakistan and to the Muslim view of this matter, but he was also the responsible Minister. He wrote:

> Respect for law and order is rapidly waning. In certain parts, large sections of the population have lost confidence in the ability of the police to protect life and property. The only relieving factor in this dark picture is that the integrity of the Aimed Forces is still unsullied. . . . It would indeed be an irreparable disaster if a Force such as this was exposed to risks that would not only weaken but ultimately destroy its worth.

Sardar Baldev Singh expressed himself strongly against discussion of the Finance Member's proposal in the Defence Committee and against suspending existing plans for reorganisation and nationalisation of the Armed Forces on the assumption of unity.

Writing to the Secretary of State on 17th April about a talk he had had with Mr. Jinnah, Lord Mountbatten recorded:

> I told him that while I remained statutorily responsible . . . for the preservation of law and order in India, I would not agree to partition of the armed forces, which had already been so weakened by nationalisation that they could not stand partition as well. I did however tell him that I would be prepared to have the matter investigated by the Defence Committee if a decision on partition were finally taken. . . .
>
> Since I was not prepared to split the armed forces until we had left, it would be necessary to keep a central organisation to control the army for the overall defence and security requirements of India; and this central organisation would have to continue to act for a long while, while the armed forces were being split.[1]

Nevertheless, on 25th April the Viceroy called a meeting of the Defence Committee, to which the papers on this subject had meanwhile been circulated as 'Top Secret and Personal'. He began by saying that in so acting he had overridden the advice of the Defence Member and Commander-in-Chief, not because he did not accept the need for complete secrecy, but because he required the Committee's views in order to report to the British Cabinet as to the future form of government he would recommend for India. 'Pakistan is an issue which must be faced, and the partition of the Armed Forces is one of its most important implications.' Both Sardar Baldev Singh and Mr. Liaqat Ali Khan agreed at the start of the debate that any decision about the Armed Forces must follow and not precede the political decision.

In the course of discussion, which was largely concerned with the many complications of partition and the need for clear terms of reference in planning, two highly important contributions were made to the general issue. The first was by Lord Mountbatten. He thought that the Armed Forces could probably complete nationalisation (i.e. Indianisation) efficiently by June 1948; alternatively, they might complete separation by the same date without

[1] *Viceroy's Personal Report* No. 3, 17th April 1947.

undue risk. But to attempt both in that time was to court great danger. He continued:

> I bear personal responsibility for law and order. I must carry this until such time as I can hand it over to one or more responsible authorities. While I bear that responsibility I have, in the last resort, the use of British troops to fall back on. After 1st June 1948 there will be no British troops. But the need for reliable and impartial armed forces may still exist. By unduly hastening the process of separation we may defeat our own ends and produce a situation in which the Armed Forces may be semi-organised and not reliable. Much as I should like to see the separation completed, I must emphasize my own doubts as to the possibility of achieving this in the time available, without weakening the Armed Forces. This I cannot possibly accept while I am responsible for law and order.

Lord Mountbatten told his staff the next day that the Indian Ministers had been 'thoroughly shaken'. The second intervention of great importance came from Field Marshal Auchinleck.

> What the discussion has brought out is that there is really no basis on which I can plan for separation. So many factors are uncertain. I do agree that I can put in hand—in broad outline— a certain amount of planning. All this can determine is the problem that will have to be tackled and the staff I shall need to do the job. As for nationalization, I agree that that can be temporarily postponed.

Thus there was agreement between Viceroy and Commander-in-Chief, despite their differences, that planning—but only planning—for communal separation in the Armed Forces could go forward, with priority for the time being over nationalisation, assuming the terminal date for either was June 1948.

It may well be asked how it came about that within a very short time these views were discarded in favour of a partition of the Armed Forces by 15th August 1947. The answer lies, of course, in the decision taken on the main constitutional issue. Field Marshal Auchinleck did not forsake his opinion of the danger of dividing the Army but he had to accept a political decision. Lord Ismay did his best to persuade Mr. Jinnah not to insist on a communal division, but to accept a division on numerical lines, keeping the regiments intact, but in vain. If, as seemed certain, the plan eventually published on 3rd June led to the establishment of Pakistan, it followed that the Forces must be divided by the date of partition. Since this would coincide with the transfer of power, Lord Mountbatten's condition that he would not acquiesce in such a weakening of the Forces while he was responsible for law and order was fulfilled; for after the transfer he would no longer be responsible. The acceptance of transfer of power on a Dominion-Status basis meant that British officers could remain, and nationalisation could be held up until after separation was completed. Moreover, it was the Viceroy's confident belief, at that stage, both that there must be an overall Indo-Pakistan defence authority—which emerged as the Joint Defence Council with limited functions—and that both Dominions would have the same Governor-General, who although strictly as powerless as a constitutional monarch could use his personal authority and his experience of military affairs, of which the Indian politicians were for the most part totally ignorant, to steer them away from conflicts and towards a common defence policy and inter-relationship of their Armed Forces. Such expectations were not in fact fulfilled, but in the light of them the risks of partitioning the forces seemed more acceptable at the time than they appear in retrospect.

The question remains whether the dangers of simultaneous partition of the Armed Forces should not have caused a delay in the transfer of power. Again, one must beware of making historical judgments with too much hindsight. The mass conflicts and migrations of August and September 1947 were foreseen by no one—neither by the Viceroy and Commander-in-Chief, nor by the Indian political leaders, nor by the Governor of the province chiefly concerned, the Punjab, who repeatedly warned the Viceroy of the need for strong military forces to quell rioting if partition were imposed by force but discounted those dangers considerably if it were partition agreed on by the parties and leaders. The Punjab Boundary Force was regarded as an adequate answer to the immediate danger.[1]

Lord Ismay, a devoted friend and former officer of the Indian Army, believed that the risk of trouble in the Army itself was perhaps the first reason for hurrying the transfer of power. At the back of his mind, he told the author not long before his death, was

[1] See below, p. 343.

'the awful thought of what might happen if the Army went wrong'. The men, he said, were hearing terrible things of what was happening to their women and children, and in their villages. 'While I would have backed their loyalty with my own life, I would not have risked the safety of my country on their continued loyalty to command at that time. We had lost the power to punish or reward, and it was quite time for us to go.' The man he blamed was Mr. Jinnah, for insisting on communal partition.

The loyalty of the Indian soldier [he said] is to the Regiment. The Regiment means everything to them. It was impossible to take two squadrons from a regiment and put in some other two squadrons, call it by the old name and number, and expect it to be the same. If regiments were to be divided into Hindus or Sikhs or Muslims, every regiment had to have a surgical operation. I said to Jinnah: 'Why not divide for the present on numerical lines—say two-thirds to India and one-third to Pakistan—and sort it out later, after perhaps a year?'[1] Your new States will need reliable institutions, especially the Army, and the Army will stand steady.' All he said was: 'Lord Ismay, we are very grateful to you for coming out to India to try to help us, but you know nothing about Hindus and you know nothing about Muslims.'

So the inevitable had to be. On 11th June Field Marshal Auchinleck put up proposals for an Armed Forces Reconstitution Committee. He himself chose and championed the word 'reconstitution' rather than 'division' or 'partition' as doing less psychological violence to the idea of solidarity implicit in any worth-while military force, let alone the historic Indian Army. On 16th June Lord Mountbatten told his staff that, in a number of talks which he had had with the Commander-in-Chief the previous weekend, the latter now appeared satisfied that the division of the Armed Forces could be carried out without vitally affecting their efficiency, provided that there was goodwill and trust, and that political pressure was not applied to hurry the process unduly. Notwith-

[1] In the course of his discussions with Ministers in London in late May 1947 Lord Mountbatten said at one stage that the division of the Armed Forces, which was involved in his new plan, would have to be made on a territorial, not a communal basis, but this idea was evidently soon abandoned.

standing the provisos, neither of which was fulfilled in the event, this was a great change from the almost passionate hostility with which Field Marshal Auchinleck had first met the idea of partitioning the Indian Army. It is a tribute, therefore, both to his adaptability to shifting political circumstances and to his loyalty to the Viceroy whose ever-hastening leadership he accepted.

It was at this staff meeting that Mr. V. P. Menon suggested bringing in Sir Chandulal Trivedi to help with the task of reconstitution. Trivedi, then Governor of Orissa, was one of the outstanding Indian members of the I.C.S., known for his toughness.[1] He had been Secretary of the War Department of the Government of India until 1946 and therefore probably knew more about military administration in India than any other Indian, and had worked closely with the Commander-in-Chief. Besides, while a Hindu having good relations with some of the Congress leaders, he was a long-standing friend of Mr. Liaqat Ali Khan. Thus he had the confidence of all three interests. This was indispensable; for the Congress leaders greatly disturbed the military, Mr. Jinnah was deeply suspicious of Field Marshal Auchinleck, and the Hindu and Muslim politicians were hardly on speaking terms. It was largely thanks to Sir Chandulal that on 30th June the Partition Council, with scarcely a murmur, adopted the proposals for reconstitution.

The principles of the operation were, first, that by 15th August India and Pakistan should each have, within their territories, effective forces, predominantly of non-Muslim and Muslim personnel respectively, under their own operational control, thereafter to be reconstituted on a permanent basis as soon as possible; secondly, that each prospective Dominion should select its three Commanders-in-Chief of Army, Navy and Air Force, to be directly responsible to the new Governments and having executive control of all forces in their territories after 15th August; thirdly, the Armed Forces should remain under the administrative (but not operational) control of the existing Commander-in-Chief until they had been finally reconstituted as distinct forces and their Governments were in a position to administer them: Field Marshal Auchinleck, in this role, would become after 15th August 'Supreme

[1] Under independence he became Governor of East Punjab, of Andhra, and of Andhra Pradesh, and Deputy Chairman of the Indian Planning Commission.

Commander', answerable to a Joint Defence Council comprising, besides himself, the Governors-General of the two Dominions and their Defence Ministers. He would have no responsibility for law and order, nor operational control over any units save those in transit from one Dominion to the other.

Within these principles, the Armed Forces Reconstitution Committee worked out the detailed plan. The first stage in reconstitution would be to move all Muslim-majority units from prospective Indian to prospective Pakistani territory, and *vice versa*, shedding if possible their minority components as they went. The next stage would be voluntary transfer of individual officers and men to the Dominion of their choice—though a Pakistan-domiciled Muslim would not be allowed to choose India, nor an India-domiciled Hindu or Sikh be allowed to choose Pakistan. The target date for the completion of reconstitution was 1st April 1948, by which time it was hoped that each Dominion would have set up its own administrative services and that central administration could be dispensed with.

In comparing these plans with what actually transpired one must recall that at the time the leaders of both main communities and parties and the British rulers and their advisers were expecting a very different relationship between the two successor Dominions from that which eventuated. They foresaw a hurried scramble to separate all that had to be separated by 15th August, a rough-and-ready job which would be trimmed up later; then a period of reflection, perhaps of reaction towards Indo-Pakistani co-operation, during which details could be put right and more stable arrangements made, while the British could still exercise, if requested, a benevolent chairmanship. If this expectation had been fulfilled, the subsequent history of India and Pakistan would have been very different.

16

Disorder in the vexed areas

1 *A joint appeal for peace*

'The whole country,' wrote Lord Mountbatten in a letter to London a week after his arrival in India, 'is in a most unsettled state. There are communal troubles in the Punjab, N.W.F.P., Bihar, Calcutta, Bombay, U.P., and even here in Delhi.' The same story continued week after week. On 17th April he reported to the Secretary of State:

> In the Punjab the Gurgaon area [near Delhi, where there had been a serious disturbance] is quieter, but there have been riots in Amritsar which have necessitated a 24-hour curfew. In the N.W.F.P., rioting, looting, and arson have been reported from Dera Ismail Khan. Half the city is in flames and there is severe communal fighting . . . the tension both in the Punjab and the N.W.F.P. is still very high. . . . In Bengal, there were more incidents in Calcutta on Sunday 13th April. In Bombay a curfew at night has been imposed, and similarly at Benares. . . .[1]

The places varied but the story did not change. As in a tinder-dry forest, fires would break out suddenly here and there, lit by a spark from the embers of earlier conflagrations and fanned by the hot wind of communal fear and hatred.

Convinced as he and all his advisers were that the only step which was likely to quieten communal strife was an early decision on how power was to be transferred, the Viceroy nevertheless believed that tension might be reduced if the leaders of the two main parties or communities were to make a joint appeal for peace. He first asked Mr. Jinnah, on 8th April, if he would sign a joint statement with the Congress renouncing the use of force for political ends. According to Lord Mountbatten's record, Mr. Jinnah tried to evade a firm answer by recalling at length his

[1] *Viceroy's Personal Report* No. 3, 17th April 1947.

speeches deploring violence. When he had finished, Lord Mountbatten said: 'Of course if you would find it embarrassing to renounce the use of force, please consider the matter closed.' There was an awkward pause before Mr. Jinnah replied: 'I should be proud to give a lead in this matter and am grateful to you for giving me this opportunity.'

The next time he came to see the Viceroy he was given a copy of the draft statement to study. As he left he asked Lord Ismay: 'Who will sign for Congress. Gandhi or Kripalani?' Lord Ismay supposed that this would have to be settled by Congress themselves. The following day Mr. Jinnah agreed to sign if Mr. Gandhi would also sign. The Viceroy put the draft to the Mahatma, who after amending the wording slightly put his signature to it there and then. Sir Eric Miéville took the document round to Mr. Jinnah, telling him that Mr. Kripalani, as President of Congress, would sign after him. Mr. Jinnah thereupon refused to sign, saying he would not put his name on the same piece of paper as an unknown nobody like Kripalani. Pandit Nehru was consulted and was furious. Mr. Gandhi passed the ball back to the Viceroy and Pandit Nehru. The latter wrote a two-page letter of protest, but finally left the decision to Lord Mountbatten, who on 15th April issued the statement over two signatures only, those of Mr. Gandhi and Mr. Jinnah. It read:

We deeply deplore the recent acts of lawlessness and violence that have brought the utmost disgrace on the fair name of India and the greater misery to innocent people, irrespective of who were the aggressors and who were the victims.

We denounce for all time the use of force to achieve political ends, and we call upon all the communities of India, to whatever persuasion they may belong, not only to refrain from all acts of violence and disorder, but also to avoid, both in speech and writing, any incitement to such acts.

The incident is related here at length, as it was by Lord Mountbatten at the time, 'to give an idea of the fantastic difficulties with which the simplest negotiations were hedged'. A matter of great public urgency on which in principle everyone concerned was agreed took a week to conclude. Pride, jealousy and suspicion crowded out statesmanship and calm consideration.

The statement was favourably received by the Press in India, though it was often accompanied or followed by provocative articles, and it seems to have had some effect in cooling tempers for a while, at least at the more sophisticated levels. But it was a superficial ointment which eased the inflammation without healing the ulcers. Moreover there was an inherent contradiction over the place of force in the Indian complex. India was passing through two great revolutions at once: the revolution of national liberation, undoing 150 years of British rule, and the revolution of Hindu-Muslim separation, undoing a millennium of Islamic conquest and Hindu reaction. No great revolution is ever accomplished without force and suffering—force often ill applied, and suffering often of the most innocent victims. The first of those two revolutions was almost complete, and violence against the British raj was no longer either needed or used, but who will say that the revolution would have been accomplished at that time but for the actual use of force in past decades, including non-violent force which could easily turn to violence, and but for its potential use in the future if the British had clung to their waning power? And who will say that without force the second revolution would have been accomplished either as it was in 1947 or, if the constitutional settlement had been other, in some subsequent upheaval? Independence and partition were alike the creatures of force. Political debate and soft persuasion alone would have achieved neither, certainly not so swiftly. It was only when violent reaction had been enough to make the outcome inevitable that the use of force could be sincerely and credibly renounced, and by then it was too late to tame the demons that had been liberated by the opening of Pandora's Box.

2 *The situation in the Punjab*

The Punjab was the key to the issue of partition, and thus to the constitutional fate of India, for it reproduced within itself an almost exact likeness of the communal situation in the whole country, though in reverse, and both the larger and the smaller issues were bound to be settled in the same broad way. In Lord Mountbatten's debates with Mr. Jinnah and other leaders of the Muslim League, the dilemma was simplified thus: 'Every argument for dividing India is an argument for dividing the Punjab, and every argument for keeping the Punjab united is an argument for retaining the unity of India'—arguments either from rational justice or from the harsh facts of communal conflict. But in terms of might-have-beens the inter-relationship was a little more subtle. If the Muslim League wanted a Pakistan of the five provinces, they would have to reconcile the Sikhs and Hindus of the Punjab to Muslim-majority rule in provincial matters, which is to say all those matters that most closely concern the ordinary citizen; and this was never to be hoped for unless they themselves could be reconciled to Hindu-majority rule in remoter matters, such as would form the minimum function of an all-India Centre. Nor could the Muslims hope for an entire five-province Pakistan without attracting some support from the Punjabi Sikhs and Hindus by attitudes and undertakings that were contrary to a demand for a specifically, militantly Muslim State. It was the attempt to square this circle which eventually brought down the Muslim leadership of the Punjab Unionists, and yielded the day to the extremists for Pakistan—Mr. Jinnah, from Bombay, and Mr. Liaqat Ali Khan, from the United Provinces—and to the inevitable conclusion of a 'moth-eaten Pakistan' and a divided Punjab. The scale of the communal slaughter and the mass migrations that followed were unforeseen, the latter by anybody, the former, it would seem, by most of those in high places, though fair warning was given by the Governor of the Punjab. In becoming the heart of a sovereign, anti-Hindu Pakistan, the Punjab became also its most suffering victim.

At the Provincial elections of 1936 the Muslim League had little success in the Punjab. The great majority of Muslim seats went to supporters of the Unionist Party, a three-community group, founded by Sir Fazl-i-Husain in the 1920s as a genuine attempt at intercommunal co-operation and representing mainly rural interests against the urban and commercial classes from which the Congress drew its principal strength in the province. A powerful Unionist Government was formed under Sir Sikander Hyat Khan, having no need of League support. As an essentially Punjabi organism, welding Muslims, Hindus and Sikhs under Muslim leadership on a provincial economic basis, the Unionist Party was inherently inimical to the League, an all-India communal body representing minority aspirations. Yet within a year Sir Sikander had taken all his Muslim Unionist members into the Muslim League.

So fateful a decision needs some probing. It can be explained as a piece of tactical trimming by Sir Sikander. The reaction to Congress Government in the Hindu-majority provinces, especially to the refusal to bring Muslim League men into the Ministries save on terms of submission to the Congress, followed by the Congress campaign to enlist the Muslim masses, had inflamed Muslim sentiment throughout India and given great impetus to Mr. Jinnah's leadership. Sir Sikander doubtless calculated that if he did not bring his followers to the League they would defect to it, leaving him isolated, as his successor in office eventually became. If so, by a tactical manoeuvre, to secure his immediate party future, he brought strategic reverse. For his accession with his Punjabi followers immediately made Mr. Jinnah the undisputed leader of the Indian Muslims, and himself the prisoner of one whom he might otherwise have confronted on level terms. Sir Sikander's motive may have been more far-seeing. Possibly he discerned, even then, that a struggle would be coming within the Muslim camp between radical and conservative ideas of the community's future, and that if it was conducted between an all-India League and provincial fragments, however well established, the radical, nationalist view, which was not his, would be likely to win. Could he not do better as a minority or alternative leader within the League than as a non-co-operator outside it? This interpretation, though the less probable, is given some credence by a later event, Sir Sikander's outward acceptance of the goal of Pakistan when the League had voted for it at Lahore in 1940, despite the fact that inwardly he was fundamentally opposed to it. Pakistan was then only an idea, perhaps only a shibboleth. To challenge it at that stage might well seem bound to force the League leadership into a deeper commitment to it, or himself into isolation, whereas if realities were given time to assert themselves it might wither or be amended in a moderate sense. And so it conceivably might, but events beyond Sir Sikander's reckoning took charge.

At first, developments leaned his way. Not without some British diplomacy, the Sikhs drew back from a threatened radicalism of their own, at once anti-British and anti-Muslim, and co-operated with the war effort and the Sikander regime. Pakistan remained a vague aspiration, and Sir Sikander continued to advocate his own version, which had much in common with the eventual Cabinet

Mission plan of 1946.[1] But in December 1942 Sir Sikander suddenly died, aged fifty, in the full flight of power.

His successor, Sir Khizar Hyat Khan Tiwana, who shared many of his views and was even more resolutely opposed to Pakistan in its full sense, took a different course. When he openly opposed Mr. Jinnah, and refused to interpret his membership of the League as allowing it to dictate to him and his followers in the Punjab, Mr. Jinnah reacted with equal vigour, both within the League, from which Sir Khizar was expelled in 1944, and in fomenting revolt among the Muslims of the Punjab. The Quit India movement of 1942 and the consequent elimination of the Congress from the active political scene had immensely strengthened Mr. Jinnah's position. Sir Khizar could hold together neither his party nor his voters. In the elections of December 1945, the Muslim Unionists were reduced to a rump of half a dozen, after several had joined the League band-wagon when the results were known. The League held 79 of the 86 Muslim seats. Nine short of an absolute majority, it needed a coalition only with one group in order to govern. But the logic of its own position prevented this. Its support for Pakistan precluded its allying with the specifically Hindu or Sikh groups, and its insistence (reflecting Mr. Jinnah's iron rule at the Centre) that the League alone could speak for Muslims precluded a working alliance either with the Congress or with the remaining few non-League Mussulmans. Eventually Sir Khizar formed a Coalition Ministry supported by Congress, Akali Sikhs and his own Muslim rump of the Unionist Party.

It was an extraordinary outcome which may well have sealed the death-warrant of that united Punjab which the Coalition purported to stand for. It threw the provincial Muslim League into frustrated and negative opposition which in the circumstances only became more and more violent in word and deed, with equal and opposite reactions among the other communities. It was a trump card in propaganda for Pakistan among the Muslims, who could say: 'Even in the Punjab, even with a Muslim majority, the wily Hindus will be able to rule you, with the connivance of Sikhs and businessmen and a few Muslim stooges: the only way out is independence for your homelands.' And it politically destroyed the remant of the Unionists, who became prisoners of the cage they themselves had constructed. What would have happened if they had held out is

[1] See p. 82 above.

a moot question. No majority Government would have been possible and the Governor would have had to impose direct rule under Section 93. Under its shelter, and particularly with the lure of office to tempt the irresolute, the provincial Muslim League might possibly have divided, some going for Pakistan and the wilderness meanwhile, others for an immediate chance of power on condition of their rejecting a carve-up of the Punjab. Alternatively, and perhaps more likely, the League might have absorbed the Muslim Unionist rump, and then have had to court some marginal Hindu support in order to secure a majority. Some observers believe that in such ways the forces of unity might have sufficiently revived to prevent partition of the province. Others held that the divisive forces were already too strong and that these political incidents had little effect on the ultimate outcome.

Inherently incapable of strong government, the Khizar Coalition Ministry seemed to go out of its way to advertise its weakness. A sequence of orders and counter-orders at the end of January 1947, concerning quasi-military auxiliaries of the Hindu and Muslim parties, and bans on meetings and processions, left it humiliated and impotent. On 3rd March Sir Khizar resigned and the Governor (Sir Evan Jenkins, who had replaced Sir Bertrand Glancy in April 1946), after going through the procedure of inviting the Nawab of Mamdot, as leader of the Muslim League, to form a Government, went into Section 93. A crisis which called for the strongest popular leadership found this key province of India without a democratic government at all.

Not only politically was the Punjab hopelessly and progressively divided. In the background of these political manoeuvres, deep communal emotions were being stirred. The end of the Khizar Ministry and the bombast of the striving political leaders touched off a train of violence which was not to end until scores of thousands had been slain. In Lahore and Amritsar mobs murdered, pillaged and burnt the people and homes of rival communities. The police, mainly Muslim, were under strength, and many Hindus fled, leaving their homes and property to destruction. In the rural Rawalpindi district, the small Sikh and Hindu minority suffered worse than anywhere else, over two thousand people being killed, most of them non-Muslim, and misery and terror being spread among those communities in wide areas of the northern Punjab. A complete breakdown of law and order was saved only by the intervention of the military. But troops cannot do the work of police or of government, and both, as forces against communalism, had been weakened in morale by this time. Though the flames of March 1947 were subdued, the embers glowed ominously, and to all who could read the signs another fierce conflagration appeared to need only a stray spark or a puff of wind. Sporadic outbreaks of violence continued both in cities and the countryside. It was estimated that casualties from the beginning of March to the beginning of August included 5,000 dead and 3,000 seriously injured, most of them in March.[1] How much blame should be laid on deliberate agitation, how much on inflammatory national politics, on administrative weakness, or on communal bias in the police or other services, can only be a matter of judgment; all these, in some measure, undoubtedly contributed to the evil.

The last breath of inter-communal politics in the Punjab had expired with the demise of the Khizar Government. When Sir Evan Jenkins talked with the Viceroy on 14th April during the Governors' Conference he reported that Sir Khizar had offered, in order to save all the turmoil of elections (which in the Governor's opinion would give the Muslim League a small overall majority), to lead his Unionist Muslims into the League and so enable them to form a Government. Lord Mountbatten and Sir Evan agreed that a communal Government would only make matters worse, and that Section 93 administration must continue.

'If,' said the Governor, 'partition of the province were imposed, four divisions of troops would be needed to prevent a civil war.' Lord Mountbatten replied that he had no intention of forcing partition; his policy was to get the parties to agree on what the partition was to be. If he succeeded in this, said Sir Evan Jenkins, and if the political leaders came down into the country and made it clear that the parties were agreed, additional troops would be much less necessary. His main pre-occupation was to get such troops as were allotted placed on a war footing, as without adequate transport and other resources for action they could not do very much. The up-shot appears in the story of the Punjab Boundary Force.

---

[1] The 'communal war of succession' in the Punjab is described more fully below, pp. 337–46.

3 The situation in Bengal

In the constitutional problems of 1947, Bengal played a peculiar part, though less dramatic or hectic than those of the Punjab and the North-West Frontier Province. Although the Bengal Presidency had a majority of Muslims, this had been whittled by the Communal Award to a minority of 119 seats out of 250 in the Legislative Assembly, against 80 'general' seats, the remainder being reserved for Anglo-Indians (4), Indian Christians (2), Europeans (11), and representatives (34) of various interests—industry and commerce, landholders, universities and labour—the majority of whom were Hindus. The balance of power was thus held by the smaller minorities. (It will be recalled that the potentially critical effect of the European vote for the Constituent Assembly caused a minor crisis in the Cabinet Mission's negotiations until the Bengal Europeans agreed to forgo it.) In the general elections of January 1946 the Muslim League won 113 seats and the Congress 87. Mr. H. S. Suhrawardy, the leader of the League Party, tried but failed to form a coalition with the Congress, and his Ministry held office with the support of independent groups. This ministry, which was in power at the time of the 'great Calcutta killing', remained until partition.

The political balance in Bengal was thus such as to suggest inter-communal compromise rather than a straight majority-minority conflict, as in the Punjab. There were more profound reasons pointing to unity rather than division of Bengal. The Presidency had been partitioned before, in Lord Curzon's Viceroyalty, to establish a Muslim-dominated province with its capital at Dacca, and the partition had been undone in 1911, largely as the result of intense and partly terrorist Hindu agitation, based both on interest and perhaps still more on an extremely powerful sentiment for Bengal as a single motherland. For this there were strong historical and cultural claims. One language was spoken and written by all the Indian communities (again unlike the contrast of Urdu, Pushtu, Punjabi and Hindi in the north-west), and the mass of the Mussulmans had sprung from native Bengali stock converted to Islam long ago by the Muslim conquerors but retaining an essentially Bengali culture. These historical forces would have seemed to tend towards making the Hindus favour unity and the Muslims lean to partition. But there were two contrary forces which greatly qualified and almost reversed the balance of interest and sentiment.

The immensely heightened communal tension throughout India overwhelmed other loyalties. On the eve of Direct Action Day, 16th August 1946, the signal for the terrible communal slaughter in Calcutta, Mr. Suhrawardy had declared that if the Congress were put into power at the Centre the result would be 'the declaration of complete independence by Bengal and the setting up of a parallel government'. It is obvious that he was assuming a Bengal controlled by its Muslim majority, as indeed he had reason to assume if the Europeans were neutralised. The Bengali Muslims wanted a united Bengal if they could control it, the Bengali Hindus wanted it only on the opposite hypothesis. There was another reason against renewal of the bygone Muslim favour for partition. The key to the trade and prosperity of the province was the city of Calcutta. Without Calcutta, East Bengal was a poor land, lacking ports, communications and industry. But Calcutta was predominantly Hindu in population, and a settlement on communal-majority lines would give it lock and stock to Hindu West Bengal. Calcutta was rich bait on provincial unity for the Bengali Muslims —worth, to many of them, more than the dubious attractions of Pakistan—whereas for the Hindus unity meant the subjection not only of the province as a whole but specifically of Calcutta to Muslim supremacy.

It has already been recorded[1] how Mr. Suhrawardy, Bengal's Chief Minister, told the Viceroy that given enough time he could persuade Bengal to remain united, outside Pakistan; how Mr. Jinnah at once approved of this with the words 'What is the use of Bengal without Calcutta?'; how the leader of the provincial Opposition, Mr. Kiran Shankar Roy, said that if the Muslims would concede joint electorates (which would give the Hindus a good chance of getting political control), as Mr. Suhrawardy had offered, 'you can practically count on unity'. The Governor of Bengal, Sir Frederick Burrows, also pressed this policy upon his Chief Minister. Sir Frederick had been in favour of placing Calcutta under joint Hindu-Muslim control, but he withdrew the idea as inconsistent with the general settlement which the Viceroy had in mind.

Nothing came of these moves. The offer of joint electorates was

[1] See p. 246. See p. 246.

never publicly confirmed. The original plan for the transfer of power included an option for Bengal to decide on independence as a unit, but this was one of the provisions which Pandit Nehru attacked as leading to the Balkanisation of India, and when Lord Mountbatten, on returning from Simla to Delhi with the revised draft plan in his pocket, saw Mr. Suhrawardy and his Revenue Minister, Mr. Fazlur Rahman, he told them that the latest proposal would merely give certain provinces or parts of provinces the option of voting for Hindustan or Pakistan, without the alternative of independence.

The Viceroy added, however, that if the Bengal Legislative Assembly were to pass a resolution asking for independence he would certainly consider it in the light of the Governor's recommendations. Mr. Suhrawardy had reported that since their previous discussion he had been conferring with Mr. Kiran Shankar Roy about keeping Bengal united, and had brought in Mr. Sarat Chandra Bose, the Socialist leader (brother of Subhas, commander of the 'Indian National Army'). They had made good progress and on the whole he was hopeful. There had been talk of declaring Bengal a Socialist Republic, on which point the Viceroy emphasised the complications of Commonwealth membership. He also warned Mr. Suhrawardy that Pandit Nehru was not in favour of an independent Bengal unless it were closely linked with India after partition, feeling, as he did, that the exigencies of partition would anyhow cause East Bengal to return to India in a few years' time. Nevertheless Lord Mountbatten promised that if an agreement were reached on a Hindu-Muslim coalition Ministry in Bengal he would do his utmost to get the national leaders, with Mr. Gandhi's help, to accept this and to agree that the final announcement should contain no reference to the partition of Bengal.

The first thing, therefore, that Lord Mountbatten did on his return from London was to send privately for Mr. Suhrawardy, to learn how things were going in Bengal. He was distressed to learn that Mr. Roy had been unable to persuade the Congress leaders to allow Bengal to vote for independence. Mr. Suhrawardy pleaded that Calcutta should be designated a free city during the period of partition, since he felt that communal tension would meanwhile be relaxed, and that with reviving confidence the Congress might eventually concur in perpetuating the arrange-

Above Devastation in the 'communal war of succession': Lord and Lady Mountbatten, with Sir Evan Jenkins (hand in pocket), Governor of the Punjab, in a stricken Punjab town, June 1947.

Below The birth of Pakistan: Mr. M. A. Jinnah, Governor-General-designate, with Lord Mountbatten, followed by Miss Jinnah and Lady Mountbatten, Karachi, 14th August, 1947.

Lord Mountbatten leaves India, 21st June 1948: last handshakes
with Pandit Nehru and Mr. C. Rajagopalachari, his successor as
Governor-General.

ment. Otherwise he feared serious riots and damage in the city. Lord Mountbatten sent Mr. V. P. Menon to see Sardar Patel and seek his agreement to six months' joint control of Calcutta. The Home Member's reply was decisive: 'Not even for six hours!'

The plan of 3rd June, which made no exceptional provision for Bengal, beyond the mechanism for deciding there and in the Punjab by sections of the provincial legislatures whether or not to partition the province, was accepted without demur. On 20th June the members of the Bengal Legislative Assembly met together and voted by 126 to 90 that if Bengal remained united it should join Pakistan. The representatives of the western, Hindu-majority part then voted to 58 to 21 that the province should be partitioned: the voting of the eastern representatives against partition was consequently null. Thus in the end it was the Hindus and the Congress who decided upon the partition of Bengal, which their forebears had so bitterly opposed.

4 The situation on the North-West Frontier

In the elections of December 1945 the Congress party won 30 out of 50 seats in the North-West Frontier Province Legislative Assembly. It was their only substantial success in Muslim India— and even there it was boosted by the weightage given to the Hindu minority, who though only 6 per cent of the population were allotted 24 per cent of the seats. Of the 38 Muslim seats, however, the Muslim League won only 17, two being held by independents and the remainder by Congress Muslims. One non-Muslim seat went to an Akali Sikh. A Congress Ministry was formed under Dr. Khan Sahib, brother of Khan Abdul Ghaffar Khan, often dubbed Badshah Khan. The predominance of the Congress in this overwhelmingly Muslim province, right up to 1947, was a cause of wonderment to outside observers. Its origins go back to the Khilafat movement of 1919, when Mr. Gandhi urged the Hindus to make common cause with the Muslims in a united mass campaign to restore the Ottoman Caliphate, uprooted by the Treaty of Sèvres, and to win self-government for India. The Congress thus became an ally of the Khilafat Committee, whose greatest strength was in the north-west. It was at this time that the Khan brothers, for a generation the outstanding political leaders of the Frontier Province, began their long career in Indian politics.

In the 1930s they harnessed the martial spirit of the Frontiersmen by forming a semi-military organisation, the Khudai Khitmatgars, commonly known as the Red Shirts, who as a shock brigade of every non-co-operation movement were a bogy to successive Governments.

Basically more important, however, was the character of the Frontier Mussulman. Independent and proud, with the attitude of the hillsman towards the man of the plains, and of the erstwhile conqueror towards the formerly conquered, he fundamentally despised the Hindu and never contemplated subjection to him. To the Frontier Muslim, home rule for India meant home rule for himself and his ancient form of tribal democracy, not submission to an all-India majority. He made allies with those having the greatest apparent power to unseat his present rulers, the British, that is to say with the Congress, not because he loved the Hindus better than the British but because he wanted to be ruled by nobody. He had few affiliations with the Muslims of the Hindu-majority provinces or Bengal, and saw little attraction in the weak and fragmentary Muslim League of the 1930s, or in the ruling oligarchy of the Punjab, his nearest neighbours. As soon as he perceived the real prospect of becoming subordinate to Hindu raj in an independent India, his allegiance began to shift. By 1947 it was evident that much of the popular support among Muslims for the Congress Ministry in the N.W.F.P. was ebbing away.

It might have ebbed faster if the provincial Muslim League had thrown up any leaders of stature. Dr. Khan Sahib stood head and shoulders above the rest of the Frontier politicians, in and out of Congress, though he had many faults, including an inhospitality rare on the Frontier, and committed many mistakes in office, which would in the end have had their own retribution, regardless of divisions on the larger scene. Sir Olaf Caroe, Governor of the N.W.F.P., described him to Lord Wavell as 'the most impressive Indian I have ever met'. He and his brother had close personal as well as political links with the all-India Congress leaders, especially Mr. Gandhi and Pandit Nehru, who believed them to be all-powerful in the Frontier Province. Maulana Abul Kalam Azad was better informed. Of the situation in 1946 he wrote, much later:

The Khan brothers were certainly right in claiming that a large section of the people in the Frontier supported them. They had, however, exaggerated the extent of their influence. This was natural, for one invariably over-estimates one's strength. Perhaps they also wished to impress on us that while there were differences in other provinces, the Frontier was solidly with Congress. In fact, however, there was quite a powerful group against the Khan brothers.

Accordingly, he strongly advised Pandit Nehru against the latter's sudden intention to pay a personal visit to the Frontier in October 1946 as 'Foreign Minister' in the Interim Government: Nehru said he must meet the tribesmen for whose relations with India he was responsible, and see for himself whether it was true, as he was constantly told, that opposition in the province was being worked up only by the machinations of anti-Congress British officials. Azad thought the risk of such a visit too great—both the risk to Nehru's life and limb, and the risk, which as a Muslim he the better appreciated, of rallying the opposition by giving them a focus for attack. In this Mr. Gandhi agreed with the Maulana. The Governor himself, Sir Olaf Caroe, went down from Peshawar to Delhi to dissuade Pandit Nehru on the same grounds. Such a visit, he urged, would not strengthen the Frontier Congress Ministry but weaken it, for the banners of Islam against the Hindu would be unfurled; if Nehru wanted a united India he should play a waiting game with the Frontier Muslims.[1] Sir Olaf added another reason of all-India import, that so politically-loaded an expedition, on the eve of the formation of a Coalition Government at the Centre, would be very ill-timed, and should, if it were nevertheless undertaken, be on all-party lines.

To all these arguments Pandit Nehru turned a deaf ear, and with that mixture of impulsiveness and obstinacy which marred his leadership on so many occasions he embarked on his Frontier tour in the company of Khan Abdul Ghaffar Khan. It came close to disaster. As the Governor had foretold, the Muslim League seized the opportunity given them to intensify their propaganda, especially among the tribesmen. One of their leaders, the Mullah

---

[1] In the Governor's mind, though not on his lips, was the story of Akbar's favourite, Raja Birbal, whom the Emperor sent in charge of a column into tribal territory in 1586: this Hindu courtier and intellectual was a red rag to the hardy, warlike Pathans, and was slain on his retreat through the passes with 8,000 of the Emperor's troops.

of Manki, was sent on a tour of tribal territory, so timed as just to precede Pandit Nehru's visit. When the latter arrived at Peshawar airport he was greeted by a large and hostile League demonstration, and had to be slipped out by a back way. Abdul Ghaffar Khan and other Congress zealots accused the Political Department of having staged this demonstration, but few believed a charge ascribing so much popular power to a few officers. In Waziristan the next day Nehru had an extremely hostile reception by the tribal leaders. Abdul Ghaffar Khan struck a provocatively wrong note with these fierce Pathans by declaring that they had all been slaves and were now going to be free. Nehru did not help matters by losing his temper, which the Maliks contrasted with his proclamation of a regime of love. They told him bluntly that they regarded Hindus as *hamsayas,* their tenants or serfs, while he called them, as recipients of Government allowances, pitiful pensioners, an insult which filled them with foreboding.

In the north of the Province the reception was even worse. The Afridis had refused to meet him, indeed to have any dealings with the Congress or the League. The Political Agent, Sahibzada Khurshid,[1] spent a dangerous day breaking up large gatherings of tribesmen at Jamrud. On their way back from the Afghan frontier, near Landi Kotal, Pandit Nehru's party were subjected to stone-throwing, and the situation was saved only by the gallantry of the Political Agent in advancing into the midst of the mêlée, and by an order to the Khyber Rifles to open fire. In the Malakand area there was more stone-throwing, Pandit Nehru and the Khan brothers being all slightly injured, and again fire had to be opened. The Deputy Commissioner, Mr. Curtis, finding the road through Mardan and Nowshera blocked by dangerous crowds, with great difficulty persuaded the party, whose courage to the point of bravado did not flag, to return by a cross-country route. At Abdul Ghaffar Khan's home near Charsadda they were greeted enthusiastically by an organised demonstration of Red Shirts, and so the tour ended. On the last evening, at Sir Olaf Caroe's invitation, Pandit Nehru came to see him: the Governor reported on their conversation thus:

He had not been badly hurt, having bruises on the ear and the chin. He made no direct charge that Political Agents had been

[1] Later Governor of the North-West Frontier Province, after independence.

behind the demonstrations, but he accused our Indian subordinates of this kind of machination. He also charged the Political Agents in the Khyber and the Malakand (both happen to be Indians), and I gathered the Deputy Commissioners of Peshawar and Mardan also, with inefficiency in having been unable to prevent the demonstrations. I told him that I resented attacks on officers who had been subjected to immense strain by his untimely tour and had been doing all that was humanly possible against an outburst of feeling to secure his safety. I said, too, that if he believed that our Indian subordinates were powerful enough to organise opposition of this nature he would believe anything. On more general questions I said that, as I had told him, a party approach to the tribal problem was bound to fail, and could not have been timed worse than was his approach. . . . If he meant to take with him party politicians, he should have attempted to induce men from all parties to go with him. His answer to this was a tirade against the League, and an assertion that it was not his wont to desert his old friends, of whom Abdul Ghaffar Khan was the chief. He also said that he was coming again as soon as he could, and then gave me a lecture on 'the authoritarian habits of the I.C.S.'. I told him that in my experience both the Indian political parties were far more authoritarian than any I.C.S. officer had ever been, and quoted, in reponse to a demand for instances, the tendencies towards one-party rule, and when in power to override the law. . . . I said it seemed to me that this tour had put out of court for a very long time any hope of bringing in the tribes into the new India peacefully and free from party lines, and that his visit had done more to strengthen communalism and the party approach on this Frontier than anything else could possibly have done. Incidentally one result is likely to be the weakening of my Ministry's position. Finally I asked him why at critical junctures he always set out on his own with preconceived and published ideas and without hearing the other side, making it hard for him to adjust his attitude later. He said he felt himself unable to comment on his own proceedings, but one thing he must impress on me, and that was that there must be a complete change in the method of Frontier control, and what he termed 'the romance of the frontier' must come to an end as soon as possible.

The Governor's considered judgment, long afterwards, was that this visit of Nehru's to the Frontier, more than anything else, made partition inevitable.

It may be doubted whether even Mr. Jinnah would not have shrunk from the prospect of a Pakistan based upon a Punjab torn between Muslims, Sikhs and Hindus, and having at its back a pro-Congress or at best divided Frontier Province, with the suspicious, opportunist tribes beyond. Both Congress and the League recognised the key importance of the Frontier to their policies, and during Lord Mountbatten's Viceroyalty it was the acutest of all bones of contention between them. The peace of the Frontier—always relative—was also of vital importance to a bloodless transfer of power in the sub-continent, and with so much explosive material, and such obvious opportunities for violence when the authorities were morally and physically weakened, it is a great tribute to those officers most concerned that the peace was on the whole maintained, and the Frontier Province was eventually incorporated in Pakistan by vote of its people without any frontier warfare or general collapse of law and order.

The only substantial change in the situation in the N.W.F.P. when Lord Mountbatten took over was that meanwhile Dr. Khan Sahib's Government had put large numbers of the Opposition in gaol. In the Governor's view it was essential that the true view of the electorate should be ascertained through fresh elections, the Province being meanwhile placed under Section 93 (Governor's rule). On the other hand, Pandit Nehru in his capacity as Minister responsible for tribal affairs was officially (though confidentially) accusing the Governor of anti-Congress partisanship and demanding his replacement. He was strongly opposed to fresh elections. The atmosphere had not been improved in the meantime by the levying of charges of misconduct against Sheikh Mahbub Ali, the Political Agent in Malakand, in failing to prevent the attack on Pandit Nehru and his party, nor by the finding of a High Court Judge completely exonerating that officer and tearing to shreds his accusers, especially Khan Abdul Ghaffar Khan, who had gone so far as to charge him and other officers, including by implication the Governor, with conspiring to murder Pandit Nehru. When, on 4th April 1947 Mr. Gandhi brought his old friend 'Badshah' Khan to see the Viceroy, the Khan denounced the Governor and all his officials, accusing him of being pro-League and hostile to Dr. Khan

Sahib's Government. (Sir Olaf Caroe's despatches in fact showed him wholly unbiased between the parties, though often critical of his Ministers for such misbehaviour as attempting to interfere with or override the processes of law.) The Viceroy had sent Lord Ismay on an exploratory mission to the Frontier, and the latter's report was considered at Lord Mountbatten's staff meeting on 2nd April. Referring to the pressure for removal of the Governor, Lord Mountbatten observed that on this particular issue, as in all others, it was necessary to face up to realities. The object, which must continually be borne in mind, was to hand over power in the most peaceful and dignified manner possible. To that end Pandit Nehru was indispensable. It had also to be realised that, unless the British members of the Services played their part to the last, there would be a loss of prestige and honour, therefore it was essential that there should be no victimisation of British officials. These two essentials were practically impossible to reconcile.

Lord Mountbatten next sought advice in a fashion which was at least unorthodox, and which he admitted he would have considered reprehensible in normal times. He sent for Lieutenant-Colonel de la Fargue, Chief Secretary to the North-West Frontier Government, who chanced to be in Delhi on his way to England on leave, and asked his confidential opinion, first of the situation in the Province and then of the Governor. Colonel de la Fargue held the beliefs that a free and clean election in the Province was more likely to return the Congress to power than the League, even if Section 93 government had been interposed; that the Governor, though having great knowledge of the Frontier, was biased against his Congress Government; and that his continuance in office was a menace to British prestige. Colonel de la Fargue was as wrong in his assessment of the electoral probabilities as he was disloyal in his strictures on his chief; if Lord Mountbatten had carried the method of personal intelligence further he would have learnt that the Chief Secretary was regarded as a man of little judgment and as being deeply involved with Dr. Khan Sahib and his faction. However, there is no evidence that his opinion weighed with the Viceroy in comparison with the assessment he was soon able to make for himself when he talked with Sir Olaf Caroe during the Governors' Conference, and when a little later he paid a memorable personal visit to the Frontier.

In the course of an hour's interview on 14th April, he told Sir

Olaf that it was only fair to warn him that the situation within the Interim Government might make his position impossible unless their attitude towards him changed. As long as Sir Olaf was Governor he could count on his full and unquestioned support, but later, he, the Viceroy, might have to discuss the situation with him. Sir Olaf asked straight out if Lord Mountbatten wanted him to resign, to which the latter replied: 'No, I don't want you to do anything until I have had time to go into the matter and I shall do nothing further without sending for you and discussing the question in a friendly and frank manner with you. I am sure we can reach a satisfactory solution, bearing in mind that my principal duty is to arrange for the peaceful and happy transfer of power to Indian hands, and that I cannot let anything or anybody stand in the way of this being achieved.' Soon afterwards, in a report to London, Lord Mountbatten wrote:

> I am convinced of Caroe's essential straightforwardness and desire to handle the very difficult situation on the Frontier in the most impartial and statesmanlike manner. But I think that at the moment he is suffering badly from nerves.[1] . . . I shall try to keep in touch with him and his Province in case the position gets worse. I do not envy him his job which I should say is the most difficult out here.[2]

During the Governors' Conference Lord Mountbatten called Pandit Nehru, Mr. Liaqat Ali Khan, Sardar Baldev Singh, Field Marshal Auchinleck and the Governor of the N.W.F.P. together and proposed that Sir Olaf be authorised to state, on his return to Peshawar, that after a recommendation about the transfer of power had been made to the British Government, and before the transfer had been effected, a general election would be held in the Province. To this procedure Pandit Nehru strongly objected, and no agreement could be reached, though Pandit Nehru did accept in prin-

[1] 'Nerves' is an ambiguous condition to diagnose or define. Certainly Sir Olaf was under great nervous strain, and may well have showed it; but equally certainly he never lost his head or succumbed to a *crise de nerfs*. After seeing him in Peshawar on 2nd April, Lord Ismay wrote in a private letter: 'The situation in both provinces' (Punjab and N.W.F.P.) 'is about as tricky as can be, and in the existing state of intense emotionalism it is very difficult to see what should be done. . . . Olaf Caroe himself looks terribly tired and strained. These Governors are lonely men. . . .'
[2] *Viceroy's Personal Report* No. 3, 17th April 1947.

ciple that it would be desirable to obtain the views of the people before a final decision was taken. The idea of a plebiscite, which eventually prevailed, can be traced to this occasion. Another meeting took place two days later between the Viceroy, Pandit Nehru, the Governor, who had been held back in Delhi, and Dr. Khan Sahib, who had been invited to fly down. Much time was wasted by Dr. Khan Sahib's charges of bias and interference against the Governor and the latter's rebuttal, but it was agreed that the Provincial Government, basing itself on the Gandhi-Jinnah appeal, should release all political prisoners not charged with violence, though processions and picketing would continue to be banned. The effect of this gesture was somewhat spoilt, in the event, by the refusal of most of the 5,000 political prisoners to leave the gaols.

As the situation still appeared critical, on 21st April Lord Mountbatten decided to go himself to the Frontier Province in a week's time. This and a short trip to the Punjab in July were the only provincial visits he paid during his Viceroyalty.

It began with a dramatic episode which may have changed the course of history in the north-west. Before his arrival a crowd of 50,000 to 100,000 Pathans,[1] all apparently supporters of the Muslim League, had gathered on the airfield, rendering a landing impossible. The Governor managed to get them to move to the open space between the fort and the railway embankment, a sort of glacis separating the city from the cantonment, near the Cunningham Bagh (now Jinnah Bagh) and only a few hundred yards from Government House. There, immediately after his arrival at midday on 28th June, the Viceroy was advised by the Governor that these demonstrators were determined to show him their grievances, would undoubtedly march on Government House, and could be prevented from storming it by the forces at his disposal only at the risk of bloodshed and heavy loss of life. Sir Olaf advised Lord Mountbatten that the only way of preventing them, risky as it might be, was for the Viceroy himself to go out and see them. Lord Mountbatten said he would go if Dr. Kahn Sahib, the Prime Minister, agreed. Dr. Khan Sahib replied: 'The Governor has collected them, but I agree you should go.' Lord and Lady Mountbatten, who courageously insisted

[1] Crowd numbers are notoriously subject to wide errors of estimation. Alan Campbell-Johnson's figure was 'well over 70,000', Sir Olaf's 100,000, Lord Mountbatten's the range recorded here.

on accompanying her husband, then drove with the Governor to the railway embankment overlooking the fort. The Viceroy was wearing a jungle-green bush shirt, which may have helped to save the day, for this is the colour worn among Muslims by Hajis, who have made the pilgrimage to Mecca. Threatening shouts filled the air: 'Pakistan Zindabad! Pakistan Zindabad!' But as Lord and Lady Mountbatten were seen on the ridge the mood began to change. Cries of 'Mountbatten Zindabad' were heard. For nearly half an hour Lord and Lady Mountbatten stood there, unable to do more, but mollifying that great concourse by their presence, their friendliness and their courage. After they left, the crowd peaceably dispersed and the crisis was over. That evening, thanking the Viceroy for his action, the General Office Commanding, the Inspector General of Police, the Deputy Commissioner of Peshawar and other officers told him that if he had not shown himself the crowd was determined to invade Government House, and that there would have followed the biggest killing the Frontier had ever known. In fact, nothing worse happened than an abortive attempt, that night, to murder the G.O.C.

The Viceroy then had to deal with the other face of Frontier politics. At Government House he met Dr. Khan Sahib and his Ministers 'at what surely must have been'—so he wrote afterwards—'one of the craziest meetings ever held with any Ministry'. The Chief Minister told Lord Mountbatten that Mr. Jinnah had no control whatever over the Muslim League on the Frontier. Who then did run it? 'The Governor and his officials.' The night before he had left Delhi, the Viceroy had been told by Mr. Jinnah that the latter had arranged for a demonstration of 100,000 of his followers in Peshawar, and he wished them to march in procession to Government House. This the Viceroy flatly forbade, though he was prepared to receive a deputation of six. Mr. Jinnah said he would issue orders to that effect. Later on the day of the great demonstration, the delegation presented itself, six from the demonstrators, six on parole from gaol (they had demanded to come under escort as prisoners, but this was refused, as they were staying in gaol by their own refusal to quit). Lord Mountbatten asked them about Mr. Jinnah. 'He is our leader,' they said. 'Do you obey him?' 'Implicitly. Was it not on his orders that we did not form a procession today?'

As to elections in the province, Lord Mountbatten took different lines with the Ministers and with the Muslim League deputation. He told the former that he would require to know whether they had a mandate from their people before he could decide the future of the province, and that he would probably go into Section 93 for at least two months to ensure that the elections were fair. When, however, the Muslim Leaguers demanded Section 93 immediately, followed by elections, he replied that he could not possibly yield to duress and that while they were trying to overthrow the provincial Government by force it must have his support. He advised them to trust him, as their leader did, to see that they got fair play in the transfer of power. (When Pandit Nehru was shown the first plan for transfer of power, he protested vehemently against its proposal to hold fresh elections in the N.W.F.P., a policy which he said was giving way to violence. 'If you force this issue on us,' he declared, 'we shall not contest the elections.')

During his second day on the Frontier the Viceroy went up the Khyber and met tribal representatives both at Landi Kotal and, on his return, at Government House. They spoke unanimously of their grievance that H.M.G. had never taken the tribes into account and that the British Prime Minister had not mentioned them in his statement of 20th February. They demanded the return of the Khyber and their tribal areas and swore that in no circumstances would they submit to Hindu domination—they would prefer to make terms with Afghanistan. Leaders of the Mahsuds and Wazirs pressed hard for Pakistan and dismissal of the Congress Government in Peshawar. There were no untoward incidents.

The Frontier Province continued to be highly disturbed in the succeeding weeks, with outbreaks of communal violence on top of an embittered political condition. The Governor and his officials succeeded, much against the odds, in preventing a major disaster, while the agitation against them in the Congress continued unabated. On 6th June, three days after the announcement of the definitive plan for the transfer of power, the Viceroy wrote to Sir Olaf Caroe. In view of the incessant allegations against him by his detractors, notwithstanding the high opinion the Viceroy had of his capacity, integrity and selfless devotion to duty under an immense strain, the time had come, said Lord Mountbatten, when he must, for the moment at any rate, replace Sir Olaf as Governor of the N.W.F.P. Lord Mountbatten had thought of a way of doing this with the least injury to Sir Olaf and without closing the door to his further employment in India (or, more likely, in Pakistan) if he so wished—a slightly disingenuous point, perhaps, in all the circumstances—namely, that he should ask for leave and remain absent until 15th August, the date of the transfer of power, and that Lieutenant-General Sir Rob Lockhart should be seconded to act for him, so that the referendum could be carried through by soldiers. Sir Olaf, agreeing with the Viceroy that 'in these momentous days, personal considerations are a small thing compared to the public weal', fell in with these proposals, though he probably had his own views as to what would best serve the public weal.[1]

It was a story that illumined many sides of Lord Mountbatten's personality and methods, many unpleasant aspects of Indian politics, and many proofs of the devoted and selfless service of the officers of the old regime, both British and Indian, civil and military. That chaos did not result from the sudden if premeditated revolution in the whole governance of the sub-continent, including its division into two nation states and the forging of new relations with the border tribes and the Princely rulers, was due, above all other causes, to their strength and resolution in conditions which would have tried the character of the best of men.

[1] A happy ending to the story confirms that Sir Olaf was the victim of transitory politics rather than his own personality or error. The Khan brothers, when the dust had settled, recognised his impartiality and worth. In 1956 Dr. Khan Sahib (in concert with President Iskander Mirza) invited him to spend three months on the Frontier as a Pakistan state guest to gather material for his book *The Pathans*. Later Abdul Ghaffar Khan ('Badshah' Khan) stayed with Sir Olaf at his home in Sussex, where the Khan sons and grandsons also visit. To cap all, in 1963 Sir Olaf was invited to India as a state guest to help co-ordinate work for the Tibetan refugees: the man who invited him was Pandit Nehru.

17

A plan for the transfer of power

1 *The evolution of a plan*

Before his talks with political leaders (other than his Cabinet
Ministers) even began the new Viceroy had decided that speed was
the essence of the matter in framing a scheme for the transfer of
power. After a week in office he wrote:

> The scene here is one of unrelieved gloom. . . . At this early
> stage I can see little common ground on which to build any
> agreed solution for the future of India. The Cabinet is fiercely
> divided on communal lines; each party has its own solution and
> does not at present show any sign of being prepared to consider
> any other. In addition, the whole country is in a most unsettled
> state. . . .
> The only conclusion that I have been able to come to is that
> unless I act quickly I may well find the real beginnings of a
> civil war on my hands. There are many who think that I have
> come out with a preconceived plan as to the transfer of power
> approved by H.M.G., which I am going to produce at the appro-
> priate moment. I have made it quite clear in my conversations
> that this is not so. But I am convinced that a fairly quick decision
> would be the only way to convert the Indian minds from their
> present emotionalism to stark realism and to counter the
> disastrous spread of strife.[1]

On 25th March Lord Ismay wrote in similar terms: 'The situation is everywhere electric and I got the feeling that the mine would
go off at any moment. It is not reason or logic that is at the back
of it all but sheer emotionalism, and emotionalism is the hardest
thing to compete with. There is very little anti-British feeling, but
inter-communal hatred is a devouring flame.' And three days later
he wrote: 'If we don't make up our minds on what we are going to

[1] *Viceroy's Personal Report* No. 1, 2nd April 1947.

do within the next two months or so, there will be pandemonium. And if we do, there may also be pandemonium. But doubtful. . . .'[1]

In his talks with the party spokesmen, and with Mahatma Gandhi, Lord Mountbatten made it clear that his mind was open, that the Cabinet Mission plan was a potential starting-point for a new settlement, one which he was bound to consider until it had been proved useless, and that partition, if it were to come, must be applied to the disputed provinces as well as all-India and must allow for the joint conduct of the essential affairs of the successor states. Beyond this he disclosed his ideas more by way of argument or leverage than as the exposition of a decided view. 'We are still running round like squirrels in a cage,' wrote Lord Ismay on 6th April, 'and are certainly nowhere nearer a solution than when we arrived.'[2] But on 17th April, after 'nearly three weeks of incessant talks', the Viceroy set down his thoughts as follows:

In the first place, I am convinced that we have got to make up our minds one way or the other in the very near future if we are to avert civil war and the risk of a complete breakdown of the administration. On this there is complete unanimity of opinion, both European and Indian, in this country. The Governors have not a shadow of doubt about it. My first conclusion, there-fore, is that our decision must be announced before the end of May at latest.

Secondly, I have very slender hopes of getting acceptance of the Cabinet Mission plan, and I am very much afraid that if any attempt is made to impose the Cabinet Mission plan on the Muslim League they will resort to arms to resist it.

Thirdly, I feel strongly that the scheme of partition should be such as will not debar the two sides from getting together, even before we transfer power, if saner counsels prevail when the bewildering complications of partition are more clearly realised.

The chances are that I will send Ismay home with the draft announcement towards the end of this month to discuss it with the Secretary of State, and try to reach the earliest possible agreement on the precise terms.

Once this is done, I plan to try to get Jinnah, Nehru, Patel, Liaqat, Baldev Singh and possibly Bhopal and Patiala, to come

[1] Letter to Lady Ismay.
[2] Letter to Lady Ismay.

and stay with me in Simla. The date at which I am aiming is 15th May. Alternatively I might aim at a rather bigger 'round table conference'. I will then make one final determined effort to secure some compromise on the basis of the Cabinet Mission plan. If I fail, I shall have to fire my last shot in the shape of our announcement of partition.

Whatever the decision may be, I feel that the central Government should be as strong as possible until we hand over. In this connection I am thinking of trying to get Jinnah to join the Cabinet. The talks in Simla would then be in the nature of a discussion of a Cabinet Committee, which I think would be all to the good.

The Governors' Conference concluded yesterday afternoon. . . . The Governors have expressed their unanimous support of the line I have taken with the various Indian leaders; and all of them urge the greatest possible speed in making a decision and an announcement; for even the quieter Provinces feel that we are sitting on the edge of a volcano and that an eruption might take place through any of the main craters—Bengal, Punjab and N.W.F.P.—at any moment, with the risk of sporadic eruptions in Assam, Bombay and Bihar.[1]

Besides the stress on urgency, three things stand out in Lord Mountbatten's view of the constitutional problem at that date. First, the hope of acceptance of an all-Indian structure on the lines of the Cabinet Mission plan had receded to a chance of last-minute salvage. Secondly, Pakistan was still regarded as a monster, from which even its champions might recoil when with all its terrors it was offered them as a reality. Thirdly, though the decision on means of transferring power must be immediate, the transfer itself would be some time ahead, perhaps June 1948, and meanwhile a strong central Government would remain under ultimate British control.

As for the constitutional plan itself, the broad ideas on which Lord Mountbatten was working were likewise threefold.

1 *Decision on separation or otherwise by provinces (or, in Bengal and the Punjab, parts of provinces delineated by communal majorities) through their legislatures.*

To his staff the Viceroy emphasised that the announcement

[1] *Viceroy's Personal Report* No. 3, 17th April 1947.

must not give the impression that partition was inevitable but rather that the question had been referred for decision by the will of the people; he had, he said, worked out the voting system with Mr. Liaqat Ali Khan.

2 *If separation was indicated, some form of central authority or Supreme Defence Council to deal with 'overall defence'.*

3 *An intermediate period while new constitutions were being worked out, and before the final transfer of power.*

As early as 8th April the Viceroy had commended Pandit Nehru's view that for this intermediate period the 1935 constitution, as modified in practice under the Interim Government, should remain in force; his Reforms Commissioner, Mr. V. P. Menon, had likewise advised most strongly that on no account should the central Government be dissolved until there were competent alternative authorities to which to hand over. In this he was undoubtedly speaking with the voice of Sardar Patel.

In this scheme there was a strong tactical element. On 22nd April Lord Mountbatten told his staff he was convinced that the Cabinet Mission plan could somehow be resurrected under a new name or form; for if the Muslims were allowed the opportunity of a separate State, they could then negotiate for a Centre on parity terms. Two days later he wrote:

I am still doing everything in my power to get the Cabinet Mission plan accepted. But . . . Jinnah and the Muslim League leaders . . . are convinced that Congress have no intention whatever of complying with the spirit of the plan. . . . Liaqat went so far as to say that it was providential that Congress had refused the plan during the time that the League had accepted it, since it was now clear that they intended to use the Cabinet Mission plan to obtain a permanent strangle-hold over the predominantly Muslim groups [of provinces].

I have already pointed out to Jinnah and the League leaders that there must be some form of Centre or Supreme Defence Council even if Pakistan comes about, and that this Centre will have to deal with practically the same subjects as the Centre envisaged in the Cabinet Mission plan, that is to say, overall defence. So we come to the ridiculous situation where Jinnah in his insistence on Pakistan is likely to get a very truncated edition of it and still have to go to some form of Centre, instead of accepting complete autonomy over Groups B and C with a somewhat similar Centre. The real difference of course lies in the fact that in the former case there would be parity at the Centre and the League could not be outvoted. But it shows what value the League sets on this parity, since to obtain it they are prepared to sacrifice the richest plums of Pakistan.

This is the one bargaining counter I have left, for it is just possible that when faced with the full stupidity of what they are doing, the League might make some gesture to accept a compromise Cabinet Mission scheme and Congress in their desire to retain some form of unity might also be more forthcoming. But I am afraid this is a very pious hope and there are no signs that I shall succeed.[1]

Lord Mountbatten set up a special committee to work on the draft plan, including an announcement by H.M.G. on how power would be transferred by June 1948, consisting of himself, Lord Ismay, Sir Eric Miéville and Sir George Abell. This group met the chief political leaders (Nehru, Patel, Jinnah, Liaqat and Baldev Singh) in succession, and without laying a formal document before them discussed with them the outline of what was proposed. The intention was to show them all the plan in general draft before Lord Ismay took it to London, but Lord Mountbatten changed his mind on this, mainly because the British Government had not yet seen the plan and might want to amend it. Eventually the draft text was shown only to Mr. Jinnah and Pandit Nehru; Sir Eric Miéville, taking it round to them as deputy for Lord Ismay, who was indisposed, in the absence of the Viceroy on his tour of the north-west, had a satisfactory interview with Pandit Nehru except as to the Frontier Province, but an unsatisfactory one with Mr. Jinnah, who protested strongly against the partition of the piovinces and demanded the immediate dissolution of the Constituent Assembly.

On 2nd May Lord Ismay flew to London with the plan and a message from the Viceroy to the Secretary of State:

It is impossible to exaggerate the need for speed. My recent tour has more than confirmed all the reports I have had from outlying

[1] *Viceroy's Personal Report* No. 4, 24th April 1947.

parts of India about the shocking deterioration that is taking place in so many Provinces. . . .

I very much hope that the Cabinet will be able to give me the necessary authority to go ahead and will be able to release Ismay after a week, for we all feel that every day now counts out here if we are to prevent the communal conflict from spreading to unmanageable proportions.

In London, Lord Ismay reported that the Viceroy had found communal feeling in India to be far more bitter than he had expected. It had become an obsession with both Hindus and Muslims and had been much intensified by the statement of 20th February. (Field Marshal Auchinleck, who was also in London, had told the Prime Minister that the situation in India was dangerous, and had strongly emphasised the need for an early decision.) The Viceroy had come to the conclusion that the prospects of agreement on anything resembling the Cabinet Mission's plan were negligible. His proposals were designed to place the responsibility for dividing India conspicuously on Indians themselves. The five Indian political leaders with whom he had discussed them had at least acquiesced in them. The plan might have to be amended in the light of developments since it was drafted. For instance, the Governor of Bengal was anxious that Bengal should have the chance of opting for independence; he and the Governor of the Punjab had advised against referenda, and the latter was no longer in favour of the Viceroy's proposals; Lord Mountbatten himself was now proposing a referendum instead of an election in the North-West Frontier Province. The Viceroy intended, when he met the Indian leaders not later than 20th May, to give them only twenty-four hours' notice of the announcement and to refuse to make any alterations of substance.

The Ministers concerned at Westminster held three meetings with Lord Ismay to consider the draft announcement. They fully accepted the need for an immediate decision and agreed with the Viceroy's time-table subject to the Parliamentary recess at Whitsun and the desirability of giving the Indian leaders forty-eight hours to consider the plan. They made a number of amendments which seemed to Lord Ismay, and appear in retrospect, of a minor character, taken separately. The point of chief importance made by the Ministers was that the announcement should explain that the plan involved only a form of notional partition, not any final demarcation of boundaries; where separation was decided upon, Boundary Commissions would determine the eventual dividing lines. They agreed that the Viceroy should be asked for further advice on the proposed Boundary Commissions, the problem of the Muslim-majority area of Sylhet in Assam, the referendum in the Frontier Province, and the options exercisable by the Indian States. In the light of his replies the Prime Minister would settle a final draft which could be put to the Cabinet on 13th May. Before that date arrived, however, events had occurred in India which caused Lord Mountbatten radically to alter his proposals and to leave the Cabinet and Lord Ismay in London in some confusion.

The provisional re-draft of the plan was received on 10th May in Simla, where the Viceroy had retired for a rest and a change from the heat of the plains. He discussed it at a staff meeting the same day.[1] According to one of those present, he was worried by the amendments made in London, which he felt had worsened the prospects of the plan's acceptance.[2] This is not confirmed by Lord Mountbatten's own records. He told the Secretary of State:

> I was greatly impressed at the speed with which Cabinet dealt with the plan which Ismay brought home, and felt every confidence in the way the matter was being dealt with in London. The new draft appeared better than ours.[3]

And he wrote, in a confidential account of his Viceroyalty after it had ended, that the new draft 'did not seem to alter any essentials'. That this was his view at the time is supported by the fact that he forthwith wrote to Pandit Nehru, Mr. Jinnah, Sardar Patel, Mr. Liaqat Ali Khan and Sardar Baldev Singh inviting them to meet him in Delhi on 17th May to 'receive a plan which His Majesty's Government had approved for the transfer of power', and gave instructions for a Press communiqué to that effect to be issued.

Nevertheless, Lord Mountbatten told his staff that he had 'an absolute hunch' that he ought to show the re-drafted plan to Pandit Nehru, who was staying as his private guest at Mashobra,

[1] The only paper in the records of staff meetings bearing that date, however, makes no reference to the telegram from London; the meeting noted in the records had presumably been held earlier in the day.
[2] V. P. Menon, *The Transfer of Power in India*, p. 361.
[3] *Viceroy's Personal Report* No. 7, 15th May 1947.

the Viceregal retreat in the hills above Simla, in strict confidence, and get his personal reactions. His staff argued against this, on the ground that it was a breach of the principle of keeping the different party leaders equally informed, or uninformed; but his 'hunch' was so strong, and his experience in South-East Asia Command had given him such confidence in his occasional intuitive decisions, that he acted upon it. Taking Pandit Nehru aside just before his guest was going to bed that evening, he gave him a copy to read, on the understanding that the Prime Minister would merely advise him as a friend as to its likely reception by the Congress.

The moment was a watershed in the history of three nations. The next morning, while Lord Mountbatten was talking with Sir Evan Jenkins about the probable reactions to the plan in the Punjab, and when he had just assured the Governor that there was every hope of securing the party leaders' acquiescence in the plan —without which Sir Evan thought large-scale riots would be inevitable—a letter arrived from Pandit Nehru which the Viceroy described as 'a bombshell of the first order'. The Indian Prime Minister had no doubt that Congress would reject the proposals in the plan, and that they would provoke deep resentment throughout India.

> Not only do they menace India but also they endanger the future relations between Britain and India. Instead of producing any sense of certainty, security and stability, they would encourage disruptive tendencies everywhere and chaos and weakness.

The whole approach, wrote Pandit Nehru, had been completely changed. The proposals involved a complete retraction by His Majesty's Government of its previous pledges, the virtual scrapping of the Constituent Assembly and abandonment of the Cabinet Mission plan. The acquiescence of the Congress in the splitting of Muslim majority provinces did not imply casting away an all-India basis of settlement, but was designed to make the Cabinet Mission plan viable without coercion, and was not at all inconsistent with an Indian Union of both separated parts. The proposals, by inviting the claims of numbers of potential successor States, including innumerable Princely States claiming independence, would lead to the Balkanisation of India, provoke civil conflict, cause a further breakdown of the central authority, and demoralise the Army, the police and the central services. Pandit Nehru added criticisms of certain specific provisions, especially regarding Baluchistan, the North-West Frontier Province and the tribes. Constructively, he urged that the Constituent Assembly should proceed with constitution-making on the basis of an all-India Union, while the League prepared its own schemes on an equal level, the two constitutions being then presented to all the provinces as a clear choice, to be made by plebiscite. 'Until those decisions are made, the Government of India must remain as one.'

Lord Mountbatten was not only dismayed. He was baffled. 'I was at first,' he wrote later, 'at a loss to understand what was at the bottom of Pandit Nehru's violent reactions. The rest of the day was spent in trying to find out what the objections were. Finally it emerged that the mere fact that the plan had been re-drafted in London had not only raised his own suspicions but would, in his opinion, make the plan less likely of acceptance by the other Congress leaders. I pointed out that the plan was not changed in the essentials from the lines I had understood him to have agreed to in Delhi. Pandit Nehru, however, insisted that the new plan was conniving at the possibility of the complete Balkanisation of India, and that there was insufficient connection between the present plan and the Cabinet Mission's plan, which he claimed was by no means dead.'[1] Indeed in conversation Pandit Nehru told the Viceroy that he did not think the plan which he had seen would be accepted by any of the parties in India, a point which reinforced Lord Mountbatten's view that, if Nehru rejected a plan on which it was essential that both the Congress and the League should agree, it would be pointless to show it to Mr. Jinnah. Comparing, in cold blood, the plan taken to London by Lord Ismay, the revised version, and the plan eventually adopted with the agreement of Pandit Nehru and the Congress, there is, as regards the mode of partition, nothing much to distinguish them, except in details and nuances, the great difference in the eventual scheme being something outside the long-term constitutional settlement, namely, the early demission of power on a Dominion Status basis. This may be counted the deciding factor in securing acceptance; it was certainly vital, though it was not by any means necessarily to the advantage of Congress and the Hindu majority, since it allowed no time for that shuddering contemplation of the enormity

---

[1] *Report on the Last Viceroyalty*. This repeats much of the language of *Viceroy's Personal Report* No. 7, 15th May 1947.

of partition which Lord Mountbatten—and, evidently, the Congress leaders—thought might still persuade the Muslims to recoil in the direction of the Cabinet Mission's plan.

Professor Tinker has argued[1] that in rejecting a plan whose close likeness he had previously accepted Nehru was exhibiting a characteristic 'amnesia'—or, as he might have put it, 'double-think'—such as he displayed in the later 1950s, when he persisted in regarding China as India's partner in international peace, founded on the famous Panch Sila or Five Points, despite her manifest aggressive intentions on the Himalayan frontier. He had accepted the inevitability of partition without relinquishing the aim of union. Persuaded by facts on the surface, in a deeper part of his mind he had never renounced the principle which the facts affronted, and his explosion was an internal one when his reading of the draft scheme made it impossible any longer to preserve these two incompatible levels of thought. But there was more than Pandit Nehru's complex and emotional personality behind his out-burst. If the changes were nuances, nuances are often important in politics, which are essentially exercises in public and political relations; and Pandit Nehru was not altogether wrong in detecting in the 'London plan' a tendency to accept fission into not merely two but probably several parts as inevitable, and to regard the seven undisputed provinces[2] as merely one of the successor States (Hindustan) of which perhaps Bengal and the larger Princedoms or groups of smaller ones might be others. The eventual concept of an India having full continuity and related to the existing Constituent Assembly, from which the Muslim-majority areas might be shed to form Pakistan, and to which most of the Princely States would adhere, was different in form and presentation, even though the mechanism of establishing it might be much the same.

That this matter did not come into the open until the eleventh hour seems strange until we reflect on the procedure which Lord Mountbatten had followed. Unlike the Cabinet Mission, he was not persuading Indians to agree among themselves, but working for a decision in which they would acquiesce. He had discussed his ideas with the leaders separately, but never hammered out a draft with

[1] Hugh Tinker, *Experiment with Freedom*, Oxford University Press, 1967, p. 112.
[2] United Provinces, Bihar, Central Provinces, Bombay, Madras, Orissa and most of Assam.

them together. He had shown the two principals the outline of his plan, but had never given them an opportunity of discussing it with him in detail. Had he done so, he would probably have been frustrated. Without doing so, he ran the risk, not of excluding their arguments, which he had heard to the full, but of missing the inflexions of their thought. The effect of the plan on Pandit Nehru, according to Mr. V. P. Menon, was to make him realise that 'if we don't behave ourselves the consequences will be disastrous', and that was why he eventually accepted partition. Had the Congress rejected the May plan, the consequences would have been calamitous: by accepting the revised plan they put the League into a position where the latter had to accept, and Lord Mountbatten's central objective, the agreement of the major parties, was secured.

But this is to cast ahead of the story. The explanatory talks between Pandit Nehru and the Viceroy came later in the day. When Lord Mountbatten received the 'bombshell' he did not waste time in wringing his hands. After seeing that Nehru's letter was forthwith telegraphed to London, he sent an A.D.C. to fetch Mr. V. P. Menon, his Reforms Commissioner, who was at the moment closeted with Nehru himself. The Viceroy's foresight in bringing Menon to Simla was now to be bountifully rewarded. The fateful hour found a man and an idea to match it.

2 *Dominion Status as the solvent*

Rao Bahadur V. P. Menon was a remarkable man in many ways. When barely more than a schoolboy, he had run away from his home in the south of India to spare his family the strain of his further education. He worked in the gold-mines of Mysore and as a teacher of English in a Muslim State. Eventually he reached Simla and got a clerical job in the government service. It was by sheer merit that he won his way to the top in an administrative system controlled by the brahminical I.C.S. He first visited England in 1931 as a lowly member of the secretariat of the India Round Table Conference, but he understood the mind of the British, and had a great affection for Britain and his British friends. A loyal servant of the Government of India and of successive Viceroys, by whom he was securely entrusted with the closest political secrets, he nevertheless was a staunch Indian patriot who equally had the confidence of political leaders, especially Sardar Patel; he greatly admired Patel as quick in understanding, clear in mind and strong in action, the civil servant's ideal Minister.

Menon became in the 1930s deputy to Sir Hawthorne Lewis, Reforms Commissioner and constitutional adviser to the Viceroy, and to his successor, the author of this book, whom he succeeded in that office late in 1942. Lord Wavell relied much on his constitutional advice, and took him to London in the spring of 1944 and again in August 1945 for his consultations with His Majesty's Government. But when Lord Mountbatten came to India with his powerful entourage, he had to rediscover Menon for himself. Though the Reforms Commissioner organised the Governors' Conference of 15th–16th April he took no part in it, nor did he even figure in the official photograph of the Conference principals and their staffs, as if the guns and the dogs had been photographed at a shoot but the head gamekeeper left out, perhaps as suspect of being on the birds' side. His status, right up to the 'moment of truth' in Simla, is illustrated by the fact that although he was the Viceroy's Constitutional Adviser he had never been shown the text of the draft plan which Lord Ismay took to London. Nothing, of course, could change the fact that he was a Hindu, and as such suspect to the Muslims: his close touch with the Congress, through Sardar Patel, was also known, and invaluable as it was to the Viceroy it affected his impartial position, especially later after the constitutional plan had been agreed and the Government of India virtually split into two halves. Lord Mountbatten, however, had realised his worth and it was to Menon that he turned when catastrophe stared him in the face upon Pandit Nehru's vehement rejection of his plan.

Menon had the advantage that he, too, did not like the plan, whose nature of course he knew, and had thought deeply about an alternative. The key to this was the early demission of power to two Dominions. This idea had a considerable past as well as a successful future, and it is necessary at this point to turn back the pages of history.

The concept of 'Dominion Status', meaning full nationhood within the British Commonwealth, had been developed after the adoption of the famous Balfour Report on Inter-Imperial Relations by the Imperial Conference of 1926. Three years later it was first applied to India, as an acknowledged objective of British policy, in a statement by Lord Irwin,[1] the Viceroy. In this, he was trailing after the (Motilal) Nehru Committee of 1928, which had drafted a constitution for India whose first article, following the Anglo-Irish treaty of 1921, had read:

India shall have the same constitutional status in the comity of nations known as the British Empire as the Dominion of Canada. . . .

But this was a demand for the present, not an aspiration for the future: by the time it became actual British policy, Indian demands had leapt further. Even Lord Irwin's words aroused indignation among right-wing British thinkers about India, although at that date Dominion Status still implied an unbreakable constitutional link. Under Conservative-dominated Governments from 1931 onward the phrase was officially avoided in the Indian context, evident though it was that the Federal constitution embodied in the Act of 1935 was capable of leading in due course to Dominion Status. The verbal caution was understandable; for while India's constitutional position had stood still, and the problem of advancing her to nationhood had grown no less, the other members of the Commonwealth had moved on, and with them their 'Dominion Status'. By convention and by law under the Statute of Westminster, 1931, it had come to embody complete constitutional freedom—demonstrable freedom to make laws for the succession to the Throne (1936) and to decide for themselves whether they were to be at war or peace (1939), and an asserted and undenied right to secede from the Commonwealth: all this sprang inexorably from the concept of equality that had been formulated in 1926. When Sir Stafford Cripps came to Delhi in February 1942 to offer India the right to frame her own constitution within the Commonwealth after the war, it was Dominion Status that he thus held out. but he legitimately called it independence. His bold public use of that word may have had some effect in reconciling Indian nationalist opinion to Dominion Status, new-style, as a means to complete national freedom, after rejecting and despising it ever since the 1920s.

The idea of advancing India to practical Dominion Status without radically altering the existing constitution had played a considerable part in exchanges between the Viceroys (both Lord Linlithgow and Lord Wavell) and the Secretary of State from 1942

[1] Later Earl of Halifax: the statement is quoted in a footnote on p. 5.

onwards, and was the basis of Mr. Amery's bold and imaginative but abandoned plan of 1944.[1] Shortly after the war had ended, under Lord Wavell's Viceroyalty, Mr. V. P. Menon as Reforms Commissioner had written a paper on the development of the 1935 constitution to embrace Dominion Status; that is to say, to eliminate arbitrary control by Governors and Governors-General and to make the Central and Provincial Governments fully responsible to their elected legislatures. He had been authorised by the Governor-General to send his plan to the India Office, and this he did, but without response. Early in 1947, during the discussions on Lord Mountbatten's impending appointment, the Secretary of State for India reported that he had received through an Indian intermediary a memorandum on the political and constitutional problem in India, following the Dominion theme, which was believed to have been written by an eminent Indian member of the I.C.S. The author was in fact Mr. V. P. Menon (not a member of the I.C.S.), the intermediary was Mr. Sudhir Gosh,[2] and the plan had been sent to the Secretary of State (through his Private Secretary) with Lord Wavell's knowledge and approval. Menon's memorandum had actually been dictated in the presence of Vallabhbhai Patel, but his name was not mentioned, lest his position in the Congress be compromised, though Menon did say he had reason to believe that Congress would accept Dominion Status, at least as an interim step. In persuading Sardar Patel, Menon had used three arguments. First, a Dominion solution would ensure a peaceful transfer of power to a strong central government (or central governments, for Menon assumed the possible partition of the country), a point which he rightly considered vital. Secondly, acceptance of Dominion Status would assure Britain's friendship and goodwill towards the Congress. Thirdly, India could continue to have the invaluable services of British civil and military officers after independence.

The Prime Minister, Mr. Attlee, impressed by the memorandum, said at a meeting held to brief Lord Mountbatten that the Act of 1935 ought to be carefully examined to see whether it could be adapted to embody Dominion-Status principles. Although this task had in fact already been done by Mr. Menon, Mr. Attlee's

[1] See above, p. 117.
[2] Menon, *The Transfer of Power in India*, p. 359, and Ghosh, *Gandhi's Emissary*, p. 204.

directive appears to have been lost in the administrative sands.

The way in which the concept of Dominion Status eventually emerged as a solvent for many of the problems inherent in the transfer of power, and as a means of accelerating the transfer without handing over to untried and hastily fabricated regimes, was strongly affected in the early stages of Lord Mountbatten's Viceroyalty by the fact that the Constituent Assembly (boycotted, of course, by the Muslims) had unanimously resolved, before he appeared on the scene, that India should be a sovereign independent republic. It is too easy to forget, in retrospect, that the *rationale* of the Commonwealth which was elaborated after India and Pakistan had gained their independence, and especially after India had successfully applied for continued membership when becoming a republic, was not familiar to administrators and politicians in early 1947.[1] It is likely that certain Indians, such as V. P. Menon, Krishna Menon, or Sir B. N. Rau, had a fuller understanding of the modern Commonwealth than many of Lord Mountbatten's British entourage, Sir Eric Miéville and Lord Ismay being among the exceptions. The Viceroy, assuming from the Constituent Assembly's vote that independent India, truncated, would leave the Commonwealth, saw as an acute problem the possibility that other parts of India might decide differently, with the result, as he saw it, that the frontier of the Commonwealth would run along new and perhaps unstable lines of demarcation across the Indian sub-continent, and that Britain would be liable, as a Commonwealth ally, to be drawn into conflicts with independent India.[2] Of course, if the Commonwealth as such ceased to be in any sense a military association, as later proved the case, fears of that sort would have been greatly mitigated, but this was early 1947, when ideas were still cast in an earlier mould.

[1] Lord Mountbatten himself had far sight on this. He is recorded as saying on 30th July 1947 that he believed the new Union of India would wish—at a time considerably later than some enthusiasts then thought probable—to elect a Head of State and perhaps call him President, without breaking ties with the Commonwealth, which by then, maybe, would be much looser.

[2] Lord Ismay, always sage, felt that if the British Government were forced into a position in which only one part of former India—presumably Pakistan—wanted to stay in the Commonwealth, it should entertain the application. In his opinion, that would be more likely to prevent a war than would a refusal to allow either part to remain in.

Accordingly, Lord Mountbatten repeatedly warded off attempts by leaders of the Muslim League or individual Princes to influence him in favour of their separatist policies by confiding to him that Pakistan or their States would want to stay in the Commonwealth after the transfer of power; his stock answer was that this was a matter for His Majesty's Government and that he was not prepared to discuss hypothetical questions about membership of the Commonwealth in circumstances which had not yet been determined. His mind ran on the possibility of a form of relationship somewhere between staying under the Crown and complete detachment. A few days after his arrival in India the Nawab of Bhopal telegraphed him that he had reason to believe, from a conversation with Mr. Jinnah, that the latter, if granted Pakistan, could be persuaded to remain in the Commonwealth—a report which the Viceroy's advisers suspected was a tactical manoeuvre. Lord Mountbatten, while reiterating that he would not discuss the issue of Commonwealth membership with representatives of different parts of India, added that it would be a different matter if Mr. Jinnah and the Princes agreed to accept the Cabinet Mission's plan on the condition of 'continued close contact with the Commonwealth'. A few days later, however, Mr. Jinnah told him direct that there was now no hope of the Muslim League's accepting the Cabinet Mission's plan. Again, in an early interview the Nawab of Palanpur asked whether there was any prospect of States' being allowed individually to remain in the Commonwealth; the Viceroy replied that he thought His Majesty's Government would consider such an application only if it came from all Indian parties jointly; it might be an application, not to remain in the Commonwealth, but 'to maintain some sort of link'.

The prospect, as seen from London, of India's forsaking her Commonwealth allegiance gave rise at this stage to a revealing episode. The British Government decided, without reference to the Viceroy, to cancel the invitation to India to become a member of the Commonwealth Advisory Committee for Defence and to exclude Indian officers from future Imperial Defence College courses, and sent a telegram to that effect to the Indian Defence Department on or about 4th April. To this procedure Lord Mountbatten took 'the gravest possible exception'; in a conversation with Field Marshal Auchinleck he used the words 'absolutely amazed' and 'unbelievable', and although the Commander-in-

Chief tried to soothe him about the practical effect he cabled a strongly-worded protest direct to the Prime Minister. This drew from Mr. Attlee an unequivocal apology and a promise not to let it happen again. Not often can a British Prime Minister have offered such humble words to a Governor-General of India.

At his daily staff meeting on 19th April, Lord Mountbatten laid down six principles or objectives which the staff members were to observe in forming ideas for his guidance on a plan for the transfer of power. One of these, which he characterised as 'the most urgent question', was 'to grant some form of Dominion Status as early as possible'.[1] And on the following day he ordered 'Planning for the grant of Dominion Status possibly by January, 1948, to continue concurrently with plans for the main decision'. It will be seen that the Viceroy was evidently thinking of a Dominion-Status plan as perhaps 'an interim measure', to be devised 'concurrently with the main decision' and capable of being granted 'as early as possible', as a sort of advance instalment. This thinking was very different from the idea that Dominion Status, in its contemporary form of complete national independence in the Commonwealth, might serve as a total solution of the problem of the transfer of power.

When they next gathered together Lord Mountbatten ruminated to his confidential staff:

A point which impresses me is that spokesmen for more than half the inhabitants of India have asked to remain in the Commonwealth. Or rather, they usually don't ask, they offer. They seem to think they are doing Britain a favour.

Do you think there is any possibility of giving Dominion Status to India—or perhaps to separate parts of India, in the near future? I want to tell you I am considering saying to Nehru that both Jinnah and the States have told me they want to re- main in the British Commonwealth and that I believe popular sentiment in the rest of the Commonwealth would not allow such a request to go unanswered.

[1] This notion had already been maturing in the Viceroy's thoughts. On 5th April, recording a conversation on that day with Field Marshal Auchinleck, he wrote: 'I then gave the Commander-in-Chief a rough outline of one of the many alternative solutions for the future set-up in India that were revolving in my mind. A feature of this scheme was the almost immediate offer of Dominion or Commonwealth status to India.'

Mr. V. P. Menon was not present, though the Viceroy had had private talks with him and may have been affected by them. What Menon would have said in response to Lord Mountbatten's question may be deduced from subsequent events.

A few days later, Lord Mountbatten returned to the earlier theme. He was personally of the opinion, he said, that if there were a united request from all Indian parties for the British to remain in India after June 1948 (which obviously could be considered only if India stayed in the Commonwealth) it should be refused if it could be refused with honour. The task facing a British Governor-General (observe the assumption not only of Dominion Status but also of the selection of a British figure to represent the Crown), as a sort of high-level umpire, with only a small team of advisers, would be fraught with frightful difficulties. (Events were to demonstrate the prescience of this forecast.) And as late as the 1st May, when the main plan was already in being and Lord Ismay was about to depart with it to London, the Viceroy told his staff that the more he thought about it the more convinced did he become that it would be disastrous to allow only, say, Pakistan to remain in the Commonwealth, and thus back up one part of present India against the other, a course that might involve Britain in war. (The occasion of the discussion was a letter from the Secretary of State for India on the question whether Princely States could be granted Dominion Status, singly or in groups, pointing out that as the States were not legally British territory they could hardly be incorporated in the British Empire.)

Lord Ismay gave his personal opinion that, if and when the time came for such a decision, it would be well-nigh impossible on both moral and material grounds to eject from the Commonwealth any part of India which asked to remain in it. He might have added constitutional grounds; for once a nation had Dominion Status under the Statute of Westminster it became co-equal with the United Kingdom and was no more subject to her wishes as regards continued membership of the Commonwealth than as regards any other aspect of its affairs, and no constitutional mechanism existed for detaching from allegiance to the Crown an equal nation which continued to proclaim it. It was Sir Eric Miéville, who had served with the Governor-General of Canada, who then suggested that, under the Statute of Westminster, all nation members of the Commonwealth would have to be consulted as to whether India or parts of it should be permitted to remain in the association.

On 1st May, as an outcome of the directive on concurrent planning, a document was circulated to the Viceroy's staff, based on a paper by V. P. Menon, entitled 'A method of transferring power to successor authorities in India which could result in a form of transitional constitution analogous to that of the Dominions'. But the bus had been missed, in the shape of the draft plan which Lord Ismay was about to take to London.

Had Menon's plan, sent to the Secretary of State in January 1947, been seriously considered either by the Government in London, or by Lord Mountbatten when Menon broached it to him at their first meeting, the whole course of the negotiations with the political leaders might have been different, and the first draft plan might never have been adopted. The Menon scheme involved separation of the Muslim-majority areas, two 'national' constitutions, each reported back to the Constituent Assembly for adoption and for consideration of any Central authority, and the immediate grant of Dominion Status to the two successor States. To have endorsed this scheme at once in his talks with political leaders would have been contrary to Lord Mountbatten's instructions to base himself on the Cabinet Mission's plan if possible; but as soon as he saw that this cock would not fight he might have turned to the dual-Dominion scheme and spared himself the crisis of the Nehru 'bombshell'.

The whole issue, however, was about to take a dramatic turn. Also on 1st May, Sir Eric Miéville reported two conversations which struck him as important. Sir Walter Monckton, then in India as legal adviser to the Nizam of Hyderabad, had been invited by Pandit Nehru to dine with him on 3rd May to discuss 'some form of continued allegiance to the Crown'. And Mr. V. P. Menon had told Sir Eric that Sardar Patel, so he had good reason to believe, might accept an offer of Dominion Status 'for the time being'.

With the Viceroy's authority, Menon discussed his ideas with Pandit Nehru during the first two days of the latter's visit to Simla as the Viceroy's guest. He got the impression that Nehru was not unfavourable. Lord Mountbatten then brought himself into the discussion, giving the Dominion Status plan a fair wind but without committing himself. Nehru thought it very desirable that there should be an early transfer of power on such a basis, if only because so long as the British Government held the reins there was a lack of realism and self-reliance in Indian politics. But the real difficulty was the threat of the partition of India. It is clear that Pandit Nehru was still thinking in terms of an interim transfer of power, to be followed by a final act which would have been affected by the greater realism of Indian political leaders when thrown on their own resources. (Indeed there is some evidence that not until weeks after the plan for demission of sovereignty on a Commonwealth basis in August 1947 had been accepted did Nehru rid his mind of the idea that the genuine demission was still dated June 1948.)

When Lord Mountbatten sent for Menon on the morning of 11th May, the latter was in fact closeted with the Indian Prime Minister, who was too upset by the fundamental faults he found in the draft constitutional plan to pay much heed to other notions. The Viceroy, who was in a very ruffled state, told Menon that he was not sorry he had shown Pandit Nehru the draft plan. If, otherwise, he had followed up his invitation to the party leaders to confer with him on it the consequences would have been disastrous. He had completely misled the British Government into thinking that the Congress leadership would accept the plan. It was characteristic of Lord Mountbatten that in the moment of calamity his thought was not how to muffle the difficulties with compromise or procrastination but how to find immediately another course whereby he could recapture the initiative and this time succeed. The Reforms Commissioner had his answer ready. The Congress would accept Dominion Status because it would mean an early transfer of power, even though it were to two Governments, and because the essential unity of India was maintained; while Mr Jinnah would also be offered Pakistan with real power at an early date, which he could hardly refuse, truncated though his Pakistan might be. When Menon dined with the Viceroy that night, having meanwhile used his private channel of communication with Sardar Vallabhbhai Patel, Lord Mountbatten had completely recovered his cheerfulness and self-confidence; for Pandit Nehru had told him that the new plan drafted in great haste by Menon during the day—he was instructed at lunch-time and given until 6 p.m. to complete the draft on which the end of the Indian Empire was to depend—would not be unacceptable to the Congress. The next morning there was a remarkable telephone conversation between

Pandit Nehru in Simla and Sardar Patel in Delhi, most of the actual talking being done (because the line was bad and the principals found it difficult to communicate) by Mr. V. P. Menon and Mr. V. Shankar, Patel's Private Secretary. Pandit Nehru was persuaded that the Dominion Status plan was acceptable but was worried about how to get it through the Congress; to which Patel instantly replied: 'Leave that to me. That is my business.'

It is understandable that Mr. Attlee and the Secretary of State, not to mention Lord Ismay, had become bewildered by the Viceroy's telegraphed reports of these developments. Ministers had fiddled with a few details of Lord Mountbatten's first plan, but not, they thought, with its substance; they had virtually dismissed it from their attention, having authorised the Prime Minister to draft the final form of the announcement (in consultation with the Secretary of State and in the light of the Viceroy's reply to certain questions) and to lay it before the Cabinet on 13th May. Yet here was its author himself wishing to withdraw it, as fundamentally unsuitable, and to substitute something quite different. British Cabinets are unaccustomed to having their business suddenly changed like a character in Alice's Wonderland. They decided that either a Cabinet Minister should go out to India, or the Viceroy should come home to explain this *volte-face* and enable a decision to be reached. Lord Mountbatten did not hesitate between these alternatives, though there was a moment when he felt that if His Majesty's Government did not accept his revised plan he would resign. On 14th May he flew to London, taking V. P. Menon with him.

Before leaving he had been at pains to make sure that this time he really could promise the consent of the Indian party leaders. The negotiation was conducted, in the first place by Menon and Sir Eric Miéville, and then by the Viceroy himself, with the five chief political figures on the basis of draft Heads of Agreement drawn up by the Reforms Commissioner. These included acceptance of the procedure for ascertaining the will of the people as to partition; transfer of power on a Dominion Status basis to one or two central Governments, responsible to their respective Constituent Assemblies; that the constitutional regime to which power was transferred should be that of the 1935 Act modified to allow Dominion independence; that in the event of partition the Armed Forces should be divided according to territorial recruitment (a different proposition, be it noted, from division by communal allegiance); and that the present Governor-General be reappointed as common Governor-General of both Dominions. No great difficulties were encountered in negotiating these points—though the document was never initialled by the party leaders—and in drawing up a new plan for approval in London. Nehru wrote that the Congress accepted it generally, provided all parties took it as a final settlement. They understood it to be a variant of the Cabinet Mission plan to meet new circumstances—an observation which must have had some incantatory value. If it were rejected by the Muslim League they insisted on enforcement of the Cabinet Mission plan. If 'during the interim period' there were to be two Dominions, the Congress would be happy to have Lord Mount-batten continue in office. Mr. Jinnah and Mr. Liaqat Ali Khan, while seeming ready to embrace the plan, refused to express this consent in writing. Jinnah knew that at last his poker hand had been called, the cards were on the table, and he could hope for nothing more. Sardar Baldev Singh, warned by V. P. Menon that unless there were partition the Punjab would have a blood-bath, told him that if Congress accepted the plan he would not stand out.

3 The reception of the plan

In London, the Cabinet endorsed the plan after the briefest of discussion. Apart from its inherent merits, they clearly had no alternative to approving a plan to which the Viceroy was committed and which had been accepted by all the main Indian parties and communities. Lord Mountbatten returned to Delhi late on Friday, 30th May. He decided not to broach the final plan to the Indian leaders before the meeting arranged for the following Monday, but he saw several of them socially meanwhile, and Mr. Jinnah in particular pressed him on the question of a referendum in Bengal. He also discussed the plan, without revealing its details, with two leading Princes, the Maharajah of Bikaner and the Nawab of Bhopal, when they lunched with him. At the meeting on the morning of 2nd June the Congress was represented by Pandit Nehru, Sardar Patel and Mr. Kripalani, the Muslim League by Mr. Jinnah, Mr. Liaqat Ali Khan and Mr. Abdur Rab Nishtar, and the Sikhs by Sardar Baldev Singh. The inclusion of Mr. Kripalani as President of the Congress, on which Pandit Nehru insisted, had threatened to wreck the whole procedure, but Mr. Jinnah was persuaded to concur, given the counterpoise of a third League spokesman.

The atmosphere was tense and Lord Mountbatten at once felt that the more he himself talked and the less opportunity he gave for debate and cross-argument the better. He began by saying that he had called such an intimate meeting—eight men sitting round a small table—in order that it could be held in a friendly atmosphere. He could recall no meeting, among those at which momentous decisions for the conduct of world war had been taken, whose deliberations could have such a profound influence on world history as those now to be taken. Before he had come to India as Viceroy, he had been led to believe that the beginning of 1948 was time enough for Parliament to legislate for the transfer of power. But from the moment of his arrival a terrific sense of urgency had been impressed upon him and he had come to realise that the sooner power was transferred and the present uncertainty ended the better it would be.

The Viceroy spoke of his regrettable failure to obtain agreement to the Cabinet Mission plan, of the impossibility of accepting the full demands of either side, and of the position of the Sikhs, about which he was greatly exercised. He had repeatedly asked the Sikh leaders whether, if Pakistan was conceded, they desired the partition of the Punjab, which would necessarily divide them, and they had confirmed that they did. In arranging the notional partition—which was entirely provisional—it had not been possible to adopt any principle other than division into Muslim-majority and other areas: it would be for the Boundary Commission to work out the best permanent solution.

Paragraph 20 of the statement, headed 'Immediate Transfer of Power', was a 'new and very important feature'. The British Prime Minister had agreed that the necessary legislation should be rushed through the present session of Parliament, and Mr. Churchill, for the Opposition, had promised to facilitate the passage of the Bill. Power would be demitted in the first instance on the basis of Dominion Status. Thereafter, the new Indian Government or Governments would be completely free to withdraw from the Commonwealth whenever they wished.

Copies of the statement of His Majesty's Government were then handed round. The Viceroy observed that since he had discussed the plan with the leaders there had been some small drafting amendments which were subject to their general concurrence. He was not seeking an immediate acceptance or categorical agreement to all the terms, but asked them to take copies to their Working Committees and let him know their reactions by midnight.

Pandit Nehru, whose confidence in Lord Mountbatten had been greatly increased by his instant success in gaining approval from the Cabinet in London, affirmed that Congress generally accepted the plan. He and Sardar Patel had been committing themselves to it step by step. In the conditions of urgency which prevailed, the leaders had to decide. A letter would be sent that evening giving the Congress Working Committee's reactions. Mr. Jinnah, true to his practice of never committing himself until forced to do so, was more difficult, and all Lord Mountbatten's tactical skill was called upon to keep him in line. The decision, said Mr. Jinnah, could not be left to the Working Committee alone. They would have to bring the people round and much explanation would be necessary. When he called on the Viceroy that night, Mr. Jinnah refused to give anything in writing. He would, he said, do all in his power to get the plan accepted, and his Working Committee were hopeful, but it would require at least a week to assemble the Council of the All-India Muslim League, which alone could constitutionally decide. Lord Mountbatten asked whether he would be justified in asking the British Prime Minister to go ahead and make his announcement on the following day. Mr. Jinnah replied yes. Lord Mountbatten, who knew that the Congress would not give its assent without that of the League, said he would tell the leaders in conference that he was satisfied with the assurances he had received from Mr. Jinnah; all he asked was that Mr. Jinnah should then nod his head. Mr. Jinnah agreed, and when the fateful moment came, and the Viceroy turned to Mr. Jinnah, Pakistan with the two provinces divided went through on the nod.

On the evening of 2nd June, a long letter arrived from Mr. Kripalani reporting acceptance of the plan by the Congress Working Committee 'in order to achieve a final settlement'. This was dependent on acceptance by the Muslim League and a clear understanding that no further claims would be put forward. The letter also referred to the need for great care in protecting the position of the Sikhs in the Punjab. (Sardar Baldev Singh wrote accepting the principle of partition as embodied in the plan but stressing that Sikh demands must be taken into account in framing the terms of reference of the Boundary Commission.) Mr. Kripalani's letter also referred to the possibility of one Dominion wishing to leave the Commonwealth while the other did not, and asked for the referendum in the North-West Frontier Province to include the alternative of independence. Lord Mountbatten and Mr. V. P. Menon discussed these points with Pandit Nehru and Sardar Patel respectively, and persuaded them to withdraw them both: the first on the ground that, if India were free to secede from the Commonwealth, Pakistan as an equal member must be equally free to remain; and the second on the ground that Pandit Nehru himself at the earlier stage had protested against the independence option for provinces, which could not now be revived for one province alone.

Accordingly there were no struggles, though there were a few recriminations, when the leaders met the Viceroy early on 3rd June and confirmed acceptance of the plan. Once more Lord Mountbatten was afraid to let the politicians speak, lest each cause others to argue, so he spoke for each of them in turn. It was to be expected, he said, that all three interests would have grave objections to some or other points in the plan, and he was gratified that they had aired them to him. Since, however, he knew enough of the situation to realise that not one of the suggestions made by the Congress or the League would be accepted by the other side, he did not propose to raise them at this meeting. Lord Mountbatten then asked all the leaders to signify their consent, which with varying degrees of grace, partisanship and clarity they did. As soon as he felt that he was entitled to go ahead he announced this decision and then threw on the table copies of a long paper which his staff had prepared over the past weeks entitled *The Administrative Consequences of Partition*,[1] indicating all that needed to be done to separate and divide the strands of government. 'The severe shock that this gave to everyone present,' wrote the Viceroy, 'would have been amusing if it was not rather tragic.'[2] He arranged to call another conference in two days' time to consider it, and then broke up the meeting as quickly as he could.

Meanwhile, however, Lord Mountbatten had been faced with another daunting task of diplomacy and persuasion. Mr. Gandhi

[1] The main draftsman of this vital document was Mr. John Christie, I.C.S.
[2] *Viceroy's Personal Report* No. 8, 5th June 1947.

had been ardently preaching at his prayer meetings against the plan for partition and in favour of imposing the Cabinet Mission's scheme—which he himself had scotched a year earlier. A rift in the Congress Working Committee seemed the certain consequence. The Viceroy apprehensively invited the Mahatma for a talk on the Monday afternoon. 'Judge,' he wrote, 'of my astonished delight on finding him enter the room with his finger on his lips to indicate that it was his day of silence.' Lord Mountbatten used his fullest art to persuade Mr. Gandhi that to enforce such a plan as that of the Cabinet Mission against the will of any community was not in accordance with non-violence, and that the way of deciding for or against partition was trusting to the will of the people. Mr. Gandhi, barred from arguing, seemed mollified, and scribbled notes in friendly terms on the backs of used envelopes. Later he made no attempt to alter or frustrate the decision of the Working Committee. To have secured the assent, however unwilling, of Mr. Gandhi, the Congress leaders and Mr. Jinnah to partition of India combined with division of the historic provinces of Bengal and the Punjab was indeed a diplomatic triumph. It could not have been achieved without the conditions of urgency and fear that prevailed in India; but without those conditions it would not have been necessary.

The British Prime Minister, having received from the Viceroy news of the plan's acceptance, made his statement in the agreed terms in the House of Commons on 3rd June. The Leader of the Opposition, Mr. Churchill, observed that the two conditions which had been foreseen at the time of the Cripps Mission in 1942—for which as Prime Minister he had been responsible—seemed to have been fulfilled, namely, that the Indian parties should agree on the settlement, and that there should be a period of Dominion Status during which the successor state or states could decide whether to remain in the Commonwealth. The Opposition, while reserving the right to criticise detail, would not oppose the implementing Bill. 'The Prime Minister,' he added, 'said that credit was due to the Viceroy. There are matters about which it is extremely difficult to form decided opinions now, but if the hopes that are contained in this declaration are borne out, great credit will indeed be due to the Viceroy, and not only to the Viceroy, but to the Prime Minister who advised the British Government to appoint him.' Hypothetical and constitutionally inaccurate as it was, this statement aligned the Opposition with the Government and the Labour Party in tribute to the endeavours of one whom they had always regarded with suspicion.

On the evening of 3rd June the Viceroy broadcast to the peoples of India. After explaining the plan he said that while it could not be perfect its success depended on the spirit of goodwill in which it was carried out. He had always felt that the transfer of power should take place at the earliest possible moment. The proposal which he had put forward, and which had been accepted, was that His Majesty's Government should transfer power immediately to one or two successor Governments, each having Dominion Status. Lord Mountbatten's use of the word 'immediately' was the first harbinger of a decision on the date for partition and independence. He was followed by the Indian leaders, Pandit Nehru speaking in Hindi and Mr. Jinnah in English, translated for him into Urdu. It was with no joy in his heart, said Nehru, that he commended the proposals, though he had no doubt in his mind that it was the right course. 'It may be that in this way we shall reach that united India sooner than otherwise.' After describing the violence in the country as shameful and revolting, he expressed his deep appreciation of the labours of the Viceroy, and paid tribute to Mr. Gandhi, who had led the nation through darkness and sorrow to the threshold of freedom. Mr. Jinnah, while admitting that the plan did not altogether meet the Muslim League point of view, and declaring that it was for the League's All-India Council to say whether it should be accepted as a settlement, also paid tribute to Lord Mountbatten. The Viceroy had impressed him as being actuated by a high sense of fairness and impartiality. It was up to everyone to help him as much as possible to achieve the transfer of power in a peaceful and orderly manner. For the Sikhs, Sardar Baldev Singh said that the plan steered a course above conflicting claims. 'It does not please everybody, not the Sikh community anyway, but it is certainly something worth while.'

This was by no means the end, however, of the business of getting equal and simultaneous acceptance of the plan by the two main parties. The Working Committee of the Congress had given its concurrence provided that the Muslim League did so also and that no further claims were put forward. The All-India Council of the Muslim League met on 9th June. Although the meeting was private, Sardar Patel was able to send the Viceroy a transcript of shorthand notes of its proceedings, presumably taken by a Congress spy. The Council, in its resolution, was of opinion that 'although it cannot agree to the partition of Bengal and the Punjab or give its consent to such partition, it has to consider His Majesty's Government's plan for the transfer of power as a whole.' It accordingly resolved to give full authority to the League's President, Mr. Jinnah, 'to accept the fundamental principles of the Plan as a compromise', leaving it to him 'to work out all the details in an equitable and just manner' and empowering him to take all steps and decisions which might be necessary in connection with the plan.

This resolution caused an uproar in Congress circles. Pandit Nehru and Sardar Patel wrote violent letters of protest to the Viceroy, expressing the fear that they would not be able to manage the All-India Congress Committee, which would have before it a draft resolution accepting the plan 'in view of its acceptance by the Muslim League Council'. Lord Mountbatten kept back Sardar Patel and Mr. Liaqat Ali Khan after a Cabinet meeting on 12th June. Patel demanded that Mr. Jinnah give a firm acceptance in writing. Liaqat retorted that the League did not want to be outmanoeuvred by Congress reservations as they had been over the Cabinet Mission plan. The Viceroy suggested as a compromise that Mr. Jinnah should write him a letter saying that he, the Qaid-i-Azam, was authorised by the League's Council to accept the plan as a compromise settlement subject to the All-India Congress Committee doing likewise. Despite appeals by Mr. Liaqat Ali Khan, and later by the Viceroy in person, Mr. Jinnah categorically refused to sign such a letter until after the Congress had decided. Once more Lord Mountbatten had to take the responsibility. He wrote to Mr. Kripalani, as President of the A.I.C.C., recording that.

Mr. Jinnah came to see me this evening to inform me officially as President of the All-India Muslim League that the Council of the A.I.M.L. had empowered him to accept the plan contained in H.M.G.'s announcement of 3rd June as a compromise. Subject to the A.I.C.C. accepting this plan, he has given me his word that he will sign a joint document on behalf of the A.I.M.L. with such representatives as the A.I.C.C. may appoint, accepting this plan as a settlement.

A copy of this letter was sent to Mr. Jinnah without drawing a contradiction, and the trick was turned. This ludicrous procedural episode shows plainly the total lack of confidence or mutual respect that ruled between the leaders of the Congress and the League, and on the other hand the trust that both of them reposed in Lord Mountbatten.

The present account is concerned with facts, not with 'might-have-beens'. But it is a fact that the Viceroy and the British Government had to consider their options if the plan upon which they agreed in May were rejected by either of the two main parties in India. Assent by the Congress seemed assured: the possibility of rejection by the League was still open. Lord Mountbatten told Ministers in London that in that event there appeared four possible courses: to hand over power to the Interim Government, with the Cabinet Mission plan as the basis of constitutional transfer; to demit power to provinces; to impose the plan in the draft announcement as an award; to refer the whole matter to the United Nations. He rejected the first two and the last of these alternatives; in his view the third was the only possible course. The Prime Minister and other Ministers agreed with him. They thought that Mr. Jinnah might be persuaded if he were told that his refusal might lead to a scheme less favourable, from his point of view, than the present one; for instance, the partition of the Punjab might be on lines more favourable to the Sikhs. In the event, however, no such arm-twisting, to which several senior advisers of the Viceroy were strongly opposed, proved necessary. The balance between contending aspirations and power complexes in India appeared to have been struck at precisely the right point.

One consenting voice had yet to be gathered in. A few days after the announcement the Viceroy was told that Mr. Gandhi was in a very wretched, emotional mood and might denounce the plan at his next prayer meeting. Lord Mountbatten asked him to come round for a talk. The Mahatma was indeed obviously very upset, and began by saying how unhappy he was at Lord Mountbatten's spoiling his life's work. The Viceroy replied that while he shared Mr. Gandhi's distress at seeing a united India apparently destroyed, he hoped to convince him that the new plan was the only possible way to achieve an early and peaceful transfer of power. Indeed it might well have been called the Gandhi plan, since all its salient points had been suggested by him.

In the first place, Mr. Gandhi had pressed the Viceroy to try to get the Cabinet Mission plan or any other retaining the unity of India accepted by all the leaders, providing that it did not involve coercion or violence. Unable, despite every effort, to follow the first part of this advice, Lord Mountbatten had followed the second part and had not insisted on enforcing a scheme with grave risk of violent resistance. Secondly, Mr. Gandhi's advice had been to leave the choice of their future to the Indian people. It was therefore he who had given Lord Mountbatten the idea of letting the provinces choose, as the simplest and fairest way of carrying out that advice. Thirdly, Mr. Gandhi had urged that the British should quit India and transfer power as soon as possible: the Viceroy was very proud to have found a solution to this most difficult problem. He understood, he said, that in the past Mr. Gandhi had not been averse to Dominion Status. The Mahatma agreed, and later sent an extract from *Harijan* of 16th December 1939, in which he had written: 'I have said to a friend that if dominion status was offered, I should take it, and expect to carry India with me.'

Mr. Gandhi was obviously impressed and mollified. At his prayer meeting he spoke mildly, and when the Working Committee's acceptance of the plan was brought before the All-India Congress Committee on 14th June he supported the resolution. Peace in the country was essential, he said. There were two other parties to the settlement, he reminded them, and if they went back on it they would have to find a new set of leaders capable not only of heading the Congress but also of forming a Government. He himself had steadfastly opposed the division of India, yet he had come before them to urge acceptance of the resolution. There were times when certain decisions, however unpalatable, had to be taken, and this was such a time.

4 *The date of the transfer of power*

No bargains or conditions (other than acceptance by the opposite party) were attached to the party leaders' compliance with the plan. Sardar Patel was speaking with faulty memory when he said in the Constituent Assembly on 10th October 1949:

I agreed to partition as a last resort. . . . I made a further condition that in two months' time power should be transferred and

an Act should be passed by Parliament in that time, if it was
guaranteed that the British Government would not interfere
with the question of the Indian States.

As regards the States, the statement of 3rd June merely reiterated
the policy of letting paramountcy lapse which had been announced
by the Cabinet Mission. The States problem apparently played
no significant part in the two meetings with the party leaders
before the plan was promulgated: discussion on this came later.
As to the time-table, it was, of course, also part of the statement
that legislation would be introduced in the current session of
Parliament (with the intention, as the Viceroy explained to the
leaders, that it should be passed by the end of July) for the transfer
of power on a Dominion Status basis 'this year', that is to say not
later than 31st December 1947. The question of a much earlier
date was indeed discussed with the party leaders on 3rd June, but
there was no bargain or condition about it. Much of the private
negotiation with Sardar Patel was done by Mr. V. P. Menon,
but he left no record of any condition about timing.

When Lord Mountbatten, in May, had met British Cabinet
Ministers in London, he had told them that certain Congress leaders now favoured His Majesty's Government's announcing, simultaneously with the plan for the transfer of power, their intention
to grant Dominion Status to India or to its two parts 'as soon as
possible in 1947'. They thought the whole scheme would be
accepted if the actual transfer of power were thereby secured
'well before the end of 1947'. The difficulties of governing India
between the date of the announcement and the effective establishment of the successor authorities rendered it advisable to make the
transition period as short as possible. Lord Mountbatten's plea
was accepted, but no date for the transfer of power was fixed; there
is some evidence that the British Government were thinking of
1st October. Lord Mountbatten, in another conversation with
British Ministers, had specified 'not later than the early autumn of
1947'.

The date actually chosen suddenly appeared, as if by accident,
during Lord Mountbatten's Press conference on 4th June. Having
made it plain that the transfer of power would be effected in 1947,
not in 1948, he added: 'I think the transfer could be about the 15th
of August.' Once mentioned, that date seems to have taken root at

once and never thereafter to have been questioned. The first mention of it in Lord Mountbatten's private papers is in a document dated 12th June describing a very contentious Cabinet meeting the previous week (presumably on 7th June), as illustrating 'the appalling difficulty with which all of us are going to be faced during the 64 days that remain until partition is achieved on the 15th August'. These are terms in which one refers to an undisputed fact. In his retrospective despatch on his Viceroyalty, dated September 1948, Lord Mountbatten wrote:

> I also raised with the leaders on 3rd June the question of the date of the transfer of power. This had been discussed at staff meetings, and the decision had been taken that as early as possible a date should be chosen. The main factor in reaching this decision was the period during which it was likely to be possible to keep the existing Interim Government functioning. The Indian leaders agreed unanimously, without any sort of reservation, to the choice of 15th August. . . . I was able to inform representatives of the Princes of this at a meeting which took place later that day. . . .

Unfortunately, the minutes of the Viceroy's staff meetings do not record any such discussion and decision, nor is consideration of the date mentioned in his own contemporary account to the Secretary of State of the meetings with Indian leaders on 2nd and 3rd June, or in the published account by Mr. V. P. Menon, who was present.[1] It is certain, however, that the date of August 15th 1947 was firmly fixed in the Viceroy's purpose and accepted without demur by the Indian leaders during the first three days in June, though exactly how and why is the subject of recollection rather than immediate record.

Granted the need for great haste, lest the Government of India fall apart, the main reason for choosing 15th August appears to have been that it was, within a day or two, the earliest possible date, working forward either from the passage of the necessary Act of Parliament,[2] the drafting of which in turn had to await the outcome of decisions taken on partition in the Punjab and Bengal, or from the initiation of work on the administrative consequences of

[1] *The Transfer of Power in India*, pp. 373–7.
[2] The Indian Independence Act received the Royal Assent on 18th July 1947.

partition, including division of the Army, or from the appointment and deliberations of the Boundary Commissions which were to draw the mutual frontiers of India and Pakistan—though the Act expressly provided that the final boundaries could be determined by the Commissions' awards either before or after the appointed day. Serious consideration of phasing does not appear to have had more than marginal effect on the Viceroy's overriding belief that the sooner partition and the transfer of power were completed the less likely would be a breakdown of central government or a recrudescence of large-scale communal disorder and rapine.[1] That 16th August was the anniversary of Direct Action Day, which launched 'the great Calcutta killing', was probably no accident; for repetition or even recollection of such an occasion, before partition but within weeks of its fulfilment, might have let loose disaster.

One unexpected difficulty assailed the choice of 15th August. The Viceroy was not warned that he should consult the astrologers before fixing the date of the transfer of power. He learned, barely a week beforehand, that they had pronounced the 15th inauspicious, though the 14th would be lucky. The difficulty was overcome by summoning the Constituent Assembly late on the evening of the 14th, and having it take over as the Legislative Assembly of independent India as midnight struck, which was apparently still an auspicious moment. The date chosen was within three days of the anniversary of Mr. Edwin Montagu's historic declaration of India's goal of responsible self-government in 1917. It had taken exactly thirty years for that policy to reach its culmination.

---

[1] 'Everybody wanted the greatest possible speed. . . . Indeed why wait? For in waiting there would be the risk of continued and increasing riots. . . . So we went ahead and fixed a date.' Lord Mountbatten, in an address to the East India Association, 29th June 1948. V. P. Menon records (*The Transfer of Power in India*, p. 396) that the problem of holding together the Interim Government 'was one of the considerations that prompted Lord Mountbatten to press for the transfer of power earlier than the stipulated period'. This must refer rather to the general need for hurry than to the precise fixing of the date in August.

18

The period of dissection

1 *The Interim Government*

The members of the Bengal and Punjab Provincial Assemblies voted in favour of partition during the last week in June. The way for division of the whole country was thus open. The Sind Assembly voted 3 to 2 for Pakistan. In Sylhet a 4 to 3 majority of the voters decided early in July in favour of joining East Bengal. A provisional line now ran, therefore, down the middle of the Punjab and along the border of Sind, and through the provinces of Bengal and Assam, on one side of which the country had a national destiny as India, on the other side as Pakistan.[1] Yet the existing Governments, provincial and central, straddled both sides of the line and had constitutional authority over their whole areas. How were these two facts to be reconciled in day-to-day government?

The Punjab was being administered under Section 93, and therefore had no problem of political bisection. In Bengal, where a Muslim Ministry was in office, the solution found was to set up a second Ministry for West Bengal, sworn in as members of the provincial Executive but having authority only in their own part of the province, while the existing Ministry, though in administrative charge of the provincial portfolios, could apply their policies only in East Bengal, unless the West Bengal Ministers agreed.

The Viceroy, pressed hard by Pandit Nehru, who had always

[1] This presupposes the adherence of the North-West Frontier Province to Pakistan. It was not until 6th to 17th July that the referendum was held there. It was boycotted by the Congress, and the vote was 289,244 for Pakistan and 2,874 against, a bare majority of the electorate of 572,798. In the conditions of the Frontier, however, a considerable percentage of normal non-voters must be admitted, and if this were only 10 per cent the majority for Pakistan would have been over 5 to 4; if 20 per cent, the majority would have been nearly 2 to 1. The total number of valid votes cast in the previous provincial election had been 375,989.

claimed that the League members of the Interim Government were there on false pretences, and who threatened resignation if they continued to share in the government of India, proposed a similar device at the Centre. The Cabinet, he recommended, should work in two committees, one consisting of Union of India members who would hold the actual portfolios but would confine their activities to the prospective area of India, the other of holders of Pakistan portfolios who would be responsible for the interests of the prospective Pakistan area. Mr. Jinnah, however, flatly refused to accept this, on the grounds that it was insulting to the Muslim League and was moreover illegal. For the latter claim he received some support from the British authorities when the point was referred to London by the Viceroy. This was fortunate, since if the plan had been pronounced legal the Viceroy would have been faced either with the resignation of the League members on his trying to apply it or by the resignation of the Congress members on his failing to do so. In the end, aided by a diplomatic telegram from Mr. Attlee, he persuaded both parties to accept deferment of the problem until after the Indian Independence Bill had been passed. Meanwhile the Interim Government continued its bickering and disjointed existence.

Three days after the passage of the Bill, a plan similar to that previously rejected was put into effect, with virtually two parallel Cabinets, one for prospective India and the other for prospective Pakistan. But by this time it was possible to bisect the administrative machine itself. The existing departments, under the Congress Ministers, would be manned only by staff who had elected to stay in India; new departments, concerned only with Pakistan, would be set up in Delhi and manned by those who had elected to join the new Dominion. Thus for exactly four weeks an embryo Cabinet and administration for Pakistan was in being under the old constitution and under the aegis of the Viceroy. Short as the period was, the early days of Pakistan might otherwise have seen governmental chaos.

2 The administrative dissection

The legal and constitutional exercise of implementing the 3rd June plan was not particularly difficult, for the Act of 1935 provided the whole framework. It was conducted, in association with the India

Office, by Mr. V. P. Menon as Reforms Commissioner, assisted by Sir George Spence,[1] formerly Secretary of the Law Department, and a lawyer sent out at Lord Mountbatten's request from London. The administrative exercise was a very different matter.

The paper on *The Administrative Consequences of Partition*, which caused a sensation when the Viceroy suddenly produced it at his meeting with the Indian leaders on 3rd June, contained a proposal that the mechanism for sorting out these matters should centre in a Partition Committee with equal representation of both sides. At the next meeting with the leaders two days later, the setting up of such a Committee was about the only point that could be agreed, as both sides took the opportunity to make political speeches. A characteristic difficulty next arose because Pandit Nehru and his Congress colleagues, who took the view that India would enjoy continuity of government and that the problem was to make provision for the separated areas, urged that the Partition Committee should be a Committee of the Cabinet; whereas Mr. Jinnah objected that the constitutional authority for these affairs was His Majesty's Government or the Governor-General himself, not the Governor-General in Council. At one stage Pandit Nehru said that, whoever the responsible authority might be, the matter had obviously nothing to do with the President of the Muslim League; therefore Mr. Jinnah was 'out of court'. Sardar Patel chipped in: 'He only came into court at all by civil disobedience.' 'In which you are an expert,' retorted Mr. Jinnah. Such was the atmosphere in which these high issues of state were considered. Mr. Jinnah eventually agreed that the Partition Committee should consist of four members of the Interim Government, two from the Congress and two from the League, but should not be described as a Cabinet Committee. Immediately after the decision for partition had been taken in the provinces, the Partition Committee gave way to a Partition Council, with full powers to reach final decisions, to consist likewise of two members from each side, who need not be Cabinet Ministers. It was unanimously agreed that Lord Mountbatten should preside over the Partition Committee

[1] Sir George Spence, though personally wishing to retire, volunteered to serve as officer on special duty in the Reforms Office, under Mr. Menon who had worked as a clerk under him a generation earlier. Such self-effacing devotion to duty was characteristic of the best of government servants in India, both British and Indian.

and Council, but he stipulated that he should have no arbitral power or responsibility.

Some sort of arbitral machinery appeared essential. It was quickly agreed that this should consist of a tribunal of three men of high judicial experience. But who should be chairman? The Secretary of State offered Sir Cyril Radcliffe,[1] who afterwards became Chairman of the Boundary Commissions. The Congress objected to having anyone from outside India, and proposed that the Federal Court become the arbitral tribunal. This Mr. Jinnah would not have. But eventually it was agreed that the tribunal should be presided over by the resigning Chief Justice of India, Sir Patrick Spens. Like a goalkeeper spending a cold afternoon behind good backs, the Tribunal proved a moral rather than a practical necessity.

At its first meeting the Partition Committee agreed to set up a Steering Committee consisting of two officials, Mr. H. M. Patel, the Cabinet Secretary, and Mr. Chaudhuri Mohammed Ali,[2] the Financial Adviser to the Military Finance Department, two exceptionally able men trusted alike by their own communities and by each other. It was also agreed that the ten expert sub-committees of the main Committee should be manned by officials. It is a tribute to the spirit and skill of the old Civil Service of India that such an immense task was carried through in so short a time and with so little friction.

The expert sub-committees, which covered the whole field of administration from departmental records to currency and national debt, from contracts to foreign relations, put up a large number of agreed recommendations, while the Steering Committee was able to reach agreement on most of the remaining issues. Only a handful of matters remained unsettled on the day of independence and partition. Even these never went to the Tribunal; for a special meeting in Delhi of representatives of the two Dominions, under Lord Mountbatten's chairmanship, agreed to remit them all to Mr. Patel and Mr. Mohammed Ali, who in every instance were able to evolve an acceptable formula. All references to the Arbitral Tribunal were then withdrawn.[3] Lord Mountbatten's tactics

[1] Later Viscount Radcliffe.
[2] Later first Secretary General of the Pakistan Government, and Prime Minister of Pakistan, 1955–6.
[3] See below, p. 503.

throughout were never to allow matters to reach a deadlock from which the parties could not resile, but instead to end debate with a proposal that the matter be further considered either by the Steering Committee or otherwise. In no case did these tactics eventually fail.

That is not to say that all went smoothly. Typical of the conflicts that arose was the affair of the printing presses. In the Partition Committee Mr. Liaqat Ali Khan asked that one of the Government of India's six presses should be moved from Delhi to Karachi, where there was only one press inadequate to the provincial Government's needs, let alone those of Pakistan. Sardar Patel refused, declaring that all six presses were fully occupied with Government of India work. To an appeal from the Viceroy he replied: 'No one asked Pakistan to secede. We do not mind their taking their property with them, but we have no intention of allowing them to injure the work of the Government of India merely because they have not enough resources of their own.' Lord Mountbatten rebuked him sternly, and later persuaded him privately to release one press to Pakistan on condition that it remained in Delhi and that the user would cease as soon as a new press had been bought and set up in Karachi. Lord Mountbatten further telegraphed London urging that such a press be supplied with the highest priority, and this was done.

Much graver, and more portentous for the future, was a dispute that arose in the Partition Council early in August over the provisional allocation of the rights, liabilities and property of the Governor-General in Council. It was obvious that the eventual division in detail would take time and that a holding order was necessary, expressly without prejudice to the final arrangements. The Viceroy accordingly drew up a draft order—to be issued on his own responsibility—providing among other things that the National Debt was to devolve upon India. When this came before the Partition Council at its last two meetings on 5th and 6th August, the Pakistan representatives objected strongly to this provision, under which Pakistan would become the debtor of the Dominion of India for Pakistan's proportionate share of the whole debt. This, they argued, would put Pakistan in a weak bargaining position in any dispute over the ultimate allocation of assets, and in particular would prejudice her claims on the existing cash balances of the Government of India.

Although Lord Mountbatten was satisfied that both common sense and convenience were on the side of his proposal, he was anxious (being now Governor-General designate of India but not of Pakistan) not to be thought to favour India's interests against Pakistan. He therefore sent the draft order to the Secretary of State and set about trying to persuade Mr. Jinnah by satisfying him that reasonable terms would be arranged for repayment of Pakistan's share of the National Debt. He also tried, but in vain, to get the Indian representatives to agree to hand over to Pakistan more than the Rs. 20 crores (£15,000,000) which they had so far accepted as Pakistan's interim allocation from the existing cash balances. Mr. Jinnah, now in Karachi, telephoned his flat refusal. The Viceroy then sent his constitutional draftsman, Mr. Cooke, to Karachi with Mr. Mohammed Ali to try to convince Mr. Jinnah that unless he put forward a compromise acceptable to India he ran the risk of starting an economic war which would probably be disastrous to a nascent Pakistan. Nothing came of this effort, except a formula about assets slightly more acceptable to Pakistan, but Lord Mountbatten contrived to get Sardar Patel to write him a letter stating that, if an order were passed making India liable for the National Debt, she would be content to recover Pakistan's proportionate share (about Rs. 200 crores, or £150,000,000) over a period of about fifty years, beginning in 1951. When the Viceroy was in Karachi on the eve of the transfer of power he again tackled Mr. Jinnah and Mr. Liaqat Ali Khan. The latter was persuaded that, in view of Sardar Patel's letter, Pakistan would not suffer under the order. Mr. Jinnah ended up by saying: 'Well, if you have put the matter in the Secretary of State's hands there is nothing more I can do about it.' The Secretary of State having approved the order, it was issued on 14th August. The position was saved in the nick of time. But this was true of so much else besides.

3 The divided Governor-Generalship

As has already been recorded, until the second week in May Lord Mountbatten was thinking in terms of India's probably leaving the Commonwealth on the transfer of power, and of Dominion Status for India or its parts as being a possible interim stage, lasting perhaps from January to June, 1948. Even if all the Indian parties, he reflected, were to agree on asking for continued membership of the Commonwealth, he saw the task of a British Governor-General, shorn of constitutional power but acting as 'a high-level umpire', as fraught with difficulties. This thought remained with him after the decision had been taken to accelerate the complete transfer of power on the basis that both India and Pakistan became Dominions within the Commonwealth. Thus he told his staff on 31st May that while it would obviously simplify many problems if both prospective Dominions were to have the same Governor-General he did not feel that the latter should have the powers of an arbitrator, and that in no circumstances would he himself accept appointment in such a role.

On the 17th May, on the eve of Lord Mountbatten's departure for London to propound his revised plan to the Cabinet, Pandit Nehru had written to him, on behalf of his Congress colleagues:

> We agree that during the interim period (i.e. until partition had been completed) the Governors-General should be common to both the States.

Lord Mountbatten's reply gracefully accepted Mr. Nehru's express wish that he should stay on, but on condition that a similar invitation must be received from the Muslim League. On the same day he saw Mr. Jinnah and Mr. Liaqat Ali Khan. The former said that while he would not commit himself he felt it would be better to have two Governors-General, together with a representative of the Crown responsible for the division of assets. He was keen that Lord Mountbatten should accept this role. The Viceroy replied that he could not think of it. An impossible situation would arise if the so-called Arbitrator were junior in status to the Governors-General, as he must be since they would be the King's representatives. Nevertheless, he invited Mr. Jinnah to send him a letter within the next two days setting out his proposal in full, for submission to His Majesty's Government. He pressed Mr. Jinnah to agree to a common Governor-General as the alternative if H.M.G. found his plan unworkable, but obtained no straight answer. The letter requested was never received, despite reminders by Sir Eric Miéville, who was deputed to telegraph it to the Viceroy in London. Consequently Mr. Jinnah's idea was canvassed informally with representatives of the India Office, who were unanimously of opinion that it was unconstitutional and unworkable. Mr. Jinnah appeared by his silence to have come to the same conclusion.

After the plan of 3rd June had been accepted, the issue became clearer. A week later Lord Mountbatten expressed to his staff the view that it was essential that the legislation to implement the plan should enable both India and Pakistan to have the same Governor-General, at any rate to begin with. His own name should in no way be associated with this provision. After careful consideration he had come to the conclusion that he could not stay as Governor-General of India alone, if Pakistan did not want the same Governor-General. It would be fatal for Mr. Jinnah to know of this decision. The Viceroy's mind was running on the lines of having, in the shape of a common Governor-General, a supreme constitutional authority who could bridge and settle by mediation the conflicts and issues inevitably arising between the two Dominions. He spoke of keeping on his present staff if he stayed in that role; he had told Mr. Attlee that were he to remain as a constitutional Governor-General he would require, not as big a staff as at present, but 'a team of high-level experts' to aid him in giving advice and guidance and acting as a mediator. He had also discussed the matter with Pandit Nehru, whose view had been that the Governor-General after the transfer of power would be in a very different position from a normal Dominion Governor-General; in the initial stages at least, his influence would count for a great deal, and he, Nehru, doubted whether the processes of partition would work satisfactorily unless Lord Mountbatten personally stayed on. Mr. V. P. Menon observed at this staff meeting that in regard to the States also an independent advisor and guide would be of the greatest benefit. Even Mr. Gandhi had said he would be willingly guided by the decisions of any committee of which Lord Ismay, for example, was Chairman.

One acute member of the Viceroy's staff said firmly that in his view the Governor-General should not be Chairman of any Committee with executive or political authority after the transfer of power. (If this counsel had been followed, history might have told a different tale of the crises in India, and between India and Pakistan, in the ten months after 15th August 1947.) Lord Mountbatten agreed that it would be out of the question for him to take the chair at meetings of either side separately: but precedent had to be dismissed in these matters. If he personally was the only man holding office in both Dominions, it might well be possible for him to take the chair at meetings between them, without a vote and only to guide discussion.

The position therefore was this: the Viceroy, assuming that both Dominions invited him—and the draft Bill had meanwhile been drawn to provide that the existing Governor-General of India, unless and until another appointment was made, should become forthwith Governor-General of each of the two Dominions—was prepared to accept the office for an interim period, not as an arbitrator but as a mediator, and as non-executive chairman, if required, of joint Indo-Pakistani organs; on no account would he become Governor-General of one Dominion alone. Pakistan, he felt, would gain the most from a joint Governor-Generalship on those lines, since she was the weaker party in many respects, the more in need of an impartial figure at the top watching the process of partition. His staff agreed with him. On those assumptions Lord Mountbatten suggested to them that Viceregal Lodge, Simla, might be considered 'neutral territory'. Although most of his staff as joint Governor-General would obviously have to be Indians and Pakistanis, he would be greatly handicapped in the difficult negotiations that would fall to him if he did not have at least Lord Ismay and Sir Eric Miéville to help him.

On the evening of 2nd July, however, Mr. Jinnah came to see the Viceroy 'to seek his advice'. He wished, he said, to have British Governors in all provinces of Pakistan except Sind, and had already appointed three British officers as chiefs of the Armed Services. The only way, he considered, in which all this could become acceptable to the people of Pakistan was that he himself should be Governor-General. Mr. Jinnah said that he had been unwilling to do this, but had been so advised by three or four intimate friends and colleagues whom he had consulted.

The Viceroy recorded sourly:

I did not know to whom Mr. Jinnah referred. But I did know that his principal friend and adviser was the Nawab of Bhopal, who had told me three days previously that Mr. Jinnah had specifically consulted him on this point, and that he had told Mr. Jinnah that he thought that it would be an act of the utmost folly to reject the chance of having a common Governor-General with a British staff until . . . the end of the partition period. It was also clear from what Mr. Liaqat Ali Khan had said that he shared the Nawab of Bhopal's view. I therefore had difficulty in not reaching the conclusion that the only adviser to whom Mr. Jinnah listened was Mr. Jinnah.

I pointed out to him that if he became the constitutional Governor-General of Pakistan his powers would be constitutionally restricted and that he would act only on advice, but that as Prime Minister he could really run Pakistan. His answer was significant. He said: 'In my position it is I who will give the advice, and others who will act on it.'[1]

Lord Mountbatten argued with him vigorously and tried for a compromise solution: that whenever the common Governor-General was not in Pakistan—which would be by far the greater part of the year, since partition work under his auspices would have to proceed in Delhi—there should be an 'officiating Governor-General'—who would presumably be Mr. Jinnah. Inserting this device in the draft Bill, he was able to say after slipping off for consultation, would have the support of Congress leaders. But Mr. Jinnah categorically refused to accept it. Lord Mountbatten, reporting to the Secretary of State two days later, described this conversation as a 'bombshell'. He could not forbear to show his wounded and hostile reaction.

> Jinnah solemnly assured me that he realised all the disadvantages of giving up the common Governor-General, that his one ambition was that I should stay on as Viceroy, or overall Governor-General, to see the partition through, but he was unable to accept any position other than that of Governor-General of Pakistan on 15th August.
>
> I asked him 'Do you realise what this will cost you?' He said sadly 'It may cost me several crores of rupees in assets', to which I replied somewhat acidly, 'It may well cost you the whole of your assets and the future of Pakistan.' I then got up and left the room.[2]

The next day Lord Mountbatten discussed the new situation with some of his staff. No minute was kept of this conversation, but from subsequent records two things are clear: first, that Lord

[1] *Report on the Last Viceroyalty.*
[2] *Viceroy's Personal Report* No. 11, 4th July 1947.

Mountbatten was personally very strongly disinclined to consider accepting the Governor-Generalship of India alone, and in this was vigorously supported by Lady Mountbatten, and secondly that the staff with one unnamed exception took the contrary view— to the surprise of Their Excellencies, since only a couple of days previously the staff had regarded such a course as unthinkable. Colonel Erskine Crum, the Conference Secretary, put down the reasons for the staff's conclusion in a paper which was considered at a regular staff meeting the next day, 4th July.

Lord Mountbatten then said that he was clear in his conscience that he had done everything in his power to put plainly before Mr. Jinnah the advantages of having the same Governor-General as India at least during the initial period. The most painful part of all this to him was that he had, quite unintentionally, deceived the Congress leadership. He clearly attached some weight to the opinion given him by the Nawab of Bhopal, that the only hope for Pakistan now was for him to stay on as Governor-General of India —and the only hope for the States too. From a personal standpoint, said Lord Mountbatten, the position was much more difficult, and he could not decide at once.

In his report of that date to London, which was taken personally to the Secretary of State by Lord Ismay, the Viceroy wrote:

> I am now in a complete quandary. I have always held the view that I should stay on with both sides or neither of them. I never dreamt that both sides would ask me to stay on with one side. My own inclination is to go, for I have always felt and said that I considered it morally wrong to stay on with only one of the two sides. But unfortunately I fear that I have unintentionally led Nehru and all the Congress leaders up the garden path and that they will never forgive me for allowing Jinnah once more to have his way. I therefore feel that this is a matter on which I require higher guidance, and have considered it essential to send Ismay to seek it.

Lord Ismay also took with him a document drawn up by the Viceroy's staff setting out 'Reasons for and against Lord Mountbatten's staying on as Governor-General of the Dominion of India'. For tactical purposes, no doubt, the defendant in that cause was given the last word. The following is a condensation of this document.

A *Against*

1 *Mixed reception in India.* People hostile to the 'Nehru-Patel clique' by whom the invitation had been extended would say that the British were trying to retain their hold.

2 *Depressing effect in Pakistan.* Muslims would feel that Lord Mountbatten had deserted them for the stronger side.

3 *Criticism by world opinion,* already hostile to partition.

4 *No real help on partition.* As Governor-General of one Dominion Lord Mountbatten could not logically be expected to act impartially on partition matters, nor would it be reasonable to ask the Government of India to allow him to be impartial.

5 *Moral objections.* The example of the Governors of Bengal and the Punjab, who had refused to stay in any capacity with either part of their partitioned provinces, had been applauded and should be followed. For Lord Mountbatten to stay on with one side only when his mission had been accomplished would be 'undignified and morally wrong'.

B *For*

1 *A personal appointment.* It would be Lord Mountbatten's personal relationship with the leaders of the two Dominions rather than his office that would be the stabilising influence.

2 *Importance to the Armed Services.* Field Marshal Auchinleck had said that if Lord Mountbatten left he would resign; other Commanders would probably follow suit, and few British officers would volunteer to remain. 'The one stable element in India, namely the Army, might well disintegrate, and riot and bloodshed on an appalling scale would result.' On the other hand, if Lord Mountbatten remained, British officers and officials would be reassured, and the partition of the Armed Forces would go through smoothly.

3 *Value in partition.* Decisions of the Partition Council and Arbitral Tribunal would have a far better chance of being implemented.

4 *Political effects.* Relations between India and Pakistan, and conditions in India itself, both of which would have great effect on the situation in South-East Asia, would be more likely to be friendly and stable.

5 *The States.* Lord Mountbatten's advice to the Indian

Government and the States Rulers on their mutual relations would be invaluable.

6 *Effect at Westminster*. The Opposition in Parliament might delay the Independence Bill if faced with the prospect of two non-British Governors-General.

7 *Pakistan's support*. Mr Jinnah had stated, and Mr. Liaqat Ali Khan had confirmed in writing, that they would welcome Lord Mountbatten's appointment as Governor-General of India.

8 *Value for Britain and the Commonwealth*. From the British point of view, in addition to the advantages derived from the above benefits to India and Pakistan, great prestige value would be gained if India had asked that her first Governor-General after independence should be British. India would then be much more likely to stay in the Commonwealth indefinitely. But 'if His Excellency were to go, and if the Indian Government were thus turned down in their application for a British Governor-General, they would be as a lover scorned'.

9 *World opinion*, so far from criticising a decision to stay, might well attack him for making a quick getaway with the job half done.

Even with hindsight it is impossible to prove or disprove the merit of these arguments. We know what happened, but we do not know what would have happened if Lord Mountbatten had not stayed as Governor-General of India. How far his presence determined what did happen is itself a matter of judgment.

One thing, however, is plain. The relations between India and Pakistan, so far from being friendly apart from disputes over implementing partition, as both the critics and the defenders assumed at the time, rapidly deteriorated as a result of events which they did not foresee—first the Punjab massacres and migrations and then the conflict in Kashmir. This lent special weight to a reason 'against' which was not made in the memorandum though it was implied in reason 4 and in the earlier objection by a staff member to Lord Mountbatten's chairing any committee with political or executive responsibility—namely, that in the event of inter-Dominion conflict the Governor-General of India would be bound, both constitutionally and implicitly in the public view, to support the cause of that nation with whose Government he was identified and was in daily contact, from which Government indeed he was obliged to accept advice even though he might disagree with it. On the other hand it is also a fact that despite those bad relations the process of partition went through without serious hitch, and that in one crucial case on the transfer of cash assets in the midst of the Kashmir conflict Lord Mountbatten's efforts on behalf of Pakistan against tensely-held Indian policy appear to have been decisive.[1]

More influential, perhaps, than the reactions of his staff were those which came from London. Lord Ismay arrived in London on 7th July. Meanwhile Mr. Jinnah had once more asked Lord Mountbatten to become Governor-General of India only and to be Chairman of the Indo-Pakistani Joint Defence Council; and Field Marshal Auchinleck had said at a Viceroy's staff meeting that he doubted whether he and other senior British officers would be able to carry on without Lord Mountbatten's advice and support. The Prime Minister and other Ministers whom Lord Ismay saw on the evening of his arrival were unanimous in favour of Lord Mountbatten's staying. Mr. Attlee observed that both parties in India clearly had complete confidence in him, Mr. Jinnah's self-nomination being only a piece of egotism, and that if the Government advised Lord Mountbatten to leave India the Congress might say that Britain was yielding to Jinnah at their expense. On the other hand, Lord Mountbatten could best influence the Congress leaders to give Pakistan a fair deal in the division of assets. But the decisive argument was that no one could compare with Lord Mountbatten in qualification to secure the successful transfer of power, which was the paramount object. To stay might react on his personal position, but in the interests of India and Pakistan he ought to complete the work that he had so ably started. The same advice was given by the Opposition leaders who were consulted the next day. Lord Ismay himself went to Chartwell, where Mr. Churchill dictated the following message to be sent to the Viceroy:

Mr. Churchill did not think that an exact symmetry and balance of the appointments at the top was important. What mattered was to find what worked best in the circumstances if Mr. Jinnah

[1] See below, p. 505.

became Governor-General of Pakistan. This would not make
him more unfriendly to our country or less dependent upon it.
Such a solution for Pakistan would make it all the more important that all possible guidance should be given to Hindustan.
Under the British constitution, which is much in vogue in India
at the present time, the King reigns but does not govern. He has,
however, an unlimited right to receive information and to give
advice which Ministers may take or reject on their own responsibility. On this basis Lord Mountbatten might be of great help to
the Hindustan Government in the next year or so and in Mr.
Churchill's opinion he ought not to withhold that aid. He can
strive to mitigate quarrels between Hindu and Muslim, safeguard the position of Princes when that is involved, and preserve
such ties of sentiment as are possible between the Government
of Hindustan and that of the other Dominions of the Crown (or
Commonwealth). It will be for Lord Mountbatten himself alone
to decide whether any point is reached where his conscientious-
ness or patriotic loyalty is involved, or when his usefulness is
exhausted.

Lord Ismay also saw His Majesty the King, who was convinced
that Lord Mountbatten should accept the Governor-Generalship
of India. Mr. Attlee cabled asking him 'most earnestly' to do so.
'I believe this to be essential,' declared the British Prime Minister,
'if the transition is to go through smoothly. You have the trust of
both parties in India and of all parties here. You need have no fear
that anyone would think it improper for you to be Governor-
General of one new Dominion or that it would reflect on your
impartiality.'

Lord Mountbatten told his staff on 9th July that he had finally
made up his mind. He wished it to be put on record, however,
though for the last time, that he was still most uneasy and unhappy
about this decision; in accepting the overpowering advice which he
had received from London, he considered he was choosing the
lesser of two evils. Pandit Nehru and Sardar Patel, he said, could
not have been more charming or approving when he had shown
them the draft of the Prime Minister's statement in Parliament.
He had insisted that this should include the formula 'at all events
for the transition period' because this left him free to choose the
date at which he could depart with honour.

4 *The Communal War of Succession*

Although there were serious communal disorders in many parts of northern India in the interval before the transfer of power, including a number of violent incidents in Calcutta, in which rioters sometimes used sten guns, by far the worst and most menacing for for the future were in the Punjab. In Gurgaon, close to Delhi, the situation was already grave when the plan was announced. The Hindus appeared to be the original aggressors against the primitive Meo (Muslim) community, though retaliation swiftly followed. Fighting proceeded on a fifty-mile front, and village after village was burnt by the rival communities; the troops available were raised from a battalion to a brigade. When the situation was discussed in Cabinet on 10th June, Congress members demanded the removal of the Deputy Commissioner, an Englishman. The Governor of the Punjab, however, supported him, and refused to make transfers under political pressure.

Meanwhile trouble was worsening rapidly in Lahore and Amritsar. Instead of mass riots, individual cases of arson and stabbing developed on a large scale. These were extremely difficult to combat in the conditions of an Indian city, either by the police, or, still more, by the military. On 23rd June Mr. Jinnah begged the Viceroy to be absolutely ruthless in suppressing disorder in Amritsar and Lahore. He said: 'I don't care whether you shoot Muslims or not, it has got to be stopped.' The next day Pandit Nehru came and spoke in a similar strain. He suggested turning over the cities to the military, withdrawing the police 'who were being accused of communal partiality' and declaring martial law. The Governor, Sir Evan Jenkins, to whom the proposal was referred, opposed this. In doing so he was following the opinions of the senior military commanders, who were in principle opposed to declaring martial law unless it were to protect their own organisation, preferring the well-tried system of providing troops 'in aid of the civil power'. Their advice to the Governor had been, in effect: 'If we take over we shall have to use your magistrates and the rest of the civil structure. We are certainly not able to replace them, and we have no reason to believe that the change would improve matters.' Moreover, Sir Evan argued, in his reply, that against 'cloak and dagger' tactics troops were helpless, and the likely failure of martial law would actually make matters worse, by drawing upon the military the same charges of bias as were levied against the police.

Discussion of these opinions in the Cabinet evoked a violent attack on all British officers, from the Governor downwards. Sardar Patel said bitingly that the British had had little difficulty in maintaining law and order when it was a question of putting down Indian freedom movements. 'It was a case,' he said, 'of the British covering up for the British.' The Governor-General called him to order and he apologised. The Muslim League members were equally vehement, saying that there would be no Lahore left for them to inherit. Finally it was agreed that the Governor of the Punjab should be invited to form a Security Committee composed of leaders of all three communities, which should among other things advise as to officials in whom they had confidence. Sir Evan Jenkins formed his Security Committee but it was soon hamstrung by Muslim non-co-operation. Consultative devices indeed had little relevance to the plague of violence, some individual and some organised, which was now raging in the Punjab.

While it is difficult to apportion blame between the communities for the Punjab disorders in the first month after the announcement of the plan for the transfer of power, from early July onwards the main instigators were certainly the Sikhs. They had suffered terribly in Rawalpindi and were thirsty for revenge. The Muslim leaders did nothing to appease them, and their own often inflamed their latent animosities. Even Sardar Baldev Singh, the Defence Member of the Central Cabinet, was reported in the Press to have said at a meeting on 8th July that, if the boundary award went against the Sikhs, they would resist it, and would not count any sacrifice too great to vindicate the honour of the Panth, though when Lord Mountbatten taxed him with this utterance he indignantly denied it. On 10th July Mr. Giani Kartar Singh, a prominent Sikh leader, openly warned Sir Evan Jenkins that if the Sikhs were not satisfied by the Boundary Commission's award they would take violent action, and would sabotage communications and canal works. When the Viceroy visited Lahore on 20th July he met the Punjab Partition Committee, and among other matters persuaded them to issue a statement, similar to one which the Central Partition Council was at his instance putting out, giving full assurances to minorities in either future Dominion, calling for peace, and declaring that violence would not be tolerated, especially in the areas affected by the boundary awards; but the publication of this statement, which was to be signed by other men of influence in the Punjab as well as members of the Partition Committee, was shelved because, significantly, other Sikh leaders refused to put their names to it. On 27th July Giani Kartar Singh was among many arrested in demonstrations around Nankana Sahib, a Sikh shrine, where several thousand Sikhs had gathered despite a ban on such an assembly.

On 5th August the Governor of the Punjab sent an officer of the Criminal Investigation Department, Mr. Savage, to see the Viceroy personally and urgently. Lord Mountbatten was called out of a Partition Council meeting, and having heard the report and returned to the Council, which was about to adjourn, kept back Mr. Jinnah, Mr. Liaqat Ali Khan and Sardar Patel, to whom the officer repeated his report. Statements made by men arrested at demonstrations had incriminated, among others, Master Tara Singh in the production of bombs and in Sikh plans to attack certain canal headworks, to wreck trains carrying Pakistan officials from Delhi to Karachi, and to assassinate Mr. Jinnah by throwing a bomb into the open car that he was expected to use for his State drive during the independence celebrations of 14th August. Mr. Jinnah and Mr. Liaqat Ali Khan immediately demanded the arrest of the Sikh leaders. Sardar Patel was against their arrest, which he thought would only precipitate trouble. Lord Mountbatten was in favour of arrest, provided that the authorities on the spot concurred. When the proposal was put to Sir Evan Jenkins he replied that he had discussed arresting Tara Singh and other Sikh leaders with Sir Chandulal Trivedi and Sir Francis Mudie, Governors designate of East and West Punjab, and they had unanimously agreed that such arrests would only cause a deterioration in the situation in the Punjab. The Viceroy felt the better able to accept this decision because he had already arranged to accompany Mr. Jinnah in the State procession on 14th August. The failure to arrest the Sikh leaders was afterwards bitterly denounced in Pakistan, in the light of all that followed, and became one of the chief Pakistani grievances against Lord Mountbatten, ranking with his alleged pro-Indian leaning in the application of partition and his part (supposed rather than known) in the Kashmir affair. Some culprit had to be found for the sufferings of Muslims in the aftermath of partition in the Punjab, and for this the Sikhs were clearly marked out: blame was then focussed upon Lord Mount-batten for failure to prevent the Sikhs from the murderous violence in which as a community they undoubtedly indulged in the sum-mer and autumn of 1947. The Viceroy's threats of the most drastic action against law-breakers while he remained responsible were known: the charge was that they remained words, not deeds. Specifically, Pakistan leaders have insisted that he ought to have ordered the arrest of Master Tara Singh and other militant Sikh leaders in July or August, and have removed the Rulers of Sikh States like Patiala who were believed to be harbouring, encoura-ging and even arming Sikh bands for violence in the Punjab.

The complicity of Patiala and other Sikh States was and still is a matter of conjecture. To depose a Ruler or take away his powers was not an action easily undertaken at any time, let alone when every organ of government, including those concerned with the States, was stretched to the limit, or when the alleged offence was his support for a cause ardently expressed by his people. It could have been done, no doubt, but whether it would have had any good effect on the situation, or instead have further inflamed the Sikhs, is very much open to debate. As for arresting the Sikh leaders in the Punjab, Lord Mountbatten had been personally in favour of it, but he accepted the deliberate advice to the contrary given him by those responsible for law and order in the Punjab, west as well as east, before and after partition. As a former Deputy Commissioner of Hoshiapur, Gurdaspur and Amritsar, Sir Evan Jenkins, the Governor, knew the Sikhs and their ways intimately, and was certainly not regarded by them as pro-Sikh or anti-Muslim. He was well aware that, once roused to fanatical action, as they had been not only by the prospect of the Punjab partition but also by their experiences in Rawalpindi, they were unlikely to be deterred either by casualties, or by arrests, or by deprivation of leaders. He believed that, with less than a fortnight to go before the transfer of power, putting the leaders behind bars would in any case be a futile and probably self-defeating exercise. Lord Mountbatten is certainly not to be blamed for accepting his advice, backed by that of Sir Chandulal Trivedi and Sir Francis Mudie.

On 4th August the Governor of the Punjab addressed to Lord Mountbatten, in response to the latter's request made on 20th July, a long memorandum on the disorders in the province, in refutation of the criticisms raised by the politicians against his government.

> There are two short answers [he wrote] to most of these criticisms. In the first place, the critics have missed the significance of what is happening in the Punjab. We are faced not with an ordinary exhibition of political or communal violence, but with a struggle between the communities for the power which we are shortly to abandon. Normal standards cannot be applied to this communal war of succession, which has subjected all sections of the population to unprecedented strains, has dissolved old loyalties and created new ones.
>
> Secondly, the critics are themselves participants in the events which they profess to deplore.

Sir Evan Jenkins here wrote of the communal attitudes adopted by Central political leaders on their visits to the Punjab, especially Sardar Baldev Singh, Sardar Patel, Mr. Liaqat Ali Khan and Mr. Ghazanfar Ali Khan. 'Moreover,' he added, 'there is very little doubt that the disturbances have in some degree been organised and paid for by persons or bodies directly or indirectly under the control of the Muslim League, the Congress, or the Akali party.'

The Governor, after rehearsing the political events which had led to the breakdown of responsible parliamentary government in the Punjab and his own assumption of power under Section 93 on 4th March, wrote that the disturbances since that date had fallen into three main phases.

Phase One, from 4th to 20th March, was characterised by rioting in the cities, including Lahore, Amritsar, Multan and Rawalpindi, and massacres of Sikhs and Hindus in rural areas of the Rawalpindi Division and Multan District, with very heavy casualties and much burning, especially in Multan and Amritsar. The urban slaughter was without precedent (in Multan City about 130 non-Muslims were killed in three hours) and the wholesale burnings and rural massacres were new, but on the whole the situation was akin to communal disturbances of the past and yielded to well-tried counter-action, order being restored everywhere by 20th March. (This was the situation which Lord Mountbatten inherited from Lord Wavell's period.)

In Phase Two, up to 9th May, there were minor incidents in many districts, serious rioting and burning in Amritsar in mid-

April with repercussions in Lahore, and the first outbreaks in Gurgaon. This period of relative quiet was used by the communities for preparations, and there was much practising with bombs.

Phase Three, from 10th May onwards, launched the 'communal war of succession'. Lahore and Amritsar suffered much incendiarism, stabbing and bombing. There was scarcely any urban rioting, all activities in the cities, including some organised raids, being conducted by 'cloak and dagger' methods. Village raiding began, and grave disturbances broke out again in Gurgaon, with very heavy casualties.

> The third phase [wrote the Governor] showed the real dimensions of the problem. The communities settled down to do the maximum amount of damage to one another while exposing the minimum expanse of surface to the troops and police. Mass terrorism of this kind offers no easy answer—troops and police can act, and sometimes act decisively, against riotous mobs: they can do little against burning, stabbing and bombing by individuals. Nor can all the King's horses and all the King's men prevent—though they may be able to punish—conflict between communities interlocked in villages over wide areas of country.

The Governor proceeded to give figures of casualties reported in all three phases by areas up to 2nd August. They were, in summary:

	Killed	Seriously Injured
Urban	1,044	2,023
Rural	3,588	550
Total	4,632	2,573

The figures, he added, were clearly incomplete, especially for Gurgaon. In his opinion, not less than 5,000 (and probably not more than 5,200) people had been killed, and not more than 3,000 seriously injured.

Basing himself on the facts that almost all the casualties in the rural areas of Rawalpindi, Attock, Jhelum and Multan were Sikh or Hindu, that perhaps two-thirds of the victims in other rural districts and a high proportion of those in Gurgaon were Muslim, while in the cities Muslim and non-Muslim casualties were probably about equal, Sir Evan Jenkins gave the following communal estimates:

	Killed	Seriously Injured
Muslim	1,200	1,500
Non-Muslim	3,800	1,500

In rural Rawalpindi alone 2,164 killings had been reported, most of them murders of Sikhs and Hindus by Muslims. Apart from Rawalpindi and neighbouring districts, where the outbreak—itself provoked by reports of massacres of Muslims in Bihar and elsewhere—had been brought to an end by 20th March, the Muslim and non-Muslim communities had thus been about equal in guilt and in suffering. Such was the Governor's report.

Revenge for Rawalpindi was now to make the pendulum swing again. As 15th August approached, the situation grew steadily worse. In and around Amritsar, the Sikhs formed large armed bands which raided Muslim-majority villages at a rate of three or four a night. These bands were well organised and often included mounted men who acted as forward scouts. Muslim bands were organised for a like purpose in Lahore District, but these were fewer, smaller and less well organised. In Amritsar city the toll of Muslim dead rose fearfully after the newly appointed Superintendent of Police, a Hindu, had ordered that all Muslim policemen should be disarmed. The Governor quickly removed him and reversed the order, but this could not bring the dead to life nor restore faith in the rapidly ebbing authority and impartiality of the police. In Lahore, where the mainspring of trouble was Muslim retaliation for the slaughter in Amritsar, the predominantly Muslim police were reported to have lost discipline in the last days of the British regime and in some cases to have joined the rioters.

Meanwhile, on 22nd July, the Partition Council had decided upon the formation, from 1st August, of a special military command in the disputed area of the Punjab. Major-General T. W. Rees was nominated Commander of what became known as the Punjab Boundary Force, with responsibility to the Supreme Commander, and through him after 15th August to the two successor Governments. He had a high officer from each of the future Indian and Pakistan armies attached to him as adviser. The Indian officer was Brigadier Dhigambir Singh, the Pakistan officer

Brigadier Mohammad Ayub Khan, who was later to become auto-
crat and President of Pakistan: he has recalled his experience in his
autobiography.[1] (Another Muslim and another Hindu adviser were
added later.) The Force comprised some 55,000 officers and men,
mostly from mixed units which had not yet been partitioned. It
was reputedly the largest military force ever collected in a specific
area in one country to keep order in time of external peace.

Although it had a high proportion of British officers, it included,
of course, no British units. Such British forces as remained in
India and Pakistan at the transfer of power were explicitly barred
from operational use. The decision to withdraw British troops from
active service, and steadily to repatriate them, before the transfer
of power was deliberately taken. If they had become involved in
partition conflicts it might have been hard to disengage. A concerted evacuation on 15th August would have been too dramatic a
display of the lapse of the established power, and might have
evoked the charge that the British cared nothing about the disorder
they might bequeath.

A fortnight after his operative command began, General Rees's
force was being bitterly criticised by both sides. On 29th August
the Joint Defence Council decided to disband it and to end the
Punjab Boundary command on 1st September. That story belongs
to the period after the transfer of power and is told in a later
chapter. But the failure of the Force to stop the communal war in
the Punjab was already apparent by 15th August. The killings and
rapine in the Punjab had mounted as the day of partition came
nearer. Sometimes the lawbreakers came into direct conflict with
the troops; more often they operated in groups far from the arm of
authority. Though the Force seemed large, it had little more than
one soldier per square mile of the territory it had to cover. It was
designed, as a military force must be, as an aid to the civil power,
but the civil power itself was rapidly disintegrating. The police
became more and more communal, and thousands deserted—
Muslims from East Pakistan and non-Muslims from West. Even
before 15th August, hundreds of thousands of people had lost or
left their homes and were on the move; after 15th August, the
stream of migration became a torrent.

On 6th August, at its last meeting, the Partition Council took up
the question of refugees, of whom there were by then very large

[1] *Friends Not Masters,* pp. 15–17.

numbers not only in the Punjab but also in Bihar, Bengal, and the North-West Frontier Province. They had in fact been encouraged by politicians to move—especially by Muslim politicians in eastern districts of the Punjab—against the counsel of Governors and Central Government. The Partition Council's decisions, aimed at 'arresting further exodus of refugees and encouraging the return of those who have already left', seem utterly pathetic in the light of what actually happened and indeed was even then happening. A great and painful exchange of populations, driven by fear, was already under way. General Rees reported that when he took over

> Communal bitterness was at a peak, and the masses were egged on and inflamed by shock-troops of resolute and well-armed men determined to fight. . . . Throughout, the killing was pre-medieval in its ferocity. Neither age nor sex was spared; mothers with babies in their arms were cut down, speared or shot, and Sikhs cried 'Rawalpindi' as they struck home. Both sides were equally merciless.[1]

No military operation could have countered this orgy of murder and hate.

On 14th August the Supreme Commander, Field Marshal Auchinleck, flew to Lahore and met General Rees and Sir Evan Jenkins. They discussed the imposition of martial law. The Governor reported that he had not enough officials left to attempt it; Rees said it would need two hundred extra officers. For martial law is still law, not unlimited licence to the military. But the mechanism of law had collapsed, and the military could not be more ruthless (even if their precarious communal discipline was capable of it) without more injury and death to the innocent than to the guilty. 'It is quite clear, and we are all agreed,' wrote Lord Mountbatten after the meeting of the Joint Defence Council on 16th August, 'that the soldiers are doing everything that is humanly possible to try and hold the situation, and that although it was decided, among other things, to reinforce the Boundary Force by two more brigades, some armour and some air, the situation is long past mere military action and requires political leadership of a high order.' But of high political leadership there was none. As Independence Day dawned in the Punjab, a few hundred exhausted and sickened British civilian and military

[1] *Report on the Punjab Boundary Force.*

officers, whose sole aim had been to protect the weak and needy, and impartially to prevent the rival communities from destroying each other, gazed upon the ruin of their hopes, and above the cries of the maimed, the homeless and the bereaved heard only the vilifying voices of the politicians who had brought about this chaos.

5 *The Boundary Commissions*

The plan of 3rd June provided that, in the event of partition, Boundary Commissions were to be set up by the Viceroy for the Punjab, Bengal and Assam-Sylhet, with terms of reference settled by him in consultation with those concerned. Two alternative forms of arbitral commission were debated by Lord Mountbatten with the political leaders. Mr. Jinnah originally favoured asking the United Nations to nominate three members of each Commission, to sit with expert assessors from India. Pandit Nehru argued that this would involve intolerable delay and that the choice of Commissioners might in the end be quite unsuitable. Agreement was eventually reached on the second scheme suggested: each Commission would have an independent chairman and four other members, all High Court judges, two nominated by the Congress and two by the League. Failing to agree on a chairman, the party leaders asked the Viceroy to seek a nomination by His Majesty's Government. The name of Sir Cyril Radcliffe, who had earlier been suggested as chairman of the Arbitral Tribunal, proved fully acceptable, and at Mr. Jinnah's instance he was made Chairman of both Commissions, with a casting vote, the parties having agreed that only one Commission was needed for Bengal and Assam. Sir Cyril, later Viscount Radcliffe, was probably the most brilliant lawyer at the English bar, and had never been involved in politics.

The terms of reference were even more difficult to decide than the membership. The Sikhs wanted them drawn widely for the Punjab, to allow for their historical and religious associations and their landed property; the Muslims wanted them drawn narrowly for the Punjab, for converse reasons, but widely for Bengal, where they still hoped for Calcutta, or a share of it, and feared the possibility of an economically unviable East Bengal. Eventually the leaders agreed on a simple formula which originated with the Congress side. The Commissions were to demarcate boundaries on the basis of ascertaining the contiguous majority areas of Muslims and non-Muslims, and in doing so to take into account also other factors. (The last clause was omitted in respect of Sylhet and the Assam boundary, but was nevertheless unanimously written in by the Bengal-Assam Commission.) The 'other factors' were not specified. Obviously they could include material considerations such as administrative viability, natural boundaries, communications, or water and irrigation systems: but it was also open to the Commissions to take into account less tangible influences. Nevertheless, their prime duty was to delimit contiguous communal-majority areas, and no wide variation from that criterion would have been within the spirit of their terms of reference. The Partition Council agreed that no direction beyond the terms of reference should be given to the Commissions, and that they should interpret these at their own discretion.

The Commissions were set up on 30th June, and on 8th July Sir Cyril Radcliffe arrived in India. After staying in New Delhi for a couple of days he visited Calcutta and Lahore, where the Commissions had already started their work. Unable to attend the simultaneous public sittings of both Commissions, he attended those of neither, but studied the daily record of their proceedings and all material submitted. His base was a house on the Viceregal estate in New Delhi, the Viceroy having decided that it would be improper for the Commission chairman to stay at Viceroy's House, where he might be thought to be under Viceregal influence. Indeed Lord Mountbatten was careful to keep personal contacts with Sir Cyril to a minimum, and to decline either to offer any interpretation of the terms of reference—which Sir Cyril certainly did not invite from anyone—or to make any third-party representations to the Commissions. For instance, he refused to see a delegation of Sikh officers brought by the Maharajah of Patiala to press their views about the Punjab boundary, but asked his Chief of Staff to explain to them that the Viceroy had nothing to do with the Boundary Commissions and that they must make their representations direct.

Sir Cyril at once consulted the party leaders—Mr. Jinnah, Pandit Nehru, Mr. Liaqat Ali Khan and Sardar Patel—as to the timing of the Commissions' reports. The question he specifically put to them was whether the importance of a decision by 15th August outweighed all other considerations, such as the inevitable roughness of such hurried work. Each and all replied that it must be made by 15th August at all costs. He also obtained, through the Viceroy, the two party leaders' agreement to inclusion of the word 'award' in the Indian Independence Bill, the award being 'the decision of the Chairman of the Commission contained in his report to the Governor-General at the conclusion of the Commission's proceedings'. The phraseology is important in view of *ex parte* claims made later that the real award was other than in the Chairman's report to the Governor-General. Neither in the Punjab nor in Bengal could the Commissioners agree on the demarcation. While he was indebted to his colleagues for their help, wrote Sir Cyril in his reports, their divergence of opinion was too wide, especially as to the significance of 'other factors' and the weight to be attached to them, for an agreed solution. On the strength of his casting vote, therefore, each of the awards was 'the decision of the Chairman of the Commission'.

In the Punjab, reported Sir Cyril, while the claims of the respective parties ranged over a wide territory, the truly debatable ground in the end proved to lie in and around the area between the Beas and Sutlej rivers on the one hand and the river Ravi on the other. Here the fixing of a boundary was complicated by the existence of vital canal systems and road-and-rail communications predicated on a single administration. There was also the stubborn geographical fact of the respective situations of Lahore and Amritsar, and the claims to each or both of those cities which either side vigorously sustained. (Lahore was allotted to Pakistan, Amritsar to India.)

In Bengal, Sir Cyril perceived that the demarcation depended upon the answers to certain basic questions, which he cited. Of these, probably the three most important were:

1 To which of the two States was the City of Calcutta to be assigned, or was it possible to divide the City between them?

2 If Calcutta as a whole must be assigned to one State, what were the latter's indispensable claims to territory such as adjacent river systems on which the life of the city and port depended?

3 Who was to have the Chittagong Hill Tracts, with their small Muslim minority but their intimate physical and economic association with East Bengal?

To none of Sir Cyril's basic questions could his colleagues agree upon the answer.

As to Sylhet and Assam, besides the 'other factors', the Commission had problems in interpreting their terms of reference. These were:

> In the event of the referendum in the District of Sylhet resulting in favour of amalgamation with Eastern Bengal, the Boundary Commission will also demarcate the Muslim majority areas of Sylhet District and the contiguous Muslim majority areas of the adjoining districts of Assam.

The Muslim Commissioners argued that, since the above instruction was subsidiary to that of demarcating the boundary in Bengal, 'adjoining districts of Assam' meant any districts of Assam that adjoined East Bengal. The Hindu Commissioners argued that the reference was only to Muslim-majority areas of Assam, other than Sylhet, which adjoined Sylhet. The Chairman, when asked to give his casting vote, supported the latter interpretation. It was also argued by the East Bengal Government that, on a true construction of the terms of reference in the light of the Indian Independence Act, the whole of the District of Sylhet must without question be allotted to East Bengal; but the claim was rejected unanimously by the Commission.

At its meeting on 22nd July the Partition Council agreed on a public statement pledging its members to accept the awards of the Boundary Commissions whatever they might be, and, as soon as they were announced, to enforce them impartially.

Nevertheless it became clear, as the publication of the awards drew near, that those pledges were not made without reservation. Early in August, Lord Ismay was given a strongly worded oral message from Mr. Liaqat Ali Khan that if Gurdaspur district in the north of the Punjab or any large part of it were allotted to India this would be regarded as a most serious fact by Mr. Jinnah and the Pakistan Government. If it turned out that such an award was a political rather than a judicial decision, it would amount to so grave a breach of faith as to imperil future friendly relations between Pakistan and Britain. (Gurdaspur district was in fact divided between India and Pakistan, broadly along the line of the river Ravi.) Lord Ismay replied that the Viceroy had nothing to do with the Boundary Commissions, and that the political leaders themselves had selected the personnel of the Commissions, drafted their terms of reference, and undertaken to implement their awards.

On the other side, Sardar Vallabhbhai Patel wrote to the Viceroy on 13th August an extraordinary letter about a deputation of the Chittagong Hill tribes who had expressed to him that morning their grave fear that their area was to be included in Pakistan. 'I have told them,' wrote Sardar Patel, 'that the proposition was so monstrous that if it should happen they would be justified in resisting to the utmost of their power and count on our maximum support in such resistance.' Personally, he thought it 'inconceivable that such a blatant breach of the terms of reference should be perpetrated'. 'Any award against the weight of local opinion and of the terms of reference, or without any referendum to ascertain the will of the people concerned, must, therefore, be construed as a collusive or partisan award and will therefore have to be repudiated by us.' (The Chittagong Hill Tracts were in fact awarded to Pakistan. No reason was given by Sir Cyril Radcliffe, but according to the Governor of Bengal, in advice to the Viceroy, the whole economic life of the people of the Hill Tracts depended upon East Bengal, and they had no communication with Assam save a few indifferent tracks through the jungle. The great majority of the population, less than a quarter of a million, were tribesmen, not Muslims certainly, but not Hindus either.)

Lord Mountbatten wrote to London a few days later about Sardar Patel's outburst: 'The one man I had regarded as a real statesman with both feet firmly on the ground, and a man of honour whose word was his bond, had turned out to be as hysterical as the rest. . . . So much for his undertaking on behalf of India to accept and implement the awards whatever they might be.'[1] The Viceroy had received warning of this storm at a meeting with his staff on 12th August, when he was informed that the award would probably allot the Chittagong Hill Tracts to Pakistan. Mr. V. P. Menon said that this would have a disastrous effect on the Congress leaders, who had been committing themselves unequivocally on the matter. If the details of the award were given them before 15th August, he thought they might well refuse to attend the meeting of the Constituent Assembly which the Viceroy was to address on that day, or the State banquet in the evening.

[1] *Viceroy's Personal Report* No 17, 16th August 1947.

Lord Mountbatten, who observed that he had never known V. P. Menon to mislead him, decided that somehow the details of the awards must be kept back from the leaders until after 15th August, and must then be discussed with them before publication.

The Viceroy had reached the conclusion some time earlier that publication of the awards must be effected as close to the date of the transfer of power as possible. Despite the great administrative disadvantages of not knowing, at the creation of the two Dominions, what their precise areas would be, with the result that the administration of potential border districts would be completely in the air, to postpone publication until after independence would not only divert odium from the British, but also avoid turning a day of rejoicing over Indian and Pakistani freedom into one of mourning over disappointed territorial hopes.

The first indication the Viceroy had that the awards were almost ready was on or about 9th August, when his Private Secretary, Sir George Abell, told him that he had obtained for the Governor of the Punjab a preliminary forecast of the Punjab award.[1] About the same time Lord Mountbatten had a private meeting with Sir Cyril Radcliffe to discuss the date on which the awards were to be announced. He asked whether Sir Cyril could hold his reports until after 15th August. Sir Cyril replied firmly that he could not delay beyond the 13th at the very latest. The Viceroy agreed that the reports should be sent to his office on the 13th. He was leaving for Karachi that afternoon and would not have time to see them until he returned on the evening of the 14th, which would automatically delay publication until the 15th or later.

This was the plan that was followed. The Bengal report was delivered, but not read by the Viceroy, on the morning of the 13th, the Punjab report not until later in the day. Lord Mountbatten was therefore able to write to Pandit Nehru and Mr. Jinnah that afternoon saying that all the reports had not been received before he left for Karachi, and calling a meeting at Viceroy's House on 16th August to decide upon the timing of publication and the method of implementing the Partition Council's undertaking to accept the awards and enforce their effect. In Karachi Lord Mountbatten struggled, in the end with success, to persuade Mr. Jinnah to let Mr. Liaqat Ali Khan come to this meeting and also to a Defence Council meeting on the same day to discuss the situation

[1] This incident is described fully below.

in the Punjab. The meeting was held at 5 p.m. on the 16th, the reports having been sent to the participants three hours earlier. The atmosphere was one of mutual indignation and protest. Neither the Congress leaders, nor the Muslims, nor Sardar Baldev Singh for the Sikhs, were in the least appreciative of any good they might have found in the awards; they could only complain bitterly of their defects. After some time, however, they perceived that there must be some merits when their rivals were equally dissatisfied, and after two hours' debate the conclusion was reached that the awards must be announced forthwith and loyally implemented.

It is alleged by some Pakistani controversialists[1] that publication of the reports was delayed while Lord Mountbatten brought pressure to bear on Sir Cyril Radcliffe to alter the awards, especially to the disadvantage of Pakistan in the northern part of the Punjab. The charge is based on a supposed disclosure of the line of the Punjab award which was subsequently altered. The foundation for the story is a letter dated 8th August from Sir George Abell to Mr. Abbott, the Private Secretary to the Governor of the Punjab, Sir Evan Jenkins, who had asked for a forecast of the Punjab award in order that he might make his administrative dispositions. (It was normal practice in India to give advance information to Provincial Governments of the contents, or likely contents, of reports liable to cause disturbances.) Sir George Abell's letter read as follows:

> I enclose a map showing roughly the boundary which Sir Cyril Radcliffe proposes to demarcate in his award, and a note by Christopher Beaumont describing it. There will not be any great change from this boundary, but it will have to be accurately defined with reference to village and *zail* boundaries in the Lahore district.
>
> The award itself is expected within the next 48 hours, and I will let you know later about the probable time of announcement. Perhaps you would ring me up if H.E. the Governor has any views on this point.

Sir Francis Mudie, Governor-designate of West Punjab, was staying with Sir Evan Jenkins around this time for the express purpose

[1] e.g., G. W. Choudhuri, *Pakistan's Relations with India 1947–66*; Chaudiri Muhammed Ali, *The Emergence of Pakistan*.

of discussing the hand-over of authority. Sir Evan recalled mentioning the advance information to him, and the map itself was given to him by Mr. Abbott, on Sir Evan's instructions. Later, after the transfer of power, he handed it to the Pakistan Prime Minister, Mr. Liaqat Ali Khan.

The first point about the letter is that the exchange of information was entirely at private-secretary level. (Beaumont was Sir Cyril Radcliffe's private secretary.) Sir Cyril was aware that such correspondence was proceeding but did not see either the letter or the map. Lord Mountbatten knew of Sir George Abell's letter, after it had been sent, but not, until much later, of its contents, and never saw the map, of which no copy was kept in the Private Secretary's files. Sir Francis Mudie saw the map but not the letter. The second point is that the forecast was clearly distinguished from 'the award itself', and purported to do no more than show 'roughly the boundary'. Sir George Abell (and implicitly Mr. Beaumont) may have under-estimated the likely variation from the line shown on the accompanying map, but this was a matter of degree. Sir Evan Jenkins' view of it is shown by the fact that in assigning local civil staffs in anticipation of the transfer of power —the Congress and the League having demanded that the hand-over should be made in India to Indian officials, in Pakistan to Pakistanis—he continued to assume that all four border districts (Gurdaspur, Amritsar, Lahore and Ferozepore) were in doubt and therefore to designate for them alternative Indian and Pakistani administrative teams. So far as Sir Cyril Radcliffe was concerned there was only one decision and one award, namely, that contained in his report to the Governor-General.

The map itself is therefore not important, but the substance of the difference between it and the award was the transfer to India of two tahsils of the Ferozepur district. On or about 11th August Sir Evan Jenkins received a cypher telegram reading 'Eliminate Salient'. He correctly understood this to refer to the Ferozepur area. The two tahsils in question were not thought by him to be of any great significance, but they were subsequently regarded as highly important by Pakistan for military and irrigation-water reasons. Lord Radcliffe, on this and all other points, has steadfastly refused to supplement or discuss his awards.

The innuendo of the Pakistani allegation has been sharpened and embittered by the claim that an important variation concerning the Gurdaspur district deliberately gave India a route into Kashmir. There is a high degree of myth in this also. The two main routes into Kashmir, via Rawalpindi and Murree and via Sialkot and the Banihal Pass, would in any case have gone to Pakistan. The Pathankot tahsil, which on any showing would have gone to India, had at that time no good road into Kashmir and Jammu, nor had the Gurdaspur tahsil, which, if it had gone to Pakistan, could have been bypassed by India in developing a new route into the State via Pathankot. The decisive action at the opening of the Kashmir warfare was accomplished by India with an airlift without over-flying any territory that could have been seriously disputed between India and Pakistan. Lord Radcliffe has denied that access to Kashmir and Jammu was at any time one of the 'other factors' affecting the award.

No evidence of the influence or pressure which Lord Mount-batten is alleged to have brought on the Chairman of the Commission in those last days has yet been produced. There was, however, one conversation, undisclosed hitherto, which might have some bearing on the point. It has been mentioned above because its primary purpose was to discuss the timing and method of publication of the Chairman's reports. It took place in Lord Ismay's house on the Viceregal estate in New Delhi over an evening drink on or about 9th August 1947. There is no contemporary record of it and the recollections of the three participants differ. On the point now under discussion Lord Mountbatten recalled, a year or so later, remarks which neither Lord Ismay nor Lord Radcliffe could recollect having been made on that occasion. It seems fairly certain, however, that at some time—probably not in that conversation, as he supposed, but more likely soon after Radcliffe arrived in India—he did make the point to Sir Cyril that the fairness of the eastern and western awards to the Muslims and non-Muslims respectively should be judged as a whole, so that disgruntlement in one area might be offset by satisfaction in another. This principle of 'balance' could conceivably have been so interpreted as to compensate, say, some concession to the Sikhs in the Punjab canal colonies by some concession to the Muslims in Assam-Sylhet. But to exemplify it thus is to show up its inherent unsoundness for an impartial arbitrator who was Chairman of two separate Commissions each with its own task, and was moreover duty-bound to obey the specific terms of reference which he had been given in demarcating the boundaries; and the author has the assurance of Lord Radcliffe that he totally rejected and ignored it in making his awards. Misguided as Lord Mountbatten's point may seem in that light, it certainly had nothing to do with the Kashmir frontier, which was not in anybody's mind at the time, nor with any particular section of the Punjab or Bengal-Assam boundaries.

The awards were as ill received by the Press in India and Pakistan respectively as they had been by the political leaders, comment concentrating on the supposed injustices done to their own side rather than benefits at the expense of the other. Detailed criticism was, however, very soon swallowed up in reaction to the migrations, riots and massacres which followed, and which were the outcome, not of any particular frontier-drawing, but of partition itself and of the communal hate which had led to it.

The boundary awards, in fact, like all the other arrangements for partition, had been made on the implicit assumption that friendly relations would subsist between the two Dominions and that the inevitable pains and anomalies of dividing a once-integrated nation-state would be mitigated by political and administrative co-operation. Sir Cyril Radcliffe expressed this need in each of his reports. That the assumption was vitiated was neither his fault nor that of the particular lines that he drew.

19

The accession of the States

The statement of 3rd June was laconic about the States: it merely
affirmed that the British Government's policy towards Indian
States remained as expressed in the Cabinet Mission's memorandum of 12th May 1946. This memorandum, based on a draft by
Sir Stafford Cripps with some amendments by Sir Conrad Corfield,
the Political Adviser, had been addressed to the Chancellor of the
Chamber of Princes. It said that when British India became independent His Majesty's Government would no longer be able to
carry out the obligations of paramountcy; as a logical consequence,
they would cease to exercise its powers. Thus all the rights surrendered by the States to the paramount power would return to
them. The void left by the lapse of political arrangements between
the States on the one side and the Crown and British India on the
other would have to be filled by their entering into a federal
relationship with the successor Government or Governments, or
by entering into 'particular political arrangements'. In suitable
cases, States might do well to form or join administrative units
large enough to fit into the new constitutional structure. In their
statement of 16th May the Cabinet Mission pronounced succinctly
that

> Paramountcy can neither be retained by the British Crown nor
> transferred to the new Government.

The States, released from paramountcy, would work out their own
relations with the successor authorities, and 'it by no means follows
that it will be identical for all the States'.

Although Lord Mountbatten discussed the future constitutional
structure of India with a number of leading Princes during his
preparatory talks, and took the chair at the conference of British
Residents in the States held soon after his arrival, he appears not
to have concentrated on the States' problem before 3rd June. It
must be remembered that almost up to the last moment he had still

hoped to revive the Cabinet Mission's plan, or a variant of it, under which the future of the States would be worked out through their participation in an autonomous Constituent Assembly. When Lord Mountbatten came to tackle the States' problem in the light of the imminent transfer of power to a partitioned India he was, perhaps naively, taken aback by its complexity and difficulty.

'Nothing had been said to me in London,' he wrote afterwards, 'to prepare me for the gravity and magnitude of the problem of the States. I had been given no inkling that this was going to be as hard, if not harder, to solve as that of British India. I was therefore hoping to deal with the future of the States after the main decision on the future of British India had been taken. Indeed this course was forced upon me by pressure of work, which also meant that full realisation of the problem only dawned on me gradually.'[1] It also meant that a constitutional revolution as radical in essence as that in British India (apart from partition) had to be accomplished in barely two months.

Lord Mountbatten had, however, been charged personally by the King, upon his appointment, with special responsibility towards the future of the States; for His Majesty knew better than anybody how much the Princes treasured their direct relations with the Crown in its human as well as its constitutional form. And when Lord Mountbatten turned to the problem of the States he took this charge very seriously. His liberty of action was of course restricted, bound as he was, not only by the announcement of 20th February and the basic policy laid down by the Cabinet Mission, but also by his letter of instructions from the Prime Minister. Mr. Attlee had given him these terms of reference:

It is, of course, important that the Indian States should adjust their relations with the authorities to whom it is intended to hand over power in British India; but, as was explicitly stated by the Cabinet Mission, His Majesty's Government do not intend to hand over their powers and obligations under paramountcy to any successor Government. It is not intended to bring paramountcy as a system to a conclusion earlier than the date of the transfer of power, but you are authorised, at such time as you think appropriate, to enter into negotiations with individual States for adjusting their relations with the Crown.

[1] *Report on the Last Viceroyalty.*

You will do your best to persuade the rulers of any Indian States in which political progress has been slow to progress rapidly towards some form of more democratic government in their States. You will also aid and assist the States in coming to fair and just arrangements with the leaders of British India as to their future relationships.

These instructions were not, of course, made public, nor were they known to his official advisers on States affairs in Delhi.

Up to 3rd June Lord Mountbatten's policy towards the States was largely negative, in the sense of discouraging ideas of Dominion Status for States or groups of States. He spoke in this sense particularly to the Nawab of Bhopal, the Chancellor of the Chamber of Princes, as well as others. Various ideas for the future of States occupied his mind—grouping, even some form of independence. But he soon decided that such thoughts made nonsense. He took a chill view of Dominion Status for Indian Princely States because he feared both the fragmentation of India and the appearance of an indefensible, irrational frontier of the Commonwealth within the sub-continent. But he also realised that, however plausible such a future might seem for certain of the largest States, it had little meaning for the vast majority, and that the destiny of all, both small and great, must depend upon their relations with the great nation or nations in which they were embedded. Such ideas, therefore, could only be a distraction from the main task before both the States and the Crown Representative.

These conversations with Rulers or their representatives did not take place in a vacuum, but in an atmosphere charged with Indian political ambition, particularly that of the Congress. On 19th April Pandit Nehru made a speech at Gwalior in which he was reported to have given the States Rulers a virtual ultimatum, either to join the Constituent Assembly or to be treated as hostile. Lord Mountbatten privately rebuked him, both for the substance of his opinion, which was contrary to the advice that he, the Viceroy, was giving and would continue to give to the Princes, namely, that they need not make up their minds until after the plan for the transfer of power was defined, or until the final stage of the Cabinet Mission's plan, and also for his demagogy, especially as a Member of the Interim Government who ought not to speak in such terms without Cabinet approval. Pandit Nehru took this castigation meekly, explaining that he was speaking in a personal capacity as President of the States' Peoples Conference, though his plea that he had been misreported did not carry him far, since his own version of his remarks was almost equally threatening towards the Princes. The Viceroy found himself agreeing, however, that in principle the Rulers ought to consult the will of their own people on the future of their States, and he afterwards advised them accordingly, both in person and through the Political Department.

The Political Department had always been deeply distrusted by Congress leaders, who regarded it as a buttress, as well as an instrument, of British power in Princely India, and as being hostile to democracy in the States, especially to the Congress-organised States' Peoples Conference. In the new phase they also believed the Political Department to be working for an independent future for the States, which they could not accept. Lord Mountbatten shared these latter suspicions. His relations with his Political Adviser, Sir Conrad Corfield, a man of strong sense of duty and moral obligation, were personally friendly:[1] he properly consulted Sir Conrad on States matters, encouraged and arranged contact between him and Pandit Nehru, and sent him to London with Lord Ismay to discuss with the Cabinet and the India Office the plan for the transfer of power as it concerned the States. But not long after 3rd June the Viceroy was led to believe that Sir Conrad and the Political Department under him were working to band the States together and to make them an independent force in the new India. In this he was mistaken, but a long talk between the two men confirmed Lord Mountbatten's view that they were pulling in different directions, and thereafter he largely ignored the Political Department in his plans and efforts for the constitutional future of the States. At the end of July, with the Viceroy's willing agreement, Sir Conrad went home on leave and retired from the Service.

The nature of their disagreement has been misunderstood by some critics of either. It was not the view of Sir Conrad Corfield or

---

[1] Their friendship was of long standing. A quarter of a century earlier, in February 1922, when Lord Louis Mountbatten was staying with Viceroy Lord Reading in Delhi and there became engaged to Miss Edwina Ashley, the Lady Mountbatten of the present story, Conrad Corfield was on the Viceroy's staff.

the Political Department that individual States or regional groups of States could have maintained national independence after the transfer of power. They held, as did Lord Mountbatten, that this was impractical: the exercise of paramountcy had welded the sub-continent into too firm a structure. Where they differed from him was in regard to the negotiation between the States and the successor Governments of British India. They believed that the threat of States' independence, if sustained up to and beyond the transfer of power, would have given the Rulers a great bargaining advantage in relation to the Congress; for such independence was what its leaders most feared. The Political Department therefore encouraged the States to present a united front in assertion of their theoretical right to independence. They regarded Lord Mountbatten's policy of pressing for a settlement with the States before the transfer of power as an improper exercise of paramountcy because it hampered the States in their negotiations for their political future, contrary to the letter and spirit of the Cabinet Mission's memorandum, which had been accepted as the basis of a final settlement, and therefore as a breach of faith with the Rulers. While they did not think that the process of adherence to the new Dominions would have been radically different if it had taken place after independence, they believed that it would have required more understanding from the Congress leaders, and that in the process of bargaining more of the values of indigenous personal rule in India might have been preserved. Lord Mountbatten believed, on the contrary, that the States would fare much worse if they delayed their negotiations until after the transfer of power, rather than reaching a settlement while the influence of the Crown and its representative on their behalf still remained.

In relation to this triangle of forces—the Viceroy, the Congress leaders, and the Political Adviser as exponent of the more traditional British policy towards the States—Mr. Jinnah and the Muslim League were not so much a fourth element of a quadrilateral as a force outside the triangle. For the States indubitably destined for association with Pakistan were very few, and the main object of Muslim policy in this sphere was, on the face of it, to secure leverage for Pakistan and embarrass India. Not least was this so in regard to Hyderabad, like Bhopal a Hindu-majority State with a Muslim ruler, whose efforts towards an independent status they therefore supported. Kashmir, a Muslim-majority State with a Hindu ruler, was not a conspicuous bone of contention at this time.[1]

Lord Mountbatten did not change his ideas on the future of the States after 3rd June, although the prospect of Dominion Status for both India and Pakistan had removed one of the objections to a like aspiration for the larger States or groups. He saw that path all the more clearly barred by a more fundamental objection—the prospect of fragmentation of India on a pattern inherently unstable and transitory; for it was based on mere historical accidents and could not hope to withstand the forces not only of modern communications, commerce and political power but also of modern democracy.

The first reactions by the States' Rulers to the plan for the transfer of power gave an inkling of what was to follow. In private talks on 2nd June, the Viceroy disclosed the gist of the new scheme separately to the Nawab of Bhopal and the Maharajah of Bikaner, who had been lunching with him. The Maharajah was delighted: the prospect of Dominion Status for the successor nation-states, with continued association with the Crown, would make the greatest difference, he said, to the Princes' entering the Constituent Assembly. The Nawab was bitterly dismayed. 'Once more,' he said, 'His Majesty's Government have left the Princes in the lurch.' They could have joined in the weak Centre envisaged by the Cabinet Mission, 'but now there will be a tight Centre, whichever Dominion we join, which will utterly destroy us'. Prophetic words! Nothing the Viceroy could say was able to shake the Nawab from his intention to stand out from the Constituent Assembly as an independent area.

On the evening of 3rd June Lord Mountbatten expounded the new plan to the States' Negotiating Committee, with Sir Conrad Corfield present to assist him.[2] In introducing it he balanced the point that had been made by the Nawab of Bhopal and that made by the Maharajah of Bikaner. When discussion began, Sir C. P.

[1] 'The Indian States will be free to negotiate agreements with Pakistan or Hindustan as considerations of contiguity or their own self-interest may dictate, or they may choose to assume complete and separate sovereign status for themselves.' Liaqat Ali Khan in *Dawn*, 22nd April 1947.
[2] The following account of the meeting is condensed from a fuller report in V. P. Menon, *Integration of the Indian States*, pp. 80–4.

Ramaswami Aiyar, the distinguished Dewan of Travancore, who was to prove a difficult man to persuade in the coming weeks, pleaded for a loosening or lapse of paramountcy before the transfer of power, in order to strengthen the bargaining power of the States and enable them to negotiate on equal terms with the prospective Dominion Governments. The Viceroy replied that in his opinion the imminent lapse of paramountcy enabled the States to negotiate on a basis of complete freedom. He would, however, consider the premature lapse of paramountcy in special cases if it could be proved that its continuance was a handicap to negotiation. The Dewan's point was opposed by the Nawab of Bhopal and was not pressed.

Sir B. L. Mitter, Dewan of Baroda, asked what would happen to economic and commercial agreements when paramountcy lapsed. Lord Mountbatten said that, in order to avoid an administrative vacuum, interim arrangements would be needed until new agreements could be negotiated. These interim arrangements could best be made on a standstill basis. Sir Conrad Corfield gave some examples. One was Army cantonments in certain States; another, through railways. Efforts were being made to persuade the Interim Government to negotiate arrangements whereby the revision of jurisdiction over these properties to the States would not affect the working of the railways or the accommodation of the Army until new agreements could be concluded. Regarding past agreements made not with the Crown but with the Government of India or provincial Governments, efforts had been made to set up an all-India consultative committee to deal with them, but the Interim Government had not agreed to this. Contractual agreements would have to be discussed with the opposite party, which might be a provincial Government.

Sir V. T. Krishnamachari, former Dewan of Baroda, then Dewan of Jaipur, called for the setting up of machinery for joint consultation in regard to existing agreements. Sir Conrad spoke hopefully of the prospect of a general standstill formula on which such joint negotiation could take place. Later in the debate it was agreed that, if the Interim Government agreed, two committees of representatives of the States likely to adhere to India and Pakistan respectively should be set up to negotiate with the two Constituent Assemblies.

The Rajah of Bilaspur asked whether the entry of States into either Constituent Assembly was a matter of free choice. Lord Mountbatten confirmed that it was. When the Rajah asked about the future of States which decided to join neither Constituent Assembly, Lord Mountbatten's reply was extremely cautious. Until, he said, it was known what shape the two Dominions would take, this was a hypothetical question which he was not prepared, at that stage, to refer to His Majesty's Government; but, whether or not a State actually joined either Dominion, it was obvious that administrative arrangements with one or other or both would be essential, and the first step was to negotiate such arrangements. While, said the Viceroy, he did not wish to give any official advice to States that were in doubt whether or not to join either Constituent Assembly, he would willingly give personal advice to anybody who asked for it. The one suggestion he would make was that, in coming to their decisions, the representatives of the States should cast their minds forward ten years and consider what the situation in India and the world was likely to be then.

Whereas the Princes and their representatives accepted the plan comparatively meekly, as it concerned the States, this was far from true of the politicians. At a meeting between the Viceroy and the chief political leaders on 13th June, at which the States were discussed and the Political Adviser was present, Pandit Nehru pursued the familiar Congress line that any Indian successor Government was entitled to assume paramountcy after the transfer of power. He vehemently denied that the States had any right to declare their independence, claiming that there was no trace of this in the Cabinet Mission's memorandum. Sir Conrad Corfield quoted the option of 'entering into particular arrangements' with the successor Governments, as the alternative to federal relationship, and argued that the phrase implied relations with autonomous units. On this point, and on Sir Conrad's alleged failure to treat non-paramountcy matters as the concern of the Government of India, Pandit Nehru attacked the Political Adviser to his face, declaring that he ought to be tried for misfeasance. 'In fact,' wrote Lord Mountbatten, 'as usual he completely lost control of himself.'[1]

Mr. Jinnah, with delight, took the opposite view, that Indian States were sovereign entities for every purpose except in so far as they had entered into treaties with the British, which were now to

[1] *Viceroy's Personal Report* No. 10, 27th June 1947.

lapse unless they were voluntarily renewed with the successor Dominions. Pandit Nehru retorted that he was not insisting that every State must join one or other Constituent Assembly, but that, if they did not, they must come to some other arrangement, which could not and should not be preceded by declarations of independence. He objected strongly to the Viceroy's proposal that the States should appoint representatives to negotiate with the appropriate successor Governments in Delhi, which he said would lead to serious delays: instead, the Government of India should, in effect, take over the existing system of dealing with the States. After a long and acrimonious discussion it was unanimously agreed among the rival political leaders and the Viceroy that the Government of India should set up a new 'States Department', to deal with all matters of common concern with the States, especially the formulation of standstill agreements covering their immediate relations after the transfer of power, and to take over from the Political Department all its responsibility not connected with paramountcy; and that a parallel Department should be set up for Pakistan. This plan was ratified a few days later on the basis of a memorandum prepared on the Viceroy's instructions by Mr. V. P. Menon in consultation with the Political Adviser, who loyally carried it out although he had strongly opposed it at the meeting, believing as he did that standstill agreements and the existing machinery should suffice for the interim period and that these new Departments would be bound in effect to usurp some of the functions of paramountcy, which His Majesty's Government had promised not to transfer to the successor Governments.

'I am glad to say,' wrote Lord Mountbatten, 'that Nehru has not been put in charge of the new States Department, which would have wrecked everything. Patel, who is essentially a realist and very sensible, is going to take it over. . . . Even better news is that V. P. Menon is to be the Secretary.' Pandit Nehru had originally nominated Mr. H. V. Ayengar as Secretary, but Sardar Patel wanted the man of his own choice, and sent for Menon who accepted after consulting the Viceroy. It meant a big sacrifice for him, for he had been virtually promised the Governorship of a major province, but Sardar Patel persuaded him that there was far more important work to be done at the Centre than in some provincial Government House, as indeed proved dramatically to be the case.[1] (Sardar Nishtar was appointed to look after the new Department for Pakistan, with Mr. Ikramullah as Secretary.) The Nawab of Bhopal 'could hardly contain himself with pleasure' at the news of these appointments, and said 'This alters the whole outlook for the States'.

The Nawab, meanwhile, had resigned the Chancellorship of the Chamber of Princes, on the ground that 'Bhopal State would, as soon as paramountcy is withdrawn, be assuming an independent status'. Another reason was that the Chamber was part of a constitutional machinery which, in his opinion, would now become *functus officio*, as indeed was true. The Political Department itself, being essentially concerned with paramountcy which was to expire within a few weeks, was now primarily engaged on self-liquidation. It had started this process in April 1947 with a conference of Residents and Political Officers at which Sir Conrad Corfield had announced a programme involving the virtual winding-up of the Department by March 1948. More than once Pandit Nehru complained that the Department had been seen burning papers, which he claimed rightly belonged to the successor Governments. Sir Conrad Corfield, taxed by the Viceroy, retorted: 'Do you mean to tell me that we must hand over reports of the private behaviour of some Maharajah years ago?' To which Lord Mountbatten replied: 'I will not stop you burning papers, but don't do it so obviously.' The matter was discussed in conference with the political leaders, whom Sir Conrad assured that nothing of permanent value would be destroyed. It was agreed that the Political Adviser should apply to the Member for Education for expert advice on the culling of records, and that those disclosing the private lives of the Rulers and the internal affairs of States should be handed over, on the transfer of power, to the High Commissioner for the United Kingdom. Nevertheless, the grievance rankled, and a sense of conflicting loyalties, interests and policies strained the relations

[1] Menon never did become a Governor, nor receive from the Indian Government the honour he deserved: after Sardar Patel's death he was allowed to pass into retirement. Lord Mountbatten, in his final Viceregal Honours List, offered him a K.C.I.E. Already possessing the C.S.I., which he valued more than the offered Knighthood because the Star of India had been almost entirely a preserve of the I.C.S. and British proconsuls, Menon politely refused an honour regarded in India as the regular reward of satisfactory service as a departmental head.

between the States Department and the Political Department during the seven weeks of their joint existence.

One of the first actions of the States Department was to stop the Crown Representative's Police Force from being dismembered, as had been proposed by the Political Department at its conference of Residents in April. This force had been established when the Political Department found that it could no longer rely on autonomous provinces to provide the police force required to fulfil the paramount power's duty of protection: the plan now was to hand over its units to particular States. After the States Ministry took hold of it, its strength was raised from one to two battalions. It was to play an important part in the vexed times that lay ahead, as a means to the virtual inheritance of paramountcy.

Mr. V. P. Menon held a position of extraordinary influence at this time. While Secretary-designate of the States Department, and indeed after he assumed the Secretaryship on 5th July, he remained Constitutional Adviser to the Viceroy and was one of the latter's principal consultants on the drafting of the Indian Independence Bill, for weeks the subject of daily telegraphic exchanges between the Governor-General and the Secretary of State. Menon had earned the complete confidence both of Lord Mountbatten and of Sardar Patel. Though his relations with Pandit Nehru were less intimate, he had been brought into close contact with the Prime Minister in the negotiations over the new plan for the transfer of power, and in that quarter likewise he was a valuable mediator.

So closely did Menon work both with Lord Mountbatten and Sardar Patel that it is difficult to be sure, from the records,[1] in what sequence their key discussions occurred, or who originated ideas or actions in regard to the States at this time. Menon describes[2] two long conversations that he had with the Sardar after his nomination to the States Department, in which they first reviewed the whole situation presented to the Indian political leadership by the imminent lapse of paramountcy, with its threat of disintegration and disorder across the map of India ('Sardar told me . . . that if we did not handle it promptly and effectively, our hard-won freedom might disappear through the States' door'), and then Menon put forward his own plan, based on an

---

[1] Including personal evidence of Lord Mountbatten and Mr. Menon tape-recorded by the author.

[2] *The Integration of the Indian States*, pp. 93–7.

idea that he had submitted to Lord Linlithgow without effect as a means to an all-India Government in 1942, namely, that all Rulers should be asked to accede to India, or in a few appropriate cases to Pakistan, for three subjects only—defence, external affairs and communications—without any financial obligation or other commitments or bargaining such as had frustrated federation in 1937–9. Sardar Patel was 'inclined to agree', and at Menon's request conveyed the proposal to Pandit Nehru, who also agreed 'if we could see it through'. Menon narrates that he then approached the Viceroy, with Sardar Patel's cordial assent, and asked for his help. Lord Mountbatten said he would think the matter over, and after an interval accepted the plan, and discussed it frankly with Sardar Patel himself.

According to Lord Mountbatten, the first time that he debated the States problem with Patel—and this must have been before the setting up of the States Ministry, since he records that he did so because Mr. Menon had told him Patel was much more interested in the States than was the Prime Minister—the Sardar told him that he need not bother about the States because after the transfer of power the States peoples would rise, depose their Rulers and throw in their lot with the Congress. The Viceroy reminded him that the States had forces, trained and equipped by the British, ranging from a division in Hyderabad to personal bodyguards in small States, which would shoot down the rebels, and that the Princes were preparing themselves, on the advice of the Political Department, against any uprisings. A civil war would result, and India would lose far more than she would gain from a peaceful settlement. Sardar Patel asked what he meant. The Viceroy replied that the peaceful settlement he had in mind was to allow the Rulers to retain their titles, extra-territorial rights and personal property or Civil List, and in return they would join a Dominion—most of them India, a few, like Bahawalpur, Pakistan—only the three subjects of defence, external affairs and communications being reserved to the Central Government. Patel said he would think it over.

When he next came to see the Viceroy, having meanwhile talked with V. P. Menon—and here the two accounts converge— Sardar Patel said 'I am prepared to accept your offer provided that you give me a full basket of apples.' 'What do you mean?' asked Lord Mountbatten. 'I'll buy a basket with 565 apples'—the computed number of States—'but if there are even two or three apples missing the deal is off.' 'This,' said the Viceroy, 'I cannot completely accept, but I will do my best. If I give you a basket with, say, 560 apples will you buy it?' 'Well, I might,' replied Patel.

Two things are clear. First, the policy of pressing for accession before 15th August on the three subjects, without financial commitment, as the alternative to confronting the States with the choice between joining a Constituent Assembly whose outcome could not be foreseen, and attempting a precarious if not spurious independence, originated as a joint decision of the Viceroy and the Indian section of the Government (specifically, Sardar Patel with Pandit Nehru's assent). When Mr. V. P. Menon told Sir Conrad Corfield of the decision 'he literally threw up his hands in surprise'. He did not then know the part the Crown Representative himself was to play. Sir Conrad, when he did learn of Lord Mountbatten's intentions, warned him that he was agreeing to use his influence as representative of the paramount power to recommend to the Rulers a bargain which could not be guaranteed after independence. The Political Adviser also considered the policy of accession within six weeks far too ambitious. He was told on behalf of the States Department that they assumed the responsibility for negotiating with the Rulers, though they would welcome assistance from the Political Department. Nor was the policy of rushed accession agreed with the Pakistan section of the Government. It was conveyed through official channels to Sardar Abdur Rab Nishtar, the Muslim League Minister for States. He made no comment, but both privately to the Viceroy and publicly Mr. Jinnah proclaimed his objection to the accession plan and his intention to guarantee the independence of States adhering to Pakistan.

Secondly, Lord Mountbatten's direct and personal assistance in securing accession was asked for by the Indian leaders, though the Viceroy certainly welcomed the request. They believed that his personality, prestige and Royal connection would be invaluable in dealing with the Princes. Besides, they had plenty of other things on their hands.

On 5th July a statement which had been drafted by V. P. Menon was issued in the name of Sardar Patel. It appealed to the Rulers to accede for the three subjects 'in which the common interests of the country are involved'. It continued:

This country with its institutions is the proud heritage of the people who inhabit it. It is an accident that some live in the States and some in British India, but all alike partake of its culture and character. . . . It is therefore better for us to make laws sitting together as friends than to make treaties as aliens. . . . The Congress are no enemies of the Princely Order, but, on the other hand, wish them and their people under their aegis all prosperity, contentment and happiness. Nor would it be my policy to conduct the relations of the new department with the States in any manner which savours of the domination of one over the other; if there would be any domination, it would be that of our mutual relations and welfare.

The tone and content of this proclamation were in striking contrast with earlier expressions of Congress policy towards the Rulers, such as Pandit Nehru's menacing speech for which he was rebuked by the Viceroy. Sardar Patel—granted his sincerity—here displayed both realism and statesmanship, qualities desperately needed in India's crisis and too often missing. It must also be recognised that the policy involved considerable immediate sacrifices from the Indian Government, not only of its previous more revolutionary political doctrine, but also of financial and material advantages which it could have expected from negotiating more complete accession or more comprehensive agreements. Equally sharp is the contrast between the statement and subsequent events, culminating in the virtual absorption of the States and the relegation of the Princely Order to the status of a non-governing aristocracy.

The broad policy having been decided upon, intensive discussion, sometimes highly contentious, was then applied to four necessary corollaries: the drafting of standstill agreements covering all non-acceded matters, the drafting of a standard instrument of accession, the construction of machinery for negotiation, and the amendment of the draft Indian Independence Bill. On negotiating mechanism, Lord Mountbatten, speaking to the Chamber of Princes as Crown Representative on 25th July, announced the formation of a Negotiating Committee consisting of ten Rulers and twelve Ministers of Princely States. This apparatus had in fact been decided upon after heated political debate. The Congress leaders would have nothing of negotiation by the British Residents and Agents in the States. To send Indian Government representatives to all the States was impossible in terms of personnel, and would have been resisted by many Rulers, who certainly could not be forced to accept them. It was agreed that there must be direct negotiation in Delhi and through correspondence. The Negotiating Committee was not a plenipotentiary representative of individual States, but was guardian of the interests of States generally in drafting the Standstill Agreements and Instruments of Accession; its strength and prestige, however, carried immense weight with all the Rulers when they were asked to sign the documents that it had approved in common form.

These were hammered out in two sub-committees between 26th and 31st July. The draft Standstill Agreement originated in the Political Department, which had been concerned with the problem, essentially in its sphere, well before 3rd June. The draft Instrument of Accession originated in the States Department. Both were agreed, with amendments, by the States Negotiating Committee by 31st July. This left exactly a fortnight for individual negotiation and signature. The standard Standstill Agreement provided that all agreements and administrative arrangements as to matters of common concern then existing between the Crown and the signatory State, as specified in a schedule, should continue until new arrangements were made. The Instrument of Accession took three forms, according to the existing status and powers of the various States. For 140 States with full powers the Instrument caused them to accede to the Dominion of India only for defence, external affairs and communications, without any financial liability. The three subjects were defined in the same terms as in the schedule to the Government of India Act 1935 listing the matters exclusively reserved to the Federation that was to be set up under the Act: borrowing this definition must have saved an enormous amount of drafting and argument.[1] For about seventy States in Kathiawar, Central India and the Simla Hills

[1] There was added a fourth class of 'Ancillary' matters, namely, 1. Elections to the Dominion Legislature; 2. Offences against laws with respect to the three central subjects; 3. Inquiries and statistics for the purposes of those subjects; 4. Jurisdiction and powers of all courts with respect to them, but not so as to confer, without the Ruler's consent, any jurisdiction or powers other than those ordinarily exercised in or in relation to the State. These items were also borrowed from the 1935 Act Schedule. They clearly limited to some extent the internal sovereignty of the acceding States.

which had never exercised full powers, the standard Instrument of Accession was such as to restrict their future powers to those they already possessed. Finally, for over 300 estates and *talukas* in Kathiawar and Gujerat, which were not in any proper sense States though ranking as such and being no part of British India, an Instrument was devised on the lines of the common-form accession but reserving all residuary powers and jurisdiction to the Central Government. In the course of discussion on the draft Indian Independence Bill, Sir Benegal Rau had pressed, with Lord Mountbatten's support, for a clause transferring to the Dominion Government the criminal and civil jurisdiction previously exercised in such miniature States by the Crown Representative, arguing that it was unthinkable to grant overnight to a petty lord of a few square miles the powers of life and death; but the Secretary of State refused to qualify the total lapse of paramountcy, no doubt because to change the principle anywhere might have endangered its acceptance everywhere.

The Instrument of Accession, while making no provision for termination by either party, had a kind of escape clause in the following terms:

> Nothing in this Instrument shall be deemed to commit me (the Ruler) in any way to acceptance of any future constitution of India or to fetter my discretion to enter into arrangements with the Government of India under any such future constitution.

The Instrument continued:

> Nothing in this Instrument affects the continuance of my sovereignty in and over this State, or, save as provided by or under this Instrument, the exercise of any powers, authority and rights now enjoyed by me as Ruler of this State.

The Instrument specifically bound the State as such and the Ruler's heirs and successors.

The actual terms of the Indian Independence Act regarding the States were short and sweeping:

> 2 (4) ... Nothing in this section[1] shall be construed as preventing the accession of Indian States to either of the new Dominions.

[1] Defining the territories of the two successor Dominions formed out of British India.

7 (1) As from the appointed day . . . (b) the suzerainty of His Majesty over the Indian States lapses, and with it all treaties and agreements in force at the date of the passing of the Act between His Majesty and the rulers of the Indian States, all functions exercisable by His Majesty at that date with respect to the Indian States, all obligations of His Majesty existing at that date towards the Indian States or the Rulers thereof, and all power, rights, authority or jurisdiction exercisable by His Majesty at that date in or in relation to Indian States by treaty, grant, usage, sufferance or otherwise.

Provided that, notwithstanding anything in paragraph (b) or paragraph (c)[1] of this sub-section, effect shall, as nearly as may be, continue to be given to the provisions of any such agreement as is therein referred to which relates to customs, transit and communications, ports and telegraphs, or other like matters, until the provisions in question are denounced by the Ruler of the Indian State or person having authority in the tribal areas on the one hand, or by the Dominion or Province or other part thereof concerned on the other hand, or are superseded by subsequent agreements.

The slate was wiped clean—even the agreements preserved by the proviso, which had been inserted under pressure from India, could be unilaterally denounced at any time by either party to them. There remained, after the passage of the Act on 17th July, only four weeks on which to write on the slate a totally new structure of relations between the successors of British India and hundreds of would-be independent States inextricably mixed up with them.

The negotiation was conducted both on the comprehensive and on the particular levels. Comprehensively, the Negotiating Committee, as recorded above, was launched in a speech by Lord Mountbatten to the Chamber of Princes on 25th July, the first and last time he addressed their assembled Highnesses. It was a splendid occasion, with the Crown Representative in full dress uniform and the Princes in their jewelled finery. Lord Mountbatten's speech, made without notes, was described by Mr. V. P. Menon as 'the apogee of persuasion'.

[1] A similar paragraph in respect of tribal areas.

The Indian Independence Act [he said] releases the States on 15th August from all their obligations to the Crown. The States have complete freedom—technically and legally they are independent. . . . But there has grown up during the period of British administration . . . a system of co-ordinated administration on all matters of common concern which meant that the sub-continent of India acted as an economic entity. That link is now to be broken. If nothing can be put in its place, only chaos can result, and that chaos, I submit, will hurt the States first.

. . . The States are theoretically free to link their future with whichever Dominion they may care. But when I say that they are at liberty to link up with either of the Dominions, may I point out that there are certain geographical compulsions which cannot be evaded. Out of something like 565 States, the vast majority are irretrievably linked geographically with the Dominion of India. . . . In the case of Pakistan, the States, although important, are not so numerous, and Mr. Jinnah . . . is prepared to negotiate the case of each State separately and individually. But in the case of India, where the overwhelming majority of the States are involved, clearly separate negotiation with each State is out of the question.

The Crown Representative then urged the need for standstill agreements, notwithstanding the proviso to Clause 7 of the Independence Act, which only gave a breathing space. He next reminded his audience of the fact that the Rulers had accepted as reasonable, fair and just the Cabinet Mission's plan for surrender to the Central Government of defence, external affairs and communications, and he elaborated on these three heads.

I am sure you will agree [he continued] that these three subjects have got to be handled for you for your convenience and advantage by a larger organisation. This seems so obvious that I was at a loss to understand why some Rulers were reluctant to accept the position. One explanation probably was that some of you were apprehensive that the Central Government would attempt to impose a financial liability on the States or encroach in other ways on their sovereignty. . . . The draft Instrument of Accession provides that the States accede to the Appropriate Dominion on three subjects only without any financial liability. Further, that Instrument contains an explicit provision that in no other matters has the Central Government any authority to encroach on the internal autonomy or sovereignty of the States.

This would, in my view, be a tremendous achievement for the States. But I must make it clear that I have still to persuade the Government of India to accept it. If all of you would co-operate with me and are ready to accede, I am confident that I can succeed in my efforts. Remember that the day of the transfer of power is very close at hand, and if you are prepared to come in, you must come in before 15th August. I have no doubt that this is in the best interests of the States. . . .

I am not asking any States to make any intolerable sacrifice on independence. My scheme leaves you with all the practical independence that you can possibly use and makes you free of all those subjects which you cannot possibly manage on your own. You cannot run away from the Dominion Government which is your neighbour any more than you can run away from the subjects for whose welfare you are responsible. Whatever your decision, I hope you feel that I have at least done my duty by the States.

Three things stand out from this masterly and momentous speech. First, the Crown Representative pronounced unequivocally that legally the States would be independent after 15th August. Secondly he committed himself without reserve to the policy of accession for the three subjects—he called it 'my scheme'. Thirdly he used as persuasive sanction the statement that the Indian Government had not yet agreed, but that he could succeed in his efforts if *all* States acceded. He added the implication that if any did not accede by 15th August they would be left out in the cold, to survive as best they could. Thus he skilfully used the probable desire of the majority to accede as leverage which they themselves would exert on their doubtful brethren to bring them into line by 15th August.

When the day for the transfer of power arrived, apart from the few States clearly destined to adhere to Pakistan, every one both great and small bar only three[1] had signed Instruments of Accession—a very full basket of apples; though two of the missing States were very large apples indeed. The three were Junagadh, Kashmir and Hyderabad. The first was little regarded at this time, and its

[1] To be accurate, two other small States in Kathiawar which, like Junagadh, had Muslim rulers had also failed to accede by 15th August, but they proved of no significance.

omission was thought to be scarcely more than an oversight. Of Kashmir and Hyderabad more will be said in this chapter, but meanwhile it is well to record some difficulties with other States which eventually acceded, for all was not as plain sailing as the broad result might seem to indicate.

Bhopal. It will be recalled that the Nawab of Bhopal had resigned as Chancellor of the Chamber of Princes because of his determination to declare the independence of the State. He refused to attend the meeting on 25th July, declaring that the Rulers 'were being invited like the Oysters to attend the tea-party with the Walrus and the Carpenter'. Though he had been mollified by the creation and personnel of the States Ministry, he persisted in this attitude, despite much personal persuasion by Lord Mountbatten, who described him in a letter as 'my second best friend in India'— the best being presumably Pandit Nehru. 'I suppose,' wrote the Viceroy, 'I have spent more time on Bhopal's case than on all the other States put together, because he is such a charming and high-principled man that it would be a tragedy if he were to wreck the State by failing to come in now.'[1] Two days previously Lord Mountbatten had had a very long talk with the Nawab, in which His Highness threatened to abdicate in favour of his daughter. 'I told him that I considered this would be a cowardly act and unfair to his daughter, and that he must stay for at least a year. . . . I do not feel that I can allow him to abdicate if I can possibly avoid this, since it would look as though I were bringing pressure to bear on him, which is far from being the case, as he himself is the first to admit.' Realising that by now the great majority of Rulers were acceding, the Nawab wavered. He first asked if he could sign a Standstill Agreement without acceding (as other States also asked) and received a firm 'No'. He then sent his Constitutional Adviser, Sir Mohammed Zafrullah Khan, to discuss the terms of the Instrument of Accession, but was told that no alterations could be conceded. At last he signed the Instrument, stipulating only that his accession should not be disclosed until ten days after the transfer of power. He wrote a generous letter to Sardar Patel, saying 'throughout I have been treated with consideration and have received understanding and courtesy from your side', and he received an equally generously-worded reply.

[1] *Viceroy's Personal Report* No 16, 8th August 1947.

Indore. The Maharajah of Indore was a very different character —young, erratic and bad-mannered. He failed even to reply to the invitation to attend the meeting of Rulers on 25th July. At Lord Mountbatten's instance, six of his fellow Mahratta Princes headed by the Maharajah Gaekwar of Baroda[1] flew to Indore on 30th July bearing a personal letter from the Viceroy urging the Ruler of Indore to come to Delhi. He declined to see them and according to the Gaekwar's account cut them stone dead in his own drawing-room. However, on 4th August he obeyed the summons, to receive from Lord Mountbatten, in the presence of the Nawab of Bhopal, whom he had brought with him, a dressing-down of painful severity. Indore, said the Crown Representative, was the only State that had done nothing at all in response to his efforts to produce the best possible future for the States, thereby displaying a lack of responsibility towards the people of the State and of courtesy to the Crown Representative. He resented the deliberate misrepresentation, which the Maharajah had made to H.H. the Gaekwar, to the effect that the invitation to Delhi conveyed a threat. The way in which the Maharajah of Indore might behave was a matter of indifference to him. The States, it was quite clear, were at liberty to do anything they liked—either take no action at all or sign standstill agreements and accede to one or other Dominion—and he did not intend to take any step which could be represented as coercion. He was not even expressing a view. Sardar Patel, he added, had informed him that he was equally indifferent to the action taken by Indore. Enough States had already decided to accede to India for the States Minister's purposes. Two months previously the terms and conditions which the future Government of India intended to offer to the States had been very different. He, the Viceroy, had 'gone into battle' and succeeded, first, in getting the States Department set up and then in persuading the leaders to accept a plan for accession on three subjects only. Both he and Sardar Patel were now being attacked for being 'pro-Prince'. It was touch and go whether Sardar Patel would get the plan through, and his private opinion was that the Sardar, in face of party extremists, could not afford to make concessions. Whereas he could guarantee the terms of the Instrument of Accession up to the transfer of power, he could do nothing to help after that date.

[1] The others were the Maharajahs of Kolhapur, Gwalior, Dhar and Dewas Junior and the Raja of Sandur.

There was no other reason for speed. If the Maharajah thought he would get better terms after 15th August, it was open to him to wait until then. His Majesty's Government had not yet given him any decision on whether or not they would recognise as international entities any States which stood out. The granting of Dominion Status had been argued *ad nauseam* and rejected. Non-acceding States, so far as he knew, would no longer retain the advantages of connection with the British Commonwealth, nor would their subjects any longer be British protected persons. Surely the difference between treaty relationship with the successor Dominion and accession lay primarily in this point. Treaties might well prove far more disadvantageous than accession.

The Maharajah did little more than make his excuses. Two important points, however, were raised by the Nawab of Bhopal. First, he observed that the option of treaty relationship was contradicted by the Congress policy of refusing standstill agreements to States which did not accede. The Viceroy said he had had no official confirmation of this, but perhaps the Congress presumed that the standstill under Clause 7 of the Independence Act would suffice to prevent chaos. It was obviously impossible to compel the new Government to enter into treaties or even standstill agreements against their will. Secondly, the Nawab asked whether the Government of India could be counted on to honour the Instruments of Accession. If they did not, replied the Viceroy, he would be in an extremely strong position to expose them, since he was remaining as Governor-General until April.

Since the Maharajah of Indore did not commit himself at this interview, the States Department were surprised to receive shortly afterwards in an ordinary postal envelope both the Instrument of Accession and the Standstill Agreement signed by him. The case of Indore is not important in itself, but the Viceroy's interview with him was fully recorded and it may be taken, minus its element of stern reproof to the Ruler for his personal conduct, as displaying the arguments used by Lord Mountbatten on other unrecorded occasions in convincing the Princes or their Ministers of the advisability of acceding. There were no threats, for he had nothing to threaten, except the withholding of his own good offices after 15th August; the disagreeable consequences of non-accession which he so forcibly emphasised were those which he saw to be inherent in the situation in India and in the British Government's policy towards the States.

Travancore. Between 20th and 22nd July Sir C. P. Ramaswamy Aiyar, Dewan of Travancore, an elder statesman of the States' world, had a succession of interviews with the Viceroy and Mr. V. P. Menon. He had been publicly proclaiming that Travancore would declare its independence, and at his first interview with Lord Mountbatten, after producing files of Press cuttings (including cartoons caricaturing himself, and cuttings implying that Mahatma Gandhi was a sex maniac), he declared that the State would never accede to India; he had indeed made preliminary terms with Mr. Jinnah, including a trade agreement. To such an agreement, the Viceroy told him, the Government of India could have no objection. Both Lord Mountbatten and Mr. Menon played on Sir C.P.'s vanity. It ought not to be said of him, of all people, said Menon, that at India's critical hour he had not made his contribution towards building a united India. Whatever might be his grievances against the Congress—who undoubtedly had been striving to stir up the people of his State—these ought not to deflect him from what he considered in the best interests of Travancore and of India as a whole. Lord Mountbatten added a sharply-pointed argument. Only that morning, he said, Sir Seth Dalmia, a millionaire Marwari supporter of the Congress, had paid five lakhs of rupees (then worth £37,500) into the Travancore Congress Party funds in anticipation of starting internal trouble after 15th August. Sir C.P. said that this was indeed a serious matter, and asked the Viceroy to write a letter to his Maharajah setting out the proposals, in order that he might take His Highness's pleasure—a significant temporising ploy, since the Maharajah would certainly do as his Dewan advised him. Shortly after his return to Travancore, Sir C.P. was violently attacked with a billhook and nearly killed. But the Maharajah telegraphed his acceptance of the Instrument of Accession, and Sardar Patel appealed to the Travancore State Congress to cry off their campaign of direct action. A few days later Lord Mountbatten wrote: 'The adherence of Travancore after all C.P.'s declarations of independence has had a profound effect on all the other States and is sure to shake the Nizam.'[1]

[1] *Viceroy's Personal Report* No. 15, 1st August 1947.

In the course of Sir C. P. Ramaswamy Aiyar's talks with the Viceroy a point of general importance was raised. What would be the position of the State, he asked, if India later decided to leave the Commonwealth; would the Maharajah have the right to secede from India and would he be allowed to remain within the Commonwealth? Lord Mountbatten told him that he could give no official opinion, but that he thought it would not be difficult for His Highness to disentangle himself from India if he had only acceded for the three central subjects, and that whereas His Majesty's Government would never have agreed to the Maharajah's entering the Commonwealth as a separate Dominion because they did not wish to Balkanise India, he (Lord Mountbatten) thought Travancore would have a different case in demanding not to be thrown out once it was in. He could, however, give no assurance beyond pointing out that unless the Maharajah acceded he would never get into the Commonwealth at all. This point was never tested in fact, for at the time of writing India remains in the Commonwealth and by now the States are so completely integrated that such recession would appear to be impossible; but the prospect of exciting a demand from States to cancel their accession, in order to remain in the Commonwealth, may have been a makeweight in determining India's policy of seeking continued Commonwealth membership at earlier times, notably in 1948 when she decided to become a Republic.

Jodhpur. The case of Jodhpur should be mentioned because it illustrates both the lengths to which Mr. Jinnah was prepared to go in order to wean States from India, and the contrary efforts of Lord Mountbatten. Jodhpur, a Rajput State abutting on Pakistan, had a predominantly Hindu population and a Hindu ruler. Its Ruler[1] had a series of meetings with Mr. Jinnah and other Muslim leaders, including the Nawab of Bhopal, and had been on the point of agreeing to join Pakistan. Mr. Jinnah had offered him the use of Karachi as a free port, free import of arms, jurisdiction over the Jodhpur–Hyderabad (Sind) railway, and a large supply of grain for famine relief, all on condition that Jodhpur would declare its independence on 15th August, and subsequently accede to

[1] The young Maharajah Hanwant Singh, who had succeeded his father, an old friend of Lord Mountbatten's, only a couple of months previously, and who was killed in an aeroplane crash in 1952.

Pakistan. The Maharajah, however, had been shaken by a reminder of realities from the Maharaj Kumar of Jaisalmer—a neighbour-ing State of the same character—who had accompanied him at his last meeting with Mr. Jinnah. The Maharaj Kumar had said that for his part he would join Pakistan on one condition, that if there were trouble between Hindus and Muslims he would not side with the Muslims. The Maharajah of Jodhpur was then summoned to Viceroy's House in Delhi. Lord Mountbatten told him that, while he was legally entitled to accede to Pakistan, he should consider seriously the consequences of doing so. It would be in conflict with the principle underlying the partition of India and could only result in communal trouble within the State. The Maharajah began by asking for a string of concessions, saying that Mr. Jinnah had handed him a blank sheet of paper on which to write all the con-cessions he wanted. Mr. Menon, in the Viceroy's presence, urged him not to be swayed by false promises, but after some argument gave him a letter conceding some of his demands, including free import of arms, food for the famine districts, and the building of a railway from Jodhpur to a port in Cutch. The States Department were in fact scared by the possibility of Jodhpur's joining Pakistan, for this might have set the trend for other Rajput States like Udaipur which would become contiguous to Pakistan through their frontiers with Jodhpur. Both Jodhpur and Jaisalmer, to-gether with Bikaner, the third large Rajputana State actually ad-joining Pakistan, whose Ruler had given a strong lead in the policy of acceding to India, signed Instruments of Accession to the Indian Dominion.[1]

Hyderabad. Hyderabad was the largest State in India, and the first in status. Its area was over 82,000 square miles and its popula-

---

[1] When the Maharajah of Jodhpur eventually came to Viceroy's House to sign the instrument of accession, he used an exceptionally large pen. Lord Mountbatten having left the room, he whipped out the nib, reveal-ing a pistol barrel, which he levelled at Mr. V. P. Menon, exclaiming, 'I refuse to accept your dictation!' Mr. Menon told him not to indulge in juvenile theatricals. The Maharajah calmed down, and later he and Mr. Menon came much to respect each other; but when Lord Mountbatten was told of the Prince's conduct he 'gave him hell'. The pistol-pen, which the Maharajah, a member of the Magic Circle, had had made for him in his 'magic and gun shop', was handed over, and was presented by Lord Mountbatten to the Magic Circle after he himself was elected to it. A story of great issues and high statesmanship had its crazy moments.

tion nearly 16,000,000. It had its own coinage and paper currency. Its Ruler, alone among the Princes, enjoyed the prefix 'His Exalted Highness', and the title 'Faithful Ally'. The people were over 85 per cent Hindu, but the public services, including the army, were the preserve of the ruling Muslim minority. Even in the newly-created Hyderabad Legislative Assembly the Muslim seats exceeded by one-sixth those open to Hindus.

Soon after 3rd June the Nizam issued a *firman* declaring that he would join neither India nor Pakistan and that on 15th August he would resume the status of an independent sovereign. (His ancestors, originally appointed as Viceroys of the Deccan, had made themselves practically independent of the Mogul throne before engaging first with the French and then with the British, though they continued to pay a nominal allegiance to the Delhi Emperor up to 1858.) His object was Dominion Status, and when he saw this frustrated by the Indian Independence Bill he protested against the abandonment of his State by its ancient ally and the severance of the loyal ties which had bound him to the King-Emperor; Sir Walter Monckton,[1] Constitutional Adviser to the Nizam, who was in India, told Lord Ismay that he might find it necessary to return to London to stir up opposition to the Independence Bill on account of its treatment of the States. However, at a meeting on 11th July between the Viceroy and his advisers on the one hand, and on the other a delegation from Hyderabad including the Nawab of Chhatari, President of the Nizam's Council (equivalent of Prime Minister), and Sir Walter Monckton, some negotiating progress was made. A stiff debate on Berar, a large part of the Nizam's dominions leased in perpetuity to the Government of India by a pact of 1902 and administered under the Central Provinces, gave rise to a proposal that the pact should be continued by a standstill agreement which, though of indefinite term, could be denounced by either party at twelve months' notice. On Dominion Status the Viceroy reiterated its rejection by His Majesty's Government. He urged on the delegation the advantages of acceding to India, and 'without implying any sort of threat, he foresaw disastrous results to the State in five or ten years' time if his advice were not taken'.

When the delegation returned on 23rd July they proposed a treaty with India covering defence, external affairs and communi-

[1] Later Viscount Monckton of Brenchley.

cations, without accession, but this the Indian Government refused to consider. The Hyderabad representatives also went to see Mr. Jinnah, with whom the Nizam had been corresponding, even committing himself not to take a decision without Mr. Jinnah's concurrence. The Muslim League leader told them that he could not agree to the Nizam's accession to India even if it were stipulated that his forces should never be used against Pakistan. 'I require Hyderabad as an active ally,' he said, 'not as a neutral in such a war.' The mood is indicated by the fact that the Nawab of Chhatari, though nominated to the States' Negotiating Committee, refused to take part in it. Early in August the Nawab and Sir Walter reported to the Viceroy that the Nizam was moving towards the idea of a treaty in the same form as the Instrument of Accession, and Sir Walter thought that having come thus far he might be induced to accede; but the extremist Muslim militants in Hyderabad, the Ittehad-ul-Muslimeen, backed by Mr. Jinnah, were trying by every possible pressure to stop him even from making a treaty. Sardar Patel again refused to accept a treaty, and Mr. Menon told Nawab Ali Yawar Jung,[1] a member of the delegation, that no accession meant no standstill agreement. The only progress made in this period was the Nizam's assenting to the appointment of an Indian politician as the new Governor of the Central Provinces and Berar, thus temporarily stabilising the constitutional position of Berar. Sir Walter Monckton asked for further time, not only to persuade the Nizam, but also to prepare for trouble from the extremist Muslim organisations in the State.

At a meeting of the future Government of India over which he presided, Lord Mountbatten pleaded for an extension of the time-limit in this exceptional case. Unless, he argued, they authorised negotiations to continue on the existing Instrument of Accession there might be violent trouble which could threaten the stability of India. An extension of two months was agreed, and Lord Mountbatten's offer of his own services in carrying on the negotiations was, to his surprise, unanimously accepted by the Indian leaders. He was also authorised to inform the Nizam in writing that he was satisfied that the leaders of the new Dominion had no intention of treating a decision by him not to accede, in the existing circumstances, as a hostile act. Lord Mountbatten remained optimistic, and in his address to the Constituent Assembly on 15th August

[1] Later Indian Ambassador in Washington.

declared that he was hopeful of reaching a solution of the Hyderabad problem satisfactory to everyone.

Kashmir. In the light of later events, it is hard to credit that at this stage the Indian leaders seemed indifferent to the accession or non-accession of Kashmir and Jammu, and that the political situation in this quarter was dominated by the intense mutual hostility between Pandit Nehru and the Maharajah's regime, headed by his Prime Minister, Pandit Kak. But so it was. The States Department made no approach at all to the Ruler. Early in June Pandit Nehru had told the Viceroy that he, Nehru, must go to Kashmir immediately to obtain the release from prison of his friend Sheikh Abdullah, leader of the Kashmir National Conference, the counterpart of the Congress in the State, and to support its popular movement. Mr. Gandhi made a similar request a few days later. Lord Mountbatten headed them off by saying that he would much prefer first to go himself and see the Maharajah, an old acquaintance from whom he had an invitation to stay. Mr. Gandhi and Pandit Nehru were both very anxious that the Maharajah should make no declaration of independence. This Lord Mountbatten urged on the Maharajah and Pandit Kak in informal conversations during his visit to Kashmir between 18th and 23rd June, and they agreed. He also pressed them to take measures to ascertain the will of their people and to announce their intention to send representatives to one Constituent Assembly or the other. The States Department, he told them, were prepared to give an assurance that if Kashmir joined Pakistan this would not be regarded as unfriendly by the Government of India. He pointed out the dangerous situation in which Kashmir would find itself if it did not have the support of · one of the two Dominions after 15th August.

Lord Mountbatten again with difficulty dissuaded Pandit Nehru from going to Kashmir,[1] but allowed that Mahatma Gandhi's going would not raise the same problems, because of his 'religious aura' and his non-governmental status. The Mahatma, on his visit to Kashmir at the end of July, fulfilled his promise to the Viceroy not to make political speeches, contenting himself with a statement on his return journey specifically giving Kashmir the choice of joining either Dominion, according to the will of its people. The

[1] See below, p. 443.

Maharajah, however, continued to procrastinate, and on 15th August had still made no decision.

Reflections. At that moment Lord Mountbatten could feel a sense of triumphant success in respect of the States. Against all the probabilities, the overwhelming majority of States had joined the new Dominions, and the constitutional chaos and insurrectionary violence that might have followed the total lapse of paramountcy had been averted. True, there were a few exceptions, two of them great principalities, and these were to cause immense and enduring conflicts; but that was in the future, and if the future could have been foreseen it could have been claimed to prove what disasters would have overtaken all India had the exceptions been the rule. True it was, also, that the policy so successfully applied was the policy of the Indian Government, and as such was both shrewd and statesmanlike, and that its success was due in no small measure to the leadership and patriotism of certain distinguished Rulers who led the way and greatly influenced their peers, especially the Maharajah Gaekwar of Baroda and Maharajah Scindia of Gwalior—Mahratta Princes—the Rajput Maharajah of Bikaner and the Sikh Maharajah of Patiala. But Lord Mountbatten had been the first to announce the policy to the Princes, he had called it 'my scheme', he had 'gone into battle' for it with the Indian leaders, overriding his Political Adviser, and above all it was he who personally pressed the negotiations in critical cases.

Here his tactics were consistent and strong. Without threatening, he emphasised most forcefully the evils that would attend the States if they did not accede by 15th August: exclusion from the Commonwealth, exposure to Congress-inspired revolts, loss of all clear status for their regimes or their subjects, the likelihood of their being obliged to accept worse terms after 15th August when he would no longer have power to help them. On the other side he stressed that they were being asked to give up no powers that they actually possessed, and that accession involved them in no commitments whatever beyond the three central subjects. In thus committing himself not only to the principle of the proto-Indian Government's policy but also to its execution, Lord Mountbatten was undoubtedly led to put himself in opposition to the proto-Pakistan Government, whose policy was not only different but hostile, namely, to offer independence to States joining themselves

to Pakistan and to dissuade as many as possible from joining India
—not only those with Muslim Rulers like Hyderabad or Bhopal,
nor only those adjacent to Pakistan like Jodhpur or Jaisalmer, but
even Hindu-ruled States embedded in India like Indore or
Travancore.

This conflict between Lord Mountbatten and Mr. Jinnah was
no doubt inevitable; for the Viceroy was still Crown Representative in relation to the Indian States, with responsibility for guiding
them at a crucial moment of their history, and if he made up his
mind that one policy was right for them and another wrong he had
the duty to press the right and oppose the wrong. Nevertheless his
attitude was influenced by the fact that after the transfer of power
he would still be Governor-General of India, with overall if wholly
constitutional responsibility for its security and welfare, and having
no such constitutional responsibility for Pakistan; hence he could
not take an equal view of the possible future of the States in relation to the two Dominions respectively after 15th August. And his
vigorous countering of Muslim League ambitions in respect of
marginal or hesitating States contributed to the suspicion which
steadily grew in Pakistan after 15th August that his policies and
feelings were loaded in favour of India. However, this was not to
blight his initial popularity on both sides of the boundary or to mar
the ceremonies, in which he played his eminent part, to celebrate
the creation of the great new Muslim State.

20

The end of the British Raj

On the afternoon of 13th August Lord and Lady Mountbatten flew to Karachi. At the airport the head of the C.I.D. in Sind warned the Viceroy that he was certain that the plot to throw a bomb into Mr. Jinnah's open car in the State procession on the following day was definitely on, and begged him not to drive with Mr. Jinnah. The Military Secretary to the new Governor-General of Pakistan reported that Mr. Jinnah was willing to go through with the drive if the Viceroy was willing. 'In that event,' said Lord Mountbatten, 'I will go with him.' The plans were not altered.

On the evening of the 13th a State banquet was held. It had been agreed that there should be two toasts but no speeches. Lord Mountbatten was therefore horrified when Mr. Jinnah stood up and, pulling a typescript from his pocket, proceeded to deliver a speech—very pro-British in tone and friendly towards Lord Mountbatten himself. At the end Mr. Jinnah proposed the health of His Majesty the King: this was apparently the last time that he was to do so, for thenceforward he steadfastly refused to propose the King's health, even when entertaining Royalty. Lord Mountbatten was obliged to make an impromptu speech in reply, proposing the health of Pakistan: few Viceroys could have dealt with such an emergency better than he,

The next morning Lord Mountbatten addressed the Pakistan Constituent Assembly. He did so from the Chair, having insisted on his rights as Viceroy on this last occasion, against Mr. Jinnah's claim to take the principal seat as President of the Assembly. Lord Mountbatten began by delivering a message of greetings and god-speed to the new Dominion of Pakistan from His Majesty the King. He continued:

Tomorrow two new sovereign States will take their place in the Commonwealth: not young nations, but heirs of old and proud civilisations . . . not immature Governments or weak, but fit to

carry their great share of responsibility for the peace and progress of the world.

The birth of Pakistan is an event in history. . . . History seems
sometimes to move with the infinite slowness of a glacier and
sometimes to rush forward in a torrent. Just now, in this part
of the world our united efforts have melted the ice and moved
some impediments in the stream, and we are carried onwards in
the full flood. There is no time to look back. There is time only
to look forward.

I wish to pay tribute to the great men, your leaders, who
helped to arrive at a peaceful solution for the transfer of power.

Here I would like to express my tribute to Mr. Jinnah. Our
close personal contact, and the mutual trust and understanding
that have grown out of it, are, I feel, the best of omens for future
good relations. He has my sincere good wishes as your new
Governor-General.

Moral courage is the truest attribute of greatness, and the men
who have allowed the paramount need for agreement and a
peaceful solution to take precedence over the hopes and claims
they so strongly held and keenly felt, have shown moral courage
in a high degree. I wish to acknowledge, too, the help of others;
of the men who advised and assisted the process of negotiation;
of the men who kept the machinery of administration running
under great difficulties, of the men who have worked day and
night to solve the innumerable problems of partition. All this
has been achieved with toil and sweat. I wish I could say also
without tears or blood, but terrible crimes have been committed.
It is justifiable to reflect, however, that far more terrible things
might have happened if the majority had not proved worthy of
the high endeavour of their leaders, or had not listened to the
great appeal which Mr. Jinnah and Mahatma Gandhi together
made, and which the respective future Governments reiterated
in a statement made by the Partition Council.

'This,' declared the Viceroy, 'is a parting between friends, who
have learned to honour and respect one another, even in disagreement. It is not an absolute parting, I rejoice to think, not an
end of comradeship.' And he concluded: 'May Pakistan flourish
always . . . may she continue in friendship with her neighbours and
with all the nations of the world.'

The State procession then took place, with Mr. Jinnah and the Viceroy—as he still was until midnight—in the leading car and Lady Mountbatten and Miss Jinnah, the Qaid-i-Azam's sister, in the following car. Along the route cries of 'Mountbatten Zindabad' mingled with those of 'Pakistan Zindabad' and 'Mahomed Ali Jinnah Zindabad'. As the procession turned in at the gates of Government House, Mr. Jinnah put his hand on Lord Mountbatten's knee and said with evident emotion 'Thank God I have brought you back alive!' Lord Mountbatten replied 'Thank God I have brought *you* back alive!' That afternoon when Mr. Jinnah bade farewell to his noble guests, he made, with considerable feeling, a declaration of eternal gratitude and friendship. 'In fact,' wrote Lord Mountbatten, 'when we all parted I felt that nothing would shake that friendship.'[1]

The Viceroy and Vicereine flew back the same day to Delhi and at twenty minutes past midnight a deputation of the President of the Indian Constituent Assembly and the Prime Minister of India called on him to announce that the Constituent Assembly had taken over power and had endorsed the request of the leaders that Lord Mountbatten should become their Governor-General. Pandit Nehru then said in ceremonious terms: 'May I submit to you the portfolios of the new Cabinet', and handed Lord Mountbatten a carefully addressed envelope. On opening it after his departure the Governor-General found it to be empty. 'I must, however, admit,' he observed later, 'that we had been through the list carefully together, previously.' In fact that exercise had formed a premature example, in the new India, of the right of a constitutional monarch or Governor-General to be informed, his duty to warn and his power to influence, even though he is bound to accept Ministerial advice. Rumours in the Press and from private sources had indicated that in forming his Cabinet Pandit Nehru intended to submit a list of old-time Congress stalwarts. It seemed to the Viceroy that this would not meet the difficult situation that would confront the new Government. He therefore made a point of discussing the composition of the Cabinet with the Prime Minister, stressing that he would be bound to accept any names submitted, but offering counsel as a friend, an offer willingly accepted. Lord Mountbatten then told Pandit Nehru that unless he got a really sound Cabinet in which young, talented and keen members pre-

[1] *Report on the Last Viceroyalty.*

dominated, he would lose a great opportunity of catching the imagination of the country; that one of his greatest weaknesses, in the Viceroy's opinion, was his personal loyalty to old friends and colleagues; and that unless he got rid of some of the older members who held office only because of their long connection with the Congress he would find himself gravely hampered. Pandit Nehru, though listening attentively, gave no indication of his reaction; but afterwards the Viceroy heard that he had immediately summoned his close Congress colleagues, torn up the list of the Cabinet he had intended to submit, and said that it was vital for the future of India that a more imaginative team should be produced.

A more extraordinary piece of advice was necessary. Pandit Nehru's first list for his post-independence Cabinet omitted the name of Sardar Vallabhbhai Patel.[1] Hearing this—no doubt from Patel himself—Mr. V. P. Menon hurried to the Viceroy and warned him, 'This will start a war of succession in the Congress Party and split the country.' Nehru had great influence with the masses, and some of the supra-political appeal of Mahatma Gandhi had rubbed off on him; but Patel, as party treasurer and chairman of the committee which selected parliamentary candidates, had immense power over the party machine, and in a show-down with Nehru he might well win. Lord Mountbatten conveyed this alarm to his Prime Minister, though he would have had no official intimation of the plan to drop 'the strong man of the Congress'.

When Pandit Nehru sent in his final list it included, besides all the Congress-nominated members of the Interim Government (except Mr. Rajagopalachari, who became Governor of West Bengal and was destined to succeed Lord Mountbatten as Governor-General[2]), three non-Congressmen: Dr. S. P. Mukherjee, leader of the Hindu Mahasabha, Mr. Shanmukham Chetty, a business man and administrator, who had been bitterly critical of the Congress, and Mr. B. R. Ambedkar, the Scheduled Caste leader; and three others from the Congress but outside the existing inner circle. The list hardly fulfilled Lord Mountbatten's specification that 'young, talented and keen' members should predomin-

[1] Possibly on the advice of Mr. Gandhi. See p. 426.
[2] Twenty years later, Mr. Rajagopalachari was still active in politics as founder and President of the Swatantra Party, formed to oppose the Congress in defence of individual liberty.

ate, but, as he remarked, 'the requirements of party politics could not entirely be done away with'.

After that midnight ceremony, the first event of the day of the transfer of power was the swearing in, first of the Governor-General by the Chief Justice, and then of the Ministers by the Governor-General. This was the prelude to a day which Lord Mountbatten described as the most remarkable and inspiring of his life. The story is best told in his own words.[1]

Description of Events on 15th August, 1947
(Written on the following day)

The 15th August has certainly turned out to be the most remarkable and inspiring day of my life. We started at 8.30 with the Swearing-In ceremony in the Durbar Hall in front of an official audience of some 500, including a number of ruling Princes. The official guests, including Ambassadors, Princes and the Cabinet, then drove in procession from Government House (ex-Viceroy's House) to the Council Chamber.

2. Never have such crowds been seen within the memory of anyone I have spoken to. Not only did they line every rooftop and vantage point, but they pressed round so thick as to become finally quite unmanageable. At the Council Chamber it had fortunately been arranged that there should be two Guards of Honour (R.I.N. and R.I.A.F.) of 100 men each. These 200 men joined with the police were just able to keep the crowd back sufficiently to let us get out of the State coach without being physically lifted out of it by the crowd.

3 The ceremony in the Council Chamber was extremely dignified and my speech was well received. Fortunately two more Guards of Honour of the Indian Army were due for the departure ceremony, and I gave orders that the four Guards of Honour were to pile arms inside the Council Chambers, and then endeavour to keep the crowd back. As we were about to depart they said that it was doubtful whether the 400 men of the Guards of Honour could keep the way clear to the coach, so Nehru went on to the roof and waved to the crowd to go back; the door was then opened and surrounded by our staff we fought our way through to the coach.

[1] Appendix to *Report on the Last Viceroy*.

4 It took us half an hour to go the short distance back, for we had to go slowly through the crowds. Once we were held up for some five minutes by the pressure of the crowds. Apart from the usual cries of 'Jai Hind' and 'Mahatma Gandhi ki jai' and 'Pandit Nehru ki jai', a surprising number shouted out 'Mountbatten ki jai', and 'Lady Mountbatten ki jai' and more than once 'Pandit Mountbatten ki jai'.

5 After lunch we decided to pay an impromptu visit to the great children's fête being held in the Roshnara Park. This visit was an unqualified success. Thousands of children gathered all round us cheering and yelling and trying to shake hands. I felt that it would be a good idea to get out of uniform and into informal surroundings for at least one of the Independence Day celebrations.

6 At 6 p.m. the great event of the day was to take place—the salutation of the new Dominion flag. This programme had originally included a ceremonial lowering of the Union Jack; but when I discussed this with Nehru he entirely agreed that this was a day they wanted everybody to be happy, and if the lowering of the Union Jack in any way offended British susceptibilities he would certainly see that it did not take place, the more so as the Union Jack would still be flown on certain days in the Dominion, such as the King's birthday.

7 A parade had been arranged of the units of the three Services, pages of orders had been issued, rehearsals had been going on for days, and seats on raised platforms had been provided. The crowds, however, were far beyond the control of the police. Some Indian officials estimate that there were 600,000 people there. But personally I doubt if there were more than a quarter of a million. At all events they thronged the processional route and if possible gave my wife and myself a greater reception than in the morning.

8 But for the admirable Bodyguard with their wonderfully trained and patient horses we should never have been able to get on to the ground. But at a slow walk they managed to breast a way through the crowd up to the appointed position opposite the Grand Stand and the Parade. There was, however, nothing to be seen of the Grand Stand, and although a row of bright

coloured pugrees in the crowd indicated where the troops had been engulfed there was no other indication of a military parade.

9 Nehru fought his way to the coach and climbed in to tell us that our daughter Pamela was safe. George Abell (my late Private Secretary) described how Nehru came to their rescue when they were being overwhelmed by the crowd, fighting like a maniac, striking people right and left and eventually taking the topee off a man who annoyed him particularly and smashing it over his head.

10 Major-General Rajendra Singh, the Delhi Area Commander, Nehru and I had a hurried consultation and we decided that the only thing to do was to hoist the flag and fire the salute and give up all other idea of the programme. This was done amid scenes of the most fantastic rejoicing, and as the flag broke a brilliant rainbow appeared in the sky, which was taken by the whole crowd as a good omen. (I had never noticed how closely a rainbow could resemble the new Dominion flag of saffron, white and green.)

11 Meanwhile danger of a large-scale accident was becoming so great that we decided that the only thing to do was to try and move the coach on through the crowd and draw the crowd with us. For this reason I invited Nehru to stay in the coach, which he did, sitting like a schoolboy on the front hood above the seats. Meanwhile refugees who had fainted or had been almost crushed under the wheels were pulled on board and we ended with four Indian ladies with their children, the Polish wife of a British officer and an Indian pressman who crawled up behind. The Bodyguard gradually opened a way through the crowd and then the whole throng began to follow us. Hundreds of thousands of people all running together is an impressive sight; several thousand ran the whole three miles back alongside the coach and behind it, being stopped finally by the police only at the gates of Government House.

12 No British or Indian whom I have since met has ever remembered crowd scenes even approaching those that were witnessed yesterday; but the significant feature is that numerous Indian observers all agreed that the reception which was

accorded to us was no whit less enthusiastic than that accorded to their own leaders. This sounds rather incredible but it appears to be a fact and was generously referred to by Nehru in his speech last night as the best omen for the future good relations between our two countries.

13 There are two other significant facts which I feel I should report. The first is that the President of the Constituent Assembly, Dr. Rajendra Prasad, invited me on behalf of the Assembly to send back a 'loyal' message of thanks to His Majesty saying that India and Britain even if their precise future relations were different would always be the greatest friends. The other is that at a State banquet of a hundred that night Nehru made a speech in the most friendly terms possible prior to proposing the toast of The King. I replied and proposed the Dominion of India.

14 Close on 3,000 people came to our evening party at Government House and stayed till after two o'clock in the morning. At this dinner and subsequent party the Ambassadors, the new Cabinet, the senior British and Indian officers of the Services, and the Ruling Princes were freely mixed. I have never experienced such a day in my life.

In his speech to the Constituent Assembly Lord Mountbatten had again given a message of greeting and goodwill from the King. He then recalled events leading up to this great day. He had not been a week in India, he said, before he realised that June 1948, which had seemed impossibly early for the transfer of power, was indeed too late. Communal tension and rioting had assumed proportions of which he had no conception when he left England. A decision, it seemed, had to be taken at the earliest moment if there were not to be a general conflagration. The plan of 3rd June, continued Lord Mountbatten, 'was evolved at every stage by a process of open diplomacy with the leaders. Its success is chiefly attributable to them. I believe that this system of open diplomacy was the only one suited to the situation.' And he here paid tribute to the wisdom and tolerance of the leaders, and to the work of Ministers and officials on the administrative consequences of partition, which had enabled the transfer of power to take place ten and a half months earlier than had been intended.

I know well [declared Lord Mountbatten] that the rejoicing which the advent of freedom brings is tempered in your hearts by the sadness that it could not come to a united India. . . . In supporting your leaders in the difficult decision which they had to take, you have displayed as much magnanimity and realism as have those patriotic statesmen themselves.

These statesmen have placed me in their debt for ever by their sympathetic understanding of my position. . . . They agreed from the outset to release me from any responsibility whatsoever for the partition of the Punjab and Bengal. It was they who selected the personnel of the Boundary Commissions including the Chairman; it was they who drew up the terms of reference; it is they who shoulder the responsibility for implementing the award. You will appreciate that had they not done this I would have been placed in an impossible position.

After referring at some length to the Indian States, and particularly to the unique position of Hyderabad,[1] Lord Mountbatten observed:

From today I am your constitutional Governor-General and I would ask you to regard me as one of yourselves, devoted wholly to the furtherance of India's interests.

His only consideration in accepting the request to stay on had been that he might continue to be of some help to India in the difficult days immediately ahead; and he said that he proposed to ask to be released in April 1948.

In his peroration, to which he came after announcing a generous policy of amnesty, including military prisoners sentenced by court-martial, Lord Mountbatten stressed the problems of reconstruction that lay in the wake of 'a treaty of peace without war', and the 'sympathetic expectancy' and goodwill with which Britain and the sister Dominions would watch India's future as a factor of the greatest international importance. And he concluded:

At this historic moment, let us not forget all that India owes to Mahatma Gandhi—the architect of her freedom through non-violence. We miss his presence here today, and would have him know how much he is in our thoughts.

Mr. President, I would like you and our other colleagues of

[1] See above, p. 382.

the late Interim Government to know how deeply I have appreciated your unfailing support and co-operation.

In your first Prime Minister, Pandit Jawaharlal Nehru, you have a world-renowned leader of courage and vision. His trust and friendship have helped me beyond measure in my task. Under his able guidance, assisted by the colleagues whom he has selected, and with the loyal co-operation of the people, India will now attain a position of strength and influence and take her rightful place in the comity of nations.

There appears, as one reads them, a distinct difference in tone between Lord Mountbatten's speech to the Pakistan Assembly and his speech to the Indian Assembly. The one, of course, was a farewell, the other the inauguration of a new relationship. There is a distinction, too, between neighbourly benevolence and parental love. For Pakistan, Lord Mountbatten was becoming the friendly Governor-General of an adjacent state; for India, he was becoming its own Governor-General, an intimate element in a new free nation. As such, he could but ask his audience to regard him 'as one of yourselves, devoted wholly to the furtherance of India's interests', though Pakistanis, reading this, must have been sharply conscious that India's interests were bound to conflict at some points with those of Pakistan.

All this, however, does not entirely explain the more formal rhetoric of the Karachi address, nor the contrast between the respectable tribute to Mr. Jinnah and the intimate praise of Mr. Gandhi and Pandit Nehru. There can be no doubt where, between the two Dominions, Lord Mountbatten's heart lay. His closest relations in day-to-day politics had been with Pandit Nehru and Sardar Patel rather than Mr. Liaqat Ali Khan. Mr. Jinnah, with whom no more than anyone else had he been able to establish any personal intimacy, had not been a member of his Government. The official Indian advisers whom he trusted most were also Hindus, whereas his principal Muslim friend and go-between, the Nawab of Bhopal, was more a problem in India than a pillar of Pakistan. For Mahatma Gandhi the last Viceroy had a real if wary affection. Such personal relationships influence a man's political attitude. But it is also clear, if only from the respective references to partition in the two speeches, that Lord Mountbatten shared the feeling of most British people involved in pre-independence

India that the breach of Indian unity, which had been the great pride of the Raj, was a sad ending forced on him by ugly necessity, rather than an act of statesmanship justified by its own merits. There may have been, besides, some lingering resentment of Mr. Jinnah's frustration of his hope of becoming Governor-General of both Dominions and of presiding over their joint destiny in the initial, formative months of their freedom.

It is unlikely, however, that many Indians or Pakistanis paid much attention to the nuances of state speeches on 15th August. They were at once intoxicated by the thought of their new nation-hood and sobered by the prospect of all the problems that it implied. There were many Indians, no doubt, who expected a millennium, having been taught incessantly that freedom from British rule was the key that would unlock the doors of social and economic advance, a prize to be ranked above all others; and many Pakistanis to whom Pakistan was a magical Promised Land. There were also some—men and women of communal or economic minorities, or of classes in the 'Establishment' favoured by the British or participating in British power—who feared what might happen under the rule of a majority or of political leaders inimical to them, leaders committed, in India, to democratic socialism, and in Pakistan to 'Islamic democracy'. For the inheritors of power, joy at the achievement of their supreme goal ruled their hearts, overcoming for Indians the pain of the partition of their country, and for many Pakistanis the grief of leaving their homes for a new land of problematic future. But for them, too, triumph was mixed with awe; for great responsibility is awesome when it has always lain upon others, even if years of struggle have been spent in wresting it from them.

For close on a century the British had been the effective sover-eign rulers of all India; for a century before that, since the battle of Plassey, they had been a territorial power of consequence in an India ruled by a swarm of autocratic princes and satraps. And now they were going, handing over to Indians the power they had so long exercised—to their own advantage, no doubt, but with bene-volence and with confident assurance and deep experience and skill. To have transmitted power in peace and order and with complete constitutional continuity was perhaps their greatest achievement and their last gift to India and Pakistan. They left also two immense assets to their successors: a strong and efficient system of public administration, and a loyal, finely-trained Army and air and sea Forces. Many British officials and military officers stayed on in the transitional period, thanks to the decision that the two new nations would remain in the Commonwealth; but even if all had gone the structure, though much weakened, would have remained. The vast majority of civil servants, some half a million in the two Dominions, were in the provincial services, which had long been wholly Indian in personnel. The so-called Secretary of State's Services—mainly the Indian Civil Service and officers of the Indian Police, about 3,000 altogether—which provided the 'iron frame' of civil administration, were by now as to a majority Indian, including many in the highest posts. Indianisation of the officer hierarchy of the Army had started later, and the top commands were all held by British officers, the most senior Indian Army officers being brigadiers. But here, too, the groundwork of training and experience in command were present, and within a few years accelerated promotion produced officers fully fit to take over from the British who had stayed on as servants of the new nations.

Nor was experience of high administrative responsibility altogether lacking on the political side. Members of the Interim Government had held office for up to nearly a year, and were no newcomers to the machine of central government. Provincial Ministers had held office for several years, before, after and in some cases during the war. Many observers, indeed, doubted whether, at the Centre, men whose lives had been spent in agitation directed to the overthrow of the existing government could at a stroke turn themselves into efficient administrators and strong decision-takers. But this was India's problem, and Pakistan's. Britain had taken her final strong decision, and her responsibility was at an end.

The question that British people could address to their consciences was whether, in this transfer of power, their duty and their pledges to the minorities and the weaker elements in Indian society had been discharged with honour. To the Muslims had been granted their supreme demand, separate nationhood. If this was not the best assurance for their future, the fault lay on Muslim heads, not British. The Indian-Christians, the Anglo-Indians, the States' Rulers, all lamented that they had been forsaken. But Britain and the Indian and Pakistani minorities alike, including the Princes, had to face the plain fact that self-government must be complete or it is not self-government. Once India and Pakistan were granted national sovereignty, no possibility remained of intervention to defend minorities or even to see that constitutional guarantees bequeathed to them were carried out. All that Britain could do upon the transfer of power was to see that the system of government she left behind was inherently balanced and likely to secure fair treatment for the weak or the few. Administratively, this was generally so. Politically, the Congress and the Muslim League were both pledged to fair play and equal treatment for minorities; the drafting of the respective permanent constitutions was deliberately and inevitably left to the Indians and Pakistanis themselves, under the rule of majority. But there was a third factor, judicial. The vital safeguard for minorities and persons is not the vote or the constitution but the rule of law. And the rule of law under a detached professional judiciary was perhaps the greatest legacy of all that Britain bequeathed in the great sub-continent. It has proved, in the twenty years that have since passed, more valuable than any constitutional safeguards, which majorities or dictatorships could erode. The rule of law, experience of democratic if subordinate government, a sound administrative mechanism with experienced personnel, and an army ranking in discipline and strength with any in the world, these were a rich endowment for the two new independent nations which were born on 15th August 1947. All were to be fully tried in the troubled times that lay ahead.

PART FOUR

The aftermath

21

Feelings after partition

After partition and the creation of Pakistan few of the leaders of the new-born nation States, save Mahatma Gandhi and some of his kind, showed that spirit of forgiveness and understanding which heals separation and binds up wounds to ambition and pride. Some time after the transfer of power Pandit Jawaharlal Nehru visited London and called on Mr. Winston Churchill at his home. Mr. R. A. Butler, arriving just as host and guest parted on the doorstep, found Mr. Churchill in tears, as was his wont when emotionally affected. 'We put that man in gaol for ten years,' he said to his colleague, 'and he bears us no malice. I could not have been so magnanimous.' Mr. Churchill erred in his judgment both of his visitor and of himself, for Churchill was the soul of magnanimity towards former foes in war and in politics, whereas Nehru, for all his readiness to forget his earlier experiences at the hands of the British, must have felt that these were all part of a contest, fought under an accepted code, in which he had won the last battle, in contrast to the defeat that he had suffered in the simultaneous war between Indian nationalism and Muslim separatism. He could forgive Churchill and the British for having harassed and imprisoned him; Jinnah and the Muslim leaders, for having robbed the Congress of a free united India, he could not so soon forgive. Bitterness, suspicion, and unreadiness to let bygones be bygones, and be friends, infected politicians on both sides of the borders who now took power, each according to his character and the opportunities he had of expressing it. Even some of the British who remained caught that mood. In some Indians hostility to Pakistan was an obsession. And from it sprang the murder of the largest-hearted of them all, Mahatma Gandhi.

In Pakistan a more generous spirit was to have been expected. The Muslim League had won its political battle against all odds, and was entering into the Promised Land. Hindu raj over the subcontinent had been broken, and the Muslims had triumphantly secured their national home. Magnanimity could have been afforded. Mr. Jinnah had told Lord Ismay in April 'with the greatest earnestness,' that, once partition had been decided upon, everyone would know exactly where they were, all troubles would cease and they would live happily ever after.[1] The Qaid-i-Azam's utterances at the time suggest a genuine desire for Indo-Pakistani friendship, which was decidedly in the interest of the smaller country, and an end to inter-communal conflict, which could only endanger the nascent nation and jeopardise the great Muslim minority still left in India. But the awakening on the morrow of partition was for many in Pakistan as painful as it was for Indian nationalists, perhaps more painful. Pakistan they had, but it was the 'moth-eaten' Pakistan that the Qaid-i-Azam had scorned; purchased at the price of vivisecting the two historic Muslim dominions of Bengal and the Punjab, it was but two spaces on a map, without a natural frontier along the new dividing lines, without a ready capital, without the apparatus of national government or much trained skill to exercise it, a weak and feeble infant, a dry-mouthed end to a romantic dream. Even so, India and the Hindus had yielded it not in friendship but grudgingly under coercion. They were feared to be hoping for its death and ready to damage it in every way. The fight to get for Pakistan her share of the assets in British India in money and material was still only half-fought. Amid such feelings of disillusionment and fear there was little soil in which reconciliation could prosper.

[1] *Viceroy's Interviews*, No. 43, 9th April 1947.

22

Massacre and migration in the north-west

While most of India and Pakistan celebrated Independence Day with peaceable rejoicing, in the Punjab it was a day of violence and terror. That afternoon, in a town of East Punjab, a mob of Sikhs were reported to have seized Muslim women, stripped and raped them, and paraded them naked through the streets, some of them being then slaughtered and burnt.[1] Across the border, on the night of 15th August a large Muslim mob burnt down a Gurdwara (Sikh temple), killing and incinerating its occupants to the number of about a score—'it was impossible to count the victims properly in the confused heap of rubble and corpses'.[2]

'It had been obvious to anybody,' wrote Lord Mountbatten, 'that there were going to be disturbances in the Punjab on the transfer of power. But I freely confess that I did not anticipate the scale and extent of what was going to happen, nor, so far as I am aware, did anyone in authority in India, Pakistan and the United Kingdom anticipate this.'[3] This was certainly true of those in high places. Even the Governor of the Punjab, who could have had no illusions as to what was going on, had based his worst predictions on the hypothesis that partition would be imposed, not agreed to

---

[1] As with many 'atrocity stories', no contemporary eye-witness account of this event can be traced.
[2] Report on the Punjab Boundary Force, by Major-General T. W. Rees.
[3] *Report of the First Governor-General of the Dominion of India.* This was addressed to His Majesty the King on 25th November 1948, five months after Lord Mountbatten vacated that office. It was, however, based textually upon twelve reports which he sent to His Majesty, at first fortnightly and then monthly, from 2nd September 1947 to 21st June 1948, virtually in continuance of his reports as Viceroy to the Secretary of State. The considered report has been frequently preferred for quotation in this section of the book, and is cited as *Report of the Governor-General*, the individual reports being given their numbers and dates.

by the parties and communities,[1] and was much less anxious if there were to be such agreement. There were less exalted observers who expected horrors and wholesale massacres, but one of them, Mr. Penderel Moon, confessed:

> I foresaw, of course, a terrific upheaval in the central districts [of the Punjab] which would have repercussions in the farthest corner of the province; but I quite failed to grasp the speed with which disturbances and displacements of population in the centre of the province would resolve themselves into a vast movement of mass migration, affecting not only the whole Punjab but adjoining areas as well. I envisaged a slower, more prolonged, more confused and chaotic agony. Punjabis in general were strangely unprepared for what was coming.[2]

Failure of foresight is not, however, to be blamed for failure to take action which could have prevented such disasters; for even looking back one can see little that the supreme authorities could have done but did not do, short of reversing the whole policy of early independence and partition. Some critics of Lord Mountbatten, especially in the Punjab, have argued that the root of the evil was the haste with which partition was performed. At the critical moment, they rightly say, government was in many respects at its weakest. Military units, civil officers, even railway officials, were either in transit or in the opposite country to that which they had opted to serve. But this aspect of those affairs cannot be isolated from the rest, and the reasons for speed, in the interest of effecting the surgery before the patient had been too much weakened by the growing communal distrust within the armed forces and all services, were regarded by the highest political figures, not only by the Viceroy, as outweighing the reasons for delay.

The key fact was the breakdown of civil government. Without effective civil authority it is impossible for an army—the sole remaining instrument of order—to prevent murders, arson and rapine committed by ordinary people against ordinary people over a vast rural area or in the alleys or bazaars of Asian cities. And

[1] See above, p. 273.
[2] Sir Penderel Moon, *Divide and Quit*, p. 93. Sir Penderel, who had served in the Indian Civil Service from 1929 to 1944, and had been Private Secretary to the Governor of the Punjab, was at the time of these troubles a Minister in Bahawalpur State.

it was these crimes, and the overmastering fears which they aroused, that provoked the universally unforeseen migrations of Muslims to Pakistan, Sikhs and Hindus to India, in and around the Punjab. Had the available military forces been concentrated sooner on protection of refugee trains and convoys the loss of lives *en route* might have been less, but probably at the expense of still worse slaughter and destruction elsewhere. Even military guards could not always prevent heavy casualties among the refugees. And the military arm itself was gravely weakened by rising communalism among the troops, excited both by what they saw with their own eyes and by the news that they had from their families and villages.

The breakdown of civil government had many causes, including the fact that new Governments of inexperienced politicians had just taken over in East and West Punjab from the Governor's rule under Section 93 which had operated since Sir Khizar Hyat Khan's resignation in early March. It was the primary factor in the failure of the Punjab Boundary Force to do all that was expected of it. The Commander of the Force painted this picture:

. . . The civil administration had been steadily deteriorating for some time. During the recent war, there had been no intake either of Europeans or of Indians of suitable calibre into the administration; and in consequence every area had become under-staffed in the higher levels, with the inevitable gradual drop in efficiency. Then came the announcement of the intention to hand over power in June 1948, and this accelerated the deterioration. British officers felt that they were not getting the same efficiency and support from subordinates who knew they would not be responsible to their present superiors much longer and that they could not hope for much promotion or reward from them. Communalism was also eating deep into the administration. The declaration advancing the date to 15th August 1947, still further accelerated the administrative decline. The British officers strove to maintain all the efficiency that they could while still present, but their days were numbered. And, in addition to the fact that Indian officials, both high and humble, were fully aware that they would not be responsible to British officers much longer, the Indian officials and police also knew that they themselves would soon be scattered and transferred to various places in India and Pakistan. So, on that account also, there was a loosening of responsibility, discipline and possible sanctions.

. . . The machinery of Government became less and less effective, until, after 15th August, in the West Punjab it almost ceased to function and, in the East Punjab, to all intents and purposes, it did cease to function.

. . . From 70 to 80 per cent of the Punjab Police was Muslim; and, having been disarmed by order of non-Muslim officials, even before 15th August, the Muslim police in East Punjab refused to continue to serve there: similarly the non-Muslim police in the West all wished to go East. The intelligence system, which had formerly been so efficient, but which had been deteriorating steadily, rapidly disintegrated. All police became completely partisan, even before partition. So, on 15th August, in the East Punjab, in the Jullundur Civil Division alone, Government was minus 7,000 policemen due to the loss of their Muslim police. And already Lahore and Amritsar were burning and given to internecine fighting: the non-Muslims were being exterminated out of Lahore, and Muslims out of Amritsar; large-scale killing of Muslims and burning of their villages was in progress in the rural areas of the Amritsar district; and the migration of refugees both ways had started.

This was the situation when the two new Dominion Governments assumed responsibility. And, directly responsible to the Supreme Commander representing the Joint Defence Council, the neutral P.B.F. was there to act in aid of Civil Power in the twelve districts. But there was but little effective Civil Government machinery to work with, other than the two new Governors and their new Ministers and a certain number of willing senior officials. These, with the best will in the world, without the necessary subordinates and functioning machinery of Government, could not produce the essential basic elements of the administration and law and order which are naturally pre-requisite to a military force detailed to act in aid of Civil Power. And, in scattered villages and hamlets spread over the 37,500 square miles of the twelve districts of the Central Punjab, the warring factions of fourteen and a half million tough Punjabis, Muslim and non-Muslim, were inextricably mixed, often occupying parts of the same village, and in the cities and towns they were even more inextricably mixed. Communal bitterness was at a peak, and the masses were egged on and inflamed by resolute men and shock-groups of well-armed men determined to fight.

In face of all this, the situation was beyond the control of the national or provincial political leaders; nevertheless, their efforts had some ameliorative effect. On the morrow of Independence Day Lord Mountbatten summoned a meeting of the Joint (i.e. Indo-Pakistan) Defence Council, of which he had been invited by both Dominion Governments to be chairman. Field Marshal Auchinleck gave a grim and graphic account of what was happening in the Punjab. It was decided to reinforce the Punjab Boundary Force. Lord Mountbatten persuaded the two Prime Ministers, Pandit Nehru and Mr. Liaqat Ali Khan, to meet at Ambala, in East Punjab, the following day, together with their Defence Ministers, the provincial Governors and Ministers, the Deputy Supreme Commander and General Rees. The disbandment of the P.B.F. was mooted by Ministers, in the light of the changed situation and the fact that it was now acting not as a military reserve but virtually as an arm of government for which the respective provinces and Dominions were responsible; but it was recognised not only that to try to split the Force communally and territorially in the midst of operations was dangerous but also that it was the only firm rock of organised authority shielding the Punjab from anarchy. It was also in effect the only day-to-day bridge of communication between the Governments on either side of the new border.

Steps were decided upon at Ambala to improve liaison between the two civil Governments and between them and the military. But the Ambala meetings did more than reach administrative decisions; above all they enabled a confrontation between the national leaders and the leaders of the Sikh community, at this time clearly the worst aggressors. Pandit Nehru himself told Lord Mountbatten later that Master Tara Singh had candidly admitted that the Sikh leaders had been inciting their followers to violence and had approved of most of what they had done, but that things had gone too far and the Sikh population was itself now in danger. Master Tara Singh and the other Sikh leaders were therefore prepared to use their influence to stop the fighting. After the Ambala meeting Tara Singh toured the East Punjab in military transport, appealing to the Sikhs to refrain from violence, but to little effect. The two Prime Ministers went on together to Lahore and Amritsar, where they issued a joint appeal for peace. Pandit Nehru, accompanied by Sardar Baldev Singh, again visited the Punjab over the weekend of 23rd–25th August, and further joint tours by the two Prime Ministers and other Indian and Pakistani Ministers on both sides of the border were arranged at the end of the month. These visits did some good, but they could neither restore the confidence of the regional minorities nor reach the scattered and uprooted people of the rural districts.

Meanwhile the future of the Punjab Boundary Force had been thrown into the melting pot. At a meeting of the Joint Defence Council on 21st August Lord Mountbatten managed to stave off a demand for the interposition of officers in the Command who would be directly responsible to their Governments, a disruptive plan which threatened to cause Field Marshal Auchinleck to resign. At another meeting on 25th August, a proposal by Lord Mountbatten to include in the communiqué a tribute to the soldiers of the Force raised a furore. There had already been some criticism of their alleged partiality, but Field Marshal Auchinleck and General Rees had defended them with much spirit. Mr. Chundrigar, a Minister of Pakistan, declared that he had never paid any tribute to the soldiers and did not intend to pay any; he would prefer to publish a warning to them that any indiscipline or failure to do their duty would be severely punished. Lord Mountbatten pointed out, with some heat, that the soldiers were all Indians or Pakistanis, apart from a few British officers, and that they were doing their utmost, under enormous strain, to stop other Indians and Pakistanis from behaving like beasts. But Mr. Chundrigar—whose attitude was paralleled by that of many senior Indian politicians—remained unshaken.

A grave conflict between the politicians and the military commanders over the Boundary Force was avoided only because at this stage Field Marshal Auchinleck himself, supported by the Commanders-in-Chief of the Indian and Pakistan armies, reached the conclusion that the Force had outlived the purpose for which it was created. A Joint Defence Council meeting at Lahore on 29th August approved a recommendation that the Force be disbanded, to be replaced by area headquarters in each of the two Punjab provinces, answerable directly to the Army Commanders-in-Chief of India and Pakistan respectively. Lord Mountbatten wrote afterwards, in a report to H.M. the King:

> I had been much opposed to this step at first, and indeed remained opposed to it from the strictly military viewpoint, because of the risk of lack of liaison and the consequent danger of actual clashes between entirely separately controlled armies operating on a recently imposed boundary under conditions approximating to civil war. But it had gradually become apparent that the political leaders of both Dominions felt that their hands were tied until this step was taken; moreover, as the communal virus had started to infect the troops themselves, and as increasingly serious reports were spread exaggerating this infection, some such measure became inevitable.[1]

The Punjab Boundary Force ceased to exist as a joint command at midnight on 31st August, and with it the last operational responsibility of Field Marshal Auchinleck and Lord Mountbatten himself. The Field Marshal's chief continuing duties were the care and repatriation of British military personnel and the completion of partition of military forces and material. Lord Mountbatten remained, however, by request, chairman of the Joint Defence Council, and later became chairman of the Defence Committee of the Indian Government.

Despite the cloud under which it fell, the Punjab Boundary Force of 55,000 Indians with a few British among their officers fully deserved the tribute that was paid to it by its Commander, General Rees:[2]

> During the first furious impact of the struggle, the P.B.F. stood firm, rock-like, in a welter of confusion and anarchy. Indeed, during the second half of August, 1947, the Civil Administration for the time being having broken down, the only effective organisation in the Punjab was the Army; and to carry on, it had to muster every officer and man that it could; even cooks and mess orderlies etc. were sent on escort duty, and the strain on Commanders and staff was very heavy. A prodigious amount of work fell on all ranks, who accepted it with commendable

[1] *Governor-General's Personal Report* No. 1, 2nd September 1947.
[2] *Report on the Punjab Boundary Force.*

cheerfulness and willingness. The troops were out day and night, often with very little rest in the notoriously trying Punjab hot weather of 1947; and at various Headquarters several staff overworked to such an extent that the doctors had to enforce rest to avoid complete breakdown in the case of some British officers. Extra officers and experienced officers would have been welcome; but with demobilisation in progress, they were hard to find.

There was ample evidence of the courage, steadfastness, and impartiality of the troops. Only one case will be mentioned, that of a Sikh Major, the O.C. of a train escort on a Muslim refugee train. He himself suffered nine wounds (three gunshot wounds and six spear wounds) in repelling attacks on the train by people of his own religion. The casualties of the Army numbered forty-four killed and wounded in August, and about the same number during the first half of September.

It was the P.B.F. alone that prevented the slaughter from getting completely out of hand; that enabled the new Governments of the newly created Provinces gradually to get into the saddle, however precariously; and that saved the refugees of both communities from extermination, and started to cope with the problems of their movement and administration. These three big achievements stand to the credit of the Force, also one less likely to be appreciated by the public—between the Government, of the two new Provinces, the P.B.F. was the only satisfactory go-between, and as the day-to-day administration of both Provinces was, to start with, still closely interlocked it would, undoubtedly have broken down without this service of liaison. And, when tempers have cooled, and men are able to get affairs into their right perspective, it is reasonably certain that credit for these very real achievements will be given to the Punjab Boundary Force, who, held together by their officers, carried out the task with relatively few exceptions, in a manner worthy of the great tradition of the old Indian Army in conditions of communal trial and strain well nigh unprecedented in the world's history.

By the beginning of September, the problem of refugees overbore every other in the Punjab and neighbouring areas. On 10th September the Emergency Committee of the Government of India decided that priority should be given to the transfer of refugees rather than the maintenance of law and order. Lord Mountbatten recorded that he agreed with this decision, because the solution of the first problem was alone likely to lead to a solution of the second. At that time it was estimated that the number of refugees in both directions could not have been less than a million and might have been two or three times that number. Travelling by train and by road, they were constantly exposed to attack by the opposite community. An air lift by military and officially hired civil aeroplanes carried thousands, but the upheaval was far beyond the capacity of such means. A vast column of Muslims was about to pass through Amritsar when Indian Army officers tried to get Master Tara Singh to guarantee its safety. As the city was full of Sikh refugees from the West in an ugly mood, he could give no such assurance. The column was diverted along canal roads, but these started to break up. A bypass was bulldozed round Amritsar but was put out of action by heavy rains. The passage through the city brought heavy casualties and bitter recrimination.

Lord and Lady Mountbatten flew over the Punjab on 21st September accompanied by Pandit Nehru and three senior Ministers and the Commander-in-Chief. Lord Mountbatten wrote afterwards to H.M. the King:

. . . The contrast between the organisation of the columns in each direction was striking. Coming from the West, a non-Muslim column, which seemed to consist entirely of Sikhs, was about to cross the Ravi; it was drawn up in good marching order along some fifty miles of road. The Sikhs had their bullock carts and flocks with them. . . . It was obviously going to be a very difficult problem to decide what to do with these vast hordes of refugees when they arrived, and laid claim to the land from which the Muslims had been expelled—a claim which was bound to conflict with that of their brethren who had already occupied it. . . .

In contrast, the Muslim columns coming from the East appeared poor and ill-organised. They looked as if they had been driven out or fled in panic, as indeed they had. Bullock carts were fewer and spread out, and not closed up as with the Sikhs. But in a way their resettlement problem on arrival was going to be easier, for although more numerous, they would have the richer holdings abandoned by the non-Muslims to take over.[1]

Gruesome attacks were made on refugee trains, by Sikhs and others. Between 20th and 23rd September, 2,700 Muslims and 600 non-Muslims were killed or wounded on trains. As a result all train movement was stopped for a while, though Master Tara Singh, prompted by a British officer, Major J. McG. Short, who had been brought out specially because of his influence with the Sikhs, issued a statement calling off the attacks. When fresh arrangements for the defence of trains had been made and the conditions were thought to be safer, floods following the heavy rains breached the lines, and it was not until the second week of October that the railway movement could be resumed. Lord Mountbatten recorded:

> The attacks on trains carrying Muslim refugees from Delhi to Lahore had mostly been made by Sikh jathas operating from the States inside East Punjab. Sardar Patel, as Minister for States, therefore got together the Rulers concerned and induced them personally to accept responsibility for the safety of movement through their own territories. He also visited Amritsar and, by meetings with the Sikh leaders and public addresses to the population, succeeded in persuading them that it was in their own interests to let the Muslim refugees through, unharmed, both by rail and road, so that the non-Muslims would be allowed, reciprocally, out of West Punjab in safety. It may here be mentioned that in the non-Sikh States bordering the Punjab, notably Bikaner, great quantities of refugees had passed through, not only in safety but with the active assistance of the Maharajah and his Government.[2]

Meanwhile a fresh focus of grave danger had appeared in Delhi itself. At the end of August Lord Mountbatten retired to Simla for a rest, and to emphasise that he now had no real responsibility and that Ministers now had to 'carry the can'. On 4th September Mr. V. P. Menon telephoned him from Delhi with the urgent message (which he said was from Sardar Patel but which in fact originated with himself) that the situation in and near the capital

---

[1] *Report of the Governor-General.*
[2] loc. cit.

had so far deteriorated in the direction of communal war that only the Governor-General's presence could save it. Lord Mountbatten returned to Delhi the next day. According to his own report to H.M. the King, after a Cabinet meeting on 6th September Nehru told him that it had been unanimously decided that an Emergency Committee of the Cabinet should be set up and invited him to take the chair. But this was less than the bare bones of the story. Mr. Alan Campbell-Johnson, writing in his diary on the same day, recorded:

> We found V. P. Menon awaiting Mountbatten with a message from Patel hoping that he will grip the situation without delay. Nehru came round immediately to enlist his active and overriding authority to deal with the emergency. . . . After Mountbatten had had two or three hours to acquaint himself fully of [sic] the scale of the crisis, he proposed that an Emergency Committee should be set up. This was at once agreed to by Nehru and Patel, and at their insistence Mountbatten accepted the chairmanship.[1]

Between the lines can be read the truth, that the Indian leaders, conscious that the situation had got beyond their inexperienced capabilities, asked the Governor-General in effect to cease from being purely constitutional and to assist in governing: 'hoping that he will *grip the situation* . . . enlist his *active and overriding authority*'. While he had been gaining experience of emergency administration at the highest level, said Pandit Nehru, his Ministers had been in prison. That barely three weeks after independence the topmost Indian politicians should have been prepared to re-entrust effective authority to a British Governor-General is an astonishing tribute to the confidence they reposed in him: it is also a tribute to their own courage and realism, which thus put an urgent practical objective before nationalist principle or personal pride.

Realising that Indian public opinion was unlikely to take such a tolerant view, Lord Mountbatten, having asked for a couple of hours to think the problem over, offered the device of an Emergency Committee over which he would preside but which would be responsible to the Cabinet, thus preserving the latter's supremacy. The plan was immediately accepted, the Cabinet

[1] *Mission with Mountbatten*, p. 178.

resolved to set up the Emergency Committee, and Lord Mountbatten was duly invited to preside over it. The Committee met
daily in Government House, with Pandit Nehru on the Governor-
General's right and Sardar Patel on his left. Lord Mountbatten's
secretariat under Colonel Erskine Crum kept the minutes and
issued instant instructions in writing on the Committee's authority.
All inter-departmental procedure was thus short-circuited. The
Committee's instructions were never questioned.

The story can be continued in Lord Mountbatten's words, in a
report to H.M. the King dated only five days later:

> My first meeting of the Emergency Committee was held four
> hours after I had been invited to join it, at 5 p.m. on Saturday,
> 6th September. Within 27 hours of then, there were a total of
> three meetings lasting in all some 8 hours and issuing over 40
> directions. . . . After a daily report on the situation by the
> Commander-in-Chief of the Indian Army or his representative
> in the map room we have had set up . . . we run through a list of
> all the points on which action has been ordered at previous meet-
> ings and obtain reports from the Ministers concerned. This
> results in events moving at more than war speed. In fact I am
> sure that we did more business and set more wheels turning in
> the first three days, than would have otherwise been done in
> several weeks. . . . We have issued orders requisitioning civilian
> transport. We have made arrangements to send the tens of
> thousands of refugees in Delhi . . . to Provinces and States.
> We have arranged for trains for them, and guards for the trains.
> . . . We have made arrangements to save and harvest the deserted
> standing crops in the Punjab. . . . We have cancelled Public
> Holidays, including Sundays. We have taken measures to keep
> at least two newspapers and the All-India Radio going in
> Delhi; to bring Government servants to their work; to get the
> telephone system on its legs again . . . to protect all diplomatic
> representatives . . . to collect and bury the corpses on the streets
> and in the hospitals. We have arranged food movements. . . .
> We have arranged for large-scale cholera injections . . . and 101
> other things.[1]

All this, and much more, including military action and emergency
legislation, was done within the space of five days. Of course it was

[1] *Governor-General's Personal Report* No. 2, 11th September 1947.

not all the Governor-General's doing: many others initiated and carried out these measures. Nevertheless, Lord Mountbatten by his vigour, decision and leadership, and Pandit Nehru and Sardar Patel by their wise abnegation, may well have saved Delhi from disaster, the Government of India from collapse, and the nation from being rent apart.

Lady Mountbatten, who became chairman of a council co-ordinating the efforts of all organisations concerned with relief, set a magnificent example to all those volunteers, men and women, British and Indian, who worked for the refugees, visiting hospitals and camps at great risk to personal safety and health, and often exposed to terrifying threats from the opposite community to that whose members they were helping. When she left India in June 1948, refugees who remembered her visits and her work clubbed together to send representatives by train bringing her little gifts made by the refugees themselves in token of their gratitude. The camps were often indescribably foul, with little shelter and no sanitation. Inert and resentful, most of the refugees seemed unable to help themselves. Catastrophic epidemics were avoided only by mass inoculation, but without the help of volunteers and voluntary societies the toll of death and disease could have been appalling.

The Emergency Committee was largely preoccupied with Delhi, especially in the early days, but it also concerned itself with the situation in East Punjab. (In the United Provinces, also threatened with a mass influx of refugees bringing with them the torch of communal warfare, the situation was kept under remarkable control by a strong provincial Government headed by Pandit Pant.) An episode recalling the controversy over martial law in the Punjab before independence was thus narrated to the King by Lord Mountbatten:

The question of the introduction of martial law in East Punjab and Delhi was one which caused a slight fracas in the Committee. It was almost decided to authorise this, when it was very wisely pointed out by [General] Lockhart that a British General would have to be the Chief Martial Law Administrator. This came as a shock to Nehru, and he—quite understandably—flared up: 'I will never tolerate it. The Indian people will never tolerate it.' I expressed my complete agreement, and the matter was dropped, but ordinances were produced giving as nearly as possible the same effect as martial law.[1]

The position of British officers was indeed invidious and painful. The General Officers commanding the Indian and Pakistan armies both reported an alarming drop in morale.

> ... The main reasons appeared to be a sickening at the appalling scenes they had witnessed on duty; a sense of frustration owing to the lack of assistance or support from the civil authorities on both sides of the border; a feeling that impartiality was now impossible and indeed not welcomed by either side; a feeling that their efforts were entirely unrecognised by either Dominion Government; and complete absence of all amenities, especially mails.
>
> 2,800 out of a total of 8,000 officers in the pre-partition Indian Army had volunteered to serve on; but now these were asking to be released from their contracts, under the three months' notice clause, in rapidly increasing numbers.[2]

It was again with great difficulty that Lord Mountbatten and Lord Ismay persuaded the Indian political leaders to take public steps to restore military morale, though this they eventually did. There was also a problem about the use of remaining British troops in the emergency. Lord Mountbatten wrote to the King:

> I was sorely tempted to ask for the agreement of His Majesty's Government and of my own Government to the use of British troops at least to protect hospitals and institutions since there was a British Brigade in Delhi. The existing secret order to British troops only permitted their use in communal disturbances to save British lives. Field Marshal Auchinleck was bitterly against any extension and was within his rights. I finally agreed with him. Later, however, volunteers from two British battalions in Delhi assisted in the running of refugee camps, and their efforts were appreciated. In fact they did much to build up and maintain the remarkably good feelings for the British which persisted right throughout the trouble and afterwards.[3]

[1] *Governor-General's Personal Report* No. 2, 11th September 1947.
[2] *Report of the Governor-General.*
[3] loc. cit.

The Pakistan Government also set up an Emergency Committee similar to the Indian one, and it was at first intended that there should be occasional joint meetings of the two committees. Both Governments later agreed that these were unnecessary while the two Prime Ministers were meeting frequently. These interchanges, however, were far from always constructive and friendly. The Pakistan Government in particular protested vehemently—to their opposite numbers, to the British Government and through them to other Dominion Governments, and in these personal meetings—that the Government of India was unwilling or powerless to restore order on its side of the frontier, and at one stage there was danger of a total rupture of relations between the two countries. Joint Defence Council meetings continued to be held, however, under Lord Mountbatten's chairmanship, and practical liaison on the military side, which was closely identified with the civil in the Punjab, was maintained through the British Army commanders and their staffs. Early in October two Ministers of the Indian Government, concerned with Relief and Rehabilitation and with liaison with the Punjab authorities, met the Prime Minister of Pakistan in Lahore, with the principal object of setting up a permanent joint Ministerial Committee to deal with refugee problems. They reported, however, that every proposal for joint organisation was opposed by the Governor of West Punjab, Sir Francis Mudie. Sir Francis's view was that consultation between himself and his opposite number in East Punjab would be futile: each of them, he argued, was responsible for the refugees in his own province, and neither could help the other. A joint Movement Control office in Lahore took care of day-to-day problems.

Lord Mountbatten found himself in an ambivalent position, which was to repeat itself still more damagingly over Kashmir. As constitutional Head of State (under the Crown) he was unable officially to represent or commit his responsible Governments or to give executive orders. But as Chairman of the Emergency Committee of the Indian Cabinet he was deeply involved in the formation and execution of policy. While his Ministers could deal with their opposite numbers in Pakistan, in dealing with Mr. Jinnah, his own opposite number, he had to revert to his constitutional position, even though Jinnah was in truth the effective head of the Pakistan Government.

Gradually the situation improved. The reopening of the rail link began to clear the Delhi camps of refugees, some of whom returned to their homes in the city. The movement on foot of refugees across the mid-Punjab frontier almost dried up in mid-November. At the end of November the Indian Emergency Committee ceased to meet. During December there were scarcely any incidents of communal violence either in India or in Pakistan, though communal tension remained acute. An event occurred in January 1948 which could have set the smouldering fires ablaze again. A party of 184 Sikhs, who were being evacuated from Upper Sind, were attacked by a vast Muslim mob while spending a night in the sanctuary of a *gurdwara* in Karachi, sixty-four of them being killed and most of the rest wounded. The mob then took to looting, particularly of non-Muslim shops in the city. When Mr. Jinnah heard what was happening, he insisted that the troops who were brought in to control the situation were to be ordered to shoot to kill, and 'not to take any prisoners' among the rioters. This instruction was not obeyed to the letter, but order was restored fairly quickly, and there were no direct repercussions. The era of large-scale massacres and mass migrations was virtually at an end. The task of resettlement and rehabilitation had only just begun.

It is impossible to be sure, even within a wide margin, how many people were killed in the communal war of August to November 1947. In the earlier stages there was no effective civil authority to report the widespread deaths; with the vast refugee movement, local records were destroyed or rendered useless. The figure of a million was popularly bandied about. The truth was probably around 200,000 men, women and children, a terrible enough total, even seen against India's 400 millions. (The Bengal famine of 1943 was believed to have killed about 1,500,000 people.) Some five million people—mostly from the Punjab and other parts of West Pakistan and from the neighbouring regions of north-west India, for migration in Bengal and Assam was on a small scale until much later—left their homes and crossed the border. The fear, the heartbreak and the destitution which this spontaneous and unforeseen upheaval spelt represented more human misery than even the fearsome toll of sudden death.

23

The last days of Mahatma Gandhi

From the Independence Day celebrations in Delhi one great Indian figure was conspicuously absent. Mahatma Gandhi had seen the occasion as one for prayer rather than rejoicing, and his presence as embarrassing; for the most honoured of Indians held no office or status, being, as he often insisted, not even 'a four-anna member of the Congress'. Accordingly he had taken himself to Bengal, where Mr. Suhrawardy, the provincial Prime Minister, shared his humble lodging among the Untouchables of Calcutta, and with him to show an example of communal fraternity to the people enraged by partition and by the tales of violence and suffering that they heard from other parts of India and Pakistan. It was in fact Mr. Suhrawardy who, in conversations with the Viceroy, when he had declared that no display of force could by itself hold the situation in a city like Calcutta, had offered to go along with Mahatma Gandhi in such a human demonstration, a proposal which went forward with Lord Mountbatten's blessing; and although there may have been a strain of self-preservation in his motive, for his own life was threatened by Hindu reaction, he earned a share in any tribute to the Mahatma's pacifying triumph. Thanks to their influence, the day of independence and division passed off peacefully in eastern India.

When towards the end of August the terrible happenings in the Punjab threatened to set Bengal alight, Mr. Gandhi entered upon a fast unto death , 'to end only if and when sanity returns to Calcutta'.

The entire police force of north Calcutta undertook a 24 hour fast in sympathy, while continuing on duty. Within four days there was complete peace. After one of Gandhiji's prayer meetings on the Calcutta maidan, thousands of Hindus and Muslims mingled and embraced one another. No word of Government could have given so much confidence and assurance as this one

man alone had inspired in the minorities on either side. Perhaps
the best description of Gandhiji's part in maintaining communal
peace in Bengal was made by Lord· Mountbatten when, in a
broadcast, he referred to Gandhiji as 'the one-man boundary
force who kept the peace while a 50,000 strong force was
swamped by riots'.[1]

Throughout the last months of 1947, while blood flowed and fire
raged in the north-west, Bengal remained, if not immune from
communal violence, no more disorderly and dangerous than at
many an earlier time. The movement of Hindus from East Bengal
and Muslims from West Bengal, which was gradually to assume
serious economic and social proportions, originated in different
causes from the terror that led to the mass migrations in the
Punjab, and belongs to another story.

It was not Bengal but the situation in the north, above all in
Delhi itself, that inspired the Mahatma's next fast. On 12th
January 1948 he announced at his prayer meeting in Delhi that he
would fast, even at the cost of his life, to restore Hindu-Muslim
unity, and would persist until the communal situation had improved throughout India and particularly in the capital. His fast
began the next morning. Lord Mountbatten, to whom Mr. Gandhi
had confided his intentions immediately after his prayer meeting,
before seeing any of his Congress intimates, to their lasting
chagrin, wrote:

> The exact reasons for Mahatma Gandhi's fast . . . will forever
> remain a mystery. . . . It·came at a time when the massacre of
> Sikhs in Karachi, and the massacre of non-Muslim refugees
> from the North-West Frontier Province in a train at Gujerat,
> seemed likely to produce reprisals in India.
>
> But it doubtless had, at least secondarily, the object of bring-
> ing Pandit Nehru and Sardar Patel . . . together once again. The
> partnership between Pandit Nehru and Sardar Patel had for
> some weeks been most uneasy, and the time had come when the
> danger of a split appeared imminent. . . . Each had been making
> speeches, often in the same place and on the same subject,
> without the least reference to the other. Each had been saying
> things with which the other did not agree. . . . Mahatma

[1] *The Transfer of Power in India*, V. P. Menon, p. 434.

Gandhi had been my chief informant about this. . . . Further-more Sardar Patel himself was in a very curious mood about the fast when he came to see me the day after it had started. He resented the fact that Mahatma Gandhi had made a 'unilateral' decision to fast, for the first time in his life, and declared that the timing was hopelessly wrong, and that the fast would have the opposite effect to what Mahatma hoped—and had, inciden-tally, put himself in an impossible position. His suggested method to improve communal relations was that every Hindu and Sikh should be removed from West Pakistan, and every Muslim removed from East Punjab and the affected neighbour-ing areas. The complete removal of the possibility of communal incidents in these areas would be the guarantee of the safety of the remaining Muslims in the rest of India.

During the fast itself, Sardar Patel was absent from Delhi, visiting first Kathiawar and later Bombay, most of the time. But it was most noticeable that his public utterances, during this period and indeed thereafter, were completely toned down, and in support of the fast.

Pandit Nehru also came to see me the morning after the fast started, and, of course, took a very different line. He could not conceal his pleasure and his admiration at Mahatma Gandhi's action, which he described as just what was needed to bring people to their senses. He revealed that he had seen Mahatma Gandhi only one hour before the announcement the previous evening and had been given no indication of his intention. He said: 'I have known Gandhi for 32 years and I can still never guarantee that I can fathom his mind.'[1]

By 16th January, the Mahatma was beginning to grow weaker. But his fast had awakened the leaders to their duty to allay com-munal fears and hatred by their utterances, their undertakings and their actions. Following a suggestion by Lord Mountbatten, the Indian Cabinet had set up a Rehabilitation Committee, which decided on various measures to improve the miserable lot of the refugees, one of the worst sources of communal infection. On 17th January Gandhi laid down seven conditions whose fulfilment could induce him to end his fast. They all concerned restoration

[1] *Report of the Governor-General.*

of the rights and safety of Muslims, primarily in Delhi. Dr. Rajendra Prasad, President of the Congress, formed an all-party Peace Committee, which pledged itself to carry out the Mahatma's conditions. On the strength of this promise, Gandhi broke his fast on 18th January.

Lord Mountbatten wrote for His Majesty the King this account of the events that followed:

> . . . The same evening he sent a message to his prayer meeting saying that, if the pledge was fulfilled, it would revive with re-doubled force 'his intense wish and prayer before God to be enabled to live the full span of life, doing service to humanity till the last moment'. 'That span,' he naively added, 'according to learned opinion is at least 125 years, some say 133.'
>
> Mahatma Gandhi's life was nearly ended two days later. Towards the end of his prayer meeting on 20th January, a bomb was thrown at him by a young Hindu extremist. My wife went round to visit him immediately on hearing of this incident. The old gentleman was quite unperturbed, saying that he thought that 'military manoeuvres' must have been taking place somewhere in the vicinity.
>
> Mahatma Gandhi was assassinated shortly after 5 p.m. on 30th January, 1948. He was shot at three times at point blank range by a man called Godse . . . Mahatma Gandhi was walk-ing to his prayer meeting when the tragedy occurred. Just as he was climbing the steps leading to the platform from where he addressed his prayer meeting, and was returning the greetings of the crowd with folded hands, Godse suddenly stepped out in front of him and fired his revolver.
>
> I had just returned from Madras and on hearing the news immediately went round to his room at Birla House, where the body had been taken. Most of my Ministers were already there, and we met together. . . .[1]

Lord Mountbatten had not been recognised in the dark until he reached the lighted door. Then a loud-voiced Hindu shouted at him: 'It was a Muslim who did it.' The Governor-General shouted back for the crowd to hear: 'You fool! Don't you know it was a Hindu?' This quietened the rising excitement. Mr. Alan Campbell-Johnson, who was with Lord Mountbatten, whispered

[1] *Report of the Governor-General.*

to him: 'How could you possibly know it was a Hindu?' 'If it wasn't,' replied Lord Mountbatten, 'we are lost anyhow, for a terrible civil war will break out.[1]

His report continued:

I took this opportunity, at Birla House, of telling Pandit Nehru and Sardar Patel that Mahatma Gandhi had taken me into his confidence on their innermost secrets, including Sardar Patel's resignation, and that I now regarded myself as having inherited the moral obligation of seeing his policy through. I trusted that his death would bring them closer together and invited them as a first step to join together in a broadcast that evening, so as not only to steady the public after the shock of the news of the Mahatma's death, but to prove from that very moment onwards that they intended to carry on his policy shoulder to shoulder.[2]

In so many words, Lord Mountbatten asked Nehru to 'kiss and make it up'. Taking him literally, they embraced with tears streaming down their cheeks. They agreed that he should instruct the Minister of Defence and the three Chiefs of Staff to organise the funeral, giving them his ideas as to how this should be done.

State mourning was declared for thirteen days. Telegrams of condolence poured in from all over the world. Statements were made by leading personalities of many nationalities. Nearly all from India bore tribute to his non-communal outlook and his equal love for the Muslims. The only one of those which in any way struck a jarring note was Mr. Jinnah's—who referred to Mahatma Gandhi as 'one of the greatest men produced by the Hindu community and a leader who commanded their universal confidence and respect'.

The following day I witnessed the departure of the funeral cortege from Birla House in the morning, and the cremation itself in the evening, in the presence of a crowd estimated at a million. . . .[3]

[1] 'The first impact of the event was terrible', wrote Mr. K. M. Munshi, who arrived just as the doctor pronounced the Mahatma dead. 'We had been told that the assailant was a Muslim. This opened up a ghastly prospect; the next day rivers of blood would flow both in India and Pakistan'. *The End of an Era*, p. 107.
[2] loc. cit.
[3] loc. cit.

So vast were the crowds at Rajghat that Lord Mountbatten feared that when the funeral pyre was lit thousands would surge towards it, forcing the eminent guests in front into the flames. He went round personally insisting that not only they but also some twenty rows of people behind them should sit on the ground. When the rush indeed started the crowd fell over the hindermost rows of the seated figures, and a perilous situaiton was saved.

During the days which followed Mahatma Gandhi's assassination, the evidence accumulated that this was not an isolated crime, but part of a wider plot whereby the assassination of Pandit Nehru and others was also planned. The subject was considered at a meeting of Governors which took place on 2nd February. . . .

On 3rd February, the Government of India passed and published two resolutions announcing that no organisations preaching violence, and no private armies would henceforth be permitted. This was at a time when demonstrations against the Hindu Mahasabha and the Rashtriya Swayam Sevak Sangh[1] were taking place all over the country, but without as yet assuming very serious proportions. The Government therefore had popular support for its actions.

On 4th February the Government declared the R.S.S.S. illegal, and large numbers of R.S.S.S. workers were arrested in many Provinces and States. This was followed by a similar declaration and similar action with regard to the Muslim League National Guards and the Khaksars, two extreme Muslim organisations. . . .

Neither the Hindu Mahasabha nor the Muslim League in India dissolved themselves. The former passed a resolution suspending its political activities, and the latter decided to draw up a new Constitution. But it was to be hoped that neither body would, in the future, be in a position once more to fan communal feelings.

On 12th February some of the ashes of Mahatma Gandhi were cast upon the waters at the point where three rivers—the Jumna, the Ganges and the mythical Saraswati—meet. Simul-

---

[1] The militant branch of the Mahasabha.

taneously others of his ashes were cast upon other sacred rivers, and upon the sea, at various places throughout India.[1]

Perhaps the Mahatma's finest hours had been in the last months of his life—in the pacification of Calcutta and Bengal at the time of crisis in August and September, and in his indefatigable campaign against communal hatred and retaliation. These, like his selfless service to the cause of the Untouchables, were the acts of one who loved his fellow men and saw in politics not an end in itself but a means to a fellowship founded on freedom, equality and brotherhood. It was as fitting as it was tragic that he should die a martyr to that humane ideal—at the hand of an assassin spurred by communal hate, while he moved undefended among a crowd of ordinary men and women to whom he was prophet, saint and father.

Sadly it has to be recorded that his example and his martyrdom, potent as they were, and appealed to as they have been ever since by the champions of peace and non-violence in India, faded in effect as time went by. Lord Mountbatten's hopes were disappointed. The 'secular state' which Pandit Nehru was determined to create and sustain, inspired by the Gandhian ideal of communal unity and understanding, has had to fight for its life in India, and even now, two decades later, is beset by enemies. Though there have been no vast holocausts—no 'great Calcutta killings' as in 1946, no Punjab massacres as in 1947—Hindu-Muslim violence has sporadically broken out, much as under British rule and in very much the same areas.

Perhaps it was fitting, too, that Mr. Gandhi should have passed from the stage soon after independence. The task of his disciples in the Congress had changed—no longer to oppose government but to govern, no longer to missionise but to administer, no longer to hold together every diverse element and class in a single national cause but to devise and impose policies which would hurt some in helping others, and could lead—some might argue, ought to lead—to division and partisanship between rival factions and opposed national parties. Mr. Gandhi himself could never have been a party man in this factional sense. A decade before his death, in a conversation with the present author in his *ashram* at Segaon, questioned about the monopolistic position of the Congress, he had replied that it was necessary to achieve independence but that

[1] loc. cit.

after independence there might well be various parties with conflicting policies. When the time came he saw things in a rather different way. He thought that the Congress should remain the embodiment of the national spirit and the champion of all non-violent causes on behalf of the masses, a watchdog for the poor, the exploited and the unfree, and should detach itself from the Government, which should seek its own party support for party causes. Oddly, he had cast Sardar Patel in the role of leader of the detached conscience of the Congress—Patel, the strong man, the tough administrator, champion of the unyielding line on Indo-Pakistani relations after partition. Perhaps the Mahatma hoped that Patel would be the first convert to the cause of universal benevolence which he was thus assigned to lead. Within a few months, Mr. Gandhi had been assassinated, and a year later Sardar Patel had died of heart disease. For sixteen years, until his own death, Pandit Nehru remained Prime Minister of India backed by a Congress which sought at one and the same time to be the governing party and the representative of the whole Indian people. The consequences, good as well as bad, of this dualism have endured through more than twenty years of nationhood. Whether Mahatma Gandhi might have resolved it, or whether his survival might have made it even stronger, can only be guessed. The great non-violent revolutionary was no more.

24

The Junagadh affair

After the transfer of power, the 'basketful of apples', which Sardar Patel had asked of the Viceroy as the price of agreeing to accession by Princely States for defence, foreign affairs and communications only, lacked three big apples, one of which might not have belonged in the basket at all. A fourth, Bhopal, though still secretively wrapped, could be counted as in the basket, for its Nawab had by private agreement lodged with Lord Mountbatten an Instrument of Accession in a sealed envelope to be handed to the Ministry of States on 25th August unless the Nawab instructed otherwise. Three days before this period of grace expired, His Highness, after a long talk with Sardar Patel, came to see Lord Mountbatten and explained why he still hesitated: he had ambitions to play a big role in the Muslim world in the future, and he feared that if he acceded Mr. Jinnah would denounce him as a traitor to the Muslim cause. The Governor-General advised him to fly at once to Karachi and have it out with Mr. Jinnah face to face. The Nawab went straight to the airport, Mr. Jinnah was sufficiently magnanimous, Bhopal acceded and its Ruler decided not to resign his *ghadi* to his daughter, as he had intended to do in order to take office in Pakistan. Loyal and true man that he was, he wrote to Lord Mountbatten:

> Now that the decision has been made, I will abide by it faithfully and will, so far as lies in my power, support and uphold the Dominion of India.

Indeed he afterwards served India well. If only the Rulers of the three missing big apples had been like the Nawab of Bhopal! All three were weak, eccentric and devious.

Only three recalcitrants out of over 550—but what a vital and dangerous trio they proved to be! Hyderabad, the greatest State of all, lodged in the heart of India, with a large majority of Hindus but ruled by a Muslim Prince whose dynasty went back to the

time of Aurangzeb. Kashmir and Jammu, the fourth largest
(Mysore and Travancore had bigger populations), a Muslim-
majority State ruled by a Hindu Maharajah, bordering both on
India and on Pakistan, occupying a strategic relationship to each,
and capable of accession to either. And Junagadh, the joker in the
pack, a seaboard State close to Pakistan, yet enmeshed with
Princely India, having a Muslim Ruler but a predominantly Hindu
population, and sacred to Hindu sentiment for two reasons—as the
death-place of the Lord Krishna and as the site of the famous
temple of Somnath, whose sacking by Mahmud of Ghazni in A.D.
1024 lingered in the folk memory of Muslim and Hindu alike
nearly a thousand years later.[1]

An air of fantasy, even of farce, overhangs the story of Junagadh
in 1947. Among other idiosyncrasies, the Nawab, whose family
had ruled the State for 200 years, loved dogs to excess. He was said
to have owned 800 of them, each with its human attendant, and to
have spent 20 lakhs of rupees (£150,000) on a wedding for two of
them, for which he proclaimed a state holiday. When he decided
to quit his State for Pakistan, he fled the palace in such a hurry
that his Begum forgot to bring her baby, and had to be left behind
at the airport. More serious was the absurd complexity of the map
of the State. Fragments of other States were embedded in Junagadh, and fragments of Junagadh were embedded in other States,
while an arm of Junagadh separated one substantial outlying portion of the Mahratta State of Baroda from another and from the
sea. Furthermore, the best of lawyers could not advise with certainty whether two considerable neighbours and feudatories of
Junagadh, Mangrol and Babariawad, were entitled to accede independently to India, or in this were subject to its suzerainty. The
Sheikh of Mangrol first signed an Instrument of Accession and
then, on returning to Mangrol from Rajkot, the principal town of
the Kathiawar region, repudiated his signature; and another poli-
tico-legal wrangle arose as to which of these decisions, if either,
had been taken under duress. Most ridiculous of all, it took the
Government of India a month to discover as a fact—and for its
military and political dispositions this was a crucial fact—whether
or not Mangrol had a common frontier with the acceded State of
Porbandar. The Maharajah of Porbandar said the two States were

---

[1] After Junagadh was taken over by the Dominion of India, the temple
was restored at great expense.

contiguous: the ex-Dewan of Mangrol said they were six miles apart. The point was referred to the military in Porbandar, who declared they were not contiguous. The States Ministry insisted that on its information they were. The Indian Regional Commissioner at Rajkot would not commit himself. The Chief of Naval Staff ventured a middle opinion, that an outlying portion of Mangrol abutted on Porbandar but not the main part. Finally the seafaring Governor-General proposed that the practical point at issue, whether Mangrol, whose people had invited such a peaceful occupation, could be entered by troops from undisputed Indian territory without violating Junagadh soil, should be settled by sending them by tank landing craft.

The comedy notwithstanding, Junagadh was inherently important as a State of 700,000 people, fronting on the ocean (though its coasts were flat and marshy, and its ports were closed in the monsoon), in the midst of the great Indian region of Kathiawar, whose chief Princes were the Maharajah of Bhavnagar and the Maharajah Jam Saheb of Nawanagar. The complexities themselves implied that its handling would be full of traps, and there was good reason to suspect that some of those traps had been deliberately laid by Pakistan. At the start of the story, all the signs were that Junagadh would eventually join India and that the Nawab favoured an association of the Kathiawar States in which he would participate. Then in May 1947, during his absence in Europe, a 'palace revolution' placed in power as his Dewan a Muslim League politician from Sind, Sir Shah Nawaz Bhutto, who was soon in correspondence with Mr. Jinnah and obeyed the latter's advice to 'keep out under all circumstances until 15th August'. On the very day of the transfer of power, without notifying the Government of India, the Junagadh Government announced that it had decided to accede to Pakistan. This decision aroused the utmost dismay, not only in Delhi, but also among the Rulers and people of the rest of Kathiawar, who saw in it a grave threat to their security and their communal peace. The Jam Saheb, the Ministry of States, the Governor-General and even the Secretary of State for India (who was visiting both Delhi and Karachi), vainly bent their best efforts to persuade either the Nawab to change his mind or the Pakistan Government to decline his accession.

Why, we may ask, should Mr. Jinnah and his Government have

been so keen to get, and have gone to such length to hold, a poor, communally divided State whose geography would make her adherence as great an embarrassment for Pakistan as her defection made it for India, even without the extravagant promises of defensive and economic help that were given in Karachi to the Nawab and his emissaries? The answer must surely be sought in Mr. Jinnah's tactical shrewdness. He must have seen—or, if he did not see, it certainly turned out—that the accession of Junagadh to Pakistan placed India in an acute dilemma from which any escape could be turned to the advantage of Pakistan. If the Indian Government acquiesced, admitting the undoubted legal right of the Ruler to decide which way to go, the precedent of a Muslim Prince taking a Hindu-majority State into Pakistan, notwithstanding geographical and communal arguments to the contrary, could be applied to the far greater prize of Hyderabad. If the Indian Government intervened with force, besides the harm that it would do itself with outside opinion, it would set up a contrary precedent, to be applied by Pakistan to Kashmir, were the latter's Maharajah to accede to India. If India demanded, as the alternative to force, a plebiscite in Junagadh, this could be adopted as a general principle which when applied to Kashimr and Jammu would, in Karachi's estimation, take the State to Pakistan.

Pandit Nehru's Government began circumspectly by protesting to Pakistan and refusing to recognise the latter's acceptance of Junagadh's accession. But pressure for action quickly mounted, from the Kathiawar Rulers and from an inflamed anti-Pakistan public opinion in India. Lord Mountbatten reported to the King:

> My chief concern as Governor-General was to prevent the Government of India from committing itself on the Junagadh issue to an act of war against what was now Pakistan territory. My own position was singularly difficult. . . . For the Governor-General of a Dominion to have acquiesced in action which might lead to a war with another Dominion would have been completely unprecedented.
>
> But at the same time I was aware that, in the wider aspect, my own physical presence as Governor-General of India was the best insurance against an actual outbreak of war with Pakistan. To have compromised my position too far over the preliminary threat of war would have undermined my final position. I was

therefore anxious to make it clear to my Government that I was not necessarily opposed to their taking all necessary precautions, military and otherwise, to safeguard their own legitimate interests.

A Cabinet meeting to consider the Junagadh situation was summoned for 5 p.m. on 17th September. I was informed that the members of the Cabinet had, prior to this meeting, decided among themselves that military action was the only answer. I accordingly sent for both the Prime Minister and the Deputy Prime Minister before the meeting. They were in a militant frame of mind—Sardar Patel very much more so than Pandit Nehru: being a native of Gujerat (the part of India next to Kathiawar), he was particularly anxious that the Government of India should not show itself weak over the Jungadh issue. . . .

With all the force of persuasion possible I advised Pandit Nehru and Sardar Patel to take no decision which the world could interpret as putting India in the wrong and Pakistan in the right, and that all the resources of negotiation should first be exhausted. . . .

Both Pandit Nehru and Sardar Patel were fortunately finally convinced of the soundness of this line of reasoning. Pandit Nehru agreed emphatically and Sardar Patel also appeared convinced. Pandit Nehru subsequently had little difficulty in carrying his Cabinet with him, as it was taken by surprise with the arguments he produced. I heard afterwards that what he said to the Cabinet was almost a word-for-word repetition of my plea to him.[1]

India's policy at this stage was to continue the maximum direct and indirect pressure on the Nawab and to station troops around Junagadh without entering any Junagadh territory. It could be described as forcible demonstration without violence. The complications arose over Junagadh's feudatories, Mangrol and Babariawad, which the Nawab claimed as his territory but which the Indian Government regarded as acceded to India.

There was another meeting between Lord Mountbatten and the two Indian statesmen on 22nd September. Meanwhile, wrote the Governor-General:

[1] *Report of the Governor-General.*

I had spoken to Mr. Liaqat Ali Khan, who was in Delhi for a meeting of the Joint Defence Council, about the situation in Junagadh. He used one phrase, which in view of my belief that the issue had been planned by Pakistan as a trap, I considered of considerable significance. This was: 'All right. Go ahead and commit an act of war and see what happens.'

Lord Ismay had also spoken to Mr. Liaqat Ali Khan. He had referred to the principle, which had already been raised in telegraphic correspondence by the Government of India to the Government of Pakistan, that a referendum should be held in Junagadh, and that the issue of the State's permanent accession should be decided according to the will of the people. Mr. Liaqat Ali Khan had asked Lord Ismay why, if it was suggested that a referendum should be held in Junagadh, one should not also be held in Kashmir.

These reports of conversations with Mr. Liaqat Ali Khan were considered at the meeting on 22nd September. Lord Ismay gave his view that one of the main objects of the Pakistan Government was to use Junagadh as a bargaining counter for Kashmir.[1]

The next series of events in Delhi had far more lasting consequences than the Junagadh affair itself. The Chiefs of Staff of the three Services, all of whom were British officers, put up a paper to the Cabinet expressing their concern 'at the possible results of the military measures being planned to protect the State of Mangrol and the jagirdars of Babariawad'. 'Military action in Kathiawar,' they wrote, 'may lead to war between the two Dominions and with the bulk of the Army involved on internal security the Army is in no position to wage war.' The three commanders then referred to the position of British officers, including themselves, serving with the Indian forces:

These officers belong to the British fighting Services and it would be impossible for any of them to take part in a war between two Dominions or to be the instrument of planning or conveying orders to others should the operations now contemplated result in such a war, or appear likely to do so.

[1] loc. cit. The tribal invasion of Kashmir followed by the State's accession to India subject to the eventual holding of a plebiscite had not yet taken place.

They ended by urging that the movement of armed forces for the projected operations be stopped and that the dispute over Junagadh be settled by negotiation.

Pandit Nehru and his Ministers protested sharply at this paper. The military, they said, were invading political ground. They were saying in effect that if a certain political decision were taken they would not carry it out: this was highly improper and disloyal. The Chiefs of Staff, while claiming that they were only doing their duty in drawing the Cabinet's attention to the facts as they saw them, admitted that their hastily-drafted paper was a mistake, and withdrew it.

In order to avert further incidents of this sort, Lord Mountbatten proposed, and it was at once accepted, that there be set up a Defence Committee of the Cabinet, after the British example, including the Prime Minister, Deputy Prime Minister, Defence Minister and other required members of the Cabinet, and with the Chiefs of Staff always in attendance. The Cabinet invited Lord Mountbatten, in view of his great military experience, to become Chairman of the Defence Committee, and to this he agreed without hesitation or reluctance. Greatly as this decision strengthened the direction of India's defence, its implications were far-reaching and harmful to Lord Mountbatten's status in regard to Pakistan and to relations between the two Dominions. For although the decisions taken were, of course, those of Ministers, and his policy was always to work for Cabinet agreement, on defence he became virtually a member of the Indian Cabinet. No longer could he say that he was only in the position of a constitutional monarch. In the vital field of defence he now presided over the formation of policy and became committed to its consequences.

By invitation of both India and Pakistan, he was also chairman of their Joint Defence Council; this evidently required that he should stay scrupulously impartial between them—so far as his constitutional position as Governor-General of India allowed—able as well to encourage or rebuke the one as the other in the framing of their defence policies, according to their joint interest. His impartiality, on the face of things, must henceforward be suspect. He could claim that the opposite held good—that as Chairman of the Joint Defence Council he could and did bring to bear upon Indian policy, through his chairmanship of the Indian Defence Committee, a moderating or impartial influence in the interests of peace and co-operation between the two Dominions. This is certainly true. It is significant that at a meeting of the Joint Defence Council on 26th November, two months later, when Lord Mountbatten took the opportunity of the Supreme Commander's departure to offer to hand over the chairmanship, this was as strongly opposed by the Pakistani as by the Indian representatives. Lord Mountbatten revealed that Mr. Winston Churchill had told him in November that, according to information he had received from Pakistan, he (Lord Mountbatten) was considered there to be biased in favour of India. Mr. Liaqat Ali Khan then declared that he would not have hesitated to inform Lord Mountbatten if at any time he had felt his conduct to be partial. Nevertheless, Mr. Churchill's informant was correct as to the views of many people in Pakistan. More and more they came to regard Lord Mountbatten as *parti pris*. When, within a month, his new position came to have momentous consequences in the Kashmir affair, their criticism began to foment into hostility.

At the first meeting of the Defence Committee of the Indian Cabinet on 30th September Pandit Nehru put in a masterly paper analysing the situation in and around Junagadh. As regards immediate action he was concerned primarily with Babariawad, now occupied by Junagadh forces though acceded to India. But he recognised the possibility that an incident here could provoke a war. 'The Government of India does not want a war with Pakistan or anyone else and would like to avoid it at almost every cost.' Pandit Nehru continued:

> Any war with Pakistan would undoubtedly end in the defeat and ruin of Pakistan provided no other nations are dragged in. At the same time it may well mean the ruin of India also for a considerable time. A war with Pakistan at this juncture would necessarily lead to very grave consequences. . . . Our international position, such as it is, would disappear.
>
> It is exceedingly likely that Pakistan also does not want war, and has taken the steps it has chiefly to irritate us and to make us take some false step so that they can appeal to U.N.O. . . .

If this appeal were made, and the United Nations issued directions or suggestions, India would 'naturally abide by those directions'. Pandit Nehru concluded:

It is desirable that the Pakistan Government as well as the public generally should be informed:

1 that we do not accept in the peculiar circumstances the accession of Junagadh to Pakistan.

2 that we entirely disagree with the claims and contentions of Pakistan in regard to Mangrol and Babariawad.

3 that the Pakistan Government must withdraw Junagadh forces from Babariawad.

4 that in response to requests made we are sending our troops to Kathiawar—both to Porbandar and other places.

5 that we are entirely opposed to war and wish to avoid it. We want an amicable settlement of this issue and we propose therefore, that wherever there is a dispute in regard to any territory, the matter should be decided by a referendum or plebiscite of the people concerned. We shall accept the result of this referendum whatever it may be as it is our desire that a decision should be made in accordance with the wishes of the people concerned. We invite the Pakistan Government, therefore, to submit the Junagadh issue to a referendum of the people of Junagadh under impartial auspices.

Thus Pandit Nehru committed himself to the general policy in the last subparagraph before the dispute over Kashmir blew up but in the knowledge that Junagadh might well be a trap designed to exploit the case of Kashmir. He repeated his commitment in a talk with Mr. Liaqat Ali Khan which Lord Mountbatten engineered, with some difficulty, after the two had lunched with him on the same day. (The Pakistan Prime Minister was in Delhi for a meeting of the Joint Defence Council.) They argued for a while about Mangrol and Babariawad, and the nature of the preventive military action which India was taking, and which Mr. Liaqat Ali Kahn thought 'savoured of pressure and the intent to commit a hostile act'. Pandit Nehru replied: 'We are determined that no hostile act should be committed by any Indian troops, but we also consider that the whole question of Junagadh must be reviewed.'

Lord Mountbatten's account of this conversation, which he had joined soon after it turned to Junagadh, in his report to the King, continues:

Mr. Liaqat Ali Khan then stated that the Government of Pakistan had spent more than a fortnight considering whether or not to accept Junagadh's offer of accession, since they realised the various difficulties which this would cause. However, in view of the fact that the Government of Junagadh was a Muslim Government and that the ports of Veraval and Karachi were within easy reach of one another, the Government of Pakistan had come to the conclusion that they should not turn down the Nawab's offer. I admitted to the Prime Minister of Pakistan the legality of his Government's acceptance of Junagadh's Instrument of Accession in the light of the Cabinet Mission's Statement of 12th May 1946; but I repeated my opinion that, however much they might be in the right legally, their action was indefensible morally and ethically, and that even from a practical point of view Veraval was closed as a port during the monsoon months.

Pandit Nehru then declared that he considered that, in difficult cases like this, the will of the people should be ascertained. He said that India would always be willing to abide by a decision obtained by a general election, a plebiscite or a referendum, provided that it was conducted in a fair and impartial manner.

I emphasised the importance of Pandit Nehru's statement to Mr. Liaqat Ali Khan, and assured him that the Government of India would abide by it, and that Pandit Nehru would agree that this policy would apply to any other State, since India would never be a party to trying to force a State to join their Dominion against the wishes of the majority of the people. Pandit Nehru nodded his head sadly. Mr. Liaqat Ali Khan's eyes sparkled. There is no doubt that both of them were thinking of Kashmir.[1]

The public statement proposed by Pandit Nehru in his Defence Committee paper was issued as a Press communiqué on 6th October. Its last paragraph read:

The Government of India wish to reaffirm that all they seek is an amicable settlement of the Junagadh issue and of the connected issues of Barbariawad and Mangrol. Any decision involving the fate of large numbers of people must necessarily depend on the wishes of these people. This is the policy which the Government of India accept in its entirety and they are of

[1] *Report of the Governor-General.*

an opinion that a dispute involving the fate of any territory should be decided by a referendum or plebiscite of the people concerned. This is a method at once democratic, peaceful and just. They suggest, therefore, that the issues regarding Junagadh should be decided by a referendum or plebiscite of the people of the State. . . .

The whole Junagadh affair, however, churned on without any move on Pakistan's part. The Government of India's patience was becoming frayed. At a Defence Committee on 21st October

Sardar Patel stated that he considered that the prolongation of delay in taking any action in Babariawad and Mangrol was placing the Government of India in serious difficulties. He reported that certain States, which had acceded to India, were now saying that, unless they were protected, they would send back their Instruments of Accession. In his opinion, the Government was giving a general impression of weakness with the States over the whole of India, and was getting into a position which would have an unfortunate effect on Hyderabad in the current negotiations with that State.[1]

After accounts had been given of oppression and terrorism in Babariawad and Mangrol, Lord Mountbatten reported to the King:

. . . eventually I came to the conclusion that I could not, short of threatening to resign myself, stay the hands of my Ministers any longer, and would have to accept with a good grace their unanimous decision that Indian troops should be sent to occupy Babariawad and Mangrol, particularly and firstly the former. . . .

I emphasised the necessity for avoiding individual acts of retaliation during the forthcoming operations. I urged that special orders should be issued to prevent any communal incidents, and that full protection should be given to minorities. I asked that every effort should be made to impress upon the troops taking part that the success of the operations depended largely upon not opening fire and upon the compactness and dignity with which they were implemented.[2]

The operation duly took place, without bloodshed, on 1st Novem-

[1] loc. cit.
[2] loc.cit.

T.G.D.—P

ber, and the administration of Babariawad and Mangrol was peacefully taken over by the Government of India.

While Pakistan stonewalled, and India fretted and toyed with force, there had been important developments both inside and outside the State. A Provisional Government of Junagadh had been proclaimed in Bombay on 25th September under the presidency of Samaldas Gandhi, a relation of the Mahatma, and had set up its headquarters in Rajkot. Though it was never recognised by the Indian Government and never assumed power in the State, it became the focus of popular agitation within Junagadh and around its borders. The Nawab saw the writing on the wall and fled to Karachi, together with his family, many of his dogs, and all the cash and negotiable assets of the State Treasury. The Dewan, Sir Shah Nawaz Bhutto, wrote miserably a few days later on 27th October, to Mr. Jinnah, telling of the drying-up of revenue from railways and customs, the shortage of food, and the fading of Muslim ardour for accession. 'Today our brethren are indifferent and cold. Muslims of Kathiawar seem to have lost all enthusiasm for Pakistan. . . . Responsible Muslims and others have come to press me to seek a solution of the impasse. . . . I should therefore suggest that you immediately arrange for a conference of the representatives of the two Dominions to decide the Junagadh issue.' There was no such response. On 5th November the Junagadh State Council decided that it was 'necessary to have a complete reorientation of the State policy and a readjustment of relations with the two Dominions even if it involves a reversal of the earlier decision to accede to Pakistan'. The Dewan was authorised to negotiate with the proper authorities.

The next chapter of the story can best be told in Lord Mountbatten's own words.

I was due to leave on 9th November for the United Kingdom to attend the wedding of Her Royal Highness Princess Elizabeth to my nephew, Lieutenant Philip Mountbatten, and in my 'handover' notes which I prepared for Mr. Rajagopalachari, who was to be acting Governor-General in my absence, I contented myself by saying that Indian forces were now being withdrawn from Kathiawar. . . .

However, on 8th November, the Dewan of Junagadh, Sir Shah Nawaz Bhutto, sent Major Harvey Jones, the Senior

Member of the Junagadh State Council, with a letter to Mr. Buch, the Indian Regional Commissioner at Rajkot. This letter requested the Government of India to take over the administration of Junagadh 'in order to save the State from complete administrative breakdown and pending an honourable settlement of the several issues involved in Junagadh's accession'. The Dewan of Junagadh . . . had telegraphed to Mr. Liaqat Ali Khan telling him that he was making this request which, he said, was supported by the public of Junagadh. . . . He had received telegraphic instructions from the Nawab, who had a short time previously flown to Karachi, to avoid bloodshed at any cost.

The Dewan of Junagadh's request was considered by Pandit Nehru, Sardar Patel and other Ministers, and they decided to comply with it. Either through a misunderstanding or purposely in order not to embarrass me (I am not sure which), I was not informed of what had happened until late in the evening of 8th November. In the meanwhile the Ministry of States had telegraphed instructions to the Regional Commissioner at Rajkot instructing him, in view of 'the complete breakdown of administration resulting in chaotic conditions in the State', to take over the administration of Junagadh forthwith and to ensure peace and order at the earliest possible moment.

Pandit Nehru and Lord Ismay were at dinner with me on 8th November, the night before my departure, when the news came through, and we immediately called in Mr. V. P. Menon and held a discussion. During this, Lord Ismay and I registered strong disapproval of India's behaviour. Pandit Nehru undertook to despatch a conciliatory telegram to Mr. Liaqat Ali Khan at once and to release it to the Press. Mr. V. P. Menon took the draft of this telegram round to Sardar Patel who, as Lord Ismay subsequently reported, 'thought we were cissies to want to send any telegram at all, but agreed to the draft subject to the omission of anything that could possibly be interpreted as friendly'.[1]

Sardar Patel had been particularly opposed to offering a referendum, but was persuaded to agree to it. In the early morning of 9th November Indian troops entered Junagadh State, occupied the capital and disarmed the State forces and police, without

[1] *Report of the Governor-General.*

resistance. The administration was taken over by the Indian Regional Commissioner.

Two days later Mr. Liaqat Ali Khan replied to Pandit Nehru's telegram. He contended that, since Junagadh had lawfully acceded to Pakistan, neither the Dewan nor even the Ruler himself could negotiate a settlement with India. India's actions were a clear violation of Pakistan territory, a breach of international law, and a direct act of hostility. He demanded that the Government of India should withdraw its forces, hand back the administration to the Nawab, and stop Indian citizens from committing acts of violence and subversion against Junagadh. Only if these conditions were fulfilled could Pakistan enter into any inter-Dominion conference. Further exchanges of telegrams left the Pakistan Government's position unchanged.

In February 1948 a referendum was held in Junagadh and the neighbouring disputed States, and resulted in an overwhelming vote for accession to India. Though pains had been taken to conduct the referendum impartially, Sir Zafrullah Khan, who was then representing Pakistan at the United Nations Security Council, denounced it as a farce. Later Junagadh was incorporated in a Union of Kathiawar States, eventually called Saurashtra. But Pakistan has never recognised the legality of its accession to India and continues to claim it as Pakistan territory.

25

Conflict in Kashmir

The fanatical concern for Kashmir which developed in India after the State's accession, and especially after this event had brought India and Pakistan into open conflict, are in sharp contrast to the comparative detachment with which the State's future was viewed in Delhi before the end of October 1947.

Before the transfer of power, the Viceroy, as Crown Representative, repeatedly urged the Maharajah to make a decision to accede to one Dominion or other, if possible before 15th August 1947; to consult the will of his people as to which Dominion it should be —though this consultation was not made a condition, nor was its method specified; and to form a more progressive and representative Government.[1] This advice was given by Lord Mountbatten personally when he visited the Maharajah in June, and was repeated on his instructions by the British Resident in Kashmir, and by Lord Ismay on his holiday in Srinagar in August. The Maharajah, however, went on procrastinating, first trying not to be obliged to hear the advice and then failing to heed it. The only positive action he took was to sign a standstill agreement with Pakistan. The States Ministry of the Government of India meanwhile was strictly passive. Kashmir was deliberately omitted from a committee of States' representatives called by the pre-independence States Department to discuss terms of accession, though Hyderabad was included.

It is widely believed in Pakistan that there was a long-matured plot in India, aided and abetted by Lord Mountbatten, to tie Kashmir to India and prevent the State's accession to Pakistan. Available documents supply no material whatever to support this myth, and indeed all the evidence indicates the contrary. There is a full and circumstantial record of an interview which Pandit Nehru had with Lord Mountbatten on 24th June 1947, shortly after the latter had returned from his visit to Kashmir. The Viceroy

[1] See above, p. 383.

recounted that the advice he had given to the Maharajah and his Prime Minister covered five points:[1]

1 That Kashmir should not decide about joining any Constituent Assembly until the Pakistan Assembly had been set up and the situation was clearer;

2 That meanwhile they should make no statement about independence or their intentions;

3 That they should enter into 'standstill' and other agreements with both India and Pakistan;

4 That eventually they should send representatives to one Constituent Assembly and join one of the two States, at least for the three central subjects;

5 That so far as possible they should consult the will of the people and do what the majority thought best for the State.

The Viceroy had the impression that both the Maharajah and Pandit Kak had separately agreed that this was sound advice; but both had stated that on account of the balance of population and Kashmir's geographical position any premature decision might have a serious effect on their internal stability. Lord Mountbatten's note of the conversation, dictated immediately afterwards, continues: 'Pandit Nehru agreed that my advice was sound and unexceptionable.'

The Prime Minister then asked what luck the Viceroy had had with Sheikh Abdullah, the Kashmir Muslim Nationalist leader, who was *incommunicado* in gaol, and Lord Mountbatten explained how accidents had prevented the talk between his wife and the Begum Sheikh Abdullah which had been hoped for as a diplomatic liaison. Nehru insisted that the problem of Kashmir would not be solved until the Sheikh was released and the people's rights restored. He felt himself called upon to devote himself to this end,

[1] It should be noted that this was before the policy of States' accession for defence, external affairs and communications only had been announced, or the policy of 'no accession', no standstill agreement'. The file of Lord Mountbatten's interviews also includes a note of a conversation with Pandit Kak, Prime Minister of Kashmir, on 22nd June in which he recalled the advice that he had given to the Maharajah: this account is entirely consistent with the five points, though its emphasis, for the Maharajah's benefit, was on the need for Kashmir to join one or other of the Constituent Assemblies if its regime was to be protected from the pressure of the Congress.

he said, and he would soon have to go to Kashmir to take up the cudgels on behalf of his friend and for the freedom of the people.

Lord Mountbatten lectured his Prime Minister severely. As both the Maharajah and Pandit Kak had urged, it would greatly add to their difficulties if they were subjected to political propaganda by visiting Congress or Muslim League leaders before a decision had been reached. Pandit Nehru, moreover, really must look to his duty to the Indian people as a whole. There were 400,000,000 in India, only 4,000,000 in Kashmir, and they might very well be going to join Pakistan in any case. Pandit Nehru, influenced by Mahatma Gandhi's offer to go to Kashmir instead, reluctantly agreed that the Viceroy was right.

The Viceroy contrived to defer the Mahatma's visit until after Pandit Kak had come to Delhi for the States' representatives meeting on 25th July. Unfortunately Pandit Kak in succeeding in persuading Mr. Gandhi, only opened the door to a peremptory decision by Pandit Nehru that he must now go himself. Lord Mountbatten, with visions of the same sort of trouble as had happened when Pandit Nehru dashed off to Kashmir during the Cabinet Mission's visit,[1] called a meeting with the Mahatma, Pandit Nehru and Sardar Patel on 29th July, at which, with painful reluctance, Nehru agreed to Mr. Gandhi's going in his place. To him, Kashmir, the home of his ancestors, meant more than any other State.

From these records it is abundantly clear, first, that the advice the Maharajah received was not to hurry but to consider the will of his people in deciding which new Dominion to join; secondly, that not only the Viceroy but also Pandit Nehru and Sardar Patel openly accepted the possibility that Kashmir might accede to Pakistan; thirdly that the Viceroy went to great lengths to prevent even an appearance of undue political pressure on Kashmir from the Congress; and finally that Pandit Nehru's personal emotions were deeply engaged, though at this stage they were more concerned with the fate of Sheikh Abdullah and the rights of the people than with the accession of the State.

After independence, a representative of the Kashmir Government who sought a lead from the States Ministry on the choice between India and Pakistan was told by the Secretary (Mr. V. P. Menon) that the Government of India could give no guidance in

[1] See above, p. 156.

the matter, and that if a formal proposal for accession was received it would be considered in the light of all the relevant factors. The Kashmir Government was also rebuffed when it sought to discuss the terms of a standstill agreement with India. Mr. Menon explained that 'we wanted time to examine its implications. . . . Moreover, our hands were already full'.[1] The States Ministry's general policy was indeed, as has been recorded, no standstill agreement without accession. It might also have aimed to force the Ruler's hand; for if he had made standstill agreements with both Dominions he might have been able to delay indefinitely making up his mind on accession.

We do not know what Pandit Nehru may have said privately to the Prime Minister of Kashmir, or to Sheikh Abdullah, or other Congress leaders to their own friends in the State. But it is significant, and indeed astonishing in the light of subsequent events, and of allegations that the accession of Kashmir was a deep-laid Indian plot, that even after the organised incursion of tribesmen into Kashmir powerful men in the Indian Cabinet still hesitated to seek or accept the Maharajah's accession.

The Maharajah, Sir Hari Singh, was an evasive vacillating man who not only failed to make up his mind about accession to India or Pakistan but did his best to avoid the pressure to decide which Lord Mountbatten was trying to exert upon him. From mid-July to mid-October 1947 the choice before him was real and open. Had he acceded to Pakistan, India could only have accepted the decision, painful though it would be, not least to Pandit Nehru. Lord Mountbatten had given the Maharajah an assurance that accession to Pakistan would not be regarded by the Government of India as a hostile act. But to the Maharajah that course was utterly repellent. To submit as a Hindu monarch to Muslim supremacy was a forbidding destiny; and he rationalised and reinforced his personal repugnance by the argument that Pakistan was a one-community theocratic state, whereas Kashmir nominally enjoyed a secular equality among all religions. The Maharajah may well have really believed in this argument, for despots have always been apt to regard their absolutism as impartial and paternal, and sectional divisions among their people as hostile to good order. He used it strongly to Lord Ismay when the latter, on Lord Mountbatten's behalf, urged him in September to make up his mind.

[1] *The Integration of the Indian States*, p. 395.

On the other hand, he feared to accede to India lest this lead to imposition of democracy in the State, or to an uncontrollable uprising among the Muslims who formed the great majority of his people. He can hardly 'have thought that the problem would vanish by being ignored, or that some *deus ex machina* would arrive to settle it plainly and happily for him. Perhaps he hoped that by procrastinating he could play off one Dominion against the other in competition for his favours, and so win special terms; or could extract from the unwillingness of either Dominion to see him join the other a chance of permanent independence for his State and his dynasty. All this is a matter of conjecture. The fact the the invasion flung him into a humiliating and craven despair, in which his paralysis of decision was broken only by prompt action by the Indian Government, suggests that weakness of will, not calculated cunning, caused his fatal inertia.

In September and October events of some importance were taking place in Kashmir, but the Government of India was too preoccupied, first with the Punjab massacres and the refugees, then with the Junagadh affair, not to mention all its other problems, to pay them close heed. There were uprisings of Muslims, especially in Poonch; sporadic for the most part, but tying down State troops, isolating their garrisons and defying the rule of government over a wide area. There was some evidence that individual Pakistanis took part, besides State subjects, and the commander of the State forces protested to Pakistan Army Headquarters about raids from across the Pakistan border by armed groups of 200 to 300 strong. On the other hand, official Pakistani spokesmen proclaimed that here was a spontaneous popular revolt against oppression by a Hindu and Sikh minority. Inter-communal violence also broke out in the Poonch and Mirpur area, where Muslims were the worst victims. There was perhaps nothing very surprising or portentous in these developments and the rival propaganda about them, in a land on the fringe of the bloodstained Punjab, but later events have cast upon them a different light.

On the evening of Friday, 24th October, the Governor-General and the Foreign Minister of Siam were guests of Pandit Nehru at dinner at the latter's house in New Delhi. During the evening Lord Mountbatten was taken aside by his host, who told him that news had come in of a large-scale invasion of tribesmen from the

North-West Frontier into Kashmir. Realising at once that a new and grave situation had arisen, Lord Mountbatten called a special meeting of the Defence Committee at 11 a.m. next morning. There an official report was received from General Lockhart, Commander-in-Chief, Indian Army,[1] who had been informed by Headquarters, Pakistan Army, in Rawalpindi that some 5,000 tribesmen had entered Kashmir three days previously from the west and had seized and burnt the town of Muzaffarabad on their way towards Srinagar.[2]

The date, the hour and the source of the information are all significant. The timing of the invasion was well calculated to place the defence of Kashmir from India at a disadvantage. Winter was beginning to close in upon the passes. The troubles in Poonch were holding down many of the Maharajah's police and soldiers. Whereas the invaders could be expected to master the central valley of Kashmir before the winter snows came, there was little margin of time left for forces to be assembled and deployed from India before the road from East Punjab became impassable. It was bad enough at the best of times. As events fell out, another hour or two's delay in holding the Defence Committee meeting of 25th October, by preventing the action that was taken on its instructions that day, might have fully vindicated such a strategy on the invaders' part—if indeed it was strategy and not accident—by allowing them to take Srinagar airfield and so oblige any Indian

[1] He had ceased to be acting Governor of the North-West Frontier Province on the transfer of power.

[2] Muzaffarabad had fallen on 22nd October. According to the appreciation of the military position which Indian Army H.Q. gave to the leader of the Kashmir expeditionary force on the 27th, the main incursion along the Kohala-Srinagar road had been made on 20th October by a force composed of a thousand-odd tribesmen from the Hazara–Murree road, about 400 Pathans said to be Afridis, and some Muslim National Guards from the Rawalpindi district of Pakistan, travelling in three hundred civilian lorries carrying surplus arms and ammunition. This information was presumably gathered by the Indian Army officer who accompanied Mr. Menon to Srinagar. It has been widely believed that the original report on the tribesmen's invasion came in a letter to General Lockhart from Sir George Cunningham, Governor of the North-West Frontier Province. This was not so. There was such a letter at that time, but it was concerned with private business except for a postscript saying, 'Some people up here have been acting very foolishly. You will know what I mean by the time this letter reaches you.'

reinforcements to advance by the slow, hazardous and probably ambushed land route in the teeth of impending winter.

That the report which set off the decisive response came from Rawalpindi confirms that the facts of the invasion were known in Pakistan before they were known in India, and were not communicated through any official civil channel.[1] The Government of Pakistan claimed to have known of the raiders' incursion only after the main body had passed. Later, when Mr. Jinnah was complaining to Lord Mountbatten of India's high-handed and unilateral action in Kashmir, he said that if, on 24th October, the Government of India had telegraphed to Karachi pointing out that a critical situation was developing in Kashmir and had suggested that Pakistan should co-operate in dealing with it, 'all the trouble would have been ended'. Remiss as the Government of India may have been in their lack of communication with Pakistan, they could have asked in reply why the Pakistan Government had not itself telegraphed Delhi to the same effect. Mr. Liaqat Ali Khan, Prime Minister of Pakistan, when taxed with knowledge of the movement of Wazirs and Mahsuds from beyond Peshawar across part of the North-West Frontier Province into Kashmir, travelling in lorries and buses, did not deny such knowledge, but said that any attempt by Pakistan authorities to interfere with the movement of tribesmen in defence of their fellow-Mussulmans would have precipitated trouble with the rest of the tribes on the Frontier. It was also

[1] General Sir Frank Messervy, Commander-in-Chief in Pakistan, aware of agitation by the tribesmen to be allowed to invade Kashmir, had strongly advised Mr. Liaqat Ali Khan against such a course. Shortly before the invasion, Sir George Cunningham asked him on the telephone what was the Pakistan Government's policy, as the Chief Minister of the N.W.F.P., Khan Abdul Qaiyum Khan, was encouraging the tribesmen to go into Kashmir and even collecting Frontier Scouts and militia transport for a tribal invasion. Thereupon Sir Frank renewed his emphatic advice to his Prime Minister before flying to London on military business. Within the next few days a conference was held in Lahore between Mr. Jinnah, Mr. Liaqat Ali Khan and Khan Quaiyum Khan. Its outcome was unknown to General Messervy, then in England, but may be presumed from actual events. After his return he sent one of his officers on some pretext to the house of the Commissioner of Rawalpindi, from which it was rumoured the operations in Kashmir were directed, to discover the Commissioner presiding over a meeting which included Badshah Gul and other tribal leaders. This evidence is of course circumstantial rather than conclusive.

a fact that the Pakistan Army was not in good order after partition, with its units scattered and its administration disjointed, and was in no shape to take on a campaign against Frontier tribesmen who were, in their own view, rescuing their co-religionists in Kashmir.

The fact that the Kashmir emergency was considered in Delhi not by the Indian Cabinet but by its Defence Committee also proved historically vital. At this body, by request of Pandit Nehru and his other Ministers, the Governor-General presided, thus acting in some sense as Prime Minister in matters of defence, though the Cabinet took responsibility and the Governor-General was constitutionally bound to accept their advice. He had been invited by the politicians to head the Defence Committee because they had realised they knew nothing about the armed forces, military administration, or problems of national defence. Thus it happened that all the key decisions of the Government of India about Kashmir at the end of October 1947 were taken under the leadership of the Governor-General, for they were decisions in terms of defence against the tribal invasion. This was to have momentous consequences; for while Lord Mountbatten could consequently be identified with the policies adopted by India in Kashmir at that time, he had neither responsibility normeans for carrying them to fulfilment in the future.

At the emergency meeting of the Defence Committee on 25th October, General Lockhart's information was supplemented by the Prime Minister. The advance guard of an invading force which had travelled in motor trucks through Muzaffarabad had reached Uri. Muslim troops of the Kashmir Army were reported to have joined the raiders (this report was later confirmed) and many Hindu and Sikh refugees had been killed. When Lord Mountbatten recalled his efforts to persuade the Maharajah to make up his mind, and said that his indecision had brought this trouble on himself, Pandit Nehru retorted that it had been largely induced by the policy of the Political Department under the previous Viceroyalty. He also complained that although the State and Defence Departments had approved Kashmir's continual requests for arms and equipment nothing had happened. The meeting then discussed how quickly a supply of arms could be flown to Kashmir. This was the first step towards an airlift which was to prove historic. It was decided to switch British Overseas Aircraft Corporation aircraft, which had been borrowed for transport of refugees, to ordinary passenger traffic, in order to release Indian civil airways machines. These would be chartered to the Government, and would be flown by Indian Army officers, collecting arms from depôts and taking them to Kashmir. The Commanders-in-Chief of the Army and Air Force were ordered to give this operation the highest possible priority. The arms were to be flown to Srinagar and delivered to the Maharajah's Government or (a notable addendum) any provisional Government which might have been set up and was not sponsored by Pakistan. That was the full extent of the military decision on Day One of a three-day drama.

Pandit Nehru then raised the question of the future policy of the Government of India towards Kashmir. Events might overwhelm them by their swiftness if no action was taken. It was clear, he said, that the raids into the State, with arms and trucks, must have had the full assistance of the Pakistan authorities. Indeed he had information (unspecified) that the invasion had been planned at a meeting in Rawalpindi a fortnight previously, and he had no doubt that happenings in Junagadh had been intended as a screen for Pakistan's operations against Kashmir. The only way in which the Maharajah's Government could save the situation was by complete co-operation with the National Conference and Sheikh Abdullah. This was the essential first step. It was of little advantage to talk of accession now. He accepted the principle that accession should be dependent on the will of the people, but agreed with Lord Mountbatten's view that the Maharajah could hardly be expected to agree to ascertain this in the midst of a revolution.

The Governor-General suggested as a possible solution that Kashmir might temporarily accede to India, which would come to its aid, subject to the proviso that the will of the people should be ascertained as soon as law and order was generally restored. Such a solution would help redress the situation in Junagadh, which everyone agreed was closely linked with that in Kashmir, and which otherwise might become a running sore. He had always thought that Junagadh might be a trap set for India to spring on herself. If she used armed intervention in Junagadh, without the Nawab's accession, Pakistan would claim the right to intervene with arms in Kashmir without the accession of the Maharajah; and the Kashmir question, which was by far the more important and dangerous, would be determined by force and war.

Pandit Nehru was not so sure about this: it might still be necessary to use force in Junagadh. It was fully agreed that they must ultimately abide by the decision of the people, but it was equally agreed that it was desirable to send help to Kashmir in the present crisis, including possible armed intervention: the question was whether a temporary accession would encourage the people to side with India or would only act as an irritant. There was bound to be propaganda to the effect that the accession was not really temporary, and tempers might be inflamed. Another Minister, who shared these doubts, suggested that the Maharajah should write to the Government of India offering accession and asking for armed assistance, and that they should reply that it was not their policy to accept accession in doubtful cases unless the people's will had first been ascertained, but that they would forthwith send armed help. Lord Mountbatten was of much the same opinion. Sardar Vallabhbhai Patel said he saw nothing to prevent India from sending armed assistance whether or not Kashmir acceded, and Pandit Nehru agreed. The Finance Minister argued that if one State interfered in the affairs of a neighbour, on the entitlement of friendly relations, another might claim to do likewise; but the Prime Minister still considered that intervention after accession, rather than before, might lead to greater complications. It is important for the subsequent story to underline that the Indian Cabinet at this stage had no enthusiasm for the accession of Kashmir, nor did they think it necessary for the sending of aid to protect the State and restore law and order.

The Defence Committee on Day One took no decision on accession. But it directed the Secretary of the Ministry of States, Mr. V. P. Menon, to fly to Srinagar that day to discuss with the Maharajah (and if possible with Sheikh Abdullah) various possibilities; first, of the Maharajah's requesting armed assistance, which might possibly be concentrated on the Jammu front; secondly, of his Government's co-operating with Sheikh Abdullah's National Conference; and thirdly, of his offering accession, which (it was recorded) would in all probability not be accepted until an opportunity had arisen to ascertain the will of the people. In anticipation of the answer on the first of these points, the Chiefs of Staff were asked to examine and prepare plans for certain possible courses of action, including flying troops to Srinagar.

As soon as an aeroplane could be made ready Menon flew off with two officers from the Army and Air Force. They found

Srinagar airport deserted. The only signs of defence were some so-called National Guards, supporters of Sheikh Abdullah. Menon made his way to the palace, where the Maharajah was in a state of panic and preparing to flee. He was in a mind to do anything the Indian Government might require or propose to save his family and his throne. It appeared that the State forces were in danger of disintegration. The tribal invaders were expected in Srinagar at any time, perhaps within twenty-four hours. After a discussion with the Prime Minister, Menon went to the rest-house to get a little sleep before flying back to Delhi. The place was deserted: he could get nothing to eat or drink nor any bedclothes. After a little fitful sleep he was awakened at 4 a.m. by someone sent by the Prime Minister, telling him to come at once to the airport. The jeep was overcrowded but they arrived and roused the pilot, who however refused to take off in mountainous country until dawn. Whereas on the previous day the airport had been empty, now it was crowded with people, all driven, it would seem, by a simultaneous wave of panic to find some means of escape. A middle-aged Hindu lady approached Menon and begged him with sobs and tears to take her two daughters with him; for themselves, she and her husband could face the danger of looting and murder that they saw approaching, but for her daughters there would be a fate worse than death if they fell into the hands of these savage Muslim invaders. When first light came and the aeroplane took off, the girls were packed on board, where they ruined by their weeping any further chance of rest for the tired V. P. Menon. The Prime Minister of Kashmir flew with them too.

In Delhi, after a bath and a shave, Menon hurried to the Defence Committee which had been called by the Governor-General. He reported on what he and his two companions had found. The tribesmen might reach Srinagar in three days' time, perhaps sooner. Quick decisions had to be taken, though some were still conditional on events to be yet determined.

Of the Kashmir State Forces, totalling about 8,000 men, one-third were Muslims and these had gone over with their arms. There were four companies of State Forces in Srinagar, while the raiders, who had reached a point only thirty-five miles away, were said to number 2,000 to 3,000, all armed and having some modern equipment and mortars. The National Conference (Sheikh Abdullah's organisation) gave the impression of meaning to put up a good fight, but the Muslim League in Srinagar was arming its members. The Prime Minister of Kashmir, Mehr Chand Mahajan, a former Judge of the Punjab High Court,[1] had been obsessed with the local situation: he had seemed to want to retire to Jammu and leave Srinagar to the mercy of the invaders. The Maharajah had completely lost his nerve. At one stage he had said he would be prepared to make a present of Kashmir to the Government of India and himself retire to Jammu. Menon advised him for his own safety to leave immediately for Jammu with his family.

After Menon had made his report, supported by a military appreciation by the Indian Army colonel who had accompanied him, the Committee, at this meeting on Day Two, at once discussed the military action required. General Lockhart said the Commander of the State Forces had asked for a battalion of Indian infantry to be sent to Srinagar that day. A Gurkha battalion was available, but objection was raised to the use of Gurkhas for such a purpose, and later in the meeting General Lockhart said that the 1st Battalion of the Sikh Regiment could be sent from Gurgaon. Transport aircraft was the limiting factor and he warned that the operation involved considerable military risk, especially if the population proved hostile. The Prime Minister discounted this danger. He believed the great majority of the population of the Vale of Kashmir would be friendly though there would be an active hostile minority. Lord Mountbatten's part in this debate can be recorded in his own words to H.M. the King:

> It was unquestionable that, if Srinagar was to be saved from pillage by the invading tribesmen, and if the couple of hundred British residents in Kashmir were not to be massacred, Indian troops would have to do the job.
>
> The Commanders pointed out the extreme hazards of flying in troops, and I added my voice to theirs. But as soon as I saw that my Ministers had made up their minds that the military risks must be accepted and Indian troops sent, I was clear that it was essential to send sufficient and in time. . . . I therefore made it my business to over-ride all the difficulties which the Commanders-in-Chief, in the course of their duty, raised to the proposal.[2]

[1] Pandit Kak had been replaced by Major-General Janak Singh and he in turn by Mr. Mahajan.

[2] *Governor-General's Personal Report* No. 5, 7th November 1947.

Lord Mountbatten had a particular reason for supporting immediate action to defend Srinagar and the Kashmir Valley. As soon as the news of the threat to the Valley had reached Delhi, Field Marshal Auchinleck had come to the Governor-General asking to be allowed to send British troops to defend the lives of the many Europeans who lived there. Lord Mountbatten had without hesitation refused. He was determined that British forces should not be involved in the affairs of independent India and Pakistan: they were present in India only on sufferance, in effect, while their repatriation proceeded, and not for any operational purpose. Auchinleck exclaimed: 'Those people will be murdered and their blood will be on your head.' 'I shall have to take that responsibility,' said Mountbatten, 'but I could not answer for what might happen if British troops became involved.' He therefore felt a special personal responsibility for ensuring that all possible military measures were taken to defend Srinagar and the Valley, and he saw those measures as dependent on accession of the State; for he feared that without it Kashmir would become a battleground between India and Pakistan. To him, armed conflict between the two Dominions in these earliest days of their independence appeared as the worst threat of all. He wrote in a report to His Majesty the King:

The accession would fully regularise the position, and reduce the risk of an armed clash with Pakistan forces to a minimum.[1]

'I shall relate a little further on,' he continued, 'how lucky it was that this accession was accepted.' The facts to which he referred will also be related a little further on in this book.

Having taken its military decisions—primarily to prepare for a troop airlift to Srinagar—the Defence Committee on Day Two turned to the political problem. According to V. P. Menon's published account, the Governor-General took the lead.

Lord Mountbatten said that it would be quite improper to move Indian troops into what was at the moment an independent country. . . . If it were true that the Maharajah was now anxious to accede to India, then Jammu and Kashmir would become part of Indian territory. This was the only basis on which Indian troops could be sent to the rescue of the State from further pillaging by the aggressors. He further expressed the strong

[1] loc. cit.

opinion that . . . accession should be conditional on the will of the people being ascertained by a plebiscite after the raiders had been driven out of the State and law and order had been restored.[1]

Members of the Defence Committee considered that the issue of accession would make little difference to the situation, though one Minister argued that immediate accession might only arouse further opposition. It was agreed that when the accession was accepted this should be subject to the proviso that a plebiscite would be held in Kashmir 'when the law and order situation allowed this'. Lord Mountbatten suggested that this plebiscite should be on three choices: to join India, to join Pakistan, or to remain independent. He also suggested that before a plebiscite was held the future defence of Kashmir should be discussed by the two Dominions in the Joint Defence Council. The Prime Minister, Pandit Nehru, observed that the Government of India would not mind Kashmir's remaining an independent country provided that it were within India's sphere of influence.

Although the Defence Committee took no decision on that morning that Kashmir's accession should be accepted—which was strictly not its business—it is clear that by the end of its discussion this was treated as a foregone conclusion. Its actual decision, apart from military directives, was to charge the Ministry of States with preparing a draft Instrument of Accession and a draft letter from the Government of India to the Maharajah, recording the conditional acceptance of this Instrument, as justification for aiding in the restoration of law and order, provided that the will of the people of Kashmir on the question of final accession were ascertained when conditions allowed this to be done.

One further decision was taken: that the Prime Minister should send a telegram to the Prime Minister of Pakistan asking that steps should be taken to stop further infiltration, so worded as not to be open to the possible interpretation that Pakistan was being asked to send armed support to Kashmir. This was the total recorded extent to which the Defence Committee considered liaison with the Pakistan Government when debating the situation in Kashmir on those crucial two days. Pakistan was tacitly assumed to be not merely a rival suitor for the adherence of Kashmir but a hostile power in all but name.

[1] *The Integration of the Indian States*, p. 399.

Later the same morning Mr. V. P. Menon flew to Jammu accompanied by the Prime Minister of the State. His own description of what ensued cannot be bettered.

On arrival at the palace I found it in a state of utter turmoil with valuable articles strewn all over the place. The Maharajah was asleep, he had left Srinagar the previous evening and had been driving all night. I woke him up and told him of what had taken place at the Defence Committee meeting. He was ready to accede at once. He then composed a letter to the Governor-General describing the pitiable plight of the State and reiterating his request for military help. He further informed the Governor-General that it was his intention to set up an interim government at once and to ask Sheikh Abdullah to carry the responsibilities in this emergency with Mehr Chand Mahajan, his Prime Minister. He concluded by saying that, if the State was to be saved, immediate assistance must be available at Srinagar. He also signed the Instrument of Accession. Just as I was leaving, he told me that before he went to sleep he had left instructions with his A.D.C. that if I came back from Delhi he was not to be disturbed, as it would mean that the Government of India had decided to come to his rescue and he should therefore be allowed to sleep in peace; but that if I failed to return it meant that everything was lost and, in that case, his A.D.C. was to shoot him in his sleep![1]

Back in Delhi, Menon attended a further meeting of the Defence Committee the same evening, at which it was decided after long discussion that the accession should be accepted, subject to the proviso that a plebiscite should be held in the State when the law and order situation allowed. Plans were finalised for the despatch of troops by air, and at first light the following morning, 27th October, the movement began. By nightfall 329 men of the 1st Battalion the Sikh Regiment under command of Lieutenant-Colonel Dewan Ranjit Rai had been flown to Srinagar.

Their orders were to secure the Srinagar Airfield, to assist the Kashmir Government (assumed to be a popular administration under Sheikh Abdullah) in maintaining law and order in Srinagar, and if possible to drive away any tribesmen who might have entered Srinagar. If failure to communicate with the airfield im-

[1] loc. cit.

plied that it had been captured by tribesmen the force was to turn back to Jammu and await orders. 'In the unlikely event' of the force's being allowed to land and finding a government sponsored by Pakistan in being, it must be re-embarked and flown back to Jammu. Six days' field ration was to be taken, and transport was to be found locally. The operation, which was dubbed JAK, was therefore improvised, local and frought with doubts.

The raiding forces, however, had not yet arrived in Srinagar and the airfield was secured. Two companies were sent out immediately towards Baramula on the road to the west, to try to stop the raiders there before they entered the Valley; but meeting with far superior forces they withdrew to a point on the road seventeen miles from Srinagar. In this operation Lieutenant-Colonel Rai was killed. But the bridgehead had been established and the capital saved. Simultaneously a force of armoured cars was sent by road, crossing the Ravi by a hastily-built pontoon bridge north of Gurdaspur, with orders to drive through Poonch and the Banihal Pass to Srinagar at the utmost speed and link up with Colonel Rai's expedition. Though the roads were terribly bad this mission was successfully accomplished. By the end of the month three more battalions of the Indian Army had reached Srinagar and the military position had been more or less stabilised. In the whole story nothing is more astonishing than the airlift of 27th October, which changed the course of history. Lord Mountbatten has said that in all his experience he had never heard of such a lift being effected at such short notice. The first directive to the Commanders-in-Chief of the Indian Army and Air Force to prepare plans for such an operation was given on the morning of 25th October. Less than forty-eight hours later, over a hundred civilian aircraft and R.I.A.F. planes had been assembled to fly troops, equipment and supplies to Srinagar. The battalion that moved was not a ready-to-go combat unit but had been engaged on internal security duties not far from Delhi.

It was unlikely that Pakistan would watch all this without re-action. On 28th October Lord Ismay, who had been in England to report to his Government and the Press on Lord Mountbatten's behalf, landed at Delhi airport and was greeted with the news about Kashmir. He was deeply shocked at the risk of war between India and Pakistan that had been exposed, and at the failure of the Indian Government to attempt any consultation or joint policy with Pakistan in face of the events in the State. While at a meeting of the Defence Committee the same day, he was called out to speak to Field Marshal Auchinleck, telephoning from Lahore. The Supreme Commander reported that he had succeeded in persuading Mr. Jinnah to cancel orders, which he had given the previous night, for Pakistani troops to be moved into Kashmir. The detailed story emerged when Field Marshal Auchinleck reached Delhi later on the 28th October. On hearing of the despatch of Indian troops to Srinagar, Mr. Jinnah had at once instructed Sir Francis Mudie, Governor of the Punjab, who was with him, to telephone General Gracey, acting Commander-in-Chief of the Pakistan Army in the absence of General Messervy, ordering him to move troops into Kashmir at once. They were to seize the pass on the Rawalpindi–Srinagar road, and then to proceed through Srinagar, where Mr. Jinnah knew Indian troops were now deployed, and occupy the Banihal Pass on the road to Jammu, thus isolating Srinagar and nullifying the Indian intervention, which could be sustained and reinforced only by that road. General Gracey had replied that he was not prepared, without the approval of the Supreme Commander, to issue orders which would inevitably lead to armed conflict between the two Dominions and the withdrawal of all British officers from their forces. An acrimonious conversation followed, in which General Gracey attributed to Sir Francis Mudie language of undiplomatic tone and imperiousness. The Governor was, of course, speaking for Mr. Jinnah, who presided over all Cabinet meetings and was undisputed head of the Pakistan Government.

It was at the General's urgent request that Field Marshal Auchinleck had flown next morning to Lahore, where he saw Mr. Jinnah with General Gracey. He emphasised a sequence of points: the legal propriety of the accession, quoting Junagadh against Pakistan; India's right to send troops in response to the Maharajah's request; the incalculable consequences of military violation of what was now territory of the Indian Union; and the extreme weakness of the Pakistan Army if British officers were withdrawn, as they would have to be from both sides. Mr. Jinnah had countermanded the orders but remained very angry, and in the Supreme Commander's view, reporting to the Chiefs of Staff in London, the situation was highly dangerous. Mr. Jinnah had agreed to Lord Auchinleck's suggestion that he and his Prime Minister should meet Lord Mountbatten, Pandit Nehru, the Maharajah of Kashmir and his Prime Minister round a table.

Lord Mountbatten was eager to accept this invitation and to go with Nehru to Lahore, though nothing more was heard of the idea that Kashmir's representatives should join in a tripartite conference. Sardar Patel, however, was strongly opposed, on the ground that, Pakistan being the aggressor, such a visitation would smack of Munich and imply an admission of guilt. 'For the Prime Minister to go crawling to Mr. Jinnah,' he said, 'when we were the stronger side and in the right would never be forgiven by the people of India.' Pandit Nehru was nevertheless inclined to go, arguing that India had not entered Kashmir for territorial acquisition and that if a peaceful solution could be found she should not stand on prestige. While this dispute was being hammered out, Nehru went sick with a high fever, and the proposed meeting was postponed. The Prime Minister eventually agreed to go to a Joint Defence Council meeting in Lahore on 1st November, but on the evening before he was due to leave he read in the papers a statement by the Pakistan Government to the effect that the accession of Kashmir had been accomplished by 'fraud and violence' and could not be accepted by Pakistan. He telephoned Lord Mountbatten to say that this was more than he could stomach, and that, if the Governor-General still insisted on taking him to Lahore, he begged not to be expected to discuss Kashmir with Mr. Jinnah. Lord Mountbatten excused him from coming, and went to Lahore without the Prime Minister, refusing himself to allow motives of personal pride or prestige to stand in the way of efforts for peace. Dog snarling at cat, and cat spitting back at dog—the interchange was all too typical of relations between India and Pakistan at this time.

In a long conference in Lahore, where Mr. Liaqat Ali Khan was ill in bed and depressed almost to the point of resigning himself to war, Mr. Jinnah's principal complaint was that the Government had failed to give the Pakistan Government timely information of the action they proposed to take in Kashmir. Lord Mountbatten replied that Pandit Nehru had telegraphed his opposite number on 26th October, immediately the decision was taken to send troops. Mr. Jinnah, having looked up his files, retorted that the telegram had arrived after the troops had landed, and did not contain any form of appeal for co-operation: it merely reported the accession and the despatch of troops. The Indian Government ought to have telegraphed on 24th October. 'If,' he said, 'they had on that date telegraphed saying that a critical situation was reported to be developing in Kashmir and they had sent in observers to confirm these reports and suggested that Pakistan should co-operate in dealing with the situation, all the trouble would have been ended by now.'[1] Lord Ismay, who was present, intervened to say that the first thing that had occurred to him on his return from England was that Pakistan should have been notified at the earliest possible moment. To the best of his recollection, Pandit Nehru had told him that Mr. Liaqat Ali Khan had been kept in touch with what was happening all the time. If this had not been done, the oversight must have been due to the pressure of events, and not because the Government of India had anything to hide. If we accept Mr. Jinnah's conclusion, the oversight was a grave misfortune.

There followed a sharply-worded interchange as to which side was responsible for the violence which in Mr. Jinnah's indictment vitiated Kashmir's accession to India. Mr. Jinnah then proposed that both sides should withdraw at once and simultaneously. When Lord Mountbatten asked how the tribesmen were to be ordered out, Mr. Jinnah replied that if India would withdraw he would 'call the whole thing off'. He would warn the tribesmen that if they did not comply he would send large forces along their lines of communication. To Lord Mountbatten's suggestion of a plebiscite in the State Mr. Jinnah objected that with Indian troops present and Sheikh Abdullah in power (he had been invited by the Maharajah to form an emergency Government) the people would be too frightened to vote for Pakistan. Lord Mountbatten then suggested a plebiscite under the auspices of the United Nations, but Mr. Jinnah pressed for one under the joint control and supervision of the two Governors-General. Lord Mountbatten had to point out the differences in their respective political positions which made this an unreal proposal. His account continues:

At the end Mr. Jinnah became extremely pessimistic and said it was quite clear that the Dominion of India was out to throttle and choke the Dominion of Pakistan at birth, and that if they continued with their oppression there would be nothing for it

[1] *Governor-General's Personal Report* No. 5, 7th November 1947.

but to face the consequences. However depressing the prospect might be he was not afraid; for the situation was already so bad that there was little that could happen to make it worse. I pointed out that war, whilst admittedly very harmful for India, would be completely disastrous for Pakistan and himself. Lord Ismay tried to cheer him up out of his depression but he was not very successful. However, we departed on good terms.[1]

Though perhaps time was gained and the heat reduced, nothing constructive came of this conference, and the problem of Kashmir slithered into its next equally unhappy phase.

The military position in the Kashmir Valley was stabilised by the capture of Baramula on 8th November, but in the Jammu and Poonch areas the Indian forces met with more serious difficulties. Lord Mountbatten's efforts to reach a peaceful settlement did not flag, save for his visit to London from 9th to 24th November for the Royal wedding. On 26th November Mr. Liaqat Ali Khan, though still unwell, came to Delhi for a meeting of the Joint Defence Council—an opportunity for the first meeting between the two Prime Ministers since 30th September. Lord Mountbatten wrote in his report to His Majesty the King:

> In the middle of the Joint Defence Council meeting itself, whilst everything was going very well, a 'Most Immediate' letter from Pandit Nehru (who was not himself present) was brought in to me. This enclosed two telegrams which he had that morning received from Mr. Liaqat Ali Khan. They were of such a nature that Pandit Nehru wrote: 'In view of what Mr. Liaqat Ali Khan has said in these telegrams, I see no particular advantage in my discussing the Kashmir situation or indeed any other matter with him.'

If Mr. Liaqat Ali Khan's intention had been to ruin any chance of further negotiations, he could not have phrased or timed his telegrams better. He accused Sheikh Abdullah, who, he must full well have known, was one of Pandit Nehru's closest friends, of being 'a Quisling and a paid agent to disrupt the Muslims of Kashmir'; and he accused the Government of India of trying to mislead the world, of evasion, of contradiction, of tyranny and of attempting to eliminate the whole Muslim population of Kashmir. In one of the telegrams (which was also

[1] loc. cit.

addressed to Mr. Attlee), he laid down, as one of the principles upon which Pakistan founded their case, the setting-up of an impartial and independent administration immediately.[1]

Lord Mountbatten saw Mr. Liaqat Ali Khan alone and told him he had been criminally foolish thus once again to jeopardise the chance of any negotiations. Having rebuked one party, he was able to placate the other, to the point of persuading Pandit Nehru to meet Mr. Liaqat Ali Khan at four o'clock that afternoon.

Pandit Nehru held forth for about three-quarters of an hour and gave a full account of events in Kashmir as he saw them. He said categorically that, if the Dominion of India had not gone to the assistance of Kashmir when called upon, not only by the Ruler but also by Sheikh Abdullah, the leader of the biggest popular party, he had no doubt whatever that the present Government of India would have been overthrown and that it would have been replaced by an irresponsible and extremist Government which, in his opinion, would probably have declared war upon Pakistan.

Mr. Liaqat Ali Khan countered this by saying that the Government of Pakistan had had their position greatly weakened by not taking strong action against India, and that he personally was being abused in the vernacular Press for failing to support Muslim interests. Apart from this, Mr. Liaqat Ali Khan did not speak very much (he was obviously tired and weak); but he managed to ask some searching questions and to make some important observations, and, in the course of the talks, gradually formulated certain proposals which Pandit Nehru said that he would consider.

These proposals, which were later formulated more exactly by Lord Ismay sitting with an official representative of each Dominion—Mr. Mohammed Ali for Pakistan, and Mr. V. P. Menon for India—formed the basis for four further discussions which the two Prime Ministers held, sometimes alone, some-times with myself and sometimes with Lord Ismay present, during the next two days. In brief they were that Pakistan should use all their influence to persuade the rebel 'Azad Kashmir' forces to cease fighting and the tribesmen and other 'invaders' to withdraw from Kashmir territory as quickly as possible, and

[1] *Report of the Governor-General.*

to prevent further incursions; that India should withdraw the bulk of their forces, leaving only small detachments of minimum strength to deal with disturbances; that the United Nations Organisation should be asked to send a Commission to hold a plebiscite in Kashmir and to recommend to the Governments of India, Pakistan and Kashmir, before it was held, steps which should be taken to ensure that it was fair and unfettered; and that certain steps which it was intended to take towards this object, such as the release of political prisoners and the return of refugees, should be published right away.[1]

It was agreed that each Prime Minister should discuss these proposals with his respective contacts in Kashmir. Mr. Liaqat Ali Khan had compromised on the objectives with which he came to Delhi—complete withdrawal by both sides, an impartial interim administration, and a plebiscite under independent auspices—but was willing to negotiate in the hope of gaining more. Lord Mountbatten's hopes, however, were soon dashed:

Two hours after Mr. Mohammed Ali's aircraft had taken off, I attended a meeting of the Defence Committee of the Indian Cabinet. This was one of the most disastrous and distressing meetings it has ever been my lot to preside over. It appeared that all the efforts of the last few days towards reaching an agreement on Kashmir were to come to naught—a circumstance which, in its turn, would surely tear to pieces the agreements on other matters and, generally, the closer co-operation which had been obtained.

The trouble had originated in a visit which Sardar Patel and Sardar Baldev Singh had paid to Jammu the previous day. The reports which they had brought back, together with independent reports that Pandit Nehru had received, had served so to embitter and infuriate the leading Ministers of my Government that they were now thinking in terms of fighting out the issue, and not holding a plebiscite, rather than of continuing negotiations.

These reports were threefold in nature. First, it was alleged that there were large concentrations of would-be invaders, including tribesmen, in specified places in West Punjab near the Jammu border. Secondly, it was alleged that Mr. Liaqat Ali

[1] loc. cit.

Khan had, on leaving Delhi, gone out of his way to encourage more raiders to enter Kashmir, and had made speeches to the effect that Pakistan would never give up Kashmir. Thirdly (and this affected India Ministers perhaps more than anything else), there were the stories, which had by now become almost commonplace, of the raiders having indulged in the most ghastly atrocities, including the wholesale murder of non-Muslims and the selling of Kashmiri girls.

Pandit Nehru declared that, in these circumstances, he would certainly not talk to Mr. Liaqat Ali Khan at Lahore about a plebiscite. All the Ministers were insistent on the most violent offensive military action being taken.[1]

Their proposals involved them in sharp conflict with their Chiefs of Staff—all British—who were obliged to emphasise the military difficulties and risks of such ventures. On the most dangerous of their demands—that a *cordon sanitaire*, or demilitarised zone, should be established along the Kashmir frontier with West Punjab, and that any observed movement within it should be attacked from the air after due notice, they were so insistent that Lord Mountbatten had to temporise by getting the proposal referred to the Joint Planning Staff. He made sure meanwhile that the report would be adverse, and so it was. The Ministers then gave up the idea without argument.

Lord Mountbatten next tried, through the lower-floor communication between his Conference Secretary and Mr. Mohammed Ali in Lahore, to persuade Mr. Liaqat Ali Khan to make a conciliatory gesture. Mr. Mohammed Ali was not hopeful:

. . . In the last two days Mr. Liaqat Ali Khan had visited Sialkot. The stories which he had heard there had completely changed the outlook of this normally placid man, who had returned in a state of excitement and emotion such as he (Mr. Mohammed Ali) could not remember having seen him in before.

These 'stories' were very similar to those which had so hardened the outlook of the India Ministers. Mr. Liaqat Ali Khan had heard that non-Muslims in Kashmir, and particularly the Sikhs, had indulged in the most ghastly atrocities; in Jammu District every single Muslim male, without exception, had been butchered; casualties ran into hundreds of thousands;

[1] loc. cit.

Muslim girls had been abducted and a large number were being kept naked in a camp by Sikhs, and were being periodically raped. . . .[1]

Mr. Mohammed Ali also told Lieutenant-Colonel Erskine Crum that he had accompanied Mr. Liaqat Ali Khan to Rawalpindi, where they had met the leaders of the 'Azad Kashmir' Government. Mr. Liaqat Ali Khan had, in his presence, put before them the outline of the draft agreement on Kashmir—in, he said, a very fair and impartial manner. They had unanimously and immediately condemned this out of hand. They had said that they were not willing to consider any terms which did not include the complete withdrawal of all Indian forces from Kashmir, and an impartial administration preceding the plebiscite. Without these, they would prefer to go on fighting.[2]

However, on 9th December, the two Prime Ministers again met on the occasion of a Joint Defence Council session in Lahore.

The first two hours or so were spent (at my instance) in mutual recriminations—which, as a method of clearing the air, served a good puprose. . . .

For nearly all the rest of the time the conversation circled round the means of attaining the object, on which both sides were agreed—namely the holding of a fair and impartial plebiscite. . . . What was to be the first step?

Pandit Nehru maintained that the first step should be a declaration by the Pakistan Government that they would use all their influence to persuade the raiders who had entered Kashmir from outside the State to withdraw—and issue an appeal to this effect; and to take steps that no further invaders should go in.

Mr. Liaqat Ali Khan pointed out that any physical measures taken to stop the raiders going in would mean that Pakistan would have to go to war with the tribes. He was not prepared to do this—not least because the people of Pakistan would not support such a step. However he did feel that he would be able to appeal to the raiders to withdraw, and stop more going in, if he had something concrete to offer them. The concrete offer

[1] This was, of course, a second-hand account of what Mr. Liaqat Ali Khan had heard: no confirmation of these rumours of atrocities on either side was forthcoming.
[2] loc. cit.

which he had primarily in mind was the promise by India of the complete withdrawal of Indian forces from Kashmir, and the setting up of an impartial administration, before the plebiscite took place. Such an impartial administration might take the form of a coalition Government, or of a neutral Administrator put in the place of Sheikh Abdullah.

Pandit Nehru's answer to this was that he could not undertake to withdraw all the Indian troops from Kashmir. If he did, the State would be at the mercy of the armed men of Poonch, who would overrun it. Chaos would ensue, and troops would have to be sent back again to restore the situation. He did not retract his offer, however, to withdraw the bulk of the Indian troops, leaving behind only small detachments to ensure the maintenance of law and order.

Pandit Nehru also reiterated that he could not promise to supersede Sheikh Abdullah's administration before the plebiscite. The administration was a matter for the people of Kashmir, not the Government of India, to decide. . . .

So the talk went on, round and round, on the whole very friendly, but with occasional outbursts, such as when Pandit Nehru flared up and declared that the only solution was to clear Kashmir with the sword, and that he would 'throw up his Prime Ministership, and take a rifle himself, and lead the men of India against the invasion'.

Eventually, after trying every means I knew to find common ground between the two parties, I realised that the deadlock was complete, and that the only way out now was to bring in some third party in some capacity or other. For this purpose, I suggested that the United Nations Organisation should be called upon.[1]

Lord Mountbatten now bent his efforts to getting the idea of reference to the United Nations accepted. Pandit Nehru was at first adamantly opposed. Under what article of the Charter, he asked, could any reference to the United Nations be made? How did Pakistan come into the picture at all? He insisted that the first step was to drive out the raiders. However, he gradually came round, and on 20th December the Indian Cabinet finally decided that India should appeal to the United Nations, accusing Pakistan

[1] loc. cit.

of helping the raiders. Pandit Nehru still refused to consider a joint application of any sort. When Mr. Liaqat Ali Khan came to Delhi the next day and was informed of India's intention, he said that this accusatory reference was far from what he had hoped for; however, if Pandit Nehru was sincere in his declared intention to proceed with a plebiscite under the United Nations when the time came, he supposed he would have to accept it, since the earlier the U.N. was brought in the better it would be. India's application to the Security Council was despatched on 1st January 1948.

Meanwhile there had been a still more dire threat of war between the two Dominions. On the eve of Christmas the military news from the Kashmiri front was grave. The garrison of Jhangar had been attacked with heavy casualties, and a relief column had to be withdrawn. The garrison at Uri, the furthest point commanded by India on the road to the north-west from Srinagar, appeared to be in danger. Lord Mountbatten concluded that if a withdrawal from Uri was enforced, thus exposing Srinagar, there was every possibility of his Government's deciding to march into West Punjab. The Governor-General therefore spent Christmas Day composing a long letter to his Prime Minister. It ran to some 2,000 words. Lord Mountbatten repeatedly emphasised that his policy, as the records showed, had always been governed by one theme—the need to stop the fighting. Having that single paramount purpose, and being aware of the grave military difficulties, as well as the moral and political objections, involved in operations intended to impose India's will on a hostile population, he expressed the strongest disagreement with the action which he now understood was contemplated in the Poonch and Mirpur areas.

When first I suggested bringing U.N.O. into this dispute, it was in order to achieve the object I have quoted above—*to stop the fighting* and to stop it *as soon as possible*. What has happened since then has only served to reinforce my views, and to increase the urgency.

I do not know in what form you are drafting the actual reference to U.N.O. But, from these Cabinet Minutes, I have gathered the impression that at present the main object seems to be to argue the case in New York.

Surely the main object should rather be to bring U.N.O. here at the earliest possible moment—to get a team nominated, to come out and deal with the business and help to stop the fighting, within a matter of days? Can we do nothing to hasten this object?

Pandit Nehru replied next day at even greater length. He claimed that his own policy had also been consistent.

From the very first date that we discussed the Kashmir issue I have laid stress on the fact that we must drive out the raiders and establish peace and order in Kashmir State. It was only then that the question of a plebiscite arose. . . . The position of inhabitants of Poonch who might have joined the raiders was different. . . . There is no desire to coerce a large section of inhabitants against their will and by force of arms. At the same time if any people carry on a war against a State even when it is on a popular basis, they have to be opposed.

While we ardently desire peace and the end of fighting, we must not be unrealistic. Our desire does not lead to peace unless something is done to that end. We have not started the fighting. We have come into the picture to oppose a well-planned invasion and I do not see how we can submit to this kind of aggression. . . .

. . . The present situation is that the Frontier Province and a considerable part of West Punjab have been turned into military training grounds where vast numbers of tribesmen, ex-service men and others are being armed and trained and then sent on to invade Kashmir. The resources of Pakistan are being employed to this end. . . . The only inference to draw from this is that the invasion of Kashmir is not an accidental affair resulting from the fanaticism or exuberance of the tribesmen, but a well-organised business with the backing of the State. . . .

The present objective is Kashmir. The next declared objective is Patiala, East Punjab and Delhi. On to Delhi is the cry all over West Punjab. . . .

From the strictly legal and constitutional point of view it is our right and duty to resist this invasion with all our forces. From the point of view of international law we can in self-defence take any military measures to resist it, including the sending of our armies across Pakistan territory to attack their bases near the Kashmir border. We have refrained from doing this because of our desire to avoid complications leading to open war. In our avoidance of this we have increased our own peril and not brought peace any nearer. . . .

. . . I have made it clear that we attach the utmost importance to Kashmir and on no account are we going to submit to an armed invasion, whatever the consequences. . . . I have said that if necessary we shall employ all the resources of India to combat this horrible method of coercing a people. Even if the whole of Kashmir State was occupied by the enemy we would fight on and would not surrender. It is only the declared will of the people of the State, ascertained under peaceful conditions of law and order, that we will accept. . . .

We shall proceed with this U.N.O. matter. But meanwhile the situation is becoming a dangerous one. Vast numbers of the enemy are entering Kashmir at many points. . . . We have taken enough risks already, we dare not take any more. . . .

My conclusion is that we should immediately proceed along two parallel lines of action:

1 Reference to U.N.O. . . .

2 Complete military preparations to meet any possible contingency that might arise. If grave danger threatens us in Kashmir or elsewhere on the West Punjab frontier then we must not hesitate to march through Pakistan territory towards the bases.

'If there had been any doubt, previously,' wrote Lord Mountbatten, 'of the danger of the situation, and how near India was to war with Pakistan, it was dispelled by this letter.' He immediately sent a message to Mr. Attlee, through the British High Commissioner, urging him to offer to fly out immediately and meet the two Prime Ministers. Mr. Attlee declined because he felt that there was no specific role he could play, beyond general conciliation. Pandit Nehru also telegraphed the British Prime Minister, at the Governor-General's suggestion, and received a prompt reply urging caution. As soon as this message was received, the Government of India forwarded their reference to the United Nations.

This was made under Article 35 of the Charter, which enables any member to bring to the attention of the Security Council a situation whose continuance is likely to endanger the maintenance of international peace. It briefly described the situation in Kashmir and the assistance received by the invaders fron Pakistan, and continued:

> ... The Government of India request the Security Council to call upon Pakistan to put an end immediately to the giving of such assistance, which is an act of aggression against India. If Pakistan does not do so, the Government of India may be compelled, in self-defence, to enter Pakistan territory, in order to take military action against the invaders. The matter is therefore one of extreme urgency and calls for immediate action by the Security Council for avoiding a breach of international peace.

It then proceeded to elaborate on the whole claim—evidence, conclusions and demands. While emphasising a desire for peace and friendship with Pakistan, it specifically reserved the right to take at any time such military action as the Government of India might think necessary in self-defence.

Fortunately, the threat to Uri faded, and with it the immediate danger of open war between India and Pakistan. The plans which the Chiefs of Staff had been instructed to prepare for the invasion of West Punjab were never made, and Lord Mountbatten persuaded Pandit Nehru not to press for them.

The Indian Government, however, was grievously disappointed by the reception of its appeal to the Security Council, which it had naively hoped would at once take India's part, without reserve, as the victim of aggression. Its representative proved no match, as contending Counsel, for Pakistan's Sir Muhammad Zafrullah Khan.[1] When the Security Council started showing signs of favouring Pakistan's proposal for a neutral administration in Kashmir while a plebiscite was prepared, Pandit Nehru told Lord Mountbatten that he now bitterly regretted going to the United Nations.

> Pandit Nehru said that he was shocked to find that power politics and not ethics were ruling the United Nations Organisation and was convinced that the United Nations Organisation was being completely run by the Americans, and that Senator Warren Austin, the American representative, had made no bones of his

---

[1] Later President of the United Nations General Assembly and a member of the International Court of Justice at The Hague.

sympathy for the Pakistan case. He considered that the United Nations Organisation did not intend to deal with the issue on its merits but merely to help Pakistan against India. He said that he thought that Mr. Noel Baker (the Secretary of State for Commonwealth Relations and the leader of the United Kingdom Delegation) had been nearly as hostile to India as Senator Warren Austin, except that he had been more polite and had wrapped up his phrases in more careful language. . . .

During the first half of February, I made repeated efforts to persuade Pandit Nehru and Sardar Patel that it was not true that power politics and not ethics were ruling the attitude of most of the members of the Security Council to the Kashmir issue. But in this I was not successful. The belief spread during the first part of February, being founded on the assumption that the United Kingdom wished to appease the cause of Muslim solidarity in the Middle East, and that the United States wished to rehabilitate their position vis-à-vis the Arabs after their advocacy of partition in Palestine.

This interpretation of events at the United Nations Organisation became coupled with feelings of bitterness towards His Majesty's Government in the United Kingdom and deep suspicion of the United Kingdom Delegation in New York. Mr. Noel Baker became particularly 'suspect'. . . .

Simultaneously an impression was starting to gain ground in India that the only two members of the Security Council who were likely to look with sympathy on her case were U.S.S.R. and Ukraine. . . .[1]

Lord Mountbatten now became involved in a double diplomatic effort, which he pursued over many weeks with his usual energy and skill; on the one hand to temper the British Government's attitude, at least so as to give more visible recognition of the force of India's case, and to reconcile their explanation, from London, of their attitude and what Mr. Noel Baker was saying at Lake Success; and on the other hand to persuade Pandit Nehru that British policy was not anti-Indian and that there was some reason and not mere prejudice or power politics behind the Security Council's debates. He was only moderately successful on either score, though he did dissuade his Prime Minister from withdraw-

[1] *Report of the Governor-General.*

ing the Indian delegation from Lake Success and from rejecting outright the Security Council's resolution.

This was passed on 3rd April 1948. It set up a Commission of five, which was to proceed at once to the Indian sub-continent and place its good offices and mediation at the disposal of the Governments of India and Pakistan, with the objects of restoring peace and order and facilitating the holding of a plebiscite by the two Governments in co-operation with one another and the Commission. The resolution went on to recommend to the two Governments certain measures 'to bring about a cessation of the fighting and to create the proper conditions for a free and impartial plebiscite'. The resolution was not accepted by either India or Pakistan. The Government of India declined to implement those recommended measures, to which their delegation had objected, but they were prepared to confer with the Commission. When Lord Mountbatten left Delhi on June 21 1948, the Commission had not yet arrived. 'Had they been able to come in my time,' he wrote, 'I could have done all in my power to smooth their task.'

One more effort by Lord Mountbatten to settle the Kashmir problem directly between the two Governments—and the most fascinating of all his attempts—had meanwhile failed.

Despite the fact that previous meetings between the Prime Ministers of India and Pakistan had not resulted in an agreement on the Kashmir problem being reached, I hoped, at the end of May, that a solution would be found at such a meeting during my last month in office.

These hopes were based on the facts that an agreement between India and Hyderabad seemed about to materialise; that the time which had elapsed since Kashmir became a bone of contention between the two Dominions had resulted in a cooling of tempers and a desire, particularly on the part of the Government of India, for a settlement out of court; and that Mr. Liaqat Ali Khan was due to come to Delhi for a meeting with Pandit Nehru. . . .

The solution of the Kashmir problem which I would have backed, had Mr. Liaqat Ali Khan come, would have been based on the partition of the State. At my request Mr. Gopalaswami Ayyangar and Mr. V. P. Menon had worked out a compromise which they said the Indian Cabinet would accept if Mr. Liaqat Ali Khan put it up. It was my intention to have suggested to Mr. Liaqat Ali Khan that he should put this forward as a proposal. I had never dared to have it raised before, because both sides had been clearly committed to an 'all or nothing' policy; and, once the partition proposal was put forward, and if it failed, it obviously could never be raised again.[1]

That two such powerful and committed exponents of India's case should have accepted a solution by partition in May 1948 is indeed an important historical fact. The partition maps were all marked up, and discussed between Pandit Nehru and the Chief of Army Staff.

But no agreement was reached between India and Hyderabad. Tempers rose again in India—though not to the extent which was to have been expected—on receipt of the news that three Pakistan Army battalions had been sent into Kashmir. And Mr. Liaqat Ali Khan, because he fell ill, did not come to Delhi.[2]

Evidence had been accumulating, and was accepted by the (British) Chiefs of Staff[3] in India, that troops of three regular Frontier Force battalions had been operating against the Indian Army in Kashmir. Pandit Nehru sent a telegram to Mr. Liaqat Ali Khan to this effect on 10th June. The Pakistan Prime Minister's reply, a week later, did not deny the charge. He wrote: 'There exists now a state dangerous to the security of Pakistan. . . . As

[1] *Report of the Governor-General.*
[2] loc. cit.
[3] The Officers commanding the three Armed Services of independent India had originally been called Commanders-in-Chief, but this title seemed to Indians too reminiscent of the British raj, when the Commander-in-Chief, India—the Jangi Lat Sahib—had been second only to the Viceroy. On Lord Mountbatten's suggestion the Service heads became Chief of the Army (or General) Staff, Naval Staff and Air Staff respectively. At first these were all British officers (General Lockhart, Admiral Hall and Air Marshal Elmhirst). Because of the disparity in age and seniority of the Indian officers who would succeed in due course, Lord Mountbatten recommended that there should be no Chief of the Defence Staff as inter-Service Chairman for at least a dozen years; but, when the time came, the obvious choice for India's first Chief of Defence Staff, General Thimayya, was *persona non grata* to the then Defence Minister, Mr. Krishna Menon, and no appointment was made.

the Indian Army approaches the North-West Frontier, the tribesmen feel directly threatened.' However this explanation might be
interpreted—and it obviously implied that the further the Indian
Army advanced and the more the raiders retreated, as they had
now been doing for some weeks, the more necessary Pakistan
found it to intervene with armed force—the fact clearly was that on
the eve of the United Nations Commission's arrival, and at the
moment of Lord Mountbatten's departure, India and Pakistan
were on the brink of undeclared war in Kashmir. One extraordinary aspect of the situation was that the armies of both nations
were commanded by British officers (Generals Bucher and Gracey)
who were in direct personal touch and had come close to arranging
a qualified *de facto* truce at the end of March. Fighting actually
stopped for several days: the truce was called off when Pandit
Nehru refused to treat with the head of the Azad Kashmir (rebel)
Government, as Mr. Liaqat Ali Khan had wished him to do.

Lord Mountbatten's personal part in the Kashmir story thus
falls into three chapters. First, his vigorous support—without
which decisive action would not have been taken in time—of his
Government in accepting accession with a plebiscite and sending
troops into the State. Secondly, his long-continued efforts to bring
the two Governments together and to stop the fighting, while he
persistently checked his Government from rash courses which
could have enlarged the dangers of open war; in these he steadfastly refused to adopt the attitudes of injured pride, affronted
legality and consequent thirst for a military solution which his
Government presented. Thirdly, his pressure on them to resort to
the United Nations and to accept that neither the Security Council
nor the British Government was evilly anti-Indian because it saw
some good in Pakistan's case. In all this, after the first move had
been made, he deserved the gratitude no less of Pakistan than of
India. But his position as Governor-General of India identified
him too much in Pakistani eyes with Indian policy for his true role
to be discerned.

There is in some ways a strange likeness between Kashmir and
Vietnam, with India playing in one place the role of the United
States in the other. The differences, of course, are obvious.
Kashmir is on India's most vulnerable frontier, Vietnam is an
ocean's breadth from America. The Kashmiris are racially
Indians, in the sense in which that term was used before the

division into India and Pakistan. No global ideology, whether of communism or of anti-colonialism, is involved in the Kashmir conflict. The status India claimed was that of sovereign, not that of ally. And there are other manifest contrasts. Nevertheless, certain parallels are remarkable: the righteous and lawful response to an appeal for help; the pressure for escalation, as the initial military objectives are not securely achieved; the constant harassing of rear areas and occupied territory by guerillas, both local and invading; the state of actual though undeclared war, with a third party also intervening in what it considers a just and democratic cause; the deadlock and stagnation and the drain not only of life and resources but also of international reputation and political self-confidence; the intense commitment of a national public to a patriotic purpose; the disillusionment with a more sceptical world opinion; the appeal to a domino theory—'if we give way here, we shall be next defeated there, and there, so we must stand to the last'; the equal intransigence on the other side; the ever more meaningless promise of 'free elections' or a plebiscite when only the incursor withdraws; the impotence of outside powers and international organs. Historians may compare the two episodes and give thanks that in fact India was not a United States nor Pakistan a China.

26

The recalcitrance of Hyderabad

The negotiations with Hyderabad between August 1947 and June 1948, when Lord Mountbatten left India, were protracted and tortuous. Lord Mountbatten's own account of them, in his final despatch to the King as Governor-General, runs to over 27,000 words. Mr. V. P. Menon's to about the same length. They had their moments of drama, even of humour, but for the most part they were wearisome, repetitive and frustrating, and they ended in failure. Repeatedly, when they seemed on the point of success, the Nizam or his emissaries raised fresh issues, or went back on points already agreed, and the process of persuasion had to begin again in an embittered and recriminatory atmosphere. Mr. Menon, pausing in his story at the moment when Lord Mountbatten (of whom he said 'the Nizam could not have had a better friend') left India, explained the failure thus:

> It was obvious to anyone conversant with current Hyderabad politics that the Laik Ali Cabinet,[1] under the control of the Razakars,[2] would agree neither to accession or to responsible government. The minority community, which was holding a virtual monopoly of all offices under the State Government, could not view with equanimity the grant of responsible government, for that would spell out the end of their privileged position. The Nizam and his advisers were possessed by the notion that India was unable to take any action against Hyderabad because her hands were full with Kashmir and other problems.[3]

[1] Mir Laik Ali had been appointed President of the Nizam's Executive Council, or Prime Minister, early in November 1947.
[2] The extreme Muslim organisation in Hyderabad. Every volunteer for the Razakars, the militant branch of the Ittehad-ul-Muslimeen, had to take an oath which included the words: 'In the name of Allah, I hereby promise that I will fight to the last to maintain the supremacy of the Muslim power in the Deccan.'
[3] *The Integration of the Indian States*, p. 369.

But it did not seem so obvious at the time. Otherwise why should Lord Mountbatten, advising and advised by the Indian Government, have spent such enormous efforts, over the whole term of his Governor-Generalship of the new India, to achieve a peaceful settlement on the basis of something like accession and of responsible government, and have repeatedly believed himself to be on the brink of success? Why should Sir Walter Monckton,[1] the Nizam's Constitutional Adviser, time and again have thrown up his work at the English Bar in order to fly out and attempt to reach a negotiated settlement.

The stakes, of course, were high, and worth a great length of candle. Hyderabad had a population of 16,000,000 and an area of over 82,000 square miles, and it lay squarely in the heartland of India. If its independence seemed vital to its Ruler, to India it seemed equally vital that the State should cast in its lot with the Dominion that surrounded it on all sides. To Lord Mountbatten it seemed vital that this conflict be settled peacefully, lest central India be set alight with communal warfare. He himself, in his concluding despatch to the King as Governor-General, offered the following reflections on the negotiations:

> . . . Possibly the main reason for their failure was that the principals on either side (i.e. the Nizam and Pandit Nehru) were never able to get together. If the Nizam could have come to Delhi and if such a meeting could have taken place, perhaps with the addition of myself in the role of a mediator, I think that an agreement could have been reached. It is equally indubitable that an agreement must have been reached if the Hyderabad Delegation had had more negotiating power and more negotiating ability. To be always going back to obtain final approval, and then always returning and raising some new issue, was very exasperating for the other side.[2]

Whether or not Lord Mountbatten was right in thinking that a direct confrontation of principals could have settled the matter, the negotiations had another weakness, which concerned himself.

When, alone among the States, Hyderabad had been allowed

[1] Later Viscount Monckton of Brenchley. In order to assert his detachment, Sir Walter refused to accept any fees from the Nizam for the protracted and personally costly services he rendered in 1947–8.
[2] *Report of the Governor-General.*

three months' grace after 15th August for decision on accession for three subjects only, he had been explicitly authorised by the Indian Government, at his own suggestion, to carry on the parleys with the State. (The concession of time stuck in the gullets of Indian Ministers, and of some Princes, because all the States had been given to understand that if they did not sign by the deadline they might get worse terms thereafter.) As a negotiator he had great personal advantages, but they had their countervailing defects. While the Nizam's emissaries never had plenipotentiary powers, nor had he. He had constantly to persuade his Ministers, especially Sardar Patel, with almost as much trouble as he expended on the Nizam and his men, to agree to any concession or variation of previous policy. Thus he was at once negotiator and mediator. It seems plain that the Nizam was bemused by this. His correspondence with the Governor-General is bespattered with references to Lord Mountbatten's connection with the Royal Family. A Prince himself, in the autocratic tradition, he imagined himself dealing with a Prince, *capax imperii*. He distrusted intensely the Hindu politicians of India. From this point of view the confrontation that was much more likely to be fruitful was one between the Nizam and Lord Mountbatten. It never took place. The Nizam would not come to Delhi, seeing himself as a suppliant before the Indian politicians, a role which he understandably scorned. He more than once pressed Lord Mountbatten to come to Hyderabad, but the Governor-General never accepted. After such an invitation on 9th May 1948 he wrote to the King:

> I did not make up my mind immediately whether or not to do this. Whilst on the one hand I was determined to leave no stone unturned towards finding a solution of the Hyderabad problem before I left, I felt that I would be in such a comparatively weak position, if my talks with the Nizam took place in Hyderabad rather than in Delhi, that it might not be worth my going. For in Delhi I would be able, at each stage of the negotiations, to consult my Government and take each further step; in Hyderabad I would be compelled to keep exactly to whatever brief I was given by my Government before departure.[1]

This was precisely Lord Mountbatten's criticism of the Hyderabad delegations who came to Delhi, but in reverse.

[1] *Governor-General's Personal Report* No. 11, 20th May 1948.

The story of the negotiations divided into three phases. The
first ended with the signature of a Standstill Agreement on 29th
November 1947: since the time-limit of two months, expiring in
mid-October, had already been overrun, and the Nizam had still
not been brought to the point of acceding, the acceptance of a
mere standstill at that stage represented a considerable concession
by the Indian Government, especially as their general policy had
been 'no accession, no standstill'. The end of the second phase,
which was characterised by increasingly violent activities and fiery
speeches by the Ittehad, was marked by an attack by a Muslim
mob, with armed Razakars and a Hyderabad policeman standing
by, on Hindus travelling by the mail train from Madras to Bombay
at Gangapur station in Hyderabad State, when at least two people
were killed and eleven seriously wounded: this was on 22nd May
1948. During this phase, which was embittered by charges and
counter-charges of breaches of the Standstill Agreement, the negotiations concentrated on an alternative demand made by the
Government of India to the Nizam: either accede, or introduce
responsible government. The third phase embraced Lord Mountbatten's final effort to secure a settlement. This centred round
draft heads of agreement drawn up by the indefatigable V. P.
Menon, who played the key role on the Indian side, sometimes as
direct negotiator, sometimes as Lord Mountbatten's right-hand
man, always as the one intermediary who could reliably represent and tirelessly persuade Sardar Patel, the Minister of
States, a much sterner and less conciliatory leader than Pandit
Nehru.

Several times during the three periods agreement was frustrated
by last-minute reactions in Hyderabad just when it seemed to be
'in the bag'. On 22nd October the Hyderabad Delegation which
had been negotiating the Standstill Agreement, and which included
the Nawab of Chhatari (then Hyderabad's Prime Minister), Sir
Walter Monckton and Sir Sultan Ahmed, returned to their headquarters with an agreed pair of documents—the agreement itself
and a collateral letter to be signed by the Nizam. His Exalted
Highness decided to refer the drafts to his Executive Council,
directing that they should sit day after day for three days to give
him their final advice; and this they did. On 25th October they
voted 6 to 3 in favour. Lord Mountbatten described the subsequent events in his despatch to H.M. the King:

Late in the evening of 25th October His Exalted Highness formally approved the decision of the Executive Council, and gave an undertaking to the members of the original Delegation that he would sign the Standstill Agreement unamended, and the collateral letter with a few minor amendments.

During the 26th, the Nizam worked on the collateral letter, and on a separate secret letter undertaking not to accede to Pakistan. This secret letter also contained two further points: first that if India decided to secede from the Commonwealth he would be at liberty to reconsider his position; and secondly that, if there was war between India and Pakistan, the Nizam would remain neutral. The two letters were typed for the Nizam's signature that evening. When the members of the Delegation went to see His Exalted Highness to collect the documents, he postponed his signature until the following morning before they were due to fly back to Delhi. No reason can be adduced for His Exalted Highness delaying his signature, since the documents were ready and the Delegation was due to leave early in the morning. On the other hand there is no evidence that bad faith was intended.

At 3 a.m. on the morning of 27th October a crowd, estimated at about 20,000, collected round the houses which the Nawab of Chhatari, Sir Sultan Ahmed and Sir Walter Monckton occupied and which were all adjacent. No Hyderabad police were seen at any time. The Ittehad-ul-Muslimeen publicly claimed the credit for having organised this crowd in order to prevent by physical force the departure of the Delegation to Delhi. There were loudspeakers in the crowd calling upon them to remain orderly and not to create a disturbance beyond preventing the Delegation from leaving. At 5 a.m. the Nawab of Chhatari managed to get into touch with the Army authorities by telephone, and the three members of the Delegation and Lady Monckton were evacuated to the house of Brigadier Gilbert of the Hyderabad State Forces.

At 8 a.m. on Monday, 27th October, the Nizam sent a message to the Delegation to the effect that they should not leave for Delhi for a few days. . . .[1]

During these few days the Nizam, though fierce in his denuncia-

[1] *Report of the Governor-General.*

tion of the Ittehad-ul-Muslimeen and its leader, Qasim Rasvi, to
the members of the Delegation, in effect gave way to him. He
summoned Qasim Rasvi, who in the presence of the Delegation
begged to be allowed to reopen negotiations, declaring that he
could make the Government of India revert to an original Hyderabad draft which they had rejected, because, he said, 'the hands of
the Indian Union are so fully occupied with their troubles elsewhere that they will be in no position to do anything to us or
refuse our demands'. (Indian troops had been flown into Kashmir
on 26th October.) The Nizam appointed a new delegation headed
by Nawab Moin Nawaz Jung, an Ittehad sympathiser, let his two
constitutional advisers depart, accepted the Nawab of Chhatari's
resignation, and appointed Mir Laik Ali in his place. The Hyderabad Government was thereafter in the power of the fanatical
Qasim Rasvi.

The new delegation failed in fact to secure any but trivial
amendments. Nevertheless, a month later the Standstill Agreement
and the collateral letter were duly signed, virtually unaltered. The
Standstill Agreement, after affirming in the preamble that it was
the aim and policy of the Indian Dominion and the Nizam to work
together in close association and amity, laid down that all agreements and administrative arrangements on matters of common
concern, including defence, external affairs and communications,
which had subsisted between the Crown and the Nizam before the
transfer of power, would continue with the Government of India.
The second article provided for an exchange of agents in Hyderabad and Delhi. By the third, the Government of India renounced
any paramountcy functions. The fourth provided for arbitration,
and the fifth fixed the period of the agreement at one year. The
Nizam's collateral letter raised a number of specific points which
Lord Mountbatten, in reply, promised would be sympathetically
considered by the Government of India. 'This means,' exclaimed
Pandit Nehru to V. P. Menon, 'we shall have peace for one year!'
Less than ten months later, following much disorder and violence
in the State, Indian forces invaded Hyderabad.

Article One of the Standstill Agreement fell far short of the
accession which India wanted, being much closer to the treaty of
association governing the three central subjects which the Hyder-
abadis had offered and Sardar Patel had flatly refused (though
whether the Nizam would have actually signed such a treaty in

September or October is an open question in the light of experience). Yet it gave the Indian Government most of the practical effect of accession, or would have done so but for the way in which Hyderabad flouted the spirit of the agreement, and indeed its letter, in all three respects: in foreign affairs by intrigues with Pakistan, to whom the State secretly arranged a loan of Rs. 20 crores (£15,000,000); in defence by building up a large semi-private army inspired by violent anti-Indian propaganda; and in communications by interfering with traffic at the borders and even (as in the Gangapur incident) through traffic by rail. There were counter-accusations, not without facts to substantiate them, of Indian breaches of the Agreement, especially in the way of an economic blockade, which if unofficial and unknown to the top Indian Ministers was real enough for Sir Walter Monckton to regard it as coercion preventing free negotiation.

The exchange of agents did not lead to smoother relations. The Agent-General for Hyderabad in Delhi, Nawab Zain Yar Jung, was indeed a rock of sense and reliability when the Hyderabadi negotiators seemed obtuse and perfidious; but Mr. K. M. Munshi, appointed as India's representative in Hyderabad, appeared to Lord Mountbatten to regard himself more as a partisan for India, and for the Hindu cause in the State, than as an agent of pacification and compromise. . . . This may have been less than fair: Mr. Munshi was an agent of the Government of India *ex parte,* not of the Governor-General as conciliator, and his ability to negotiate was limited by the cold-shouldering he received from the Nizam's Government. Mr. V. P. Menon had high praise for him. His instructions were to work for accession. He recalled a talk with Mahatma Gandhi at the time of his appointment.[1]

'I want you to promise me that you will exercise your utmost skill in order to bring about a settlement', he said.

I gave the promise, but asked him how long the negotiations should continue. 'Should they last interminably?' I asked.

He laughed. He guessed what was passing in my mind. 'Shall we say for three or four months?' 'And if they fail, what then?' 'There will be no alternative but to bring things to an end (*to pacchi puru karej chhutako chhe*),' was his cryptic reply.

[1] *The End of an Era,* by K. M. Munshi (Bharatiya Vidya Bhavan, Bombay, 1957).

This insistence that patience in peaceful negotiation was not inexhaustible recurs through the successive phases of Indian policy.

Sir Walter Monckton returned several times to the scene, despite the way in which he had been treated, and took a leading part in negotiations which continued almost unremittingly. He did not always share Lord Mountbatten's confidence in the *bona fides* of the Indian side, though he was more readily persuaded of it than they were of the good faith of the Nizam, of Mir Laik Ali, or of the egregious Qasim Rasvi, who among other inflammatory statements proclaimed in February 1948:

> I urge that negotiations should immediately be commenced for an agreement with Pakistan and that the present negotiations with the Indian Union should be discontinued forthwith.

> We must ask the [Hyderabad] Government to tear the Standstill Agreement into pieces at once and throw it into the waste-paper basket. The Government are trying to do so and I offer them a further opportunity. But so far as the Indian Union is concerned I cannot grant more than one month's time. This declaration of mine can be taken as a declaration of war.

On 28th March, less than a month after returning to England with the thought that further negotiations would be a waste of time, Sir Walter was in Hyderabad again, and on 6th April came to Delhi. What then happened can be recorded in Lord Mountbatten's words:

> Before his arrival he sent me a letter declining my invitation to stay at Government House, as he had invariably done in the past. As I was not due to return from a week-end in Simla until the following day, I sent my Conference Secretary, Lieutenant-Colonel Erskine Crum, round to see him.

> When first the results of this interview were reported to me I could not understand what had happened. Sir Walter Monckton had talked to Lieutenant-Colonel Erskine Crum about the imminence of a 'show-down'; about a date between 10th and 15th April as ' "D" day'; about a forthcoming 'bitter public controversy' in which he and I were apparently to be involved; about preparations for a publicity campaign in the United Kingdom having been made—he mentioned specifically Mr. Churchill and the whole of the Opposition Front Bench; and that the front

pages of two leading London newspapers would be available to help him; about the fact that he was receiving no pay for his present assignment 'because it might look awkward'; and about his intention to return to Hyderabad in two days' time and there await developments, ready to fight to the last—not with the sword, but with his voice and pen.

The outline of what Sir Walter Monckton had said was reported to me in Simla by telephone. On my instructions my staff made enquiries about the reported 'show-down' and ' "D" day'. . . . They were unable to obtain any information to substantiate what Sir Walter Monckton apparently feared was about to happen. General Bucher did, however, say that the Area Commander at Jubbulpore had given an unauthorised Press conference a fortnight previously and was reported to have made some wild statements in regard to Hyderabad. . . .

I saw Sir Walter Monckton myself immediately on my return to Delhi on 7th April. I asked him what his expected 'show-down' was. He replied by saying that for the last three months very few goods of any nature had been imported into Hyderabad, and that demurrage charges of Rs. 80 lakhs had already been incurred. He went on to say that he had reason to believe that India now intended formally to break off relations with Hyderabad, to denounce the Standstill Agreement and to declare an official economic blockade; as a result of this there would be a 'flare-up' in Hyderabad and an excuse for Indian troops to march in. Sir Walter Monckton added that Mr. Munshi, the Indian Agent-General in Hyderabad, had been openly hinting at the probability of such events and naming various dates for 'D' day.

I asked Sir Walter Monckton whether he intended to arraign me personally. He replied in the affirmative and quoted a letter which I had written to the Nizam on 12th August, 1947, saying that I was satisfied that the future Government of India had no intention of applying improper pressure against Hyderabad; this, Sir Walter Monckton suggested, directly implicated me.

This forthright declaration by Sir Walter Monckton cleared the air. After it, I had a comparatively easy task to persuade him that the Government of India had never even contemplated taking the various steps which he feared, and that they were not a party to the present stoppage in the flow of goods. I expressed my own regret that this stoppage should have occurred, and said that I was sure that Pandit Nehru shared this. I gave my opinion that the stoppage had come about in much the same way as the delay to the movement of military stores from India to Pakistan had been caused, by the unilateral action, from motives of misguided patriotism, by officers and officials on the lower levels, possibly encouraged by Provincial Ministers, and presumably Mr. Munshi (whose activities I mistrusted).

The assurances which I had given to Sir Walter Monckton were repeated to him by Pandit Nehru, first in an interview with him alone and later in my presence. . . . Our assurances apparently convinced Sir Walter Monckton; anyway I was later informed that he telegraphed to his Secretary, whom he had sent back to London, to call off the preparations for the publicity campaign which had been laid on. Sir Walter Monckton also stated, in an interview with Pandit Nehru and myself, that he fully appreciated and understood that circumstances might arise in which the Government of India might be forced to take action in the event of an extreme deterioration of the situation in Hyderabad, owing to the activities of the Ittehad. . . .

When Sir Walter Monckton left on 9th April, he said he had the intention of advising the Nizam to introduce responsible and representative Government at an early date. He said that he also meant to advise His Exalted Highness to arrest Qasim Razvi. . . .[1]

Neither of these courses, if they were urged by Sir Walter, was taken by the Nizam. Although negotiations went on, the atmosphere deteriorated further and the parties seemed to have reached deadlock.

The Gangapur incident, by chance, occurred the day before Mir Laik Ali arrived again in Delhi to reopen negotiations, apparently at the Nizam's instance following a visit by Mr. Alan Campbell-Johnson as Lord Mountbatten's personal envoy.

Mr. Campbell-Johnson [wrote the Governor-General] had gained the impression that the Nizam was searching furtively and anxiously for an honourable settlement, and was likely to take a final stand both on the accession and the representative Government issues by 1st June. He described the Nizam as a Ruler of the old school, with no liking for the limitations of a

[1] *Report of the Governor-General.*

Constitutional monarch: the tighter the corner, the more the Nizam would fall back on prerogatives. Mr. Campbell-Johnson said that he did not believe that the Nizam would accept an accession solution which made him anything other than the factual executive of law and custom inside his own State. He added that any appreciation of the Nizam's attitude would have to take into account the fact that the prospects of all the other Princes did not interest him at all, and that he regarded them merely as impotent noblemen.[1]

Mr. Campbell-Johnson also reported his significant impression that the Nizam was hoping to do better with Lord Mountbatten's successor-designate as Governor-General—Mr. C. R. Rajagopalachari, a South Indian—than he had done with Lord Mountbatten himself.

From this time on there were serious, though difficult and fragile, negotiations focussing, not on accession, but on an approach to responsible government in Hyderabad, which the Indian Ministers believed would not only break the power of the Ittehad and the Razakars but must lead before long to accession or its equivalent. Lord Mountbatten wrung a number of concessions from a reluctant Sardar Patel—who had had a serious heart attack on 5th March and conducted his work from a sick-bed in Mussoorie, mainly through Mr. V. P. Menon. The latter, at Mir Laik Ali's request after a strenuous meeting between them during the night of 25th–26th May, drew up draft Heads of Agreement. These, a brief, compact document, were to form a 'package deal' with a draft *firman*, or decree, to be issued simultaneously by the Nizam. In their final shape, dated 15th June, the Heads of Agreement provided that:

The Nizam's Government agreed to pass, at the request of the Government of India, legislation similar to that of India on any matter of defence, external affairs and communications (as specified in a schedule).

The Hyderabad army would be fixed at a strength of 20,000 plus a maximum of 8,000 irregulars. The Razakars would be progressively disbanded.

India would not station forces in the State except in a proclaimed general emergency.

Hyderabad's external relations with any foreign country, apart

[1] *Report of the Governor-General.*

from trade agencies, would be conducted by the Government of India.

In the *firman* the Nizam would declare:

I have now decided to consult the will of my people upon the question whether Hyderabad should accede to India. I shall therefore take a plebiscite on the basis of adult franchise . . . under the supervision of some impartial and independent body. I shall accept the result of the plebiscite whatever it may be.

But I am satisfied that more is required . . . in order to restore confidence and tranquillity. . . . It is my intention to introduce responsible government in Hyderabad and to that end to establish a Constituent Assembly early in 1949. In the meantime, there should be a reconstitution of my Government as a result of which a new Interim Government will be formed, in consultation with the leaders of the major political parties.

It was on this last clause that the Government of India had yielded most ground, having originally insisted that at least one half of the new Executive Council must be non-Muslim, but they had given way on other points too. No doubt they calculated that eventual responsible government and a plebiscite on accession would achieve all that they wanted, but their conciliatory attitude shows that at this stage at least they were content to wait patiently for the ripe plum to drop.[1]

[1] The following story shows that Lord Mountbatten's personality and persuasion also influenced them decisively. The Governor-General went up to Mussoorie to say goodbye to the convalescent Sardar Patel. He asked the States Minister if he would initial his consent to a draft of the Heads of Agreement incorporating some Hyderabadi amendments. 'Never!' exclaimed Patel. After a couple of hours came the time for a final parting. Patel spoke emotionally of the debt India owed to Lord Mountbatten: 'How can we prove to you our love and gratitude?' Lord Mountbatten replied: 'If you are sincere, sign this document.' 'Does agreement with Hyderabad mean so much to you?' 'Yes, because India's good name is at stake.' Patel initialled the draft and embraced Lord Mountbatten with tears.

Pandit Nehru and Mr. V. P. Menon had also gone to Mussoorie for that farewell luncheon. Sir Walter Monckton had begged Menon beforehand not to oppose the new draft (which he knew Menon thought went too far) if Sardar Patel agreed to it. Menon promised, with the condition that if the Minister asked for his opinion he must give it. Patel asked him no questions.

The Nizam, however, would not sign. He asked for further amendments, all of which had already been worked over and rejected. Lord Mountbatten sent him a long, firm but reasoned refusal.

I finished off this communication, which Sir Walter Monckton read out to the Nizam and which he himself had helped to draft, as follows: 'To sum up, I cannot bring myself to believe that it is Your Exalted Highness' intention to reject this settlement, which it has taken so many hours and so much effort to reach, for the four reasons which you have quoted as having been put forward by your Council. If this is your serious intention, I cannot help thinking that the world will regard your Council's reasons as a disingenuous subterfuge to avoid honestly admitting that they are unwilling to undertake the other steps for which the agreement provides, including, for instance, the disbandment of the Razakars.'

Sir Walter Monckton arrived at Hyderabad at 6.30 a.m. on 17th June. At 1.15 p.m. he sent a telephone message: 'Lost.'[1]

Although further eleventh-hour efforts were made by Lord Mountbatten and Sir Walter to persuade the Nizam, that was the end of the road.

The chief negotiators felt that they had done their best. Pandit Nehru, according to Lord Mountbatten, told the Indian Cabinet —all of whom bar the Prime Minister thought that too much had been conceded to Hyderabad—that he considered Sir Walter Monckton had done a fine job of work. Sir Walter, though a powerful advocate and a staunch fighter for the causes he espoused, was by nature a pacifier and conciliator, always able to see both sides of an issue. No one was better filled to engineer a balanced diplomatic settlement.

Sir Walter Monckton independently paid the highest tribute to Pandit Nehru, too, saying that he had been much impressed by the qualities which he had exhibited during the last fortnight of negotiations. . . . Indeed Sir Walter volunteered to me, in the presence of Lieutenant-Colonel Erskine Crum, his belief that Pandit Nehru, Mr. Menon and myself had done everything in our power to find a reasonable solution, and his intention always to bear this in mind and never to tolerate criticisms, in his presence, of the part which we three had played. . . .[2]

[1] *Report of the Governor-General.*   [2] loc. cit.

It is worth recapitulating the main concessions that the Government of India made to Hyderabad in respect of its set policy towards the States. First, it granted Hyderabad a substantial period of grace for accession after 15th August 1947. Secondly, it broke its determination not to sign a standstill agreement without accession. Thirdly, in the final offer which the Nizam rejected, it did not even demand accession, only certain limitations on the Nizam's sovereignty. To have gained so much yet to throw it all overboard seems like madness on his part. He was indeed more than a little eccentric. One of the richest men in the world, he dressed shabbily and did all his work in a dismal little office looking on a courtyard and furnished with a plain table and kitchen chairs. By what process of decision he put himself and his kingdom in pawn to Qasim Rasvi and the Razakars, who are the real villains of the story, can only be guessed. Despite his miserliness and his erratic switching from one set of advisers to another, he attracted widespread loyalty in his State and the affection of men like Sir Walter Monckton. If ever a man accomplished his own downfall, it was he.

On 21st June Lord Mountbatten left India and ceased to be Governor-General. For the invasion of Hyderabad six months later he had no responsibility. But the military operation had its origins in his time. His relationship to it can best be described in his own words in his despatch to the King:

> From 8th to 16th March I was away from Delhi visiting Burma, Orissa, West Bengal and Assam. During my absence a further development in regard to Hyderabad took place: I was not informed of this until some days after my return. In a private conversation with Lieutenant-General E. N. Goddard, who was General Officer Commanding, Southern Command, he asked me what I thought of Operation 'POLO'. This was the first indication which I received that a military plan had been prepared for the movement of Indian troops into Hyderabad (and I must say that the name chosen for it could hardly have been better calculated to add insult to injury to me personally).[1]
>
> I at once sent for General Bucher, the Commander-in-Chief, and asked him what Operation 'POLO' was all about; but he was almost as much in the dark as I was, as he had only just

[1] The choice of this name was quite inadvertent, and was not meant to refer to any person: it seems to have originated in the polo fame of Hyderabad (Golconda) in Indian Army circles.

returned from a visit to London. It was eventually, however, explained that all that had been intended in preparing this plan was to be ready in case a massacre of Hindus took place in Hyderabad in circumstances in which the Government of India could no longer forbear from intervention; and that somehow these instructions had come to be misinterpreted, particularly in Southern Command. General Bucher informed me that he was taking every opportunity to point out to the Ministers of the Government of India the military difficulties of invading Hyderabad, especially in view of the internal security problems which the consequent communal troubles all over South India seemed likely to produce.

At my next interview with Pandit Nehru I gave him my opinion of the probable national and international repercussions of Operation 'POLO' being implemented. Pandit Nehru expressed surprise that I did not know about the plan and that I should be so upset about it. However, he undertook to take personal control of the situation and later assured me that there was nothing to worry about. It was made clear that the only movement of troops which had in fact taken place was of one brigade to Bangalore; this had been at the suggestion of Lieutenant-General Sir Archibald Nye, the Governor of Madras and in connection with the general stability of the South of India. Pandit Nehru gave instructions that this brigade was to remain concentrated, and not to be spread about in an ostentatious fashion around the Hyderabad border. Preparations had been made for the movement of the Indian Armoured Division to the South of India from Ranchi[1]—but there was no sign as yet of this move being carried out.[2]

General Bucher, who had returned from London on 8th March, was 'in the dark' about any intention to invade Hyderabad as an early operation, but not about the existence of the precautionary POLO plan. This plan had been based on an 'appreciation' called for by Southern Command in February, and by the time of which Lord Mountbatten was writing was equally familiar to army commanders and to Indian Cabinet members and high officials. On 15th March, well before his talk with Lord Mountbatten, General Bucher had written to the Defence Secretary giving warning of the

[1] A slip for Jhansi, it seems.
[2] *Report of the Governor-General.*

depletion of forces in the North-West which the plan must entail, and observing that the launching of a comparatively large-scale and long-range offensive into Hyderabad, on the lines of Operation POLO, in addition to existing commitments, would constitute an over-burden, and would, to say the least, be strategically imprudent. General Bucher regarded it as 'contingency planning', yet another precaution, such as the Chiefs of Staff were habitually asked to take, to meet yet another threatening situation. He was astonished that Lord Mountbatten had not heard of it. The ambivalence of the latter's position is plain: on the one hand he was Chairman of the Defence Committee of the Cabinet and prime mover in negotiations with Hyderabad, while on the other he was constitutional Governor-General with no administrative responsibility, no department, no executive staff. It was therefore quite possible, even likely, for things to happen at Ministerial and top official or Service level of which he was unaware and about which it was nobody's explicit duty to inform him.

On 24th April, at a meeting of the All-India Congress Committee in Bombay, Hyderabad was discussed in open session.

... I was horrified to see, on opening the newspapers the following day, under the headlines 'War or Accession', that Pandit Nehru was reported to have said: 'There are two courses now open to Hyderabad—war or accession. War is a prolonged affair, and if we resort to it, many new problems may arise. We have therefore been trying to solve this problem by negotiation, but that does not mean we are afraid of following the path of war....'

I was at Ootacamund at the time of Pandit Nehru's statement, and wrote to him asking whether he had been correctly quoted, since I could not believe that he had been. I saw him immediately on my return to Delhi, and he said that he had been as horrified as me to see the report. He assured me that he had been completely mis-reported and had never mentioned 'war' or 'accession'; the error was due to the fact that he had been speaking in Hindustani and had not been properly understood by the Madrassi stenographer who was taking down the record....

I urged Pandit Nehru to take any steps he considered appropriate to repudiate the report. Subsequently, on 1st May, he held a Press Conference to clear this matter up. At this he said that 'India had never talked in terms of forcing by military methods any State to accession'; and declared that the two alternatives before Hyderabad, in his opinion, were either accession or 'some form of subsidiary association'.[1]

It is difficult to accept Pandit Nehru's explanation. So gross a distortion of what he had said on a matter of vital importance would plainly have called for an immediate sharp denial, without any prodding or delay. The Madrassi stenographer does not make a convincing scapegoat.

The next time the question of military operations arose, Lord Mountbatten's distress had been tempered.

. . . On 19th April, Pandit Nehru had sent a letter to Sardar Baldev Singh, the Defence Minister, which was in effect an order that certain troops, including the Indian Armoured Division, should be moved to concentration areas around Hyderabad. For some days, nobody passed these orders on. . . . Major-General Chaudhuri, the officiating Chief of Staff (who had also been designated Commander of the Armoured Division) so far from passing on the orders wrote a paper trying to prove the impracticability of taking any military action against Hyderabad until the autumn. However, two days after General Bucher returned from tour on 25th April, the necessary orders were issued—he felt that he could delay no longer—and the move started—though slowly and to the Poona area rather than direct to concentration areas.[2]

[1] loc. cit.
[2] There are some errors of detail in this account of events: (a) Only part of the Armoured Division was to be moved; (b) Major-General Chaudhuri was Chief of the General Staff under General Bucher, Chief of Army Staff; (c) the document considered by the Defence Committee was an appreciation by the Joint Planning Staff, with a covering memorandum by the three Chiefs of Staff (General Bucher, who asked for a meeting of the Defence Committee to consider it, Admiral Hall and Air Marshal Mukerjee) and with a memo. from General Chaudhuri to the Commander-in-Chief as an appendix. The Chiefs of Staff concluded that acceptance of an operational liability in Hyderabad was, for the present, a hazardous military gamble and a violation of many of the principles of war. Whether it was a violation of the principles of peace was not, of course, their responsibility, but Sardar Patel's view had been made quite clear. He argued that unless Hyderabad accepted the Government of India's demands intervention would have to take place eventually, and that the risks were less than those involved in a Muslim rebellion in south India, which he believed to be brewing.

I was asked to preside at a meeting of the Defence Committee on 13th May. At this Major-General Chaudhuri's paper, with the comments of the Chiefs of Staff added, formed the basis of the main item on the Agenda. The conclusion of this paper was that, unless a political decision made it inescapable, operations against Hyderabad should be postponed until after the monsoon, which was due to start between 7th and 21st June and end in September. The Chiefs of Staff, in their covering memorandum, drew particular attention to the political and economic effects which the adoption of a 'scorched earth' policy by Hyderabad would have. . . .

The point of view put forward by Pandit Nehru, and, more strongly, by Mr. Menon on behalf of Sardar Patel, was more or less as follows: 'The Chiefs of Staff tell us that, if we move into Hyderabad, we will be very short of troops for internal security purposes in the rest of the country, to deal with whatever repercussions may occur. But it is not, in the final analysis, the action of an Army which maintains law and order—look at the Punjab last August, when a concentration of 55,000 men was unable to stop the massacres. It is rather the prestige of the Government backed by potential armed action which keeps the people in order. We believe that at the moment the prestige of the Government is sufficiently high for us to take action against Hyderabad and to maintain internal law and order at the same time. If the Government delays action against Hyderabad much longer, then its prestige will fall to such an extent that no amount of troops will be sufficient for internal security.'

The meeting lasted for three hours. In the end the decision reached was that military preparations should go forward, but that ten days' notice would be required by the Army (after the units concerned had arrived in their new areas) to implement any aggressive operation. In the meanwhile these units were not to be concentrated at the planned starting-point, but were to be spread out round the border in order to try to stop the border incidents which were continually occurring.

I accepted this decision. Pandit Nehru said openly at the meeting, and subsequently assured me privately, that he would not allow any orders to be given for operations to start unless there really was an event, such as a wholesale massacre of Hindus, within the State, which would patently justify, in the eyes of the world, action by the Government of India. I was confident that nothing would happen at all events before I left, and that thereafter the monsoon would be an important factor.[1]

Whether or not it be considered that the events in Hyderabad 'patently justified, in the eyes of the world' military action against the State, it was decided upon on 9th September 1948 and began at dawn on the 13th. Although the occasion was the disorder in and on the borders of the State—holding up of trains, murder, arson and looting, from which missionaries and other foreigners were not exempt—and the invasion was preceded by an initial ultimatum demanding the return in force of Indian troops to Secunderabad to restore order, a demand which the Nizam indignantly rejected, another factor exciting the politicians and diluting the Service objections had been the news, recorded in early July, that a big gun-running operation under the command of British adventurers was being mounted by night into Hyderabad from aerodromes in Pakistan, though without the Pakistan Government's official cognisance. All was over within a week. The cost in casualties included some 800 killed, mostly members of the less disciplined and trained Hyderabad forces. They might have been much greater but for the Indian Army's good luck at the start, in capturing an officer who was on his way with orders to blow the bridges. The invasion, under the command of Major-General Chaudhuri, was still called Operation POLO.

[1] *Report of the Governor-General.*

27

The integration of the States

In July 1948 the Government of India issued a White Paper on Indian States. Folded at the back were two maps, the one showing the patchwork of principalities as they existed at the transfer of power, the other 'The progress of political reorganisation of States according to integration and merger schemes up to 31st May 1948'. It was an astonishing transmutation, into order out of chaos, to have been accomplished in less than ten months. Apart from the disputed Kashmir and the unacceded Hyderabad, a number of big States remained at that time separate units—the larger Rajput States in the north-west, Mayurbhanj,[1] Cooch Behar, the border States in the north-east; Mysore, Travancore and Cochin in the south, Bhopal in the Deccan, Baroda in the west and a few others. But by far the majority of the former separate States were classified on the second map as 'integrated into unions' (Patiala and East Punjab States in the north, Saurashtra—Kathiawar—in the west, Rajasthan, Matsya, Madhya Pradesh and Vindhya Pradesh in central India), or as 'merged into provinces' (mainly the small States of Orissa, Central Provinces and Bombay), or as 'integrated into a centrally-administered unit' (Punjab Hill States and Kutch).

The story of their transformation—which was later to go much further—though falling within the period of Lord Mountbatten's Governor-Generalship, need not be told in every detail here, partly because it has already been fully recorded by V. P. Menon[2] and more compactly in the White Paper, partly because the policy was worked out and administered by the States Department without detailed consultation with the Governor-General or even with the Indian Cabinet. (According to a second-hand account, Sardar Patel's report of the action he had taken towards the Orissa and Chattisgarh States, which was the first and decisive move, as well as the most questionable, was 'approved' at a Cabinet meeting

[1] Later merged with Orissa.
[2] *The Integration of the Indian States*, Longmans 1956.

after one minute's explanation and no comment, though it is true that Mr. Menon had been at pains to explain it beforehand to Pandit Nehru and Mr. Gandhi.) Nevertheless the general policy was applauded by Lord Mountbatten and indeed he claimed it as his own.

> . . . I had personally originated the idea on the basis of the mediatised princely families in Germany. Subsequently I found that a paper on the subject which had been prepared by Sir Francis Wylie, who had been Political Adviser before my arrival in India, also helped to formulate my views. . . .

> . . . Although it was I who had originated the idea, and though Sardar Patel was nominally in charge of the States Ministry, the credit for working out the details and dealing with the individual Rulers must go almost entirely to Mr. V. P. Menon, the Secretary of the States Ministry. Any suspicions which anyone might have had that he was putting excessive pressure on any Rulers to induce them to sign the various Instruments would have been amply dissipated if they could have heard the unanimous praise which the Rulers showered on Mr. V. P. Menon. . . .[1]

Although Lord Mountbatten may personally have originated the idea of merger, it was not in pursuit of general ideas but in the day-to-day task of dealing with political disorder that the practice of merger began. The Orissa and Chattisgarh (Central Provinces) States had long been a problem. They were mostly small—there were forty-one of them, of which only Mayurbhanj (which was left out of the first merger) and Bastar, with a population of over half a million, were of any size. They were not deep-rooted—their origins were obscure, they had not been recognised as States by the British Crown until 1863 in Orissa and 1888 in Chattisgarh, and their administration had often been taken over by the Political Department when there were minor heirs or for other reasons. Their people were mostly poor and ignorant, many being aborigines; but some of them overlay valuable mineral deposits and were adjacent to important economic areas. They were scattered haphazard in the territory of British Indian provinces, especially in Orissa. After the transfer of power all sorts of difficulties arose.

[1] *Report of the Governor-General.*

A movement for responsible government produced some ludicrous results in such small and unsophisticated units. Some of the States spontaneously formed an Eastern States Union for their common purposes, a structure which was inherently unviable, if only because its constituent States were physically separated, spoke different languages, and could hardly administer their own territories, let alone support a constitutional superstructure. In the State of Nilgiri, in particular, there was serious disorder involving violent struggle between aborigines and Hindu inhabitants. The States Ministry at Delhi decided to grasp the nettle.

Three options were open to them: to recognise and enlarge the voluntary Eastern States Union; to establish administrative co-operation between the States and the surrounding provinces; or to merge them with those provinces. After much discussion Sardar Patel firmly decided upon the last alternative. The first he quickly dismissed. The second he thought would only lead to constant friction, especially over the smaller States. The chosen policy had a history: in 1940 the Secretary of State for India (Lord Zetland) had envisaged that the Orissa States should ultimately become an integral part of Orissa province, and this was also the advice of Sir Hawthorne Lewis, one of V. P. Menon's predecessors as Reforms Commissioner and later Governor of Orissa. The decision was not taken without qualms. Mr. Menon recorded:

. . . I pointed out to Sardar that the proposed merger of the States was contrary to the assurances held out in his own statement of 5 July and in Lord Mountbatten's address to the Chamber of Princes on 25 July 1947. It was true that, at that time, we were anxious by the policy of accession on three subjects to preserve the integrity of the country, thus preventing the States from becoming so many 'Ulsters' in the body politic. Nevertheless, a guarantee once given could not be lightly set aside, unless it could be proved that there were overwhelming considerations which were demonstrably in the interests of the country. The fact of the matter was that we did not realise that the weakness in the States' structure was the smaller States. While admitting the force of my arguments, Sardar felt he could not be a party to an attempt to perpetuate something that was inherently incapable of survival. The ultimate test of fitness for the survival of any State was its capacity to secure the well-being of its subjects. He was quite sure that the Orissa States' rulers could not do this. Further, the compulsion of events had brought about altered circumstances and, by implementing their policy of merger, the Government of India would only be saving the rulers from the fury of their subjects newly awakened to a consciousness of their rights.[1]

Accordingly, Sardar Patel and Mr. Menon set out for Cuttack, the provincial capital, where the Orissa States Rulers had been summoned.

They began by tackling the smaller States, known as B and C States, presenting the Rulers with a draft agreement for merger, drawn up by the Law Ministry in Delhi, which later served as a model for other mergers. By this instrument, in substance, the Ruler gave up all his governing powers in return for a guaranteed, tax-free privy purse, scaled according to the revenues of his State, subject to a maximum of Rs. 10 lakhs (£75,000), together with his palaces and certain other property, his personal privileges and those of his immediate family.

The meeting with the B and C Rulers went on all through the morning of 14th December 1947. Sardar Patel told them that if they did not heed his advice they would be ousted by their discontented peoples, and when they came to Delhi for help he might no longer be in a position to give it. Though there was some discontent, especially with the amounts of the privy purses, that same evening all the Rulers who had been present signed the agreement. The A State Rulers were much harder nuts to crack. They debated with the Indian Government representatives all through the afternoon of that day, and then agreed to meet again at 10 p.m. It was evident at the interval that they were averse to signing. The late session was conducted by Mr. Menon in the absence of Sardar Patel, who was angry as well as disappointed. The Rulers were still obdurate and the meeting again adjourned. Menon's account continues:

It was now midnight and Sardar was leaving the next morning for Nagpur. If no agreement were reached with the rulers of the 'A' class States before he left, there was every likelihood that their attitude would stiffen. And failure with these rulers would affect disastrously our negotiations with the Chattigarh rulers whom we were to meet the next day. Indeed, all our plans would

[1] *The Integration of the Indian State*, p. 159.

go awry unless something was done to bring round these rulers.

I took the Rajah of Dhenkanal into my confidence. He was an important 'A' class ruler, but in view of the Prajamandal agitation for responsible government he could not maintain his position inside his State without the support of the Government of India. He readily agreed to the merger of his State when I promised him that, in that event, all his demands, such as were considered reasonable, would be conceded. I then requested him to go and inform the Maharajah of Patna and others of his decision to merge his State with Orissa, adding that if they did not follow his example the Government of India would be compelled, in the conditions prevailing in Orissa, to take over the administration of their States.

The Rajah of Dhenkanal must have conveyed the message, for the Maharajah of Patna came to see me in the very early hours of the morning. We had a frank talk. . . . I told the Maharajah that it would not be long before the agitation spread to his State. . . . If the rulers would not realise their responsibilities the Government of India could not forget theirs. . . . The Maharajah asked me whether the Government of India were really serious about taking over the administration of the States and whether I would put this down in writing. I told him that, in the circumstances explained by me, the Government of India would have no option but to do so and that I would certainly record as much in writing.

After this discussion, the Maharajah of Patna brought in the other rulers. We then began consideration of the agreement clause by clause.[1]

After further long discussion, and the grant of some concessions, the Rulers all signed. The copies to which they put their names, wrote Menon, 'were so full of corrections and amendments that they looked like galley proofs after correction by the proof reader. We had no time to get the agreement retyped.' The meeting had been in almost continuous session from ten at night to nine in the morning. After this, Mr. Menon gave the Maharajah of Patna his promised letter:

I am glad that you have signed the agreement. I mentioned to you the peculiar position which your State occupied among the

[1] Op. cit., pp. 166-7

Orissa States. The Government of India are most anxious to maintain law and order. We cannot allow your State to create problems for the Government of Orissa and if you had not signed the agreement, we would have been compelled to take over the administration of your State.

It is evident that Mr. Menon had no authority to write this letter or to threaten the Rulers as he had done during the night,[1] though Sardar Patel immediately approved his actions when he reported to his Minister at the railway station. Menon had been gravely apprehensive about the Sardar's decision to come to Cuttack, for he thought that, if he himself went alone and failed, the task could then be taken up at the higher level, whereas if Patel went and failed there could be no further recourse, and in his view final failure would be disastrous. In the early hours he had therefore been desperate. Lord Mountbatten, when he learnt of the merger, wrote to the Minister of State congratulating him on 'the extremely statesmanlike way in which he dealt with potential trouble'. He was quite unaware of the letter or of the strong-arm tactics that had been employed.

Patel and Menon travelled on to Nagpur, capital of the Central Provinces, where on 18th December the Chattisgarh Rulers likewise signed a merger agreement, after another long debate. They had been specially anxious about their financial compensation. One of them asked that the privy purse be granted in perpetuity. Sardar Patel assured him that the agreement embodied a guarantee by the Government of India and that the intention was to incorporate it in the new constitution.

Nervousness and anxiety about these developments were manifest at a conference of a score of Princes or their Dewans or other representatives which Lord Mountbatten called in Delhi on 7th

---

[1] He told the author, in a tape-recorded talk in 1964, that the message he had asked the Rajah of Dhenkanal to convey to the Maharajah of Patna, and repeated to the Maharajah himself when the latter came to his bungalow in the small hours, was that if the Rulers did not sign he was going to issue orders there and then that they must remain in Cuttack and that as soon as sufficient numbers of reserve police could be assembled the States Ministry was going to occupy their States. He confessed that this was high-handed and against his conscience, but he was convinced that it was necessary to anticipate disorders which would have compelled such occupation within a year. 'It was like giving medicine to a child who doesn't like it but whom you know it will do good.'

January, but the Governor-General comforted them. The mediatisation of German States, he said, in which his own ancestral
Grand Duchy of Hesse had been involved, had enabled minor
States to become viable by merging with bigger kingdoms or grand
duchies. He was personally very much in favour of the system of
mediatisation or merger. There was no intention of applying
the merger device to the larger States. Indeed they should welcome
it as applied to their smaller brethren because all States would
stand condemned by the example of the worst. Mr. Menon backed
this by recalling that Mayurbhanj, the largest of the Orissa States,
had been left out of the merger: their Highnesses might have been
less impressed had they been able to foresee that nine months
later, at its own insistent request, Mayurbhanj would also be
integrated into Orissa, its experiment with responsible government
having resulted only in the dispersal of its cash reserves.

After the Orissa and Chattisgarh mergers, the way was open for
rapid pursuit of the States Ministry's policy of integration. The
next construction, however, the Union of Kathiawar (later called
by its ancient name of Saurashtra), was of a very different order.
Here, as well as scores of minor States, which clearly had no independent future, were famous and proud principalities like
Bhavnagar, Nawanagar or Morvi, ruled by Maharajahs who were
statesmen and men of the world. There was no question of their
being namelessly dissolved into a province. The States Ministry
did indeed toy with the idea of administrative attachment or
merger, at least of the smaller states, with Bombay, but rejected it
in favour of a separate, constitutionally-governed Union of States,
though it kept at the back of its mind the ultimate objective of
creating an all-embracing Gujerati province,[1] a proposition from
which the Kathiawar Rulers visibly recoiled.

The whole process of putting the proposal for Union to the
States' Rulers, obtaining their consent in principle, then presenting, debating and amending the draft covenant by which they were
to give up their birthright as autocrats, fixing their privy purses
(which were on a higher scale than in the Eastern States or,
subsequently, anywhere else in India), and securing the signatures
of the major States' Rulers, occupied only five days of intensive

[1] This was achieved in May 1960, when Bombay was split into Maha-
rashtra and Gujerat, the latter including the former Saurashtra Union
and Kutch.

work at the Residency in Rajkot, from the morning of the 17th to the night of the 21st January 1948. It was entirely conducted by Mr. V. P. Menon, without prior consultation with the Prime Minister and largely on his own responsibility, for the pace was too hot for continuous contact with his Minister, Sardar Patel. It was a much greater feat than his all-night session with the Orissa Rulers. Here no bullying tactics would serve: sophisticated and confident Princes had to be persuaded by argument and the logic of events. The most telling fact was that one of their number, and the greatest, the Maharajah of Bhavnagar, had just conceded responsible government in his State. The others perceived that they would soon be obliged to follow his example, and that even if such a system were to prove viable for such comparatively small units their future would then be in the hands of their popular Assemblies and Ministers, who might demand merger in a form far less palatable and less careful of the Rulers' personal interests. Led by the Jam Saheb of Nawanagar, who eventually became Rajpramukh or Head of State of the Union, their Highnesses fell into line, and the Union of Kathiawar, exercising all the powers of its States, including the power to set up its own constituent assembly, came formally into being on 15th February 1948.

The Maharajah Jam Saheb, on that inaugural occasion, declared:

> The point that I wish to make on behalf of my Order in Kathiawar is this: it is not as if we were tired monarchs who were fanned to rest. It is not as if we have been bullied into submission. We have by our own free volition pooled our sovereignties and covenanted to create this new State so that the United State of Kathiawar and the unity of India may be more fully achieved and so that our people may have that form of government which is today most acceptable to them and which I hope and pray will prove beneficial to them.

One accomplished scheme of merger into provinces, one accomplished scheme of union of States—the pattern was now set. The Deccan States (except Kolhapur) were merged into Bombay, and two States into Madras, in February 1948, the Gujerat States into Bombay and three small States into East Punjab in March. The East Punjab Hill States were merged into a centrally-administered unit, Himachal Pradesh, in April, and Kutch likewise in June. The Unions of Matsya (Alwar, Bharatpur, Dholpur and Karauli) and of Rajasthan (Bikaner, Jodhpur, Jaipur and others in Rajputana) were formed in March, those of Vindhya Pradesh (Bundelkhand and Bagelkhand States) and Madhya Pradesh (Gwalior, Indore and Malwa) in April, that of Patiala and East Punjab States in May 1948. Five months, from the Orissa merger onwards, had revolutionised the map of India. This period, Mr. Menon's five days with the Kathiawar Rulers, and the two months within which all but a handful of States had signed Instruments of Accession to India, may be contrasted with the snail-like moves towards minor mergers under the aegis of the old Political Department or the two fruitless years of negotiation to bring the Princes into federation under the 1935 Act. Two radical differences lay behind that contrast: first, the revolutionary effect of democratic self-government around and in the States, and their deprivation of a maternal British paramountcy which protected them from the changing world; secondly, the adoption of a clear, inflexible policy, and the driving of it into effect under relentless pressure. Before the transfer of power, responsibility for such clear inflexible policy towards the States in India was shared between Lord Mountbatten and Sardar Patel: after the transfer, though he had the concurrence and encouragement of the Governor-General, it is Patel who stands to take the praise or blame.

As the Political Department had foreseen, in advising Lord Mountbatten against the policy of accession for three subjects only, it could not stop but inexorably rolled on. Each stage in the process had its own logic. Once the pattern had been set by the accessions and Unions, the Government of India found that the calibre both of Ministers and of civil servants in the States and Unions was often lamentably low. They therefore negotiated with the Rulers and Rajpramukhs a right of 'superintendence, direction and control' in the interest of bringing the whole country up to an acceptable administrative standard. Next they asked themselves what would happen if popular government in the States and Unions broke down; and they accordingly negotiated a virtual equivalent of the old Section 93 in relation to British Indian provinces, namely, the right of the Ruler or Rajpramukh in such circumstances to take over the government of the State or Union, acting in reponsibility to the States Ministry in Delhi. By these measures the Indian Government virtually re-created for itself the powers of paramountcy without its obligations.

28

The completion of partition

1 *The machinery of partition*

Two major pieces of apparatus were constructed to continue and complete the process of dividing the governmental fabric of the country after the transfer of power. On the civil side the Partition Council, at Ministerial level, remained in being, together with its official Steering Committee. Closely related to it was the Arbitral Tribunal, under the Chairmanship of the former Chief Justice of India, Sir Patrick Spens,[1] established to give final adjudication on disputed matters referred to it. On the military side a Joint Defence Council was set up to complete the division of the Armed Forces and their plant, equipment and stores; to control the general administration, discipline, pay, food, clothing and medical services of the Armed Forces for an interim period; and to control any forces overseas and any force operating under joint command in disturbed areas near the new frontiers (that is, in practice, the Punjab Boundary Force). The Joint Defence Council was thus partly an executive body, with the Supreme Commander (Field Marshal Auchinleck) as its executive agent, whereas the Partition Council was conciliatory only and without executive power.

Lord Mountbatten, though invited by the two new Governments to continue as Chairman of the Partition Council, declined to do so, because he felt that sooner or later he would in that capacity incur the dissatisfaction of one side or the other and lose his impartial status. The senior representative of the Dominion in which each meeting was held took the chair. In fact, so well did the civil substructure of partition work that no cases were finally submitted by the Council to the Arbitral Tribunal. The latter did, however, adjudicate a number of matters referred to it by the affected provinces; only in a small minority of cases was the independent chairman obliged to arbitrate. The realistic and

[1] Later Lord Spens.

balanced contributions of civil servants and judges, in the process of splitting the country, make a striking contrast with the fevered conflicts of politicians.

2 *Two civil disputes*

All this did not mean, however, either that there were no serious disputes on civil issues or that Lord Mountbatten was without influence in resolving them. Two examples will suffice to show how effective his intervention could be. In both cases he decisively used his power of persuasion upon the Government of India to abandon policies gravely injurious to Pakistan.

The first concerned the division of the cash assets of the pre-partition Government of India. These amounted to about Rs. 400 crores,[1] of which Rs. 20 crores had been allocated to Pakistan as a preliminary cash balance. The distribution of the rest was tied up with the sharing of the uncovered debt, the terms on which Pakistan would repay her share of this, the apportionment of India's sterling assets, and responsibility for pensions. On 26th November (a month after the outbreak of fighting in Kashmir) Lord Mountbatten took the opportunity of a successful Joint Defence Council meeting in Delhi to get the representatives of Pakistan and India, both Ministerial and official, to work together to settle all these matters and two others which were causing trouble, the division of surplus military stores and a settlement over ordnance factories which could not be physically divided. The strong persuasion that he used on both sides separately resulted in a comprehensive 'package deal' covering all the issues mentioned. Pakistan's share of the cash assets was fixed at Rs. 75 crores, of which, therefore, Rs. 55 crores remained to be paid.

In the middle of December, however, the Government of India decided not to implement the various financial agreements until there was a settlement on Kashmir. This policy, of which warning had been given, was particularly sponsored by Sardar Patel but was endorsed by Pandit Nehru and the whole Cabinet. When Mr. Liaqat Ali Khan was in Delhi for a Joint Defence Council meeting on 21st December, Lord Mountbatten tackled him alone before the two Prime Ministers met, and tried to calm him down. At their meeting Pandit Nehru said that his Government had no

[1] £300,000,000: a crore of rupees was worth £750,000.

intention of repudiating the financial agreements, but could not bring themselves to agree to release money to Pakistan while there was virtual war between the two Dominions. After the Joint Defence Council had met, Lord Mountbatten held back the Indian Ministers and sent for two others concerned, and tried his best to persuade them to lift the embargo on implementation of the financial pact. He was unable to move them an inch. While they acknowledged the pact to be binding, they argued that it had not been well received in India, and that public opinion would never stand for handing over money which might be used to prosecute a war against Indian troops in Kashmir. Lord Mountbatten had to break this news to Mr. Mohammed Ali, the Pakistan Secretary-General. Admitting that the original Rs. 20 crores was almost exhausted, Mr. Mohammed Ali said he was sure that all Pakistan government servants and officers would forgo their pay while their Government was raising a loan elsewhere, rather than 'submit to India's blackmail'. Mr. Liaqat Ali Khan, when he heard what had happened, was greatly upset. He refused, he said, to be put under financial pressure over Kashmir, nor would he be able to yield any point in the Kashmir discussions if his people could accuse him of having done it in exchange for money—which in any case was Pakistan's legal due. There the matter rested, unhappily, for a while, though the Reserve Bank of India, with the Government's approval, advanced a loan of Rs. 10 crores to Pakistan, enough to last two months.

On 12th January, the day before he started his fast,[1] Mr. Gandhi came to see Lord Mountbatten and asked what he thought about India's refusal to pay over the Rs. 55 crores. The Governor-General told him he viewed it as unstatesmanlike and unwise, and as the only conscious act taken, to his knowledge, by the Government of India which he regarded as dishonourable. Mr. Gandhi expressed regret that he had not earlier appreciated the significance of the affair, or he would have done something about it. After Lord Mountbatten had reviewed the whole story, the Mahatma said that he was convinced the only honourable course was for the Government of India to pay over the Rs. 55 crores forthwith, and that he would take the matter up with Pandit Nehru and Sardar Patel. He told two touching little personal stories to illustrate his recognition that afterthoughts, however prompt,

[1] See above, p. 420.

could not give absolution from a written promise. The next day
Lord Mountbatten saw Sardar Patel and to him also he used the
word 'dishonourable'. Patel protested. Clear notice had been given
to Pakistan, within two hours of the meeting at which the cash
agreement had been reached, that India intended to link implementation with a settlement in Kashmir. If the Government of
Pakistan had not accepted this caveat it would not have signed,
several days later, a letter withdrawing the various financial
matters from the Arbitral Tribunal. Lord Mountbatten withdrew
the word 'dishonourable', while doubling his emphasis on 'unstatesmanlike and unwise', and passed a message to this effect to
Mahatma Gandhi. The latter's approach to Pandit Nehru and
Sardar Patel proved irresistible during a fast in which his life was
in danger, and which he declined to break until they adopted the
'honourable' course towards the cash balances. On 16th December
the Government of India decided to pass orders releasing the
Rs. 55 crores to Pakistan. The gesture was ill-received by Indian
public opinion. Sardar Baldev Singh told Lord Mountbatten that
the Government had received a severe blow to its prestige, and that
only the absence of an organised Opposition had enabled it to
survive. It was widely believed that Mr. Gandhi's fast had been
the leverage of pressure on the Government; so this righting of
a palpable wrong may well have been a proximate cause of his
assassination by a rabid Hindu extremist.

The second incident concerned canal waters. The head-works
of certain canals which served the Lahore and Montgomery districts of West Punjab had been placed in India by the Boundary
Commission. Sir Cyril Radcliffe had suggested that they be jointly
operated, but the East Punjab Government had refused this.
However, an interim agreement had been concluded, to operate
until 31st March 1948. When it expired, the East Punjab Government shut off the water, arguing that Ministers from West Punjab
had failed to come to frame a new agreement, that the water should
be paid for, and that in any case they needed most of it themselves.
At a meeting of Ministerial representatives from India and
Pakistan on 3rd May Dr. Ambedkar, for India, insisted that no
water could be supplied until Pakistan accepted India's legal claim
that all the water belonged to East Punjab, who had the right to do
with it as they wished. The chief Pakistan representative, Mr.
Ghulam Mohammed, came to see Lord Mountbatten after the

meeting had broken down on this point. The Governor-General immediately telephoned Pandit Nehru, and expressed his disgust that miserable peasants and refugees were being made to suffer while such a matter was under negotiation. Pandit Nehru agreed and undertook to get the conference going again and break the deadlock. Mr. Ghulam Mohammed, who a few weeks later was to denounce Lord Mountbatten publicly as an enemy of Pakistan, expressed his gratitude in extravagant terms, declaring that this incident, after the affair of the Rs. 55 crores and other events, was absolute proof of Lord Mountbatten's friendship for his country. The Governor-General replied: 'You are wrong. I am not trying to befriend Pakistan. I am trying to create friendly conditions throughout the sub-continent.' The next day an interim settlement was amicably reached, the water was immediately released, and a large area of West Punjab was saved from famine.

3 The Joint Defence Council

The Joint Defence Council, of which Lord Mountbatten had accepted the Chairmanship, accomplished a vast deal of work on the practical details of dividing the Armed Forces and their material. In the latter respect the most controversial subject in the early months was the ordnance factories. In respect of personnel, inter-Dominion movement of troops was plagued by the communal disorders that were raging. So inflamed were the tribesmen on the frontier by tales of massacres of Muslims that the withdrawal of each battalion of Hindu or Sikh troops from the northwest had become an operation of war. In one such encounter, the casualties had included twenty soldiers and ninety-four tribesmen killed. Nevertheless, the interchange of units proceeded steadily.

As time went on, however, the work of the Joint Defence Council became snarled in the Indo-Pakistani conflicts over Junagadh and Kashmir, and in the mounting Indian feeling against the Supreme Commander, Field Marshal Auchinleck, and his headquarters, which Sardar Patel described to the Governor-General as 'throttling the initiative of Headquarters Indian Army, and acting as the advanced outpost of Pakistan'. Lord Mountbatten protested at this remark, expressing his conviction that the Supreme Commander's Headquarters were acting fairly and impartially, and that Field Marshal Auchinleck's own integrity was beyond doubt or dispute. Sardar Patel replied: 'They may think that they are acting impartially, but as they are all mentally pro-Pakistan they are in fact out to help Pakistan at every turn.' Sardar Patel himself was so mentally anti-Pakistan that he was hardly a good judge of impartiality. Lord Mountbatten had in fact heard reports of counter-charges by the Pakistan Government, who alleged that Headquarters Indian Army were 'sitting on top of the Supreme Commander and influencing his decisions'.

Field Marshal Auchinleck's position was bound up with that of the British officers who continued serving with the Indian and Pakistani forces and who were ultimately responsible to him except for operational command (bar the Punjab Boundary Force while it lasted). The original intention had been that the Supreme Commander's role would continue until 15th August 1948 when the British officers' one-year contracts with the Dominion Governments expired, but the date was advanced to April 1948, when the special powers of the Governors-General were due to lapse. Field Marshal Auchinleck himself offered to bring the date forward further, to the end of 1947, provided that three months' notice to terminate the existing contracts was given by 1st October and the British officers were offered new contracts with either Dominion. These notices were given and the terms of new contracts were drafted by each Dominion Government and negotiated with the British Government in London. A great many officers had meanwhile decided to leave because of the hostile political atmosphere that surrounded them, particularly in India.

When Sardar Patel, in a talk with the Governor-General in which he vehemently attacked the Indian Army—Indian officers as well as British—for its alleged inability to think and act as a national force instead of an instrument of imperial rule, insisted that any fresh contracts offered must include their willingness to fight against Pakistan, Lord Mountbatten contradicted him. Except, he said, for a few adventurers who would not mind severing their connection with the Commonwealth, officers could not be expected to sign such a contract. He warned Sardar Patel, as he had more than once warned the Joint Defence Council, that so long as India and Pakistan remained in the Commonwealth all British officers were bound to be withdrawn in the event of a war between them.

On 26th September Lord Mountbatten sent Field Marshal

Auchinleck a letter[1] which he described as probably the most difficult that he had ever had to write in his life.

As you know, I have always held the view that it was absolutely essential in the interests both of India and of England that you should remain at the military helm, not only until the transfer of power, but also until the reconstitution of the Armed Forces had been substantially completed. You have proved a tower of strength: and I do not know what I should have done without you. I have, as you know, always tried to fight your battles with the greatest vigour against all criticism, from whichever quarter it may have come.

I admit that I was anxious as to what your position would be after the transfer of power: but when the Joint Defence Council accepted my proposal to make you Supreme Commander in charge of a Supreme Headquarters, I hoped that we had succeeded in devising an arrangement which would satisfy the desire of both the new Dominions to have forces under their own operational control, with effect from August 15, and which, at the same time, would ensure central administrative control over all the forces in the sub-continent of India during the process of reconstitution. I had hoped, in particular, that your own position was safeguarded by the fact that you were not to have any operational control, and that, even in the administrative field, you would be carrying out the directions of the Joint Defence Council.

Alas, my hopes were very soon shaken. . . .

There is no doubt in my mind that Indian Ministers resent the fact that at the head of the Supreme Headquarters there should be a man of your very high rank and great personal prestige and reputation—so immeasurably superior in these respects to their own Commander-in-Chief. I should be a poor friend if I did not admit that this resentment, which was initially directed against your position, has inevitably turned against yourself. . . .

I have argued the case with the Indian leaders at great length. I have pointed out that you have no operational command over the Armed Forces of either Dominion, and that Lockhart, Elmhurst and Hall[2] are responsible solely to the Indian Cabinet.

[1] Reproduced *in extenso* in *Auchinleck* by John Connell, pp. 915–19.
[2] The three Chiefs of Staff.

I have explained that everything that you do in the administrative field is subject to the approval of the Joint Defence Council. I have emphasised that you are responsible to His Majesty's Government for all the British officers now serving in India, as well as for the British troops who are awaiting withdrawal. I have reminded them of your unparalleled services to India and to the Indian Army, and of the deep personal regard which they entertained for you in the past.

I am sorry to say that I have completely failed to convince them . . . and the point has now been reached when I can no longer prevent them from putting up an official proposal to the Joint Defence Council that the Supreme Headquarters should be abolished. . . .

The discussion of a proposal of this kind in the Joint Defence Council would be absolutely deplorable. . . .

But, above all, my dear Claude, I should simply hate to contemplate a discussion if your great name became the subject of bitter controversy, and in the course of which imputations might be made which, though palpably unjustified, could not but cast a slur on your reputation and prestige. This must be avoided at almost any cost and I can see only one way out of the dilemma. . .

. . . my suggestion is that you should yourself write a letter to me as Chairman of the Joint Defence Council proposing the winding up of Supreme Headquarters as soon as the major units have been transferred to their respective Dominions and its replacement by an organisation with a less high-sounding title and headed by much less high-ranking officers. . . .

Lord Mountbatten wrote that he had taken the opportunity of the presence of the Secretary of State (Lord Listowel) in India to discuss the matter with him. He concluded by telling the Field Marshal that at his instance Mr. Attlee was ready to recommend to His Majesty the award of a peerage to Sir Claude if he wished. In a postscript Lord Mountbatten added that Lord Ismay had asked to be released within the next month or two, 'for he too feels that as an "impartial" official he will soon be subject to similar criticism'.[1] Lord Ismay, a very old friend of the Field Marshal,

[1] Lord Mountbatten had released his senior British staff on 15th August, and carried on with a reduced personal and official staff, but had begged Lord Ismay to remain to help him particularly on defence matters and in

in a letter of the same date, added his own supporting advice. 'I feel,' he wrote, 'as strongly as I have ever felt anything in my life that you in a big way, and I in a much smaller way, are now in a completely impossible position, by reason of our lack of power.'

Field Marshal Auchinleck refused the peerage. But after unbosoming himself to the Prime Minister and Chiefs of Staff in London he accepted Lord Mountbatten's advice. In mid-October he put in a paper to the Joint Defence Council recommending the closing of his headquarters by 30th November. This proposal was vehemently opposed by Mr. Liaqat Ali Khan, who was under the false impression that the Supreme Commander could overrule the Indian Government on the transfer of military stores due to Pakistan, or at least that his orders were more likely to be obeyed than theirs. The matter was referred to the British Government, who reluctantly came to the conclusion that in the circumstances of which they had been made aware they had no option but to withdraw the officers and other ranks forming Supreme Commander's Headquarters, including the Supreme Commander himself. In consequence the Headquarters automatically ceased to exist on 30th November.

Field Marshal Auchinleck's last decisive act in India was to warn Mr. Jinnah of the consequences—including immediate withdrawal of all British officers—of his orders to General Gracey on 27th October to invade Kashmir.[1] Thereafter by his own wish he faded inconspicuously from the scene. In a farewell letter Lord Mountbatten wrote:

. . . No one could have done more for India over an entire life's career devoted to her Army and nobody contributed more to help find a peaceful and acceptable solution. I hope you will not let the fact that impartiality is no longer respected by many Indians make you feel that you have somehow failed—history will show very much the reverse. . . .

Sir Claude Auchinleck had had to shoulder, in the course of 1947,

his dealings with Pakistan. Lord Ismay was anxious to be released, being long overdue for a rest, having served the War Cabinet in a highly exacting post throughout the war, but had followed the call of duty in going out to India. He confessed that six months with Lord Mountbatten had exhausted him more than six years with Winston Churchill.

[1] See above, p. 457.

two of the harshest tasks imposed on any man by those tumultuous events. The devoted 'father' of the Indian Army, to whose growth into one of the finest military instruments in the world he had contributed as much as anybody, he was obliged to preside over its dismantlement and to watch its infection with the communal disease that politicians had spread and from which had it been proud to be immune. Then, left with high responsibility but with minimal power, he had found himself, once the hero of his men of all faiths, the butt of ignorant and bitter personal attack for his alleged partiality on the one hand for India and the Hindus, on the other for Pakistan and the Muslims. Can it be wondered that occasionally he lost his temper and himself spoke bitter words? But, utterly loyal and devoted to duty as he was, he never forced an issue in public, and bowed to the painful exigencies of a political earthquake. Never were his wisdom, and his sympathy with Indian aspirations and feelings, better exemplified than in his memorandum of February 1946 on the Indian National Army trials.[1]

The Joint Defence Council continued in being, with the senior Service Chief of each Dominion attending in place of the Supreme Commander. At a meeting in mid-March Lord Mountbatten raised the question of the Council's own future, for it was due, under the Order creating it, to expire on 1st April. He wrote afterwards to H.M. the King:

My original idea had been that the Council should continue in its existing form for at least another year—and I secretly hoped for ever. It could carry on under my chairmanship (if both sides so wished) until I left, and then under the chairmanship of the Prime Minister of the Dominion in which each successive meeting took place. It was in my mind that its scope might indeed expand, to cover financial and economic matters also, and eventually External Affairs and Communications, which would mean the 'virtual accession' of the two Dominions to one another, on the same basis as the States. But I had talked the matter over the previous evening with Mr. Liaqat Ali Khan and Pandit Nehru, and they had decided that the need for the Council as such no longer existed, since nearly all the functions for which it had been created, with the exception of the movement of stores, had been virtually completed. I did not feel that the time was pro-

[1] See above, p. 252.

pitious to press the continuance, let alone expansion, of the Council.

Nevertheless, the value of the Joint Defence Council as a means whereby the two Prime Ministers had been able to meet at regular intervals could not be overlooked and I felt it necessary to do all that lay in my power to ensure that such meetings would continue in the future. Accordingly I obtained the two Prime Ministers' agreement that they should thereafter meet at approximately monthly intervals to discuss all matters of common concern and interest. It was agreed that those meetings would be attended by other Ministers of the two Governments as necessary.[1]

Here is recorded the disappointment, not of a mere administrative intention, but of a great hope which had illumined Lord Mountbatten's thought on the transfer of power from May 1947 onwards. He had been obliged to accept partition, but at the back of his mind had always been the idea that severance would be followed by amity and reconciliation, and that the logic of common needs would gradually lead the two Dominions into structural association—virtual accession, as he put it in the above passage—for their joint purposes. The Joint Defence Council was to be the root from which this tree of unity and co-operation was to grow. The hope withered, blasted by the Punjab disorders and poisoned by the strife over Junagadh and Kashmir. It is astonishing that the root he had planted survived so long. But it was never to send up its expected new life, and at his departure it had already perished.

4 The broader strategic picture

One other hope of a like order was also dashed in those days. Shortly before the transfer of power, the British Government had proposed to send out a delegation of the Chiefs of Staff to discuss with the successor Governments matters of mutual defence interest to themselves and the rest of the Commonwelath.[2] The offer had

[1] *Report of the Governor-General.*
[2] This was in accordance with Lord Mountbatten's Letter of Instructions, which enjoined him to point out to the Indian leaders 'the need for continued collaboration in the security of the Indian Ocean area'. See Appendix I.

been declined by both proto-Governments because of their many preoccupations at that time. It was decided that the delegation should negotiate with the Joint Defence Council after the transfer of power. Although the offer was renewed later, its acceptance was again deferred. At a meeting of the Joint Defence Council on 8th December, the Prime Ministers of India and Pakistan—prompted previously by Lord Mountbatten—formally invited him to put up a paper on joint defence against external aggression. His idea was that, if this development could be publicised, world opinion would see that, however India and Pakistan abused each other in public, at least they intended to stand together against any external aggressor. Lord Mountbatten presented his paper at a meeting a fortnight later.

> In this I recommended that the Joint Defence Council should decide that it was a suitably constituted body, particularly now both Prime Ministers were attending all meetings, to deal with this matter on the highest level; that the Chiefs of Staff of the two Dominions should have a meeting to 'start the ball rolling'; and that a decision should be made on when it seemed likely to that the time would be ripe for the Delegation, which the British Chiefs of Staff Committee had promised to send out to discuss matters of mutual defence interest, should arrive. . . .
> (I still hoped to arrange for their arrival during the time I was still in India.)
>
> The reaction to this paper was disappointing, but not unexpected in the prevailing atmosphere. Both Prime Ministers now took the line that it would be valueless to pursue the question of joint defence until their Governments were more in line politically. They pointed out that defence policy could not stand on its own but was intimately connected with foreign policy; and that the necessary preliminary to detailed discussions between the two Dominions of the former, was some degree of co-ordination of the latter.
>
> So far as the British Chiefs of Staff Delegation was concerned, the two Prime Ministers were also of the view that the two Dominion Governments must be in some measure of preliminary agreement on the matters which this intended to raise, before it came out.[1]

[1] loc. cit.

It is not surprising that despite the drafting of a letter to the British Chiefs of Staff asking them what points they wished to raise, and (also in India) of a reply which would not tread on Indian or Pakistani corns, no formal delegation ever came out. Commonwealth-wide collaboration on the defence of the two Dominions, such as it was, proceeded at lower and less political levels. It is not surprising because, quite apart from their local preoccupations and mutual enmity, neither the Government of India nor the Government of Pakistan accepted the assumption of the British Chiefs of Staff that those Governments were concerned with the defence of the Commonwealth, or even of the Indian Ocean theatre in which they resided. At a meeting in London shortly before the transfer of power at which Lord Ismay was present, one of the Chiefs of Staff talked of 'our requirements' and pooh-poohed the Viceroy's objections to discussing them with the Indian leaders at that time. He was sat on by Mr. Attlee, but the phrase showed how little he, and presumably his colleagues, realised either the outlook of Indian politicians or the implications of independence. After the transfer of power, Pakistan pursued a policy of military co-operation with the West, in her own interest, but showed no concern for any defence obligations or dangers outside her own area; while India, under Pandit Nehru's leadership, quickly adopted a policy of non-alignment and neutrality.

The consequences, not only of these new national policies, but also of the disappearance of the Indian Empire as the bulwark of Commonwealth defence east of Suez, so far from being foreseen at the time, were still not fully recognised by Britain and her allies twenty years later. The whole Indian Ocean basin had been, on the defence map of the world, a British lake. Japan's invasion from the east during World War II exposed the weakness of the system, but her defeat restored the position that British power controlled not only the central mass of the Indian sub-continent but also all the key entrances to the Indian Ocean—the Cape of Good Hope, the Suez Canal, the Persian Gulf, the north-west and north-east frontiers of India, Singapore, north Australia. This fact was so deeply embedded in the concepts of British strategic thinkers that they could hardly imagine its disappearance. But apart from Australia and South Africa the whole system depended upon India—as a source of troops, as a base for all three Services, as a supply area, as a training ground and barracks for a large part of the British Army as well as her own, and as the source of money to pay for the larger defence of the sub-continent as the British raj saw it, including the whole maintenance of British forces on Indian soil. With the independence of India and Pakistan, the absorption of their military strength in confronting each other, and their lack of interest in wider international security, the whole system ceased to be viable in the long run. Few perceived in 1947 what a radical upset of strategic assumptions independence was bound to cause. Two decades later the transfer of power was still throwing out its ripples in the actual or prospective withdrawal of British forces not only from the Suez Canal—abandoned in 1955 —but also from Aden, Singapore and the Persian Gulf. The ultimate consequences for the world balance of power have yet to be seen.

29

Envoi

When Lord and Lady Mountbatten left India on 21st June 1948 the demonstrations of Indian affection and regard were reminiscent of those astonishing events which they had experienced on Independence Day ten months earlier. 'It was borne in on them,' wrote Mr. Alan Campbell-Johnson, 'with overwhelming emphasis that India's people and Government had recognised the meaning of their mission and the sincerity of their endeavours, and were hailing them as liberators and friends.'[1] Half a million people were reckoned to have thronged them as they drove to receive an address from the Delhi Municipality, along the historic Chandni Chowk in Old Delhi, and then at the site of Mahatma Gandhi's funeral pyre. At a state banquet on their last evening, Pandit Nehru spoke with moving sincerity:

> Used as I am to these vast demonstrations here, I was much affected and I wondered how it was that an Englishman and Englishwoman could become so popular in India during this brief period of time. . . . A period certainly of achievement and success in some measure, but also a period of sorrow and disaster. . . . Obviously this was not connected so much with what had happened, but rather with the good faith, the friendship and love of India that these two possessed. . . . You may have many gifts and presents, but there is nothing more real or

[1] *Mission with Mountbatten*, p. 350. That this was no flash in the pan of volatile enthusiasm was shown when Lord Mountbatten visited India fifteen years later, in April 1963. No processional plans nor special announcement had been made: the party was due to make a night drive from Vera Cruz airport to Bombay dockyard. But the whole route from start to finish was lined with cheering people, in some places up to ten deep, and seeing this Lord Mountbatten left his saloon car for the leading police jeep, and stood all the rest of the way, acknowledging the greetings of the crowd. He had passed into the popular consciousness of India as a liberator, perhaps the liberator, of the nation.

precious than the love and affection of the people. You have seen yourself, Sir and Madam, how that love and affection work. It is difficult for me or anyone to judge of what we have done during the last year or so. We are too near to it and too intimately connected with events. Maybe we have made many mistakes, you and we. Historians' a generation or two hence will perhaps be able to judge what we have done right and what we have done wrong. Nevertheless, whether we did right or wrong, the test, perhaps the right test, is whether we tried to do right or did not. . . . I do believe that we did try to do right, and I am convinced that you tried to do the right thing by India, and therefore many of our sins will be forgiven us and many of our errors also.

The massive silver tray that was then presented 'with affection and good wishes and a token of friendship', inscribed by all the members of the Indian Cabinet, Governors of Provinces and the President of the Constituent Assembly, bears most of the famous names of Indian public life of those days: Nehru, Patel, Rajagopalachari, Azad, Baldev Singh, Ambedkar, Aney, S. P. Mookherjee, Sarojini Naidu, Rajendra Prasad. . . . In response, Lord Mountbatten had a still nobler and no less touching presentation to make. Drawing aside the British and Indian flags which had concealed two alcoves, he disclosed the magnificent service of gold plate which had been given by the Goldsmiths' Company of the City of London to King George V for use by the Viceroy. Its impending return to England had saddened Indian statesmen and officials. Now Lord Mountbatten presented it to the Government of India as a gift from His Majesty King George VI, as 'a symbol of the friendship of all English men and women, and indeed of all the people in the United Kingdom, to the people of India'.

The tributes to Lord Mountbatten had indeed been earned not only by his personal qualities but equally by his service to independent India. Having established her freedom and that of Pakistan, he had presided over her Government through as hard and tumultuous times as any new State could have experienced. When recalling the things that he strove but failed to do—establish friendship between India and Pakistan, stop the war in Kashmir, reach a settlement with Hyderabad—it is well to recall not only the things that he succeeded in doing, and they were massive, but also the immense problems and difficulties that faced the newly independent India: partition along two frontiers, with its concomitant violence and herds of refugees; rebuilding of the machine of government at the Centre and in the halves of partitioned provinces; revolutionary changes in the relationships with hundreds of Princely States. It is perhaps more remarkable that order and peace generally survived than that they lapsed in some places and at some times. For his guidance, his leadership and in critical respects his action, in steering India through those turbulent rapids, Lord Mountbatten entirely deserved the admiration of India, as Mr. Jinnah and his supporters earned the praise of Pakistan for their equal labours in like circumstances—easier in regard to the States, more difficult in the establishment of national government where none had been before. Those were days to test the most courageous of spirits and the greatest of men. Who was great, who petty, who bold, who weak, through those hard trials, let the finger of history point, in these pages and hereafter.

PART FIVE

Retrospect

Alternative to partition?

Looking back on the story of the Great Divide, its prelude, its climax and its aftermath, one is beset by many questions that admit no confident answer, perhaps no answer at all. Was partition the best solution of the three-cornered problem? If, in the end, it was the only solution, when did it become so? What other answers might have been found? Was the manner of Britain's withdrawal from India wise and fair? Or was it too precipitate, and negligent of her pledges and duty to those people, majorities as well as minorities, whom history had confided to her care? In such speculations there can be no certainty and no proof. All that follows here is but opinion, capable of contradiction, but it is opinion founded upon the facts that have been narrated.

To the eyes of most British people in 1947, as to those of most Indians, the partition of the sub-continent was a deplorable end to the Indian Empire. The unity of India, more complete and secure than under any Indian raj in history, was a cause of just British pride. One strong central government, one system and rule of law, one network of communications and economic intercourse, one army and other forces keeping one frontier within which peace and order reigned—these were great creations which the British profoundly felt ought to be bequeathed to Indian democracy when their own control was handed on. Up to the last moment, when within a few weeks of the fateful decision Lord Mountbatten could write of 'this mad Pakistan', partition seemed, to most of the British concerned, essentially an evil to be averted if possible. But now, from a little greater distance in time, we can perceive that perhaps they took too short and too self-centred an historical view. A hundred years ago, all the sub-continent had been brought under one hand; but the hand was alien, and in the history of Asia a century is a short span. Three hundred years ago, when European power had not penetrated beyond a few ports, most of India bowed the knee to the Mogul throne, though there were also many independent kingdoms: nearly a thousand years ago, the struggle of Hindu and Muslim for mastery in India had already begun. There was no inherent reason for assuming that an alien creation, even one so beneficent as political unity, would or necessarily ought to survive the departure of the aliens.

We can also now see, as a fact, that the prophets of Pakistan's instant decrepitude and perhaps collapse, for want of economic resources, political experience or national cohesion, were wrong. (They included many Congressmen who accepted partition because they thought it carried the quick-maturing seeds of its own decay.) They underrated the emotions that had given rise to the Muslim separatist movement, the sense of national pride and identity that grows under such a revolutionary challenge, and the vested interest in national power which becomes a supreme motive for those who share in it. They may have missed the key fact— pointed out by Mr. B. R. Ambedkar as early as 1942—that Pakistan could possess that most basic of all assets for a poor country striving to develop, a self-sufficiency in food. East Bengal was always weak, but its very weakness made it cling the tighter to the richer western part of the nation. Pakistan, today, two decades from its birth, politically disturbed as it may be, has such a distinct national character, policy and place in the world that its existence now seems inevitable, and, being inevitable, right.

It is true that Pakistan's political experience has been chastening. Generals Iskander Mirza and Ayub Khan were not alone in thinking that if her initial democratic system had continued she might have fallen apart, at least into East and West components. But this is only speculation, though the danger remains.

No one can now claim, as many did in 1947, that partition was wrong because Pakistan would be a failure. Nor can anyone prove, though he may certainly claim, that union after independence would have been a success. The forces that caused partition were present in India and would not have been diminished—indeed they might well have been strengthened—by the departure of the British. Though their success in 1947 was owed above all to one man, other Muslim leaders might have arisen to defy 'Hindu raj'. Political unity bequeathed by a lapsed imperialism is inherently fragile, as many an example has subsequently shown—Nigeria, Congo, Laos, Vietnam, Cyprus. A great bonus to disruption was offered in the scheme for continued unity of India that came closest to acceptance in 1946–7, the Cabinet Mission's plan, by the 'escape clause' allowing the whole confederal system in effect to go into the melting pot again after ten years. In ten years, the prospect of power falling from British hands caused the Pakistan movement to grow from almost nothing to its triumph; in ten years more, what might not the prospect of another struggle have done to disrupt and destroy the whole system of Indian union, if those had been its terms? Recalling both the immense boost given to Muslim consciousness by provincial autonomy in 1937–9, and the troubles that free India herself has faced with the language issue and provincial recalcitrance, we can hardly reckon the chances of indefinite survival of an all-India constitutional union after 1947 higher than fifty-fifty. If partition was not the best solution then, it was at least a solution capable of enduring, and it might have imposed itself later after a still more devastating struggle.

Yet, when we look now at India and Pakistan, barely restrained from war, wasting their substance in mutual armed hostility which weighs down their economic and social advance like leaden boots, deprived of that immense prestige and physical strength in the world which would have belonged to an independent heir to the whole Indian Empire, we cannot but sympathise with the British opinion of those days that partition was inherently dangerous and misguided, and was to be averted by any right and reasonable means.

Could it, then, have been rightly and reasonably averted? The path to an answer runs through a jungle of ifs and buts. Perhaps the most certain proposition is that Britain's transfer of power came too late to avoid partition. How much too late is more difficult to assess. Perhaps only a year, perhaps ten years or more. Lord Wavell was surely right in the idea behind his Simla conference of 1945—an idea which others had held before him—that if as a first step a national government were formed, with genuine power demitted from the British, the constitutional problem would in the course of time become more tractable. Experience of the eventual Interim Government argues the contrary, but that was two years later—after the end of the war, after the Indian elections, after the breakdown of the Cabinet Mission, after the Great Calcutta Killing. Much else in the story of British rule in India, especially the chapter on provincial self-government, shows that real political power, once offered, is rarely refused, and once shared is rarely resigned by any who share in it. It is a fair conclusion that, if Britain could have demitted more power sooner, the forces holding Hindus and Muslims and others together at the Centre would have had a stronger chance of success, and the rising forces of division would have been forestalled.

Though the constitution of 1935 was a great act of state, it was behind the times, and by 1939 it was much further behind than when it was first conceived. The opportunities of a new sharing of power in India that were presented by the outbreak of war and again in 1940 were wasted for want of courage or imagination, and of understanding of Indian facts and feelings in high British places. The opportunity of 1942 was misconceived, primarily because the importance of short-run sharing of political power was underrated by comparison with that of devising a long-run constitutional formula.

Between 1935 and 1946, even between 1942 and 1946, much had happened to make the task of holding India together by national government with Dominion powers much more difficult. The way in which the Congress exploited its electoral success in 1937 was the first blow. Next, the war and all its consequences were a disaster for India's progress to a united independence. The withdrawal of the Congress from provincial governments, its rejection of the Cripps Offer, and its Quit India campaign, set its cause back by years and gave an immense advantage to its opponents, above all the Muslim League. Every Congress error was irreversibly exploited by Mr. Jinnah. The wartime inertia of British policy (except abortively in 1942) and the negativism of the Congress left a vacuum for Muslim separatism to expand. Never was the Gandhian leadership less relevant to practical politics, never did the Congress need more to recognise its own shortcomings. Had it perceived the new political realities it might have made a better bargain with the League and the British over sharing central power at Simla in 1945 than it could have made in any later negotiation; for on his side Mr. Jinnah had not yet found and tested his full strength. And the chance of forming a genuine all-community Government of a united India was never again so strong.

Even a year later, if the Cabinet Mission had been armed with stronger authority and a more certain policy, something like its confederal, three-tier plan might have gone through, clumsy as it was. Whether it would have been a success is another matter, for it was inherently delicate and contrived. Earlier chapters have told how close the Cabinet Mission plan came to acceptance, how long Mr. Jinnah remained torn between the entire but not sovereign Pakistan which the plan gave him and the sovereign but 'moth-eaten' Pakistan which he eventually carried off, and how the powerful impulses for unity of the Punjab and of Bengal were little by little lost. To the failure of the Mission many causes contributed: their own method and terms of reference, the obduracy of Indian political leaders in staking the lesser cause against the greater, the utter elusiveness of Mahatma Gandhi. But while hope still lingered the fatal blow was struck by Jawaharlal Nehru, in the speech in which he made clear that the Congress would accept the plan only to destroy it, by seeking to demolish the system of grouping of provinces which was its essence. Muslim confidence in compromise could hardly survive such a wound. The episode showed how far the formula was from registering a real meeting of minds between the Congress and the League. They met only when forced together by the imminence of British departure and the fear of taking over an India in chaos. It is the plain fact that partition was the only constitutional plan ever agreed to by all the main Indian parties. It is also the fact that partition and the subsequent migrations did eliminate the major minority problem both in India and in Pakistan, even at the price of so much blood and tears.

Given the basic and rival objectives of the three great participants in the struggle—of the British, stable government; of the Congress, national independence; of the League, Muslim security from 'Hindu raj'—all three share in responsibility for bringing about the situation that confronted all concerned in 1947. Perhaps the Congress leaders made the worst errors: if so, in the upshot they paid the most dearly in sacrifice of their ideals.

The possibility of any other answer than total partition was extremely remote by the time of Lord Mountbatten's appointment, and was rendered even more improbable by his terms of reference, which in effect committed His Majesty's Government to transferring power to two or more successors if it failed to get agreement to transferring power to one. Only one stratagem seems, in retrospect, to have been capable of bringing such a possibility nearer: to offer Mr. Jinnah, straight away, and without argument, a sovereign Pakistan shorn of Hindu-majority areas of Bengal and the Punjab, and to throw at once upon him the onus of accepting it, or trimming his sails, or putting up his own proposals for the minimal co-operative Centre which was evidently still within range of his contemplation at that stage. Then a new tactical situation might have been created from which a constructive compromise could conceivably have emerged. But one must not press the advantages of hindsight too far, and so swift a decision, before testing Indian opinion all round, was inconsistent both with Lord Mountbatten's instructions and with the method of work which he set out to pursue and to which he was temperamentally wedded. Given those considerations, the solution he reached was in its broad outline the only one that was possible.

Lord Mountbatten appraised

In assessing Lord Mountbatten's personal role in the dénouement of 1947 we must start by recalling the facts with which he had to deal, from the moment when he started to debate with Mr. Attlee and other Ministers the terms of his own appointment. It was certain that British rule must end soon—certain because of British pledges, because British will to pay the price of its continuance was lacking, and because the means of British government in India itself were rapidly degenerating. In India it was certain that partition in some form must be an element in the solution—some form of Muslim territorial autonomy, any qualification being on a basis of equal status.

All this being so, one may see in Lord Mountbatten only the agent of forces far beyond his control, the canoeist negotiating fierce rapids who may steer his vessel off one rock after another but can no more control its direction or its destination than he can deflect or subdue the torrent in which he is caught. But so determinist a view of Lord Mountbatten's Viceroyalty is far from satisfying. Within the limits set by the facts, many were the alternatives that might have issued from his plenipotentiary regime. British rule in India might have ended in ignominy, in hatred, in violently-contested retreat. India and Pakistan might have cut all ties with Britain and the Crown. The internal dissention that followed in the sub-continent might have been greater or less. The handling of the States problem might have been very different. Instead of a transfer of power under the existing constitutional system, constituent assemblies might have been set to work, with the British Parliament eventually ratifying their products. The full time-limit of June 1948 might have been approached before Britain handed over power. Seen in this comparative light, his achievement, by any reckoning, and however qualified, was very great.

The scenes of enthusiasm and goodwill amid which the last

British Viceroyalty of India expired must be contrasted with the deadlock and despair that preceded its beginning. Lord Mountbatten's primary achievement was finding a way out of the menacing dead-end into which Indian politics had been driven in the winter of 1946–7. The path was not opened without the dynamite of partition; but the hands of the Congress, the Muslim League and the British had all by consent fired that explosion, and the escape from the blind alley had been made in good order. Above all, the responsibility for deciding the shape of India's future had been unmistakably placed where it belonged, and where British policy had striven to place it, upon the Indians themselves. Thus it came about that a century and a half of imperial rule was ended, not with violence and shame, but with constitutional rectitude and mutual amity between the former rulers and ruled. This extraordinary event was to be an example for the whole process— far swifter than anyone then foresaw—of dismantling the British Empire in the cause of self-rule.

Regardless of personalities, success would have been impossible without a new Viceroy. It required a new start and a new man, free of past commitments, past prejudices and past suspicions. It also needed a man with fresh and larger powers, such as no previous Viceroy, as the temporary incumbent of British overlordship, had ever possessed, powers implicit in the pledge that this was the last Viceroyalty and that if no agreed means of transferring sovereignty could be found the means would be imposed—necessarily, upon the advice and with the authority of the Viceroy himself.

Armed with those powers and the same charter, other men of strong character, quick decision, energy and imagination could no doubt have achieved the end prescribed. But to achieve it by persuasion and with mutual friendship needed qualities which are rare in political leaders, still rarer in administrators, but which Lord Mountbatten possessed in high degree: courage, resilience, personal charm, freedom from pomposity, readiness to listen, an out-giving personality.

He had, of course, defects as well. He was impetuous, and without such steady counsellors as Lord Ismay or V. P. Menon he might have made mistakes which he actually avoided: some of the most debatable of his actions may be traced to a certain impulsiveness, the counterpart of an astonishing speed of decision and adaptability to new events. A sailor of proven bravery in war, he was never afraid to take risks, and if occasionally the risks seemed too great this was a reflection alike of his courage and of his incurable optimism. During the twenty weeks of his Viceroyalty his mind and actions were mastered by his determination to obtain a major political solution by agreement: for the sake of that aim he was prepared if need be to sacrifice minor policies, inconvenient obstacles and even good men. Like many another great leader, he had, too, a streak of vanity which made him over-sensitive alike to praise and to criticism. It is hard not to see in the contrast between his relations with Mr. Jinnah and with Pandit Nehru a counterpart of the difference between the cold argumentation and the affectionate hero-worship that the two men presented to him. At the same time, Lord Mountbatten was a good judge of character and had both respect and friendship for Sardar Patel, who was certainly no flatterer, and with whom he had more than one stand-up verbal fight.[1] If he enjoyed friendship and frankness he gave as much as he took. His whole method was one of personal relations and free, unsecretive discussion.

British criticism of his policies—apart from the main issue of partition—has focussed upon three aspects: the speed and timing of the transfer of power, which it is alleged contributed to the bloodshed and misery that followed in some parts of the new Dominions; the want of any provision for the lesser minorities or other British obligations or trusts; and his policies towards the States, both before and after the transfer of power.

On the issue of speed and timing, Lord Mountbatten's own considered reasons were recorded in a chapter, headed Conclusions, of his considered despatch, addressed in September 1948 to those who had received his weekly Personal Reports as Viceroy, and entitled *Report on the Last Viceroyalty*. That chapter is reproduced in full as an Appendix to this book and needs no gloss. He argues that the military preparations in the Punjab were the utmost that could have been made, and that military action alone could not in any case succeed in such conditions without political action. 'I do not consider,' he wrote, 'that further political action could have been taken if power had been transferred at a later date.' The top political leaders were fully aware of the danger which threatened.

[1] 'Dickie doesn't object to one speaking one's mind, even when it is working directly opposite to his; so even a heated argument leaves no ill will.' Lord Ismay in a letter to his wife.

'But,' he added, and it is a point that has been emphasised in an earlier chapter in this book, 'not one of us, and indeed, so far as I know, no one in India, Pakistan or the United Kingdom anticipated the exact form and magnitude of what was to follow.' After debating the vexed question of handling the Sikh leaders, Lord Mountbatten referred to the run-down of the whole civil administration, which it is plain in retrospect would have made the dangers progressively worse. He then discussed the contention that an organised transfer of populations could have anticipated the panic flight that actually happened. Finally he cited five constructive reasons why the advantages of an early transfer of power far outweighed the disadvantages, and concluded:

> But all these circumstances were of little account in relation to the primary consideration of all—namely, that the difficulties which seemed likely to be encountered, and in the event were encountered in no small measure, between the date of His Majesty's Government's announcement on 3rd June and the actual transfer of power, rendered it advisable to make this period as short as possible. I am genuinely convinced that it would not have been possible to have kept the Interim Government of India functioning without one or other Party resigning and all the repercussions which that would have brought about, for a week, let alone a month, longer than was done. The August transfer of power was inherent in the Partition solution quite apart from any introduction of Dominion status.
>
> The decision of the major political parties in India to implement the 3rd June Plan represented their first agreement on the method of taking over power. If the implementation was to take place at all, speed seemed essential; delay might have plunged the whole Indian sub-continent, and not the Punjab alone, into disruption and chaos.

None of this can be gainsaid. Perhaps the weak link in the chain is the failure to foresee the scale and nature of the violence that would follow partition. This was certainly not Lord Mountbatten's failure alone, but that of most of his official advisers and of the politicians too. More prescient warning by Punjabi officers could perhaps have been heeded. But, even if forewarned, it is hard to see how the authorities could have been much better forearmed. Delay in the transfer of power would have helped only if, first, advantage could have been taken of it to improve the military and civil dispositions; secondly, if the interval were one of political calm and an allaying of communal fears and hates; and, thirdly, if the strength and reliability of the forces of law and order—civil administrators, police, the Army—would be enhanced with time, rather than deteriorating further. All these conditions appear to the historian most dubious. The fact was that the forces of law and order were themselves becoming more and more communal and unreliable. If the Army, the last disciplined instrument of impartiality and system, had cracked, immeasurable disaster could have followed.

There can be no better witness as to the state and relevance of the Indian Army than General Lord Ismay, who had served in it for twenty-three years, had once been Military Secretary to the Viceroy (Lord Willingdon) and was Lord Mountbatten's closest and sagest counsellor. In a tape-recorded talk with the author in January 1965 he said:

> Probably the Indian Army was then [after the Second World War] the finest all-round army in the world. . . . But it still centred round its British officers and its regiments. The British officers had less and less control, but the regiment meant a tremendous lot to them.
>
> Now we come to the period of partition. It was no good saying it was a rotten idea. We had got to get agreement. Jinnah was insistent that the Army was going to be divided on communal lines. . . . That meant that you were going to break down two things. The security that comes from having mixed units, that safeguard went. The other great asset that was lost was that the regiment, the thing for which they lived and fought, was also going to disappear. How was this going to affect them? . . .
>
> Even before partition, or the transfer of power, men were already writing to their commanders saying 'I want to go home: these riots are taking place and my family are being killed.'
>
> I had all this at the back of my mind but somehow I was completely confident that the Army would stand firm. Looking back on it I cannot think why. They had no reason to be: their best British officers had gone, they knew they were going, they had

nothing to keep them staunch, they were going to fall into the hands of people like Nehru who didn't appreciate them at all. Yet they stood firm.

The first people who looked like going were the Viceroy's Bodyguard, of all people. The Commandant came to me and said that the Indian officers said they were going to start shooting each other, the P.M.s [Punjabi Muslims] and the Sikhs. I got him to go down and harangue them. I told him not to dismiss them until they had given their promise that they wouldn't shoot, and if they wouldn't promise I would come. They knew me. He came back and said 'They are surly as anything but they promise they won't shoot.' I met them on duty in this riot-stricken town [Delhi]. You saw a section of Sikhs and a section of P.M.s working together in armoured cars. They wouldn't speak to each other. I went to see the P.M.s off to Karachi. There was not a single Sikh to see them off. They went off 'in Coventry', hated. The comradeship of twenty years was finished, killed already. So I don't know how we got through.

I feel no one has made enough of the very grave risk we ran with the Army. I don't believe the Army would have stayed if we had hung on any longer. If the Army had gone wrong, if the Army had started shooting, there's just no limit to what the casualties would have been. It would have been a holocaust which one just can't imagine.

Asked whether the Punjab Boundary Force might have been better organised and deployed, had the nature of the violence and migrations been foreseen, Lord Ismay gave a qualified 'Yes'. Would it have been better to have an interlude before the boundary was finally drawn, say a week or two? Lord Ismay replied:

The trouble is that they [the Indian leaders] were absolutely unreasonable. You only had to have a little bit of reason, of charity, of commonsense, in those two men, Jinnah and Nehru, and the sub-continent of India now would be all completely friendly. . . . We had lost the initiative. We had lost all authority. The sawdust was running out of the doll hour by hour. There was nothing you could do. . . . You can't bluff if you have nothing to bluff with. We hadn't anything. . . .

We really did take a most terrific chance with the Indian Army—and it came off.

The conclusion must be that delay in the transfer of power would only have made the underlying dangers worse, and that Lord Mountbatten's insistence on the utmost speed was fully justified. With greater foresight, an all-out effort to strengthen the civil and police administration in the Punjab, alongside the military arm, might perhaps have bettered the situation, but the material available was lamentably weak. The price that was paid in bloodshed and misery was paid not for any British decision but for the inflaming of communal emotions that had been proceeding for months and years past.

One other criticism may be made, with perhaps more validity. Although the Cabinet Mission plan had to be thrown overboard, it was still Lord Mountbatten's hope and resolve that a rudimentary Centre would survive partition, for defence and all that went with it. Two means were thought to assure this—a common Governor-Generalship for the initial period, an intention frustrated by Mr. Jinnah, and the Joint Defence Council, which though operative for six months after the transfer of power was undermined in its general and long-term purpose by the enmity between the two Dominions after the Punjab troubles and the Kashmir conflict.[1] The criticism is that, in the period between the decision of 3rd June and the actual severance, more should have been done to create and strengthen the co-operative mechanism between Pakistan and India; that in working out the consequences of partition too little attention was given to construction, by contrast with all that was devoted to division; and that a little more time would have made a greater constructive effort possible. It may be so, though one must recall the atmosphere and attitudes of mind of those days, and must not suppose that with the best of will and direction from the top things could have been accomplished which were contrary to the spirit and the political possibilities of that highly emotional, bitterly divisive period. Perhaps a joint communications board, a joint economic council or other such instruments could have been devised, though how they could have been staffed and organised at a time of acute shortage of administrative manpower is a very doubtful question. But who will say, in the light of the estrangement between the two Dominions that followed upon the Punjab massacres and the Junagadh and

[1] Another bridge was the position of the Supreme Commander, but this was inherently transitory.

Kashmir affairs, that such institutions would eventually have met a better fate than the Joint Defence Council?

The speed of movement between the adoption of a broad constitutional plan and the actual transfer of power also had an obvious bearing on the issue of safeguards and obligations towards lesser minorities. There simply was no time to enter into negotiations with the two Dominions-designate on behalf of minor communities or special interests. But the bearing, though palpable, was not of fundamental importance. Such negotiations, had time and temper allowed them, would have been inherently futile if conceived in terms of Britain's providing after independence for protection such as she could exercise only when she was the ruling power. A nation's independence must imply freedom to care for its peoples of all persuasions in its own way. No sovereign state voluntarily acquiesces, even by way of treaty, in commitments to other countries in regard to its own internal affairs. The most that British authority could do for minorities like Indian Christians, Anglo-Indians, Parsees, Buddhists, primitive tribes or Scheduled Castes in a final transfer of power was to see that the packs of constitutional cards which Britain left on the table for Indians and Pakistanis to play were not stacked against them. As it happened, though more by accident than by design, this was done in the most effective way that could have been found, namely, by handing over power under the existing constitution and laws, with all the favour they gave to communities towards which the British felt a special obligation, leaving to the new Dominions the onus of making any change to the detriment of those communities.

Theoretically, pressure could have been brought to bear upon the Indian Constituent Assembly during the last months of British rule to entrench certain protective clauses in the constitution: but the history of involuntary entrenchment, for instance in South Africa, discourages faith that such devices would be more permanent and effective than self-imposed restraints. The Constituent Assembly, as almost its first act, had voted a declaration of fundamental rights which was as realistic a constitutional provision as any that British influence might have written in.

In the 'secular state' which Pandit Nehru insisted independent India should be, the lesser minorities did not fare badly in the first two decades after the transfer of power. Anglo-Indians continued to enjoy (though on an expiring lease) their special quotas of jobs.

Christian missionaries naturally found a more discouraging atmosphere and less money, but they continued their pastoral and
educational work, and the higher educational standards of those
who went to their schools, both Indians and Anglo-Indians, served
them well in a competitive market for employment. As time wore
on, however, Christians, Anglo-Indians and other minority communities felt the pressure of the communal solidarity of major
groups, linguistic and regional as well as religious; and for all who
had shared to some extent in the standards and ways of life of the
British the adjustment to being but elements in an Indian India
was often painful. Yet it is impossible to say that any action that
could have been taken by Britain at the time of independence
would in the end have bettered their lot.

One community suffered most directly from the settlement, the
Sikhs, whom partition divided and whom it deprived of some of
their best lands. But partition was their own wish, and none of
their leaders ever repudiated Sardar Baldev Singh's acceptance of
it in their name. Their only constructive demand, not seriously
pressed, was for a state or province of their own—Sikhistan or
Khalistan. This was quite out of the question in 1947. There was
not a single district of the Punjab in which they had a majority.
When the dust of partition had settled and the great migrations
had ended, their demand for national identity was renewed, and
was at length partially granted in a re-drawing of state boundaries
twenty years later. But this was something that could come about
only at the hands of an Indian regime.

The Princely States are a far more difficult and complex matter,
 hough the same basic principle applied to them as to the minorities—that independence and intervention were contradictory
concepts. It followed that once India and Pakistan were independent the States must make their own way with the democratic
neighbours that surrounded them, without any possibility, thereafter, of external support from Britain, save conceivably in a few
rare geographical cases. To that principle and its consequence,
obvious as they were, most of the Princes and their counsellors
remained seemingly blind until a late hour, burying their heads in
the sand of repeated British utterances about standing by the
Crown's treaties and obligations towards the States,[1] which were

[1] For example, in January 1943, replying to a letter from the Chancellor of
the Chamber of Princes, who had voiced their Highnesses' anxiety about

no doubt echoed by officers of the Political Department and British Residents in their advice to individual States.

Granted that Indian independence must render Britain incapable of exercising either the rights or the obligations of her paramountcy, which depended upon her control of British India, three solutions of principle were theoretically open to His Majesty's Government: to abandon paramountcy altogether, to transfer paramountcy, including the treaty obligations, to the successor Indian Governments or Government, or to offer to conclude, while paramountcy lasted, fresh treaties with the States consistent with the new situation. The last alternative was never remotely viable for all the States, and even for the largest it could have little practical meaning. The second alternative was as bitterly opposed by the Princes as it was vociferously demanded by Indian politicians. The Cabinet Mission came down firmly for the first, the total lapse of paramountcy.[1] The Princes then had just a year, before the adoption of the plan of 3rd June 1947, to adjust their minds and their policies to the early prospect of paramountcy's demise.

Bound by it as he strictly was, Lord Mountbatten had again three theoretical possibilities before him. One was to leave the States to make for themselves the best bargains they could with the successor Dominions upon or after the transfer of power, relying upon the theoretical independence which would follow the lapse of their treaties as the mainstay of their negotiating position. This was broadly the policy of the Political Department, combined with an effort to get the Princes to present a united front to the Congress and at the same time to modernise and constitutionalise their regimes. It was rejected by Lord Mountbatten. It was certainly contrary to his temperament to sit back and let the States fend for themselves after his Viceregal authority had ended, and he held

the effect of the Cripps Offer, the Political Department wrote that, subject to the necessary adaptation of treaties by usage and sufferance to changing conditions, the fulfilment of the fundamental obligations arising out of their treaties and *sanads* remained an integral part of the policy of His Majesty's Government. As late as January 1946, addressing the Chamber of Princes, Lord Wavell assured them that no changes in their relationship with the Crown or the rights guaranteed to them by treaties or engagements would be initiated without their consent.
[1] See above, p. 148

such a policy to be inconsistent with the special charge laid personally upon him by the King to care for the Princely States.

He also regarded it as unrealistic. The Political Department itself admitted that in the long run independence was not practical politics. The bargaining threat of it was therefore a bluff which could be called by the player with the stronger cards. Even in respect of short-run bargaining, the Rulers had far too little time to put themselves and their autocratic regimes into a posture in which to meet the full forces of Indian democracy and political independence, and they were far too divided among themselves, both great and small, to unite in a joint stand against the Congress-controlled Government of India.

If this objection to a hands-off policy was sound, it applied with equal force to the second policy theoretically open to Lord Mountbatten, to encourage and assist the States in uniting to form, alone or in groups, new independent nation-states of their own. The idea had a discouraging history. After the Cripps Offer of 1942, Mr. V. P. Menon recorded:

> Much adverse criticism had appeared at the time in a section of the Indian press about the demand of the Rulers that the non-acceding States should be allowed to form a Union of their own. It was alleged that the Rulers had been instigated to make this demand by the Political Department with the connivance of the Viceroy. When the matter came up for consideration, the Secretary of State felt at first blush that the question was one which must be faced, however reluctantly, and that the Rulers' suggestion deserved sympathetic consideration. H. V. Hodson, my predecessor as Reforms Commissioner, and later I myself, opposed the proposal. Lord Linlithgow accepted our advice and told the Secretary of State that a separate Union of States was just not practical politics and that it was not worth wasting time considering it. He was emphatic that it would be disingenuous to encourage the States to go on thinking along those lines.[1]

The author may be exposed as *parti pris,* but at least Lord Mountbatten was not the first Viceroy to reject the idea of a separate States' Dominion. Nor did it receive, in his time, any support from the Political Department.

As regards the vast majority of States it was obviously quite

[1] *The Integration of the Indian States,* p. 54.

unworkable. Even as applied to a few great States like Hyderabad, Mysore and Kashmir, it had no assurance whatever of durability. The history of relations between India and Pakistan gives no encouragement to the belief that they and such hypothetical Princely Dominions would have settled down amicably as equal neighbours. Pakistan had at least a communal identity, a political ethos and large Armed Forces to sustain her independence. The States had none of these. They would have been no more able to prevent 'subversion' by democratic forces from former British India after the transfer of power than they were before, indeed less able. Their administrative independence was highly qualified, their political independence would soon have become a myth, and their formal independence was unlikely to survive their democratisation for long. A possible exception was Kashmir, whose geographical and communal situation might have held her suspended between India and Pakistan, if her independence had been guaranteed by both.

Lord Mountbatten accordingly turned to the last possibility, to encourage and help the States, while his authority as Viceroy lasted, to make terms forthwith for accession to the new independent Dominions. The terms available to them were better for his influence than they might otherwise have been. He certainly pressed his encouragement very far, perhaps too far having regard to the Princes' habituation to doing what they were told by the Representative of the Crown. But the only sanction he could exercise was to underline the dangerous consequences that might ensue after the transfer of power if they failed to take his advice, and these they were perfectly capable of perceiving for themselves. If he vigorously pushed them onward, it cannot be said that he let them down, unless the proposition is accepted that their nominal independence after the transfer of power would have extracted better terms from the Congress.

It is to his conduct in relation to the States after 15th August 1947, when he was Governor-General of independent India, that the more telling criticism can be addressed. The impetus of his perfectly valid pre-independence policy carried him forward into actions that were less than valid for a constitutional Head of State. That this was so stemmed from the unique confidence that the Indian Government reposed in him, expressed in his chairmanship of the Defence Committee of the Cabinet (which directly embroiled him in the military action towards Junagadh and Kashmir) and in their entrusting to him the negotiations with Hyderabad. Over Kashmir his leadership was decisive in adoption of the policy of accepting accession subject to an eventual plebiscite and of immediately sending troops into the State: in this, and thereafter, his prime and unexceptionable object was to avoid war between the two Dominions and, as he repeatedly urged, to 'stop the fighting'. The reference to the United Nations as peacekeeper was made under his strong pressure. Ultimate failure in that peaceable object may, however, be traced to the lapse in communication between the India and Pakistan Governments in the critical two days of decision, a lapse which horrified Lord Ismay. Had Lord Mountbatten remained detached as constitutional Governor-General—a trusted consultant but not an executive—his first thought would surely have been to communicate at once with his opposite number in Pakistan and try to frame a mutually agreed policy towards the situation created by the tribesmen's invasion, an effort which might or might not have succeeded. Had he been Governor-General of both Dominions the likelihood of joint action or mutual agreement would have been much higher still: that he was not was not his fault.

In Junagadh the actual take-over was ordered, to his disgruntlement, without reference to him. But it is hard to see how he could have done otherwise than concur in it: constitutionally he had a right to be informed but no power to oppose, and in any event matters had gone so far that such action had become inevitable. The invasion of Hyderabad happened after he had left India, but again he had concurred, though with reluctance, in the military preparations for the eventual 'police action'. He had done his utmost, for the most part in harmony with Sir Walter Monckton, the Nizam's adviser, to secure an agreement between Hyderabad and India, and at several points had substantially moderated his Government's policy, but he had failed. The problem was an intensely difficult one, in which to become involved was to court great risks. Lord Mountbatten was no man to shrink from political risks, any more than from military. The criticism which cannot altogether be allayed is that as constitutional Governor-General he took too many.

If, it may further be asked, his influence with the Nehru Government and the confidence they placed in him were so great, must he not also take responsibility for the development of their constructive policy for the merger and integration of the Indian States? In general, he approved that policy, and must be answerable for such encouragement as he gave it, but it is quite clear that its implementation went on without his full knowledge, let alone agreement. In particular, he knew nothing of the midnight arm-twisting tactics that had secured the critical first merger of the Orissa States. It was from these early moves that there inexorably began the dethroning of the Princes and the virtual disappearance of the States as political entities.

Reflecting on the whole story of the aftermath of the transfer of power, one can make two broad observations. First, Lord Mountbatten's Governor-Generalship of independent India must be judged as a whole. Against the criticisms that have been levied, especially in Pakistan and in some circles in Britain, must be set his salvation of Delhi when its disorders threatened to bring chaos to India, his great and successful efforts to secure fairness for Pakistan in the division of assets, his support for every endeavour to lessen the Punjab disasters, his pressure for a peaceful solution in Kashmir, his untiring work for a compromise over Hyderabad, and his persistent steering of the new, untried Government of India on a steady and moderate course. It is unbelievable that a Governor-General of a different order—presumably a Hindu politician rich in seniority and respect but short in experience of government—could have done nearly so much for the good of both the new nations. Any man who takes responsibility assumes risks: he must accept the odium for his failures, even when they were beyond his control, but he is equally entitled to the credit and praise for his successes, even when they consist in no more than avoidance of worse troubles than those which the circumstances actually brought to pass. And Lord Mountbatten's successes as Governor-General after the transfer of power were very great.

Secondly, all this period, like partition and the transfer of power themselves, must be viewed in the perspective of centuries-long history. Like them, it is but a passing scene in a huge panorama of the rise and decline of empires, peoples and doctrines. It illustrates certain historical themes: it did not initiate any. The Great Divide, which by separating Britain from all India undid two centuries of imperialism, and by separating India and Pakistan imposed a draconian solution to a still more ancient problem of Hindu-Muslim rivalry for power, could not be expected to leave all other things as they were. The great migrations between the two successor states seem now a natural consequence of the partition, hideously dis-figured as it was in the north-west by bloodshed and rapine; and the demise of the Princely autocracies now seems equally bound to have followed the withdrawal of the imperial hand which had sheltered and supported them amid all the hostile trends and ideologies of the age. Even now, the direct consequences of the Great Divide within the sub-continent have not all matured: linguistic and regional conflicts, strife on the tribal fringe, the Indo-Pakistani confrontation itself, are all continuing expressions of re-adjustment after that stupendous historical trauma. We could not expect of the men who led in this revolutionary time that they should have withstood forces far stronger than any policy, any Government, any administrative machine. Though they were not puppets, mere corks on a torrent flooding from a burst dam, they could act only within their powers. A later historian will be able to judge them more fairly than we can judge them today. There were great men among them, and Lord Mountbatten was among the greatest.

An historian of contemporary events is neither a soothsayer to foretell nor a god to deliver judgment. He can only seek and express the truth as it is given to him to see it. More of the truth about the revolutionary happenings in this book will duly come to be known; for the present, let the story stand.

Appendix I

THE PRIME MINISTER'S LETTER

OF INSTRUCTIONS TO LORD MOUNTBATTEN

10 Downing Street, Whitehall.
March 1947

My dear Mountbatten,

The statement which was issued at the time of the announcement of your appointment sets out the policy of the Government and the principles in accordance with which the transfer of power to Indian hands should be effected.

My colleagues of the Cabinet Mission and I have discussed with you the general lines of your approach to the problems which will confront you in India. It will, I think, be useful to you to have on record the salient points which you should have in mind in dealing with the situation. I have, therefore, set them down here.

It is the definite objective of His Majesty's Government to obtain a unitary Government for British India and the Indian States, if possible within the British Commonwealth, through the medium of a Constituent Assembly, set up and run in accordance with the Cabinet Mission's plan, and you should do the utmost in your power to persuade all Parties to work together to this end, and advise His Majesty's Government, in the light of developments, as to the steps that will have to be taken.

Since, however, this plan can only become operative in respect of British India by agreement between the major Parties, there can be no question of compelling either major Party to accept it.

If by 1st October you consider that there is no prospect of reaching a settlement on the basis of a unitary Government for British India, either with or without the co-operation of the Indian States, you should report to His Majesty's Government on the steps which you consider should be taken for the handing over of power on the due date.

It is, of course, important that the Indian States should adjust their relations with the authorities to whom it is intended to hand over power in British India; but as was explicitly stated by the Cabinet Mission, His Majesty's Government do not intend to hand over their powers and obligations under paramountcy to any successor Government. It is not intended to bring paramountcy as a system to a conclusion earlier than the date of the final transfer of power, but you are authorised, at such time as you think appropriate, to enter into negotiations with individual States for adjusting their relations with the Crown.

You will do your best to persuade the rulers of any Indian States in which political progress has been slow to progress rapidly towards some form of more democratic government in their States. You will also aid and assist the States in coming to fair and just arrangements with the leaders of British India as to their future relationships.

The date fixed for the transfer of power is a flexible one to within one month; but you should aim at 1st June, 1948, as the effective date for the transfer of power.

In your relations with the Interim Government you will be guided by the general terms of the Viceroy's letter of 30th May, 1946, to the President of the Congress Party, and of the statement made by the Secretary of State for India in the House of Lords on 13th March 1947. These statements made it clear that, while the Interim Government would not have the same powers as a Dominion Government, His Majesty's Government would treat the Interim Government with the same consultation and consideration as a Dominion Government, and give it the greatest possible freedom in the day to day exercise of the administration of the country.

It is essential that there should be the fullest co-operation with the Indian leaders in all steps that are taken as to the withdrawal of British power so that the process may go forward as smoothly as possible.

The keynote of your administration should therefore be the closest co-operation with the Indians and you should make it clear to the whole of the Secretary of State's Services that this is so, and that it is their duty to their countries to work to this end.

You should take every opportunity of stressing the importance of ensuring that the transfer of power is effected with full regard to the defence requirements of India. In the first place you will impress upon the Indian leaders the great importance of avoiding any breach in the continuity of the Indian Army and of maintaining the organisation of defence on an all Indian basis. Secondly, you will point out the need for continued collaboration in the security of the Indian Ocean area for which provision might be made in an agreement between the two countries. At a suitable date His Majesty's Government would be ready to send military and other experts to India to assist in discussing the terms of such an agreement.

You will no doubt inform Provincial Governors of the substance of this letter.

Yours sincerely,
(signed) C. R. ATTLEE

Admiral the Right Hon. the Viscount Mountbatten
  of Burma, K.G., G.C.S.I., G.C.I.E., G.C.V.O.,
  K.C.B., D.S.O.

Appendix II

LORD MOUNTBATTEN'S 'CONCLUSIONS'

APPENDED TO HIS 'REPORT ON THE LAST

VICEROYALTY' SUBMITTED TO HIS MAJESTY'S

GOVERNMENT IN SEPTEMBER 1948

1 The appalling communal disturbances which shook the Punjab during the two months which followed the transfer of power have raised the two questions whether power was transferred too quickly and whether adequate counter preparations were made. These questions are in a way interdependent, because it may be argued that more time before the transfer of power would have allowed of more adequate preparations being made.

2 So far as military preparations were concerned, it is doubtful whether more could have been done had more time been available. The Punjab Boundary Force, which was gathered together in the areas which it was considered were most likely to be affected, was about the largest force that has ever been concentrated in one place in time of peace. It was of approximately the size which Sir Evan Jenkins, the Governor of the Punjab, had estimated would be required to prevent civil war, and was composed of all arms, including armoured and artillery support.

3 Air Force Squadrons were sent to the Punjab too. It had been my hope that an opportunity might be offered for air action, as nothing in the military way could have had a greater morale effect on the trouble-makers. But the form of the disturbances did not allow of this. At a Joint Defence Council meeting after the transfer of power it was unanimously decided not to use aircraft offensively, because of the difficulty of distinguishing rioter from refugee. Aircraft were useful, though, for reconnaissance.

4 British troops were not used in the disturbances which followed the transfer of power. The instructions of His Majesty's Government were

that they were only to be used to protect European lives, nor were their services asked for by either Dominion Government. If they had been used to combat communal disturbances they would doubtless have incurred the odium of both sides as had happened in the case of Sir Cyril Radcliffe. That would have had a most deleterious effect on relations between the United Kingdom and the two new Dominions, but this might have been worth while if thousands of innocent lives had been saved. Indeed, after the transfer of power I was tempted to ask His Majesty's Government that British troops might be used in the riots. His Majesty's Government might or might not have agreed. But this would have been irrelevant because, as I found not altogether to my surprise, no Indian leader of any party would have agreed.

5 In any case it would have been a task of the utmost military difficulty to have maintained a larger number of soldiers in the Punjab. The reconstitution of the Armed Forces, which was proceeding before the transfer of power at the request of the leaders of both sides, would have been seriously delayed if more units had been sent to the Punjab. But both these were minor considerations in comparison to the fact that to have stationed a larger proportion of the available Army in this one Province would have involved weakening the garrisons in the rest of the sub-continent. Although it was apparent that communal warfare was more likely to start in the Punjab than anywhere else, the danger of outbreaks in other Provinces, particularly in Bengal, and on the borders of Hyderabad, seemed very real.

6 Indeed after the transfer of power there were disturbances in other parts of the sub-continent, especially in Calcutta, where the second largest concentration of troops was available. The Calcutta riots were stopped by the immense influence exerted by Mahatma Gandhi on the spot, assisted by Mr. Suhrawardy.

7 Military action alone cannot stop large-scale communal disturbances in the Indian sub-continent. The form of the disturbances, and the areas involved, make the soldiers' task an almost impossible one. It is only political action, backed up by military action or the threat thereof, which can bring the people to their senses and stop them murdering one another.

8 I do not consider that further political action could have been taken if power had been transferred at a later date. It had proved impossible to get out of Section 93 Government in the Punjab except by the transfer of power. Every effort had been made to bring the dangers of the situation home to the top rank political leaders, and they were as fully aware as I was of the danger which threatened. But not one of us, and indeed, so far as I know, no one in India, Pakistan or the United Kingdom anticipated the exact form and magnitude of what was to follow.

9 My threats to the Sikh Rulers and leaders may now appear to have been empty; it is doubtful, however, if any other approach to them would have been more successful. The Sikh leaders in the East of the Punjab, and the Muslim leaders in the West, had encouraged and armed their supporters. It was from them that the political leadership was lacking. A typical example was the resignation of the Khan of Mamdot from the Punjab Security Committee. The constant requests from the Sikhs for partition, and their insistence that they should be allowed to retain the bargaining power of being able to make up their own minds which way they should go, were further examples. The Provincial Muslim and Provincial Sikh political leadership was in the hands of unbalanced and seemingly unintelligent men.

10 The Sikh leaders might have been arrested. When this step was suggested, I was not averse to it. The decision not to arrest them was taken in view of the unanimous advice of Sir Evan Jenkins, Sir Chandulal Trivedi and Sir Francis Mudie—the last two in their respective capacities as Governors-designate of East and West Punjab. They stated that such arrests would only make matters worse. It seemed out of the question to over-rule the advice of the men on the spot. As it turned out they were probably right. However guilty Master Tara Singh and his colleagues may have been to start with, they appeared to do their genuine best later on to call their followers to heel and to stop the killings.

11 The extent of the complicity of these Sikh leaders in encouraging preparations may never be determined. The only direct evidence which I received of the part which they were alleged to be playing was from Mr. Savage at the meeting on 5th August. This was due to the run-down of the British Intelligence Organisation, which was functioning far below its previous well-known competence.

12 This run-down was common to the whole civil administration. The greatest handicap under which the new Governments, Provincial and Central, worked after the 15th August was a great lack of adequate and competent civil administration. The Government of India had made no efforts to retain the services of British officials, and the Government of Pakistan had not made very great efforts. The Governor and I had done what we could to ensure that really competent Indian officials were made available for the most dangerous districts of the Punjab.

13 It had proved impossible, despite the Governor's best efforts, to get out of Section 93 administration. I am convinced that, if he had allowed the Muslim League to form a Ministry, the disturbances would have been precipitated and might have prejudiced the whole operation of transferring power.

14 It may be said that one step which could have been taken in the Punjab, had the transfer of power been at a later date, and which might

have precluded communal disturbances, was a properly organised wholesale transfer of population from each half of the Province. Pandit Nehru and Mr. Jinnah turned down the suggestion that even a start should be made on planning for this, and were supported in this decision by all of their followers with whom I discussed this suggestion.

15 This decision may perhaps be criticised, especially as the population transferred themselves on their own and completed the moves within about three months after the two new Dominions had come into being. These moves were carried out in appalling circumstances. Most of the migrants went on foot; there were few who were able to take many of their belongings; some were murdered on the way. But surely it was the very fact that it took place in such appalling circumstances that made its so rapid completion possible. Few families whose forbears have lived for generations in one place will uproot themselves, leaving most of their worldly goods behind, on the threat of danger. Mass killings and the fear of reprisals alone could have produced a mass transfer of population.

16 Furthermore, such a transfer of population seemed, from the point of view of the two future Dominion Governments, much against their own interests. The Muslims in East Punjab were a poor but most necessary part of the community. The Sikhs and particularly the Hindus of West Punjab seemed an almost essential part of the community, especially in the towns. It would have been very difficult for Pandit Nehru and Mr. Jinnah to have agreed to a wholesale transfer of population, quite apart from whether such a decision could have been put into effect successfully.

17 The decision to transfer power on 15th August was not made hurriedly. An immense amount of thought was given to this part of the problem, and the conclusion was reached that the advantages of an early transfer far outweighed the disadvantages. Mention has been made of these advantages in the body of the Report, but perhaps they are worthy of repetition here. They were as follows:

1 It seemed that an early transfer of actual power well short of the original time limit of June, 1948, would be likely to make for lasting goodwill between the United Kingdom and the successor Governments in India.

2 If the transitional Dominion status worked well, it might prove to be acceptable as a permanent arrangement.

3 It would be in accordance with the expressed desires of both parties —by Congress that there should be a transitional period of Dominion status for the new India, and by the Muslim League that Pakistan should form a part of the British Commonwealth; and the leaders expressed themselves as unanimously in favour of the date of 15th August.

4 It would place the responsibility for administration on the shoulders of the successor authorities and enable them to build up their own administrative machinery before the existing one had completely run down; a later date would have meant an even more complete lack of civil administration.

5 It seemed likely, by lessening the urgency for framing new constitutions, to increase the chances of really workable and sound ones being worked out; and it would make possible, in the meanwhile, administrative continuity within the framework of the Government of India Act, 1935, which was perhaps the greatest single legislative achievement of the British in India.

18 But all these circumstances were of little account in relation to the primary consideration of all—namely, that the difficulties which seemed likely to be encountered, and in the event were encountered in no small measure, between the date of His Majesty's Government's announcement on 3rd June and the actual transfer of power, rendered it advisable to make this period as short as possible. I am genuinely convinced that it would not have been possible to have kept the Interim Government of India functioning without one or other Party resigning and all the repercussions which that would have brought about, for a week, let alone a month, longer than was done. The August transfer of power was inherent in the Partition solution quite apart from any introduction of Dominion status.

19 The decision of the major political parties in India to implement the 3rd June Plan represented their first agreement on the method of taking over power. If the implementation was to take place at all, speed seemed essential; delay might have plunged the whole Indian sub-continent, and not the Punjab only, into disruption and chaos. It seemed that the only possible alternative to a quick transfer of power was to reopen recruitment of British officials to the Indian Civil Service and Indian Police, and to bring in a large number of British Army Divisions to hold down the country.

Index